Gale Encyclopedia of
World History: War

Gale Encyclopedia of World History: War

VOLUME 1

GALE
CENGAGE Learning

Detroit • New York • San Francisco • New Haven, Conn • Waterville, Maine • London

Gale Encyclopedia of World History: War

Project Editors: Anne Marie Hacht and Dwayne D. Hayes

Editorial: Ira Mark Milne

Rights Acquisition and Management: Margaret Chamberlain-Gaston, Vernon English, Aja Perales, and Robyn Young

Composition: Evi Abou-El-Seoud

Manufacturing: Wendy Blurton

Imaging: Lezlie Light

Product Design: Jennifer Wahi

For product information and technology assistance, contact us at
Gale Customer Support, 1-800-877-4253.
For permission to use material from this text or product,
submit all requests online at **www.cengage.com/permissions.**
Further permissions questions can be emailed to
permissionrequest@cengage.com

Cover photographs reproduced by permission of Bettmann/Corbis (picture of Macedonian troops in formation of hoplites) and Henri Bureau/Sygma/Corbis (picture of soldier watching oil refineries burn in Iran).

While every effort has been made to ensure the reliability of the information presented in this publication, Gale, a part of Cengage Learning, does not guarantee the accuracy of the data contained herein. Gale accepts no payment for listing; and inclusion in the publication of any organization, agency, institution, publication, service, or individual does not imply endorsement of the editors or publisher. Errors brought to the attention of the publisher and verified to the satisfaction of the publisher will be corrected in future editions.

Library of Congress Cataloging-in-Publication Data

Gale encyclopedia of U.S. history : war / editorial, Anne Marie Hacht, Dwayne D. Hayes.
    p. cm. --
    Includes bibliographical references and index.
    ISBN 978-1-4144-3148-2 (set) -- ISBN 978-1-4144-3149-9 (vol. 1) --
ISBN 978-1-4144-3150-5 (vol. 2)
    1. Military history--Encyclopedias. 2. Battles--Encyclopedias. 3. World history--Encyclopedias. 4. Military art and science--History--Encyclopedias. 5. War and civilization--Encyclopedias. I. Hacht, Anne Marie. II. Hayes, Dwayne D. III. Gale Group. IV. Title: Encyclopedia of world history : war.

D25.A2G35 2008
355.003--dc22   2007034399

Gale
27500 Drake Rd.
Farmington Hills, MI, 48331-3535

978-1-4144-3148-2 (set)   1-4144-3148-1 (set)
978-1-4144-3149-9 (vol. 1)   1-4144-3149-X (vol. 1)
978-1-4144-3150-5 (vol. 2)   1-4144-3150-3 (vol. 2)

This title is also available as an e-book.
ISBN-13: 978-1-4144-3151-2 ISBN-10: 1-4144-3151-1
Contact your Gale sales representative for ordering information.

Printed in the United States of America
1 2 3 4 5 6 7 11 10 09 08

Contents

VOLUME 2

Contents

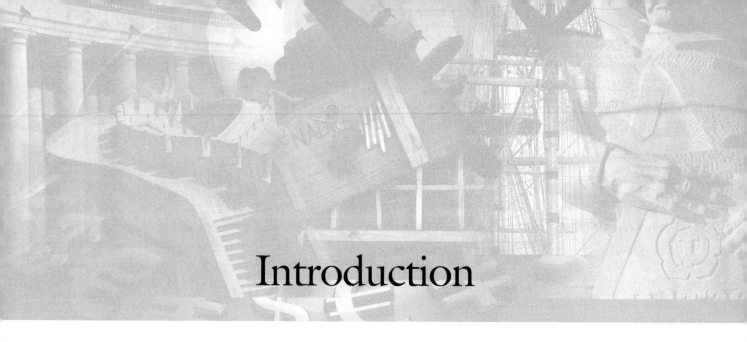

Introduction

How To Use This Book

The history of recorded conflict stretches back five thousand years, but it is likely that humans had begun making war on each other long before that. In fact, it is quite conceivable that people have been killing each other in an organized fashion for the entire fifty-thousand-year span of modern *Homo sapiens*. What is certain is that there is not a corner of the inhabited globe that has not been touched by war, and that as a general rule war has been fought on an increasingly grander scale, culminating in the once inconceivable concepts of world wars and the specter of complete annihilation.

The superficial motives for war can be quite complex at times, but the fundamental causes have largely remained unchanged over the millennia. The nineteenth century military thinker Carl von Clausewitz even went so far as to proclaim that all war is simply the ultimate extension of politics. Others would add to that motive the further pressures of economics and demographics—in other words, lack of, or desire for more resources, along with growing populations, can force populations to make war on each other.

Like the motivations for going to war, the fundamentals of waging it have changed very little from the dawn of history. Time-tested strategies (such as, in the words of Nathan Bedford Forrest, "getting there firstest with the mostest") and classic tactical maneuvers (such as double envelopment) have been winning wars and battles since the days of Ancient Egypt and remain the foundation of armed conflict, even in this day and age of mechanized, computerized warfare.

Organization

To study how humanity has moved from tribal skirmishes fought with copper-tipped spears and hurled stones to global conflicts fought in the shadow of the threat of nuclear holocaust is to study the rise and fall of the greatest civilizations and to follow the personal dramas of men and women whose personal decisions and beliefs impacted the very course of human history. *The Gale Encyclopedia of World History: War* aims to assist the student and generalist reader interested in studying the most significant conflicts of the past, and to impart an appreciation for the sweep and scale of the subject of military history—for to study the history of war is to study the history of humanity.

Accordingly, each section of this book covers a different war or period of warfare, organized chronologically, and opens with an overview of each conflict, featuring biographies of major figures who, through actions either brilliant or ill-advised, contributed to the conflict's eventual resolution. The reader will see how the simple drama of human lives, the split-second battlefield decision, or the moment of critical hesitation, can have a lasting impact on the course of history.

After the biographies of major figures, the key battles that weave together to tell the story of the war will be examined. The full variety of methods of waging war, and of the opposing generals' tactics, oftentimes startlingly different, being borne out by the soldiers on the battlefield, will be in full evidence here. Readers will discover for themselves the old military truism that "no plan survives contact with the enemy."

In order to better understand the tools that enabled soldiers to fight battles, and to chart the impact of evolving technology on the battlefield, each section also includes articles on the "key elements of warcraft," in-depth examinations of the weaponry and logistical innovations that brought victory to those who employed them and changed the face of warfare for all time.

What's Inside

The book opens with an examination of the first great empire, that of the Assyrians, who set the pattern for the rise and fall of all empires to follow and were the first to introduce concepts of professional armies, psychological warfare, and methodical siegecraft.

The rising dominance of Greek culture in the Mediterranean is next to be examined, first in the great East-West clash of the Persian Wars, including the famous battles of Thermopylae and Salamis, then in the conquests of Alexander the Great, who returned the Persians' invasion with interest and spread the foundation of Western civilization from the Nile to the Indus.

The rise and fall of Rome covers two chapters, looking at the greatest empire of the ancient world and how it got that way, then examining the great barbarian invasions of the fourth and fifth centuries and the beginning of the "Dark Ages."

The Medieval period kicks off with an overview of the explosion of Islam and its dominance over the Near East and North Africa, along with the crucial battles that turned the tide away from Europe. The age of the dominance of the mounted warrior covers several chapters, starting with the dark days of Viking raids and the conquest of England before moving on to the centuries-long conflict known as the Crusades.

The Middle Ages come to an end with two devastating wars. The largest empire of all time is examined with a chapter on the Mongol Conquests, while the chapter on the Hundred Years War traces the end of the knight's battlefield dominance and the origin of the modern nation-states of Europe.

Islam's second great period of expansion is covered in two chapters. The first, on the Rise and Decline of the Ottoman Empire, sees a resurgence of western conquests, including the final fall of the last vestiges of the Roman Empire leading up to the conquest of Constantinople in 1453. The Mogul Conquests of India, meanwhile, examine Islam's spread into south Asia.

Warfare in the so-called "Age of Reason" brought battles on an unprecedented scale and sweeping changes that destroyed entire civilizations. The chapters on the Conquest of the Americas and the Religious Wars in Europe examine the monumental developments that changed the way people on both sides of the Atlantic thought about the world and the violent upheavals that resulted.

On the other side of the world, the foundations of modern Japan were being forged in a series of wars between powerful feudal lords, under whose guidance Japanese warfare changed forever. So bloody and costly were the wars, Japan entered into a two-century-long period of conservative isolationism that would permanently affect the future of Asia and that region's relationship with Europe.

Even as Japan began its long isolation, the mid-seventeenth century saw Europe consumed with war. The Thirty Years War involved nearly all the great Continental powers and dynasties of the time in what began as a war of ideologies and ended in a conflict of pure politics and alliances of convenience, changing the politics of European warfare and setting Germany's unification back two hundred years.

A separate chapter examines how, as the Thirty Years War lurched to a conclusion, England, which had remained aloof of the conflict, was itself sucked into a civil war that would result in the murder of a king and the foundation of a short-lived republic.

Although England's monarchy was restored, the English Civil War marked only the beginning of a nearly century-long period of dynastic struggles across Europe that spread into the colonies of the New World as well. The chapter on these Dynastic Wars covers the first great alliances between modern European nation-states, marking the beginning of a constantly shifting pattern of international politics that would dictate world affairs for the next two centuries.

The section on the Seven Years War covers what has sometimes been called the first true "world war," as it involved all the major powers of Europe as well as their global colonies. By the war's end, the balance of power in Europe had been permanently altered, with the foundations of the British Empire (and in particular its domination of India) firmly established.

Although the Seven Years War resulted in England's domination of North America, the seeds of revolution in the American colonies were laid by the costs incurred by the conflict. The American Revolution chapter examines the origins of a future superpower, the United States.

Inspired by the ideals of the American Revolution, the French Revolution toppled its own monarchy in a bloody reign of terror. The other monarchies of Europe, fearful of witnessing a spread of such extremism, responded in force. Out of the crucible of those wars rose Napoleon Bonaparte, the greatest general modern Europe had yet seen and the man who would give his name to the wars of the age, Europe's bloodiest to date.

The following chapter returns again to the United States, which would be torn apart by an even bloodier conflict, the American Civil War, over forty years after the end of the Napoleonic Wars. The war between North and South would permanently redefine America's economy and political system and give birth to some of its most enduring heroes and legends.

The Crimean War was Europe's first major conflict after the Napoleonic Wars, witnessing once again a multinational alliance going to war to preserve the balance of power on the continent. Perhaps the greatest legacy of the war came from the reforms spearheaded by Florence Nightingale, who led the efforts to sanitize and improve battlefield medicine.

The other great post-Napoleonic conflicts arose in South America as, one by one, Spain's colonies, led in large part by "the Liberator" Simón Bolívar, fought successfully for liberation from their increasingly weak European master.

In the century of relative peace following the wars of Napoleon, Europe turned its military attention outward towards the rest of the world. Although Europe had established colonies around the world from the fifteenth century onward, the nineteenth century was a time of rampant colonial expansion. By 1900, nearly all of Africa had been divvied up between the great powers of Europe, as had large portions of Asia and Oceania. The British Empire—on at least a portion of which, it was said, the sun was always shining—was at its peak of power. The chapter covering this colonial expansion also includes a look at the Boer Wars of South Africa.

Even as the great powers of Europe were cementing their colonial empires, the "War to End All Wars" would erupt back home, spelling the beginning of the end for European dominance. World War I was the first war to reap the true horrors of industrialization and mechanization—troops were gassed, bombed, shelled, and machine-gunned in previously unthinkable numbers.

The hope held out by some that the First World War would prove so horrible and costly as to prevent the thought of ever fighting another would soon be dashed, most visibly in the three-year-long Spanish Civil War. This chapter will examine how Spain's civil war marked the first time the new post-war ideologies of communism, fascism, and Western-style democracy clashed on the battlefield, and the bloody results that were an indication of the ferocity such new political systems could bring out.

The Second World War, which began the same year Spain's war ended, was a global clash of ideologies and the deadliest conflict in history. World War II nearly ruined the once-great colonial powers of Europe and cast the United States and the Soviet Union as the new global superpowers. Thanks to a reluctance to engage in direct nuclear confrontation, the Cold War was fought between the USSR and the United States by proxy. The Korean War was the first such conflict, fought between the communist North, backed by the Soviet Union and China, and the democratic South, which was saved from total annihilation by troops from the newly-formed United Nations.

Another theater of the Cold War conflict is covered in the chapter on the Vietnam War, which erupted in the wake of Europe's colonial withdrawal but then became a proxy war between Communism and the West. Left weakened and fractured by years of imperialistic exploitation, many of the emerging countries of the so-called "Third

World" became ideological battlegrounds as indigenous factions fought amongst each other, aided by either by Western powers or by Communist states.

Another post-colonial region, the Middle East, ends the journey through world conflict, first with a look at the devastating Iran-Iraq War and the continuing impact that conflict has had on world events, and finally with a chapter on the new form of warfare, international terrorism. Included is a look at the events of September 11 and the War on Terror that followed.

Conclusion

It is hoped that by studying the stories contained in this volume, the reader can glean an understanding of the mighty tides of war that have so often helped to shape the world of today. By studying the evolution of tactics and strategy and the ever-increasing integration of technology and industry into the process of waging warfare, the reader will also hopefully gain an insight into the nature of war and its place in the twenty-first century, and the highly personal impact it has on everyone's lives.

At the very least, it is hoped that the reader will appreciate the great drama and sacrifice contained within the following chapters and will come to recognize the tremendous cost of war for those who wage it.

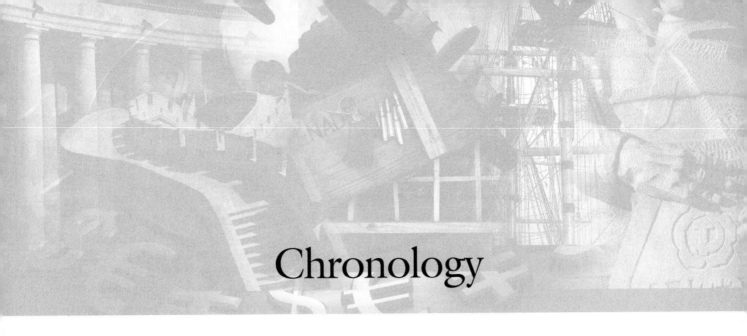

Chronology

c. 75,000 BCE:
    First specialized stone tools, including spear tips, developed.

c. 50,000 BCE:
    Homo sapiens sapiens, modern man, appears.

c. 20,000 BCE:
    Bow and arrow probably developed, although some theories hold that it did not appear until as late as 8,000 BCE. Beginning of agriculture as last Ice Age begins to recede.

c. 10,000 BCE:
    With the full withdrawal of the glaciers, the Holocene period begins. Rise of modern human civilization. Houses of mud brick constructed in the first cities.

c. 8,000 BCE:
    Earliest known wall constructed around Jericho.

c. 4,000 BCE:
    Ur and Babylon founded. Sumerians begin to use wheeled vehicles. Around the same time, Central Asian horsemen begin migrating into Central Europe, spreading Indo-European language and belief systems.

c. 3,100 BCE:
    Cuneiform writing developed in Sumeria.

2,697 BCE:
    Traditional date of "The Yellow Emperor", Huang Ti, the legendary first emperor of China, coming to the throne.

c. 2,625 BCE:
    Egyptian Pharaoh Cheops, builder of the Great Pyramid, dies.

c. 2,500 BCE:
    Bow and arrow first used in warfare.

2,279 BCE:
    Sumeria and Akkad united under Sargon the Great; first known empire.

c. 1,750 BCE:
    Code of Hammurabi, a set of laws, established in Babylon.

c. 1,600 BCE:
    Aryan (Indo-European) invasion of India.

c. 1,500 BCE:
    Pharaoh Thutmoses III conquers Canaan and Egyptian civilization reaches its greatest point of expansion. Domesticated horses introduced to Egyptian and Chinese civilizations around this time by Central Asian horsemen.

c. 1,200 BCE:
    Canaan conquered by Hebrews under Joshua.

1,184 BCE:
    Likely date for historical Trojan War.

c. 1,025 BCE:
    Unified kingdom of Israel under Saul, David, and Solomon.

c. 900 BCE:
    Hunting from chariots a favorite sport in Egypt and Mesopotamia.

776 BCE:
    First recorded Olympic Games.

753 BCE:
    Date of the traditional founding of Rome.

c. 705 BCE:
    Assyrian Empire reaches height of power under Sennacherib.

701 BCE:

Babylon razed by Assyrians. The city will be rebuilt within a generation.

671 BCE:

Egypt conquered by Assyria.

c. 600 BCE:

Confucius, Buddha, Zoroaster, Lao-tse, the Hebrew prophets, and Greek philosophers and artists all active around the same time. "Hanging Gardens of Babylon" built. Rome declared a republic.

594 BCE:

Solon pushes through democratic reforms in Athens.

529 BCE:

Rise of Persian Empire under Cyrus the Great.

490 BCE:

Greeks defeat Persians at Battle of Marathon.

480 BCE:

Second Persian invasion of Greece. Battle of Thermopylae. Battle of Salamis.

479 BCE:

Battle of Plataea ends Persian Wars, marks beginning of Greek Golden Age.

431 BCE:

Beginning of Peloponnesian War between Athens and Sparta.

401 BCE:

Ten thousand Greek mercenaries fight their way home through the heart of the Persian Empire after ending up on the wrong side of a dynastic struggle.

390 BCE:

Rome sacked by invading Gauls.

356 BCE:

Philip II becomes king of Macedon.

338 BCE:

Philip defeats Athenians and Thebans, establishes Macedonian domination of Greece.

336 BCE:

Philip assassinated, succeeded by son Alexander.

332 BCE:

Egypt conquered by Alexander's army; Alexandria founded.

330 BCE:

Persian Empire totally conquered by Alexander.

326 BCE:

Alexander reaches the Indus River, but is then forced to turn back by generals.

323 BCE:

Death of Alexander.

319 BCE:

Chandragupta Maurya reconquers Macedonian possessions in the Indus Valley and founds the Mauryan dynasty.

c. 275 BCE:

Babylon abandoned.

264 BCE:

Beginning of First Punic War between Rome and Carthage.

260 BCE:

King Asoka of India renounces violence and becomes a Buddhist following a particularly bloody conquest.

219 BCE:

Beginning of Second Punic War between Rome and Carthage.

218 BCE:

Hannibal crosses Alps, defeats Scipio.

202 BCE:

Scipio Africanus defeats Hannibal at Zama.

197 BCE:

Macedon defeated by Rome, Greek city states fall under Roman domination.

149 BCE:

Beginning of Third Punic War.

147 BCE:

Carthage leveled by Scipio the Younger.

114 BCE:

Old Silk Road opens up trade between China and Europe.

c. 100 BCE:

Great Wall of China completed.

71 BCE: Slave revolt in Italy led by Spartacus.

54 BCE: Britain invaded by Julius Caesar; British tribes agree to pay tribute to Rome.

50 BCE: Julius Caesar completes his conquest of Gaul.

49 BCE: Caesar crosses Rubicon, begins civil war with Pompey.

44 BCE: Julius Caesar assassinated.

31 BCE:

Marc Antony and Cleopatra defeated by Julius Caesar's appointed heir, Octavian.

30 BCE: Octavian, retitled Caesar Augustus, becomes first Roman emperor.

6 BCE: Judea annexed by Rome.

4 BCE: Probable date of birth of Jesus Christ.

9CE: Invading Roman legions destroyed by German tribes at the Battle of Teutoburg Forest.

30CE: Probable date of Christ's crucifixion.

43CE: Roman invasion of Britain; Londinium founded.

60 CE:

British queen Boudicca (or Boadicea) leads unsuccessful rebellion against Rome.

64 CE: Great Fire of Rome. Christians persecuted on Emperor Nero's orders.

70 CE: Jewish Revolt against Rome. Jerusalem destroyed.

98 CE: Beginning of Trajan's reign, under whom the Roman Empire will reach its greatest extent.

c. 110: Paper first used for writing in China.

125: Hadrian's Wall built in northern Britain.

164: A great plague begins to sweep through the Roman Empire, permanently weakening it.

c. 200: Bishop of Rome begins to gain papal authority.

212: Roman citizenship granted to every freeborn subject of the empire.

257: Goths invade Black Sea region, Franks invade Spain, Alemanni and Suevi invade Italy.

268: Goths sack Athens, Sparta, and Corinth.

285: Roman Empire divided into Western and Eastern halves.

303: Beginning of last Christian persecutions.

306: Constantine the Great becomes Western Roman emperor, then unites the two empires.

313: Edict of Milan establishes tolerance of Christians.

330: Constantinople founded.

337: Constantine baptized a Christian on his deathbed.

340: Rome split again into two empires.

360: Scrolls begin to be replaced by books. Huns invade Europe. Picts and Scots cross Hadrian's Wall.

402: Roman legions withdraw from Britain.

410: Rome sacked by Goths led by Alaric. Saxon invasions of Britain begin.

411: Saint Augustine writes *City of God*.

425: German kingdoms established throughout Western empire.

451: Atilla the Hun invades Gaul.

453: Atilla dies after ravaging northern Italy and threatening Rome.

476: Last Western Roman emperor deposed by barbarian Odoacer; end of Western Empire.

507: Frankish kingdom expands under King Clovis.

517: Buddhism begins spreading into central China.

527: Beginning of the reign of Justinian the Great, Emperor of the Eastern Roman Empire.

535: Eastern general Belisarius destroys Ostrogoth kingdom in Italy. Resurgence of Eastern Roman Empire.

543: Europe ravaged by plagues and earthquakes.

c. 550: The crucifix becomes ornamental art in Constantinople.

c. 570: Muhammad, founder of Islam, born.

587: First Buddhist monastery founded in Japan.

614: Persians conquer Damascus and Jerusalem, take the reported True Cross as war booty.

616: Persians conquer Egypt.

622: The Hegira: Muhammad flees from Mecca to Medina. Year One on the Muslim calendar.

633: Arabs invade Persia, conquering Syria and Iraq. Jerusalem, Antioch, and Alexandria, all important Christian centers, are also overrun.

639: Muslims invade Egypt.

641: Persian Empire ceases to exist after Muslim conquest under Omar.

649: First naval battles between Byzantines and Arabs. Greek fire is used shortly thereafter.

673: First Arab attack on Constantinople.

686: Last pagan kingdom in Britain converts to Christianity.

697: Arabs destroy Carthage, drive Byzantines out of North Africa.

711: Roderic, last king of the Visigoths, defeated by invading Arabs; Spain now almost entirely controlled by Muslims.

720: Muslim armies cross the Pyrenees into France, take Narbonne.

732: Frankish leader Charles Martel defeats Arabs at battles of Tours and Poitiers, halts westward Arab expansion.

771: Charlemagne becomes sole ruler of Frankish kingdom.

778: Basques defeat Charlemagne at Battle of Roncesvalles.

793: First Viking attack on Britain at Lindisfarne Monastery.

800: Charlemagne crowned first Holy Roman Emperor.

804: Frankish Empire extends to the Elbe River.

812: First paper money issued in China.

814: Death of Charlemagne, decline of his Western Empire.

817: Charlemagne's successor, Louis the Pious, divides the empire among his three sons.

825: Muslim conquest of Sicily begins.

838: Arabs sack Marseilles, move into southern Italy.

840: Dublin founded by Viking settlers.

843: Frankish Empire formally divided into three kingdoms by Treaty of Verdun.

846: Arabs sack Rome, plunder the Vatican.

850: Vikings establish Rus civilization centered on Kiev. Trading with Constantinople and the Khazars begins.

859: Norse raids in the Mediterranean.

861: Iceland discovered by Viking sailors.

865: Constantinople attacked by Rus Vikings. Norse kingdom of York established in England.

871: Danes occupy London. Alfred the Great becomes king of Wessex.

878: Alfred defeats Danes at Edington.

879: The Pope and the Patriarch of Constantinople excommunicate each other.

890: Alfred the Great establishes an English militia and navy, encourages growth of market towns.

895: Magyars under leadership of Arpad enter Hungary.

900: Reconquest of Spain begins under Alfonso II of Castile. Greenland discovered by Norse.

907: Magyar raids into Germany and Italy.

911: Holy Roman Emperor becomes an elected position.

939: Revolts against Japanese Emperor set off two-hundred-year period of civil war.

955: Magyars and Slavs defeated by Otto of Germany.

964: Mayan empire founded.

975: Arabic numerals, imported from India, introduced to Europe.

1008: Mahmud of Gazni defeats Hindus in India.

1013: King Ethelred the Unready flees England, which comes under Danish control.

1016: Canute of Denmark assumes English throne upon Ethelred's death.

1035: Death of Canute. His empire is divided among his three sons.

1041: Movable type invented in China.

1066: Harold II crowned in England. Defeats Norse invaders at Stamford bridge on September 25, then is in turn defeated by William of Normandy at Hastings on October 14.

1071: Byzantine Emperor Romanus V defeated and captured by Seljuk Turks at Manzikert.

1094: Spanish leader El Cid takes Valencia from the Moors.

1095: Pope Urban II proclaims the First Crusade at the Council of Clermont.

1099: Crusaders take Jerusalem.

1145: Pope Eugene III proclaims the Second Crusade.

1147: Second Crusade fails.

1150: Paper manufacture begins in Spain.

1151: Chess arrives in England.

1183: Muslim leader Saladin takes Aleppo from Christians.

1187: Saladin annihilates Crusader army at Hattin, takes Jerusalem.

1189: Richard the Lionheart leads Third Crusade, which fails to retake Jerusalem.

1192: Richard completes a truce with Saladin guaranteeing access for Christian pilgrims.

1202: Fourth Crusade begins, which conquers Constantinople in 1204 at Venice's behest. The numeral zero is introduced to Europe by Leonardo Fibonacci.

1206: Genghis Khan declared chief prince of the Mongols.

1208: Beginning of Albigensian Crusade against Cathar heretics in Southern France.

1212: Children's Crusade ends with thousands of children sold into slavery.

1214: Peking conquered by Genghis Khan.

1215: English King John puts his seal on the Magna Carta at Runnymede.

1221: First use of shrapnel in bombs by Chinese.

1223: Mongols invade Russia.

1228: Francis of Assisi canonized.

1236: Mongol leader Kublai Khan conquers China.

1240: Mongol conquest of Russia completed.

1241: Mongols defeat Germans at Battle of Liegnitz, invade Poland and Hungary, then withdraw upon death of Ughetai Khan.

1258: Mongols take Baghdad, overthrow Caliphate.

1260: Travels of Italian explorer Marco Polo begin.

1274: Mongol invasion of Japan turned back by typhoons.

1281: Second Mongol invasion fleet once again destroyed by typhoons, which the Japanese call "divine winds", or *kamikaze.*

1288: First known gun made in China.

1297: Scottish victory over English at Stirling Bridge.

1298: Marco Polo's account of his journeys is published.

1302: First "Estates General" called in France.

1314: Scots led by Robert the Bruce rout English army at Battle of Bannockburn.

1327: Completion of the 1,100 mile Grand Canal in China.

1333: Edward III takes English throne.

1337: Beginning of Hundred Years' War between France and England.

1347: Black Death ravages Europe for the next three years. One third of Europe's population dies.

1356: Edward the Black Prince defeats French at Battle of Poitiers, captures King John of France.

1363: Warlord Tamerlane begins conquest of Asia.

1364: Aztec capital of Tenochtitlan built.

1415: English led by King Henry V defeat French at Agincourt.

1420: Treaty of Troyes grants Henry V heir apparent status to France, but Henry dies in 1422 before he can take the French crown.

1429: French peasant Joan of Arc raises Siege of Orleans. She is captured and burned at the stake two years later.

1441: Portugal begins West African slave trade.

1448: Ottoman ruler Murad II wins decisive Battle of Kosovo over Serbs.

1453: Turks take Constantinople, ending the Byzantine Empire. England and France formally end Hundred Years' War. England loses all Continental possessions except Calais. Gutenberg prints first bible at Mainz.

1455: Wars of the Roses begin in England.

1463: Turks conquer Bosnia.

1486: Spanish Inquisition begins.

1485: Englishman Henry Tudor defeats and kills Richard III, ending the Wars of the Roses. Beginning of Tudor dynasty.

1492: Granada, last Muslim kingdom in Spain, conquered by Spanish. Jews given three months to leave the country. Christopher Columbus, financed by Spain, discovers "New World."

1493: Portugal and Spain, with papal support, divide the world between themselves.

1495: Leonardo da Vinci begins work on *The Last Supper.*

1507: The name "America" first applied to the New World.

1508: Michaelangelo begins painting the ceiling of the Sistine Chapel.

1517: Martin Luther posts his 95 theses in protest against the Church, beginning the Protestant Reformation. Turks take Cairo.

1521: 1521Turkish leader Suleiman I takes Belgrade, begins moving against Hungary. Aztec nation destroyed by Hernán Cortés.

1522: Turkish ruler Suleiman takes Rhodes from the Knights of St. John.

1525: Battle of Pavia: first mass use of muskets by Spanish.

1526: Sultan Suleiman defeats Hungarians, takes Buda.

1529: Turks lay siege to Vienna, but are forced to raise siege.

1542: First European contact with Japan.

1556: Akbar the Great becomes Mogul emperor.

1567: Oda Nobunaga deposes Japanese shogunate.

1581: Akbar the Great conquers Afghanistan.

1582: In Japan, Toyotomi Hideyoshi assumes power after death of Nobunaga. Pope Gregory reforms the calendar by dropping eleven days in October.

1588: Spanish Armada defeated by English.

1592: Japanese invasion of Korea fails.

1595: English army abandons use of bow in war.

1598: Tokugawa Ieyasu restores shogunate in Japan.

1600: East India Company founded in England.

1611: King James Bible published.

1618: The Defenestration of Prague, in which two Imperial Regents are thrown out a window, begins the Thirty Years War.

1620: The *Mayflower,* a ship carrying Puritan settlers, leaves England and lands in Massachusetts.

1622: Treaty of Montpellier ends Huguenot rebellion in France.

1626: Dutch colony of New Amsterdam (New York) founded.

1628: Construction of Taj Mahal begins.

1646: English Civil War ends with Oliver Cromwell triumphant; King Charles I captured while trying to escape.

1648: Peace of Westphalia brings Thirty Years War to end.

1649: King Charles I tried by Parliament and executed.

1653: Oliver Cromwell named Lord Protector of England.

1660: Following death of Cromwell, Parliament invites Charles II to return.

1663: Turks invade Transylvania and Hungary.

1667: First use of hand grenades.

1671: Turks declare war on Poland.

c. 1680: Dodo extinct.

1683: Turks begin siege of Vienna; lifted after three months by Polish army. Greatest extent of Ottoman power in Europe.

1688: The "Glorious Revolution" deposes James II of England and brings in William and Mary as king and queen.

1690: Calcutta founded by English in India.

1692: Beginning of Salem witch trials.

1697: Peter the Great of Russia travels Europe in disguise.

1700: Great Northern War begins with Saxon invasion of Livonia.

1701: War of Spanish Succession begins.

1704: Duke of Marlborough wins victory over French and Bavarians at Blenheim.

1706: Marlborough conquers Spanish Netherlands.

1707: England and Scotland united as Great Britain.

1709: Peter the Great defeats Charles XII at Poltava.

1739: Sack of Delhi by Persians.

1740: Frederick the Great introduces freedom of the press and freedom of worship in Prussia.

1756: Britain declares war on France, outbreak of Seven Years War. One hundred British soldiers die in the "Black Hole of Calcutta." Frederick the Great defeats Saxons.

1757: Prussians defeat Austrians at Prague, then are defeated at Kolin, then once again defeat Austrians at Rossback and Leuthen. Robert Clive wins Battle of Plassey in India; beginning of British Empire on the subcontinent.

1759: British take Quebec from France.

1764: Mozart writes his first symphony at the age of eight.

1767: British taxes on American colonies lead to American trade embargo.

1775: Battles of Lexington and Concord begin the American Revolution.

1783: Revolutionary War ends with Treaty of Paris.

1788: French king Louis XVI calls the Estates General for the first time since 1613.

1789: Beginning of French Revolution. George Washington sworn in as first American president.

1793: In France, Louis XVI and Marie Antoinette executed; Reign of Terror begins.

1795: Metric system adopted in France.

1796: French general Napoleon Bonaparte defeats Austrians.

1798: Napoleon campaigns in Italy and Egypt. French fleet destroyed at Alexandria by British captain Horatio Nelson.

1799: Napoleon becomes Consul of France.

1800: Eli Whitney makes the first muskets with interchangeable parts.

1804: Napoleon crowned Emperor in Paris.

1805: Austro-Russian forces defeated by Napoleon at Austerlitz.

1806: Prussia declares war on France and is defeated at Jena and Auerstadt.

1809: British general Arthur Wellesley scores victories against France fighting in Spain.

1812: Napoleon invades Russia. Defeats Russians at Borodino and takes Moscow, but is forced to retreat. United States declares war on Britain. Publication of *Grimm's Fairy Tales*.

1813: In the "Battle of the Nations" at Leipzig, Napoleon defeated.

1814: Napoleon exiled to Elba on April 11. British burn Washington, D.C.

1815: Americans defeat British at Battle of New Orleans after peace has been declared. Napoleon returns to power, subsequently defeated by allied Anglo-Dutch and Prussian armies at Battle of Waterloo.

1821: Simón Bolívar secures Venezuela's independence after defeating Spanish army at Carabobo.

1831: French Foreign Legion founded to help control French possessions in Africa.

1836: Boers begin the "Great Trek" in South Africa.

1837: British queen Victoria begins her reign.

1842: British gain control of Hong Kong after First Opium War.

1843: Maori Wars against Britain begin in New Zealand.

1848: Revolutions in Paris, Venice, Berlin, Milan, Parma, Rome, and Vienna. *Communist Manifesto* published by Karl Marx and Friedrich Engels.

1849: British defeat Sikhs, annex Punjab region in India. Gold Rush begins in California.

1850: Taiping Rebellion in China. The fourteen-year war will result in the deaths of over twenty million people.

1853: Turkey declares war on Russia; beginning of Crimean War. France and Britain join Turkey's side the following year.

1859: British naturalist Charles Darwin's *Origin of the Species* published.

1861: American Civil War begins.

1863: July 1–3: Battle of Gettysburg, turning point of Civil War in favor of Union. French capture Mexico City and set up Archduke Maximilian as Emperor.

1864: Union general Sherman's "March to the Sea" and the burning of Atlanta.

1865: President Abraham Lincoln assassinated. End of the American Civil War.

1866: Alfred Nobel invents dynamite.

1867: Dual monarchy of Austria-Hungary established.

1870: Franco-Prussian War begins. French ruler Napoleon III defeated at Sedan.

1871: France surrenders Alsace-Lorraine to Prussia. German Empire proclaimed.

1876: General George Custer killed at Little Big Horn by Native Americans. Telephone invented.

1877: Russo-Turkish War breaks power of Ottoman Empire in Europe for good.

1879: British massacred by Zulus at Isandlwana in Januray; go on to defeat Zulu king Cetshwayo in July.

1882: British bombard Alexandria, occupy the Suez Canal.

1884: Berlin West Africa Conference kicks off the "Scramble for Africa".

1885: British General Charles "Chinese" Gordon killed at Khartoum.

1888: "Jack the Ripper" murders in London.

1889: Eiffel Tower built in Paris.

1890: Sioux chief Sitting Bull arrested and killed at Pine Ridge. Three hundred more Sioux massacred at Wounded Knee.

1895: First Sino-Japanese War ends with Chinese defeat and installation of a puppet ruler in Korea.

1898: Spanish-American War grants the United States control of Cuba, Puerto Rico, and the Philippines.

1899: Second Boer War begins.

1903: Wright Brothers make their first airplane flight.

1904: Russo-Japanese War ends in surprise Japanese victory.

1912: Balkan Wars between Turkey and Eastern European nations.

1914: June 28: Archduke Franz Ferdinand of Austria assassinated by Serbs in Sarajevo, touching off First World War.

1916: First use of tanks in war.

1917: United States declares war on Germany. Russia's Czar Nicholas abdicates on March 16. Lenin takes power on November 7.

1918: Armistice goes into effect on November 11. Worldwide influenza epidemic begins; by 1920, it will have killed twenty million.

1922: Benito Mussolini forms Fascist government in Italy.

1925: Adolf Hitler publishes Volume 1 of *Mein Kampf.*

1929: Collapse of American stock market, beginning of Great Depression.

1933: Hitler becomes Chancellor of Germany.

1936: Spanish Civil War begins with Francisco Franco's attempted coup.

1937: Japanese take several Chinese cities during Second Sino-Japanese War. Chinese Nationalists and Communists unite to repel the invaders.

1938: Led by Hitler, Germany occupies Austria and the Sudetenland.

1939: Germany invades Poland on September 1, beginning World War II.

1940: Germany invades Denmark, Norway, the Netherlands, Belgium, Luxembourg, and France; German troops enter Paris on June 14. Britain left to stand alone against Nazi threat and the Battle of Britain air campaign.

1941: War in North Africa between Britain and Germany and Italy. Germany invades the

Soviet Union in June. Japan bombs Pearl Harbor on December 7, bringing the United States into the war.

1942: Americans defeat Japanese at Midway. U.S. troops land in North Africa. Germany begins its "Final Solution" by sending millions of Jews to gas chambers.

1943: In the Soviet Union, the Battle of Stalingrad turns tide against Germany. Battle of Kursk in July is the largest tank engagement ever fought. Allies land in Sicily and Italy falls soon afterwards, but is quickly occupied by German troops.

1944: June 6: "D-day", Allied landings in Normandy. The Soviet army launches a major offensive in July, capturing 100,000 Germans at Minsk. Attempt on Hitler's life fails. U.S. invasion of the Philippines.

1945: Okinawa captured. Russians take Berlin and meet Western Allies at the Elbe River. Germany surrenders on May 8. First atomic bomb attacks against Hiroshima and Nagasaki, August 6 and 9. Japan surrenders on August 14, ending the Second World War.

1947: India granted independence, divided into India and Pakistan.

1948: State of Israel proclaimed.

1949: China becomes a Communist republic.

1950: North Korea invades the South on June 25. American Douglas MacArthur commands U.N. forces and retakes Seoul, crosses into North Korea, then is forced to retreat when China enters the war.

1951: Seoul once again taken and lost by North Korea. Border re-established at 38th parallel.

1954: The first volume of *The Lord of the Rings* by J.R.R. Tolkien is published.

1962: Cuban Missile Crisis nearly sets off World War Three.

1964: Escalation of American involvement in Vietnam.

1967: Six-Day War between Israel and Arab nations ends in resounding Israeli victory.

1968: Assassinations of Martin Luther King, Jr. and Robert F. Kennedy. Riots in Paris. Soviet invasion of Czechoslovakia. Tet Offensive in Vietnam.

1971: Indochina conflict expands into Laos and Cambodia.

1972: Arab terrorists kill two Israeli athletes at the Munich Olympic games.

1973: Last U.S. forces withdrawn from Vietnam. The South will fall to the North two years later.

1979: Shah of Iran deposed, Ayatollah Khomeini takes power. Hostages taken at the U.S. embassy in Teheran. Soviets invade Afghanistan.

1980: Iraq invades Iran.

1981: Iranian hostages freed.

1982: Britain defeats Argentina in the Falklands War. Israel invades Lebanon.

1983: 237 U.S. Marines killed in Beirut terrorist bombing.

1988: Pan Am 747 explodes over Lockerbie, Scotland, due to terrorist bomb, killing 270. End of Iran-Iraq War.

1990: Collapse of Soviet Union begins. Iraq invades Kuwait. United States and allies deploy to Saudi Arabia and prepare for war.

1991: Iraq defeated after one-hundred-hour ground war, Kuwait liberated. Warsaw Pact dissolved. Soviet Union officially broken up on December 25.

1993: Terrorists detonate 1,100-pound bomb under World Trade Center; six killed, 1,000 wounded.

1994: Rwandan genocide; at least 800,000 killed. International terrorist "Carlos the Jackal" captured.

1995: November 4: Israeli Prime Minister Yitzhak Rabin assassinated at peace rally by a Jewish extremist.

1998: August 20: U.S. cruise missile attacks on suspected terrorist bases in Afghanistan and chemical weapons factory in Sudan.

2001: September 11: Terrorists hijack and fly three commercial airliners into both towers of the World Trade Center and the Pentagon. A fourth plane crashes in Pennsylvania during a struggle between the passengers and hijackers. Nearly three thousand killed in the largest terrorist attack on American soil in history. Afghanistan invaded October 7.

2003: March 18: Iraq invaded by American forces. Major combat operations declared over by

May 1. Iraqi insurgency begins. Saddam Hussein captured on December 30.

2004: April: First Fallujah marks turning point in perception and tone of war.

2006: Former Iraqi dictator Saddam Hussein executed.

2007: U.S. Coalition casualties for Iraq invasion and occupation top four thousand.

Glossary

A

ARMY: From the Latin *armata*, or "act of arming," a term that describes any land-based military force and sometimes including other branches of service as well. In modern military usage, an army is defined as a group of two or more corps. During the World Wars, the massive scale of the conflicts often saw armies being organized in turn to form Army Groups.

B

BARRAGE: A coordinated mass of artillery fire, often fired indirectly.

BATTALION: In modern military usage, a grouping of multiple companies totaling around one thousand soldiers. The smallest unit considered capable of independent, unsupported action.

BAYONET: A dagger-length blade fitted to the end of a rifle or musket. Originally developed to arm slow-firing guns with a secondary use in close combat, turning the firearm into a spear, the use of bayonet tactics was taught in European-style armies from the mid-seventeenth to the mid-twentieth century.

BEACHHEAD: A small footing gained by an army landing on enemy shores or crossing a river. Often the target of determined counterattacks.

BRIGADE: First developed by Swedish king Gustavus Adolphus during the Thirty Years War, the brigade was originally an early version of a combined arms task force consisting of several regiments of infantry, cavalry, and artillery. Modern usage places the brigade roughly on par with the regiment in terms of size.

C

CALIBER: The diameter of the bore, or inside, of a gun's barrel. Can be expressed in millimeters (i.e., 9 mm) or fractions of an inch (i.e., .50 caliber, meaning half-inch bore).

CAMPAIGN: A series of military operations, often designed towards a single objective.

CAVALRY: Soldiers who move and fight primarily from horseback. Does not generally extend to troops who use mounts to move into battle but dismount to fight, who are instead referred to as "mounted infantry."

CIVILIANS: Also called noncombatants, any non-enlisted person. As war became increasingly driven by industry in the late nineteenth and early twentieth centuries, civilians became targets of armies and the weapons of war.

COLUMN: Defined as a formation in which the files are longer than the ranks. As it is quite vulnerable to flank attacks and enfilade fire, the column is most often used on the march, although at times it has been used, most notably by French Revolutionary armies, as a method of attack.

COMPANY: A military unit consisting of platoons, usually three or four in number, totaling anywhere from 100–200 enlisted men and officers.

CORPS: An organization of two or more divisions, grouped in turn to form armies.

D

DEFILADE: A position that protects a unit from direct enemy fire.

DIVISION: A concept that first emerged during the Seven Years War of the mid-eighteenth century, the division organizes ten to twenty thousand soldiers into a single unit, forming the building block of larger armies and corps. Napoleon Bonaparte was the first general to fully adopt the divisional system; by the end of the Napoleonic Wars, all of Europe's armies would be organized by divisions, as are all modern armies.

E

ENFILADE: Also known as "flanking fire", the condition whereby a unit's flank becomes exposed to enemy fire, exposing troops beyond the front rank.

ENLISTED MAN: A term used in modern military organization to refer to the lowest ranking soldiers, often including non-commissioned officers.

F

FILE: A line of troops standing one in front of another. Multiple files form a column.

FLANK: As a noun, flank is a term used to describe the side of a military unit. As a verb, the action of moving against an enemy's side or rear.

FLYING COLUMN: An *ad hoc* unit created from hand-picked troops, usually all mounted and traveling light, with the express intent of ensuring mobility and speed. Often used during attempted relief operations.

FRONT: Also called a battlefront, this is the point along which two opposing forces meet. The term can be applied to anything from local engagements up to entire theaters of war.

G

GRAPESHOT: Also called cannister, a type of ammunition for cannons that consists of a sack or can filled with metal balls, effectively turning the cannon into a giant shotgun. Designed for use up close against infantry.

GRENADE: An explosive devise originally designed to be hurled by hand, which also sends shards of metal flying through the air.

GRENADIER: Originally applied to soldiers who were trained in the throwing of grenades in the seventeenth century, the term quickly became generalized to apply to a type of elite soldier.

I

INFANTRY: The backbone of most armies throughout history, the infantry is characterized by soldiers who fight and move primarily or exclusively on foot and who are armed with relatively light weapons such as spears or rifles.

IRREGULAR: A soldier trained in non-standard military techniques, often making use of loose, open deployments.

N

NO MAN'S LAND: The ground between opposing forces along a front. Can be anywhere from a few yards to a mile or more in width.

NON-COMMISSIONED OFFICER: Commonly abbreviated NCO, an enlisted man given battlefield authority by a commissioned officer. The most well-known "noncom" rank is sergeant.

O

OFFICER: Also called a commissioned officer, these are individuals vested (or "commissioned") with the ability to issue commands on the battlefield. Up until relatively recently, commissions were commonly bought and sold and did not necessarily reflect actual military skill.

P

PALISADE: A wooden fence, often constructed of tree trunks lined up side by side and sunk into the ground.

PHALANX: Developed by the Ancient Greeks, a mass formation of troops wielding long spears, the phalanx dominated ancient warfare for several centuries.

PLATOON: Originally used to describe a small detachment of men, the platoon evolved into a modern military unit usually consisting of two to four squads totaling thirty to fifty soldiers. Usually led by a low-ranking commissioned officer such as a lieutenant.

R

RANK: A line of soldiers standing shoulder to shoulder. Most regular military units up until the First World War were trained to fight in ranks.

REDOUBT: A small, self-contained fortification, often placed just outside a larger fort and used to guard vulnerable approaches to that structure.

REGIMENT: The first post-feudal military unit, developed as armies became increasingly professional and organized during the sixteenth century. Early regiments often acted as independent military entities, conducting their own recruiting and commissioning their own officers. The modern British Army still has traces of this "regimental system" in its training and deployment of its units. Modern regiments vary widely in size depending on the army and their perceived tactical usefulness and range, anywhere from a few hundred up to three thousand soldiers.

REGULAR: Term used to distinguish trained soldiers who follow commonly accepted forms of military organization and tactical deployment.

S

SQUAD: In modern military organization, the smallest recognized unit on a battlefield, most often consisting of between eight and fourteen soldiers. Called a "section" in British and Commonwealth armies.

STRATEGY: The deployment and movement of large units, from divisions up through entire army groups, to achieve a military goal.

T

TACTICS: Military methods for defeating an enemy in individual battles.

Introduction to the Assyrian Conquests (853 BCE–612 BCE)

The Assyrian Empire was the world's first great empire and the first nation to make warfare and militarism a central facet of its foreign and domestic policies. A force to be reckoned with for over seven centuries, the Assyrian Empire experienced many ups and downs, attaining its greatest heights of power and dominance during the ninth through the seventh centuries BCE before imploding spectacularly, perishing under the booted heel of vengeful conquerors in 612 BCE.

The traditional heartland of Assyria was centered on the Tigris River in what is now northern Iraq. Bordered by the expansionist Hittite Empire to the west and the Babylonians to the south, and constantly harried by nomadic tribes to the north and east, Assyria developed a militaristic culture early on.

The Assyrians took a unique approach to warfare. While other armies of the day traditionally gave preeminence to the swift chariot, the Assyrians deployed heavily armored infantry and ingenious siege engines. Off the battlefield, they relied on a combination of doggedness and intimidation, becoming masters of psychological warfare.

Assyria enjoyed two distinct periods of regional dominance. The first period, often referred to as the Middle Assyrian period, lasted from roughly 1350 to 1200 BCE During this time, Assyria conquered its neighbors, clashed with the Hittites, and annexed the ancient kingdom of Babylon.

In the wake of the collapse of the Hittite Empire, Assyrian ruler Tiglath-Pileser I (1115–1077 BCE) inaugurated a new period of expansionism that saw the Assyrians extend their empire to the Mediterranean coast. A succession of weak rulers temporarily stalled the Assyrian war machine, but by the reign of Ashurnasirpal II (883–859 BCE), the Assyrians were aggressively expanding their empire in every direction. They would continue to do so as a matter of policy for the next two centuries during a period commonly called the Neo-Assyrian Empire.

That period also marks the full flowering of two vastly different aspects of the Assyrian culture. On the one hand, the infamous tools of Assyrian psychological warfare were perfected: the deportations, mass beheadings, and gruesome atrocities, all meant to send a message to those who would oppose the empire's will. On the other hand, Assyrian art, architecture, and learning all reached new heights during the Neo-Assyrian period.

Although known for their warlike society, Assyrians put great emphasis on piety and record keeping. Much of our understanding of Babylonian mythology comes from Assyrian records. Additionally, Assyrians were well known for their grand palaces and feats of engineering: aqueducts and canals watered the capital at Nineveh and the Assyrians were the first to lay a system of paved roads across the Near East to facilitate travel and administration (as well as warfare), a system that served later empires well.

Despite all these triumphs, Babylon remained a thorn in the Assyrians' side; the Babylonians had never accepted foreign rule. After trying a variety of solutions, in 689 BCE the Assyrians finally razed the ancient city of Babylon. It was an extreme measure, even in those extreme times, and Babylon was soon allowed to rebuild.

It was a resurgent Babylon that would lead an allied army against Assyria, sacking the capital of Nineveh (across the river from modern-day Mosul, Iraq) in 612 BCE and bringing a sudden end to what was once the most powerful empire on Earth. The Assyrians built their power on a foundation of terror and retribution, and that is what led directly to their downfall.

The Assyrian Conquests
(853 BCE–612 BCE)

🌐 Major Figures

King Ahab of Israel

Ahab (birth and death dates unknown), king of Israel in the middle of the ninth century BCE, is perhaps best remembered for the Biblical account of his marriage to the Phoenician princess Jezebel and the bloody revolution that eventually resulted from that union. But in his own time, the people of the Near East primarily knew him as one of the twelve allied generals who checked, albeit briefly, the relentless advance of the Assyrian war machine at the Battle of Qarqar.

The Political Climate in Ahab's Time At the time of Ahab's rule, the ancient Hebrew tribes were split into two kingdoms. Ahab ruled Israel, the "Northern Kingdom," which was centered on Samaria, a hilltop city chosen by Ahab's father Omri as the new capital.

Throughout its turbulent history, the Northern Kingdom saw the passage of many "dynasties," many of which only lasted as long as the kingship of one or two kings—in the case of the House of Zimri, all of seven days! Ahab had the fortune to be the son of the founder of one of Israel's more successful dynasties.

During Ahab's life, Israel became a player on the international scene, garnering mention in contemporary Assyrian documents. With its increased recognition came wealth, particularly after Ahab cemented an alliance through marriage with the rich Phoenician city-state of Tyre on the Mediterranean coast. The economic connection to Phoenicia's vast mercantile empire brought fabulous wealth to Samaria. It also brought a religious influence that would eventually spell the doom of the House of Omri.

While Ahab was honoring his wife by constructing a temple to the Ba'al ("lord") of Tyre, most likely the god Melkart, he was also busy shoring up good relations with his many neighbors. The region known as the Levant that today encompasses Israel, the Palestinian territories, Lebanon, Syria, and Jordan was in Ahab's day a patchwork of small kingdoms and city-states. These states had arisen after the fall of the Hittite Empire had left a power vacuum in the region, and they spent most of their time warring with each other.

The most powerful city-state in the region was Damascus, and it was with Damascus that Israel had the most strained relations. Nevertheless, the bickering states had enough of a sense of self-preservation to band together in the face of the approaching Assyrians, whose empire was swiftly overshadowing the region.

Assyria on the Move The Assyrian heartland is in modern-day northern Iraq and was in ancient times surrounded by more powerful nations. Initially as a method of self-preservation, the Assyrians developed the most warlike culture yet seen and began conquering their neighbors. Soon self-preservation turned to greed, and conquest, no longer defensively motivated, became a state policy. By the middle of the ninth century, the Assyrians, who were just entering into their last and greatest phase (the so-called Neo-Assyrian Empire) under Shalmaneser III, had turned their gaze to the fractured Levant.

In one of the earliest examples of psychological warfare and propaganda, Assyria had consciously built a reputation for brutality and cruelty, knowing that a fearsome reputation would more often than not compel potential resisters to surrender without a fight. Of course, this approach can backfire and inspire one's enemies to band together and put up a fierce fight rather than submit—and this is precisely what happened as Shalmaneser marched his armies into Syria.

Ahab and the Battle of Qarqar Strangely, the Old Testament is silent on Israel's participation in the alliance and ensuing battle. Our chief source is an Assyrian *stele* (carved stone monument) that provides detailed lists of the twelve allied armies that stood against the Assyrians at the Battle of Qarqar in 853 BCE

It would appear that Damascus was the leader of the alliance, but Ahab provided a sizeable contribution of

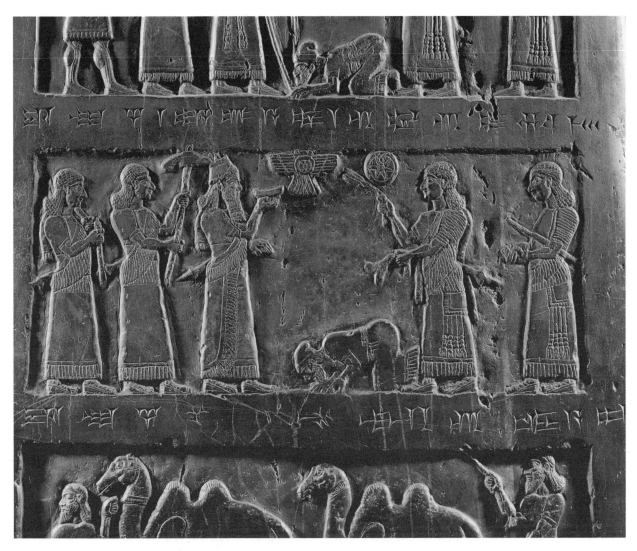

Detail from an Assyrian stele depicting Jehu of Israel paying tribute to King Shalmaneser III.   *Erich Lessing/Art Resource, NY*

troops, about half as many as Damascus. The battle took place near the town of Qarqar on the Orontes River in modern-day Syria. Although the stele makes a claim that the Assyrians emerged victorious, their advance was apparently checked.

It would be another decade before Assyria was able to lay siege to Damascus and begin raiding Israel proper. By that time the alliance of Qarqar had long since disintegrated and the Assyrians soon added the divided city-states of Syria to their growing empire. Israel was next in the line of conquest.

Ahab's Legacy Ahab was long gone by the time Assyria took Israel. He probably died only a few years after Qarqar and was succeeded by his son Ahaziah. The House of Omri disintegrated as the foreign influence, both religious and political, of Ahab's widow Jezebel inspired a bloody revolution led by Jehu, a captain in the Israelite army. Ahab's children were beheaded, Jezebel murdered. Ahab's line was extinguished.

Tiglath-Pileser III

Tiglath-Pileser III (ruled 745–727 BCE) is widely regarded as one of the greatest kings in the centuries-long history of the Assyrian empire. His reign marks a high point for the so-called Neo-Assyrian Empire, both militarily and culturally. Under his leadership Assyria finally defeated the Kingdom of Urartu, their longtime enemy. More importantly, Tiglath-Pileser III reformed Assyria's imperial administration and is the king most likely responsible for creating a network of paved roads and messengers, a network that would outlive the Assyrian Empire by many centuries.

Rise to Power Historians are unsure of Tiglath-Pileser's exact birth date. He came to power in 745 BCE, apparently as a result of a palace coup that overthrew the previous king, Ashur-Nirari V. It is also likely that he took the name Tiglath-Pileser when he ascended to the throne, a common practice in the Assyrian monarchy.

He is also referred to in the Old Testament as Pul, which might have been the name he took when he assumed personal kingship over Babylonia in 729 BCE.

Babylonia Although the Assyrians numbered the ancient state of Babylonia as one of their first conquests, their southern cousins were never comfortable with Assyrian rule. Because of close linguistic and cultural ties, as well as the capital city Babylon's status as a holy place, Assyrian kings were reluctant to deal with the periodic Babylonian revolts in their customarily harsh manner.

When Tiglath-Pileser III assumed the Assyrian crown, Babylonia had been operating in a state of near anarchy for some fifty years. One of the new king's first acts was to take an army south, restore order, and install a new governor. Babylonia was pacified for the time being.

War with Urartu Urartu, also known as the Kingdom of Van, was centered in modern-day Armenia. It had been steadily expanding, taking advantage of a series of weak Assyrian kings and annexing the city-states of Syria. This southern expansion had cut off Assyria's access to the iron mines of Anatolia (modern Turkey). Tiglath-Pileser III prepared an expedition to win back the lost Assyrian territories and finally put an end to his troublesome northern neighbor.

The Assyrians defeated Sarduris, King of Urartu, and his Syrian allies in 742 BCE and the flow of iron from the west was restored. Tiglath-Pileser extracted tribute from the Phoenician city-states of Tyre and Byblos, rich mercantile cities on the Mediterranean coast, and from Israel.

Military Intervention in Judah It was to the Hebrew kingdoms that Tiglath-Pileser next turned his attention. Ever since the death of Solomon in the middle of the tenth century, there had been two kingdoms: Israel in the north and Judah in the south. Israel was by far the dominant one of the pair, enjoying sea access, a lucrative trade relationship with the Phoenicians, and strategic placement on north-south and east-west trade routes.

Judah, landlocked and with a smaller population and less arable land, was poor and often turned to its more powerful neighbors for protection. In 734 BCE, King Ahaz of Judah was feeling sufficiently put-upon by both Israel and the great Syrian city-state of Damascus to appeal to Tiglath-Pileser III for help. The Assyrian king was only too happy to oblige and marched his armies, fresh from their victory over Sarduris, south.

King Pekah of Israel, knowing he could not stand up to the might of Assyria, submitted quickly, but Damascus shut its gates and prepared for a siege. Despite their mastery of siegecraft, it took the Assyrians two years to take the city. When they did, in 732 BCE, they subjected the city to the usual round of atrocities that lay in store for any town that dared oppose Assyria. Damascus was ruined, its independence lost for centuries to come.

Invasion of Urartu With his campaigns in the west wrapped up, Tiglath-Pileser III turned his attention back to Urartu. Although it had lost its southern possessions, the Kingdom of Van still posed a real threat to Assyrian interests. The king led his army into the mountainous north, looting and ravaging the countryside. Some Assyrians may have marched as far north as the Caspian Sea, bringing ruin in their wake as the main force besieged the capital-fortress at Van.

Van never did fall to the Assyrians, but the damage was done. The depredations of the invaders caused a major disruption from which Urartu would never recover. Assyria's northern border was finally secure.

Innovations in the Infrastructure After so many years of campaigning, Tiglath-Pileser III apparently felt it necessary to turn his attention to the upkeep of his vast empire, and he did this ably. Ancient roads were often little better than footpaths, making overland travel slow and difficult. Tiglath-Pileser saw that a speedy and reliable system of roads would make administration much easier and ordered the construction of a network of royal roads, wide lanes paved with limestone.

To this network Tiglath-Pileser added a system of messengers who operated in relays, much like the Pony Express of the Old West. Travel time throughout the empire improved dramatically, and messages could be conveyed to their destinations in days instead of weeks.

This system worked so well that it actually outlived the Assyrian Empire itself, which fell in 612 BCE The later empires of the Near East—the Neo-Babylonians, the Persians, the Macedonian successor states—would continue to use, expand, and improve upon the system developed by Tiglath-Pileser III.

Babylonia Revisited The reign of Tiglath-Pileser III began with trouble in Babylonia and ended the same way. In the 730s BCE, a local usurper named Ukin-zer seized the Babylonian throne and incited an uprising against Assyria. Tiglath-Pileser led his army south one more time and put down the revolt with great severity.

At this point, the Assyrians had tried a variety of solutions to placate the restive Babylonians, such as installing local governors and puppet kings, using government-appointed eunuch viceroys, and so forth. Tiglath-Pileser decided on a new strategy: he had himself crowned King of Babylonia and Assyria, uniting the two thrones for the first time in history.

Ultimately this solution would not work any better than any of the others and Babylonia would continue to be a thorn in Assyria's side, but Tiglath-Pileser III would not be around to see the failure of his last innovation. He died in 727 BCE, two years after taking the Babylonian crown.

Sargon II

The reign of Sargon II (?–705 BCE), king of Assyria from 722 BCE to his death in 705 BCE, marked a continuation

A winged bull from from Nimrud, Assyria.   *Public Domain*

of the growing power of the resurgent Neo-Assyrian Empire. Sargon II's reign looms large in Biblical history, as it marks the end of the ancient Kingdom of Israel and the origin of the tale of the "Ten Lost Tribes."

Sargon the Usurper   All indications point to Sargon II coming to power through a coup, usurping the power of King Shalmanassar V in 722 BCE A close examination of the evidence further indicates that Sargon was most likely not of royal blood, or even a palace insider.

Sargon II, lacking the proper royal pedigree, tried to establish his legitimacy in other ways, starting with the name "Sargon," which literally means "legitimate king" and was the name of the first great Mesopotamian empire builder, a Sumerian who conquered vast swaths of land sixteen hundred years before.

About a decade into his reign, Sargon II even went so far as to build his own capital city, most likely to get

away from the entrenched political factions in the traditional capital of Ashur. Dur-Sharrukin (or "Fort Sargon"), also called Khorsabad, not only became Sargon's refuge but a source of national prestige as well.

Dur-Sharrukin was dominated by the royal palace, a magnificent structure of brick, wood, precious stones and metals, and ivory. The city also featured a magnificent park filled with exotic trees and a variety of temples dedicated to different Assyrian gods. To populate the city, Sargon relocated subjects from around the empire, particularly from recently conquered lands, a common practice in ancient Assyria.

The Destruction of Israel   It was this practice of deportation and resettlement that sealed the fate of the northern Kingdom of Israel and the ten Hebrew tribes who lived within its borders. Although the Old Testament attributes the destruction of Israel to Sargon's predecessor, it is likely that it was Sargon himself who finally captured the Hebrew capital of Samaria and completed deporting the native inhabitants to other parts of the empire.

The legend of the Ten Lost Tribes—the residents of Israel who vanish from the historical record after the Assyrian conquest—has been a source of debate and controversy ever since. Just what happened to the tribes will most likely never be known. What is known is that upon winning the town after a three-year siege, Sargon rebuilt Samaria and resettled it with Syrians and Arabs, who, by melding their own practices with Jewish tradition, became known as the Samaritans.

In 720 BCE, Sargon II also won a major victory in the region at Qarqar, the site of a famous battle that took place over a century earlier when a coalition of twelve local kings had briefly checked the Assyrian advance. Sargon won a decisive victory over another coalition force, this time made up of armies from the states of Arpad, Simirra, Damascus, Samaria, and Hamath. In the wake of the battle the Assyrians found themselves masters of Syria. Sargon made the former Kingdom of Hamath into an Assyrian province.

Expedition in Urartu

After his successful campaigns in Palestine and Syria, Sargon II next turned his attention to that perennial Assyrian enemy, the Kingdom of Urartu. Centered on Lake Van and straddling modern-day Armenia and Turkey, Urartu's rugged terrain and mountaintop fortresses had long challenged would-be Assyrian conquerors.

Sargon's record of his campaign provides a detailed account of how the Assyrians conducted their military expeditions. Recorded in the form of a letter from Sargon to the chief Assyrian god, Assur, the account is written from the perspective of a defender of Urartu observing the Assyrian army as it invades and conquers his land. Whether written by Sargon himself or a creative court scribe, the account's format is without precedent in Assyrian records and makes for a very readable tale.

Launched in 714 BCE, the campaign into Urartu marked Sargon's eighth military undertaking. It was traditional for Neo-Assyrian kings to lead their army on a military expedition once a year, every year of their reign. Sargon chose Urartu as his target that year because the northern kingdom had been weakened by invasions of the Cimmerians, horse nomads who had moved from what is now southern Russia into the region of modern Azerbaijan by the end of the eighth century BCE

Sargon's foe, King Rusas of Urartu, met the Assyrians in battle in a steep-sided mountain valley. Rusas, who had fought a nearly continuous war against Assyria since the days of Tiglath-Pilesser III, was defeated decisively. Put to flight, the king was forced into hiding as Sargon and his army plundered the countryside mercilessly and annexed the territory of Musasir, fixing an annual tribute on the remainder of Urartu from that point on.

Babylonia and the Rise of Merodach-Baladan

Having won a decisive victory in the north, Sargon's next major campaign would be aimed squarely at Babylonia, which had been in open revolt against Assyrian rule since Sargon took the throne. Babylonia, despite sharing extremely close linguistic, cultural, and religious ties with Assyria, had never fully accepted the Assyrians as their imperial overlords and rebellion was a constant problem.

Tiglath-Pilesser III had instituted a dual monarchy, uniting his crown with Babylonia's in an attempt to both placate and awe the Babylonians. The move, like most Assyrian solutions to the "Babylonia problem," proved to be only a temporary fix. In 721 BCE, as Sargon II was busy consolidating his power, a certain Merodach-Baladan led an uprising in Babylonia and was proclaimed king. Merodach-Baladan would prove a persistent foe of the empire for years to come, vexing both Sargon II and his son and heir, Sennacherib, eventually driving Sennacherib to take the extreme measure of razing Babylon completely.

When he took the throne, Sargon decided to let Merodach-Baladan have his kingdom for the time being—there were frontiers to secure and internal rivalries to stamp out before he could take his army south. By 710 BCE, with the west subjugated and Urartu in ruins, Sargon II launched an expedition against Babylon from Dur-Sharrukin. Babylon was taken and Merodach-Baladan was taken prisoner, at least for the time being. The fact that he shows up in later chronicles has led some to speculate that reports of his capture were simply Assyrian propaganda and that the rebel leader had actually fled to the southern swamps at the mouth of the Euphrates.

Assyrian Zenith

Whatever Merodach-Baladan's fate, the year 710 BCE marked the Assyrian Empire's high point. The seven kings of the island of Cyprus submitted tribute to Sargon that year, as did the legendary King Midas of Phrygia, who was having his own trouble with the Cimmerians. All of Assyria's long-time enemies, from Urartu in the north to Egypt in the south, were pacified. Sargon II could look out over an empire at the height of its power and influence.

The manner of Sargon's death is unclear, but it is most likely he fell in battle against the Cimmerians in 705 BCE In his seventeen years as king, Sargon II had expanded the empire and brought his many enemies to heel. Although his reign was cut short, his legacy was safe. His son and heir, Sennacherib, is remembered as an able general and great patron of art and architecture who held on to and expanded upon his father's conquests while simultaneously increasing Assyrian power and prestige.

A photomechanical print of Sennacherib, King of Assyria.
© *Bettmann/Corbis*

Sennacherib

King Sennacherib (ruled 705–681 BCE) was one of the "four great kings" who led Assyria during the last century of that empire's existence. Although he spent most of his reign fighting to hold together the conquests of his father, Sargon II, Sennacherib also managed to turn his capital at Nineveh into one of the jewels of the Near East.

Babylonian Trouble, Part I Although he was not the eldest son, Sennacherib was chosen by his father Sargon II to succeed to the throne of the mighty Assyrian empire. The crown had scarcely been placed on the heir's head when revolts broke out across the region.

Babylonia, that old hotbed of insurrection, rose up against Assyria under the leadership of the would-be king, Merodach-Baladan. The rebellion was put down with little difficulty, although Merodach-Baladan escaped ahead of Sennacherib's army, fleeing to the marshlands of the Persian Gulf.

Rebellion in the West Meanwhile, the petty kingdoms of Syria and Palestine, encouraged by Egypt, refused to pay tribute to the new king and so, having scarcely stamped out one fire, Sennacherib was compelled to march west to extinguish these new blazes of rebellion.

Thanks to the Assyrian mastery of siegecraft, the city-states of Ascalon and Sidon were quickly taken and the Assyrians turned their attention to Judah, the last Hebrew kingdom.

Sargon II had completed the conquest of Israel, long an Assyrian tributary, and deported the "Ten Lost Tribes." Judah, with its capital at Jerusalem, had so far escaped its northern neighbor's fate. After the Assyrians had quickly taken strategically important towns like Lachish, reducing them to smoking ruin, the previously rebellious Judean king Hezekiah proved quite willing to negotiate when Sennacherib showed up at the walls of Jerusalem. He is quoted in the Bible as saying: "I have done wrong. Leave me, and I will pay whatever tribute you impose on me."

An emergency tax was levied and Sennacherib left Judea. He turned his army south, intending to march into Egypt to punish that kingdom for its role in stirring up insurrection. The expedition was a failure, however. It is unknown why his army turned back, although a plague among the troops is the most likely explanation.

Babylonian Trouble, Part II Babylonia, meanwhile, continued to simmer. A second rebellion was quickly put down and Sennacherib installed his son, Assur-nadin-shum, as governor.

Suspecting that the rabble-rouser Merodach-Baladan had stirred up the latest revolt, Sennacherib built a fleet at Nineveh, his capital in the far north on the banks of the Tigris River. He sailed the ships downriver, dragging them overland to the Eurphrates at one point, before reaching the Persian Gulf.

In a series of sea battles, Sennecherib pacified the coastal communities of the Gulf, burning several towns in the process.

Meanwhile, the governorship of the king's son was not working out as planned. Assur-nadin-shum's appointment was just the latest in a long line of Assyrian attempts to find a way to effectively rule Babylonia, attempts that included merging the kingships of Assyria and Babylonia into one. Nothing had worked.

The Destruction of Babylon Assur-nadin-shum was deposed and murdered in 689 BCE. This proved the last straw for Sennecherib, who assembled an army and marched on the holy city of Babylon. The cultural pre-eminence that Babylon enjoyed in the ancient world, as well as the close linguistic and religious ties the Assyrians had to their southern cousins, had spared the city the full wrath of the empire. No longer. Sennecherib took the city, razed it to the ground, and flooded it, proclaiming that it could not be rebuilt for at least eighty years.

This action shocked the ancient world. Babylon was once the seat of a great empire itself and still maintained a reputation as a major cultural center and seat of learning. Nevertheless, Sennecherib's extreme action accomplished what none of his predecessors' efforts had. The smoldering embers of Babylonian revolution were finally extinguished.

ASSYRIAN ALABASTER RELIEFS

The ancient Assyrians are famous for their great carved stone reliefs. A standard element of palatial decoration during the Neo-Assyrian Empire (ninth to seventh centuries BCE), these stone reliefs were originally painted in bright, garish colors, the better to stand out in the dimly-lit palace corridors where they were hung.

Beards and hair were painted pitch black, blades and tongues bright red. Other colors used included rich blues and stark whites. Traces of the paint still linger in the deeper grooves on the carved surfaces. The rest has been scoured away by the elements and the ravages of time.

Although the reliefs often depicted kings returning from conquest or conferring with bird-headed gods, the best known Assyrian reliefs depict massive winged bulls with human heads. Commonly called *lamia* or *cherubim*, these monstrous creatures tower above the viewer in stately silence. They were often found guarding gates and entryways and they certainly do make for intimidating guardians.

In the end, the lamia could not hold back the collapse of the Assyrian Empire. Buried in sand, the carvings would lay undisturbed until the nineteenth and twentieth centuries CE, when European archaeologists dug them up and shipped them back to their museums in London, New York, Paris, and Berlin, where most of them remain to this day.

The Glory of Nineveh   Although he earned his reputation as a ruthless general, Sennecherib was also responsible for one of the greatest cultural projects of the Neo-Assyrian period: the rebuilding of Nineveh.

Long a cult center of the goddess Ishtar, Nineveh had enjoyed a rather scholarly reputation before Sennecherib chose it as his new capital. Once established in the city, the king undertook a massive overhaul of the ancient town. He expanded and strengthened the walls, building fifteen magnificent gates to provide access. In one of the great engineering feats of the time, he built an aqueduct twenty-five miles long to bring fresh water from the hills into the city.

Buildings were knocked down to accommodate new street construction, turning dark and twisting alleyways into sunlit avenues. The city was suddenly dotted with grand plazas, parks, and orchards. Through the city, running in a straight line, was a broad ceremonial boulevard paved with bright limestone.

Sennecherib's palace sprawled over eight acres and featured botanical and zoological gardens and man-made wetlands stocked with cranes and wild pigs for hunting.

A Violent End, A Violent Legacy   Like many who came before him and many who would come after him, Sennecherib both lived by the blade and died by it. In

681 BCE, he was stabbed to death while at prayer by two of his sons. The Bible describes the incident: "When he was worshiping in the temple of his god Nisroch, his sons Adram-melech and Sharezer slew him with the sword and fled into the land of Ararat."

Evidently the motivation was jealousy of the heir-apparent, Esar-haddon, who did indeed become king upon his father's death.

Sennecherib's legacy lived on in the grandiosity of Nineveh, which would remain the capital of the empire right up until the fall of Assyria in 612 BCE, when the city was burned and leveled by an allied army that included a resurgent Babylonia thirsty for vengeance.

Ashurbanipal

Ashurbanipal (ruled c. 668–626 BCE) was the last great king of Assyria. One of that Empire's few scholarly kings, the documents collected in his library are responsible for most of the knowledge concerning the culture and history of the region. Ashurbanipal's military campaigns, although successful in the short-term, ultimately began a series of events that would see the mighty Assyrian Empire in ruins a mere fourteen years after his death.

Like most Assyrian kings, Ashurbanipal was adept at the military arts, being skilled in the sword, spear, and bow and arrow, as well as hunting and falconry. He differed from many of his predecessors, however, by demonstrating the other legendary "divine" quality of the Assyrian king: wisdom. His love of learning and his cultural innovations earned him widespread fame, such that the Greeks would remember him—as King Sardanapalus—centuries after his death.

Campaigns   Like all Assyrian kings, Ashurbanipal's reign is marked with one military campaign after another. His first task was to subjugate the Phoenician island-city of Tyre, which had been withstanding a siege laid by Ashurbanipal's father, Esarhaddon. The city surrendered shortly after the new king took the throne and the Assyrian Empire added both the rich city-state and territories in northern Syria to its ever-expanding borders.

The other conflict inherited from Esarhaddon was with Egypt, a recent addition to the empire. The deposed pharaoh, Tarku, had returned and led an uprising that Esarhaddon had been unable to put down before his death.

Ashurbanipal assembled a massive army, drawing troops from twenty-two provinces and sent Tarku fleeing south to Nubia once again as his army sacked and razed the city Thebes, carrying off the riches of the ancient capital.

However, Egypt was not pacified—the governors the king installed soon stirred their Egyptian subjects to revolt and Ashurbanipal had to return yet again, sacking the cities of Sais, Mendes, and Tanis in the usual thorough Assyrian fashion. One of the Egyptian rebels, Necho, so impressed Ashurbanipal that he was appointed regional governor. Necho would later lead an Egyptian army in support of the crumbling Assyrian Empire in 612 BCE.

Closer to home, Ashurbanipal would spend much of his time fighting in the south of his empire, in and around Babylonia, that perennial source of trouble and rebellion. The king's adversary came in the form of his brother, Shamash-shum-ukin, who had been named governor of Babylonia by Esarhaddon.

Shamash-shum-ukin attempted to stir up revolt in Babylonia, but his attempt failed. Only managing to gain the support of the king of Elam, who just as quickly abandoned him, Shamash-shum-ukin chose to die in the flaming wreckage of his palace in Babylon as Ashurbanipal took the city after a long, brutal siege. Ashurbanipal took the Babylonian crown, taking the name of Kandalanu in 647 BCE after his brother's failed revolt and then turned his attentions to Elam.

Centered on the city of Susa and perched at the edge of the Iranian plateau, Elam had long served as a buffer region against the nomads and hillmen of the east, the expanding country of the Medes in particular. In a series of campaigns, Ashurbanipal destroyed Elam, but in so doing he eliminated this buffer. This would have dire consequences for the empire after his death.

Disappointing Legacy Despite his long reign, and his status as the last great Assyrian king, Ashurbanipal left his empire on the edge of collapse. The legacy of learning Ashurbanipal attempted to establish died with him—the chronicles of Assyrian history end with Ashurbanipal, leaving great gaps in the record of his two successors, the last kings of Assyria. Within fourteen years of his death, the Assyrian capital of Nineveh would lay in ruins due in large part to events that played out during his reign.

There were indications of trouble even before the end of Ashurbanipal's time on the throne. Egypt would rise in revolt shortly before his death. The destruction of Elam left Assyria wide open to invasion by the Medes, who would ally with the Babylonians and bring down the greatest empire the world had yet seen.

⊕ Major Battles

Qarqar, 853 BCE

Sometime in the year 853 BCE near the town of Qarqar in modern-day Syria, a coalition of twelve allied kings fielded their combined armies in a bid to stop the relentless advance of a war machine that was threatening to absorb their corner of the Near East. The Assyrian Empire was on the march, and had set its eyes on the squabbling city-states of the Levant (modern Syria, Jordan, Israel, Palestine and Lebanon). The Battle of Qarqar would mark a point where the seemingly unstoppable Assyrian army and the ambitions of its king were

---

THE FIRST LIBRARY

In the seventh century BCE Ashurbanipal founded the first actual library in the world, stocked with shelves and shelves of clay tablets on a wide range of subjects. It was a systematically collected selection of material, put together by one of Assyria's few literate kings.

Ashurbanipal's library collection—with subjects ranging from word lists to bilingual vocabularies to Babylonian literature like the EPIC OF GILGAMESH—proved instrumental in modern deciphering of cuneiform (an ancient form of writing) and in preserving ancient Babylonian myths and stories.

---

checked, and the Assyrian domination of the region delayed by about a century.

The town of Qarqar (also spelled Karkar) was located on the Orontes river in the Kingdom of Hamath, one of many small kingdoms and city-states that dotted the Levant in the ninth century BCE. The various kings of this region spent most of their military efforts in petty wars with each other, but as the Assyrian Empire entered a new phase of expansionism, the wisdom of presenting a united front must have become obvious.

Present knowledge of the alliance, down to the relative amount of troops each king provided, is owed to the Assyrians, who were inveterate record keepers. An Assyrian *stele*, or carved stone monument, commemorates the battle and presents a roll call of the various enemies faced by the would-be conquerors. The stele lists approximate numbers for each allied faction, but these are almost certainly inflated. What we can determine, however, is who fought at the battle and the relative number of troops they contributed.

The Alliance The leader of the coalition, and the faction with the biggest individual contribution of troops, was the city-state of Damascus, led by King Hadadezer I. Damascus was the greatest local power in the region outside of the Phoenician city of Tyre, which stayed out of the battle. Several Phoenician cities did send troops, however: Byblos, Irqata, Arvad, Usanat, and Siannu are all listed on the stele with minor contributions to the army—the Phoenicians' strength lay in their navies, not their armies.

The two biggest contributions to the allied effort after Damascus were courtesy of King Irhuleni of Hamath—whose land was being most directly threatened, after all—and King Ahab of Israel. Israel's army was about half the size of the Damascene force.

Composition of the Assyrian Army The king would have personally commanded the Assyrian army that met this motley alliance on the field of battle in 853 BCE, with the assistance of a field marshal whose job it was to

Relief from the palace of Sennacherib shows Assyrians impaling Jewish defenders of Lachish after the fall of the city. *Erich Lessing/ Art Resource, NY*

coordinate the fifty-man companies that made up the overall force. Each company, commanded by a mace-wielding officer, was further broken down into groups of ten men. This level of organization and discipline was one of the keys of Assyrian success.

The well-drilled, disciplined infantry formed the backbone of the Assyrian army, a rarity in the days of armies dominated by massed chariots. The Assyrians did employ chariots as well, but assigned them a supporting role.

The bulk of the infantry was armed with a variety of weapons, from spears to swords to battle-axes. They were supported by teams of archer-spearmen: a trio of warriors, one armed with a bow as tall as himself, another armed with a shield large enough for the archer to hide behind, and a third armed with a spear in case the enemy got too close for arrows.

This attention to mutual defense reflects another key to Assyrian success at Qarqar and elsewhere: the relatively high priority the army put on protecting its troops. The development of armor in battle was a slow process due to its expense, and most armies at the time were very lightly armored as a result. But even the lowliest skirmisher in the Assyrian army wore hardened leather, and the main infantry troops were often provided with "scale" armor, a type of metallic armor

resembling fish scales, as well as distinctive conical metal helmets that increased the soldiers' apparent height while providing protection.

Qarqar: Its Outcome and Consequences Perhaps it was due to the fact that there were twelve enemy kings to target that the Assyrians were not able to secure a decisive victory at Qarqar. Their stele claims the battle was a victory, but the actions of Shalmaneser's army after the battle and Assyrian activity in the region for the next decade would suggest that, at best, the battle was fought to a stalemate.

In light of the apparent invincibility of the Assyrian army, a draw is perhaps the best result the allies could have realistically expected. In the end, Qarqar merely delayed the Assyrians in their bid to become masters of the region, which they gradually accomplished over the next 150 years, picking off one territory after another.

Lachish, 701 BCE

The Battle of Lachish provides a detailed example of the Assyrian method of taking a fortified city, as well as what fate awaited those unfortunate people whose stone walls proved insufficient in the face of the Assyrian war machine.

King Sennacherib invaded the Hebrew kingdom of Judea, a subordinate state that had risen in revolt, in 701 BCE. Judea's capital of Jerusalem was best approached from the coast; Lachish was a fortified town that guarded the passes leading to the highlands around Jerusalem. It would need to be taken before Sennacherib could besiege the Judean capital.

Knowledge of the siege of Lachish comes from an abundance of sources from both sides involved. The Old Testament refers to the siege in two places, and there are several accounts in Assyrian annals, as well as a detailed carved relief from Nineveh that portrays the course of the siege in sequential art, like an early graphic novel.

Assyrian military operations emphasized speed. The Assyrians preferred to take cities through guile and diplomacy if possible. Failing that, an attempt to take the city by quick assault would follow. Lachish apparently resisted both these methods, as the Assyrians were obliged to settle in for a long siege.

Jerusalem While the main army was besieging Lachish, a detachment of Assyrian soldiers bypassed the city and made its way to Jerusalem. The account in the Old Testament provides an example of another aspect of Assyrian siegecraft, in which an officer positions himself outside the city and shouts a message aimed at the garrison within, trying to persuade them to open the city gates without a fight. According to the Bible, the Assyrians shouted this message from Sennecherib: "Now do not let Hezekiah deceive you and mislead you like this. Do not believe him, for no god of any nation or kingdom has been able to deliver his people from my hand or the hand of my fathers. How much less will your god deliver you from my hand!"

Although the people of Jerusalem did not open their gates, King Hezekiah did open up a dialogue with Sennecherib that eventually resulted in payment of an emergency tribute to the Assyrians in exchange for a cessation of hostilities. Unfortunately for the citizens of Lachish, this tribute would not be delivered in time to save their city or themselves.

The Course of the Siege

As the Assyrians approached Lachish, they met a column of refugees offering tribute—most likely people from the surrounding countryside who were unwilling or unable to hole up behind the walls of the city.

Following standard procedure, the Assyrians assaulted the town as soon as they arrived. Archers and slingers provided covering fire as the heavily armored Assyrian infantry moved up to the walls with ladders and armored tower/battering rams. The defenders of Lachish would most likely have defended their walls with "wolves"—looped lengths of chain meant to catch the heads of battering rams—and fire in the form of boiling liquids and flaming arrows.

The initial assault failed and the engineers set to building a ramp, a tactic occasionally practiced by the Assyrians that involved heaping earth up against a portion of the enemy wall, slowly creating an inclined pathway to the top of the battlements.

As they built their ramp, the engineers were protected by archer teams who fired from behind shield-bearers holding massive shields the size of a man. The archers' bows themselves were nearly the same size and had terrific range and power. It was the archers' job to use their powerful bows to sweep the battlements clear of defenders and allow the engineers to do their job.

The ramp was eventually completed and the Assyrian army, probably led by covered battering rams to knock away any last remaining bit of wall, flooded into the city. At modern-day Tell ed-Duweir, the probable site of Lachish, the ramp can be seen even today, leading up to the artificial mound that marks the foundation of the former city. The grass-covered artificial hill seems peaceful now, but archaeologists have uncovered hundreds of arrowheads at the point where the ramp meets the mound—the defenders of Lachish did not give in without a fierce fight.

They fought fiercely not simply out of honor or duty, but because they were no doubt aware of the fate that awaited them if the Assyrians took the town. The Assyrians did take the town, and the fate of the defenders is well chronicled in Assyrian carvings.

The Defenders' Fate

The Assyrian stele commemorating the siege shows wagons laden with booty and columns of captive citizens being led off, back to Assyria, as the town leaders are skinned alive at the roadside. A

HADADEZER, KING OF DAMASCUS

Hadadezer (birth and death date unknown), also known as Adad-Idri to the Assyrians or Ben-Hadad II to the Hebrews, was the leader of the coalition that fought the Assyrians at Qarqar in 853 BCE All three versions of his name refer to the god Hadad, a storm god analogous to the ancient Greek god Zeus.

Damascus was the preeminent local power in the region at the time of Qarqar, and Hadadezer fought to keep it so. After leading the coalition that checked the Assyrian advance, he fought at least six more battles against Shalmaneser, sometimes with his ally King Irhuleni of Hamath and sometimes on his own.

His willingness to stand up to the Assyrian advance, along with his crafty diplomatic skills, ensured the survival of Damascus as an independent state for another century.

The Hadadezer who fought at Qarqar was *not* the same Hadadezer who fought King David and the Israelites in the Old Testament.

nearby cave recently excavated by archaeologists was found to contain 1500 skulls, likely the remains of beheaded defenders of Lachish.

After capture, the captives were taken before Sennecherib, where some are shown in the carving begging for their lives while their compatriots simultaneously have their throats slit. Those who managed to survive this hellish experience were most likely doomed to a life of slavery.

Nineveh, 612 BCE

The fall of Nineveh in 612 BCE marked the effective destruction of the Assyrian Empire. The end came quickly and, for the Assyrians at least, unexpectedly. In less than a decade the greatest empire the world had yet seen fell from its position of dominion into utter ruin and oblivion.

The Importance of Nineveh

Nineveh, due to its central importance towards the end of the empire, is often thought of as the traditional Assyrian capital, but in fact Assyrian kings had largely ignored the city until the last century of the Neo-Assyrian period. Prior to the residency of the great king Ashurbanipal, the city was most well-known as a cult center of the goddess Ishtar.

The king most responsible for transforming Nineveh into the political center of the empire was Sennacherib, who turned the city into an urban jewel crisscrossed with broad avenues, wide plazas, magnificent palaces, and rich temples. He also strengthened and expanded the city's walls, making it, in common estimation, virtually impregnable.

The walls traced an eight-mile perimeter and were up to 150 feet thick in places. Sin-sharra-ishkun, the

Relief from the palace of Sennacherib shows a warrior wearing the distinctive Assyrian peaked helmet. *Erich Lessing/Art Resource, NY*

Assyrian king who would witness the crumbling of the empire, had just a few years before the fall of the city reinforced and repaired the walls, making them stronger than ever.

The walls featured fifteen gates, each a miniature fortress in its own right. The so-called Shamash Gate has been completely excavated and provides an excellent example of the sort of defenses that surrounded each entrance to the city: the fifteen-foot-wide gate was protected by six towers built of mud and fired bricks and faced with limestone slabs. Crenellated battlements topped the towers and the approach to the gate was broken up by two moats.

Babylonian Resurgence

Babylonia had long been a hotbed of insurrection and discontent. Sennecherib was so exasperated with the region, he had the capital city, Babylon, razed in 689 BCE. Such was the importance of Babylon as a religious and cultural center that the city was allowed to rebuild after Sennecherib's death in 681 BCE By 626 BCE the city was once again up to its old tricks, as a succession of weak Assyrian kings had allowed the Babylonians to form a new breakaway government, the so-called Chaldean dynasty, under the leadership of Nabopolassar.

The Assyrians moved to suppress the rebellion, ushering in nearly a decade of warfare. Although a majority of Babylonian cities had supported Assyrian rule, the ensuing wars against the Chaldeans, with the attendant famine and misery that they spread, pushed more and more people toward siding with Nabopolassar.

A letter from an official in the Babylonian town of Nippur shows how desperate things were getting for the pro-Assyrian faction: "The king well knows that people hate us everywhere on account of our allegiance to Assyria. We are not safe anywhere; wherever we might go we would be killed. People say, 'Why did you submit to Assyria?' We have now locked our gates tight and do not go out of town . . . ."

By the year 616 BCE, Nabopolassar had rallied most of the towns in southern Mesopotamia to his cause. The army he now led constituted a major threat to Assyrian power, a threat that was ably demonstrated at the Battle of Gablini, when, after a march up the Euphrates River, the Chaldeans and their allies defeated the Assyrian army.

Sensing weakness, an army of Medes, hill people from the Iranian plateau, invaded Assyria that same year and defeated another Assyrian army at Arrapkha, near Kirkuk in modern-day Iraq.

Such was the threat constituted by the resurgent Babylonians that the Egyptians, another traditional enemy of Assyria who had been partially subjugated by the empire only fifty years before, pledged their support to Sin-sharra-ishkun and sent units to his army while they began assembling an army of their own.

Thus reinforced, Sin-sharra-ishkun marched his army south again, attempting to corral Nabopolasser's army as it marched back down the Euphrates. The Chaldeans made it to Tikrit ahead of the Assyrians and took shelter behind its walls. The Assyrians assaulted the city for ten straight days, but were unable to dislodge the Babylonian forces within. The Assyrians were forced to withdraw.

Meanwhile, the Medes were still on the move. In 614 BCE, under the leadership of Cyraxes, they sacked the ancient Assyrian capital of Ashur. Nabopolasser, arriving at the scene of the battle as the city crumbled in flames, struck a formal alliance with Cyraxes.

The End Draws Near

Despite these setbacks, all indications are that the Assyrians did not sense their impending doom. The year after the sacking of Ashur, the Assyrians forced the allied army south, with Sin-sharra-ishkun pursuing them all the way. Meanwhile, back in the home country, life went on as usual. An indication of how lightly the Babylonian-Medean threat was taken can be seen in the fact that the defenses of a key fortress on the Assyrian border were dismantled that year to begin a series of renovations on the structure.

Nonetheless, the allied Babylonian-Medean army, after the setbacks of 613 BCE, was ready to march north again in 612 BCE. Along with it marched the so-called

The massive walls of Nineveh. *Randy Olson/National Geographic/Getty Images*

"tribal hordes," hillmen and horse nomads (most likely Scythians) bent on vengeance and plunder.

Nineveh Falls The city of Nineveh was besieged for three months. The Assyrians, masters and innovators of advanced siegecraft, found themselves victimized by the very tactics they had pioneered. It has been theorized that the Babylonians finally gained access to the city by breaking the dams on the Khosr River, which had been diverted around the city. The resulting flood would have knocked holes in the otherwise impenetrable walls.

The Babylonian Chronicle, a series of tablets recording ancient Babylonian history, describes Nineveh as being "turned into a ruin heap." The government fled and Sin-sharra-ishkun vanished from history.

The probable crown prince, Ashur-uballit II, holds the dubious honor of being the last king of Assyria. His government retreated to the city of Harran, where it languished for another four years, rulers in nothing more than name.

The Assyrian Empire, held together by bonds of violence and terror, disintegrated nearly overnight. For its part in supporting Assyria, Egypt suffered as well. Sending their main army north in 610 BCE, the Egyptians under the leadership of Pharaoh Necho II defeated a Judean army at Megiddo. The Egyptians then met up

with the remnants of the Assyrian army, which by this point had been ousted from Harran and had retreated to Carchemish. The allied Egyptian-Assyrian army was defeated once and for all in 605 BCE by the legendary Babylonian king, Nebuchadrezzer II. The Assyrian empire completely ceased to exist at this point, and Egyptian power in the ancient Near East was ended for good as well.

With no lofty kings or imperial riches to encourage their growth, the great cities of Assyria were soon abandoned. By the time of the rise of the Persian Empire, a little over a century later, the Assyrian Empire was but a memory, its once great palaces and cities reduced to ghostly ruins.

⊕ Key Elements of Warcraft

Siege Warfare

The Assyrians hold a place in history and the popular imagination as a warlike society and as one of the most aggressively militaristic empires of all time. Perhaps most emblematic of the Assyrian war machine was the revolutionary new brand of siege warfare developed and refined

This Neo-Assyrian relief shows Assyrian warriors scaling a city wall with ladders. *Erich Lessing/Art Resource, NY*

by the empire over several centuries. The Assyrians' contribution to siegecraft long outlived their own empire.

The Near East boasts the oldest known walled city, Jericho, which was enclosed by a stone wall as early as the ninth millennium BCE It should come as no surprise, then, that the armies of the region had been working out systems for conquering walled cities since before the dawn of recorded history.

As the Assyrian Empire rose to power in the first millennium BCE, the conventional method for taking a walled city was to simply surround it and starve it out, or to somehow make contact with a traitor within the walls and persuade him to open the gates. The problem was, starving a garrison could take years if the city was placed over a deep well and well stocked with provisions.

The Assyrian military philosophy prized speed in all things, and it was probably their desire to extend this philosophy into the realm of sieges that led to their revolutionary developments.

Assyrian Engineers The Assyrian army always marched with a unit of dedicated engineers. They existed almost exclusively to ensure speedy and successful sieges, but they could also be of use on the march. The engineer unit, like military engineers of today, cut roads through hostile wilderness and constructed pontoon bridges over otherwise unfordable rivers.

The engineers marched in what was probably the first dedicated "siege train," a column of wagons laden with materials for besieging enemy fortifications. Thus, the army could come off the march and lay siege to a city or fortress almost immediately. And once the siege began, the true power of the corps of engineers would be revealed.

Siege Weapons and Tactics Building on Sumerian and Babylonian ideas, the Assyrians developed a variety of new weapons and tactics for dealing with seemingly impregnable walls. Perhaps best known of these new inventions was the "ramming tower," a sort of primitive tank featuring a covered battering ram with a tower on top. The ram would be wheeled up to the perimeter of the fortification and could be elevated to attack different heights of the wall. The tower would be stocked with a unit of archers who would pour arrows onto the defenders on top of the wall. The whole construction was covered with leather or animal hides to provide protection to the crew working the ram.

Sometimes before launching an assault, an officer would approach to within hailing distance of the threatened town and shout to the soldiers of the garrison within, exhorting them to ignore their leader and open the gates. Thanks to the Assyrians' fearsome reputation for atrocities, this often worked.

Assuming a deal could not be reached and the city or fortress held out against the initial assault, the Assyrians would settle in for a siege. Engineers would begin tunneling under the walls in an effort to undermine their foundations. Archers would fire flaming arrows into the city to sow panic and disorder. If the wall had wooden gates (as most did), a brave unit of engineers would rush forward under fire from the defenders and try to set the gates alight.

A tactic that was sometimes employed to great effect, as at Lachish, Judea, in 701 BCE, was to build a great earthen ramp up against the side of the wall. This would be done under constant harassment from the defenders and at great risk, but if the ramp was completed it virtually ensured an Assyrian victory, as it would allow the invaders to simply run up and over the walls themselves. Nearly eight hundred years after Lachish, the Romans took another Jewish fortress, Masada, using the exact same tactic. The earthen ramp was a favorite of the Romans, the ancient world's other great masters of the siege.

Every ancient empire that followed the Assyrians, from the Babylonians to the Persians to the Macedonian successor states and beyond, all used and improved upon the siege techniques pioneered by the Assyrians. Many of their basic siege tactics were still being practiced long into the Middle Ages, two millennia after the last inhabitants of a walled town quailed at the sound of an approaching Assyrian army.

This bas-relief from the palace of Nimrod shows an Assyrian battering ram assaulting a city's walls as the archers in its tower rain arrows on the defenders.   *Erich Lessing/Art Resource, NY*

⊕ Impact of the Assyrian Empire

The Assyrian Empire left its mark on world history in many ways, but it is most remembered today as brutal and militaristic. The Assyrians did indeed make their presence felt through war—and it was through war that they sealed their own doom—but they were also responsible for establishing systems of administration and scholarship that would be emulated by almost every empire that followed them.

Perhaps the best example of this is the Assyrian road network. A system of paved roads that connected one end of the empire to the other and a whole corps of messengers to ride those roads in relays allowed for swift communication and administration, as well as rapid movement of armies in times of unrest. Every successful ancient empire, from the Persians to the Romans, would emulate this system.

The Assyrians, although not necessarily great scholars themselves, also made major contributions to the world of learning. The first ever systematically collected library was located in the Assyrian capital of Nineveh, and it is thanks to Assyrian records that we know much of ancient Near Eastern history and mythology, as well as details of economic and domestic life. All was carefully preserved on clay tablets. The clay tablets themselves, many of which were bilingual vocabularies, enabled archaeologists in the nineteenth century CE to decode ancient cuneiform writing, thus unlocking the secrets contained within.

One area of science in which the Assyrians did excel was engineering. Nineveh, for example, was protected by a double bank of walls eight miles in circumference and received its water from an aqueduct twenty-five miles long, a major feat of engineering in its day.

Of course, what Assyrian engineers are perhaps best remembered for is their military endeavors. The Assyrians were masters of siegecraft and introduced techniques never before seen that were to play an integral part in sieges for centuries to come. Prior to the Assyrians, walled towns were virtually impregnable. The only option for the would-be besieger was often simply surrounding the city and starving the inhabitants, a costly proposition. The Assyrian innovations—especially siege towers and battering rams—suddenly made siege warfare much more viable and made town walls seem a lot less reassuring.

Assyrians also introduced psychological warfare to the military world. Assyrian kings preferred to acquire territories through diplomacy. When this proved unfeasible, the army would march forth and besiege an enemy town, often choosing a site that would be relatively easy to take. Upon taking the town, the Assyrians would engage in all manner of atrocities, beheading, impaling, flaying, and roasting the luckless townsfolk. Any survivors would then be sent into a life of slavery, save for one or two who would be sent off to the enemy capital to report in gruesome detail the fate that befell his town. Meanwhile, in perhaps the first recorded examples of wartime propaganda, the Assyrians would carve a record of their deeds and erect it at the site of the siege so travelers would read the news and carry it abroad.

In this way the Assyrians consciously cultivated their fearsome reputation, knowing that more often than not they could force a potential enemy to surrender without a fight for fear of suffering the full wrath of their army.

But in many ways, the fate of the Assyrian Empire impact can be taken as an example of what not to do—their record of atrocities inspired coalitions to form against them, as at the Battle of Qarqar in 853 BCE. Their administration of conquered provinces diverted all surplus wealth to Assyria and offered little in return, resulting in an almost continuous stream of insurrections and plots against the empire, especially in Babylon, a hotbed of unrest whose periodic uprisings vexed Assyrian kings throughout the whole of the empire's history. Many later empires, the Roman Empire in particular, would take this to heart, administering their subjects with a gentle hand whenever possible.

BIBLIOGRAPHY

Books

Boardman, Johns, et al., eds. *Cambridge Ancient History, 2nd Edition, Volume III, Part 2.* Cambridge: Cambridge University Press, 1991.

The Holy Bible. Anaheim, CA: Foundation Publications, 2001.

Perry, Marvin, Joseph R. Peden and Theodore H. Von Laue, eds., *Sources of the Western Tradition, Vol. I: From Ancient Times to the Enlightenment*, 2nd ed., Boston: Houghton Mifflin, 1991.

Introduction to the Greek-Persian Wars (490 BCE–479 BCE)

From 490 to 479 BCE, the scattered city-states of Greece clashed with the mighty empire of Persia in a series of encounters that saw the emergence of Greek military dominance and a unified Grecian culture.

The origins of the Persian Wars lay in the support offered by Athens to Greek rebels in Western Anatolia (modern-day Turkey) in a region known as Ionia, which was part of the Persian Empire.

The Persian king, Darius I, incensed at foreign intervention in what he saw as an internal issue, was determined to teach the upstart Greeks a lesson. Landing at Marathon in 490 BCE, the Persians were defeated by Greek hoplites, heavily armored citizen-soldiers—the first time a Western force had emerged victorious over an Eastern army.

Darius died soon after the defeat at Marathon, but his son and successor, Xerxes, vowed to carry on his father's mission and conquer Greece. In 480 BCE, he raised a massive army, numbering anywhere from 100,000 to 1,000,000 men (ancient sources are vague, but there can no doubt that it was the largest army assembled up to that point) and prepared an impressive fleet of some 1,200 ships.

It was at the pass of Thermopylae, a tiny strip of land between the mountains and the sea, where Xerxes' army first came up against Greek resistance. A tiny force (albeit somewhat larger than the 300 of legend), led by King Leonidas of Sparta, blocked the way, buying time for the rest of the Greek army to prepare for the invasion. The Persians spent three days trying to break through the Spartan lines with wave after wave of frontal assaults. In the end, they outflanked and overran the Greek position. Leonidas and his men fought to the last.

Meanwhile, the mighty Persian fleet had encountered storms and battle losses that reduced its number nearly by half. It was, nevertheless, still a force to be reckoned with, and much of Greece, including Athens, fell to the advancing Persians.

A brilliantly executed, improbable Greek victory at Salamis seemed to turn the tide in the Greeks' favor, but Xerxes felt confident enough of the Persian position to take half his army and return home, leaving his brother-in-law Mardonius to finish off the Greeks the following year. Instead, Mardonius went down to death and defeat at Plataea (479 BCE), and the Persians were forced out. The Greeks and Persians continued to have skirmishes for thirty more years, but the Persians never again landed on the Greek mainland. In 449 BCE, war-weary Athens struck the Peace of Callias, which marked a formal end to hostilities with Persia.

Plataea marked the beginning of the Classical Era of Greece. Athens took up the war against Persia on distant shores, building a maritime empire even as it rebuilt its war-torn city. Meanwhile, across Greece the wars had created a new sense of shared culture and heritage known as *Hellas*.

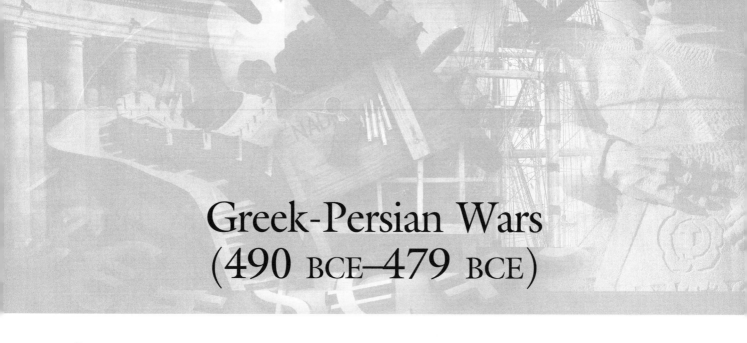

Greek-Persian Wars (490 BCE–479 BCE)

🌐 Major Figures

Darius

When Darius I (549 BCE–486 BCE) became king of the Persian Empire in 522 BCE, he inherited an empire in transition.

The Rise of the Persian Empire Although the Persians, who called themselves Irani, were an ancient people, the Persian Empire was quite new. Officially founded in 547 BCE by Cyrus the Great after his successful rebellion against the Medean Empire, the Persian Empire had grown by leaps and bounds over the ensuing twenty-five years.

Cyrus added the ancient kingdoms of Assyria, Lydia (inheritor of the Hittite Empire), and Babylon to his Medean conquests, then took control of Palestine before dying in 529 BCE. His successor, Cambysses, conquered Egypt during his brief seven-year reign, then died on the way home.

Cambysses' death created a power vacuum in Persia that was made worse by a rather bizarre twist involving fratricide and pretenders to the throne.

Darius Seizes Power The main historical source for what happened after Cambysses's death is Darius's own account of events, and there is some scholarly doubt over whether Darius was really the heroic liberator he claimed to be. What can be certain is that prior to his departure for Egypt, Cambysses's brother Bardiya (known as Smerdis to the Greeks) died. The story goes that Cambysses himself, concerned that his brother would try to seize the throne in his absence, had Bardiya killed.

So it was that when Cambysses himself died, there was no heir apparent. The story takes a strange turn at this point, however. A *magian*, or high priest, by the name of Gaumata claimed that he was none other than Bardiya, who had not died after all.

Despite the rather obvious deception (one story relates that, although they looked similar, Gaumata had his ears cut off some years previously), Gaumata seemed poised to get away with his back-door usurpation: apparently the other nobles at court were too cowed to do anything about his plot for fear of violent reprisal.

Enter Darius. With the help of six co-conspirators, Darius made a claim to the throne. He was the son of a minor branch of the royal line, the Achaemnids, and was not even the oldest member of his immediate family, but he was ambitious.

Darius himself killed the imposter Gaumata and took the throne, which by this point was resting upon very shaky foundations. Over the next year Darius fought nineteen battles against various rebellious provinces in an effort to consolidate his power. By 521 BCE, his rule was unquestioned.

His accomplishments were immortalized on the Rock of Behistun. Rising out of the surrounding plains and situated near a major east-west trade route, the rock to this day bears Darius's triumphant inscriptions 200 feet above the ground. Written in three languages, the inscriptions proudly tell the story of Darius's fight for the throne. But Darius's great reign had only just begun.

Darius as Military Leader In contrast to his two predecessors, Darius is not noted for his military conquests. He focused on consolidating and improving the inner workings of the far-flung empire.

Nevertheless, Darius did lead several expeditions. The first, from 519 BCE–518 BCE, was to Egypt, where rebellion still stirred. Two years later, Darius found himself at the other end of his empire, campaigning in the Indus River valley (modern day Pakistan). Adding a portion of India to the Persian Empire proved a wise move. The revenue generated from that region was reportedly several hundred pounds of gold dust per year.

Darius also campaigned against the Scythians, horse nomads whose territory ranged from Central Asia to southern Europe. The ancient Greek historian Herodotus reports that one of the expeditions, dated to 514 BCE,

This enamelled tile relief from the fifth century BCE shows a Persian warrior armed with bow and spear. *Erich Lessing/Art Resource, NY*

took place north of the Danube River, which would make it one of the first Persian campaigns on European soil. During this campaign, Darius made use of his Greek subjects, including one Miltiades, the Athenian who would later defeat the Persian invasion at Marathon.

Darius's Scythian adventures came to nothing. The mounted nomad-archers refused to give battle, and, after suffering weeks of guerrilla attacks, the Persians went home.

Darius as Ruler It was at home in his empire that Darius truly came into his own. Although an administrative system had been evolving in Persia since the foundation of the empire, Darius was the first king to regulate and codify what would come to be known as the *satrapy* system.

A satrapy was basically a province arranged along ethnic or cultural lines. The rulers of each satrapy, the *satraps*, were chosen from the local populace in order to avoid the appearance of imperial domination. In fact, Persian policy was to keep things as "normal" as possible in their many subject kingdoms. Local religions were allowed to flourish. For example, after conquering Babylon, the Persians allowed the Jews to return to Palestine and encouraged them to rebuild the Temple of Solomon.

All that was asked in return was for the satrap to collect a certain amount of "tribute" each year and pass the earnings on to the Persians. Of course, the Persians were not naïve, and a sophisticated royal spy network referred to as "the king's eyes and ears" closely monitored each satrapy.

Darius is also credited with constructing the Royal Road, a sort of ancient superhighway that ran from Sardis in modern-day Turkey to Susa, one of the four Persian capitals, a length of 1700 miles. A normal journey along the road took about three months, but the king also established a system of couriers who, like the riders of the Pony Express of the American West, would ride in horse relays of twenty miles per horse. This system allowed a message to travel the distance from Sardis to Susa in about a week's time.

Darius and the Greeks It was at the extreme western end of the Royal Road, at the provincial capital of Sardis, that Darius first encountered what could be called his "Greek problem." The western coast of Anatolia (modern-day Turkey), then known as Ionia, was ethnically Greek. In 499 BCE, the Ionians rose in revolt, probably encouraged by the local satrap in a politically motivated power grab. However, the rebellion quickly grew beyond the satrap's control and turned into a movement for total independence from the Persian Empire.

The Ionians sent for help from mainland Greece. The Athenians agreed to help, as did the nearby city of Eretria, which had a large Ionian population.

The Greek expedition sailed across the Aegean and marched inland to Sardis, taking the city and burning it. When word of this foreign intervention reached Darius's ears, the king became incensed. He vowed that as soon as he had put down the Ionians, he would punish the Athenians for their temerity. It took six years to finally extinguish the fire of rebellion in Ionia, and every night during that time Darius had his attendant remind him three times during dinner to "remember the Athenians."

The last Ionian stronghold, Miletus, fell in 493 BCE and was nearly razed to the ground. By the following year Darius had an expedition ready to take the fight to mainland Greece. Unfortunately for Darius, the ships carrying the army were wrecked off the Mount Athos peninsula in Thessaly, in the extreme north of Greece. The expedition did manage, however, to secure the submission of Macedonia and Thrace before heading home.

Two years after his first attempted invasion, Darius was ready to try again. He sent a fleet directly across the Aegean this time, conquering the many Greek islands that dot that sea. Upon reaching the mainland, the Persians first landed at Eretria, which fell within a week, but the Persians were defeated soon after at Marathon.

ZOROASTRIANISM

Zoroastrianism, the traditional religion of Persia, is based on the teaching of the prophet Zoroaster (or Zarathustra). Unlike other ancient faiths featuring many gods and goddesses of various natural forces, Zoroastrianism posited only one god, Ahura-Mazda, the benevolent creator of the universe. Many scholars consider it to be the first monotheistic (one-god) religion. Angra Maiyu, or Ahriman, is the name of the "destructive spirit" in the Zoroastrian faith, a force similar to the devil in Judeo-Christian theology. Zoroastrians believe in free will and the practice of good thoughts and good deeds. Though it was once the official religion of the Persian Empire, Zoroastrianism was supplanted by Islam in the seventh century CE, and today is actively practiced by fewer than 150,000 people worldwide.

Darius was not ready to give up on his dream of vengeance against the Greeks, but his time soon ran out. He died in 486 BCE at the age of sixty-four in the midst of planning a third expedition. His son and heir, Xerxes, would attempt to carry on his father's dream, but meet with defeat at Salamis and Plataea.

Legacy The reign of Darius I was pivotal for Persia. He expanded the boundaries of the empire somewhat, adding the Indus Valley, Macedonia, Thrace, and the Aegean Islands. But it is as an administrator and builder that he is remembered. He regulated weights, measures, and coinage. He built grand palaces at Persepolis, his new capital, and left behind inscriptions chronicling his great deeds. He was also the first Persian king to publicly acknowledge the new religion of Zoroastrianism.

It was in the name of Zoroastrianism's primary god, Ahura-Mazda, that Darius left this advice for future rulers of the state he helped consolidate:

"King Darius states: King, whoever you are, who may arise after me, protect yourself well from lies. Do not trust the man who lies.... Believe what I did and tell the truth to the people. Do not conceal [it]. If you do not conceal these matters, but you do tell the people, may Ahura-Mazda protect you."

Xerxes

When he ascended to the throne of the Persian Empire in 486 BCE, Xerxes (520 BCE–465 BCE) could not have known that in a scant seven years he would be responsible for one of the greatest military defeats in history. But the Persian defeat at the hands of the Greeks during the so-called Persian Wars was only one chapter of a reign plagued by strife and setbacks.

Early Life, First Years as King Born in 520 BCE, Xerxes was the son of the Persian king Darius I, and was tapped from childhood to succeed his father. Although he was not the eldest of Darius's children, he was the eldest son of the king's favorite wife. Little is known of his life prior to his ascent to the throne, although there is evidence that he was the viceroy of Babylonia during his early adulthood, perhaps as a means to prepare him for the responsibilities of rule.

When Darius died, Xerxes was immediately confronted with an ongoing revolt in Egypt and would soon have to deal with an uprising in Babylonia as well. He seems to have put down the rebellions quickly and, when necessary, ruthlessly. After Babylon revolted a second time in 482 BCE, Xerxes tore down the temple ziggurats (towers) of the city and defaced the statues of the local gods.

Along with rebellious provinces, Xerxes inherited something else from his father: the desire to crush Greece, which had proven a continual thorn in the western side of the Persian Empire. Darius had launched two expeditions targeting Greece in 492 BCE and 490 BCE. The first foundered in stormy seas off the Mount Athos peninsula; the second was turned back at the Battle of Marathon. Xerxes was determined to make good on the third attempt and set about assembling one of the largest armies the world had yet seen in an effort to guarantee victory.

Xerxes' Army The ancient Greek historian Herodotus calculated that the Persian army, when all personnel and camp followers were factored in, numbered some five million individuals. Modern scholarship estimates a total closer to 300,000, with about 120,000 comprising the main body of the army. Xerxes assembled a fleet to match his army, some 1,200 ships strong.

The composition of the army was also unlike anything previously seen, drawing units from all over the empire—from the Indus River valley, with its soldiers clad in "tree-wool" (cotton), to Nubia (southern Egypt) and all points in between. The army even included a sizeable number of Greeks, mostly Ionians from the west coast of modern-day Turkey.

The core of Xerxes' army was his personal bodyguard of 10,000, the "Immortals," so called because the unit was always maintained at that precise number of soldiers, even while on campaign.

Xerxes' Strategy The Greeks were small in number, but had won a reputation as excellent sailors and fearsome warriors. The Persians had felt defeat at Greek hands ten years earlier at Marathon despite outnumbering the Greeks in that battle. Clearly, Xerxes' strategy was to stack the odds so far in his favor that quantity would have to win out over quality.

The patient Xerxes paid heed to past defeats and took several years to prepare carefully for his invasion. His knew his army was too big to sail across the sea, so his plan was to march across the Bosporus, the strait separating Europe from Asia Minor, then on to Greece proper. Xerxes had two great pontoon bridges, bridges laid across the backs of lashed-together boats, built across the Bosporus at its narrowest point. Remembering what the treacherous Mount Athos had done to his father's fleet in 492 BCE, he ordered a canal dug across the base of the peninsula. It took three years to dig the canal. Finally ready for attack, Xerxes sought divine sanction for his mission by ordering the sacrifice of 1,000 head of cattle. Then he and his army set off for Greece.

Xerxes Invades Greece Xerxes first met Greek resistance at the Pass of Thermopylae. The famous band of 300 Spartans under King Leonidas were supported by about 4,000 allied troops and stopped the whole of the Persian army for over a week, including nearly three days of fierce close combat. Thermopylae was Xerxes' first encounter with the quality of Greek fighters, and he could count it a victory despite losing thousands of troops in the effort. He marched south and occupied Athens, with the Greek armies retreating before his advance.

The key to victory now seemed to rest not in a land engagement but on the clash of navies. If Xerxes could crush Greek naval power, his own ships could blockade the remaining third of Greece, the Spartan homeland known as the Peloponnesus. Troops could be landed at will. The war would be all but over.

The Greek fleet had gathered in the Bay of Salamis, between the island of the same name and the Athenian port of Piraeus. The Greek fleet was weakened by bickering and fractiousness and was outnumbered by the Persians to boot. Xerxes had only to blockade the fleet inside the bay and the Greeks were sure to turn on each other.

It was at this point that the crafty Athenian leader Themistocles sent a secret communication to the Persian king designed to look like an attempt at treachery. In the message, Themistocles simply told Xerxes the Greek fleet was in perilously weak condition. Overanxious for a victory, Xerxes fell for Themistocles' ruse and ordered an attack. So confident was he of victory, he even set up a throne on a nearby mountaintop from which to watch the battle and take notes on which admirals did well and which did poorly.

But instead of watching an easy Persian victory, Xerxes was forced to observe as his fleet went down to defeat. As much as one-third of the Persian fleet was sunk. Unable to swim, most of the sailors of the sinking ships drowned. Xerxes' overanxious attack, in which his fleet's great size worked against it, gave the Greeks control of the seas and the initiative in the war. The next year, the Persians would be defeated once and for all at Plataea.

After Salamis Nervous about the possibility of another rebellion in Babylon, Xerxes took about half his army and returned to Sardis. Without control of the seas, he would not be able to maintain his supply lines for the full invasion army. The vast numbers of soldiers upon whom he had depended turned into more of a hindrance than a help. The outnumbered Greeks had found ways to turn the size of the Persian force against itself.

For the Persians, the wars in Greece were ultimately a sideshow. The empire went on. Official peace was eventually declared with the Greeks about thirty years after Salamis, although the Persians would continue to meddle in Aegean politics and wars.

As for Xerxes, he proved not nearly as durable as his realm. He took no further part in the wars with Greece or the political maneuverings of his generals and governors. Often drunk, he retreated to his palaces, embittered and focused on grand building projects.

Fifteen years after Salamis, in 465 BCE, Xerxes was assassinated in a palace coup led by the captain of the guard, Artabanus. The kingdom fell to civil war between Artabanus and Xerxes' three sons, one of whom, Artaxerxes, eventually won the throne. Even in death, Xerxes' legacy was one of violence, bloodshed, and death.

Datis

There is little that is actually known about the Persian general named Datis (birth and death dates unknown), leader of the expedition against the Greeks that ended in defeat at Marathon in 490 BCE. Most of our information comes via the Greek historian Herodotus, although there are also inscriptions and palace records that help fill in the blanks.

Early Military Career Datis was a Mede from the mountainous northern region of Mesopotamia and was clearly one of the top generals in the army of the Persian king, Darius I. His name first appears in connection with the Ionian revolt, a six-year struggle between the ethnically Greek Ionians of the west coast of modern-day Turkey and their Persian overlords. Datis is historically credited with capturing the key Ionian island of Rhodes in 495 BCE and with leading the Persian fleet to victory at the battle of Lade in 494 BCE.

Lade marked the beginning of the siege of Miletus, the last holdout of Ionian resistance. Within a year, Miletus had been taken amidst much blood and fire, and the Ionian rebellion was officially put to rest.

When the Ionians had first risen against the Persians in 499 BCE, help had come from the mainland Greek cities of Athens and Eretria. Darius swore vengeance on the foreign cities for intervening, and in 490 BCE launched an expedition across the Aegean Sea with Datis and another Persian commander, Artaphernes, in charge of the forces.

The Expedition of 490 BCE The expedition had three goals: to punish Athens and Eretria for their involvement in Ionia, to restore the deposed Athenian tyrant Hippias as a Persian puppet ruler, and to incorporate the many Aegean islands into the Persian Empire, thus creating a buffer zone between Persia and Greece.

A painting on terracotta of a Greek hoplite, running with a sheild, at the Acropolis Museum, Athens, Greece. *© Ganni Dagli Orti/Corbis*

This last objective had been a Persian goal for nearly a decade, having first been attempted in 499 BCE under the command of Artaphernes's father. That campaign was cut short by the more pressing matter of the Ionian revolt, and the Aegean islands remained free for the time being.

Datis and Artaphernes met with considerably more success in 490 BCE, taking every island that stood in their way, including the vital trading center of Naxos and the island of Delos, site of a major Apollo cult. As the Persians associated Apollo with their Zoroastrian god Ahura-Mazda, Datis made a great sacrifice to thank the god for the expedition's success so far.

Marathon Upon reaching the Greek mainland, Datis first laid siege to the city of Eretria, which fell within a week. Its citizens were enslaved and eventually sent back to Babylon for a life in captivity.

After the fall of Eretria, Datis landed at the plain of Marathon, a site north of Athens that Hippias advised would be favorable terrain for the superior Persian cavalry.

Meanwhile, the Athenians had assembled a force of about 10,000 hoplites, heavy infantry clad in bronze armor and wielding spears, to oppose the Persian army, which was anywhere from twice as big to six times the size, but made up almost exclusively of lightly armored archers and light cavalry.

The Greeks blocked the road south to Athens but did not attack. A standoff ensued over the next five days

before the Greeks, under their general Miltiades, charged the Persian army and broke it. It has been theorized that the Greeks charged when they did because the Persian cavalry, to which the Greek phalanx (body of troops) was most vulnerable, was not in the area, or was perhaps boarding the ships in preparation for departing to another landing point.

What is known is that after the defeat, Datis sailed his fleet around to the south of Athens with an eye to taking the Athenian port town of Piraeus, but found the port blocked by the victorious troops of Marathon, who had raced home to secure the city. With no apparent landing point, Datis turned back for Persia.

Legacy Most of the goals of his expedition had been accomplished, but the defeat at Marathon would have the largest impact on world events. The Persians had never lost a land battle against a regular army, and the defeat had a profound effect on Persian authority and power.

Although some sources claim Datis was killed at Marathon, this is unlikely. His exact date of death is unknown. All that is certain is that he did not participate in the Persian invasion of Greece tens years after Marathon in 480 BCE, although two of his sons did serve as generals in that great army. As for their father, he emerges only briefly from the mists of history and, despite his string of successes as a general, is best remembered for one of the most momentous defeats in the ancient world.

Miltiades

Miltiades (c. 549 BCE–489 BCE) was an Athenian general and adventurer who is best remembered as the victorious commander of the Battle of Marathon.

Early Military Career An Athenian aristocrat, Miltiades first made a name for himself serving as a magistrate under the tyrant Hippias. Around 516 BCE, he set himself up as tyrant of the Greek colonies in the Chersonese, an area now known as the Gallipoli Peninsula in Turkey. In Miltiades's day, Thracians, a relatively uncivilized people the Greeks looked down upon as little better than wild men, dominated the area, and Miltiades ruled with an iron fist.

The Chersonese fell under the dominion of the Persian Empire, and Miltiades marched with the army of the Persian king Darius during an expedition against the nomadic Scythians north of the Danube River. According to the ancient Greek historian Herodotus, Miltiades considered burning the Persians' bridge over the mighty Danube, thus stranding the army and their king, but this could very well have been an attempt to paint the hero of Marathon as reluctantly serving under his future enemies, a Greek patriot through and through.

When the other Greeks in the Persian Empire did rise against Darius, Miltiades fought on their side, taking the island of Lemnos, which he later gave to Athens.

In Command at Marathon Persia eventually suppressed the Greek rebels, and Miltiades returned to Athens, where he faced a cool reception due to his tyrannical rule of the Chersonese. In fact, he was soon brought to trial for his actions, but charges against him were dropped. The Athenians, aware that Darius was preparing a punitive campaign against them for their involvement in the Greek revolts, needed someone like Miltiades, an experienced general with inside knowledge of how the Persian army fought and operated. In July of 490 BCE, as the Persian invasion fleet was making its way across the Aegean towards Athens, Miltiades was elected one of ten generals for the year.

The Athenians sent word to Sparta, the greatest Greek military power of the day, requesting help against the Persians. The Spartans replied that they would be unable to help out right away because they were in the middle of a religious festival.

Miltiades suggested marching out immediately rather than hiding behind Athens's city walls. The Greek force numbered around 10,000 and faced a Persian army at least twice that size. Miltiades and his fellow generals, having blocked the Persians from advancing beyond their landing site at Marathon, were unsure of how to proceed. For five days the Greeks held their ground.

It was Miltiades who finally proposed a bold plan: the Greeks, who excelled at close combat, should charge the Persians, who relied on their archers and cavalry. Forced into close quarters, the Greeks would negate the Persians' preferred method of fighting. Furthermore, Miltiades proposed to leave the Greek center weak and to strengthen the wings, thus setting up a trap for the Persians in which their numbers would work against them.

By a one-vote margin, his idea won approval from the other generals. The Greeks charged.

Miltiades' plan went off without a hitch. The weak Greek center gave way, the Persians surged forward, and the Greek wings swung in like great pincers, striking the Persian flanks and causing panic in their ranks. Thanks to Miltiades, Marathon was a triumph, with the Greeks losing a mere 192 men to the Persians' 6,400.

After Marathon Miltiades was showered with praise upon his return to Athens and was the natural choice to lead further expeditions against the Persian-occupied Aegean islands. However, his star rapidly fell. During an attack on the Persian-held island of Paros, Miltiades was wounded and the attack was driven off. Returning to Athens, he was condemned and fined for his failure, dying soon after from his wound.

Despite this ignominious end, Miltiades is today remembered as a military genius who showed the Greeks they could defeat the mighty Persian army, inventing the tactic of "double envelopment" in the process.

Leonidas

The legendary hero King Leonidas (?–480 BCE), defender of Thermopylae, remains largely an enigma to modern

The modern statue of King Leonidas stands defiant at Thermopylae. *Foto Marburg/Art Resource, NY*

scholarship. His birth date could range anywhere between 530 and 500 BCE, which would place his age at the time of death somewhere between twenty and fifty years old.

The main source of information on Leonidas is the ancient Greek historian Herodotus, who reports that Leonidas was born to the Spartan king Anaxandrides and came to rule Sparta through an unlikely sequence of events.

Leonidas, King of Sparta Anaxandrides had taken a wife who had produced no sons. As such, the Spartan council ordered him to take a second wife, a very unusual decree in Greek society. Anaxandrides dutifully married again and soon had a son by the name of Cleomenes. Ironically, the king's first wife then began producing sons, three to be precise: Dorieus, Leonidas and Cleombrotus.

Although Dorieus would have been the king had his father not remarried, Cleomenes took the throne instead, which was unfortunate, since consensus held Dorieus to be the better qualified of the two to rule by far. So upset was Dorieus at the hand fate had dealt him that he left Sparta for good and was soon killed during an overseas adventure.

Cleomenes, who was mentally unsound and might have actually been developmentally disabled, died sometime around 487 BCE. Leonidas, who had married Cleomenes' daughter (and his own half-niece) was next in line for succession and so became king, or rather coking, for Sparta was ruled by two men at all times.

Cleomenes had shared the throne with one Demaratus, but an internal feud had driven Demaratus to join with the Persians. A new king named Leotychides filled the vacant position.

The Role of the Spartan King

As kings, both Leonidas and Leotychides functioned as rulers and high priests, the military and spiritual leaders of their city. Spartan kings were expected to be true leaders, setting the example for those that followed them.

In the militaristic society of Sparta, that example was often by necessity quite extreme, as evidenced by Leonidas's decision to personally lead a hand-picked band of his 300 best warriors (and a few thousand allies) north to Thermopylae to provide a stopgap defense against the massive Persian army that was bearing down on Greece in the year 480 BCE. It was a mission from which none of the Spartans would return.

But Leonidas and his men were not mere lambs to the Persian slaughter—Herodotus claims 20,000 Persians died in nearly three days of fighting against the vastly outnumbered Spartans. Leonidas's leadership was critical to the Greek resistance, and it continued to serve as an example even after he died.

The victorious Persians set Leonidas's head on a pike and marched south. After the wars, the Spartans recovered their king's remains and bore them back home where he was given a hero's burial.

After the Persian army was defeated at Plataea in 479 BCE, the Spartan commander Pausanias had this to say about his deceased king: "For Leonidas, whom you bid me avenge, I tell you he has been greatly avenged; he has found great honor in these countless souls here—both he himself and the others who died at Thermopylae."

Themistocles

Themistocles (c. 524 BCE–460 BCE), was the leader perhaps most directly responsible for the Greek victory in the Persian Wars. Little is known of his early life, save a story related by the biographer Plutarch, writing some 600 years later.

Plutarch writes that a young Themistocles was walking down the street when the Athenian tyrant Peisistratus approached from the other direction. When Themistocles' tutor cautioned him to make way, Themistocles responded, "Isn't the road wide enough for him?"

Regardless of the truth of this story, it illustrates the biting wisdom that came so naturally to Themistocles and that would mark him out as a clever, wily leader of men in the mold of Odysseus of old. It also gives a hint of the great streak of pride that would eventually see Themistocles make enemies of all his allies.

Early Political Career

The famous democracy of Athens was just blossoming at the dawn of the fifth century BCE after two generations of tyrannical rule. There are hints that Themistocles was involved with the city government, perhaps pushing through plans to fortify the Athenian port town of Piraeus.

It is not until 483 BCE that Themistocles definitively enters the historical record. Athens had recently received an influx of wealth thanks to the discovery of new veins of silver in its mines. There was considerable debate in the city as to what to do with all the newfound revenue. The most popular plan involved dividing up the money equally among all the citizens of Athens, a dividend that would have been equal to a month's pay for most people.

Themistocles had a better idea. After the Athenian victory at Marathon in 490 BCE, many Greeks had assumed the Persians would no longer pose a threat. Themistocles was not so sure, and felt the best defense for Athens was a strong navy. He introduced a plan to more than double the size of the Athenian navy. The consummate politician, Themistocles was able to convince the citizens of Athens, who were still stinging from a recent naval defeat at the hands of the island state of Aegina, to back his plan.

In 480 BCE, the last of the new Athenian warships slipped into the harbor of Piraeus just as the Persians, under their king Xerxes, launched a massive invasion of Greece.

As a Military Leader

Thanks to Themistocles' navy, Athens had become the preeminent Greek naval power. Nevertheless, the Spartans were appointed commanders of the allied fleet, which first engaged the Persians off Cape Artemisium at the same time as the famous land battle at nearby Thermopylae was occurring. The Greek fleet was driven back, but not before inflicting serious losses on the Persians.

As he retreated with the fleet, Themistocles left a message in every port he stopped in, addressed to his fellow Greeks who were serving in the Persian navy. His message entreated them to come over to the Greek side, or at least not fight as fiercely against their brethren as Xerxes might like.

Although his messages did not win any converts, there is evidence that it sowed mistrust between the Greek and non-Greek generals in the Persian fleet. But Themistocles' trickery was just getting started.

The Greek navy, made up of ships from a multitude of independent city-states, was under constant threat of breaking up due to internal rivalries. Themistocles kept the various factions together as best he could, using every trick his clever political mind could muster, but he knew that time was of the essence. A battle with the

Persians needed to be forced so the squabbling Greeks could unify against a common enemy.

Once Xerxes found the Greek fleet at anchor in the narrow Bay of Salamis, his own fleet hung back. The narrow bay did not favor the massive Persian fleet, which needed the open ocean to make its numbers count.

In order to force a confrontation, Themistocles dispatched a servant to Xerxes bearing a message: the Greek fleet was on the verge of dissolution. They were apt to break up and go home any day now.

Xerxes, anxious to defeat the whole Greek fleet in one blow, ordered the bay blockaded and attacked at dawn. And, just as Themistocles had planned, the Persian numbers worked against them. The Greek fleet, led by the brand new state-of-the-art Athenian navy, outfought and outmaneuvered the Persians, sinking upwards of a third of the fleet.

The victory at Salamis was the turning point of the Persian Wars. The Greeks had won naval superiority and would go on to defeat the Persian army the following year at Plataea.

Ups and Downs after the War From his shipbuilding initiative, to his efforts to hold the fleet together, to his cunning trickery, the Greek victory over the Persians was owed almost entirely to Themistocles, and he seemed to know it. In the wake of the war, offended that his fellow Athenians did not do enough to honor him, Themistocles departed for Sparta, where he was honored with an olive branch, the "finest chariot in Sparta," and much merry-making. For his journey back to Athens, an honor guard of 300 Spartans accompanied Themistocles to their border.

Once back in Athens, Themistocles encountered a delegation from Sparta that was lobbying hard to prevent the Athenians from rebuilding their city wall, which only stood in a few spots after the Persians razed the city. According to the Spartans, a wall only served to defend an enemy who takes your city. Sparta had no wall, the Spartans argued, and neither should Athens.

Secretly telling his fellow citizens to devote every man, woman, and child to the task of rebuilding the wall, Themistocles returned to Sparta to "negotiate."

Once in Sparta, Themistocles stalled and played for time. First he claimed that he was waiting on other Athenian delegates who were unaccountably late. When word reached Sparta that Athens was rebuilding her walls, Themistocles dismissed the reports as wild rumors. He then encouraged the Spartans to send another delegation to see for themselves, sending word ahead to Athens to delay the delegation as much as possible on their journey to the city.

Eventually, of course, the truth was revealed. Not only had Athens rebuilt its walls, they now stood taller and thicker than before. What was more, the fortified port of Piraeus was now connected to Athens by a seven-mile long walled corridor and the city wall in general encompassed a larger area.

Amazingly, Themistocles extricated himself from Sparta with little overt hostility. He explained to his hosts that time and again during the war, Athens had demonstrated superior judgment, and always acted in the service of the greater good for Greece. The city walls, he continued, were simply the latest manifestation of that beneficent judgment. The Spartans let him go, albeit with considerably less enthusiasm than the last time he had departed that city.

As with many wartime leaders, Themistocles saw his popularity at home decline in peacetime. He may have exacerbated matters with his rather arrogant personality and constant need for recognition. Apparently tired of having him around, his fellow Athenians ostracized, or formally banished, Themistocles in 472 BCE, eight years after the victory of Salamis.

In theory, when an Athenian was ostracized, he had to stay away from the city for ten years, but his property and social standing were left untouched and he was free to return at the end of the exile, his reputation intact. Unfortunately for Themistocles, things did not work out quite so cleanly.

Themistocles wandered from city to city, trying to find a place to settle, but was dogged by accusations from the Spartans that he was conspiring with the Persians. Unwilling to harbor an enemy of Sparta, no city would put up with him for long. Back in Athens, the allegations of deals with the enemy led to Themistocles being branded a traitor. His property was confiscated and his citizenship revoked.

Later Life and Legacy The victor of Salamis eventually found himself in Asia Minor, where, in an ironic twist, his former enemies, the Persians, took him in. They made him governor of the province of Magnesia, which he ruled until his death. There exist today Magnesian coins bearing Themistocles' likeness.

There are two versions of Themistocles' death. One has him committing suicide by drinking bull's blood so that he would not have to lead an army against his fellow Greeks. The other, much more likely, story finds him dying of old age sometime around 460 BCE.

However he died, Themistocles left behind a towering legacy. Without his shipbuilding program and leadership, victory at Salamis is very hard to imagine. Without victory at Salamis, the Greek army would have almost certainly been defeated. Whatever his personal faults, Themistocles is more directly responsible for Greek victory in the Persian Wars than any other single person.

Mardonius

Best known for his role in the defeat at the Battle of Plataea in 479 BCE, the Persian general Mardonius (?–479 BCE) was nevertheless a capable military leader who had the misfortune to lead two campaigns that each ended in disaster.

Early Life   When Darius I became king of Persia in 522 BCE, he relied on the assistance of six co-conspirators who helped him seize the crown. One of these noblemen, Gobryas, married Darius's sister, and it is from this union that Mardonius most likely was born.

The first Persian encounter with the mainland Greeks came when the ethnically Greek region of the Persian Empire known as Ionia rose up in revolt and Athens sent troops to assist the rebels, burning the provincial capital of Sardis.

Governor of Ionia   Darius put down the revolt over a six-year period, oftentimes quite brutally, and he assigned Mardonius to patch the subjugated province back together. All evidence indicates that Mardonius was a just and capable administrator, and that he even instituted democratic reform in the Ionian cities.

As Mardonius got Ionia back on its feet, Darius was busy planning an expedition to Greece with the objective of punishing the city-states that had sent aid to the rebels. Mardonius, perhaps due to his capable work in Ionia, was put in charge of the first expedition in 492 BCE.

The First Persian Invasion   The expedition never made it to Greece: the fleet was wrecked upon the storm-tossed peninsula of Mount Athos. Mardonius made the best of a bad situation and used his army to win the submission of the northern Greek state of Macedonia and the semi-civilized region of Thrace, possibly venturing as far north as the Danube in the process. These acquisitions would prove vital to later Persian campaigns in Europe, as they provided a natural staging area for armies assembling at the extreme western edge of the mighty empire.

Serving Under Xerxes   When Darius died in 486 BCE, Mardonius's cousin and brother-in-law, Xerxes, succeeded to the throne. Xerxes intended from the very start of his reign to carry out his father's plans to invade Greece, and Mardonius wholeheartedly supported the idea. A great army began assembling at Sardis. After a brief pause to put down a rebellion in Babylon, Xerxes was ready to launch his invasion. In 480 BCE the army set out, with Mardonius as one of six generals serving under the king.

After taking northern Greece with no difficulty, the Persian army hit its first snag at Thermopylae, where a vastly outnumbered Spartan force held them up for a week. Nonetheless, the Persians pressed on and occupied Athens and central Greece. Shortly thereafter, the Persian navy was defeated at Salamis and Xerxes retired to Asia Minor with about half his army. He named Mardonius commander of the Persian army in Greece, which probably numbered about 150,000.

Prelude to Plataea   Over the winter, Mardonius attempted to win the Athenians over to his side. He retired to north-central Greece and offered to give the Athenians their city back, as well as a preeminent position in Greece, if they would only acknowledge Xerxes as their king. The Athenians, living in exile, would have none of it.

As winter turned to spring, the Athenians refused a second similar offer and Mardonius moved back to Athens. He razed the city to the ground, leveling every building in the town and covering the ruins with dirt.

Meanwhile, Sparta had begun assembling a great Greek army after the Athenians spurred them to action by threatening to turn their fleet over to Mardonius. Nearly every city in Greece not already under Persian domination contributed units to the army, which numbered about 100,000 men. The Greeks marched towards Athens in the summer of 479 BCE.

Plataea   Mardonius met the Greeks near the town of Plataea and a game of brinkmanship began. Neither side wanted to initiate the attack. Although his Greek allies suggested using the gold and silver of northern Greece to bribe his enemies, Mardonius was looking for a battle.

He finally got one when he misinterpreted Greek troop movement for a retreat and ordered his army forward. He personally led a cavalry attack on the Spartan-held right, and it was at some point during the fighting that Mardonius was killed.

It is perhaps a mark of his personal leadership qualities that as soon as Mardonius perished, his army began to fall apart. The Spartans drove back their attackers and a general retreat was soon sounded. The Greeks had triumphed and the greatly reduced Persian army limped back to Asia Minor along the old invasion route.

Several towns near the battlefield competed for the honor of burying Mardonius. It was a sign of respect for the Persian general that the Greeks would want to do such a thing, but it was an ironic end for Mardonius. As a Zoroastrian (follower of the traditional relgion of Persia, Zoroastrianism), he would have preferred his body to be left for the vultures and would have seen burial as sacrilege.

⊕ Major Battles

Marathon, 490 BCE

Origins   The origins of the Battle of Marathon, one of the most decisive battles in world history, lay in a provincial revolt at the extreme western edge of the sprawling Persian Empire. The region known as Ionia, located along the west coast of Anatolia (modern-day Turkey), was primarily Greek in population but had been subject to Persian rule since the defeat of King Croesus of Lydia in 546 BCE.

A ruined temple near Marathon, Greece. © Charles Best/Alamy

In 499 BCE, the Ionians rebelled against their Persian overlords, and it is here that the chain of events that would lead to Marathon began.

At the dawn of the fifth century BCE, the legendary democracy of Athens was in its infancy. In fact, although technically ruled by an assembly, de facto tyrants had dominated Athenian politics for many years. The Athenians, with the help of Sparta, drove out their last tyrant, Hippias, in 510 BCE.

With Hippias gone, Athenian politics began to assume a much more democratic appearance. One of the major reforms of this time was the granting of citizenship to all men residing in the countryside surrounding Athens, a region known as Attica. Significantly, there was a sizeable population of Ionians living in Attica, and once they gained the ability to participate in the political process, Ionian concerns quickly became Athenian concerns.

So it was that when the Ionians in Anatolia rose against Persia, Athens voted to send military assistance. The nearby city of Eretria, which had a large Ionian population, also voted to send ships and troops. Sparta, the greatest military power in Greece, decided to remain neutral on the issue and sent no assistance.

The joint Athenian-Eretrian force numbered twenty-five ships (twenty from Athens and five from Eretria) and quickly made its presence felt after landing in Ionia. The Greeks marched inland to the Persian provincial capital of Sardis and put the city to the torch.

Darius Swears Vengeance on Greece

When word reached the Persian king, Darius, that foreign Greeks had intervened in what he considered an internal dispute, he was outraged. Never mind that the Athenian expedition had been defeated and scattered shortly after razing Sardis, or that a pro-peace movement quickly gained traction back home in Athens; Darius determined to teach the foreign Greeks a lesson as soon as he had dealt with the rebellious Ionians.

The Ionian revolt was crushed by 493 BCE with the sacking of the Ionian capital of Miletos, an event so brutal that the peace movement in Athens quickly lost support. In the meantime Darius, determined to keep his goal of punishing the Greeks foremost in his mind, had instructed a servant to remind him three times during every dinner to "remember the Athenians."

The First Expedition

Darius certainly did not forget the Athenians, and by 492 BCE had prepared a punitive expedition that he sent by ship along the rugged coast of Thrace (a region now split by modern-day Greece and Turkey). Unfortunately for the Persians, this first expedition ran afoul of a storm off the coast of Mount Athos and was wrecked. The mission was not a total loss—before heading home, the shipwrecked Persian army extracted submission from Thrace and Macedonia (another northern Greek kingdom).

The Second Expedition

It took Darius two years to assemble another invasion fleet, and in 490 BCE this new force set out on a more direct route, landing first at Eretria. The army consisted of some 26,000 Persians, and the city of Eretria fell in flames to the invaders within a week.

Leaving some of the army to occupy the ruined city, the Persian commanders sailed on to Marathon, a site about twenty-six miles north of Athens. Traveling with them was none other than the exiled tyrant, Hippias. He knew Marathon would make a good staging point for an expedition against Athens (his own father, Peisistratos, had used the site to land an army some fifty years earlier) and Darius had promised to return Hippias to power once the Persians subjugated the upstart Athenians.

The Greek Response

In response to the Persian threat, the Athenians had assembled a force of hoplites, heavily

THE MODERN MARATHON

Modern marathon races take their name and length from the famous Marathon-to-Athens run made by Phiddipides. In 1896, when the modern Olympic games were inaugurated in Athens, the first Olympic marathon course was set to cover what was believed to have been Phiddipides's original course from the battlefield of Marathon.

armored citizen-soldiers, 9,000 strong. To this they added an allied contingent of 1,000 hoplites from neighboring Plataea.

These 10,000 Greeks marched out against an invading force that was probably twice as large. The Athenian commander, Miltiades, dispatched the runner Phiddipides to distant Sparta to call for aid, but the Spartans refused on the grounds that they were in the middle of a month-long religious festival. The Athenians were on their own.

The Battle It was late September. The Athenian force formed up on a ridge overlooking the Persian positions on the beachhead below. The Greeks relied on shock and the press of close combat; the Persians preferred to stand off and use their bows. Knowing this, Miltiades devised a plan: the Greeks, deployed with a weak center and strong wings, were to run at full speed for the Persian lines, minimizing the time available for the Persians to use their bows.

As battle was joined, the Persians broke through the weakened Greek center and began pressing forward. As they did so, the Greek wings swung inward in a great "pincer" movement, hitting the Persians in the flanks and breaking them. The Persian army disintegrated, some soldiers fleeing back toward their ships, others into the nearby marshes. At the end of the day, the Persians had lost some 6,400 men to the Greeks' 192.

Militiades once again dispatched his runner Phiddipides, this time to carry the good news of victory to Athens. Phiddipides did so, running the twenty-six miles without stopping. Upon arriving in Athens, he had just enough time to gasp out word of the victory before dying of exhaustion.

The Impact of Marathon The battle of Marathon marked the first time a Western army had defeated an Eastern force in battle, and was a tremendous boost for the fledgling Athenian democracy. Winning the victory without Sparta's aid proved to the Athenians that they could stand on their own.

But Athens, and indeed all of Greece, still had much hardship to look forward to in the short term. Darius died in 486 BCE while planning another invasion of Greece. His son and successor, Xerxes, set about carry-

ing out his father's plans. Within ten years of Marathon, the Greeks would find themselves once again defending their homeland against a massive invading army. The Persian Wars had just begun.

Thermopylae, 480 BCE

In the summer of 480 BCE, a Persian army, perhaps numbering in the millions, crossed a pontoon bridge at the Hellespont, the narrow channel of water separating Europe from Asia Minor, and marched towards Greece. Meanwhile, a small force of Spartans and their allies marched north from the Peloponnesus, the mountainous peninsula that constitutes southern Greece, determined to stop the invaders. The two armies would meet at a narrow pass called Thermopylae in one of the most famous battles of the ancient world.

The Road to Thermopylae As word of the Persian invasion reached the Greek mainland, the Greek city-states, usually occupied with squabbling amongst themselves, came together for a conference at Corinth. Sparta, as the premier military power in the region, was appointed leader of the coalition. A plan was drafted to defend the north of Greece at the Pass of Tempe, but this was quickly abandoned. The Persians were moving faster than anticipated through the rugged Greek countryside. Xerxes had come prepared and had a whole division of axemen leading the army, hacking paths through dense forests.

Sparta had a unique form of government. Technically a monarchy, it was ruled by two kings. In 480 BCE, Leotychides, who had assumed the throne after the traitor king Demaratus had been exiled, ruled Sparta with Leonidas. The two Spartan kings and their Peloponnesian allies next advocated a plan to set up a defensive line at the Isthmus of Corinth, the narrow strip of land that connects the Peloponnesus to the rest of Greece. This plan proved unpopular, however, as it would have meant abandoning most of Greece to the Persians.

A third plan was formulated: Leonidas would take a handpicked force of 300 hoplites, heavily armored soldiers, north to the pass of Thermopylae and establish a defensive line on the eastern coast road. The Spartans were in the midst of a religious festival, but once that was over they would send the bulk of their army north to join Leonidas. This plan met with approval, as it was assumed that the Persians would not reach Thermopylae before the main Greek army arrived. Nevertheless, Leonidas selected only unmarried, childless men for his 300. Perhaps he sensed they would be marching to their death.

The 300 Spartans of legend were never alone. Allied hoplites, 4,000 strong, joined them immediately. As they marched north, other city-states in the path of the invading Persians added what units they could: 700 Thespians, 400 Thebans, 1,000 Locrians and 1,000 Phocians. Thus, by the time Leonidas reached Thermopylae, he had an army of between 7,000 and 8,000 hoplites under his command.

The Hot Gates Thermopylae was an ideal site for mounting a defense. Named for the nearby hot springs (Thermopylae literally means "hot gates"), it was a site where the eastern coast road traced a narrow path between mountains and the sea. The Greek fleet had followed Leonidas north, as the sea also formed a natural choke point at nearby Cape Artemisium. Man and nature alike protected Leonidas's flanks. There was even an ancient wall that stretched across the pass, the site of previous battles between the local Phocians. Leonidas ordered the wall reinforced and sent scouts out.

It is at this point that he most likely learned of the one weakness of the pass: there was a path through the mountains, the Anapaea Path that wound around Thermopylae and came out behind the Spartan position. The Phocians volunteered to guard the path, as they were on their home territory and would be most familiar with the local terrain. Leonidas consented.

The Persians Arrive Meanwhile, other scouts brought word that the Persians were much closer than anticipated. It quickly became clear that the Spartans could expect a fight, and soon. In fact, the first Persian scouts began to appear within days of the Spartans' arrival. To show their contempt for the enemy, the Greeks engaged in athletic games and had their hair dressed for war in full view of the scouts.

When Xerxes first received word of the Greek presence at Thermopylae and their open disdain for the approaching threat, he turned to his Greek advisor, the exiled Spartan king Demaratus. There was perhaps no one better qualified to explain to Xerxes just what he was up against: the very elite of Greek soldiery.

In spite of their displays in front of the Persian scouts, the Spartans held a council with their allies to determine a course of action: to retreat or to hold. Leonidas, with Phocian and Locrian support, opted to stand and fight. Nevertheless, he sent messengers to other city-states asking for extra troops.

The main Persian army arrived at Thermopylae, then waited, most likely to allow their supply train to catch up. Xerxes sent threats of total annihilation to the Greeks. His arrows, he said, would be so thick they would block out the sun. "All the better to fight in the shade," replied the Spartan hero Dieneces, or so says the ancient Greek historian Herodotus.

The Battle: Day One When it became clear that the Greeks were not about to surrender, Xerxes launched his attack the morning of the fifth day. Leading the attack were the Mede and Cissian divisions, lightly armored warriors from the mountains of northern Mesopotamia. The fighting lasted all morning. The Persian attack was stopped cold, no match for the heavily armed Greeks.

PERSIANS IN BATTLE

The army that Darius, and later Xerxes, fielded was a reflection of the diversity of cultures encompassed by the far-flung empire.

The infantry was primarily drawn from northern Mesopotamia and was lightly armored, carrying only a wicker shield and no body armor. Their primary weapon was the bow, but they also carried short spears and daggers. The elite of the Persian army was a unit known as the "Immortals," the king's royal guard.

The Persians also deployed cavalry, horse archers recruited from the plains of central Asia and modern-day Afghanistan. Some of the cavalry also carried axes.

In battle, the Persians preferred to rely on their superior archery to sow death and confusion in the enemy ranks, then charge in only when the opponent was at the breaking point.

That afternoon Xerxes sent in his "Immortals," an elite bodyguard of 10,000 soldiers. The narrowness of the pass once again prevented the Persians from making use of their massive numerical superiority, and the Immortals, too, proved no match for the Greeks. In fact, three times over the course of the afternoon, the Spartans drove the Persians completely out of the pass and Xerxes was forced to abandon his observation post for fear of being overrun.

At the end of the first day, the Persians had made no progress and left only heaps of bodies in the pass.

The Battle: Day Two Xerxes had no choice but to launch further frontal assaults throughout the course of the following day. The Greeks fought in rotation, allowing some units to rest before rejoining the fray. The second day ended much as the first. However, it was at this point that Xerxes received a stroke of luck.

A local Greek named Ephialtes, whose name became as infamous in the ancient world as Benedict Arnold's is today, approached the Persian king with an offer to guide troops through the treacherous Anapaea Path in exchange for a hefty reward. Xerxes readily accepted and immediately sent his Immortals on a nighttime march into the mountains.

The Phocians, who had been guarding the path for two whole days with no sign of enemy action, were caught unawares by the swiftly moving Persian column. After pelting the Greeks with a volley of arrows, the Immortals pressed on, bypassing the Phocian position altogether.

The Battle: Day Three At dawn of the third day, Leonidas received reports of Persian movement in the mountains. It became clear that their position would soon be attacked from both ends. Another council was called. Leonidas vowed to fight on with his Spartans,

Leonidas leads the Spartan charge against the Persian army at Thermopylae.   © *Bettmann/Corbis*

declaring that it would be dishonorable to retreat. The Thespians vowed to fight alongside the Spartans, as it would be dishonorable to desert their allies. The other allied commanders, however, decided that discretion was the better part of valor, and opted to retreat. Leonidas let them go, except for the Thebans, whom he suspected might go over to the Persians if allowed to leave.

As the allies withdrew, those soldiers remaining sat down to their last meal. According to Herodotus, Leonidas instructed his soldiers, "Eat hearty, lads, for today we dine in Hades."

The Persian frontal assault started around midmorning, led by two of Xerxes' brothers. The Greek defenders were down to about 1,000 men. Leonidas, knowing it was only a matter of time before the Immortals appeared behind him, marched the Greeks forward, beyond the Phocian wall into the wider portion of the pass. Here he was able to fully deploy his forces, all the better to engage and kill as many Persians as possible. The Spartans were determined to sell their lives dearly.

For their part, the Persian soldiers knew that the already determined Spartans would be fighting with the ferocity of a cornered lion, and it is said that they had to

be driven into battle with their masters' whips behind them. A human wave crashed on the Greek lines.

It was just as the Persians feared. According to Herodotus, "the Greeks, knowing that their own death was coming to them from the men who had circled the mountain, put forth their very utmost strength against the barbarians; they fought in a frenzy, with no regard to their lives."

As bodies piled up, Persian and Greek alike, the Spartans fought on. They fought until their spears shattered, then drew their iron swords and continued. Both of Xerxes' brothers were killed in the melee, as was Leonidas. The Spartans fought back four Persian waves to secure their king's body.

It was around this time that the Immortals were first spotted marching in from behind the Greek position, having emerged from the Anapaea Path. Now under the leadership of Dieneces, the Greeks withdrew to a hill overlooking the Phocian wall, preparing to make their final stand. As the enemy encircled the hill, the Thebans deserted to the Persian side, just as Leonidas had feared they would. Then the Persians came at the last defenders of Thermopylae who, according to

Herodotus, "defended themselves with daggers—those who had any left—yes, and with their hands and teeth."

As the sun set over the battlefield at the end of the third day, the Persians stood in victory. Leonidas's head was placed on a pike and the Persians marched south.

It is not known exactly how many Persians died in the effort to take the pass (Herodotus estimates about 20,000 Persians were killed), but there can be no doubt that the battle cost Xerxes dearly. He had expended lives, resources, and, perhaps most importantly of all, time. It was already late in the campaigning season, and the Persians would be unable to bring the Greek armies to battle before the close of the year.

When the two sides did meet in battle the following year at Plataea, the sacrifice of Thermopylae provided a rallying cry and an example for the Greeks—the Spartans in particular. The Persians were defeated for good at Plataea, thanks in no small part to the sacrifice at the "Hot Gates."

The Battle of Thermopylae attained mythical status almost immediately. Leonidas's remains were located forty years after the battle and borne back to Sparta for a royal burial. A lion statue was erected at the hill where the Spartans made their last stand. On it were two inscriptions. The first read, "Here is the place they fought, four thousand from Peloponesus, and here, on the other side, three hundred ten thousands against." The second inscription was dedicated to the Spartans in particular: "Go tell the Spartans, stranger passing by, that here obedient to words we lie."

Today the lion statue is long gone, but a statue of a hoplite, holding his weapons out in front of him, has replaced it. At the base is carved the soldier's defiant words to the Persians: "Come and get them."

Salamis, 480 BCE

The road to Salamis began ten years before the battle, with the Greek victory at the battle of Marathon. The first Persian invasion, under King Darius, was halted on the beach twenty-six miles north of Athens, and most Greeks breathed a sigh of relief, happy to believe that the Persians would trouble them no more. When Darius died in 486 BCE, the threat seemed to have truly evaporated.

However, Darius's son and successor, Xerxes, set to work planning a massive invasion that would dwarf the first effort. As word of the preparation began to filter back to Greece, some astute individuals in Athens recognized the need for preparedness.

Themistocles's Navy One such individual was Themistocles, a statesman known for his wisdom and cleverness. When the silver mines near Athens hit a particularly rich vein, many Athenians wanted to distribute the surplus revenue among all Athenians as a one-time dividend. Themistocles, however, thought the money could be more wisely spent building up the navy, and he managed

GREEK MILITARY CULTURE

Greek warfare placed a huge emphasis on courage and willpower. The standard Greek fighting formation, the phalanx, relied on unflinching courage in combat and was only as strong as its weakest soldier. Furthermore, soldiers relied on their comrades for protection and guidance in the noisy confusion of combat.

It was therefore in the best interest of any phalanx to be comprised of a tightly knit band of soldiers. One of the reasons Sparta enjoyed so much success in war was its militaristic society that nurtured such bonds; they venerated courage in battle above all else. Even in Greek states that did not maintain anything near the rigid martial discipline of Sparta, phalanxes were often grouped by tribe or similar kin groups.

The famous "Sacred Band" of Thebes was composed of 150 pederastic couples and enjoyed an unbeaten record in war for forty years. When it was finally defeated, the unit fought to the last man, such was their level of devotion to the unit and each other.

Scholars and soldiers alike have called Greek warfare the "purest" form of combat. Sparta took this "purity" to its extreme, practically worshiping war, but every Greek state recognized the importance of martial discipline and courage. Greek military culture indelibly shaped Greek ideals and beliefs.

to convince his fellow citizens of this. From 483 BCE to 480 BCE, the Athenian navy grew by one hundred triremes (Greek war ships).

The Persian Fleet Approaches When Xerxes launched his invasion force in 480 BCE, a mighty fleet of more than 1,000 ships sailed along the flank of the massive Persian army as it made its way from Asia Minor toward Greece.

At the Hellespont, the narrow channel of water that separates Asia and Europe, naval engineers built a massive pontoon bridge to allow the Persian army to cross. As the fleet paralleled the army's progress, a canal was dug to bridge the storm-tossed peninsula of Mt. Athos, where an earlier Persian invasion had shipwrecked in 492 BCE. Wide enough for two ships to sail abreast, the canal existed solely for the purpose of creating a shortcut across an inconvenient finger of land, a monument to Persian hubris, or foolish pride, said later Greek chroniclers.

As the Persian invasion force made its way south into the Greek peninsula, a line of resistance was drawn up at the tip of the Greek island of Euboea, which sits just off the Greek coast. The narrow channel between the island and the mainland would prove an ideal chokepoint in which the Persian navy would be unable to bring its superior numbers to bear, much as the Spartans on land were simultaneously garrisoning the narrow mountain pass of Thermopylae.

The Battle of Salamis with men on triremes firing arrows.   *Public Domain*

Cape Artemesium   According to tradition, the Greek fleet met the Persians off Cape Artemesium on the same day as the Spartan-led Greeks met the Persian army at the legendary Battle of Thermopylae. After three days of fighting, as the Spartans were overrun on land, the Greek navy turned south, having inflicted serious damage on the Persian fleet while taking heavy casualties in return. The Persian fleet was delayed when it ran into storms off the coast of Euboea that reportedly sank 200 ships, compounding the loss from battle.

Divine Salamis   As the Persian army marched south and prepared to take Athens, the Oracle at Delphi (a priestess at the temple of the sun god Apollo supposedly possessed of the gift of prophecy) predicted that "divine Salamis" would bring death to the "children of men" and that the Greeks would find salvation behind a "wooden wall."

With these predictions in mind, the Greeks met for council at Salamis, a large island just opposite Athens's seaport of Piraeus. As refugees fled from Athens to Salamis ahead of the advancing Persians, the leaders from the various allied Greek states fell to bickering. The Spartans were in favor of retreating to the southern peninsula known as the Peloponnesus, their homeland.

There, they argued, they could construct a wall at the narrow Isthmus of Corinth, the only point of access to the Peloponnesus, and hold the Persians off indefinitely.

Themistocles, who was leading the Athenian contingent of the fleet, argued that as long as the Persians retained superiority on the seas, a wall would not stop them from landing troops somewhere else on the peninsula. Furthermore, he offered that the "wooden wall" of the Delphic Oracle's prophecy referred to a wall of Greek ships, not a literal wall. He won some converts with this argument, but tensions remained high and Themistocles feared that the Greek fleet might disintegrate even as the Persian fleet arrived in the region and dropped anchor at nearby islands.

The Greek Trap   Themistocles realized it was in the Greeks's best interest to initiate a battle quickly, so, in the guise of offering to turn traitor against his fellow Greeks, he sent a servant to meet with Xerxes. The servant delivered Themistolces' message: the Greeks were fighting among themselves and the alliance would soon disintegrate. If Xerxes attacked right away, he could bag the whole squabbling Greek navy in one battle.

Xerxes took the bait. He sent squadrons to blockade the two exits from Salamis Bay and had them patrol throughout the night to catch any fleeing Greek ships. Meanwhile, within the bay, the Greek ships remained at anchor, their crews sleeping. At dawn the Battle of Salamis would begin.

The Battle As the day began, Xerxes watched from a golden throne atop a nearby mountain as 200 Egyptian ships blocked the western exit from Salamis Bay and the remainder of the fleet (which may have been brought back up to a strength of 1,000 ships), consisting of Phoenician, Cypriot, and Ionian Greek ships, was stationed at the eastern exit. Leaving a thirty-ship squadron to guard against the Egyptians, the Greek fleet rowed out toward the main Persian fleet.

As soon as the Persian fleet entered the bay, the Greek fleet began reversing itself, rowing toward the shore and drawing the Persians into the narrow part of the bay where their numbers and their slower ships would be a disadvantage, as they had been at Cape Artemesium.

The Greek fleet was divided into three squadrons. The Athenians led the center and left. The Spartans, despite their lack of experience with naval engagements, were given command of the fleet and deployed on the right, the traditional location for commanders of ancient forces.

As the bay narrowed to less than 1,300 yards in width, the Persian fleet could only present a front of about one hundred ships. Nevertheless, the Persians, mindful of their king's watchful gaze, rushed headlong toward the Greeks. It was at this point that the Greeks sprung their trap.

Taking advantage of their triremes' speed and maneuverability, the Greeks wreaked havoc among the Persian ships, ramming them and sending their hoplite (a heavily armored citizen-soldier) marines aboard to engage with the unarmored Persian sailors. As the Persian ships slipped beneath the waves, many of their crewmembers, unable to swim, drowned.

Xerxes watched the whole debacle from his mountaintop post and by the end of the day could count at least a third of his fleet sunk and thousands of sailors drowned; the Greeks, in comparison, had lost forty ships. In his rush to secure a victory, Xerxes ensured his defeat. Had he simply blockaded the bay, the Greek fleet would have almost certainly fallen to infighting.

Salamis was without a doubt the most decisive battle of the Persian Wars. Without naval superiority and unable to guarantee a reliable chain of supply, Xerxes had to withdraw the bulk his massive army from Greece, leaving his brother-in-law Mardonius to continue the campaign the following year. The Persians were decisively defeated at the simultaneous land and naval battles of Plataea and Mycale, respectively, on the same day the following year. The Athenian navy became the premier naval power in the Eastern Mediterranean, eventually building an empire of allies and colonies. The Persians would never threaten mainland Greece again.

TRIREMES

The Greek navies of the Persian Wars were made up of a type of ship known as a trireme.

Representing the cutting edge of naval technology at the time, the trireme was a narrow, sleekly built vessel 120 feet long powered by 170 oarsmen seated in three banks on both sides of the ship.

The ship was reportedly able to achieve speeds of upwards of seven knots (about as fast as a racing yacht) and was highly maneuverable, able to turn sharply and put on tremendous bursts of speed.

All this speed and maneuverability served one purpose: to drive the trireme's massive bronze-tipped ram into the sides of enemy vessels. The focus during a Greek naval battle was to sink as many ships as possible with the ram, and the trireme excelled at this task.

Triremes also carried a complement of marines to engage in ship-to-ship fighting should the ramming vessel become entangled with its target.

While other navies tended to crew their ships with archers, Greek ships were crewed with armored hoplites for close combat. Upon ramming an enemy ship, the Greek trireme could disgorge a unit of soldiers to clear its decks, effectively turning the naval battle into a land battle in the process.

Plataea, 479 BCE

The Battle of Plataea was the final, decisive defeat of the invading Persian forces by the Greeks. It is considered a turning point in Western civilization, as the rout of the Persians cleared the way for the blossoming of Greek culture.

After Salamis In the wake of the Greek naval victory at Salamis in 480 BCE, the Persian war machine ground to a temporary halt. Without control of the seas to guarantee reliable re-supply of his immense army, Xerxes withdrew with perhaps half his troops to Asia Minor. The troops he left behind were tasked, along with their new general Mardonius (Xerxes' half-brother and leader of the first ill-fated Persian invasion of Greece in 492 BCE), with conquering the one third of Greece that remained out of their grasp as the year came to a close.

The problem was that this lower third, the Peloponnesian peninsula, was only accessible via the narrow Isthmus of Corinth and was the domain of the Spartans, perhaps the ablest warriors in the ancient world. The Spartans, for their part, were content to sit behind a wall at the Isthmus and let the Persians come to them.

The Athenians, whose ships had led the Greeks to victory at Salamis, were anxious to take the fight to the Persians, who were occupying Athens and laying waste to the surrounding countryside of Attica.

A Corinthian hoplite's bronze helmet, mid-fifth century BCE.   *HIP/Art Resource, NY*

Meanwhile Mardonius, who was a cagier and more patient commander than his king, marched out of Athens. Macedon, a northern Greek state, had been subjugated to the Persians since 492 BCE, and Mardonius sent the Macedonian king Alexander I to negotiate with the Athenians, hoping to turn them against the Spartans by offering them autonomous government and assistance with rebuilding shattered Athens.

The Athenians instead met with the Spartans and representatives of every Greek state that had not yet been conquered by or gone over to the Persians. The Spartans tried their standard excuse, claiming that a religious festival would prevent them from fighting, but the Athenians were determined. It took a winter's worth of arguing, but eventually the Athenians convinced the Spartans to lead an army north and take the fight to the Persians.

When Mardonius received word that the Greeks were assembling an army, he re-occupied Athens and razed it to the ground, covering every last brick in dirt. He then marched his army to Thebes, a Greek state that had willingly allied itself with the Persians at Thermopylae the year before.

The March to Plataea   The army that marched out of Sparta in the spring of 479 BCE was of a size never before mustered by that martial *polis* (city state). Consisting of hoplites, heavily armored infantry, the Spartan army also brought most of its helots, or slaves, along, too, acting in the role of light infantry.

Leading the Spartans and the whole Greek army was Pausanias, who was regent, or acting leader, for the young son of the Spartan co-king Leonidas, who had fallen heroically in battle at Thermopylae the year before.

Once all the allied states had joined up, the Greek force numbered more than 100,000, a massive army by any standards and most likely the largest army the Greeks had ever fielded up to that point. The numbers of the Persian force they were marching against are unknown, but it was most likely at least equal to the Greeks and might have been upwards of three times the size.

The two armies came together near a town called Plataea on the plains north of Athens. The battle that ensued actually unfolded over a series of phases, marked by maneuver and countermaneuver and much skirmishing prior to the actual pitched battle.

The First Phase The Persians, whose army boasted a large cavalry contingent, camped on the plains, excellent terrain for mounted troops. The Greeks, who had no mounted elements, camped in the hills overlooking the plains, the better to discourage cavalry attacks.

Mardonius sent his cavalry against the Greeks anyway, who repulsed the mounted attack, killing the Persian cavalry commander in the process. Mardonius had hoped to at least draw the Greeks into battle, but they maintained their lines.

The Second Phase Nevertheless, the Greeks were obliged to come down out of the hills after their water supplies began to dwindle. They made camp near the Asopos River, keeping a low line of hills between their position and the Persian camp. A series of skirmishes broke out over the next three days as neither side wanted to be the first to initiate a full-blown battle.

During this time, in a daring raid, Mardonius captured 500 wagons making their way across the open plains. The Greeks were faced with running out of supplies, a situation that became dire when the Persians managed to poison the local water supply. Pausanias decided to move camp again, this time retreating back towards the hills with the twin objectives of finding a fresh source of water and shortening his supply lines.

In order to avoid detection, Pausanias ordered the relocation to start after nightfall. The maneuvers did not go smoothly, and many units, the Corinthians in particular, became lost in the darkness and ended up at the town of Plataea itself rather than the intended rallying point. As the sun rose, the Greek forces were stretched out across the plains and Mardonius saw his opportunity . . . or so he thought.

The Third Phase From the Persian position, it looked like large elements of the Greek army were in retreat. This was exactly what Mardonius had been counting on—he had been told of the rivalrous and argumentative nature of the Greek allies and of the possibility that the army might disintegrate. The Persian commander mustered his army and charged the far-flung Greek positions, thinking he was riding down an army on the verge of collapse.

It came as quite a shock to the Persians, then, when they encountered fierce Greek resistance. On the Greek left, the Athenians and their allies clashed arms with Persian cavalry and Theban Greek hoplites. On the Greek right, the Spartans came under attack from a massive Persian contingent of infantry and cavalry, with Mardonius himself leading the horse charge.

The troops the Spartans fought were as varied as the empire they hailed from: Medes from what is now Iran, Bactrians from modern-day Afghanistan, Indians, Egyptians—the roll call read like a list of the subjugated states of the Persian Empire.

Against this diverse force, the Spartans held their ground but were unable to advance. The Corinthians, far to the rear and sheltering behind the walls of Plataea, saw the Spartans were hard-pressed and marched forth to aid their allies. The Persians were forced to split their attention between the Spartans and the approaching Corinthians, and in this moment of confusion, the Spartans pressed forward, killing Mardonius and routing the Persian cavalry.

Meanwhile, the Athenians on the other end of the field were faring equally well and pushing back their attackers. In the Persian center, the second-in-command, a man by the name of Artabazos, saw how the battle was going and sounded the retreat.

With the Greeks, and in particular the Spartans, hot on their heels, the Persian retreat turned into a rout. Most of the Persian losses that day occurred during the headlong flight from the enemy as the Spartans and their allies pursued relentlessly, cutting down any enemy that got in their way.

The Greeks Triumphant The Persians quit the field entirely, and the Greeks took the Persian camp and all the riches of that far-flung empire that it contained. As the Greeks marveled at the sumptuous fabrics and gilded finery, Pausanias wondered aloud why the rich Persians would be so determined to come so far to rob the Greeks of their poverty.

The same day as Plataea, the Greek navy followed up its victory at Salamis by destroying the remainder of the Persian fleet at Mycale. The Persian menace had been neutralized once and for all. Never again would a Persian army set foot on the Greek mainland.

Casualty figures for Plataea are vague. The Persians probably lost a third of their army, which could very well equate to hundreds of thousands dead. The Greeks lost anywhere from 1,500 to 10,000 men. Even the most conservative casualty estimates mark Plataea as one of the bloodiest battles in history, and certainly the bloodiest up to that point. The Greeks had purchased their autonomy at an enormous price in suffering and blood.

⊕ Key Elements of Warcraft

Hoplites and the Phalanx

The backbone of the ancient Greek army was always the phalanx, a dense formation of heavily armored soldiers called hoplites. At the time of the Persian Wars, most Greek armies consisted exclusively of hoplites fighting in phalanxes.

The Hoplite's Armor The hoplite derived his name from his massive shield, called a *hoplon*. A curved wooden shield plated with bronze on the outside and leather on the interior, the hoplon weighed about fifteen pounds and covered the hoplite from his shoulders to his thighs.

The hoplite also wore a heavy suit of armor, called a *panoply*. This initially consisted of a bronze cuirass, a hinged, bell-shaped corset that protected the warrior's torso. The hoplite also wore a bronze helmet, often topped with a fearsome crest of dyed horsehair, and bronze greaves, fitted plates that protected his lower legs.

As can be imagined, all this metal tended to weigh the soldier down. It is estimated that a full panoply, plus shield, could weigh as much as sixty-five pounds. Additionally, the armor was quite expensive, and each hoplite was responsible for his own equipment. Purchasing a full panoply was perhaps the equivalent of buying a new car today, so it should come as no surprise that most Greek hoplites were noblemen or otherwise well-off.

For all the protection it offered, the hoplite's armor was not ideal. In addition to the weight, the cuirass and helmet were seriously lacking in ventilation or comfort. Many Greek warriors grew their hair long to provide some measure of padding for their hard metal helmets. The helmets also restricted vision and, to an even greater degree, hearing.

Over time, a lighter, cheaper cuirass made of glued layers of linen was developed and helmets were constantly refined to make them easier to wear in battle while still granting adequate protection. These innovations increased the pool of recruits available to Greek armies and, over time, Greek battles became larger and larger.

The Hoplite's Weapons The primary weapon of the hoplite was the spear. Ranging in length from six to ten feet, the spear was tipped at one end with an iron head and at the other with a spiked bronze counter-weight. The counter-weight could also double as spearhead when the other end of the spear broke (which often happened). Once fighting got too close for spears to be effective, the hoplite would draw his iron sword, with which he could both slash and thrust.

The Phalanx On his own, the Greek hoplite was a fearsome warrior, but when placed in a phalanx, he became nearly unstoppable. Lining up in units of six to ten rows, shields locked together, the phalanx had one objective: march forward, get to grips with the enemy, and break him. This goal required every hoplite to maintain his place in line and not falter. The slightest gap in the lines would open the entire phalanx to disaster once in the press of combat.

As soon as a phalanx contacted the enemy, the front ranks would begin thrusting with their spears, aiming for the necks, legs, and groins of their enemy. The back rows would push against the row in front of them with their shields. Thus, the best warriors were generally deployed in the front and rear rows, the better to fight and push, respectively.

Aside from the need for absolute order, the other weakness of the phalanx was its right side. Shields were

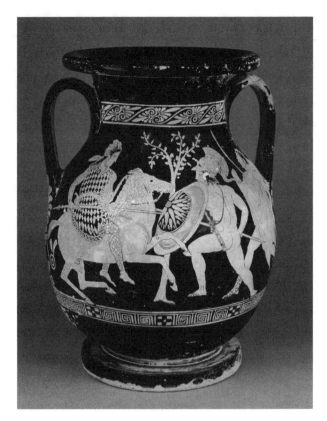

Ancient Greek vase depicting a hoplite engaging a Persian cavalryman. *Erich Lessing/Art Resource, NY*

carried in the left hand, which meant that every soldier in the unit was dependant on his "right hand man" to protect him. The extreme right side of the phalanx, obviously, had no protection and was extremely vulnerable to attacks from that direction. The position of honor on any Greek battlefield was on the right flank, as only the most steadfast units were placed there.

The experience of combat in a Greek phalanx must have tested the nerve of even the most steadfast warrior. Encased in heavy bronze, sweating profusely in the hot Mediterranean sun—most fighting went on during the summer—the hoplite's helmet would further restrict his vision and hearing to the point that he usually could only hear the trumpets and shouted cries of his unit commander, and even these not well. Several Greek battles were decided by a unit misunderstanding its orders and executing a maneuver that left it vulnerable. Weighed down by heavy armor, rapidly dehydrating, and encased in a sense-stealing helmet, the hoplite became even more reliant on his comrades for protection and support during battle.

The Greeks in Battle The typical Greek battle began with a standoff lasting anywhere from a few minutes to several hours. The phalanxes of the opposing armies would line up and attempt to intimidate the enemy. Shouted threats and challenges were not uncommon, nor was involuntary voiding of bowels or swooning, as recorded by several ancient observers.

If neither side quit the field, the two sides would begin to march towards each other. At about one hundred yards (or more, as at the Battle of Marathon) the phalanxes would break into a trot. The resulting crash as the two sides met must have been deafening. It was here that the hoplite's mettle was further tested. It was common for Greek soldiers before battle to drink double or more of their daily wine ration, all the better to dull the pain of wounds and steel the nerves.

The nature of Greek combat bred a society that put a premium on courage and martial prowess. After busily fighting among themselves for centuries, when the Persian Wars thrust the Greeks onto the world stage, they found that they had evolved a method of fighting that was almost unstoppable in its time and would come to dominate warfare for centuries to come.

⊕ Impact of the Greek-Persian Wars

The impact of the Persian Wars on world history is immeasurable. They are the definitive clash between east and west in antiquity and in many ways saw a passing of the historical initiative from the Ancient Near East to the burgeoning West, initially centered on the Mediterranean and Greece in particular.

What is more, the Persian Wars not only represented a major turning point in Greek history, they also marked the beginning of the end for the mighty Persian Empire. When Alexander the Great marched into the Persian Empire some 150 years after Marathon, he was consciously repaying the Persians for the imperial ambitions of Darius I and Xerxes. Thus, Greek culture was not only saved by the wars, it was eventually disseminated to the very regions that once sought to subjugate it.

Many historians believe Salamis to be the most decisive battle of all time. Had the Greeks lost, a Persian victory on land would have been practically assured. And had the Greeks fallen to the Persians, the foundations of Western culture—concepts of individual rights and democracy as well as Greek philosophy and culture—would have been snuffed out while still in their infancy. Considering the massive effect Western civilization has had on the rest of the world, it is fair to say that changing the foundations of Western culture would fundamentally alter world history as well.

The battle of Plataea in 479 BCE marked the beginning of the Classical Age in Greece. The great ancient societies of Athens and Sparta and Ancient Greek culture in general emerged from the crucible of invasion. Greek culture was unified, and Greeks began to view it as the superior culture in the world. Athens entered its Golden Age and saw the likes of Pericles and Socrates walking its cobbled streets.

Athens found itself the preeminent naval power of the ancient world after the Persian Wars. Heading the Delian League, an association of *polei*, or city-states, from around the Aegean, the Athenians quashed the last enclaves of Persian resistance in northern Greece, drove the Persians out of Cyprus, took Byzantium (later Constantinople, and still later Istanbul), and liberated Ionia, an ethnically Greek region in what is now western Turkey.

Thanks to her gains in the wars against Persia, Athens's power grew to the point that the Delian League effectively became the Athenian Empire, creating a natural power struggle with the Spartan-led Hellenic League. Beginning in 431 BCE, Sparta and Athens went to war.

The Peloponnesian War (431-404 BCE) marked the decline of Classical Greece and, unfortunately, the end to any chance of greater Greek political unity. At the end of the fifth century BCE, the Greeks were embroiled in a devastating war but could look back to a time when they had put aside their petty rivalries and stood united against a foreign menace.

As the Greek states bled each other dry, Persia reasserted its control over Ionia and held it for some sixty years before, once again, the Greeks marched to defend their brethren in Anatolia, this time under the leadership of Philip of Macedon.

Phillip was assassinated before he could get his campaign under way, but his son, Alexander III, known as "the Great," carried on the campaign in a bizarre sort of reversal of Xerxes carrying on Darius's invasion plans 160 years earlier.

Alexander, of course, went on to liberate not only Ionia, but to destroy the Persian Empire completely and bring Hellenic culture to the banks of the Indus River. The chain of events set in motion by the Ionian revolt and Athenian intervention at the dawn of the fifth century BCE had come full circle. Without the Persian Wars, Greek culture would not have coalesced, matured, and then spread across the known world.

See also **Conquests of Alexander the Great**

BIBLIOGRAPHY

Book

Hanson, V.D. Ed. *Hoplites: The Classical Battle Experience.* London and New York: Routledge, 1991.

Periodical

Isserlin, B.S.J., et al., "The Canal of Xerxes on the Mount Athos Peninsula." *Annual of the British School at Athens 89.* (1994).

Web Site

Herodotus. G. C. Macauly, trans. History of Herodotus. <http://www.sacred-texts.com/cla/hh/index.htm> (accessed April 2, 2007).

Introduction to the Conquests of Alexander the Great (334 BCE–323 BCE)

By the middle of the fourth century BCE, the Greek city-states found themselves threatened not by the Persians, who had been their principle rival during the previous century, but fellow Greek-speakers to the north, in Macedon. So far as the citizens of the southern city-states were concerned, Macedonians were barbarians speaking a loutish dialect of Greek. Whether they were barbarians or not, the Athenian statesman Demosthenes warned in a series of speeches called the *Phillipics* about the danger of the growing power of the Macedonian kingdom. The kingdom at this time was ruled by Philip II, who had spent three years of his youth as a hostage in the Greek city of Thebes, where he gained a Greek education.

After becoming king, Philip II took advantage of the political instability to his south. He expanded first into territories that gave him access to vast natural resources, which he deployed to strengthen his position in terms of military force and alliances. The city-states were embroiled in two major conflicts at the time. The Social War (357–355 BCE) pitted Athens against several of its subject cities and the city of Byzantium and resulted in a weakened Athens. The Third Sacred War (356–346 BCE) was even more damaging. The city of Phocis seized the treasury of the temple of Apollo at Delphi, leading not only to another war among the southern city-states but to an excuse for Philip to invade Greece for the honor of the god. He forced most of the Greek city-states (with the notable exception of Sparta) into the Corinthian League.

Philip died before being able to lead the League into battle against the Persians. This feat was left to his son, Alexander II, known as Alexander the Great, a man with a genius for conquest. The Persian Empire was still a major power, ruling most of the territories of modern Iran, Iraq, Afghanistan, Turkey, the Levant, and Egypt. All would soon fall to Alexander. He invaded Asia Minor in 334 BCE purportedly to free the Greek colonies there from despotic Persian rule, but in fact went on to dominate the region himself. He drove Darius III, the Persian king, back into Mesopotamia after the Battle of Issus in 333 BCE and defeated him definitively at the Battle of Gaugamela two years later. In between he took the Levant and Egypt, and after went on to India. Despite some notable successes, such as the Battle of the Hydaspes, India ultimately stymied Alexander and he was forced to return to the west. After a brief illness, he died in Babylon in 323 BCE.

At its height, Alexander's empire stretched from Greece to India, but he founded no dynasty. His successors were his officials, who divided up his conquests and went on to fight a series of four wars called the Wars of the Successors (or the Wars of the Diadochi, 322–301 BCE). Though his empire disintegrated, Alexander's fame grew with each passing generation. Ancient Romans venerated him. Medieval French poets celebrated him in verse. And his legend appears in more than eighty languages, from Icelandic to Malay.

The Conquests of Alexander the Great (334 BCE–323 BCE)

🌐 Major Figures

Philip II of Macedon

Philip II (382–336 BCE) was the king of Macedon, a kingdom in northern Greece, 359–336 BCE. He created the kingdom that Alexander the Great went on to expand into an empire in Asia and North Africa.

Philip's Youth   Philip was the third and last of King Amyntas III's sons to succeed to the throne of Macedon. Although the Macedonians spoke a Greek dialect, their southern neighbors in the Greek city-states considered them to be barbarians. From 390 to 379 BCE, Amyntas endured a tumultuous reign during which the neighboring Illyrians ousted him from Macedon. He had to regain his kingdom by paying the Illyrians tribute and by marrying an Illyrian princess, Eurydice, who gave birth to Philip in 382 BCE. When Amyntas died in 370 BCE, one of his older sons, Alexander II, assumed the throne and dispatched Philip as a hostage to the Illyrians. From 368 until 365 BCE, Philip lived as a hostage to Thebes, a powerful Greek city-state that had supported Alexander II during a civil war. There he received a traditional Greek education, both intellectual and physical. The Thebans were unable to prevent Alexander's assassination, though they did support his eventual successor, Perdikkas, a brother one year older than Philip. Perdikkas ruled Macedon until he and four thousand of his men perished in battle against the Illyrian king Bardylis in 359 BCE. This left a young son, Amyntas IV, as heir to the throne. Then twenty-three, Philip began his reign as his cousin's regent but was soon formally recognized as rightful king of Macedon.

Philip as King   Philip successfully contended with rival Macedonian claimants to the kingship and then dealt with hostile neighbors, the Paeonians and Illyrians. His early victories gave him lands rich in natural resources and population, making them vital to his military might. Some of these acquisitions were further cemented by diplomatic marriages, and by 357 BCE he had taken Olympias (also known as Olympia), a Molossian princess, as one of his wives. She gave birth to his eldest child, Alexander (later known as Alexander the Great), the following year.

Philip seized the Athenian colony of Amphipolis in 357 BCE. This gave him the region of Mount Pangaeus, famous for its fabulously productive gold and silver mines. With such resources Philip was well supplied with the means to pressure individuals or states with bribes. This gold and silver also allowed Philip to maintain a disciplined standing army. He perfected the phalanx, introducing the use of a very long pike (the *sarissa*) and integrating cavalry and light infantry troops with heavily armored phalanxes.

The Taking of Greece   Philip continued his territorial expansions, attacking Athenian colonies in the northern Aegean Sea and losing his right eye in the siege of Methone (356 BCE). Meanwhile, southern Greece was in the throes of the Third Sacred War (356–346 BCE). This conflict began when the city of Phocis raided the treasury of the temple at Delphi to finance its defence against Thebes. The Greek city-states broke into Theban and Phocian alliances, with Sparta and Athens siding with Phocis.

In 353 BCE, Philip joined the conflict on the side of Thebes, where he had received his formal Greek education. After some minor setbacks, in 352 BCE he defeated the Phocians and their allies at the Battle of the Crocus Plain and was rewarded with the presidency of the Thasallian League. Not satisfied, he then went on to invade Thrace in that same year. He seized the members of the Chalcidian League in 349 and 348 BCE.

His actions had not gone unnoticed by the other Greek states. The young Athenian statesman Demosthenes delivered his First Philippic address in 351 BCE, in which he warned that now was the time to defeat the Macedonian king, but it was already too late. As the Third Sacred War drew to a close in 346 BCE, the Phocians surrendered to Philip, giving him not only their

In this Greek tetradrachm, Alexander wears the skinned head of an elephant in place of his more typical lion's head, commemorating his victory over the army of King Porus. *Bildarchiv Preussischer Kulturbesitz/Art Resource, NY*

territory but their seats in the Delphic Amphictyony, the league that supported the temple of Apollo at Delphi. However, all was not settled in Greece. An anti-Macedonian party was on the rise, led by Demosthenes.

In 341 BCE, Athens broke a peace treaty with Philip. Philip besieged the coastal cities Perinthus and Byzantium in the winter of 341–340 BCE, threatening the sea route by which Athens received most of its grain supply. This prompted the Artaxerxes III Ochus, king of the vast Persian Empire in Asia, to send aid to these cities because Persian trade routes were also threatened. Philip was unhappy with this interference and his failure to take these cities. His seizure of 240 Athenian grain ships finally caused Athens to declare war. After campaigns in the Balkans, Philip invaded Greece in 339 BCE. The combined forces of former rivals Athens and Thebes confronted the Macedonian king at the Battle of Chaeronea in August of the following year. Philip's eighteen-year-old son Alexander participated in this battle, destroying the Theban lines.

The Last Years The victorious Philip forged the defeated Greek states into the Corinthian League. With such united strength under his dominating leadership, Philip declared war on the Persian Empire. Before departing on campaign, Philip married his seventh wife. This resulted in the estrangement of Olympias and her son Alexander. Philip came to regret his actions and reunited with his son, but in 336 BCE Philip was murdered by Pausanias, one of his bodyguards. It has been speculated that Olympias and Alexander played a role in Philip's assassination, but the motive might have been a personal grudge held by Pausa-

nias. In any case, Philip's appointed heir took full advantage of the legacy his father's death gave him.

Alexander the Great

Alexander the Great (356–323 BCE) was king of Macedon from 336 to 323 BCE and leader of the Corinthian League of Greek city-states. He went on to conquer the Persian Empire, proving himself to be one of the greatest military leaders of the ancient world.

In the summer of 356 BCE, Alexander was born to Olympias, a Molossian princess who was one of several women married to King Philip of Macedon. Probably the eldest son, Alexander enjoyed a well-rounded education at the Macedonian court, in both martial and intellectual subjects. For three years, the famed Greek philosopher Aristotle numbered Alexander among his pupils, and he prepared for Alexander a condensed version of the *Iliad*, Homer's epic poem of the Trojan War. Alexander's mother had impressed upon her son that through her he was descended from Achilles, Greek hero of that war. This deeply impressed the passionate Alexander, who carried Aristotle's "Casket *Iliad*" wherever he went.

Early Battles In 340 BCE, Alexander left Aristotle's school to return to the royal court at Pella where, although only sixteen, he served as regent while his father attacked the coastal cities of Byzantium and Perinthus. In his father's absence, he put down a revolt by the Maedi in northern Macedon, renamed their chief city "Alexandroupolis," and settled Greeks in the territory. He joined his father's campaign against Athens and Thebes in 338 BCE, leading a key cavalry charge in the Battle of Chaeronea. This victory allowed Philip to forge the Greek city-states into an alliance known as the Corinthian League. Under Philip's leadership, the league then prepared for war against the Persian Empire.

Before embarking on that campaign, Philip married a seventh wife. A relative of the new wife gravely insulted Alexander and Olympias, and, in a drunken rage, Philip threatened to kill his wife and son, who fled to Molossia, Olympias's home region. Regretting that he had united Greece but divided his own family, the king reconciled with Alexander. Following Philip's assassination in 336 BCE, Alexander had to put down a rival claimant to the throne, as well as various other uprisings. After Alexander's brutal treatment of the Greek city-state of Thebes, the renewed Corinthian League agreed to accept him as *hegemon* (leader). He would lead the invasion of the Persian Empire, ostensibly to free the Greek colonies in Asia Minor from the despotic rule of King Darius III.

Early Victories in Asia The invasion began in 334 BCE, when Alexander's mostly Macedonian troops (probably numbering about 43,000 infantry and 6,000 cavalry) crossed the Hellespont (the narrow strait that

This marble bust of Alexander the Great was excavated at the ancient city of Pergamum (modern Bergama), in eastern Turkey, where one of his successors, Lysimachus, founded a kingdom. *Erich Lessing/Art Resource, NY*

separates Europe from Asia) into Asia Minor. He paused at Troy to honor the heroes of the *Iliad* and to sacrifice to the goddess Athena. He intended to turn south to free the Greek colonies but could not ignore the Persian forces that had gathered along the banks of a river to the northwest. The first encounter between the Macedonian and Persian armies occurred at the Battle of the Granicus. The Persians lost, and as Alexander began his advance, the important city of Sardis and its surrounding territories surrendered to him.

He took the cities of Miletus, Halicarnassus, and other regions in western Asia until arriving at Gordium, the capital of Phrygia, where he wintered. In his wake Alexander installed satraps (governors) who poured what would have been Darius's taxes into Alexander's coffers. This wealth financed the campaigns of his expanding empire. Rumors of miraculous signs sprang up, prophesying Alexander's conquest of Asia.

May of 333 BCE found Alexander's forces on the march again. As before, Persian forces were massing, this time at Issus (near the modern border of Turkey and Syria). Alexander advanced quickly across southern Asia Minor, nominally claiming the lands through which he passed

without stationing garrisons or officials. Alexander fell ill along the route but recovered before engaging the opposition at the Battle of Issus. Despite the Persian advantage in numbers, Alexander achieved yet another decisive victory. Darius fled to Mesopotamia (modern Iraq), although this meant abandoning his mother, wife, and children to the mercy of the Macedonian forces. Alexander treated his royal hostages respectfully but rebuffed an offer from Darius to ransom them.

Rather than enter Mesopotamia, where the Persian king began to rebuild his forces, Alexander swung south into Syria. He besieged the island city of Tyre (in modern Lebanon) while his second in command, Parmenion, campaigned farther inland. Once Tyre and then Gaza fell, Alexander entered Egypt in the winter of 332–331 BCE. Glad to be rid of Persian domination, the Egyptians offered no resistance. Alexander himself laid out the plans for the port city of Alexandria. He made a pilgrimage through the Western Desert to the oracle at the Siwa Oasis. Even the Greeks respected this oracle of the Egyptian god Ammon, identified by the Greeks with their own supreme god, Zeus. The oracle declared Alexander to be a son of the god, confirming what Alexander himself likely already believed.

The End of the Persian Empire The time had finally arrived to pursue Darius again. Darius offered Alexander a large concession of territory, a vast sum in ransom, a daughter in marriage, and a promise of alliance. Alexander, who in the exchange of letters referred to himself as "King of Asia," had other ideas. He wanted to subjugate Darius as a vassal in a Macedonian empire.

Darius chose to make his next stand at the highly defensible position of Gaugamela, a plain situated between a river and a tall hill. In September of 331 BCE the armies met, and the outcome of the Battle at Gaugamela was the same as the Battle at Issus. Alexander triumphed and Darius retreated, but this time Alexander did not hesitate to follow the Persian king. Even so, he failed to catch him.

The cities of Babylon and Susa surrendered to Alexander without a fight. He married Darius's eldest daughter and arranged a mass marriage between Persian noblewomen and members of his court, a decision not entirely popular with his men. He next undertook a winter crossing of the Zagros mountains to achieve Persis, heart and namesake of the Persian Empire. Here he met ultimately unsuccessful resistance. After the capital city Persepolis surrendered, he allowed his troops to loot it. The men were massacred, the women enslaved, and the palace was burned. Alexander moved on to Ecbatana, where Darius had established a new capital. Darius fled it in advance of the conqueror's arrival. Alexander finally caught up with him in 330 BCE, but only after the Persian king had been assassinated by one of his own satraps, Bessus. Alexander accorded Darius a royal burial and campaigned against Bessus, whom he turned over to Persian authorities for execution.

Alexander's campaigns took him eastward into Bactria. When he had finally put down Bessus and Bessus's allies, he married a Bactrian princess, Roxane. In 326 BCE Alexander survived an attempted assassination by several young noblemen who were perhaps inspired by what was seen as Alexander's increasing despotism. Through the course of his conquests, Alexander had honored and even adopted local customs. He wore Persian dress at court. Perhaps even worse, as far as his men were concerned, he demanded that others bow to him. This was an everyday gesture to a superior in Persia, where it had no religious overtones, but in Greece only gods, not kings, were greeted with such bows.

Into India and Back Later that year Alexander led his troops toward India. He variously met with surrender and resistance. He crossed the Indus River in the spring of 326 BCE. Alexander then defeated King Porus at the Battle of the Hydaspes. Deeply impressed by Porus's courage, he kept Porus on as his vassal ruler in the region. Further campaigns in India were undertaken, but growing dissatisfaction among his forces ultimately persuaded Alexander to return to the west. When he arrived at Carmania (in southeastern Iran) after an arduous desert passage, unfavorable news greeted him. Some of his satraps were rebelling. In retaliation he executed the offenders and ordered the remaining satraps and his generals to dismiss their mercenary forces but not their native troops. These decisions and Alexander's "orientalized" ways cultivated mistrust and contributed to the instability of the empire's leadership.

The End of the Macedonian Empire Intending to conquer Arabia, the Caspian Sea region, and perhaps more of Africa, Alexander set out for Babylon. There, in the late spring of 323 BCE, he fell ill, probably with malaria. After suffering for eleven days, he died. Alexander the Great was mummified, and his body was brought to Egypt.

Although Roxane gave birth to his son shortly thereafter, Alexander the Great's empire died with him. His hard-won territories were sliced up among squabbling successors and, at the age of thirteen, his son, Alexander IV Aegus, was murdered.

King Darius III Codomannus

Darius III Codomannus (c. 370–330 B.C.E) ruled the Persian Empire from 336 to 330 BCE and was the principle adversary of Alexander the Great.

Troubled Beginnings Darius was born to Sisygambis, who, like her husband Arsanes, was a member of the Persian royal family. Known as Codomannus before becoming king, he distinguished himself as a general in a campaign near the Caspian Sea against a tribe known as

---

INSPIRATIONS FROM ALEXANDER

The impressive deeds and complex character of the historical Alexander inspired the creation of legendary Alexanders, who were variously philosopher-kings or tyrants. In medieval times, Alexander appears as a devil figure, but he was also as one of the Nine Worthies, heroes of the past symbolizing knightly virtues. Especially during the twentieth century, Alexander began to figure in popular novels. Perhaps the most influential, and best known, of these are Mary Renault's *Fire from Heaven* (1969), *The Persian Boy* (1972), and *Funeral Games* (1981). He inspired film makers, too, resulting in such movies as *Alexander the Great* (1956, starring Richard Burton) and *Alexander* (2004, directed by Oliver Stone). Alexander has also featured in music, from George Frideric Handel's opera *Alessandro* (1726) to the song "Alexander the Great" by the heavy-metal band Iron Maiden. Interest in Alexander has spread far beyond Europe and the United States, with notable contributions coming from India (*Sikander*, 1941, film) and Japan (*Alexander Senki*, 1997, animated television series).

---

the Cardusii. This occurred during the reign of Artaxerxes III Ochus, who made his cousin Codomannus satrap (governor) of Armenia. A high-ranking minister and eunuch named Bagoas poisoned Artaxerxes III to install Artaxerxes's son, Arses, on the throne as a puppet king. Arses proved to be too independent, however, and Bagoas also poisoned him in 336 BCE. Bagoas next placed Codomannus on the throne as Darius III. Darius was no more eager than Arses to have Bagoas as the power behind the throne. When the minister attempted a third assassination, Darius switched cups. This put an end to Bagoas the kingmaker.

Although Alexander the Great campaigned against him under the pretext of freeing Greek colonies in Asia Minor from the rule of an unjust king, later historians credited Darius with a mild disposition and a sense of decency. And his reign, despite its troubled origin, showed early promise. Darius returned Egypt to Persian rule by defeating an Egyptian king named Khababash and he put down a revolt in Babylon.

Confronting the Macedonian Army Judging from his lack of preparation against an invasion, Darius did not anticipate the danger posed by Alexander, the young king of Macedon who crossed into Asia in 334 BCE. Darius's generals, including the Greek mercenary Memnon, led their forces into their first battle against Alexander at the Granicus River, and were defeated. Memnon died suddenly the next year. Deprived of his skilled general, Darius moved against the young king too late. He was soundly beaten at the Battle at Issus (in the

Alexander is depicted in a mosaic found in the Roman city of Pompeii confronting the Persian King Darius III at the Battle of Issus, in which the two rulers met face to face for the first time.   *Erich Lessing / Art Resource, NY*

vicinity of the modern Turkish/Syrian border) in the autumn of 333 BCE. Unwilling to surrender, Darius abandoned the battlefield, leaving behind his family, including his wife Stateira, his mother, and his children (including Darius's six-year-old heir, Ochus), whom he subsequently attempted to ransom. His offers of a daughter's hand in marriage and the Persian Empire west of the Euphrates did not satisfy Alexander. The Macedonian wanted Darius on the throne of Persia, but as a vassal king, subordinate to Alexander. Darius refused, so Alexander continued his campaigns.

Gaugamela and Its Aftermath In 331 BCE, Darius attempted to stop Alexander at the Gaugamela (near modern-day Mosul, Iraq), but here again he was forced to flee, either from personal cowardice, according to Greek sources, or because his army deserted him, according to Persian sources. This time he went to Ecbatana (modern Hamadan, Iran). The capital Persepolis and other Persian cities fell to the advancing Macedonians, depriving Darius of his financial resources.

Darius's forces were insufficient to meet the approaching Macedonians at Ecbatana. As Alexander continued his acquisitive pursuit, hoping to capture Darius alive, Darius retreated eastward to Parthia (northeastern Iran). The local satraps doubted Darius's leadership, preferring that of the satrap Bessus. In 330 BCE, Darius's allies arrested him. Bessus, a blood relative, ordered him executed and set himself up as King Artaxerxes V. Bessus was ultimately defeated by Alexander in Bactria (northern Afghanistan). The usurper was brought before the Persian council and executed for regicide. Alexander, who had married Darius's eldest daughter, Stateira, in 331 BCE, accorded his dead father-in-law and enemy a lavish burial in Persepolis.

Porus

Porus (?–c. 317 BCE) ruled a kingdom in India between the Hydaspes and Acesinces Rivers (modern Jhelum and Chenab). He was defeated by Alexander the Great in 326 BCE but became a loyal vassal in Alexander's short-lived empire.

Alexander the Great Arrives in India Porus was remarkable for his great height (he was likely about six feet tall, a remarkable size for the era), handsomeness, and spirit. In 326 BCE, his unfriendly neighbor, King Omphis (or Ambhi) of Taxila formed an alliance with Alexander the Great, the young Macedonian king. Alexander had recently defeated the Persian Empire and was expanding his own empire eastward. Although another enemy of Omphis, King Abisares, also willingly submitted to Alexander, Porus refused to do so. Instead, he readied his army along the Hydaspes River and stationed his son upstream with more troops. Confident that the river, swollen with monsoon rains, would provide an additional deterrent to the invaders, Porus waited for Alexander. He was yet another ruler who underestimated Alexander's abilities and determination.

Victory in Defeat Alexander succeeded in crossing the river, defeating first Porus's son and then Porus himself at the Battle of the Hydaspes. Even with the imposing presence of two hundred trained war elephants, Porus's outnumbered troops were no match for the Macedonian army. The Indian king fought valiantly, remaining on the field even after Alexander had routed his army. Finally, wounded and virtually alone, Porus had to surrender. Alexander held games in honor of his victory and later had coins struck to commemorate it. However, Porus's old enemy Omphis could not savor his neighbor's defeat. The honorable and courageous behavior that Porus had displayed on the battlefield had greatly impressed the Macedonian conqueror. In 325 BCE, Alexander installed him as a vassal ruler of his former kingdom. Moreover, after campaigning in the rich, forested territory northeast of Porus's domain, Alexander assigned this new land to Porus, too. Unlike other satraps (governors) he had appointed elsewhere, Alexander did not assign Porus any Macedonian officials or garrisons with which to exert his authority. Porus could exercise his own power, with his own local troops, in Alexander's name.

This sudden increase in Porus's power alarmed one of his relatives, a neighboring king also named Porus, who had submitted to Alexander prior to the Battle of the Hydaspes. This second Porus now withdrew his forces eastward across the Hydraotes (Ravi) River. Alexander pursued him in appalling weather, planting garrisons along the way, and finally besieged the city of Sangala (near modern Lahore). The first Porus joined Alexander with fresh troops, and together the Indian and Macedonian forces razed Sangala and massacred the inhabitants. This territory and its numerous cities were also added to the first Porus's domain.

Although the deaths of Alexander and of his successor Perdikkas resulted in the division of Alexander's hard-won empire, Porus retained his important position as guardian of this eastern border region. However, sometime between 321 and 315 BCE, Eudamus, who commanded the Macedonian army in Taxila, assassinated Porus so that he could claim the king's 120 war elephants.

⊕ Major Battles

The Granicus

The Granicus is a river with steep banks that flows through the plain of Adrasteia, in northwestern Anatolia (Turkey). It was the site of the first battle between the forces of Alexander the Great of Macedon and Darius III of Persia in 334 BCE.

Alexander Arrives In the early spring of 334 BCE, when Alexander the Great landed in Asia Minor, the Persian generals convened a meeting at Zeleia, in northwest Anatolia (modern Turkey), to determine the best course of action against the young would-be invader. There were obvious strengths and weaknesses in both forces. The Persians had 20,000 mounted troops, with about the same number of Greek mercenaries. Ancient sources record that Alexander brought with him an army of between 4,000 and 5,000 cavalry and 30,000 to 43,000 infantry. Among the assembled Persian generals was a Greek, Memnon of Rhodes, one of the ablest commanders in the army of Darius III. He suggested stopping the enemy's advance by laying waste to the fodder in advance of Alexander, thus starving the troops. However, the satrap (governor) of this particular territory persuaded the other commanders to a plan of direct engagement. The Persians selected the plain of Adrasteia as the location to assemble their forces.

Alexander arrived in Asia near the ancient site of Troy. Having learned that the Persians were to the northwest, he postponed his intended liberation of the Greek colonies to the south. For three days his army marched toward the plain of Adrasteia, where the defending Persian cavalry was arrayed east of the Granicus in a line about a mile and a half long. Their Greek infantry mercenaries were stationed on a hill some distance behind them.

Ancient accounts of the battle, and the deployment of the Persian forces, differ. Most modern historians follow the detailed description given by Arrian, who wrote that the Persian cavalry lined the riverbank. The Granicus, swollen and swift with spring rains, and its steep, muddy banks alarmed Alexander's officers. Over their objections, Alexander led an afternoon charge across the dangerous river under a hail of enemy missiles.

The Battle The Macedonian forces were deployed under the command of Alexander on the right wing and his second in command, Parmenion, on the left. In the middle, evenly divided between the wings, were six phalanxes of heavy infantry, flanked by cavalry and light infantry. The extreme left of the Macedonian line moved first in a costly advance that cut Memnon's forces off from the principal battle and drew off some of the Persian heavy cavalry from the center of the line. Next came Alexander himself, in a helmet capped by white feathers, an obvious target at the head of his cavalry. If the Persians could kill Alexander, they would throw the invaders into confusion and bring about a rout, or so Darius's officers assumed.

Alexander and his cavalry took advantage of the gap in the center of Persian lines, but this charge put Alexander in a vulnerable position. The fighting of this battle was less cavalry charge and more mounted hand-to-hand combat. In the midst of a furious melee, one of the Persian commanders, either Spithridates or his brother Rhoesaces, struck Alexander from behind with an ax. This blow to his helmet temporarily incapacitated the king, but before the Persian could land a second, fatal blow, the attacker lost his arm to a strike from Cleitus the Black, a veteran commander. While Alexander recovered his wits from the shock, his forces and Parmenion's continued to bear down upon the defenders. The Persian army that intended to rout the Macedonian army by slaying Alexander found itself virtually leaderless. Against the continued onslaught, the Persians broke ranks and fled. One surviving Persian commander, Aristes, felt such guilt for the loss that he later committed suicide.

The Greek mercenaries in Persian employ, considered traitors to their fellow Greeks, were not so fortunate as the cavalry. They retreated to higher ground. Although Memnon and some others escaped, most were trapped by another merciless Macedonian advance. The two thousand survivors were shipped back to Macedon as slaves. These men were freed two years later at the behest of other members of the Corinthian League.

As reward for their ultimate sacrifice, Alexander declared that the families of the dead among his own forces would be spared both taxes and obligation for further military service. To secure the material results of this victory, Alexander appointed one of his Macedonian officers as satrap of the region. From this riverbank, where he showed both the Persians and his own troops what they were capable of accomplishing, Alexander went on to acquire much of southwestern Asia and Egypt.

Issus

In 333 BCE, Alexander the Great, king of Macedon, and Darius III, king of Persia, met on the battlefield for the first time at Issus, a town near the northeast corner of the Mediterranean Sea near the modern town of Iskenderun, Turkey. The result was a Macedonian victory and the beginning of the end of the Persian Empire.

Darius Leads the Charge The year before, Alexander had landed in Asia and achieved victory over Persian forces at the Battle of the Granicus and other locations in western Anatolia (Turkey). He went on to occupy Cilicia, a rich region in southern Anatolia, before pressing

The vigor and violence of Hellenistic art appealed to the Romans. Here, a Gaul commits suicide, after killing his wife, rather than face defeat at the hands of King Attalus I of Pergamum. © *Museo Nazionale Romano, Rome, Italy/Giraudon/The Bridgeman Art Library*

on toward Syria. He dispatched Parmenion, his second in command, to secure the passes into Syria. Even after Parmenion had dealt with the Persian stations along the way, Alexander's progress was delayed for several weeks while the king recovered at Tarsus, in western Cilicia, from a serious illness that nearly killed him. Once recovered, and after a campaign westward along the coast, Alexander resumed his progress eastward. Along the way, he received intelligence that the Persian forces were at a certain Syrian town, probably near modern Aleppo.

Darius had assembled an army consisting of not only his own troops but also including as many as 30,000 Greek mercenaries. One exaggerated ancient account numbered his total forces at 600,000. This figure is improbable, but it is certain Darius commanded a vast army, one much larger than the army led by Alexander. One of his Greek generals, Memnon, had died unexpectedly of illness, but he had another Greek commander, the Athenian-born Charidemus, to rely on. Like Memnon, Charidemus was not popular with the other commanders, who did not support his suggestion that he take half the Persian army to attack the Macedonians while Darius remained behind in Babylon with the other half. This disagreement led to a heated argument that in turn led to Charidemus's execution. The Persian army moved out against the Macedonians early in the summer of 333 BCE. In addition to the fighting and support troops, Darius's wife, children, and mother traveled with the king. The delay in Alexander's advance prompted Darius to believe that the invaders wanted to avoid a pitched battle. He, on the other hand, hoped to take advantage of the expansive plains of eastern Cilicia, which would give the advantage to his huge number of troops.

Logistics of supply brought Darius onto Alexander's chosen ground. Darius was dependent on supplies brought overland, while Alexander, who had by now moved into the hilly coastal plain south of Darius's forces, had the advantage of the sea routes. Rather than move directly against Alexander, Darius went first to Issus where he slew the sick and wounded men Alexander had left behind there, and he cut Alexander from the land routes to his forces stationed back in Cilicia. This move caught Alexander by surprise. With the majority of his forces—perhaps leaving some behind to guard the south, in case of a Persian attack from that direction—the Macedonian king marched back north, where Darius was waiting at the Pinarus River. Unlike the Granicus, its banks were shallow and rocky, and would afford a crossing for cavalry.

The Battle As at the Granicus, the Persians waited for the Macedonians on the far side of a river. This time, King Darius rode his chariot in the center of the front line, surrounded by his personal guard and flanked by infantry, with cavalry stationed at the far right of the line, nearest the sea. The Greeks came down to the Pinarus in a mass of phalanxes, followed by infantry, followed by cavalry. As room permitted, they fanned out over the uneven plain, with Alexander leading the right and Parmenion the left, as at the Granicus. Cavalry made up the left wing and most of the right, while between them stood phalanxes and light infantry. Other light infantry and archers remained stationed higher on the hill, obliquely to the right.

The Persians may have made the first move, a cavalry charge across the river against Parmenion's vastly outnumbered cavalry and infantry. At about this same time, the Macedonian phalanxes struck against Darius's Greek mercenaries. This did not go well for the Macedonians at first, and Alexander was forced to send in his Thassalian cavalry to outflank the left wing of the Persian cavalry. Alexander was then able to launch a successful rout of the mounted enemy.

Rather than pursue the fleeing Persians, Alexander intended to press on to the center of the Persian line, to take Darius himself. During the battle, Darius fled the field. Some Greek historians state that he did so before the battle, but more likely the Persian king held his ground until his forces gave way around him. His retreat shattered the morale of his own troops, which also broke and ran. Darius's Greek mercenaries, who had been holding the Macedonian phalanxes at the river, were now pressured not only by the phalanxes but also by a cavalry charge on their left. They too broke. News that Darius had deserted the field spread to the Persian cavalry on the right, which also fled, plowing through their own infantry as everyone tried, like their king, to escape.

The retreat resulted in more losses than had the battle. Ancient historians say that 100,000 Persian troops died, a figure that is certainly too high but reflects what was surely an enormous loss. Alexander sustained losses of probably about 450 men.

Alexander seized Darius's baggage trains at Issus and at Damascus. Through this acquisition he came by an enormous amount of wealth and also Darius's own family, whom he treated as royal guests rather than mere hostages. Later, Darius would attempt, and fail, to ransom them.

From Issus, Darius fled back to Mesopotamia, where he would gather the forces to make another stand, this time at Gaugamela. Alexander, meanwhile, went on to conquer the Levant and Egypt, and, eventually, the rest of Darius's empire.

Gaugamela

Also called the Battle of Arbela, the Battle of Gaugamela was the last, and unsuccessful, stand of King Darius III of Persia against the invasion of Alexander the Great, king of Macedon, in 331 BCE.

Darius Prepares Alexander had wrested from Darius the western portion of his empire, but the east still belonged to the Persian king, and he drew from this region to renew his army. Although he had lost most of his Greek infantry, he retained access to the cavalries of Bactria and Sogdiana, as well as troops from India and grasslands to the north. He gathered his new forces at Babylon but moved them, and himself, to a plain in Assyria called Gaugamela, which lay between the Bumelus (Gomil) River and Zagros foothills, east of the modern city of Mosul, Iraq. His men harvested crops that might otherwise have supported Alexander's approaching army. He also prepared the ground at Gaugamela for the conflict, making it flat enough so that his chariots would have an advantage. He had brought with him two hundred scythed chariots, equipped with blades attached to the wheels to mow down cavalry and infantry. About fifteen war elephants stood at his disposal, but these animals were withdrawn before the battle.

Alexander began his march from Tyre in the middle of summer, 331 BCE, knowing that Darius was headed for the Assyrian plains with an army far larger than he had fielded at Issus. Alexander found the crossing of the Tigris River sufficiently taxing to delay further advance for two days. On their second night, September 20, the shadow of the earth eclipsed the moon. Alexander offered sacrifice to the moon, the sun, and the earth on that night and took the eclipse as a good omen. For the Persians, however, a lunar eclipse was an ill omen, and the event may have undermined their morale.

Alexander encountered some advance Persian cavalry, about one thousand in number. Most escaped, but a few taken captive revealed Darius's position and the nature of his forces. By one ancient account, Alexander acquired the Persian battle orders. Once again Alexander rested his troops, this time for four days, and examined the battlefield, where the Persians were waiting in plain sight.

The Battle The Persian intent was to break the Macedonian line while maintaining their own. Darius was positioned at the center, flanked by cavalry and infantry. Chariots and more cavalry were stationed ahead, more infantry behind. The Macedonian army was divided, as earlier engagements, with Parmenion commanding the left and Alexander the right. Both ends of the Macedonian line, mostly cavalry, were angled back from the rest of the line, to prevent the line from being outflanked. In the center, as usual, Alexander stationed the phalanxes. Because Alexander had aligned his position with Darius's, the left of the Persian line extended beyond the right of the Macedonian, leaving the latter liable to an attack from its flank.

Alexander led an advance of cavalry to the right, drawing the Persian line away from the prepared battleground. Parmenion, meanwhile, was left with his forces to contend with the bulk of the Persian forces. The central phalanx was forced to remain behind to strengthen Parmenion. Darius's Persian and Indian forces penetrated through the resulting gap in the Macedonian line to Alexander's baggage train, from which Macedonian reserves had to repulse them. But he had less luck with his scythed chariots, which were evaded and diverted, and the horses slain, by Alexander's infantry and grooms.

The movement of the Persian forces, led by the satrap of Bactria, Bessus, finally created a gap in the Persian lines. Alexander led a charge into it, enlarging the hole before making a flank attack while the phalanxes attacked the Persian line from the front. This drove the Persians backward and finally broke their formation. Bessus retreated with his men in an orderly fashion.

King Darius fled during the fighting. Alexander pursued, so that Parmenion, who was having difficulty with the right wing of Darius's army, was unable to send word of his troubled situation. However, once again news of Darius's flight, and that of his center and left wing, landed a blow upon the morale of the remaining Persians, who may have been already rattled by the eclipse several nights before. Parmenion's troops, notably the Thessalian cavalry, pressed the Persian forces hard enough to rout the right wing. The final engagement of the battle occurred when Alexander and his men, having given up the pursuit of Darius, met mem-

Hector of Troy and Alexander the Great by Giacomo Jaquerio. Alexander honored Hector as a hero. *Scala/Art Resource, NY*

bers of the retreating Persian army. In this battle, some sixty members of Alexander's cavalry lost their lives.

Despite the numerical mismatch in forces, Alexander achieved yet another decisive victory. This was to be Darius's final battle against the Macedonians. He fled to Arbela, then headed farther eastward with Bessus and some of his troops. Many others in the Persian army fled to Babylon, which Alexander later seized. Alexander failed to catch up with Darius at Arbela, but the next year the Persian ruler would be dead, murdered by Bessus.

Hydaspes

Alexander the Great defeated the Indian ruler, King Porus, at the Battle of the Hydaspes in the spring of 326 BCE. After his victory here, Alexander established the easternmost borders of the Macedonian Empire.

Onward to Punjab Having already conquered the bulk of the Persian Empire, the army of Alexander the Great crossed into the Punjab (an area around the modern border of India and Pakistan) in 326 BCE, to begin what he hoped would be the conquest of the rest of Asia.

Omphis (Ambhi), king of Taxila, had already bowed to Alexander's rule and greeted him on the eastern shore of the Indus, which the Macedonian army crossed by means of a bridge and boats built from local materials. At Omphis's capital, games and festivities celebrated the foreigners' arrival, but not all of Omphis's neighbors were so pleased. King Porus refused to submit and assembled an army on the banks of the Hydaspes (Jhelum) River, east of the Indus. Porus knew that Alexander's army outnumbered his own and he hoped that the river, which had few crossings and was running fast with spring snowmelt and the early monsoon, would prove to be an ally.

The Battle Finding the ford of the river blocked on the eastern side by Porus's army, Alexander established his camp here. The Indian king included up to two hundred war elephants among his troops, which comprised four thousand cavalry, three hundred chariots, and thirty thousand infantry, and, of course, the river. Alexander gave the appearance of being prepared to wait for the waters of the river to recede in the autumn. Although they were outnumbered by the Macedonian forces (which seems not to have been at full strength), the Indians succeeded in holding the ford and the other potential river crossings upstream.

Alexander called for the boats that he had used to cross the Indus. They were dismantled and brought to the Hydaspes, where they were secretly reassembled near Alexander's chosen crossing site near an island that would shield them from enemy view. One night during a storm, Alexander moved to make the crossing. He left one of his commanders, Craterus, with troops at the ford base camp. He brought other troops along the bank upstream, to cross at other locations and occupy Porus's army while he himself crossed from behind the island. The discovery of another small branch of the river, unknown to Alexander, delayed their crossing and arrival on the western bank. Once they had landed, they met a force of chariots and cavalry commanded by Porus's son. The chariots were at a great disadvantage in the mud, and Alexander destroyed his opponents, including Porus's son, but some escaped back to the Indian king to inform him of Alexander's approach on the eastern side of the Hydapes.

Porus, who rode an elephant, withdrew most of his troops from the ford to meet Alexander, leaving some behind to continue thwarting Craterus's advance. When the two armies met, Porus's cavalry and chariots were in front, followed by the war elephants, and lastly the infantry. Alexander's' cavalry rode up to screen his infantry in order to give them time to prepare for battle. Alexander's cavalry on the right moved to attack Porus's left. Porus's right wing swung to reinforce the point of attack, which resulted in Alexander's advancing his left wing of cavalry in pursuit of them. The Indian cavalry and chariotry retreated behind the elephants. The rain hampered the Indian archers' attacks, but not the Macedonian use of their long pikes, which they put to effective use against the elephants. Many of the mahouts (elephant drivers) were forcibly removed from their animals, resulting in unmanned elephants on the battlefield. In the resulting chaos, Alexander's forces destroyed or routed almost all of Porus's forces except Porus himself. Finally, wounded, the Indian king had to surrender. The victory was overwhelming, but Alexander suffered a personal loss: his favorite horse, the famed Bucephalus, died during the action.

Alexander celebrated his victory with athletic competitions and the foundation of two settlements, Nicaea and Bucephala, the remains of which have yet to be identified archaeologically. The valiant Porus impressed Alexander so much that he allowed the defeated king to govern his own country, but as a vassal subject to Alexander. He also rewarded him with further territories, making Porus guardian of the eastern borders of the empire.

Alexander went on to take more of India, but the campaign was, in the end, not especially successful and India did not long remain under Macedonian rule.

⊕ Key Elements of Warcraft

War Elephants

Elephants were probably first used as beasts of burden in about 2000 BCE. During the next millennium, they came into use as living war machines, and armies have used them into the twenty-first century CE.

Elephants as Weapons Both the Indian elephant (*Elephas maximus*) and the African elephant (*Loxodonta africana*) have been used in war. Unlike horses or pigs, elephants are not domesticated. To be used as work animals they must be captured in the wild and then trained. Although they do have tough skin, for military purposes it could also be covered with armor of hide or leather, sometimes supplemented with metal plates or rings. Elephants must have a driver, commonly referred to by the Indian term *mahout*. The mahout is usually in addition to the fighting men who ride the elephant, commonly in a structure, such as a wooden or woven box or something more elaborate, mounted on the animal's back.

Unless trained otherwise, horses are frightened of elephants, making elephants effective against cavalry and chariotry. In addition, their enormous size is of great psychological value against enemy infantry. They can serve as walking artillery platforms or attack combatants directly using their powerful trunk and their tusks, which can be armed with metal blades. They are capable of tearing down structures, and the animals' bulk allows them to act as breakwaters to facilitate a river crossing.

Elephants often went to battle wearing some form of armor. The example here is from India, eighteenth century CE. *Erich Lessing/Art Resource, NY*

Tactics against War Elephants Certain offensive and defensive steps can be taken against war elephants. Trenches are effective. Stakes planted in the ground or mounted on wagons can prevent a charge, and sharp implements, such as caltrops, can keep elephants from advancing, grabbing, or pushing. Such devices might also be used by infantry. Dismounting a mahout, by means of a long pike or a grappling hook or by otherwise killing him, removes an elephant from enemy control but also creates a rogue element on the battlefield.

Missiles fired by catapults, like the Roman *carroballista*, are effective offense weaponry against elephants, as are modern artillery and gunfire. Fire provides another defensive weapon. Setting wagons or even live pigs alight among elephants can disrupt an attack.

War Elephants through History Armies throughout the ancient world, especially in Asia, made use of these animals as living war machines. The Chinese armies of the Shang and Zhou dynasties (1523–256 BCE) employed them. Both the Assyrians and their successors, the Persians, confronted elephants in the Indian armies, beginning in the ninth century BCE. The Persians themselves employed elephants against the invading army of the Macedonian king Alexander the Great. About fifteen of the animals

were in the initial front line for the Battle of Gaugamela (331 BCE), but for some reason they were sent back to the Persian baggage train, where Alexander's general, Parmenion, seized them after the battle. About two hundred elephants played a much more critical, if ultimately unsuccessful, role against Alexander when he fought against the Indian king Porus at the Hydaspes River. The Macedonian infantry managed to unseat many of the mahouts and wounded the elephants by means of their long pikes (called *sarissae*). Despite being witness to the liabilities of war elephants, Alexander continued to include them into his own army, and after his death they played important, and more successful, roles in the wars of his successors. At the Battle of Ipsus (301 BCE), the elephant corps of Seleucus I shattered not only the army of Antigonus the One-Eye but the potential of a united Macedonian empire. In 276 BCE, they helped the Seleucid king Antiochus I thwart an invasion of Asia Minor by Gauls.

Pyrrhus, king of Epirus and relative of Alexander the Great, invaded Italy with twenty elephants in his army in 280 BCE, to the great alarm of the defending Romans, to whom the animals were new. The famed Roman legions were still some time in the future, and the arms at hand were initially inadequate against the pachyderms. The Romans later deployed flames and other countermeasures successfully against them. Another enemy of Rome, Carthage in North Africa, also turned elephants against Rome, though during the initial encounter, the siege of Agrigentum (262 BCE), the Carthaginians so badly deployed the animals that they were worse than useless. A Spartan mercenary, Xanthippus, led Carthage and its elephants to a victory seven years later, resulting in a defeat for the Romans that thereafter made them wary of the creatures until the Roman general Metellus employed a trench to defeat them at Panormus.

Hamilcar Barca, ruler of Carthage, seized the Iberian peninsula with the aid of elephants. His son and successor, Hannibal, famously crossed the Alps into Italy with the animals, though in the end only a single elephant, named Surus, survived. Fighting the Romans back on North African soil, at Zama in 202 BCE, he fielded eighty elephants, intending to simply charge them at the Roman line, letting their bulk, rather than any mounted archery, do the damage. Commanded by Scipio, the Roman army managed to frighten and wound many of the pachyderms, and dismounted the mahouts of others, resulting in a Roman victory that ended the Second Punic War.

The Roman Republic went on to field elephants against the successors of Alexander in the east, the Iberian tribes in the west, and on Italian soil during the civil war with Julius Caesar (49 BCE). The Roman Empire sent elephants into campaigns in Europe, but, unlike their Parthian and later Sassinid neighbors in Persia, it seldom employed war elephants during this period.

Elephants in combat unnerved the Romans, but they achieved a victory against the Carthaginians anyway at the Battle of Zama, depicted in this sixteenth-century CE tapestry. *© Louvre, Paris, France/Peter Willi/The Bridgeman Art Library*

Armies resisting the advance of Mohammed and Islam made use of elephants in both western Asia and India. The Muslim Ghaznavid Empire of the tenth through eleventh centuries CE had elephants in its forces. The Indians used them to repel Kublai Khan's Mongols in the thirteenth century CE but a hundred years later another Mongol ruler, Tamerlane, defeated India's elephants. Elephants continued to figure in the warfare of Asia into the twenty-first century CE, with Myanmar being the last remaining state to include elephants in its armed forces.

The Holy Roman Emperor Frederick II numbered a single elephant in his thirteenth century CE army, which he sent into battle against the Italians, but for the most part, after antiquity, European encounters with war elephants took place on Asian soil. Colonial armies made use of them as transport, especially for artillery, through the twentieth century CE.

⊕ Impact of the Conquests of Alexander the Great

Alexander the Great's conquests destroyed the Persian Empire, but his own empire did not remain unified after his death. His successors fought a number of wars, resulting in several Hellenistic kingdoms in western Asia, northeast Africa, and southeastern Europe. Despite this rupture, his conquests had spread Greeks and Greek culture throughout Asia and led to the Hellenistic Age, generally defined as the period between the death of Alexander in 323 BCE and the demise of the last Hellenistic kingdom in 33 BCE.

New trade routes, notably the sea route to India, were opened during the period of rule by Alexander's successors. The use of coinage and a monetary economy became standard. Visual, literary, and dramatic arts flourished in the multicultural hotbed of Hellenistic cities. From the dialogue of comedy to the drapery portrayed on statuary, the idealistic forms of Classical Greece were replaced by more realistic and individualistic models. The quests for realism and understanding were undertaken by philosophers and scientists of the age, including Alexander's tutor Aristotle. Great advances in astronomy and mathematics were achieved, in part by such brilliant men as Euclid and Archimedes, but also through Babylonian scholarship. The science of medicine made important advances as well. The syncretism of eastern and western religious practices contributed to the proliferation of mystery religions, in which individuals underwent secret rites of passage, notably those of Isis and Mithras and at least some branches of early Christianity.

Many peoples chafed, however, under Hellenistic rule, which had the effect of placing a class of ruling foreigners over local populations. Even in the Seleucid Empire, which seemed to take particular pains to integrate Asians and Greeks, the former retained a second-class status. In Egypt, rebellions led to brief but independent reigns of native Egyptian pharaohs in Thebes. In Judea, Judas Maccabaeus led a revolt when the Seleucid king, Antiochus IV, tried to merge the Jewish religion with the Greek worship of Zeus, thus splitting the Jews into pro- and anti-Hellenic factions. In many areas, the local people (even the wealthy and educated) did not take up Hellenistic culture. In Persia, this fragmented the Seleucid Empire.

The fractured Hellenized regions weakened as Rome was consolidating its power. Rome conquered the Hellenistic kingdoms, reducing them to mere provinces, and what Rome could not reach (for example, Bactria, now northern Afghanistan) eventually fell apart to internal and other external forces. The Ptolemies were the last to succumb to the might of Rome, in 33 BCE, when Cleopatra VII and Marcus Antonius lost to Octavian at the Battle of Actium.

Hellenistic culture outlasted the Hellenistic kingdoms, however, persisting under Roman rule. Greek as the *lingua franca* throughout Alexander's former empire. The Roman conquerors, for their part, were more than a little impressed with the man whose former empire they came to dominate: they practically worshipped him. It is reported that when Julius Caesar saw a statue of Alexander the Great in Gades (modern Cadiz, Spain), he wept with envy. Roman general and political leader Pompey acquired a robe once belonging to Alexander and wore it as a symbol of greatness. Emperor Caligula, never a mentally stable man, even robbed Alexander's tomb and took to wearing his armor. The Romans happily appropriated the Hellenistic culture spawned by Alexander, spreading it throughout western Europe as far north as Britain.

Introduction to the Rise of Rome (3rd century BCE to 2nd century CE)

The site of Rome on the Tiber River in Italy was inhabited as early as the eighth century BCE Initially ruled by a king, Rome became a republic (a political system in which citizens control the government) in 509 BCE and began to expand by dominating or battling other societies on the Italian peninsula. Rome built up its strength slowly, first taking over southern Etruria (a region in what is now northern Italy). Gauls (Celtic tribesman from the north) sacked and occupied the city in 386 BCE, then overran the Etrurians. But the gradual development of the Roman Empire was not derailed for long.

Eventually, Rome dominated most of Italy. Its former enemies were welcomed into the Roman army, and different levels of citizenship were extended to territories and allied states. In 268 BCE, Rome's military might would meet its first significant challenge from Carthage, the capital city of the Phoenicians in Africa. At stake was control of the Mediterranean Sea, a body of water vital to the military and economic well-being of Rome.

The wars between Rome and Carthage were called the Punic Wars—the term "Punic" comes from the Roman word *Poeni*, meaning "Phoenicia." The First Punic War began when Rome invaded Sicily, then under Carthaginian control. After twenty-three years of fighting, Carthage ceded control of Sicily to Rome in 243 BCE

The Second Punic War was waged by the formidable Carthaginian commander Hannibal, who defeated Romans at the Battle of Trebia, the Battle of Lake Trasimeno, and the Battle of Cannae. In spite of these victories, Hannibal was eventually forced into submitting to a punitive peace treaty after the Battle of Zama in 201 BCE Hostilities broke out again fifty years later, and this time the results were decisive. The Third Punic War lasted only five years and ended with the complete destruction of the city of Carthage. Rome had begun the Punic Wars as a power localized in Italy; 120 years of fighting later, Rome controlled most of the Mediterranean, including North Africa, and was on its way to becoming an empire.

The evolution of the Roman Empire was marked both by great territorial expansion and internal strife, as many in Rome hungered for the power and riches associated with newly conquered territories. When Julius Caesar came to power in the first century BCE, Rome's empire included the Iberian peninsula, Greece, and Asia Minor. Caesar spent eight years conquering Gaul (now France and Belgium) as a general in the Roman army, then brought his army home, provoked a civil war (which he won), and promptly had himself declared dictator for life, effectively ending the republic. His heir Augustus became the first Roman emperor, and Augustus's successors continued to expand Rome's reach until the second century BCE, when Emperor Trajan ruled a gigantic domain stretching from Britain to Arabia, from the Danube River to the coast of North Africa.

Following Trajan, Roman emperors built permanent fortifications to protect, but not expand, the borders of the Empire. The second century CE was one of peace, but towards its end, border skirmishes, civil war, and power struggles in the military signaled the eventual fragmentation and decline of the Roman Empire.

The Rise of Rome
(3rd century BCE to 2nd century CE)

⊕ Major Figures

Hannibal

Hannibal (247–183 BCE) led Carthage against Rome during the Second Punic War. He is best known for his brilliant strategies and for leading his troops and war elephants south across the near-impassable Alps to invade Italy, considered one of the most impressive feats in ancient military history.

Prelude to the Second Punic War The First Punic War ended in 241 BCE. Three years later, Rome took control of the islands of Sardinia and Corsica, then turned most of Sicily into the first tribute-paying Roman province. Rome expanded to the north and east as well. Carthage, meanwhile, consolidated its power in Spain under General Hamilcar Barca, Hannibal's father. Hannibal inherited his father's position at the age of twenty-six. He set off the Second Punic War when he laid siege to Saguntum for eight months. Saguntum, in northern Spain, was an ally of Rome.

Invasion of Italy Hannibal expected Rome to declare war in response to Saguntum's destruction, and he planned an invasion of Italy from the north. He led forty thousand troops and between thirty-five and fifty war elephants across the Pyrenees into Gaul (modern-day France). In Gaul, Hannibal added local tribal warriors to his mercenaries and outran the two Roman consuls sent to stop him, brothers Publius and Gnaeus Scipio. Over fifteen days in the early fall of 218 BCE, Hannibal crossed the Alps into Italy, battling early snow, rough terrain, and other hardships. He lost more than a third of his men and elephants in the effort.

Early Battles in Italy Relying on his Numidian cavalry, Hannibal defeated Roman troops at the River Ticinus in what is now Switzerland. Publius Scipio was wounded and withdrew to the Trebia River, a tributary of the Po. Hannibal followed and fought the Battle of the Trebia, winning another victory for Carthage. By spring, the Carthaginians entered Etruria (northern Italy) and won the Battle of Lake Trasimeno. In 216 BCE, Hannibal handed Rome the worst defeat it had ever suffered at the Battle of Cannae. As he hoped, many Roman-held cities in Italy rebelled and joined forces with him.

Problems Faced by Hannibal Hannibal was not able to take full advantage of these victories because he had no reinforcements for his depleted troops. In Spain, the Scipio brothers and their legions tied up Carthaginian armies until both brothers were killed in 211 BCE. Hannibal made the southern Italian city of Capua his base, but in a few years Rome was strong enough to lay siege to it. In response, Hannibal marched on Rome, hoping that his brother Hasdrubal would arrive with fresh troops from Spain.

Hasdrubal's men and elephants crossed the Alps, but were defeated by a Roman force before they could reach Hannibal. Hasdrubal was killed, and his head was thrown before Hannibal's outpost. Hannibal fought on for four more years without winning any substantial victories. After fifteen years in Italy, he was called back to Africa to defend the city of Carthage in 203 BCE.

The Battle of Zama and Surrender The final battle of the Second Punic War in 202 BCE was named Zama for the place where Hannibal camped. The battle site itself was a plain southwest of Carthage. Roman historian Polybius writes that Scipio and Hannibal met at the Battle of Zama and fought: "the Carthaginians for their own safety and control of Libya, and the Romans for the empire and domination of the world." Hannibal's great victories were fifteen years behind him. The size of his army was impressive—he commanded forty thousand men and eighty elephants—but his men were inexperienced. Half his soldiers fell to Scipio's slightly smaller, but better trained, force.

The peace treaty in 201 BCE forced Carthage to pay heavy fines for fifty years and hand over all their elephants, but the Carthaginians were allowed to keep their cities.

Scipio Africanus, who defeated Hannibal. © *The Print Collector/ Alamy*

Hannibal's Later Life and Death
Hannibal lived another eighteen years after the defeat at Zama. In 197 BCE he was elected civic magistrate and worked for social reforms. He fled Carthage two years later when Roman sources accused him of conspiring against Rome with the King of Syria, Antiochus III. Hannibal stayed at Ephasus in Syria until Antiochus was defeated by Rome some years later.

The kings of Armenia and Bithynia hosted Hannibal as well. He fought at the side of the king of Bithynia against Pergamum, a Roman ally. When, in 183 BCE, the Roman senate demanded that the king give up Hannibal, the Carthaginian general poisoned himself rather than submit.

Julius Caesar

Julius Caesar (100–44 BCE): general, proconsul, and eventually dictator of Rome, affected the lives and fortunes of millions of people as he led the Roman army to war and conquest. His influence and the civil war he began ended the fabled Roman republic and pushed Rome toward becoming an empire.

Early Life and Career
Gaius Julius Caesar was born in July of 100 BCE to a patrician (noble) Roman family. The Julian family was well connected but not wealthy, although they claimed to trace their ancestry back to the goddess Venus. Much of what we know about Caesar comes from his own writings and those of his friend Cicero, as well as later historians in Greece and Rome.

He married for the first time while in his teens and was immediately caught up in political rivalries not of his making. He left Rome and enjoyed an eventful career in the army. As an officer, he was decorated for bravery during the siege of Mytilene, a Greek city. Pirates kidnapped the young Caesar; a suitable ransom was paid and they released him. Not one to forgive, Caesar gathered troops and pursued his erstwhile abductors. When he caught them, he had them crucified.

Before returning to Rome, Caesar traveled to the Roman province of Asia Minor, took command of local troops, and fought off an invasion by King Mithridates of Pontus—all on his own initiative, without orders. His daring acts and talent as a speaker and advocate prepared the way for him to enter politics in Rome.

Political and Military Achievements
Caesar was elected tribune (magistrate) in 73 BCE, and many religious and state offices followed. He spent lavishly, as was expected of Roman politicians, and formed advantageous alliances (including two more marriages; his first wife died and he divorced his second). Caesar worked and bribed his way up the political ladder, increasing his prominence and influence. In 61 BCE he went to Spain as proconsul (governor) for a year. During that time he raised the Tenth Legion and conquered new territory for Rome.

Back in Rome, Caesar formed an alliance with the fabulously wealthy Crassus and the noted general Pompey. Their alliance came to be known as the First Triumvirate. Pompey married Caesar's only legitimate child, Julia, as well. Caesar supported his two partners with legislation and favors, and they secured for him a five-year appointment, later extended, as proconsul of two provinces: Illyricum and Cisalpine Gaul (northern Italy south of the Alps). Caesar then spent eight years in the conquest of Gaul (modern-day France), a vast land beyond his province. The campaigns enriched him and added greatly to Rome's growing domain.

Civil War
Pompey's wife Julia died while Caesar was in Gaul, and Crassas was killed during his own military campaign. Pompey and Caesar became rivals for power in Rome. Both men were skilled commanders, but the Roman Senate supported Pompey. In disobedience to senate orders, Caesar rode south with his army, crossing the Rubicon, a river that separated Italy from Cisalpine Gaul. This act started a civil war, as Caesar knew it would. The phrase "crossing the Rubicon" has since come to mean going past the point of no return.

During Caesar's rule as dictator, many coins were struck in Rome with his image.   *The Granger Collection, New York. Reproduced by permission*

The armies of Caesar and Pompey met in a decisive battle at Pharsalus, Greece, in 48 BCE Caesar had four battle-hardened legions, including the tenth, and three new legions. Pompey had three times as many men, but Caesar's troops fought fiercely and Pompey's forces were defeated. Pompey fled to Egypt and was killed by agents of the pharaoh (Egyptian king).

Caesar in the East   Caesar pursued Pompey to Egypt, and after Pompey's death he became involved in a war between the two claimants to the throne of Egypt, Cleopatra VII and her younger brother (and husband) Ptolemy XIII. Caesar not only won the throne for Cleopatra, but became her lover as well, and she bore him a son. He then fought a brief war with the son of Mithridates in Asia Minor. He described this action to the

Roman Senate in his famous quote, "I came, I saw, I conquered."

Caesar in Rome   Caesar became dictator in 46 BCE and instituted reforms in Rome, many of them aimed at consolidating his own power. He tripled the number of senators, changed tax structures, and tried to reduce unemployment by forcing estate owners to employ free men in 1:2 proportion to their slaves. He revised the calendar, making a year 365 days long—and naming his birth month after himself. Caesar held multiple offices and took to wearing purple, which was considered the color of gods and kings. He also had coins struck with his own image; Roman currency had never carried the likeness of a living Roman before.

Assassination His growing power led sixty Roman politicians to plot to kill Julius Caesar on March 15, 44 BCE They attacked him with knives as he entered the senate building and stabbed him twenty-three times. The assassins included former supporters and even Decimus Brutus, the son of Caesar's favorite mistress. Many of the conspirators believed that Caesar had become a tyrant and must die so that the Roman Republic could be revived.

The assassins fled and hid after Caesar's murder, but two days later the senate granted them amnesty. Caesar received a public funeral, and sentiment turned against the conspirators. Most left Rome. In the following year, Caesar's heir and nephew Octavian (Augustus Caesar) began a series of civil wars to punish Caesar's killers and establish himself as the first Roman Emperor.

Vercingetorix

Vercingetorix (?–46 BCE) was a prince of the Arverni tribe who emerged as a war leader during the conquest of Gaul by Julius Caesar. Vercingetorix united the many Celtic tribes of Gaul to fight the Roman invasion and is considered one of France's earliest national heroes.

Noble Origins Vercingetorix was the son of Celtillus, an Arverni ruler who (according to Caesar) had been killed by his peers for seeking to rule all of Gaul. Tribes in Gaul chose their rulers from the nobility, but kingship was not necessarily passed from father to son. Caesar's writings assert that Vercingetorix was "a young man whose abilities were second to none." The prince, probably born in the 70s BCE, no doubt received the training of both a warrior and a nobleman as he grew up.

Encouraged by an act of rebellion against the Romans in a neighboring land, Vercingetorix tried to rouse his own people to fight the Romans in 53 BCE. His uncle, Gobannitio, and other nobles discouraged him, then expelled him from the principal town of Gergovia. Undeterred, Vercingetorix assembled a motley collection of vagabonds as followers and soon won over most of the Arverni tribe to his cause and was proclaimed king.

Vercingetorix (the *rix* at the end of his name means "king") formed alliances with most of the neighboring tribes of central Gaul, as far north as the Parisii (who settled what is now Paris), and west to the sea. All agreed to send warriors, horses, and weapons to the new king on certain dates. Caesar reported that Vercingetorix used severe punishments and torture to control his subjects. Most of our information about Vercingetorix comes

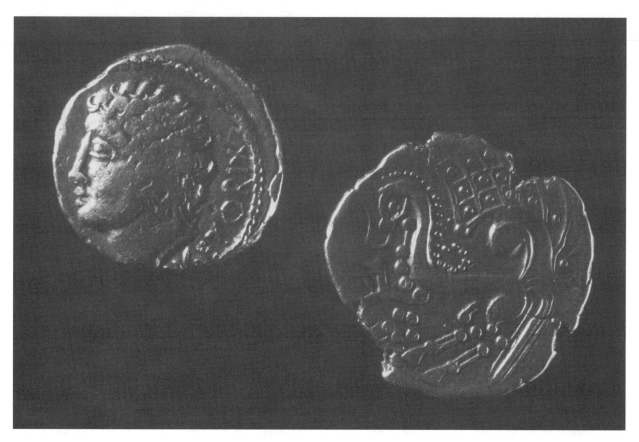

Coins from the first century BCE may be the only images made of Vercingetorix during his lifetime. *The Granger Collection, New York. Reproduced by permission*

from Caesar's book *De Bello Gallico*, but Caesar, who viewed Gauls as his enemies, may have exaggerated or slanted his reports.

Attacking Allies In the winter of 52 BCE, Vercingetorix's armies attacked and harried Roman allies among the Ruteni, Bituriges, and other tribes, forcing them to switch allegiance. He believed that snow would keep Caesar out of central Gaul for weeks, but the Romans crossed the Cevennes Mountains with a cavalry force and infantry raised in Cisalpine Gaul. Vercingetorix held his forces together and retreated to Arverni territory. He then attacked Gorgobina, a Boii tribal center with ties to Rome.

Caesar summoned his legions from their winter camps and attacked the towns of Vercingetorix's allies. This drew the Celtic army from Gorgobina. The two sides fought in Bituriges territory. Caesar backed up his own forces with four hundred German cavalry, forcing the Gauls to retreat.

Siege at Avaricum Vercingetorix proposed that the Gallic tribes burn their own towns to deprive the Romans of food and supplies. He persuaded his followers that giving up their own property was a worthwhile sacrifice, arguing that if they failed to drive out the Romans they would be killed and their families enslaved. The plan was accepted, but the Bituriges pleaded to spare the city of Avaricum (Bourges), because it was inaccessible except by one narrow road. Vercingetorix gave in to this request.

While his army suffered from hunger, Caesar laid siege to Avaricum and built up earthworks and two large towers. Vercingetorix camped nearby with his army, but could not lift the siege. The tribes questioned Vercingetorix's loyalty to their Gallic confederation at that point, but he regained their support by portraying the Roman army as desperate, starved, and depleted. After nearly a month, Caesar overran Avaricum during a storm and later reported that all but eight hundred men, women, and children of the population of forty thousand were killed.

Gergovia With winter ending, Vercingetorix sent emissaries out to renew alliances and led his army to Gergovia. The legions followed. Caesar ordered trenches and siege works built and tried unsuccessfully to lure his enemies from the high ground. He finally withdrew. The Roman and Gallic armies clashed in a fierce cavalry battle in Lingones tribal territory; Rome, with newly recruited German troops, routed the Gauls.

Alesia Caesar pursued Vercingetorix's forces to Alesia, a hilltop stronghold. He surrounded the Gauls with eight camps stretching for ten miles. The Roman fortifications included walls and a series of ditches fifteen and twenty feet wide, some with rows of spikes buried in them. Vercingetorix had provisions for only thirty days,

No statues of Vercingetorix were made during his lifetime. This image was crafted in 1865 and stands in Bourgogne, France, near the site of Alesia. *© Robert Harding Picture Library Ltd/Alamy*

so he sent cavalry out before Rome's siege works were complete. When the food ran out, Vercingetorix and his commanders sent noncombatants from Alesia.

A pan-Gallic army of 250,000 arrived to fight the Romans from outside Alesia. Despite its impressive size, the Gallic army was routed and destroyed. Vercingetorix, facing defeat, gathered his commanders and told them to decide whether to hand him over to Rome or put him to death themselves. They, in turn, sent envoys to Caesar.

Imprisonment and Death Vercingetorix surrendered to Caesar and was taken to Rome as a prisoner. There he languished in prison for nearly five years, until Caesar led him around in a belated twenty-day "triumph," or victory celebration. After this final parade, Vercingetorix was executed.

Trajan

Trajan (c. 52 or 53 CE–117 CE) was a general and emperor whose conquests in northeastern Europe and

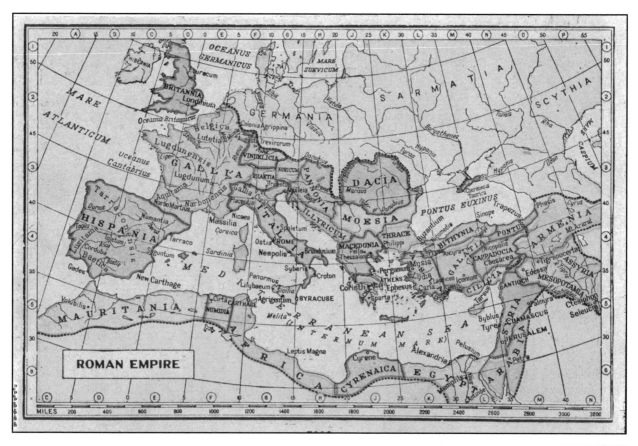

Under Trajan, the Empire reached its greatest size. This map shows the regions of the Roman Empire with the names used 2,000 years ago. © *Mary Evans Picture Library/Alamy*

the Middle East brought the Roman Empire to its largest size. After a successful military career, Trajan, who was raised in Hispania (what is now Spain) became Rome's first non-Italian Emperor in 98 CE, reigning till his death in 117 CE

Early Military Career Trajan's father was a magistrate in southern Hispania who rose through the political ranks to become governor of Hispania, then proconsul (governor) of Syria. Trajan, whose full name was Marcus Ulpius Nerva Traianus, enjoyed the benefits and training of a provincial aristocrat. He entered the army while still a teenager and served under his father in Syria before being posted back to Hispania.

Trajan served in Rome's legions under the Emperor Domitian. He was a tribune (senior military officer) from 71 to 81 CE, rising to praetor, or field commander, in 87 CE Two years later, he became legionary commander in Syria. In 91 CE he was appointed consul of the relatively new province of Lower Germany. Rome's control of all these areas was constantly challenged, and Trajan's military and administrative skills were honed and sharpened with action and experience. His career kept him away from Rome and its political rivalries.

Trajan married Pompeia Plotina, a woman of Roman Gaul, but they had no children. The historian Dio Cassius—born nearly forty years after Trajan's death—claimed that Trajan preferred attractive young men to women, but the source of his information is unknown and may simply be gossip.

Trajan: A Popular Choice for Emperor The Emperor Domitian was murdered in 96 CE He had been popular with the army but hated by the senate and is remembered for both reforms and cruelty. The senate selected the former consul Nerva to be the next emperor. Nerva was not loved by the army, so he wisely chose Trajan, a military hero, as his heir and successor. Nerva, elderly and childless, died of a fever after only seventeen months in office, and Trajan took the throne.

Military Conquests of Trajan Rome's territory expanded under Trajan, an emperor with military expertise. After the Dacian Campaign, in which Trajan pushed into the kingdom of Dacia, the Empire's borders stretched north of the Danube River for the first time, to include what is now Romania, part of Bulgaria, Hungary, and Moldava. The areas of modern-day Jordan and northern Arabia, east of the Sinai, came under the Empire's rule by 107 CE. During

Roman ideals of beauty and efficiency dominated local customs. These Roman arches were built in the Carthaginian (or Phoenician) city of Tyre, in modern-day Lebanon. *© Paul Almasy/Corbis*

that campaign, Trajan annexed the Nabataen kingdom, whose capital was Petra.

During the period of peace that lasted from 107 to 113 CE, Trajan held games to celebrate the completion of many civic projects, such as his forum, an aqueduct, and public baths. One such celebration, a gladiator festival at the Colisseum, an enormous arena that had been completed in 80 CE, lasted three months. Reportedly, five million spectators were entertained by the carnage

and gore and up to eleven thousand people died in the arena.

Trajan's Final Campaigns Rome's acquisition of Mesopotamia (modern Iraq and parts of Iran) as a province is not well documented. Trajan sailed and marched to Asia Minor when he was sixty years old, and his wife accompanied him. He was determined to enforce a treaty that the Parthians had violated when they appointed a ruler for Armenia that Rome had not approved. Trajan's campaign, called the Parthian War, was waged with troops from Syria, Egypt, Judea, Arabia, and Europe. Trajan subdued Armenia and established fortifications, including the harbor at Trabzon, along the southern coast of the Black Sea. He then pursued the Parthian king Osroes as far as the Persian Gulf. There, so the story goes, Trajan lamented his advanced age because it stopped him from marching on to India and following in the footsteps of Alexander the Great.

Before he could return to Rome after his successes in the Middle East, revolts against Roman rule broke out. Trajan quickly put down rebellions in several places, including Mesopotamia and Judea. In Syria, he suffered a stroke, then recovered somewhat and sailed for Rome. His health forced the ship to stop in Cilicia (now southeastern Turkey), where he died in August 117 CE.

Trajan's Legacy Trajan named Hadrian his successor while on his deathbed. His ashes were carried back to Rome and placed at the base of the one-hundred-foot column erected to commemorate his Dacian War.

Nerva, Trajan, and Hadrian were the first three of the so-called "Five Good Emperors" of Rome. Trajan's military accomplishments often overshadow his civic works, but Trajan set Rome on sound financial footing and opened the senate and the equestrian (knightly) class to non-Italian citizens of Rome. He repaved the Appian Way, built a new harbor near Rome, improved the aqueducts, and erected libraries, baths, and courthouses. He fought corruption in the cities and provinces, which expanded Rome's power. In many ways, Rome under Trajan was Rome at its peak.

⊕ Major Battles

Mylae, 260 BCE

The Roman victory at the Battle of Mylae in 260 BCE was the first for the newly built Roman navy, and it signaled the slow transfer of sea power from Carthage to Rome during the First Punic War.

Background of the First Punic War The First Punic War began as a fight for control of the sea between Sicily and Italy. Hiero II, tyrant of Syracuse, directed an attack on Messina, ruled by the Mamartines. Messina asked Rome and Carthage for aid. Carthage sent troops and ships. This alarmed Rome, as Messina controlled the straight between the tip of Italy and the island of Sicily. Rome borrowed ships and sent an army, and a war began that would last for twenty-three years.

Rome Builds Ships Roman legions won victories on land, but could not challenge the Carthaginians at sea. Three years into the war, in 261 BCE, Rome began the construction of 120 warships. Most were quinqueremes: galleys with five men on each oar. Quinqueremes required crews of three hundred men. A few ships were triremes, with three banks of oars on each side. Rome

had never built ships before, but they threw themselves into the endeavor boldly and with "unbelievable daring," according to the historian Polybius.

Rome recruited and trained oarsmen on land while the ships were being built, so that they could rush into battle as soon as the vessels were completed. The first fleet of seventeen ships sailed from Messina for the island of Lipara, off the northeast coast of Sicily. There, a Carthaginian fleet trapped them in the harbor. The crew panicked and abandoned the ships. Commander Gnaeus Cornelius Scipio surrendered and was taken prisoner—a debacle that earned him the nickname *Asino* (donkey).

Innovation and Victory After this defeat, an anonymous Roman shipwright invented a unique feature called a *corvus* (meaning "raven"). The corvus was a gangplank with an iron spike on one end. While sailing, the corvus was lashed to a mast, out of the way. During an attack, though, the corvus could be pivoted, dropped, and hooked to an enemy vessel, allowing Roman soldiers to quickly board and overcome their opponents.

After the defeat at Lipara, Rome's second consul, Gaius Duilius, took command of the rest of the ships. The Carthaginians were ravaging the city of Mylae (now called Milazzo), which sat on a peninsula on the northeast coast of Sicily. Duilius sailed for Mylae. The two navies met at sea; the Carthaginian commanders were at first scornful of Roman seamanship. Once the corvi were put into use, though, Duilius's navy captured thirty Carthaginian vessels, including the flagship. Thirteen enemy ships were sunk as well. Hannibal Gisco, the commander, was forced to flee in a small rowboat. (This was not Hannibal Barca, the general who crossed the Alps during the Second Punic War.)

Aftermath of the Battle of Mylae Duilius, the first successful Roman admiral, then proceeded to Segesta to lift a siege and captured Macela. Returning to Rome as a hero, he enjoyed a triumphal parade in which the prows of the captured ships were displayed. Hannibal Gisco was crucified by his own people for his incompetence in losing the battle.

The Carthaginian fleet was still formidable, however, and new ships were built. The war dragged on and the Romans suffered a major naval defeat at the Battle of Drepana twelve years later. By this time, both sides were nearly bankrupt, but refused to surrender. A peace treaty was finally signed in 241 BCE.

Drepana, 249 BCE

The naval Battle of Drepana, fought between Rome and Carthage in 249 BCE, was a devastating loss for Rome. Rome eventually rebuilt its navy and ended the First Punic War by defeating Carthage in a later battle in the same area.

Early Success of Rome's Navy The First Punic War, which was fought between Carthage and Rome for

A drawing of the Battle of Mylae, showing the corvus, or gangplank, that the Romans use to board Carthaginian ships.   © *North Wind Picture Archives/Alamy*

control of the Mediterranean, began in 264 BCE The Roman navy enjoyed early victories in Sicily at the Battle of Mylae in 261 BCE and later at Ecnomus in 256 BCE, mostly due to the development and use of the corvus, which was a spiked gangplank that allowed the Romans to board and overcome the crew on enemy ships.

The War Drags On   After fifteen years of war, the treasuries of both Rome and Carthage were depleted, and the people could not afford any more taxes. Both sides were tired of war, but not ready to give up. Rome's fleet of ships had been destroyed in storms several times. By this point in the war, Carthage knew how to avoid the corvus, and so the Roman ships were less effective. Using what vessels were available, Rome blockaded the port of Lilybaeum, but Carthaginian sailors easily ran the blockade. Rome was humiliated.

A Botched Surprise   In 249 BCE, Consul Claudius Pulcher reasoned that an attack on the Carthaginian fleet would be unexpected and therefore successful. He decided to sail from Lilybaeum by night and attack Drepana (today's Trapani in western Sicily), where Carthage's ships were garrisoned. The attack was a disaster, however. The Romans could not keep their own ships in battle formation in the darkness. When dawn broke, their line was scattered across the harbor.

The Carthaginian fleet was not in the harbor anyway. Under the command of Adhurbal, Carthage's faster ships and more experienced crews captured over ninety of the scattered Roman vessels. Consul Pulcher escaped, but returned to Rome in disgrace. Stories spread that Pulcher had recklessly ignored omens of bad luck on the morning of battle. The thirty Roman ships that got away from Adhurbal's men were destroyed by a storm.

Return to Drepana   The war continued until 241 BCE, but Rome withdrew from naval battles for seven years. Eventually, wealthy citizens funded the building of two hundred new ships, most of them quinqueremes (galleys manned by over three hundred men), hoping to finally end the war. Under Gaius Lutatius Catulus, the new navy besieged Drepana and Lilybaeum once more.

This time, the battle went in Rome's favor. Off the Aegates Islands, Roman quinqueremes sank fifty Carthaginian ships loaded with supplies and captured seventy more. Carthage gave up Sicily and signed a peace treaty that inflicted punitive fines and taxes. Dissatisfaction with this treaty contributed to outbreak of war again twenty-three years later.

Trebia, 218 BCE

During the Second Punic War, the Carthaginian general Hannibal (247–183), defeated the Romans in three major battles in northern Italy. The Battle of Trebia (or Trebbia) was the first of these clashes.

Before the Battle In 218 BCE, Hannibal led his men and war elephants across the Alps to invade Italy. The trek cost him at least a third of his force. (The main historical sources, Roman writers Livy and Polybius, differ widely in their estimates of Hannibal's army.) Whether he had twenty thousand or forty thousand men, though, he easily defeated a Roman detachment at the River Ticinus. Hannibal then moved his troops into Placentia (present-day Piacenza) and positioned them defensively west of the Trebia River. Because of his victory at Ticinus, tribal warriors and mercenaries joined his ranks, increasing his numbers.

Consul Titus Sempronius Longus led a Roman army toward Africa to fight Carthage. He was called back by a frantic Senate and dispatched to northern Italy to stop Hannibal. Once Sempronius arrived in Italy, Publius Scipio, the commander who had been wounded at Ticinus, cautioned him against bold moves. Sempronius did not listen. He encamped both Scipio's army and his own along the eastern side of the Trebia.

Hannibal's Plan Knowing of Sempronius' reputation for rashness, Hannibal planned an ambush. He put his brother Mago in charge of two thousand troops who hid at night among brambles and thorn bushes on a flat, treeless plain through which an offshoot of the Trebia River cut deeply.

The Battle: December 18, 218 BCE In the morning, Hannibal's Numidian cavalry attacked and retreated, luring the Roman forces out of their camp in spite of threatening snow and rain. Sempronius sent his entire force, more than forty thousand men, assuming they would easily defeat the enemy. The Roman troops had not even eaten their morning meal. They crossed the Trebia, getting soaked as they did so—hardly ideal conditions under which to engage a powerful enemy.

Hannibal deployed his largely mercenary army in two flanks, each equipped with war elephants. His cavalry troops far outnumbered the Roman cavalry and outflanked them. The Roman cavalry was forced back as the day wore on, and the infantry was left unprotected. As Hannibal hoped, the Roman infantry rushed into the river. Mago's hidden troops then rose in ambush and the Romans were unable to climb up the steep banks to escape. An estimated twenty thousand Roman troops died or were injured in the battle.

It fell to the wounded Scipio to lead the surviving troops back across the Po River to Cremona, to winter in relative safety. Sempronius escaped with his life, but his reputation was ruined. Rome elected two new consuls

the following year who would confront Hannibal once more at the Battle of Lake Trasimeno.

Lake Trasimeno, 217 BCE

During the Second Punic War, the Carthaginian general Hannibal (247–183 BCE) gained control of northern Italy. The Battle of Lake Trasimeno (or Lake Trasimene) was the second of three successful fights waged by Hannibal and took place in June of 217 BCE.

Before the Battle Hannibal had crossed the Alps in winter to invade and conquer Roman territory. With a depleted army supplemented by mercenaries and tribal enemies of Rome, Hannibal won battles—first in a skirmish at Ticinus, then at the larger Battle of Trebia. The anxious Roman Senate elected consuls Gaius Flaminius and Gnaeus Servilius Geminus and then sent them with newly raised legions to guard the Apennine Mountains, which run north-south along the Italian peninsula. Traveling separately, these generals took over the demoralized armies of the wounded Publius Scipio and the unsuccessful Titus Sempronius Longus.

THE WAR IN AFRICA

The First Punic War was waged mostly in Sicily, but commencing in 256 BCE, Rome threatened Carthage in Africa as well. The goal was to bring the battles closer to the Carthaginian homeland, which was located near the modern city of Tunis, Tunisia.

Under the leadership of consul Atilius Regulus, a Roman fleet of 350 ships attacked the coast of Libya. This moved the war onto Carthaginian territory. Greco-Roman historian Appian reported that Regulus captured two hundred Libyan towns, the citizens of which hated their Carthaginian overlords and eagerly surrendered. However, the general Xanthippus, a Spartan working for Carthage, used a hundred war elephants to defeat and slaughter the Romans near the city of Tunis. Only five hundred Romans survived, and consul Regulus was taken prisoner.

Rome's navy successfully engaged the Carthaginians off the coast of Libya again. The Romans rescued most of their five hundred soldiers still in Africa, but not the commander, Regulus.

Five years passed. The poet Horace, who lived two centuries later, wrote this story: "When the Carthaginians wished to negotiate for peace, they sent Regulus to Rome—under guard, to assure his return to captivity. Regulus, contrary to his instructions, urged Rome to keep fighting. When he returned to Carthage, he was punished and killed by being shut inside a cage full of spikes."

Xanthippus, the successful general from Sparta, did not fare much better. According to Appian, after receiving honor and rewards for his victory, the Carthaginians had Xanthippus murdered on the voyage back to Sparta. Apparently, the Carthaginians did not want to share the glory of their defeat of Rome in Africa.

After the last of three Punic Wars fought with Carthage over 120 long years, Rome destroyed the city. These ruins of Carthage are in Tunisia. *© Ken Welsh/Alamy*

Hannibal wanted to fight one army at a time, so he tried to lure Flaminius into battle before his army could join that of Servilius. Hannibal raided and attacked the land near Apulia until Flaminius, ignoring all his advisors, decided to pursue and engage Hannibal's forces.

Hannibal's Strategy at Lake Trasimeno

Lake Trasimeno was less than ninety miles north of Rome. Hannibal picked the north shore of the lake as an ambush site. There, the road forced men to march between high hills on either side and ascend toward a steep ridge. Hannibal sent some of his men far ahead to light fires, tricking the Romans into thinking that their enemies were camped much further away.

Throughout the night, Hannibal arranged his armies for battle. On the ridge at the east end of the road, Spanish and Libyan soldiers waited to charge down toward the Romans. To block a retreat, he deployed cavalry and Gallic (Celtic) allies in a line hidden by the forested hills, so that they could run and block the road

after the legions passed. On the sides of the road, slingers and pikemen hid in the hills, waiting the signal to attack.

The Battle: June 23, 217 BCE

Flaminius had pushed his men hard the previous day, not letting them make camp until late at night. In the morning, they hurried east along the road. Fog blocked their view. Hannibal waited until all the Roman troops were between and below his own forces before giving the signal to attack from all sides.

The Romans, taken by surprise, could not counterattack. Cavalry pressed their lines from the front and rear, while the Carthaginian troops harried the Romans from all sides. Polybius writes, "While they were still considering what they ought to do, they were being killed without knowing how."

Flaminius, in the rear, died at the hands of the Celtic warriors. In all, 15,000 Romans, or two full legions, were killed on the road along the north shore of Lake Trasimeno, many during hand-to-hand combat.

The Aftermath Horrified by yet another defeat, the Roman Senate elected a dictator: Fabius Maximus. He carried out religious rites, which eased Roman minds (it was rumored that Flaminius had ignored these rites and thus had been doomed to failure by the gods). However well-favored, Fabius Maximus could not solve the problem of Hannibal either: his policy was rather to avoid battle, and he allowed Hannibal to ravage central and northern Italy. He aversion to action earned him the nickname the "Delayer." Many Romans were disgusted by this policy of avoidance, and new consuls were elected. Rome would face Hannibal yet again, this time at Cannae.

Cannae, 216 BCE

The Battle of Cannae in 216 BCE, between Rome and Carthage, was the third of three major confrontations during the Second Punic War. No other single day of combat in Europe, ancient or modern, ever inflicted so many casualties.

The Second Punic War The Carthaginian commander Hannibal crossed the Alps in late fall 218 BCE to invade and conquer Roman territory in Italy. Hannibal quickly engaged and defeated Roman armies in a skirmish at Ticinus, the Battle of Trebia, and the Battle of Lake Trasimeno.

After such heavy losses, Rome elected a dictator, Fabius Maximus. Fabius applied a policy of following Hannibal's armies but avoiding battle, which earned him the title *Cunctator*—the "Delayer." He allowed Hannibal's troops to pillage the Italian countryside without interference from Roman legions. Some Romans thought this a wise strategy, but many others considered it not only cowardly, but costly as well.

Varro and Paullus When Fabius's term as dictator ended, the senate elected two new consuls to lead the army: Gaius Terentius Varro and Lucius Aemilius Paullus. With the senate's encouragement, the men quickly took command of the eight consular legions and an equal number of allies southeast of Rome near the Adriatic Sea. They decided to make a stand and attack Hannibal at the hilltop village of Cannae, in Apulia.

Varro and Paullus took turns commanding their legions, auxiliaries, and allies, which numbered 6,000 cavalry and 80,000 infantry. Paullus argued against fighting at Cannae, but when Varro took his turn at command, he deployed the troops at sunrise. The Roman forces ranged along a river, most facing south and deeply massed in the center. Hannibal had a larger cavalry, about 10,000 from Numidia, Gaul, and Spain, but only 40,000 infantry made up of Celts, Spaniards, Libyans, and Carthaginians. He split his force into three groups. A thin line faced the Romans across the river, while most of his cavalry were positioned left and right.

The Battle In the early morning, the worst fighting took place on the left flank, where Hannibal's Spanish and Celtic cavalry dismounted and forced the Romans into hand-to-hand fighting. As the day wore on, Rome threw more legions against this force and pushed them back. The center of the Roman line, where most legionaries were positioned, forced their way across the river and broke through the Carthaginian lines.

Hannibal had anticipated the the frontal attack. The Romans were caught between groups of skilled Libyan fighters, armed heavily in spoils taken from previous battles with the legions. In addition, the wind blew dust directly at the Romans, blinding them.

Hannibal's brothers Hasdrubal and Mago commanded different groups. While the Libyans pressed in on the Romans from left and right in a double enveloping maneuver, Hasdrubal led his men to attack the Romans from the rear. Paullus was killed in the fighting, along with many officers. Only 70 of the 6,000 cavalry escaped the slaughter with Varro. While Hannibal lost fewer than 6,000 men (most of them Celtic troops), 70,000 soldiers and allies of Rome died that day.

Before the battle, Paullus had left 8,000 troops to guard a distant camp. These troops were captured. A deputation was sent to Rome, but Rome refused to ransom the men. Instead, the senate passed a resolution saying that the army must "Conquer or Die!" The 8,000 men were sold into slavery by Hannibal.

In the wake of this terrible defeat, Fabius Maximus's old policy of avoiding battle seemed, in retrospect, quite wise. The historian Polybius reported that most Romans gave up on the idea of supremacy in Italy and lived in fear that Hannibal would attack their city at any moment. He never did; without reinforcements from Carthage or Spain, Hannibal was unable to follow up on his victories and the Second Punic War dragged on for years.

Siege of Syracuse, 213 BCE

The Greek city of Syracuse had retained its independence from Rome for years, but when Syracuse supported Carthage during the Second Punic War, Rome laid siege to the city in 213 BCE. Although its defenses were designed by the great inventor Archimedes, Syracuse eventually fell.

Syracuse's Rulers Syracuse, a large Greek city on the southeast coast of the island of Sicily, warred with Carthage for centuries over territory on the island. From 270 through 215 BCE, Syracuse flourished under the leadership of Hiero II, also called Hieron II. Hiero came to power by defeating the Mamartines in the Battle of Mylae. Like many rulers of Syracuse, Hiero was a tyrant. In those times the word simply meant a man who held the power of a dictator, usually with the support of his people.

Site of the grave of Archimedes in Syracuse, Sicily. © *CuboImages srl/Alamy*

Hiero allied with Rome during the First Punic War, although most of Sicily was under Carthaginian control until the Battle of Deprana. That naval battle ended the war in 241 BCE and made Sicily a Roman province. When Hiero died during the Second Punic War and his position as tyrant passed to his grandson Hieronymus, the Carthaginian general Hannibal was invading Italy and defeating the Romans handily in battle after battle.

War with Rome Hieronymus opened negotiations with Hannibal, but was assassinated by pro-Roman agents after one year as tyrant. Civil war erupted in Syracuse and after much bloodshed two brothers emerged as rulers: Hippocrates and Epicydes, of Carthaginian descent and sympathy. Alarmed, Rome sent Appius Claudius Pulcher to command land forces, and Marcus Claudius Marcellus in charge of a naval fleet, to stop Syracuse from aiding Carthage.

Marcellus sailed with his fleet to the Sicilian city of Leontini, where Hieronymus had been killed. There, he captured Carthaginian sympathizers and beheaded some of them. Reports of great slaughter were carried to Syracuse ahead of Marcellus; whether the stories were true is not known. Marcellus prepared to lay siege to Syracuse. His sixty ships were manned with archers, slingers, and javelin throwers. Appius's land troops carried ropes and ladders to scale the city walls. But their initial attacks failed, due to the ingenuity of Syracuse's great inventor, Archimedes.

Rome Takes the City The Romans had siege engines with wicker screens for protection and concealment, but were unable to deploy them against Archimedes' defenses. After eight months of failure, Appius and Marcellus split their forces: some remained to blockade the city while others took to raiding the towns and countryside throughout Sicily. The Romans seemed neither able to breach the city walls nor to stop supplies from reaching the city, so the siege dragged on until luck finally turned in favor of the Romans. The Syracusans neglected their defenses during a festival dedicated to the goddess Artemis, which gave Rome the opportunity to conquer the city. The historian Livy says that Marcellus noticed a tower in which he could hide his troops during the celebrations.

Exact details have not survived about how Syracuse fell. Roman soldiers swept through the city, and several stories were told about how the aged Archimedes was killed. A popular version had him so absorbed in a mathematical problem that he did not notice his enemy about to strike. Marcellus took the small planetarium that Archimedes had built back to Rome as a trophy.

Conquest of Gaul, 58–50 BCE

Julius Caesar's conquest of Gaul altered the map of Europe and brought power and wealth to Rome from both slaves and loot. The conquest also enriched Caesar himself and established him as a successful military leader. His exploits in Gaul (which covered the areas we now call France, Belgium, the Netherlands, Luxembourg, Switzerland, and part of Germany) set the stage for Roman civil war and the development of the Roman Empire.

A Brief History of Gaul and Rome Rome considered the Celtic tribes of Europe its enemies, at least since 390 BCE, when a force led by the Celtic warrior Brennus sacked and occupied Rome itself. Celts fought Romans during the Punic Wars, and afterward Rome drove the Celts from the Italian peninsula. The Celts of Iberia (Spain) battled Rome throughout the second century BCE and were eventually conquered. In 118 BCE, Rome established a province, Cisalpine Gaul, in what is today northern Italy. The Celtic tribes of Gaul remained independent until the invasion of Julius Caesar and his legions.

Julius Caesar Begins the Conquest Julius Caesar became proconsul of both Illyricum and Cisalpine Gaul in 58 BCE. From the beginning, Caesar meant to use this position to amass wealth, victories, and prestige, so he watched for opportunities. When the Helvetian tribe, with a population of 368,000, began a westward migration that skirted Roman territory, Caesar led six legions into Gaul to stop them. Allying with local tribes like the Aedui, he quickly defeated the Helvetians. He forced one-third of them back to their old territories; the other two-thirds were either killed or enslaved.

An assembly of Gallic leaders then asked Caesar to rid them of an invader named Ariovistus and his Suebi followers. The Romans pursued and defeated Ariovistus's army. Rather than returning to Roman territory, Caesar quartered his legions in Gaul for the winter.

Conquest and Rebellion In the following year, Caesar raised two more legions and marched to Gaul's Belgic area, north of the Seine River. Confronted with forty thousand legionaries and twenty thousand auxiliary troops, most of the Belgic tribes surrendered to Caesar without fighting. The Nervii, however, battled fiercely and Caesar admitted that victory "rested on a knife-edge." Although the Nervii fought until only five hundred of their sixty thousand warriors remained alive, Rome was victorious in the end. In 56 BCE, Caesar turned his attention to the west, defeating the seagoing Veneti tribe with his own navy and subduing much of Aquitaine (what is now southwestern France).

ARCHIMEDES

Archimedes, who was born in Syracuse and was probably in his seventies during the siege of Syracuse, was one of the greatest inventors, mathematicians, and scientists of any age. He developed formulae to determine the volume of cones, cylinders, spheres, and other shapes, and the properties of parabolas. He discovered the law of hydrostatics (water displacement) while sitting in his bath, according to one story. His inventions included the water screw, which was used to deliver water to irrigate fields, and a model planetarium.

Archimedes's genius was put to the test when Rome attacked Syracuse in 213 BCE He used pulleys and catapults to hurl beams, stones, and weights onto the Roman ships in the harbor. He is said to have designed a system of mirrors that set fire to the enemy's sails; scientists argue to this day whether or not it could have happened. Another invention of Archimedes was a crane with a grappling hook that swung out into the harbor to crash into and sink the Roman ships.

Syracuse eventually fell to the Romans and Archimedes was killed by a legionary who likely did not recognize the old man. The historian Plutarch wrote that, "Marcellus was distressed, and turned away from the slayer as from a polluted person, and sought out the relatives of Archimedes to do them honor."

Roman armies traveled as far north as the Netherlands in 55 BCE and battled German tribes. The legions built a bridge across the Rhine, burned and terrorized the Sugambri for two weeks, then crossed back into Gaul and tore down the bridge. Towards the end of the campaign season, having learned that British allies were reinforcing the warriors of Gaul, Caesar sailed with two legions to Britain, but soon returned. In 54 BCE, he again crossed the English Channel, this time with five legions, and established treaties with several tribes.

The legions returned and settled into winter quarters in Gaul, but food shortages in the Belgic region increased resentment towards Rome. A Celtic force under Ambiorix ambushed and massacred five cohorts—most of Caesar's Fourteenth Legion. Other tribes attacked a Roman camp, and only a quickly assembled rescue mission led by Caesar lifted the siege and stopped the rebellion from spreading further.

Gaul Unites Following yet another year of fighting in the north of Gaul and across the Rhine, Caesar faced his most formidable foreign opponent in Vercingetorix, an Arverni chieftain who was able to unite many of Gaul's tribes against Rome. Caesar claimed that Vercingetorix used torture and death threats to control his warriors and portrayed Vercingetorix as a leader of vagabonds.

The famous mathematician and scientist Archimedes reportedly used a system of mirrors to set fire to the Roman ships besieging Syracuse. © *The Print Collector/Alamy*

Vercingetorix, however, proved himself a skilled warrior and commander.

Caesar learned of Vercingetorix and his confederacy during the winter, while cut off from the legions. He crossed snow-covered mountains with allies and troops from Cisalpine Gaul to get to Vercingetorix's own territory. While Vercingetorix attacked Caesar's Celtic allies, Caesar summoned his legions from their winter camps and attacked the towns of Vercingetorix's allies. Roman troops burned and sacked Cenabum (today's Orleans), a trading town of the Carnutes, before drawing the rebel forces out to engage him. Rome won that fight, so Vercingetorix changed his strategy.

The Gauls decided to burn their towns to deprive the legions of food and supplies. In Bituriges territory, only Avaricum (Bourges) was spared because it was believed to be impregnable. With his army suffering from hunger, Caesar laid siege to Avaricum, building earthworks and two large towers. After many weeks, Caesar took Avaricum and killed nearly forty thousand men, women, and children.

The struggle moved to Gergovia, where Caesar failed to oust Vercingetorix from his home fortress. Rome suffered a blow when its former allies, the Aedui, joined the Gallic rebellion as well. Caesar requisitioned thousands more troops from Cisalpine Gaul as well as cavalry and infantry from Germany. A disastrous cavalry loss caused the Gauls to withdraw to Alesia where a final siege took place.

Final Battles Caesar surrounded Alesia with eight camps and built up massive fortifications. Vercingetorix sent for reinforcements, and an intertribal army of up to 250,000 men arrived to batter the Roman positions from the outside. Roman men and siege works held out, though, and starvation forced the eventual surrender of Vercingetorix.

A romantic statue of Boudicca, chief of the Iceni tribe, stands in London.   © *Richard Wareham Fotografie/Alamy*

Rebellions and uprisings in Gaul continued through the next winter, and Caesar attacked the Bituriges, the Carnutes, and the Belgic tribes. Only in 50 BCE did Caesar return to Cisalpine Gaul and eventually to Rome. The Greek historian Plutarch estimated that Caesar's campaigns in Gaul killed a million people and enslaved another million.

Conquest of Britain, 43–138 CE

Since the time of Julius Caesar, Britain had been a tributary of Rome—paying so much into the imperial coffers, in fact, that Rome judged it made no economic sense to take over the region, since it would make less in taxes than in tribute. In 43 CE, however, Rome changed its mind and invaded. Once Rome forced Britain into the Empire, the island became the westernmost outpost of Roman rule. In three and a half centuries of occupation, Britain's original Celtic tribal leadership was effectively destroyed, and its culture dramatically changed.

Background and Initial Invasion   Julius Caesar made two forays into Britain, resulting not in conquest, but in expanded contact and trade with the Celtic tribes that lived there. Roman legions did not return to the island to conquer it until the Emperor Claudius's reign,

almost one hundred years later. Claudius, who was not a popular choice for emperor, needed a military victory to support and validate his authority.

In 43 CE, Claudius sent a large fleet which landed in what is now Kent and took the tribes in the area by surprise. Claudius then sailed to Britain himself, so that he would be in command as his armies captured Colchester (then called Camulodunum). This earned him a celebratory triumph in Rome and the prestige he sought. The actual warfare was left in the capable hands of General Aulus Plautius and his forty thousand troops.

Conquest and Accommodation   General Vespasian, who later became Emperor, led a legion through the south, while other commanders fought in the east and the Midlands. Within ten years, the Romans had effective control of most of south Britain, except for Wales in the west. In some cases, Rome accepted tribute from powerful tribal rulers and allowed those chieftains independence. This freed the Roman military leaders to concentrate their forces in the west, where they faced fierce resistance.

The Conquest in the North   In 78 CE, Vespasian, now Emperor of Rome, appointed an able administrator

BOUDICCA'S REBELLION

East Anglia erupted in revolt in 61 CE, led by the Iceni tribe under the Celtic queen Boudicca. Prasutagus, Boudicca's husband and chief of the Iceni, had allied with Rome and maintained his tribe's independence. When he died, his daughters were raped and his widow flogged by the Romans. The Iceni rose up in arms, along with the Trinovantes tribe, and tried to expel the invaders.

Boudicca led successful attacks on the Romans in Londinium (London) and Verulamium (St. Albans), before confronting a massive Roman force in the Midlands. The Roman army was led by governor Suetonius Paulinus, who had been campaigning in Wales, and who had destroyed the druidic (druids were Celtic priests) sanctuary at Anglesey. In the final battle, more than 150,000 people died, both Romans and Britons, but the victory went to Rome. Boudicca perished and the Romans killed thousands more Britons in punitive raids. A famine struck the land as well, effectively halting armed resistance to Roman rule in the southeast.

named Agricola as governor of Britain. Agricola finally subdued Wales, introduced reforms, and pushed Roman control to its furthest point north, into Scotland. There, he defeated the Caledonian tribe decisively in 84 CE at the Battle of Mons Graupius.

Forty years later, Emperor Hadrian built the stone and turf wall across Scotland that bears his name today, marking the Roman Empire's northern boundary just south of territory controlled by the Pictish tribes. Hadrian's Wall once stretched 73 miles and included 158 towers, 16 forts, and 80 gated milecastles (small forts). In 138 CE, Hadrian's successor, Antoninus Pius, pushed 80 miles further north and began the Antonine Wall. The extended border could not be held, though. When Hadrian's Wall was constructed, approximately fifty thousand Roman soldiers were in Britain, but the empire could not afford to maintain the number. By 180 CE, the Romans were pushed back to Hadrian's Wall, which remained the border until the fourth century CE.

The End of the Occupation Like other Roman provinces, most of Britain became Romanized over the years, and as the empire declined, so did its provinces. Possibly as few as four thousand Roman troops remained in Britain by the end of the fourth century. Information is sparse, but by 410 CE, Roman officials in Britain knew they were responsible for their own security. Tribal conflicts consumed the island, with German tribes invading while Romans either fled or joined Celtic forces to hold on to their lands.

Dacian Campaigns, 101–106 CE

The Dacian Campaign was a series of wars waged by the Roman Emperor Trajan that pushed across the Danube River into modern-day Romania. Roman victory turned Dacia into a Roman province and brought tremendous wealth to the Empire.

Background of the Dacian Wars The Roman Empire in 101 CE extended to the Danube River, which runs from the Black Forest in Germany to the Black Sea. The rich Dacian kingdom counted the Black Sea as its eastern boundary. Dacia extended south into modern Bulgaria and west across the Carpathian Mountains into Hungary, an area then called Pannonia. Fighting and raids between Rome and Dacia had gone on for years.

The Emperor Domitian had defeated the Dacians and entered into a peace treaty with them in 89 CE, making the Dacian king Decebalus a client of Rome. The peace was an uneasy one, however; the Dacians continued to raid in Roman territory.

The First Campaign Trajan became emperor in 98 CE. His background was in the military, having served in Syria and as governor of Lower Germany. Trajan studied the problem of supplying a large army and made careful plans before starting his war against Dacia. Not much information exists about how and why the war started, though clearly Dacia was perceived as a threat to Rome. Dacia also made an attractive target because of its gold and silver mines.

Trajan employed the services of Apollodorus of Damascus, a brilliant engineer. Apollodorus designed and built a bridge to cross the Danube and completed roadworks begun a century before. Trajan led his legions in person as they crossed the Danube into Dacia.

The Second Battle of Tapae In 101 CE, Trajan's army of fourteen legions defeated the Dacians under King Decebalus at Tapae. Few details are known, but the victory had a symbolic aspect. Fourteen years earlier, an entire legion under the command of Cornelius Fuscus had been wiped out by a Dacian army at the same spot.

After this victory, Trajan decided to wait until the following spring to press further. Decebalus led a coalition of tribes to cross the frozen Danube and raid Roman territory to the south, but the ice gave way under the weight of the army. Rome and Dacia fought two more battles that winter, including the Battle of Adamclisi. Rome claimed victory, but losses on both sides were heavy.

A Temporary Peace Trajan left Decebalus in power after the Battle of Adamclisi, which leads some historians to wonder just how decisive Rome's victory had been. Border raids and incursions on Roman territory continued. By 105 CE, Emperor Trajan decided to wage a war of total conquest against the Dacians.

The Second Dacian Campaign Apollodorus designed another bridge to cross the Danube. This stone bridge

Trajan's Column still stands in Rome, with its 155 panels showing the progression of the war in Dacia. © *Alex Timaios Photography/ Alamy*

spanned more than 3,600 feet and stood for a thousand years. Its entrances are still visible on the riverbanks. He also designed a twelve-mile cantilevered supply route, carved into the Carpathians, to ensure supplies for the Roman legions. By the next summer, the legions were besieging Sarmizegethusa, the Dacian capital. They forced its downfall by destroying the water pipes that supplied the city's water. The Romans then burned Sarmizegethusa.

An informant told the Romans that the gold of Decebalus's treasury had been hidden in the River Sargesia. Tons of gold and silver were found and confiscated by Rome. Trajan's camp, called Porolissum, guarded the main passage through the Carpathian mountains. There, Rome and the Dacians met one last time. The result was Roman victory in 106 CE.

The Dacian kingdom became a Roman province and today carries the name Romania. Roman legionaries settled there; the Dacian capital Sarmizegethusa was rebuilt and named Ulpia Traiana—today it is called Varhely. A huge memorial column was built in Rome and carved with detailed scenes of the Dacian Campaign, but no text.

A Final Discovery On Trajan's Column, one carving shows Decebalus committing suicide as a Roman soldier rides forward to stop him. In 1965, the tombstone of a Roman soldier named Tiberius Claudius Maximus was discovered in Greece. The entire career of this cavalry officer was described on the tombstone, including the line, "I captured Decebalus." Tiberius Claudius Maximus may well have been the soldier depicted on Trajan's Column.

⊕ Key Elements of Warcraft

The Professional Army

The Legions of the Republic The Roman army, like most armies of its day, started out as a citizen militia with men enlisting for short campaigns, expecting to serve no more than one year. Soldiers had to be citizens, meaning men of property, and they provided their own arms. Even during the Punic Wars, when troops were paid for the first time, the army of Rome was still a militia.

The standard legionary unit before 100 BCE was the century. It may have originally been one hundred men, which would explain the name. In all recorded instances, though, a century was made up of sixty to eighty men. Two centuries made up a maniple, and thirty maniples made one legion. The first cohort of any legion (a cohort is three maniples) included the most experienced and skilled fighters. Tribunes, the high-ranking officers of the legion, were usually political appointees and members of the nobility.

Conquest Changes the Army As the Roman Republic grew, so did its need for armed men who could serve for longer stretches of time. During the third and second centuries B.C.E, economic changes meant fewer men of property were available to fill military needs. While no one is sure exactly when Rome's army became "professional," Gaius Marius is usually credited with reforming the army and turning it into the legionary forces that became the backbone of Roman conquest and control.

Army Reforms By allowing landless men to enter the military, Marius created a "client army." Generals became responsible for acquiring land to distribute to their soldiers. The unforeseen (at least by Marius) consequence of this was that soldiers owed their loyalty now to their general, rather than to Rome. In addition, these new soldiers fought to earn their pay, rather than to protect their homes.

Marius may not have been responsible for all the changes the army underwent at this time. The eagle, or *aquila* in Latin, became the standard for all of the legions. One writer says gladiatorial instructors (gladiators were fighters who engaged in combat for public entertainment) were used to teach the recruits to fight. Another major change was that the standard unit of men became the cohort, rather than the maniple. A cohort consisted of three maniples, and there were ten cohorts in a legion. A maniple was made up of two centuries, or

Re-enactors in Italy show how a cohort looked in action, with realistic armor, javelins (pilum), and shields.   © *Jochen Tack/Alamy*

about 160 men. A legion, then, was 4,800 men (160 times 3 maniples times 10 cohorts).

Each century, led by a centurion, was further divided into *contubernia* of eight men who shared a tent together. Another reform was that all soldiers carried their own baggage and cooked their own meals. This made the army more mobile. The legionary soldiers were called "Marius's Mules." By Julius Caesar's time, legionaries customarily served for twenty years or sixteen campaigns.

The Imperial Army and its Equipment

Besides the legions, the Roman Empire's army included auxiliaries. These were foreign troops, consisting of allies who were not Roman citizens. Usually, they carried light-arms, such as bows, slings, and javelins. Often an army had as many auxiliaries as legionaries. A small portion of both the legions and auxiliaries were comprised of mounted cavalry.

Equipment became standardized after Marius' time. Legionaries wore armor to protect their chest and back—either chainmail, metal scales, or metal bands. Helmets, greaves, and a leather skirt completed the protection. Each legionary carried a heavy curved shield made of wood and covered with leather and metal. Swords and javelins were of regulation length.

The Army on the Move

The necessity of moving and feeding a force of several thousand men through forests and fields made for difficult logistics. As Rome's wars were carried out on the frontier, the army foraged for food or demanded supplies from the local populace—demands that could leave a region to starve during the winter.

At night, the army's camp was surrounded by wide ditches, palisades, and towers. Often a camp was abandoned after one night, and fifteen miles further along the road, another camp was built for the next night. Written accounts survive about the efficiency with which a Roman camp was erected. Every man knew his job, and the tents and fortifications went up in just a couple of hours.

Reforms of Augustus

As Augustus became emperor and the Roman Republic transformed into an empire, the Roman legions changed too. They became a standing army, readied for defense and peacekeeping as well as conquest. Legions were posted to border areas and provinces on a permanent basis. Augustus set up a military treasury to distribute both the pay and retirement funds to legionaries. Augustus also began the practice of awarding Roman citizenship to auxiliaries who served for twenty-five years.

A terracotta war elephant from the period of the Punic wars.
© *Scala/Art Resource, NY*

🌐 Impact on World History

The conquests of the Roman Republic and the Roman Empire tied together much of Europe, the Middle East, Egypt, and North Africa with a common language, law code, and shared customs. This shared Roman influence laid the groundwork for Western civilization as it is today.

A Culture of Administration

Rome's constant militarism and conquests were unique. While vast empires such as Alexander the Great's collapsed or fragmented after the death of a strong leader, Rome held its far-flung provinces together for many generations. It did so by building up a strong but flexible governing structure, and by creating transportation and administrative networks. These permitted Rome and its provinces to live in relative security.

Rome combined its military achievements and conquests, professional army, and political organization into a culture that prized law, order, and administration. Unlike other conquering powers, Rome achieved peace after conquest by imposing order and sharing citizenship. This served as the foundation for future civilizations and states,

many of whom who looked back to Rome as an example of a strong, benevolent, and productive world power.

Arts, Architecture, Science, and Religion   Rome modeled many of its artistic and societal norms on those of Greece. Greek architectural forms, deities, philosophy, and politics were all adopted and adapted by Rome. In Rome, artistic achievement was appreciated and could be shared through a vast network of commerce and exchange. Again, Greek ideals of beauty predominated. Once standards of aesthetics and intellectual concepts were accepted by the ruling elite in Rome, the entire Empire embraced and imitated them. After the conquest of Gaul, for example, towns with Roman baths, stone aqueducts, and forums sprang up throughout Gaul (modern France). Statuary became Romanized and less abstract. The same process of "Romanization" took place in most Roman provinces.

Customs and Law   The changes were not entirely aesthetic. Writing became the mode of communication in formerly illiterate lands. Women lost legal standing in the few places where they had enjoyed it. Roman virtues and habits often supplanted indigenous customs. Those who wished to prosper learned Latin, and that language endured as the language of commerce and politics for well over a thousand years and eventually developed into such modern languages as French, Spanish, Italian, Portuguese, and Romanian.

Maintaining an empire of conquered peoples required constant refinement and codification of the law. A process had been in place since before Punic Wars that modified Roman laws so that new territories and citizens could become part of the empire. Roman law, which would continue to be modified through Emperor Justinian's reign in the sixth century CE, became the basis of legal systems throughout western Europe.

As a republic, and later as an empire, Rome created a stable and protected society in which its institutions could grow and develop. While the authority of the state could be repressive and cruel, there can be no doubt that the relative stability of the Roman Empire allowed art, literature, and libraries to flourish in areas that, before and after the Roman Empire, were plagued by tribal warfare.

Assimilation had its brutal side as well. In Judaea, where religious leaders resisted Roman rule, Rome responded to revolt with the total destruction of the Jewish temple. In other areas, rich cultures that had lasted centuries simply disappeared with their languages, art, beliefs, and homes, to be supplanted by the stone structures and Latin inscriptions favored by their conquerors.

BIBLIOGRAPHY

Books

Dillon, Matthew, and Lynda Garland. *Ancient Rome: From the Early Republic to the Assassination of Julius Caesar.* New York: Routledge, Taylor and Francis Group, 2005.

Julius Caesar. *The Gallic War*, translated by Carolyn Hammond. Oxford: Oxford University Press, 1996.

Polybius. *The Histories*. Internet Public History Sourcebook. <http://www.fordham.edu/halsall/ancient/asbookfull.html> (accessed March 22, 2007).

Introduction to the Invasions of Rome (4th and 5th centuries CE)

The reign of Trajan (98–117 CE) marked the high point of Rome's glory. Over the next three hundred years, Rome lost territory and strength, although its influence still pervaded every village and farm in the region. Even when the empire was still strong, power had already shifted from Rome to the eastern capital of Constantinople (Istanbul), the "New Rome."

The influx of multiple "barbarian" groups had a profound effect on Rome between the first and fifth centuries CE. Asiatic tribes and chieftains pushed other groups westward into collisions with Rome. Huns in what is now Russia and Ukraine drove Gothic tribes to cross the Danube, either as invaders or immigrants. Such large numbers were not always peacefully absorbed, yet the Goths, who eventually settled in Spain and Gaul (France), did not wish to destroy Rome. Neither did most so-called barbarians, as the long existence of the empire allowed trade, spread culture and language, and offered protection. Instead, the newcomers wished to secure a favorable place within the empire. Even Attila, the warlike leader of the Huns, sought conquest and wealth rather than total destruction.

Many barbarian tribes became integrated into Roman society by becoming members of its military. By the fourth century, most of Rome's frontier army was composed of Germans, Gauls, and other barbarians. Leadership positions switched slowly from Roman officers to men who had learned Latin as a second language. Up to the middle of the fourth century, Rome pursued preemptive campaigns along the Danube and Rhine to control the Germanic tribes there. At that point, the empire was recruiting troops from beyond the frontier, from tribes who had either been defeated or simply desired peace. After that point, armies were usually summoned to hot spots to repel attacks, leaving large stretches of the border undefended.

The inability to defend its own borders was just one sign of the Western Empire's slide from glory. The gap between the two Roman empires became even more pronounced in the fifth century, when a succession of puppet emperors in the hands of manipulative military generals further weakened the West. In 476, the Scirian leader Odovacar (or Odoacer) overthrew the last Western emperor and took control. Traditionally, that date represents the end of the Western Roman Empire.

Rome did not simply collapse, however. Odovacar, in his turn, was overthrown by Theodoric; this Ostrogothic king ruled until 526, supported by an army of German—not Roman—forces. The infrastructure of the Western Empire fell apart after Theodoric's death, as wars ravaged much of Italy. Plague and famine contributed to the misery, and the population of the city of Rome dropped to fifty thousand people.

In contrast, the Eastern Roman Empire stood for another thousand years. However, after the reign of its extravagant and powerful sixth century emperor, Justinian, its territory decreased until the Byzantine city of Constantinople fell to the Ottoman Turks in 1453.

Invasions of Rome
(4th and 5th centuries CE)

✪ Major Figures

Constantine

Constantine the Great (ca. 280–337) is credited with being the first Christian emperor of Rome. He removed restrictions against Christians in the Empire, convened the Council of Nicaea to settle issues of Christian doctrine, and relocated the capital of the Roman Empire to Constantinople—a city formerly called Byzantium, and today known as Istanbul.

A Divided Empire Constantine was born in the Balkans in what is now Serbia, around 280. In the years following Constantine's birth, Emperor Diocletian enacted many reforms to keep the Roman Empire from collapsing. One such reform was to divide the Empire in half and appoint a co-emperor in the West, while Diocletian ruled in the East. The two emperors, Diocletian and Maximian, then appointed junior emperors to succeed them.

Constantine's father, Constantius Chlorus, had distinguished himself in battle and risen in importance in Roman society. He left Constantine's mother (an innkeeper's daughter) to marry the daughter or stepdaughter of Maximian and was then appointed junior emperor. Constantine benefited from his father's position; when Diocletian and Maximian retired in 305, Constantius Chlorus became Emperor of the West. He died a year later while campaigning in Britain with his son, and his legions proclaimed Constantine the new junior emperor.

Constantine Wages Civil War Political intrigues and murder followed, as no fewer than six would-be emperors claimed the throne, including Constantine. Maximian returned from retirement to ally with Constantine, who divorced his first wife to marry Maximian's daughter Fausta. This made Constantine a brother-in-law to his widowed stepmother. In a few years, when Maximian turned against him, Constantine had the former emperor strangled. He then entered into a civil war with Maximian's son, Maxentius.

The Battle of Milvian Bridge Constantine and Maxentius met with their troops at the Milvian Bridge of Rome in 312. The bridge, built two hundred years earlier, spanned the Tiber River and is now called the Ponte Milvio.

Constantine told the historian Eusebius that he saw a vision the day before the battle: a cross appeared on the sun with the words *in hoc signo vinces* ("in this sign shall you conquer"). Knowing the cross was a Christian symbol, he had his men draw another Christian symbol, the labarum, on their shields. His troops were victorious, and Maxentius drowned in the Tiber.

Constantine as a Champion of Christianity Constantine co-ruled the Empire for ten years with a man named Licinius, but they eventually fought each other for ultimate control. In two brief years of truce, however, much was accomplished. Licinius and Constantine agreed on the Edict of Milan, legalizing Christianity and returning property taken from congregations. On the day the Edict was proclaimed, Licinius married Constantine's half-sister.

Both the Roman Catholic and Coptic Orthodox Churches consider Helena, the mother of Constantine, to be a saint. This innkeeper's daughter is believed to have found the True Cross of Christ and to have had great influence in her son's life. The historical record shows that Constantine himself was ambiguous about Christianity. He respected it, defended it, and facilitated debate and discussion over its principals. However, he did not allow himself to be baptized until he was on his deathbed.

Political Actions Civil conflicts broke out between the two emperors until Constantine beat Licinius decisively in 323. He spared Licinius's life for his sister's sake, but then changed his mind and had Licinius executed the following year. After Licinius's death, Constantine ruled as the only emperor and eventually moved the seat of the government to Byzantium.

Bust of Constantine. *Public Domain*

Constantine furthered Diocletian's separation of the powers of the military from the civilian government. With the army, Constantine is credited with creating a central force called the *comitatensis*, to be held in reserve within the Empire (rather than on the frontier). He also increased the number of barbarian soldiers in the army, a practice that would continue after him. In the early fourth century, the army included half a million men and was highly mobile. New laws bound sons of veterans to army service, much like other laws that forced farmers, shipbuilders, and workers to stay with their occupations for life and made their jobs hereditary.

Constantine financed his ventures—including the building of his new city Constantinople—through taxes, custom duties, and by plundering pagan temples. A new

gold coin, the solidus, was introduced, and it remained the standard unit of exchange for centuries.

Absolute Power Many of Constantine's actions seem at odds with his reputation as a supporter of Christianity. In 325, he convened the First Ecumenical Council of Nicaea and took sides as issues were discussed. The Arian controversy was rejected and the Nicean Creed adopted as a statement of official Christian beliefs. In the following year, Constantine had his oldest son executed for unknown reasons. His eleven-year-old nephew was also killed. Iin the following year, Constantine's wife Fausta was deliberately drowned.

Constantine died in May 337, having profoundly affected the lives of all in the Roman Empire. In his reign, power shifted from West to East; now favored, Christianity would soon become the state religion. In keeping with the violence of his personal life, however, many of his relatives were lynched by the army when Constantine died, leaving only three sons and two nephews alive.

Alatheus

Alatheus was a leader of the Greuthungi, a Gothic tribe, and the guardian of the young king of that tribe. In 378 CE Alatheus led his cavalry and soldiers to aid the Tervingi during the Battle of Adrianople.

Alatheus's People The Greuthungi inhabited a territory located north of the Tervingi, another Gothic tribe. The Greuthungi became known as the Ostrogoths in the fifth century CE. Where the tribe actually originated and lived is unknown.

The Roman historian Ammianus Marcellinus claimed that the Greuthungi were ruled by a warlike and feared king, Ermanaric. This ruler committed suicide when his land was overrun by the Huns and Alans around 370 CE, and the new king, Vithimir, was killed in battle. The king's son, Videric, was too young to lead, so care of the tribe was left to the chieftains Alatheus and Saphrax. These two regents led the Greuthungi west to the Dneister River in today's Moldava, probably to escape the Huns.

Alliance with the Tervingi The Tervingi, also pushed out of their homeland, asked permission of Rome to cross the Danube into the Empire. The Greuthungi arrived a few months later and also petitioned to cross. The Tervingi were allowed into the Empire, but the Greuthungi were not—the reason is not known. The Greuthungi under Alatheus, however, crossed in boats without permission and made camps out of sight of the Roman forts.

The Battle of Ad Salices The Tervingi, badly treated by the Romans near the Danube, revolted and terrorized the Roman province of Haemimont for nearly two years. Alatheus and Saphrax allied with the Tervingi, whose leader was Fritigern. In the late summer of 377, the first

DIOCLETIAN'S REFORMS

The problems that drove Diocletian to split the leadership of the Empire were extreme. Historians often refer to them as "The Crises of the Third Century." For five decades, civil wars and anarchy had weakened the government, invasions had chipped away at the borders, and inflation and insecurity had damaged the economy.

Diocletian appointed a co-emperor with military experience because he believed the Empire had become too large to be defended and ruled by one man. To reinforce their shared authority, religious rituals tying the emperors to Jupiter and Hercules were introduced. Christians refused to participate in these rituals, which prompted a new round of persecutions against them.

Other major reforms of Diocletian included breaking the Empire's provinces into smaller units, thus reducing the influence of local officials. He also separated the powers of civilian and military officials throughout the Empire. At the time, all legions were posted along the frontier and received their pay and supplies through their commanders. As part of his plan to rebuild the frontier defenses, Diocletian took that responsibility away from the officers and broke the army into smaller units.

The Eastern capital was moved from Rome to Nicomedia, a city in Asia Minor, while the Western capital became Milan. The reforms, along with economic measures such as price-fixing, improved efficiency in the Empire, increased security, and stabilized the government.

substantial fighting between Roman soldiers and the Goths took place, probably in modern Romania, at *Ad Salices* (Latin for "the Willows").

The Roman force was jointly commanded by Richomeres, a general deployed by Gratian, the Roman Emperor of the West, and two generals sent by Emperor Valens of the East. The fighting was fierce, but neither side won a clear victory. The Goths retreated to the mountains for the winter. Other skirmishes followed, but the historical record depends largely on Ammianus's account. The whereabouts of Alatheus and his followers are not mentioned often.

Later Battles   The Goths delivered a stunning defeat to Rome at the Battle of Adrianople the following year. Alatheus and Saphrax led both the Greuthungi and a unit of Alans in that battle. Although they had been out foraging for food, they returned to camp just as the battle began. They immediately charged into the Roman left flank and joined in annihilating the enemy.

Only one historian, Jordanes, offers more information about Alatheus. As he wrote in the sixth century, his account may not be reliable. Jordanes reported that several years later, under the reign of Theodosius, Alatheus—still acting with Saphrax—rode to Pannonia

(Hungary) with part of the Gothic force, while Fritigern of the Tervingi led the rest of the troops to other areas.

Theodosius

Theodosius the Great (346–395 CE) became Roman Emperor of the East in 379, just after an unexpected and—to the Romans—terrifying military loss in the Battle of Adrianople. During his fifteen-year reign, he restored stability, making peace with the Goths and allowing them to settle in Thrace. Theodosius also actively promoted Christianity in the Empire.

Early Career   Born in Spain in January 346, Theodosius was named for his father, a general in the Roman army. The younger Theodosius also found success in the army, defending Rome's frontier along the Danube River in the Balkans. By age thirty, Theodosius had risen to *dux Moesiae* (military commander of the province of Moesia) when his family fell out of political favor. His father was executed, and Theodosius returned to Spain.

Back in his home country, Theodosius married and his first son, Arcadius, was born. Far away, the Emperor Valens died during the Battle of Adrianople, the worst defeat the Empire had ever suffered. The Western Emperor, Gratian—who had likely ordered the death of the elder Theodosius—summoned the younger Theodosius back to the Balkans to deal with the crisis. Gothic tribes were rampaging through the province of Haemimont (eastern Bulgaria). It took two years, but Theodosius and his armies were eventually able to restore Roman rule.

Emperor Theodosius   History does not give us many details, but somehow Theodosius became Emperor of the East in 379. He raised new troops to replace those lost at Adrianople and fought the Goths in several provinces: Thrace (western Bulgaria), Macedonia, Thessaly (Greece), and Pannonia (Hungary). Not until the following year was Theodosius able to visit Constantinople (Istanbul), his imperial capital.

With little help from Gratian, Theodosius negotiated for peace with the Goths. In October 382, Theodosius granted them lands in Thrace and allowed them to keep their tribal leaders. Over the next decade, many Goths served in Theodosius's legions.

Actions as Emperor   After becoming Emperor, Theodosius underwent baptism in 380. He then expelled the Arian bishop of Constantinople (Arians believed that Jesus was a lesser deity than God Himself) and installed his own candidate who would uphold the Nicene doctrine of the Trinity.

While revolt in Arabia and possible war with Persia faced Theodosius in the east, a general named Magnus Maximus seized control in Britain, Spain, and Gaul. Maximus proclaimed himself Emperor, and Gratian's own troops defected to Maximus. Gratian was assassinated in 383.

Hieroglyphics describe the military exploits of Theodosius I.
© TongRo Image Stock/Alamy

Five years later, Maximus invaded Italy. Theodosius's position was fairly strong; he commanded strong forces and had signed a treaty with Persia. Theodosius confronted Maximus in Pannonia, fighting two battles to defeat him. After Maximus died, Theodosius traveled to Rome and pardoned many of Maximus's followers and troops, thus enhancing his own popularity and strength. Theodosius married Galla, the sister of both the late Western Emperor Gratian and his successor, Valentinian II.

While in Rome, Theodosius learned that the military governor of Thessalonica had been assassinated. In retaliation, he allowed the massacre of seven thousand people by the army. Ambrose, Bishop of Milan (later St. Ambrose), excommunicated the Emperor over this. Theodosius was forced to bow to Ambrose, do penance, and ask forgiveness before being allowed back into the church. Ambrose is credited with influencing the Emperor's "Theodosian Decrees," which disbanded the Vestal Virgins and halted many vestiges of pagan practices in the Empire (including the Olympic Games).

Battle of Frigidus Theodosius had named his general Arbogast as guardian of Valentinian II, who was fifteen or sixteen years old. In 392, the young emperor was found dead; whether he hung himself or was murdered remains an open question. Arbogast proclaimed Eugenius, a pagan scholar, as the new Western Emperor. Theodosius led an army west to confront Arbogast. His youngest son Honorius accompanied him, and several thousand Gothic troops followed him. One of the Gothic commanders was Alaric, who would later turn against Rome. Both sides used barbarian troops in the battle: Arbogast employed Franks, while Huns as well as Goths rode with Theodosius.

On September 5, 394, Theodosius and Arbogast fought in the Julian Alps at the Frigidus River (today's Slovenia). On that first day, Theodosius lost ten thousand men in a direct, frontal attack. On the second day, a strong wind from the east blew against Arbogast. Spears and arrows hurled by Arbogast's troops did not reach Theodosius's soldiers, but the weapons of the Christian army flew with more force, powered by the same wind. Theodosius was victorious; Eugenius was beheaded and Arbogast committed suicide. The battle was seen by many as a clash of Christians against pagans.

After Eugenius's death, Theodosius named his own son Honorius as Western co-Emperor, with Stilicho, a trusted general of half-Vandal heritage, as his guardian. Stilicho had fought with Theodosius at Frigidus and was married to Theodosius's niece.

Theodosius died in Milan of congestive heart failure on January 17, 395—just after his forty-eighth birthday.

Stilicho

Executed in 408 CE, Stilicho served as general, ambassador, advisor, guardian, and consul to the Western Roman Empire. Although his roles within the empire are well-documented, whether he labored in order to save Rome or for the advancement of his own family is not clear.

Stilicho's Rise to Power Stilicho was born into a family both German and Roman: his father was of the Vandal tribe, and his mother carried Roman citizenship. Stilicho distinguished himself in the army under emperor Theodosius, and he proved himself an able diplomat as envoy to Persia around the year 384. After Stilicho raised and commanded troops during the Battle of Frigidus, Theodosius appointed him *magister utriusque militae* ("master of both services"), which put him in charge of both the cavalry and infantry of the Western Empire. Stilicho married Serena, who was a niece of Theodosius.

Before Theodosius died in 395, he named Stilicho the protector of his two sons. The youngest, Honorius, was only ten when he became Emperor of the West. His brother Arcadius, Emperor of the East, was probably seventeen. Throughout his life, Arcadius remained the

Madonna and Child are surrounded by twelve angels in a fresco in the Church of Saint Saviour in Chora, Istanbul, Turkey. © *Archivo Iconografico, S.A./Corbis*

tool of manipulative advisors such as his prefect, Rufinus.

Immediate Problems The Empire was not strong and faced threats on several borders: Franks gathered along the Rhine, Alaric—a former ally—led Goths across the Danube, and Germanic tribes raided throughout Pannonia (Hungary).

Stilicho led an army of combined forces from the East and West to suppress the Goths, but Arcadius recalled his forces based on the advice of Rufinus. This forced Stilicho to withdraw. When the Eastern forces returned to Constantinople, however, they surrounded and killed Rufinus, probably on Stilicho's orders.

Putting Down Revolts Within a year, Stilicho led troops against Alaric once again, but a revolt in North Africa forced him to abandon the campaign. Grain from North Africa was vital to the West, but Gildo, the governor there, refused to send it, threatening to ship the grain

to the Eastern Empire instead. Gildo had once murdered his own brother's sons, so Stilicho sent an army under Gildo's brother to defeat the governor. The victory was quick: Gildo's forces put up no resistance and Gildo himself committed suicide rather than face his brother's vengeance.

Goths Invade Italy Stilicho was appointed consul in Rome and Honorius, the Western Emperor, married Stilicho's daughter. Military affairs, however, demanded Stilicho'a attention. In 401, he gathered troops to travel north of the Alps and confront the Vandals and their leader Radagaisus. While this fight raged, Honorius, in Milan, became the target of Alaric and the Goths. Stilicho defeated the Vandals, then brought in troops from the Rhine frontier and Britain to battle Alaric in early 402.

On April 6 of that year, Alaric and Stilicho fought at Pollentia. Although the Romans occupied the Goths' camp, no clear victory was won. A negotiated treaty forced Alaric out of Italy, but he returned the next year to attack Verona. Stilicho fought him once more, winning the battle but again allowing Alaric to negotiate for his life. Honorius celebrated with a triumph in Rome.

Germanic tribes under Radagaisus invaded Italy in 405. They ravaged the countryside for six months; Stilicho was forced to add Hunnic mercenaries to his small army to stop them. Gaul was invaded by Germans the following year. While Stilicho's attention was on a power struggle with the Eastern Empire, the Roman army in Britain crowned a new "emperor" who invaded Gaul from the West.

Stilicho's Downfall   Alaric, now an ally, demanded an exorbitant four thousand pounds of gold for his military help to the Empire. Stilicho used his influence to secure payment for Alaric. He likely wanted to use Alaric's army to reclaim Gaul, but his influence was waning. The many problems of the Empire were blamed on him. As a result of his Vandal heritage, most Romans distrusted him.

Arcadius, Emperor of the East, died in 408. Honorius was convinced that Stilicho plotted to put his own son on the Eastern throne, so he had Stilicho arrested and beheaded on August 22 that same year. This single death was not enough, however: Stilicho's son was murdered as well, his estates were confiscated, and the families of barbarian soldiers throughout the Empire were massacred. The Senate even ordered the strangulation of Stilicho's widow.

In the wake of Stilicho's death and the anti-German massacre that followed, thousands of angry Goths, Vandals, former Roman soldiers, and escaped slaves flocked to Alaric as he marched on Rome. Though he had fought to preserve the Empire, Stilicho's legacy helped lead to its destruction.

Alaric

Alaric, a Gothic chieftain, fought for and against the Roman Empire under Stilicho and Emperor Theodosius. He broke with the Empire completely in 408 CE to march on Rome, sacking the city two years later.

Early Life   Alaric's early life is largely undocumented. A sixth century writer, Jordanes, constructed an aristocratic Visigoth heritage for him, but the accuracy of his work is debated. Alaric was among the many Goths who fought with Emperor Theodosius in the Battle of Frigidus in 394. His age can only be guessed.

Stilicho, guardian of Theodosius's ten-year-old son, sent Alaric and his auxiliaries east the following year, to lands given them in 382. Alaric left angry; he felt he deserved a command or promotion for his part in the Battle of Frigidus. Soon, he led a growing group of Goths in revolt against Rome.

Battles with Stilicho   The rebels marched to Constantinople (Istanbul), capital of the Eastern Roman Empire. Emperor Arcadius sent his prefect to bribe Alaric into

CHANGES IN THE ROMAN ARMY

In the third and fourth centuries CE, Diocletian and Constantine developed a mobile army to guard the frontiers. While a typical legion still numbered around six thousand strong, it was now broken up into units of one thousand men, and these units were deployed to different provinces. The soldiers themselves were recruited from the tribes of Gaul, Germany, Thrace, the Balkans, and Asia Minor. (Regardless of their origin, from the third century onwards all legionaries were Roman citizens.) Auxiliaries were no longer associated with the legions, and even the cavalry was commanded separately.

The intent was to create a field army that could be dispatched to trouble spots quickly. By the late fourth century, though, the constant threats to the Empire's borders made the entire frontier a trouble spot. The reduced size of the army impacted all leaders of the late Empire, including Stilicho. When troops were needed for defense or war, they had to be taken from forts along the frontier, leaving other parts of the Empire vulnerable to attack.

withdrawing. Alaric and the Goths pillaged throughout Macedonia and Thessaly (Greece) until Stilicho led a combined army of troops from the Eastern and Western Empires to stop them. Arcadius ordered his troops home, however, so Stilicho returned to the west.

The Goths pushed further south into Greece. Alaric spared Athens but sacked Sparta, Corinth, and other cities. In 397, Stilicho sailed to Greece but again retreated to put down a revolt in Africa. The Eastern Emperor granted Alaric a military position in his empire: according to one account, Alaric became governor of Illyricum (Albanian, Bosnian, Croatian, and Slovenian lands today).

In late 401, Alaric led his troops into Italy. History does not record the reason for this march. He besieged the city of Milan. Stilicho assembled an army the following spring, and the two met in battle at Pollentia on Easter Sunday. Stilicho captured Alaric's wife and children along with a great deal of plunder, but the victory was not decisive. A truce followed, and Alaric agreed to leave Italy. He stayed out for only a year, however, then he and Stilicho fought again in Verona.

Change of Allegiance   Neither side won, leading historians to wonder if Stilicho truly wanted to crush Alaric. The Gothic army was strong and fierce—Stilicho may have hoped for an alliance with the Goths during their battles, and indeed, that is what happened. In 405, Alaric became an ally of Rome as Stilicho fought other invaders along the frontier. Stilicho now recognized Alaric as military governor of Illyricum.

This nineteenth-century illustration titled "Alaric Before Rome" shows Alaric overlooking the city before sacking it in 410. *Public Domain*

Two years later, Alaric grew impatient with the Western Empire once more. He marched his troops to Noricum (Austria) and demanded four thousand pounds of gold as payment for his military services. Stilicho, who needed Alaric's army to defeat an usurper in Gaul (France), convinced the Senate to pay. Unfortunately, this turned the Emperor against him. Stilicho was assassinated, and a backlash of murderous attacks on Germanic troops and families, including Goths, killed thousands in Italy.

The First Siege of Rome

The Germanic soldiers who escaped the slaughter fled to Alaric in Noricum. In the fall, Alaric marched south with up to forty thousand troops, meeting little resistance as he passed through Italy. He camped his army around Rome, blockading the Tiber.

Plague hit the city, adding to the misery of famine caused by the blockade, and corpses piled up in the streets. Devastated, Rome negotiated, promising five thousand pounds of gold, thirty thousand pounds of silver, and other riches if Alaric would leave. In addition, the Emperor in Ravenna promised to negotiate for ter-ritory and hostages. Alaric agreed, accepted the treasure, and withdrew—but stayed in Italy.

The Second Siege

The Emperor did nothing. Athaulf, Alaric's brother-in-law, joined him with more men. Alaric made further demands, which the Emperor refused. He lowered his demands and the Emperor refused again. Alaric surrounded Rome and blockaded its ports once more. The city surrendered, granted titles to Alaric and his brother, and accepted a puppet emperor, Priscus Attalus.

The Third Siege

Alaric's faux emperor had his own agenda, so in 410 Alaric removed the pretender and journeyed to Ravenna to negotiate with the real Emperor. On the way, he was attacked by a Gothic general, Sarus, who was loyal to Rome. Alaric defeated Sarus and then returned to Rome, convinced that the Emperor was behind Sarus's attack. Alaric entered the city on August 24 and turned his troops loose for three days to loot, rape, and burn. Among the captives taken was Galla Placidia, the Emperor's sister, who later became the wife of Athaulf.

Having captured Rome, Alaric continued south, but he died at Cosenza in Calabria that year. Athaulf became leader of the Goths. His followers diverted the river Basunto so that a grave could be dug in the riverbed to house Alaric's body and some of his wealth; the grave has never been found.

Attila

Attila (ca. 406–453 CE), the terrifying leader of the nomadic Huns, was called the "Scourge of God" in his day. He defeated armies of the Eastern Roman Empire, threatened the Western Roman Empire, and seized large chunks of territory, but his heirs were unable to hold on to his conquests after his death.

The Huns

Aggressive and nomadic, the Asiatic Huns herded sheep and gathered food on the march. They spent so much time on horseback that some contemporary commentators wrote that they lived on their small, fast horses. When in battle, the ferocious Huns took no prisoners. The Roman Empire first noticed them when Hunnish attacks forced Gothic tribes to seek safety and new homes in Roman territory in 376 CE The influx of Goths led to the Battle of Adrianople, a military disaster for Rome.

A series of strong rulers united the Hunnish clans and led them out of the Central Asian steppes to take lands from other tribes. Rugila (or Rua) was one such leader. Upon his death in 434, he left his kingdom to two nephews, Attila and Bleda. In the following year, with the Huns in control of the province of Pannonia, Rome signed a treaty with Attila called the Peace of Margus. In it, Rome promised a yearly tribute of seven hundred pounds of gold to the Huns—a good indication of just how much the Empire feared these mounted warriors.

War Against the East For five years, Attila fought elsewhere and ignored the Empire. In 441, he led his troops across the Danube and plundered Roman cities in the Balkans, one after the other, making his way to Constantinople (Istanbul). A few towns tried to defend themselves, and at least one battle was fought in Thrace, but Attila triumphed over all Roman efforts. Emperor Theodosius II had built new walls around the city but was forced to negotiate with the Huns, who tripled the annual tribute and demanded six thousand pounds of gold immediately.

When the Empire complied, Attila's forces withdrew. Shortly after this, Attila had his brother Bleda killed and became sole leader of the Huns.

Battles in the West In 450 Attila asked to marry Honoria, the sister of the Western Emperor. She had sent her ring to Attila, beseeching him to help her avoid an unwanted marriage. Attila's request was refused, so he allied with the Vandals and prepared for war with the Western Empire. Attila waged a bloody and destructive campaign through the Rhine Valley, crossing lands in what is now northern Germany, Belgium, and France. The Roman general Aetius, who had lived among the Huns and once been Attila's friend, raised an army of Romans and Visigoths to meet the Huns at the Battle of Chalons in Gaul (France). Aetius was victorious, though the Visigothic king was killed.

The Huns recovered sufficiently to attack Italy itself a year later. After the city of Aquileia on the Adriatic Sea was razed to the ground, Attila led his army through other northern cities and towns. He occupied Milan and threatened Rome, but Pope Leo I and two senators journeyed north and pleaded successfully for Rome to be spared. The Pope is given credit for convincing Attila to return to Pannonia.

Death of Attila Attila had several wives, and in 453 he took another bride. He was no longer young though, and after much feasting and drinking, he passed out on his wedding bed and died of a hemorrhage. His sons divided his empire between them. The Huns remained a nomadic people and without a strong leader to unite them, the lands they had seized soon fell into chaos.

Theodoric

Theodoric the Great (ca. 453–526) was king of the Ostrogoths, or "West Goths." As the second Germanic king to rule the former Western Roman Empire (reigning from 493 until his death), Theodoric kept order and peace in Italy. After his death, the structure of the former Empire collapsed amid war, disease, and famine.

Rise to Power The Ostrogoths were descended from the Greuthungi tribe that crossed into the West Roman Empire in the late fourth century CE Theodoric, as the son of king Theudimir, was sent as a hostage to the Eastern Empire capital of Constantinople (Istanbul). This practice was common; the presence of noble children ensured

---

DINNER WITH ATTILA

Priscus, a Roman historian, accompanied the Roman ambassador to visit Attila on at least three occasions. Much of his work was lost, but a personal description (Attila was short, flat-nosed, and had gray in his beard) and other details have survived the centuries because they were quoted by other writers. Here are a few lines from Priscus's long discourse on a banquet given by Attila. Two of Attila's sons were present, as well as Hunnish and Scythian noblemen and envoys from both the Eastern and Western Roman Empires.

> A luxurious meal, served on silver plate, had been made ready for us and the barbarian guests, but Attila ate nothing but meat on a wooden trencher. In everything else, too, he showed himself temperate; his cup was of wood, while to the guests were given goblets of gold and silver. His dress, too, was quite simple, affecting only to be clean. The sword he carried at his side, the latchets of his Scythian shoes, the bridle of his horse were not adorned . . .

---

cooperation and peace between lands and usually resulted in a good education for the child and mutual understanding between different societies. After ten years at the Imperial court, Theodoric returned to Pannonia (Hungary) and his people in 471.

Theudimir died three years later and Theodoric became king. Like his father, Theodoric invaded other lands to expand his holdings, and his conquests were recognized by the Eastern Roman Emperor, Zeno. Theodoric also waged war against Imperial provinces in the Balkans, but he sometimes allied with those provinces against other lands. In 488, Zeno commissioned Theodoric to conquer Italy, which had fallen to the German King Odovacar twelve years earlier.

Theodoric Takes Italy Years passed before Theodoric and his people, who numbered over one hundred thousand, eradicated all of Odovacar's supporters. The Scirian king had allies, but he was defeated in several battles in northern Italy. He retreated to Ravenna and then emerged to fight again. Theodoric concocted a secret plot with citizens who favored him over Odovacar, and on a set date, they rose up and massacred Odovacar's troops in cities throughout the north.

Odovacar still did not surrender, so Theodoric laid siege to Ravenna for two and a half years. Finally, Ravenna's bishop arranged a treaty by which both kings would share power. Theodoric agreed, entered Ravenna, and killed Odovacar with his own hands—during the banquet that celebrated their treaty. Odovacar's remaining troops were killed as well.

The Hagia Sophia, once an early Christian church, was converted to a mosque after the Turkish invasion in 1453.   *Archive Photos, Inc./Getty Images*

Theodoric as King   Theodoric ruled over two groups: his own Ostrogoths and the Roman citizens of Italy. From a religious standpoint, the Ostrogoths were largely Arians, believing in a slightly different version of Christianity than the Romans. Over his thirty-three year reign, Theodoric managed to keep peace between factions, most of the time.

He placated the Roman citizens of Italy by carefully acting as a governor rather than as a king towards them. To restore the lands and cities devastated by war, he launched public works programs and especially beautified Ravenna, his chosen base. He settled the Ostrogoths in Italy, ruling that they be given one-third of Roman estates, but left it to a Roman senator to accomplish the turnover. Two court systems were maintained: one for the Romans, and one for the Goths. The Eastern Emperor recognized Theodoric as military governor. The Roman Senate continued to meet, but the army was now composed entirely of Goths.

Later Years   One incident stands out to mar Theodoric's legacy. The philosopher Boethius served as one of Theodoric's ministers. He fell out of favor, possibly because Theodoric was an Arian Christian, while Boethius, like many Romans, followed the Nicene Creed. In 523, the Eastern Emperor Justin declared Arianism ille-

gal in his domain. Theodoric accused Boethius of conspiring with the Eastern Emperor against him and threw Boethius into prison. Boethius wrote his most famous work, the *Consolation of Philosophy*, while in prison. He was executed in 524. His father-in-law Symmachus, as well as other statesmen, met the same fate.

Theodoric died in 526. Although he could act with suspicion and cruelty, he is remembered chiefly for protecting Italy and sustaining its institutions for years after the Western Roman Empire ceased to exist.

✪ Major Battles

Adrianople, 378

On August 9, 378 CE, the Goths defeated the army of the Eastern Roman Empire under Emperor Valens, inflicting the worst military loss on the Romans since the empire began. To many scholars, this battle in the province of Haemimont (modern Bulgaria) signaled the beginning of the end for the Roman Empire.

Goths Cross the Danube   Two years before the great battle, Huns—a group previously unknown to Rome—attacked and pillaged the Gothic homeland. The Huns drove a large group of Goths to the Danube River,

Selimiye Mosque, Edirne, Turkey. *© Chris Hellier/Corbis*

which was the border of the Roman Empire. The Tervingi, the principal tribe of refugees, begged for permission to cross into the Empire, live peacefully, and serve as auxiliaries in the Roman army. Permission was granted, perhaps because the Emperor Valens was preparing for war against Persia; more allies and auxiliaries could only help.

Tens of thousands of the Tervingi crossed into Roman territory. Once there, local Roman officials abused the Tervingi, starving and enslaving some of them. Fritigern, a Tervingi chieftain, revolted and led his people away. He defeated the initial Roman force sent to contain them.

Alarmed, Emperor Valens made a temporary peace in Persia and sent his generals Saturninus, Trajanus, and Profuturus to stop the Goths. His nephew Gratian, Emperor of the West, sent able commanders as well. Their small successes only made Fritigern more determined to hold his people together.

Rampaging through the countryside of Haemimont, Fritigern was joined by other tribes, rebels, escaped slaves, and even Gothic soldiers who abandoned their posts with the Roman armies. The Roman commander Saturninus blocked them in mountain passes, attempting to starve the Goths, but new allies—including the Huns—helped the Tervingi move south.

The Battle Approaches   Emperor Valens left Constantinople with at least fifteen thousand troops (and perhaps twice that number) behind him by the time he reached Adrianople. His scouts reported that the Goths numbered only ten thousand, but this was a fatal error, as in fact, the Goths may have outnumbered the Roman force. Fritigern, however, sent an emissary seeking peace to Valens, asking only for land for his people.

Valens refused the offer. He had already decided not to wait for his co-emperor Gratian and the Western Roman army. A jealous man, Valens desired a quick, glorious victory, and he did not want to share it. On August 9, 378 CE, Valens marched his army out of Adrianople to meet the Goths on a nearby ridge. Both sides stalled throughout the morning. Valens may have thought better of waiting for Gratian's troops, while Fritigern hoped the Greuthungi and Alan cavalry under Alatheus and Saphrax would return from a foraging expedition. Buying time, Fritigern offered peace once more, then set fire to the grasslands.

Rome Defeated   One band of Imperial Guards advanced without orders and engaged the Goths and battle began in earnest. Because of this mistake and the sudden arrival of the mounted Greuthungi and their allies, Roman discipline broke and the fighting was disordered. The Roman left flank was cut off and surrounded by the enemy, and most of the soldiers were killed.

After hours of fighting, Rome's auxiliaries fled, and several generals abandoned the field. Many others died; Rome lost at least two-thirds of its army that day. Valens, after losing most of his bodyguard, sought protection with a field unit but was eventually killed. After hearing of the loss, Gratian retreated to the West and left the area to the Goths.

After the battle, contemporary accounts paint a picture of an empire shocked to its core. Many Roman citizens reacted with fury; Gothic auxiliaries in the Roman army were massacred, and Goths in Roman cities were also killed. For other Romans, the defeat was seen as the judgment of long-neglected gods. Not until Gratian summoned Theodosius from Spain and asked him to calm the Balkans was order restored.

Chalons

The Battle of Chalons in 451 CE was a rare defeat for Attila, leader of the Huns. After terrorizing both the Eastern and Western Roman Empire for years, the Huns were turned away from Gaul by the Roman general Aetius and his combined Roman, Alanic, and Visigothic troops.

Theodoric I is slain by Attila's forces in the Battle of Chalons 451. *© Classic Image/Alamy*

An Excuse for War In 450, Augusta Honoria—the thirty-year-old sister of Valentinian III, the Western Roman Emperor—wrote to Attila and asked him to help her escape betrothal to a man she loathed. There is no evidence that Honoria had ever met Attila; she probably turned to him to spite her brother. Attila chose to interpret this as a marriage proposal. In a message addressed not to Valentinian but to the Eastern Roman Emperor, Attila demanded Honoria's hand and half the Western Empire. He must have expected that his proposal would be rejected by the furious Valentinian, and it was.

Using the rebuff as a pretext to wage war, Attila assembled not only Hunnish troops but also Vandals led by their king, Gaiseric. Other Germanic allies included Gepids from Dacia under King Arderic, Ostrogoths under three chieftains, and assorted bands of Rugians, Scirians, and Heruls. As Attila rampaged west and north, Burgundians and even some Franks fought and pillaged with him along the Rhine into present-day Germany, Belgium, and France.

The Empire Confronts Attila Whether or not Attila actually led his cavalry to Paris, he did ride to Orleans, a larger city than Paris in the fifth century, intending to attack. By this time, though, Aetius, the Empire's military governor of Gaul (France), had assembled an army to confront Attila. The force included Alanic and Celtic tribes from Armorica (Brittany), Salian Franks, Ripuarians, and Burgundians. Much of Aetius's strength lay in the Visigoths, led by their King Theodoric and his son Thorismud. In the summer of 451, the presence of this army under Aetius and Theodoric was enough to drive Attila from Orleans, and there was no battle.

Aetius pursued Attila to what is now the Champagne region of France, near Troyes. The exact site where Aetius and Attila battled is not known, so the battle is referred to by several names. Besides being called the Battle of Chalons, it is also known as the Battle of Troyes, of the Catalaunian Fields, or of the Mauriac Plain.

Fight for the High Ground Attila placed his Huns in the center of a line of battle. In the afternoon, Aetius faced him. He put the Alans in the center, because he did not trust them. Aetius flanked the Alans on the left, while Theodoric and the Visigoths fought on the right side. The two sides engaged in the afternoon and kept fighting through the evening. Theodoric was killed, but Aetius was able to take the high ground of the ridge.

Fighting continued the next day as Aetius's men overran Attila's camp. According to one story, Attila had a funeral pyre built behind the lines, so that if capture looked likely, he could immolate himself rather than submit. Casualty figures vary and are likely unreliable. One historian (Jordanes, who wrote in the sixth

Snow Warriors on horseback.   © *Adam Parker/Alamy*

century) said 165,000 men fell during the fight, but that is probably an exaggerated number.

Although the Battle of Chalons was often painted as the miraculous victory of a united Roman force against bloodthirsty barbarians, the lineup of tribes presents a more complex picture. Loyalties shifted, and both Rome and the Huns were willing to fight alongside anyone on a temporary basis to gain victory.

Aetius weakened Attila by showing that he and his Huns were not unstoppable. After the battle, Aetius sent Thorismud home to protect his claim to the Visigothic kingship, and he disbanded his Frankish allies as well. Attila retreated but pursued his claim to Honoria by invading Italy the next year.

✪ Key Elements of Warcraft

Mounted Soldiers

For centuries, cavalry troops played only a small role in the Roman legions. At the Battle of Cannae in 216 BCE, for example, only six thousand of Rome's eighty thou-

sand troops were on horseback. (In that battle, the soldiers dismounted to fight, only to be quickly overcome by the larger and more effective Numidian light cavalry deployed by the Carthaginian commander, Hannibal.) Julius Caesar used only about three hundred cavalry troops in each of his legions—which were composed of up to six thousand men. Caesar used cavalry for skirmishes and pursuits, but he clearly considered the mounted men unreliable.

Changes in the Empire's Cavalry   Under Augustus Caesar in the first century CE, each Roman legion had only 120 cavalry troops. Auxiliary and mercenary cavalry units increased, though, and by the time of Trajan, just after 100 CE, two types of cavalry existed: light, quick, and deadly archers, as well as more heavily armored horsemen who fought with spears and swords. By the third century CE, Emperor Diocletian had expanded the cavalry, using it as a mobile force to support the frontier garrisons.

Outside Influences   In the fourth century CE, Huns drove Gothic tribes into the Roman Empire. Like an earlier enemy of Rome (the Sarmatians), mounted Huns sped towards their targets in a wedge formation, breaking at the last minute to dash, feint, shoot arrows, and inflict damage quickly before wheeling away. The Goths adopted some of the Hun practices, and at the Battle of Adrianople, the sudden attack of Gothic cavalry devastated Roman infantry.

As it had many times before when faced with a military setback, Rome adjusted. Fifty years later, in 428 CE, cavalry comprised one-seventh of the troops stationed in Italy and Gaul and nearly half of the troops in North Africa. Cavalry troops were heavily recruited from Rome's former enemies: the Gauls, Goths, Burgundians, and Huns.

The mounted riders of Rome had no stirrups; they gripped their horses with their knees while thrusting with lances and swords. Evidence of horseshoes is found by the fourth century CE in Continental Europe (the Celts of Britain had developed horseshoes three hundred years earlier).

After the Western Empire Fell

In the middle of the sixth century CE, Justinian, Emperor of the East, sent his general Belisarius to reconquer Italy, North Africa, and other former provinces. For a brief time, the Roman Empire was restored. Belisarius relied on his expert cavalry troops, who were now heavily protected with helmets, mail shirts, and greaves. They fought with bows, shooting while controlling the horses with their knees. In a reversal of earlier policy, foot soldiers were now perceived as weak and ineffective.

Stirrups

Stirrups probably developed in Asia, in either India or China, as early as the first century CE Persians and Avars used them by 694 CE, but metal stirrups remained unknown in the west. Historians think that Viking traders introduced stirrups to Europe; they were in use by the ninth century CE Although they no doubt gave archers leverage and more control while shooting, mounted warriors had proven effective and deadly without stirrups for centuries.

By the eleventh century CE, cavalry soldiers wore even more protective clothing, including steel boots, gauntlets, and jointed armor. The age of the medieval knight had arrived.

✪ Impact on World History

Network of Cities

Rome created an urbanized empire. Each province had a *metropolis* ("mother city"), a capital with forums, baths, temples, and often a theater. Roads connected villages, which often grew to become larger towns. Cities housed up to twenty thousand people—an unprecedented development. One million lived in Rome itself. Although problems arose—such as inflation, sanitation issues, and food shortages, for example—for centuries these new cities symbolized the efficiency and centrality of Roman administration.

Of course, the conquered and absorbed provinces frequently lost their previous cultures and mythologies. In many cases, tribal structures, dialects, and traditions were wiped out. Only a few hundred words of the language of Gaul is known, for example, and most Gallic beliefs and teachings have been lost. For centuries the Empire imposed its single language throughout the Mediterranean area, along with its preferred writings, laws, arts, and customs. Roman ideals and traditions—not Gallic, Gothic, or Scythian—still affect the world today.

Reforms Create Changes in Society

The reforms of Diocletian and Constantine solved "the crisis of the third century," a set of severe military, civil, and economic problems that threatened to destroy the Empire. In the fourth century CE, prosperity followed these reforms. A new upper class developed: a wealthy and educated elite that lived in villas throughout the Empire. Another change wrought by Constantine, the legalization of Christianity, had an even longer-lasting impact.

Once the emperor favored Christianity, citizens from Britain to Africa and Armenia openly embraced it. The Empire was united by urbanization, the efficient systems of roads and communication, a common language (Latin), and bureaucracy. The infrastructure was in place to diffuse the religion, its gospels, and other new ideas to all parts of the Empire.

Romans and Barbarians

By the fifth century CE, many barbarians (Germanic, Frankish, Gallic, and other tribal groups) had been absorbed into the Empire. By their dress, speech, education, and wealth, they were often indistinguishable from Romans. Outsiders invaded and fought for power in violent struggles until the Western Empire began to disintegrate into smaller kingdoms. The leaders of those kingdoms, however, tried to preserve the infrastructure that Rome had built over the centuries. They realized that an efficient and prosperous economy benefited both conquerors and citizens.

After the death of Theodoric in 526, disease, famine, and poverty fell on once-prosperous lands. The organized Western Roman Empire—which had kept its citizens safe and allowed many people to rise and flourish, and which had celebrated learning and achievement—was over. Although gone from the material world, it became enshrined both as a glorious past and as the embodiment of the ideal society for the future.

Legacies

Roman ideals of beauty, art, and virtue profoundly influence art and philosophy to this day. Rome's eventual acceptance of Christianity impacted the entire world for two millennia, and Latin is the basis for many of Euope's languages. The militarism of Rome has been the model of many conquerors throughout history.

In the shorter term, Rome united much of Europe with its language, roads, and with its Christian fervor, setting the stage for the institutions of the Middle Ages to slowly develop out of the chaos of the Western Empire's fall.

Rome's impact can also be measured by what has been lost. Religions, languages, art forms, mythologies, ethical codes, and teachings disappeared because of Rome. Millions of people died in Rome's wars. Rome shaped the world people now live in, but it often did so violently.

BIBLIOGRAPHY

Books

Brown, Peter. *The Rise of Western Christendom*. Malden, Mass: Blackwell, 1997.

Burns, Thomas S. *Barbarians Within the Gates of Rome*. Bloomington: Indiana University Press, 1994.

Bury, J.B. *History of the Later Roman Empire*. New York: Dover, 1931, rev. 1958.

Collins, Roger. *Early Medieval Europe 300–1000*. New York: St. Martin's Press, 1991.

Kulikowski, Michael. *Rome's Gothic Wars*. J. C. Gieben: New York: Cambridge University Press, 2007.

Nicasie, N.J. *Twilight of Empire*. J.C. Gieben: Amsterdam, 1998.

Introduction to the Expansion of Islam (600–1200)

In the seventh century, Islam burst out of the peripheral region of Arabia and quickly established itself as a major force in the world. The Arabs, converts to the new religion, soon overwhelmed much of the Byzantine Empire and its rival, the Sasanian (also spelled Sassanian) Empire of Persia. From there, the Arabs swept across North Africa and into Spain. In the east, the Arabs defeated the Tang Empire of China in Central Asia while also expanding into Northern India. Within a hundred years of the death of Muhammad the Prophet (the founder of Islam), a unified Islamic state stretched from the Atlantic Ocean to the Himalayan Mountains. While the Arabs created the Islamic world, others continued to expand and change it in a variety of ways.

While the rise of Islam is often thought of in terms of zealous, camel-riding Bedouins sweeping through the Middle East and converting all to Islam at the point of the sword, the reality is much different. Islam began as a religion of the Arabs. Initially, while Muslims did conquer modern Syria, Palestine, Egypt, and Iraq, these territories had few Arabs at the time. As a result of this, the Muslims had little interest in gaining converts. Furthermore, as the booty gathered was distributed to all Muslims, economically they had little interest in gaining converts as it would lessen their own share of plunder.

Many Christians in these regions welcomed the Arabs as liberators, for their demands of tribute and taxes were less onerous than those of the Christian Byzantine state. Furthermore, as many did not agree with the teachings of the Church based in Constantinople, the Syrian and Egyptian Christians were often persecuted. The Muslims allowed them to practice their religion as "People of the Book," as they did with other religions that possessed a sacred text, be it the Bible, the Torah, or the Indian Vedas. As a result, many found the rule of the caliph (the deputy of the Prophet and of God) to be much better than that of their previous rulers.

A unified empire was short-lived. The Umayyad Dynasty (661–750) became overextended and ceased to expand. A rebellion arose in the east, and the Abbasids (750–1258) replaced the Umayyads, although North Africa fell from the Abbasid orbit. The Umayyads remained in Spain (756–1031) while a Shia Muslim state under the Fatimid Dynasty (909–1171) arose in North Africa and Egypt. Thus for several centuries, there were three individuals claiming to rule on behalf of God.

Even so, centralized rule continued to diminish as the caliph's power, regardless of which state, became more titular than real. Influence and power shifted from the caliphs to the sultans (a title meaning "one who wields power"). Initially, sultans were governors ruling on behalf of their caliph. However, increasingly along the frontiers of the Islamic world, the sultans were the real authority. Furthermore, a new powerful element entered the Islamic world beginning in the ninth century—Turks.

The Turks first appeared as slave soldiers, but then increasing numbers of Turkic nomads entered the Middle East from Central Asia. Primarily horse-archers, the Turks replaced the Arabs as the new military elite. As a consequence of this change, new empires emerged throughout the region; the region also began to fragment politically until the twelfth and thirteenth centuries, when new forces entered the region in the form of the Crusades from the West and the Mongol invasions from the East.

Expansion of Islam (600–1200)

⊕ Major Figures

Muhammad

The founder of a major religion typically is not a military leader. However, Muhammad (c. 570–632), the Prophet of Islam, was both a man of god and a man of war. Out of necessity, Muhammad went from being a merchant and prophet to being a military leader in order not only to defend his faith, but to defend those who joined his revolutionary religion.

Life Before Gabriel Muhammad was born into the Quraysh tribe, which was centered on the important pilgrimage site of Mecca. Mecca was important not only because it was on the trade routes running through Arabia but also because it housed the Kaaba, thought to be the house of Abraham. However, it had also become the house of many idols, such as those belonging to several tribes within the region.

As a youth, Muhammad was an orphan raised by his uncle, Abu Talib. Under his care, Muhammad became a merchant and entered the employ of Khadijah, a wealthy widow. In 595, the two were married. Muhammad became renown through the region for his business acumen as well as his character.

An Angel Speaks to Muhammad In 610, Muhammad began to receive revelations from the angel Gabriel who informed Muhammad that he was the last prophet of God. These revelations ultimately became the Quran (Koran), the fundamental book of Islam.

After being convinced that he had not gone mad, Muhammad accepted his role as prophet and began to attract followers. However, because of his insistence on monotheism, Muhammad also attracted enemies. The only-one-god concept went directly against a mainstay of the Meccan economy; namely, the pilgrimage trade to the idols of Mecca. Eventually not only were his followers persecuted, but Muhammad himself was targeted. After his uncle Abu Talib and his wife died in

619, the clans of Mecca decided to murder Muhammad for being a divisive and corrupting influence in society.

Fortunately for Muhammad, he had learned of the plot and escaped to the city of Yathrid (now known as Medina), located north of Mecca. There, the leading tribes accepted his followers and offered him protection. Muhammad fled there in 622, which marks year one of the Islamic calendar.

The Prophet Fights Medina is where Muhammad began his military career, mainly out of self-defense. The Meccans would not tolerate his existence, and Muhammad did nothing to discourage this feeling as he raided Meccan sponsored caravans. His raids began out of need, but then expanded as war broke out. Initially, however, Muhammad's raids were ineffective as most of his men were city dwellers and not well versed in warfare. Muhammad then began to establish relations with local Bedouin tribes, after which the caravan attacks became successful.

The first major battle was at Bedr, along the caravan route to Syria. In January 624, Muhammad marched with slightly more than three hundred men toward Bedr, hoping to intercept a larger caravan returning from Syria. While he expected to have to deal with only thirty caravan guards, he encountered a Meccan force three times his size that had arrived to escort the caravan to Mecca.

The Meccans were divided on whether to fight or not as they had secured the caravan. However, the hawk party won out and they attacked Muhammad's party. After some skirmishing by various champions, the battle began in earnest. The Muslims held their lines and shot arrows at the Meccans. The Meccans advanced toward the sun and over sand dunes against the Muslims. In the end, the discipline and the ardor of the Muslims—who truly saw it as a life-or-death struggle—won out. The half-hearted attack collapsed and the Muslims routed the Meccans, thus gaining an important victory for the Muslims.

The Quran, or Koran, the holy book of Islam. *The Art Archive/Private Collection/Eileen Tweedy. Reproduced by permission*

The next battle took place at Uhud in January 625, near Medina. Muhammad's depredations on the caravans had increased, so a new Meccan force of three thousand men was sent to deal with the marauders. There was little threat to the city of Medina itself, as its high walls were sufficient to protect it against the Meccans who had no practical siege experience. However, the Muslim youth, still riding the elation of the victory at Bedr, sought battle. With a force of seven hundred men, Muhammad led his men forth. His key unit consisted of archers that he stationed on the left flank of his army with explicit orders not to leave their post. The right flank was guarded by a spur of Mount Uhud.

The battle consisted primarily of a mass melee. Meccan horsemen did try to turn the Muslim flank, but were kept at bay by the strategically placed archers. A sudden charge finally broke the Meccan lines. However, rather than pursue and crush their enemies, the Muslims' discipline broke and they began looting the Meccan camp. The archers who had secured the Muslim flank then joined in.

At this point, Khalid ibn al-Walid, who would later become perhaps the greatest Arab commander, rallied the Meccans and counterattacked and defeated the Muslims. Muhammad suffered multiple wounds in the combat, but he and his followers escaped to the safety of Mount Uhud, which was more defensible. Nonetheless, victory went to Mecca on that day.

The Conflict Continues After Uhud, Muhammad swore revenge for the death of his uncle, Hamza. He was also repulsed by the mutilation of bodies that the Meccans carried out. Although Muhammad did do the same to thirty members of the Quraysh in revenge for Hamza, he ultimately forbade the mutilation of the dead, which had been a custom in the Arabian Peninsula.

Even though he was once defeated, Muhammad pressed on with his raiding. Caravans and tribes allied to Mecca were targets. Muhammad clearly viewed the conflict with Mecca as one of life and death. Muhammad's successful raiding also began to attract support from more Bedouin tribes. Although they may have accepted Islam, their main interest was financial rewards through raiding. The threat increased to the point that in early 627, the Meccans finally gathered an army of ten thousand to smite down Muhammad once and for all.

THE DROMEDARY CAMEL

Although Arabian horses are known throughout the world, the initial Arab conquests would not have been possible without camels. The dromedary camel (*Camelus dromedaries*), serving as a draught animal as well as a riding animal, allowed the Muslims not only to consolidate the Arabian peninsula, but also to strike at the Sasanid and Byzantine Empires through the inhospitable deserts rather than just through obvious routes.

As the so-called "ship of the desert," a camel could go days without water and travel through deserts where horses would not survive. In addition, camels could travel—if properly trained and conditioned—almost one hundred miles a day. Khalid ibn al-Walid's advance from Iraq to the Syrian front would not have been possible without the dromedary camel. Indeed, even the Prophet Muhammad rode them into battle.

The news quickly reached Medina. Resisting three thousand men was one thing, but ten thousand was quite another; there was a real possibility Medina would fall. Fortunately for the Muslims, among them was a Persian convert to Islam (and former slave) named Salman who suggested digging a ditch and building a breastwork to better fortify the town. Considering that the Arabs on either side had no siege expertise, this was revolutionary. Even Muhammad joined in the digging and they completed it just before the arrival of the Meccan forces.

The new fortifications nonplussed the Meccans. The Bedouin allies of the Meccans had little desire to camp and wait out the Muslims. With rations growing short, many Bedouins departed. After twenty days with only a little skirmishing, the Meccans and their allies broke camp and departed. For the Muslims, it was another sign that God was on their side. The victory only increased the prestige of Muhammad and decreased that of Quraysh in Mecca.

Muhammad Takes Mecca Thus in early 630, Muhammad marched on Mecca, and the city surrendered without a fight. In return for its submission, Muhammad did not allow his men to pillage the city. The only damage they did was to smash all of the idols around the Kaaba, showing to all of the Meccans, that indeed, *Allahu akbar*, or "God is greater than their gods."

After this, most of the Arab peninsula came under Muhammad's control and raiding parties struck at the Byzantine and Sasanid Empire. One reason for this was to keep the often quarrelsome tribes occupied by attacking someone else rather than each other. Although Muhammad died in 632, his accomplishments as a military commander are overshadowed only by his accomplishments as a religious leader.

Khalid ibn al-Walid

Khalid ibn al-Walid (c. 590–642) was the primary Arab general during the first phase of the Arab conquests in the seventh century. Later known as *Sayf Allah* ("the Sword of God"), Khalid initially fought against Muhammad and the early Muslim community.

Not an Early Convert Like most Meccans, Khalid initially opposed the teachings of Muhammad. He was present on the side of the Meccans at the Battle of Uhud in 625, and was crucial to the Meccan victory there as he led the counterattack against the Muslims. Nonetheless, he converted to Islam in either 627 or 629. Historians are unsure of exactly when Khalid converted, but it is known that he was among the Muslims in 630 when the city of Mecca surrendered to Muhammad. He was also involved in raids into Byzantine territory in 629, including successfully leading a raiding party back to Medina after its commander had been killed.

When Muhammad died in 632, there was not a clear line of succession to the leadership. Many of the tribes that had submitted to Muhammad saw their agreement as one between Muhammad and their tribal leaders, so after his death, any agreements were ended. Thus when Abu Bakr, who ruled from 632 to 634, became the caliph or successor to Muhammad, he sent Khalid on several missions to quell the rebellions in what became known as the *Hurub al-Riddah*, or War of Apostasy. (Also adding to this turmoil was the appearance of many new prophets, who probably hoped to emulate the success that Muhammad had.)

Khalid quickly brought the rebels in the north and northeast of Arabia under control. In 632, while in the Nejd desert, he defeated the Asad, Tayyi, and Tamim tribes in several encounters. Then in 633, he entered eastern Arabia and crushed the Hanifa tribe, led by Musailima, a newly proclaimed prophet, at the Battle of Aqraba.

Expansion of the Faith As Khalid demonstrated exceptional military prowess, he was placed in charge of an army to invade modern day Iraq in 634. There, Khalid brought other Arab tribes and towns under his control as well as moving north along the Euphrates to take control of the important trading nexus of Dumat al-Jandal. Soon he received word from Abu Bakr to assist Arab operations in Syria, part of the Byzantine Empire. To hasten his march, Khalid crossed the Syrian desert, thought by the Byzantines to be impassable.

Khalid's exact role in Syria is unclear. Some sources place him as the primary commander, while others indicate that he was a lieutenant to Abu Ubayda ibn al-Jarrah. Some believe that initially his success led Abu Bakr to promote him to supreme command of the Muslim army in Syria, and later he was demoted. Nonetheless, Khalid led troops in all of the major battles including the capture of Damascus and Hims as well as the battle of Yarmuk. Khalid' meteoric rise and success on the battlefield earned him the sobriquet of *Sayf Allah*, although later sources refer to him with the less prestigious title of *Sayf Rasul Allah*, or the "Sword of the Messenger of God."

A New Caliph Demotes the Old Guard After the death of Caliph Abu Bakr in 634, Khalid's fortunes waned. The new caliph, Umar ibn al-Khattab, was not as enamored with Khalid as his predecessor. Umar demoted Khalid, despite Khalid's victory over the Byzantines at the first Battle of Yarmouk in 634. It is not clear if he was demoted from the primary commander or just as one of the commanders. Umar did it because he wanted to make sure that Khalid remembered that his success in battle came from God and not to consider himself infallible.

The general, however, was not removed from Syria. He led troops in northern Syria as a lieutenant of Abu Ubayda and fought at the second Battle of Yarmouk in 636 and at the sieges of Jerusalem and Aleppo. After the Byzantines evacuated Syria, Khalid then led numerous raids during the summer on the frontier with the Byzantines until his death in 642.

When not participating in the raids, he lived a semi-retired life in Hims, located in modern Syria, where he died. As with his status with Caliph Umar, even Khalid's death is immersed with speculation. Some scholars believe that Khalid was actually assassinated by Muawiya—a future caliph who was governor of Damascus at the time—out of envy of Khalid's glory.

Ali

Ali ibn abi Talib (c. 600–661), who ruled as the fourth caliph between 656–661, was a cousin of the prophet Muhammad. Ali was one of the first converts to Islam, and because of this, he was one of Muhammad's trusted companions. In addition, Ali became Muhammad's son-in-law with his marriage to Fatima (606–632), the daughter of Muhammad.

Islam in Its Infancy Ali's value as an aide to Muhammad became apparent in 622. Warned of an assassination plot against Muhammad, Ali stayed behind in Mecca, posing as the prophet while Muhammad escaped. The assassins were about to stab Ali when they realized their mistake; rather than risk invoking a blood feud with Ali's relatives, the assassins spared his life. Ali later joined Muhammad in the hills surrounding Mecca and fled with him to Medina.

During war with Mecca, Ali rose to the forefront of the champions of Islam. He distinguished himself in single combat at Bedr (624), Uhud (625), and then at the Battle of the Ditch (627). Because of his close relationship to Muhammad and his prowess in battle, he seemed a logical successor to Muhammad. However, Muhammad did not leave instructions concerning who should lead after his death in 632. Thus Ali was

Roland is surrounded by fighting Saracens, while guarding the pass at Roncesvalles in the Pyrenees. *Hulton Archive/Getty Images*

overlooked while Abu Bakr, another close friend of Muhammad, took charge in the middle of the crisis of Muhammad's death.

Troubles As Caliph It was not until 656 that Ali came to power as the fourth caliph. His rise to power also caused a major crisis within Islam. His predecessor, Uthman ibn Affan, was assassinated by men dissatisfied with his policies of nepotism. Once in power, Ali did nothing to bring these men to justice, thus giving the impression to many that he approved of the assassination. The Umayyad clan, of which Uthman had been a member, was incensed against Ali for not avenging their relative. (Many Umayyads were governors, with the most powerful being Muawiya, the governor of Syria.)

Ali also had to deal with a rebellion of Zubayr, Talha, and Aisha (a wife of Muhammad). Zubayr and Talha, two companions of Muhammad and only slightly less prestigious than Ali at the time, were frustrated that Ali had not taken any action against the murderers of Uthman and for not dealing with unruly Bedouin tribes. However, their anger was not the same as the Umayyads;

rather, they were upset that Ali was not quick at restoring law and order. Although they had sworn allegiance to Ali, they now began to have second doubts. Aisha, however, simply disliked Ali.

Zubayr and Talha departed Medina (the capital of the nascent Arab empire) for Mecca and found ample support against Ali. Thus a rebellion began. The rebels left Mecca with three thousand men and headed toward Basra in southern Iraq where Talha and Zubayr had additional supporters.

In the autumn of 656, Ali marched toward Iraq to deal with the rebellion. The Battle of the Camel (so called because Aisha, mounted in a camel litter, encouraged her troops at the battle) took place near Basra in 656. Ali had a bit more than ten thousand men and slightly outnumbered Zubayr and Talha.

Ali attempted to avoid battle, as it would pit Muslim against Muslim, something that Muhammad had strictly prohibited. Ultimately, negotiations failed and the battle began. In the end, Zubayr and Talha died and Ali was victorious. Aisha and her camel were a rallying point, but Ali undermined it by having a chosen warrior hamstring the camel. Its collapse signaled the end of the rebellion. Aisha was sent back to Medina where she lived until her death sometime in the late 670s.

Against The Umayyads The next threat was from Muawiya. This came to a head at the Battle of Siffin, near Raqqa in Iraq, in the spring of 657. According to the sources, the armies were roughly equal, approaching fifty thousand men each.

The battle was slow paced due to a reluctance to fight, as again both sides were hesitant to pit Muslim against Muslim. There was some negotiation, but in the eyes of Muawiya, there was little to discuss.

Ali challenged Muawiya to single combat, but Muawiya excused himself from it. Skirmishing began and by the middle of summer, a full battle took place. After two days of fighting, the Syrian army was slowly pushed back. Ultimately, another truce came as a result of Syrian soldiers putting the Quran on their lances and demanding that the word of God decide the battle. Both sides agreed.

Ali had no choice but to once again go to arbitration. This time, Muawiya used another tactic. He no longer insisted on whether Ali supported the murders of Uthman, but whether Ali should be the caliph. The basic issue was that a caliph must mete out justice, and because Ali did nothing, Muawiya's contention was that Ali was not fit to rule.

Arbitration concluded that neither Ali nor Muawiya could claim the caliphate and that the people would choose a new leader. However, the arbitrator for Muawiya, after denouncing Ali, immediately nominated Muawiya. Ali then rejected the decision.

Ironically, if Ali had simply continued the battle, he most likely would have emerged victorious. Instead, he

listened to the rank and file and settled for arbitration. As a result, Muawiya became the unofficial caliph in Damascus and Ali remained in his position in his new capital of Kufa, in Iraq.

Ali was killed in 661 while exiting a mosque in Kufa by one of his former followers, Abd al-Rahman ibn Muljam. Ibn Muljam and other ardent supporters had been disgusted by Ali's willingness to negotiate a settlement and left him, forming the Islamic sect known has Kharajis. A small but radical group, the Kharajis viewed themselves as the only true Muslims and considered Ali a traitor to Islam for dealing with Muawiya.

Yazid I

The second Umayyad caliph, Yazid ibn Muawiya (c. 645–683) was a key figure in the split in Islam that created the divisions of Sunni and Shi'a Islam. He was a competent military leader, having served as a commander during his father's siege of Constantinople in 669. However, Yazid I is best known for his role in the rise of Shi'a Islam and for having a disastrous reign.

Succession Troubles Traditionally, the position of caliph, the successor to the Prophet Muhammad as the leader of the Muslim community, was an elected position; the most qualified figure in terms of leadership and personal piety was chosen. Muawiya, the governor of Syria ascended the caliphal throne after the death of Ali, the fourth caliph, in 656. During his fairly effective rule, Muawiya made Yazid (his son) his successor.

Securing support for Yazid was difficult, particularly as it went against tribal tradition. Many tribes were not interested in seeing a member of the Kalb tribe—the tribe of Yazid and his father—hold such a prominent post. Nonetheless, Muawiya succeeded in gaining support for his son, allowing Yazid to become caliph in 680, the year of Muawiya's death.

Despite Muawiya's efforts, after his death Yazid faced numerous rebellions. The greatest threat came from Husayn ibn Ali (626–680) and Abd Allah ibn al-Zubayr (d. 692), who was the grandson of the second caliph (Abu Bakr) and also related to Muhammad. Both men rebelled almost instantly.

Husayn's rebellion was not unexpected. Muawiya's challenge to the authority of Ali at the Battle of Siffin (657) and the subsequent rise of the Umayyad Caliphate created a rift between the two factions. Indeed, Husayn's elder brother was told not to meddle in politics in a thinly veiled threat by Muawiya. With Yazid's reign, Husayn decided that the time had come to assert his family's claim to be the rightful rulers of the Islamic empire. Thus he and a small band of followers marched toward Kufa in Iraq to start a rebellion.

Learning of these plans, Yazid quickly sent a large force to intercept them. The Umayyad forces intercepted them at Karbala, in Iraq, only twenty miles from Kufa.

On October 10, 680, despite being vastly outnumbered, Husayn fought until he and his supporters were all dead.

This battle transformed Husayn and the *Shiat Ali* (Partisans of Ali) into martyrs. It also transformed a political faction who supported the claims of the family of Ali to the throne into a religious sect. The battle remains a centerpiece of Shi'a theology, known as Ashura, and is a holiday in which the martyrdom of Husayn is remembered.

Zubayr's Rebellion A graver threat to Yazid's power came from the heart of Arabia where Ibn al-Zubayr rallied tribes who opposed Umayyad rule. Many tribes opposed the idea of dynastic rule since it violated tradition, but the event that formed a rebellion against Yazid was due to his policies. In 683, Yazid promulgated an order to confiscate land in the holy city of Medina. This struck at many leaders who opposed him; a rebellion arose, and Umayyad supporters were driven from the city. At the same time, Ibn al-Zubayr was proclaimed caliph in Mecca, a direct challenge to Yazid.

Yazid sent an army to Medina. They easily crushed the Medinans at the Battle of al-Harra. Then the Umayyad army marched on Mecca. Many scholars think that the rebellion would have been crushed then, but Yazid died in 683, and the siege was ended.

Ibn al-Zubayr then became the problem of Yazid's successor. Ultimately, the unfinished conclusion of the siege allowed Ibn al-Zubayr to consolidate his strength and gain support throughout the empire. In addition, other rebellions broke out among the Shi'a and other sects such as the Kharijites. Most provinces recognized Ibn al-Zubayr as the caliph. He continued to be a thorn to the Umayyads until he was killed in 692.

Conflicts Internal and External Perhaps Yazid's reputation would be better if he had not died during the middle of a rebellion. However, Ibn al-Zubayr's rebellion was not the only military difficulty Yazid encountered.

In eastern Persia, Arab armies were defeated in the regions of Sistan and Zabulistan after running over most of Persia with relative ease. Furthermore, a Berber revolt in North Africa threatened Umayyad control in North Africa. Finally, the Byzantines were on the offensive and threatening northern Syria. Yazid successfully stymied their efforts by building additional fortresses, but it prevented him from dealing with threats such as Ibn al-Zubayr.

In the end, Yazid's reign is difficult to assess due to his early death. With rebellions throughout the empire, it would have been difficult for anyone to succeed in such a short frame of time.

Charles Martel

Charles Martel (c. 686–741) was the mayor of the palace of the Frankish Merovingian kingdom (consisting of France and parts of Germany). Although the Merovingians were the titular rulers, they had lost real power to

Charles Martel, King of the Franks, at the Battle of Poitiers 732. *Public Domain*

the Frankish aristocracy, led by the mayors of the palace. Martel claimed his place in history by defeating Muslim invaders from Spain at the Battle of Poitiers (also known as the Battle of Tours).

The Long Shot Charles, who gained his sobriquet or nickname of "Martel" or "Hammer" after his death, was an unlikely leader. He was not a legitimate heir to the position of mayor, being the son of Alpaida, a lesser wife. (It was not uncommon during this period for the rulers to have several wives in order to secure a male heir.) However, Martel defeated various claimants to the throne and was accepted as mayor of the palace in 718.

As it was an immense realm, administering the kingdom was difficult. Furthermore, Martel was surrounded by enemies: pagan Saxons and Germans, Lombards, and Muslims. After securing power, he launched a number of attacks against the Saxons and Germans to discourage them from invading. Martel also had to deal with recalcitrant nobles in southern France.

Checking the Muslims However, the greatest task at hand for Charles was across the Pyrenees Mountains. This was the location of the Muslim kingdom of al-Andalus, created in 711 with the conquest of Spain. It was not long thereafter before Muslim raiders entered France. Gradually they began to occupy the southern coastline as well. During Charles's reign as mayor, the Muslims began to extend their raids further north into central France.

In 732, Charles countered their attacks with a resounding victory somewhere between the modern locations of Tours and Poitiers, for which he was posthumously given the title of Martel. Although raids continued afterwards, Charles's domains were not seriously threatened afterwards as he took steps to ensure their security.

His victory allowed him to consolidate his authority in the region of Aquitaine. On his frontier he fought other battles with the Muslims, but also brought the regions of Burgundy and Provence under his control as the nobles there often allied with the Muslims against him. During one of these conflicts, Martel recaptured Avignon in 737 and defeated Muslim armies at Narbonne and at Corbieres in the same year.

Martel also formed an alliance with the neighboring Lombards in modern day Switzerland and northern Italy. This was an odd match as the Lombards and Franks had clashed before. Furthermore, the Lombards encroached on lands held by the Papacy in Italy. Although Charles was a strong supporter of the Church, it was clear that his interests lay more in the defense of his realm rather than just religion. Indeed, Charles appointed and dismissed bishops while using the Church's wealth to fund his wars.

Legacy of the Hammer   Charles Martel eventually became the founder of the Carolingian dynasty. However, this was not due to strategic planning. When the Merovingian king Theodoric IV died in 737, Charles did not replace him as had been the practice. Charles did not claim the throne himself, but after his death in 741, his son Pepin assumed his responsibilities and eventually took the title of king in 751.

Abd al-Rahman

Although the Umayyad dynasty continued in Spain after the Abbasid Revolution in 750, the rulers of al-Andalus, as Spain was called, it did not claim the title of caliph. This changed under Abd al-Rahman III (891–961), who revitalized Umayyad power and was the first to reclaim the title of caliph. Based in the great city of Cordoba, which rivaled Constantinople and Baghdad in splendor, Abd al-Rahman III built a powerful state and dealt with Muslim and Christian opponents.

Life in the Iberian Outback   Becaues of al-Andalus' distance from the center of Islamic power in the Middle East, it developed differently. Conquered in 711 by Berbers and Arabs from North Africa, al-Andalus became a bastion of Umayyad power after the Abbasid revolution of 750. Initially the Umayyads there claimed the title of emir or commander, which gave a token nod of recognition to the Abbasids as the titular ruler. However, the Umayyads remained independent under the

leadership of Abd al-Rahman I, who ruled from 756 to 788.

While Abd al-Rahman I provided unity, this fragmented after the death of Abd al-Rahman II in 852 due to factionalization between Berbers, Arabs, Muwallads (Spanish converts to Islam), Mozarabs (Spaniards who adopted Arabic language and customs), and the Jewish population. In addition, there was strife on the border between al-Andalus and the Christian north.

A Single City to Start With   When Abd al-Rahman III inherited the throne from his grandfather (Abd Allah) in 912, the ruler really only controlled Cordoba. Abd al-Rahman was of mixed ancestry, his mother was a Christian of either Frankish or Basque origins. As a result, he was born with a fair complexion and blonde or red hair, which he at times dyed. Even in his youth he was known for his bravery and intellect, qualities that served him well as he ascended the throne.

Almost immediately Abd al-Rahman began to restore Umayyad authority. In 912 and 913, he regained control over many of the provincial centers, including Seville. He then moved against Umar ibn-Hafsun, who since 883 had acted as an independent ruler near Malaga. Despite Abd al-Rahman's efforts, Umar (who had converted to Christianity) successfully resisted him in the mountains. Although Umar died in 917, his sons carried out the resistance until 928. The defeat of the Hafsun family led to the submission of other rebels. By 932, Abd al-Rahman succeeded in unifying al-Andalus again.

Now secure in his rule, Abd al-Rahman took another step to increase his authority in his kingdom and beyond, as he adopted the title of caliph on January 16, 929. By doing so, al-Rahman placed himself on the same level of authority of the Abbasid ruler in Baghdad. This title made al-Rahman not only the secular ruler, but in theory, the ultimate religious authority in the kingdom. This was not a new innovation, as in North Africa the Fatimids (909–1171), a Shi'a Muslim dynasty, had also claimed the caliphate.

Against the Christians   During his unification of al-Andalus, Abd al-Rahman had to deal with an invasion from the Christian kingdoms of Navarre and Leon. After the Christians defeated his border forces at San Esteban de Gormaz in 917, the Muslim ruler had to abandon his campaign and lead his army to the frontier. Once there, Abd al-Rahman gained the offensive, recapturing lost territory and then crushing the combined forces of Leon and Navarre on July 26, 920, at the Battle of Valdejunquera.

Afterwards, Abd al-Rahman was determined to punish the Christian kingdoms, so he sacked Pamplona in Navarre in 924. Even this did not secure his border. In 930, Ramiro II of Leon invaded al-Andalus and pillaged the Duero and Ebro river valleys.

Abd al-Rahman's subsequent invasions to punish Leon ended in failure. At Simancas in 939, Ramiro's forces defeated Abd al-Rahman's larger army on August 1. It is recorded that afterwards, Abd al-Rahman never personally led his armies again. However, conflict between the Christian kingdoms of Leon, Navarre, and Castile negated any real threat to al-Andalus.

Although he did not lead armies against them, Abd al-Rahman was still effective in manipulating the Christian rulers through diplomacy. Despite the threat from the north, this did not prevent Abd al-Rahman from having cordial relations with other Christian states, such as the Byzantine Empire or the Holy Roman Empire.

Afterwards, Abd al-Rahman's reign was relatively quiet. In terms of religion, he was a moderate who based his policies on matters of maintaining control rather than religious dogma. He would brook no challenge to his authority from his Christian or Muslim subjects and neighbors. After his death in 961, al-Andalus slowly declined and eventually disappeared as a unified state by 1031.

Mahmud of Ghazni

Mahmud of Ghazni (c. 971–1030) was the third ruler of an empire based in Afghanistan. Although theoretically subordinate to the Abbasid caliph in Baghdad, Mahmud established a vast empire that influenced events in the eastern Islamic world and was crucial to the spread of Islam or Islamic influences into Central Asia and India.

Empire Building The Ghaznavid Empire, which lasted from 977 to1186, emerged from the ruins of its predecessor, the Samanid Empire. Located in Central Asia, this earlier empire lasted from 900 to 999. Alptigin, the Samanid governor of Ghazni in Afghanistan, founded an empire in the waning days of the Samanid dynasty. As the Ghaznavids expanded, ruling elites in conquered territories were often replaced with mamluks loyal to the ruler.

Although Alptigin is the nominal founder of the empire, it was his *ghulam* (slave), Sebuktigin, who truly raised the banner of empire in 977 by usurping power. Sebuktigin initially ruled as a governor of the Samanids, ruling much of Afghanistan. His son, Mahmud, served as one of his military commanders and conquered Khurasan (northeastern Iran) and part of Afghanistan.

Unlike his own rise to the throne, Sebuktigin envisioned a hereditary successor, namely one of his sons. For ambiguous reasons, he chose his son Ismail, even though Ismail possessed neither the administrative skill nor the martial abilities of Mahmud.

After Sebuktigin's death, Mahmud did not want to deprive his brother; at the same time, Mahmud wanted his claim to the throne recognized. Mahmud asserted his superior administrative and military experience as legitimate reasons why he, and not Ismail, should be the ruler. This was a calculated maneuver, as this fact would be in the minds of the military commanders or emirs.

MAMLUKS AND GHULAMS

An important component of virtually all Islamic armies were the mamluks or ghulams. Both terms refer to someone who is owned, or a slave. However, they are terms that were generally specific to a soldier who had been enslaved in his youth and taught the ways of war. Often, mamluks were manumitted upon completing their military education. Others remained in servitude for their entire lives; however, they could become governors and generals.

Military slaves came from all regions bordering the Islamic world, but the preferred slaves were Turks from Central Asia. Beginning in the ninth century, these were purchased in increasing numbers. Turks became the preferred military slaves as their nomadic upbringing instilled a heartiness that other slaves lacked. Furthermore, they were already proficient in horsemanship and archery, skills that many of the other races lacked or were less adept at as a whole.

One of the primary reasons slaves formed a preferred corps was that as a privileged group, they owed everything to their master. Also, as outsiders, they did not have conflicting tribal and kinship ties that often conflicted with the military goals of kings. However, over time the mamluks established their own states. The Ghaznavid Empire, the Sultanate of Delhi, and the Mamluk Sultanate of Egypt and Syria are the prime examples of this phenomenon.

When mediation failed, Mahmud resorted to war and defeated his brother. Ismail was then kept under house arrest away from the center of power.

Opportunities in War After his victory, the Samanids confirmed Mahmud—who was still technically a vassal of the Samanids—in his position and possessions. The one exception was the region of Khurasan, which was given to the emir of Bukhara, a person named Begtuzun.

In retrospect, Khurasan was not a good gift to bestow. With his new territory, Begtuzun was then powerful enough to depose emir Abul Harith Mansur, the Samanid sultan, and raise another Samanid to the throne. Mahmud used this opportunity to attack Begtuzun, legitimatizing his attack against another Muslim ruler by defending the rightful Samanid ruler. Initially, the conflict ended unresolved, but war resumed and Mahmud emerged as the victor.

After his victory, Mahmud sent a report to the Abbasid caliph in Baghdad, al-Qadir Billah. In return, the caliph sent Mahmud a patent of sovereignty over Khurasan in 999. His investiture by the caliph led to further correspondence between Ghazni and Baghdad; indeed, many of Mahmud 's actions often seemed designed in order to gain recognition and legitimacy from Baghdad, or at least it was a benefit.

In October 999, the Qarakhanids, a Turkic dynasty in Central Asia, ended the feeble remnants of the Samanids. Bukhara fell before them, but some of the Samanids escaped to Khwarazm where they attempted to establish a new power base. From Khwarazm they tried to regain Khurasan from Mahmud, but the Ghaznavid ruler (and alleged vassal of the Samanids) soundly defeated them.

Connection to the Caliph

Mahmud continually strove to legitimate his reign. In particular, the caliph's approval was crucial, so Mahmud undertook three actions in order to maintain this close relationship. The first measure was to include the caliph's name on his coins. Second, a share of the plunder from Mahmud went to Baghdad as a gift from the Ghaznavid ruler. Finally, Mahmud depicted himself in his correspondence with Baghdad as a *ghazi*, or holy warrior, as he campaigned not only against Hindus in India, but also against Shi'a elements in Iran. The latter also served another purpose in that it enabled Mahmud and later Ghaznavids to portray themselves as defenders of Sunnism.

Although Mahmud depicted himself as a ghazi and undertook frequent expeditions into India and against the Shi'a, he was not a fanatical Muslim. He did not plunder the Hindus during periods of peace, and a separate quarter for them existed in Ghazni. Furthermore, as Hindu troops comprised a significant part of his army (a tribute from vassal Hindu princes), Mahmud could ill afford to alienate them. His legitimacy over the Hindu princes was due not only to his martial prowess, but also his just rule. While Mahmud encouraged the spread of Islam into India, he only acted as a ghazi during war. Once peace had been established, Mahmud proved himself to be a tolerant ruler.

The Ghaznavid Army

Under Mahmud, the army was the central institution of the state. It is estimated that the Ghaznavid army maintained a standing force of 35,000–55,000 soldiers with over a thousand elephants. Of course, this force could be increased by levies and auxiliaries.

The core of the Ghaznavid army consisted of mamluks. Although they were comprised of a wide variety of ethnicities, the majority were Turks. The Ghaznavid sultans attempted—with only moderate success—to prevent the accumulation of mamluk corps among provincial governors, as they might rival their own power.

Elephants, collected as tribute from Indian princes or as plunder, were also extensively used in battle. Indeed, the Ghaznavids were the first among Islamic states to deploy elephant tactical units in battle, including formations of one hundred elephants. Commanders were assigned elephants as command centers, giving them a vantage point in which to view the battlefield.

Although the elephants were intimidating, the primary arm of the military was the cavalry, including heavy and light forces. Infantry also formed a large percentage of the military, but it was primarily used in siege operations.

Shield of Islam

With campaigns against Shi'ites in Iran, Hindus in India, and infidel Turks in Central Asia, the Ghaznavids served as the defenders of orthodoxy until the Turkic Seljuks supplanted them.

Toghril Beg

Toghril Beg (c. 990–1063) was the founder of the Seljuk Empire, which at its height stretched from modern Afghanistan into Turkey. He was the grandson of Seljuk, the namesake of the Seljuk tribe (a subset of the Ghuzz Turks from Central Asia).

Rise of the Seljuks

The Ghuzz Turks converted to Islam in the tenth century and became increasingly involved in the struggles between the Ghaznavid and Qarakhanid empires in Central Asia. This conflict helped give birth to the Seljuk state.

During the wars between the Ghaznavids and Qarakhanids, the Seljuks and other Ghuzz Turks were displaced. One branch moved into Khurasan, where Mahmud of Ghazni kept them on a short leash. Toghril Beg and his brother Chaghri led the rest of the Seljuks to Khwarazm, south of the Aral Sea, in 1034. However, they were eventually forced to flee to Khurasan due to increasing pressure from other Ghuzz tribes in 1035–1036.

In 1037, the Seljuks were able to take over the towns of Merv, Nishapur, and Herat. These were all vassals of the Ghaznavids, now ruled by sultan Masud. Masud attempted to bring the Seljuks to heel in 1040, but he was crushed at the Battle of Dandanqan. After this, the Persian territory of the Ghaznavids was lost forever to the Seljuks.

Westward Expansion

With the defeat of the Ghaznavids, the Seljuks were now a major power in the region. Following steppe custom, Toghril and his brother divided the realm between themselves to rule, although in theory it remained a single state. Toghril's portion of the empire was the western regions.

With no major powers to oppose him, Toghril quickly acquired more territory. Much of Persia or modern Iran submitted to his authority, although taking cities through sieges remained difficult as the Seljuks had little experience in these matters. (Their most effective tactic was to blockade a city.) Toghril's troops also began to raid into Transcaucasia (modern Azerbaijan, Armenia, and Georgia). This eventually paid off as he gained the homage of many of the local lords by 1054.

Toghril gained new influence in 1055 when he took over Baghdad. The Buyids (932), an Iranian Shi'a dynasty, controlled much of western Persia as well as Baghdad. The

Abbasid caliph was still the titular lord of the region, but in reality the caliphs held power in name only.

In 1054, Toghril received an invitation from Caliph al-Qaim to liberate Baghdad from the Buyids. Toghril accepted the invitation and moved against the Buyids, deposing them in 1055. This victory was aided by dissent against Buyid rule in Baghdad and the fact that the Buyids, whose army was primarily infantry, could not resist the Seljuk horse archers.

Toghril the Sultan Once Baghdad was liberated, Toghril received the title of sultan. He was honored by the caliph and recognized as the caliph's deputy. Despite his power and titles, not everyone was happy with Toghril's power. In 1059, his cousin Ibrahim ibn Inal rebelled, in collusion with the commander of the caliph's army, a person named Besairi. While Toghril dealt with his cousin, Besairi occupied Baghdad and removed the caliph from power.

Toghril dealt with each of his attackers in turn. Ibrahim ibn Inal met Toghril in Battle at Rai (near modern Teheran). Toghril emerged victorious and executed his cousin. He then marched against Baghdad, defeating the Abbasid general before the walls of the city. In early 1060, Toghril brought the caliph back to Baghdad.

Now, things had substantially changed. Although the caliph had sought to make the Seljuk leader his subordinate and military muscle, the caliph was clearly at the mercy of Toghril. In the eyes of the people, Toghril saved Sunni Islam and restored the caliphate; in reality, the caliph was once again a puppet of a greater power.

In the course of his life, Toghril went from being a refugee to the leader of a great empire. He successfully held off threats to his power from internal and external forces. Furthermore, as his tribe were fairly recent converts, his role as the champion of Islam gave Toghril further legitimacy as a ruler.

Alp Arslan

Alp Arslan ("Lion Hero" in Turkic) (1029–1072) was the great-grandson of Seljuk, the chieftain of the Ghuzz Turkic tribes that migrated from Central Asia into Iran in the eleventh century. A product of that migration, Arslan was born in the Persian province of Khurasan and became the second Seljuk sultan.

Path to Ascension Alp Arslan was the nephew of the Seljuk sultan Toghril Beg and the son of Chaghri Beg. He began his career as a lieutenant for his father, who commanded the Seljuk armies in Khurasan. When Chaghri died (sometime in 1059 or 1060), Alp Arslan stepped into his father's position. For the next three years, he was a loyal general for his uncle Toghril. However, when Toghril died in 1063, Alp Arslan ascended the throne. Not unexpectedly, his claim to the throne was challenged, but against all rivals—such as his cousin

Detail of ornate tilework in the Friday Mosque in Isfahan, Iran. Construction on the mosque began in 771. *© Robert Harding Picture Library Ltd./Alamy*

Suleiman and his father's cousin, Kutulmish—Alp Arslan emerged victorious.

Alp Arslan's reign was pivotal to the Seljuks, as he actively encouraged the move from a nomadic kingdom to a more sedentary existence. He also increased the authority of the government over the frequently autonomous Turkic tribes. Resentment to this played a role in the rebellions. However, Alp Arslan found outlets for the tribe's frustration by directing them against neighboring Christian states as well as the (Shi'a Muslim) Fatimid caliphate in Egypt and Syria

Empire Building When not suppressing family rebellions, Alp Arslan attempted to expand the Seljuk Sultanate. In 1064 and 1068, his armies invaded the Christian regions of Georgia and Armenia. While he did not conquer them, he did force their rulers to recognize Seljuk suzerainty and pay tribute. Then in 1065 he crossed the Amu Darya and brought the region known as Mawarannahr (the territory between the Amu Darya and Syr Darya rivers) under his authority. Five years later, Alp

Arslan began to extend Seljuk dominion into Syria, capturing the city of Aleppo in 1070. Henceforth, Syria was dominated by the Seljuks, while the Fatimids generally controlled the coastline of the Levant.

Now in Syria, Alp Arslan was in a position to rival the Byzantine Empire. Indeed, as new Turkic nomads entered his domains, Alp Arslan sent them to the Byzantine border. There they could raid the Byzantines while not causing trouble in his own domains.

Naturally, this provoked a Byzantine reaction and in 1071, Emperor Romanus IV Diogenes invaded Seljuk territory. Alp Arslan met him in battle and crushed the Byzantines at Manzikert on August 26, 1071. This victory was the pinnacle of Alp Arslan's career as it opened Anatolia (modern Turkey) to Seljuk conquest. However, it would be decades before Seljuk authority dominated the region, as Alp Arslan did not take immediate advantage of the power vacuum.

The campaign against the Byzantines was not Alp Arslan's last venture. In 1072, he was once again in Central Asia campaigning. While interviewing a captive commander, he was stabbed. While he did not die immediately, Alp Arslan finally succumbed on November 24, 1072, and was succeeded by his son, Malik Shah.

Although Alp Arslan is considered one of the greatest of the Seljuk sultans, his primary focus was on military affairs. The actual running of the empire was handled by his vizier, or prime minister, Nizam al-Mulk, a Persian. Nizam al-Mulk's involvement was crucial; he provided stability for the state not only in government but by creating military fiefs. This meant that Alp Arslan's troops had financial support and could severely limit their pillaging of the populace.

Muhammad of Ghur

Muizz al-Din Muhammad (c. 1160–1206), known more popularly as Muhammad of Ghur, raised the Ghurid Empire—based in the city of Ghur, located in modern Afghanistan—to its pinnacle. Muhammad accomplished this with the help of his elder brother, Ghiyath al-Din.

An Island in a Ghaznavid Sea
The Ghurid Sultans came from the Shansab family who, according to legend, were converted to Islam by Caliph Ali, who invested them with the authority to rule the region of Ghur. Ghur was notable for not being part of the larger Ghaznavid Empire around it. Mahmud of Ghazni led three campaigns against Ghur, but never successfully conquered the region. The area around Ghur finally became a vassal as various chieftains jockeying for power sought Ghaznavid support.

After the Seljuk's victory at Dandanqan in 1040 over the Ghaznavids, the situation altered. Bereft of their Persian domains, the Ghaznavid's power waned while the Ghurids became more active. In 1150, the Suri tribe from Ghur sacked Ghazni. Later, the Ghaznavids were forced to abandon Afghanistan and take residence in the city of Lahore, in modern Pakistan.

With the Ghaznavids now in Lahore, Muhammad and Ghiyath al-Din dominated Afghanistan. The two amiably divided their realm between them with Ghiyath al-Din ruling from Ghur northward, while Muhammad ruled from Ghazni to India.

Assisted by their equally capable brother Shihab al-Din Muhammad, the brothers competed with the nascent state of Khwarazm for dominance in the eastern Islamic world. With the collapse of the Seljuk state in the mid-twelfth century, Khwarazm and Ghur, both former Seljuk vassals, were in excellent position to replace it.

The Ghurids Grow
Early on, the brothers expanded their realm into Khurasan and eastern Persia. Meanwhile, Muhammad also carried on the *ghazi* tradition began by the Ghaznavids in northern India. While doing so, the brothers earned the appreciation of the Abbasid caliphs, who were nervous about the Khwarazm's westward expansion toward Baghdad.

Although Muhammad participated in some of the battles, his elder brother Ghiyath al-Din primarily fought the Khwarazmians. Clashes with the Khwarazmians began over possession of the city of Heart in western Afghanistan. Not only did Ghiyath al-Din defeat the Khwarazmian prince Sultan Shah in 1190, but he then overran most of Khurasan. In 1198, the city of Balkh in northern Afghanistan also came into Ghurid possession.

That same year war arose between Ghur and Khwarazm and Kara Kitai. (This latter central Asian polity was founded by Kitans, members of the Liao Dynasty of northern China.) Urged on by Caliph al-Nasir, the Ghurids defeated the Kara Kitans at Guzgan and then Sultan Tekish of Khwarazm at Herat in decisive battles. Ghiyath al-Din followed up his victories by overrunning the rest of Khurasan in 1200, after the death of Sultan Tekish. Ghiyath al-Din died in 1203, leaving his brother Muhammad the sole ruler of the realm.

Campaigns on the Subcontinent
While Ghiyath al-Din had been occupied with the Khwarazmians, Muhammad campaigned in India. In 1186, he invaded the Punjab and captured Lahore, thus ending the Ghaznavid dynasty. Afterwards his domain bordered that of Prithviraj III, ruler of a powerful Hindu state. Muhammad and Prithviraj fought twice. In the first battle in 1191, Muhammad was captured but released. In the second, Muhammad finally vanquished him in 1192.

With the victory at Tarain, the North India plain was now open to Ghurid forces. Thus from 1193 to 1203, Muhammad focused most of his attention on expanding into the Ganges River basin. Here he was viewed as a *ghazi*, as he fought various Hindu kings.

In 1204, Muhammad had to focus his attention back in Afghanistan. Sultan Ala al-Din Muhammad II had consolidated his position in Khwarazm after succeeding his father, Tekish. He now sought revenge against the Ghurids. The two Muhammads first clashed in 1204 with Muhammad of Ghur as the victor. Muhammad then began to plunder the region of Khwarazm. This forced Muhammad Khwarazm to appeal to his suzerains, the Kara Kitans, for aid.

The two Muhammads met again in battle at Hezarasp. With the Kara Kitan reinforcements, Muhammad of Khwarazm won this round. Kara Kitan forces forced the Ghurids out of Khwarazm and then defeated Muhammad of Ghur again at Andkhoi, near Balkh. These defeats were the undoing for the Ghurids.

The Ghurids Wither Although Muhammad of Ghur successfully resisted further Khwarazmian expansion, he was assassinated in the Punjab while putting down an insurrection in 1206. Unfortunately, his successors could not withstand Muhammad of Khwarazm who seized Ghur and Herat immediately after Muhammad's death in 1206. The conquest of Ghurid territory in Afghanistan was complete in 1215.

The Ghurids, however, held onto their Indian territory. It was later absorbed into the Delhi Sultanate, founded by one of Muhammad of Ghur's mamluks.

Prithviraj III

Prithviraj III (1168–1192) came to the throne of the Chauhan dynasty as a child. Although he became the greatest ruler of that family, it was also during his reign that his powerful Hindu state was overrun by Muslim invaders from Afghanistan.

The Boy Grabs the Reins of Power After ascending the throne at his capital of Ajmer in 1178, Prithviraj set about consolidating his realm. Several rebellions broke out as recalcitrant rulers viewed the rule of the young king as an opportune time to assert their independence. Relying on the advice of his generals, Prithviraj successfully quelled the revolts.

At the same time he was quelling the rebellions, Prithviraj became concerned about the rise of the Ghurid dynasty in Afghanistan. Beginning in 1178, the Ghurids under Muhammad of Ghur were increasingly active in the subcontinent. In response, Prithviraj began fortifying his frontier against them.

The Muslim threat and rebellions were not Prithviraj's only concern. One of his goals was to increase the lands held by the Chauhan dynasty in northern India. Thus he also had to deal with other Indian *rajputs* (princely rulers), such as the Chalukyas of Gujarat and the Chandellas of Jejakbhukti.

His efforts against other Indian rulers came to an end, however, when Muhammad of Ghur commenced an invasion by attacking the Chauhan frontier fortresses. Prithviraj's army met the Ghurid forces at Tarain in 1191. Not only did he defeat the Ghurid forces, but Muhammad became Prithviraj's prisoner.

No Good Deed Goes Unpunished Prithviraj was a remarkable leader who was known not only for his valor, but also for his honorable actions. He released Muhammad on the condition of peace. Thinking that the Ghurid threat had passed, Prithviraj resumed his wars against other Hindu princes in an unsuccessful campaign against King Jayachandra of Kanauj.

However, Prithviraj's trust in the Ghurids was misplaced. The unsuccessful campaign against Jayachandra opened the door for the Ghurids, who took advantage of Prithviraj's weakness and invaded. At the second Battle of Tarain in 1192, Muhammad prevailed and took Prithviraj prisoner. Unlike his rival, Muhammad did not release his prisoner; instead, he imprisoned him in the fortress of Ghazni, where he died in 1192.

Popular legend has Muhammad blinding Prithviraj and keeping the Indian king as a source of amusement for his court. In this tale, Prithviraj eventually gains his revenge by participating in an archery contest despite his blindness. With his blindness, the prisoner's hearing had improved. Listening for Muhammad's voice, Prithviraj ultimately shoots and kills his tormentor. In reality, however, Muhammad did not die until 1206, long after his armies overran and absorbed Prithviraj's realm into the Ghurid Empire.

⊕ Major Battles

Yarmuk, August 20, 636

The Battle of Yarmuk was a key turning point in the war between the Arabs and the Byzantines for control of Syria. By 635, the Muslim armies had conquered virtually all of Palestine and what is today Jordan, driving the Byzantine armies before them. The final confrontation for the fate of Syria occurred at a river in northern Jordan that flows through the Golan Heights and into Jordan River.

Impasse at the Pass In response to the Arab victories, Byzantine Emperor Heraclius mustered a new army comprised of Byzantine regulars, Armenian infantry, and light Arab cavalry. (The horsemen were from the Bani Ghassani, a client state of the Byzantines.) This army was led by the general Theodorus. The Arab forces in Syria led by Khalid ibn al-Walid withdrew.

As Theodorus's force marched, the Arabs in Syria (led by Khalid ibn al-Walid) abandoned that polity and withdrew through the Deraa pass in the Golan Heights. It is possible that Khalid hoped that Theodorus would follow them into the open. However, the Byzantine general did not comply. Instead, the Byzantines decided to hold the pass, as it was the most strategic entrance into Syria.

Upon realizing this, Khalid stopped his retreat and laid siege to the Byzantine's fortified positions near the Yarmuk River. While the pass was ideal for an army,

Roncesvalles landscape. © *Bildarchiv Monheim/GmbH/Alamy*

many rifts and other passes existed, thus allowing raiding parties to infiltrate Syria and pillage.

The siege lasted for four months. The Arabs made few direct attacks on the Byzantine position, preferring to simply raid and fight the occasional skirmish. In the meantime, strains between the multi-ethnic components of the Byzantine army began to show. Meanwhile, the Arabs continued to wait.

An Arab Storm Small parties of horsemen had routinely entered Syria behind Byzantine lines. While initially they had just raided, over time they also cut Byzantine routes of communication by seizing the bridge that crossed the Yarmuk River.

The attack came rather unexpectedly in the middle of a sand storm. (Some scholars dispute this, believing it to be an excuse for the loss created by Byzantine writers after the fact.) On August 20, the main Arab force rushed the Byzantine fortifications during the sand storm. The Byzantines, already with low morale and desertions, panicked during the surprise attack and broke. The Arabs pursued and annihilated many during the retreat. Several accounts of the battle mention that many of the Byzantines were killed from falling into the ravines of the Golan Heights and into the river.

Regardless of whether or not the sand storm played a role in the battle, the end result was the same. The battle was decisive, and the large Byzantine army had been decimated. With its annihilation, Syria was open to conquest, and resistance collapsed before the Arab advance.

With no or little threat to them, the Arab forces split and quickly dominated Syria, with an occasional encounter with a garrison. Syria, however, was lost to the Byzantines. Indeed, once Heraclius realized the magnitude of the defeat, he did not attempt to regain it.

Qadisiyya, 637

The Battle of Qadisiyya in 637 opened the Persian Sasanid Empire to the Arab armies. Although Muslim forces had made good progress against the Sasanids, Rustem—the Sasanid general in charge—successfully pushed them back into the Arabian Desert. This led to an escalation of conflict as new Arab armies marched northeast toward modern Iraq.

Opposing Sides Muster The new Arab army was led by Saad ibn Abi Waqqas, a veteran of many battles and a cousin of the Prophet Muhammad. In the autumn of 636, Saad set out from Medina with four thousand men.

This force was bolstered by new contingents from Medina periodically, as Caliph Umar ibn al-Khattab sent new troops as they gathered. While the Arab forces mustered, Saad spent three months in northeastern Arabia training his men.

In December 636 or January 647, Saad began his advance toward the Euphrates River. It is estimated that by the time that Saad made his push, he had accumulated thirty thousand men, including a solid core of veterans who had fought alongside Muhammad.

Meanwhile, the Persians knew that the Arabs would be back, so Rustem, the Sasanid general, gathered his army as well. The exact number of this force is unknown except that it was larger than the Arab army. In addition, he possessed thirty-three elephants.

Rustem's plan was to hold the east bank of the Euphrates, forcing the Arabs to come to him and into the cultivated lands of the empire, where all of the advantages were to the benefit of the Persians. Meanwhile, Saad hoped to keep the desert to his back, thus making retreat easy, as the Persians could not follow them far into the desert sands.

Both generals knew the proper way for their armies to fight, but what would draw the other out?

A Headstrong King

The key was the Sasanid king, Yazdegerd, who had only recently come to the throne. Young and ambitious, Yazdegerd ignored the advice of Rustem and ordered him to take the battle to the Arabs. Rustem obliged, but reluctantly. Meanwhile, Arab raiders began marauding along the western bank of the Euphrates.

In the spring of 637, the armies met in battle. Saad drew his army up in the plain of Qadisiyya. The Arab general did not actively fight in the ranks. Instead, he remained in a building near the field due to illness. However, the building was positioned where he could see the battle and send messages to his commanders.

His right flank was protected by marshes, and the desert was to his rear. Meanwhile, the Sasanid army crossed the Euphrates, which in that particular area was divided into small streams, and then formed their ranks before the Arabs.

The Persians initiated combat by advancing and apparently ignoring various Arab heroes who sought personal combat. As the Sasanids advanced, the elephants emerged with archers in their *howdahs*, (towers mounted on their backs). The elephants broke the ranks of several tribal units, both the Bani Bajeela and Bani Asad. Although the latter fought bravely, they suffered heavy casualties. However, other Arab units stood fast with their archers focusing on the men in the howdahs while swordsmen tried to either gut the elephants or to cut the girths of the howdahs, causing them to fall off.

Through these methods, the elephant threat was nullified. As darkness fell, the Arab army had survived the first day of the battle, although it came close to collapsing.

The Arabs Get Reinforced

The second day of battle began with both sides removing the dead from the battlefield under a truce. Not until the afternoon did the armies resume combat. The Arabs also received reinforcements from Syria. These were veterans of campaigns against both the Sasanids and the Byzantines—these were the men that Khalid had led across the Syrian desert to fight in Syria a few years earlier. Caliph Umar had recalled them for the new campaign against the Sasanids. Even though Khalid was not with them, the arrival of their vanguard revived the morale of the Arabs. This time the Arabs were more aggressive and charged the enemy quite often. Nonetheless, by the end of the second day of battle, the Persians still held firm.

On the third day of battle, the main body of reinforcements from Syria arrived. This helped to offset the demoralizing reappearance of the Sasanid elephant corps. This time, the Arabs tried new tactics. Rather than attempting to fight them on horseback, Qaqaa, the leader of the Syrian troops, engaged them with lances while on foot. Although his men suffered high casualties, they blinded several elephants, causing them to stampede. Although the stampede trampled troops on both sides, eventually the elephants exited the battlefield. After the beasts had left, the fighting resumed and continued until nightfall.

The Final Day

Although there was a lull in the fighting, the Bedouin began to make night attacks on the Sasanid lines. Thus when dawn arrived, the fighting continued throughout the day. As dusk approached, the Arabs made a final charge. The Persian center collapsed and the Arabs reached Rustem, whom they slew. Although some Sasanid troops held their ground, the majority of the army fled. Those who stayed were killed to the last man.

The Arabs do not appear to have pursued those who fled, perhaps due to the last contingent who fought. However, they had suffered approximately twenty-five percent casualties, high by any standard, so it is not too surprising. Furthermore, the riches found in the enemy camp were attractive to all warriors.

Although the Arabs did not pursue the Sasanids, the battle of Qadisiyya opened the Sasanid Empire to them. The morale and core of the Sasanid army had been devastated at Qadisiyya, and the loss of Rustem was a mortal blow. The young king Yazdegerd lacked the experience necessary to rally his military. After Qadisiyya, the Arabs would cross the Euphrates and conquer the rest of the Sasanid Empire—which stretched from the Euphrates to modern Afghanistan—in a few years.

The Battle of Poitiers. © *Visual Arts Library (London)/Alamy*

Constantinople, Seventh and Eight Centuries

During the period of Islamic expansion, there were several sieges of the Byzantine capital of Constantinople. During the period of the Umayyad Empire (656–750), three sieges were attempted. The sieges not only demonstrated the military power of the Umayyads, but also the great defenses, determination, and vibrancy of the Byzantine Empire.

Take Constantinople: Take One The first Muslim assault on the environs of Constantinople began sometime between 670 and 672. The sources are murky on when the siege initiated; nonetheless, during this period the Umayyad navy seized several coastal towns in Anatolia (modern Turkey), including the town of Cyzicus on the Sea of Marmara.

The actual siege began in 674. With the provinces of Syria and Egypt lost to the Muslims, and heavy raiding and invasions in eastern Anatolia, it appeared that the Byzantine Empire was on the verge of collapse.

Most of the fighting took place in the summers when troops were available for a fighting season, although the Arabs kept troops in the vicinity for five years. Because of manpower issues as well as the superb walls and defenses of the city, it eventually became apparent to the Umayyad forces that they could not penetrate the walls. Their siege engines and catapults could not break through. Furthermore, the Arab attackers both on land and at sea had no answer for the Byzantine's secret weapon: Greek fire, a substance similar to napalm.

In 678, the Arabs abandoned their siege. Afterwards, the bulk of the Arab fleet was destroyed in a storm, so the siege was not renewed for some time.

Take Constantinople: Take Two The more spectacular siege of Constantinople was the second attack by the Umayyads. Despite the efforts of Muawiya, who ordered the first one, the attack by Caliph Sulayman ibn Abd al-Malik made the more determined effort. The Umayyads also choose their timing quite well.

In 715, Constantinople had been sacked by Bulgars, and then for the next two years, it was wracked by two civil wars. Thus it was weak from not only internal foment, but wars with the Bulgars and the Muslims. To the Umayyad court, the Byzantine Empire seemed particularly weak and Constantinople's famous defenses vulnerable. Indeed, even as Caliph Sulayman and his brother Maslamah (who would lead the attack) gathered their forces, another violent coup struck the Byzantine Empire.

With the internecine wars within the capital, it seemed that the Umayyads would succeed. However, the coup brought Emperor Leo III to the throne. Leo was not just royalty, but also a talented general who had considerable experience at fighting the Arab armies from his service in Anatolia.

Maslamah led the Umayyad army and fleet to Constantinople and began the siege in July 717. However, as his army began their encirclement of the city, they suddenly found themselves without naval support. Leo had waited until the Arab ships came into narrow confines and then attacked with every Byzantine ship available and from all of the harbors, striking the Muslims from multiple points.

The situation did not improve for the besieging land troops when Bulgarian raiders struck the Muslim camp. To make matters worse, Leo also improved the walls of the city, and one of the worst winters in Byzantine history occurred that year. The besieging army dwindled from disease and casualties. One such victim was Caliph Sulayman, who died while campaigning in Anatolia.

Take Constantinople: Take Three In 718, it appeared that the Arabs would have better fortunes. Another Umayyad fleet arrived from Egypt. It seemed that they would be able to blockade the city. However, the Coptic Christian sailors who manned the fleet mutinied, thereby denying the Umayyad army naval assistance yet again.

Additional help did not arrive from Syria either. Originally, Arab troops were to cross Anatolia to reinforce the besiegers. Byzantine troops stationed in Anatolia, however, defeated them and forced them into Syria.

Nonetheless, the Muslims continued their siege despite the hardships. Yet the situation only grew worse as inclement weather continued and epidemics broke out. Then, as if acting as the final straw to break the camel's back, the volcano near the port of Thera erupted, pummeling the besiegers with waves.

The new Caliph, Umar II, realized the folly of continuing the siege and ordered the army to withdraw. Leo emerged as the victor and brought the Byzantine Empire back from its deathbed to a resurgence of power. For the Umayyads, the resounding defeat and series of natural disasters eroded the confidence of many of its subjects. While not a direct reason for their downfall in 750, the

defeat at Constantinople clearly demonstrated that all was not well within the empire.

Covadonga, 722

The Battle of Covadonga (from the Latin *Cova Dominica* or "Cavern of the Lady") is an example of a minor incident that gains more importance through the process of history and memory. In Spain, the Battle of Covadonga is remembered as the "cradle of the Reconquest" and the beginning of the recovery of Spain from the Moors (as the Muslims of Spain were known), who had conquered Spain in 711. In reality, however, historians believe that the Battle of Covadonga was little more that a small encounter between Asturian warriors in northern Spain and a small Moorish army.

A Good Story, But Not a Truthful One According to the Spanish chronicles, Don Pelayo—a nobleman from the mountains of Asturias in northern Spain—and his small band of supporters were forced into a cave on Mount Auseva by a Moorish army numbering around 200,000 men. Don Pelayo and his men prayed to the Virgin Mary for protection and then came out to fight the Muslims.

Despite being vastly outnumbered, Don Pelayo not only won, but did so through divine agency. The arrows and spears of the Muslims bounced off the mountain and killed most of the Moors. Then, the Cross of Victory appeared in the Heavens above Don Pelayo and gave them hope. More divine intervention occurred as an avalanche of rocks crushed the remaining sixty thousand Moors. After the victory, the warriors made Don Pelayo their king.

The problem with this is that the Moors never assembled an army of this size at any point in their seven hundred years in Spain, even at the peak of their power. It is questionable if they ever had more than one hundred thousand soldiers at any given point in the entire kingdom. (When reading any chronicle, unusually large numbers typically means "They had a lot more soldiers than we had.")

Not as Exciting, But Closer to the Truth The reality of the battle is that Don Pelayo did begin an insurrection against the Moors, quite possibly because the Umayyad governor of Spain, Anbasa ibn Suhaym al-Kalbi, had doubled taxes for non-Muslims. With a band of guerillas, Don Pelayo attacked Muslim outposts and refused to pay tribute to the Moors.

Naturally, the Umayyad governor in Spain could not tolerate such actions and responded by reinforcing his garrison there. However, viewed through Moorish eyes, Don Pelayo's actions were not a serious threat to Muslim power. Don Pelayo could not expel the Muslims, but then, the Moors could not stop his insurgency either, especially as their primary focus was elsewhere in France. Thus with few available troops, the Muslims had to tolerate their inability to end the Asturian's actions.

TOURS OR POITERS?

The Battle of Poitiers, or Tours, was fought between Frankish and Muslim armies in 732. This single conflict has two names because the battle was actually fought somewhere between the two locations. Traditionally, it was called the Battle of Tours, but more recent historical trends have dubbed it the Battle of Poitiers.

The confusion in naming stems from the fact that it is not clear where the battle was fought. The Muslim army was on its way to Tours when Charles Martel intercepted it near Poitiers. Thus the initial naming was due to a literal reading of the sources. The sources stated that the Muslim army was headed toward Tours, so it was assumed that the battle took place there or nearby. However, more recent studies have determined that Charles Martel' army encountered the Muslims long before they reached Tours, and much closer to Poitiers.

However, after the Moorish defeat at Toulouse in 721, governor Anbasa felt a victory was needed to restore his army's morale; crushing a minor rebellion would provide the necessary tonic. The general Al-Kama (or Alqama) led a force into the region, but Don Pelayo fled to the mountains and successfully defeated his pursuers. Al-Kama was killed in the battle.

Pelayo's successful defense led to a general insurrection among the populace, which successfully drove the Muslims from the region. Another Moorish expedition also failed to quell the uprising; thereafter, Asturias remained an independent kingdom.

Covadonga as Propaganda

The significance of the battle has little to do with history. Christian Spanish chroniclers—both royal and monastic writers, writing two hundred years after the battle occurred—transformed the battle into an epic encounter complete with a victory showing God's favor. This retelling gave legitimacy to the Asturian monarchy as well as a historic marker to the expulsion of the Moors. Placing the birth of the monarchy at this battle also removed the stigma of the collapse of the Visigothic kingdoms with the Arab conquest in 711.

Regardless of the mythology, the Battle of Covadonga was a victory for the Spaniards and placed the monarchy in a more heroic setting, whereas the scenes of divine intervention legitimized the rulers and their efforts against the Muslims in the eyes of the people. The actual battle was a small affair, but it mobilized the population against the Moors, and an occupation will not succeed if the populace is against it.

Poitiers (Tours), October 732

In this conflict, Frankish leader Charles Martel met a Muslim army led by Abd al-Rahman I somewhere between Tours and Poitiers. The defeat of the Muslim army marked an end to significant threats of continuing Arab expansion northward into Europe.

Arab Treasure Seekers

The Muslim army was not one of conquest, but rather a raiding party. With the defeat of the nobility of southern France in 732, Muslim raiders had drifted further north seeking more plunder. Charles Martel, the Frankish mayor of the palace of the Merovingian dynasty, moved to counter these actions.

Charles Martel marched quickly and often off the road, thus arriving ahead of the Muslims. This allowed him to select the terrain to his benefit. As the two forces met, the first seven days were spent skirmishing while maneuvering for position. Charles had arranged his men in a square. His position was good as trees and a hill hindered the Muslim cavalry. While the armies made their feints, additional Frankish infantry arrived, ranging from militias to veterans of previous campaigns.

Ultimately, Abd al-Rahman made the first move, probably because as long as Charles remained in the area, the Arab raiding expedition was threatened. The Muslim cavalry charged, but the Frankish heavy infantry did not break.

Throughout the day, the Muslim cavalry charged, but could not break the disciplined Frankish infantry. However, the Franks lacked sufficient cavalry to pursue the Muslim cavalry. This meant any advantage gained was lost, and it allowed Abd al-Rahman to regroup.

Frankish Treasure Seekers

The real shift in the battle occurred behind the lines of battle. Frankish scouts had circled behind the Muslim lines and began to pillage their camp, rich with goods from previous raids. This caused some units from the Umayyad forces to withdraw to defend the camp. Because of communication issues, other units began to withdraw as well, and everything almost turned into a general retreat. Abd al-Rahman tried to rally his troops, but in the course of doing so, he became surrounded and was killed.

As night fell, both sides retired to their camps. When the Franks prepared for battle on the following morning, they discovered the Muslim camp empty; they had retreated under the cover of darkness.

Although the Battle of Poitiers was not a resounding victory, it still was significant for Charles. Muslim raiding parties continued for a few years, but any advance into northern France was checked. The victory also helped Charles secure and consolidate his power. Over time, the legend of the battle (a victory over the "infidel") helped give legitimacy to Charles's reign as well as that of his successors.

Although the Frankish victory was important, it was not quite the epic victory that some historians have made it out to be. If the Muslims had won, Arabic would not have become the language of Oxford as Edward Gibbons (the famous eighteenth-century historian) surmised, and Europe would not have become an appendage of the Muslim world. However, Charles Martel's victory did help him secure power within France. Furthermore, it deterred other raiding parties, as the Arabs learned that fighting the Franks was not an easy proposition.

Talas, July 751

The Battle of Talas, fought between the Arab armies of the Abbasid caliphate and the Tang Empire of China, gave the Muslims mastery of Central Asia. The pivotal battle enabled the Islamic penetration of the region, and it gave the Muslims control of an economically important trade zone: the heart of the Silk Road.

Growing Empires Collide The Tang desired the region not only because of the trade opportunities, but also to protect the western regions of their empire from the Turks and the nascent Tibetan Empire. However, the Arab expansion also began to reach out into Central Asia, conquering the Sasanid Empire between 637 and 652. Afterwards, the Muslims did not attempt to cross the Amu Darya river, except for occasional raids, while they assimilated the newly conquered territories.

During the next century however, skirmishing became more frequent. Most of the fights, however, took place between proxies of both empires as they tried to avoid conflict that might escalate into a full-fledged war.

Nonetheless, events did lead to war. With the expansion of the Tibetan empire, the Tang became more active in Central Asia to prevent it from succumbing to the Tibetans. The Tang general, Gao Xianzhi, led several expeditions. Although the war with Tibet (750–751) was a costly one far from the core of the Tang Empire, the Tang emerged victorious. Now, Gao Xianzhi turned his attention toward the Turks.

Turks had slowly migrated into the region since the seventh century. For the most part however, there was not a unified state or confederation, but rather individuals ruling commercial towns by the oases. Gao Xianzhi seized the city of Tashkent and then executed the Turkic ruler. The ruler's son fled and submitted to the Arabs. In return for his submission, Ziyad ibn Salih led the Abbasid forces in the region to meet the Tang army.

Little Known Except for the Outcome Unfortunately, the details of the battle are very vague, as sources vary widely on even the number of troops involved. Nonetheless, all agree on the end result after reportedly five days of battle: Gao Xianzhi and his army were crushed by the Arabs. The Arabs were aided when the Qarluq Turks, who served as auxiliary troops for the Tang, switched sides. Although defeated, Gao Xianzhi was able to extricate himself and the remnants of his army from Talas.

Although the Tang maintained their garrisons in modern Xinjiang for some years, the region remained independent of Chinese rule until the Qing Dynasty (1644–1912). Although Manchu—not Chinese—in origin, the Qing Empire was based and ruled from China.

Roncesvalles, August 778

The Battle of Roncesvalles was a resounding setback for the great Frankish king Charlemagne, who ruled from 768 to 814. The battle, part of Charlemagne's campaign against the Muslims of Spain, did not actually include Charlemagne. Instead, the conflict at Roncesvalles was a battle between the Franks and the Basque.

Charlemagne Heads South In 778, Charlemagne invaded Spain, hoping to bring the emirate of Saragossa under his control. Along the way, the Frankish king captured the Christian city of Pamplona, which was part of the emirate of Saragossa. Previously, Charlemagne had entered into discussions with representatives of Saragossa toward a peaceful transition in exchange for protection against the emirate of Cordoba.

However, when Charlemagne arrived, the situation had changed. Cordoba had attempted to subdue Saragossa, but forces led by the governor of Saragossa, Husayn ibn Yahya al-Ansari, emerged victorious. Emboldened by this victory, al-Ansari no longer felt the need for Charlemagne's protection. Therefore, when Charlemagne arrived, al-Ansari had no intention of becoming a subordinate of the Frankish ruler.

It is not clear if Charlemagne besieged the city or only conducted negotiations. In any case, Charlemagne did not stay long at Saragossa; he had received news of trouble on his border along the Rhine River. With the Saxons in revolt, Charlemagne needed to return north, so he left without gaining the city.

As they retreated through the territory of the Basques, the Franks were ambushed by a Muslim force near Pamplona. This was defeated, and Charlemagne then razed the walls of Pamplona, a Basque city under Muslim rule.

A Clear Outcome for Murkier Reasons The Basques attacked the Franks at the village of Roncesvalles in August 778. Their reasons for doing so are not fully understood. Perhaps it was because of the sacking of Pamplona, or perhaps the simple opportunity to plunder. Nonetheless, the Basques ambushed the Frankish army as it crossed the mountains.

Although the Franks had the most powerful army in Western Europe, the Basques were renowned mountain warriors fighting in familiar terrain. In addition, they struck in the early evening and from ambush, two more advantageous factors. As a result, the Franks suffered heavy casualties in what may have been a running fight, with the Franks essentially running a gauntlet.

One of the Frankish dead was Hroudland, lord of Breton. He is also known as Roland of the epic poem *The Song of Roland*. This battle became the basis of the epic poem, but with the Basques being transformed into Muslims to fit the beginning of the Crusading era.

Roman ruins at Hamat Gader, Israel, in the Yarmuk Valley.   *© Avi Horovitz/Alamy*

Dandanqan, May 23, 1040

The Battle of Dandanqan was a pivotal battle for dominance in the eastern part of the Islamic world, pitting the newly arrived Seljuks against the established Ghaznavid Empire. The winner, the Seljuks, became the dominant power in Iran, while the Ghaznavids became a peripheral state.

Immigration Troubles   Since 1031, Masud, the son of Mahmud the Great, ruled the Ghaznavid Empire, which stretched from the Amu Darya river to the Indus River valley. In the northwestern regions of his empire, Masud had to deal with the arrival of the Seljuks, nomads who crossed the Amu Darya in the early eleventh century during Mahmud's reign.

Mahmud had kept them in check. During the 1030s, however, the Seljuks and other Ghuzz Turks began to enter the empire in increasing numbers and threatened to overrun the regions of Khurasan (today part of Iran and Afghanistan) and Khwarazm (the region south of the Aral Sea).

It is possible that the matter could have been resolved peacefully; the Seljuk leader, Toghril Beg, did request land in Khurasan from Masud. Masud, however, refused the request. As a result, Toghril seized the city of Nishapur in 1038. Forced to deal with this growing menace to his realm, Masud led his army from Afghanistan toward the city of Merv.

Although the capture of Nishapur was a bold action, Toghril Beg also courted disaster in doing so. By drawing the wrath of the powerful Ghaznavid army, he also risked the destruction of his tribe. Knowing that Masud preferred battle to diplomacy, Toghril knew he had to avoid fighting Masud on his terms.

Skirmishes Before the Main Event   On the march, Masud's forces were constantly harassed by attacks from the Seljuks. This not only undermined the morale and discipline of Masud's army, but also prevented Masud from procuring adequate supplies of food and, more importantly, water.

Eventually, the reportedly fifty-thousand-man Ghaznavid army met a smaller (twenty thousand), but more mobile force of Seljuks—under the leadership of Toghril Beg and his brother, Chaghri—on the steppe of Dandanqan, near Merv. Tired from the long march and dehydrated on the arid steppe, the Ghaznavid forces were defeated. Sultan Masud barely escaped the disastrous encounter with a hundred men. Masud was unable to recover Khurasan from the Seljuks. Indeed, this may have cost him the throne, for while marching into India, he was assassinated.

For the Seljuks, the victory at Dandanqan gave them complete control of Khurasan and eastern Iran. From this victory, the Seljuks then went on to dominate all of Iran; being recent converts to Islam, they became allies of the Abbasid caliphs. Dandanqan was the crucible in which the Seljuk Empire was forged.

Manzikert, August 1071

A resounding defeat of the Byzantine Empire by Seljuk Turks under the leadership of Alp Arslan, the Battle of Manzikert helped solidify the presence of Islam (and the Turks) in Anatolia.

From Nomads to Farmers As the Seljuk Empire expanded westward, its main efforts were partially fueled by recently arrived Turkic nomads. By the reign of Alp Arslan (who ruled from 1063 to 1072), the Seljuks had largely settled down, becoming sedentary rather than remaining nomads. The army had received military land grants that produced a form of salary. The idea was that if these soldiers received a regular payment, then they would be less likely to pillage villages and towns.

The downside of this was that more nomads entered the empire from Central Asia. To maintain stability in Persia, the Seljuks sent these nomads westward. Here they could satisfy their avarice by plundering the frontiers of the Byzantine Empire, but also provide religious legitimacy for the Seljuks by serving as *ghazis*, or holy warriors.

Naturally, the attacks on the Byzantine frontier drew the ire of the Byzantine emperor, Romanus Diogenes IV. In addition, the Seljuks forced Armenia, a traditional client state of the Byzantines, to pay tribute to Alp Arslan. Finally, the Seljuks captured the fortresses of Akhlat and Manzikert. In response to all these belligerent actions, Romanus Diogenes led his army of approximately forty thousand men eastward.

The Byzantine army successfully recaptured Akhlat and then marched against Manzikert. During the siege, Alp Arslan's army arrived. The Byzantines expected a normal battle between the two large armies. Having come to the throne in 1068, Diogenes had little experience in fighting the Turks, who rarely stood and fought. Instead, they used their mobility and archery to keep the Byzantines on the defensive and harass them when they advanced.

For the Byzantines, Dissension Leads to Destruction Eventually, gaps opened in the Byzantine ranks and

THE SONG OF ROLAND

The Song of Roland is a French epic that was composed around 1100. Its influence was immense, as its values and ideas of chivalry and warfare penetrated the mindset of the French nobles during the Crusading period. In many ways, it also became a propaganda piece.

Unlike the real battle of Roncevalles, the epic is placed during Charlemagne's seven year campaign against the Muslims in Spain. At the siege of Saragossa, King Marsile of Saragossa offers to become the emperor's vassal in exchange for peace. The Franks are divided as to whether or not to accept an infidel as a vassal. Roland, the hero of the epic, convinces his uncle Charlemagne to press the campaign to its conclusion. Meanwhile, Roland's stepfather Ganelon argues for accepting the peace.

Ganelon eventually wins out but is nominated by Roland to carry out the dangerous task of negotiating with King Marsile. Because of this, Ganelon conspires with the enemy to gain vengeance. Upon his return, he arranges for Roland to lead the rearguard of the army as it vacates Andalusia. The rearguard is ambushed once it reaches the village of Roncevalles.

The climax of the epic is whether or not Roland will sound the Oliphant, a trumpet whose call can be heard for miles, thereby alerting Charlemagne of danger. Out of honor, Roland is reluctant to sound the horn. In the end, the rearguard is eliminated except for Roland. As the enemy closes on him, Roland finally sounds the Oliphant before he dies.

The Muslim army, however, suffers heavy casualties, so it retreats before Charlemagne can arrive. Charlemagne then leads his army back against King Marsile in what becomes a cataclysmic battle between Christendom and infidels. In the end, Charlemagne is victorious against the Muslims; Ganelon is executed; and the angel Gabriel appears in Charlemagne's dreams commanding him to new wars against the pagans.

As the poem was written at the time of the Crusades, it served to reinforce ideas of valor and honor, but also the superiority of Christianity and the perfidy of non-Christians. Furthermore, with Charlemagne and the heroism of Roland at the center of an epic struggle, it made the case for a view of the Franks as the new chosen people. While the epic has very little to do with actual events in the eighth century, it clearly depicts the mindset of the French aristocracy of the eleventh and twelfth centuries and their views toward Islam.

Romanus Diogenes had to order a withdrawal. At this point the Turks increased their pressure on the Byzantines. Romanus Diogenes then ordered the army to stand and fight. However, the commander of his rear guard, Andronicus Ducas (a rival of the emperor), ignored his orders and continued marching to the Byzantine camp. This betrayal allowed the Seljuks to surround and annihilate the main army.

Although the Byzantines had suffered defeat, the military was still strong enough to repel attacks. Unfortunately, the defeat made them vulnerable in other ways. Central Anatolia was now open to attack, and this was the core recruiting ground for the Byzantines. Furthermore, Armenia, an important source of mercenaries, was now isolated from the Byzantines. The end result was that over time, the military weakened as it lost important resources.

Seed of the Crusades More Turks began to settle in the region, gradually leading not only to the Islamization of Anatolia, but also the Turkicization. Eventually, the Turks took Nicaea, a city only a hundred miles from Constantinople.

The desire to regain these lands also led to the Crusades as the Byzantines appealed to Pope Urban II in 1095 for aid. They had hoped for a few hundred mercenaries, but instead received thousands of knights and noncombatants, filled with religious zeal and not at all under Byzantine control.

Tarain, 1191 and 1192

Two battles took place at Tarain. (The correct spelling is Taraori, but it has entered the English language as Tarain.) Both battles involved the same participants, Muhammad of Ghur and Prithviraj III. These two conflicts ultimately determined the future of three kingdoms.

Round One The first battle took place in 1191 as Muhammad of Ghur attempted to expand the Ghurid Empire into India. Having conquered the Punjab and destroyed the Ghaznavid dynasty that had taken refuge there, Muhammad then turned east toward the Hindu kingdoms in the plains of northern India. His first target was the fortress of Bhatinda, on the frontier of the Punjab.

As the Ghurid forces moved forward, King Prithviraj, whose kingdom was based on his capitals of Ajmer and Delhi, attempted to stop the invasion. His army encountered the Ghurids at Tarain, near the town of Thanesar.

Details of the battle are scant, but ultimately the Ghurid wings broke against the Indian charge. Muhammad still held the center, but was wounded in the battle and fell from his horse. With the collapse of the Ghurid flanks and the possible death of the ruler, the Ghurid army was routed.

Taken prisoner, Muhammad was brought before Prithviraj and humbly begged for his freedom. Prithviraj, known for his honor, did not heed the advice of his advisors and released the Muslim ruler.

The Rematch This proved to be a mistake. Muhammad learned from his previous encounter with the Indians and invaded again in 1192, so the two rulers fought at Tarain once more. However, the Ghurids knew much more about Hindu tactics than they first did. For example, it was now known that the Hindus traditionally fought only between dawn and dusk. Furthermore,

before a battle it was common for the rulers to try and settle the matter diplomatically.

Both these points would be used against the Hindus by the Ghurid leader. Prithviraj offered a truce on the condition that Muhammad withdraw his army. Muhammad deceived Prithviraj by accepting the truce. Muhammad then took advantage of Prithviraj's honor (again) by attacking at dawn, catching the Hindus completely off guard.

Waves of horse archers struck the Rajput army. Although the Indian forces attempted to rally, the surprise attack proved devastating. The only effective Indian force was archers stationed in towers on the back of elephants. However, the Ghurid cavalry simply retreated before them, luring them away from the main army.

Eventually, Muhammad's heavy cavalry hit the Rajput lines. Prithviraj's army was defeated and routed. Prithviraj fought a running battle back, but was eventually captured. Muhammad, being more of a pragmatist than a man bound strictly to honor, blinded Prithviraj and imprisoned him in Ghazni rather than release him.

Aftereffects of Tarain The two battles determined the future of three kingdoms. For Prithviraj's kingdom, it was destroyed. The defeat at Tarain opened northern India to the Ghurids and Islamic domination. For the Ghurids, the victory not only allowed them to expand into India, but it allowed them to survive as the Khwar-azmian Empire drove the Ghurids from Afghanistan in 1206 after the death of Muhammad of Ghur.

Eventually the Ghurids declined, and from its ashes emerged the Sultanate of Delhi, a new Muslim kingdom that was firmly based in India. It was established by Qutb al-Din Aybak, one of Muhammad's generals, and lasted until 1526.

⊕ Key Elements of Warcraft

Greek Fire

One of the most effective and intriguing weapons used in the Middle Ages was Greek fire. It was developed around 673 by a Byzantine named Callinicus, an architect from Heliopolis (modern Baalbek in Syria). As Callinicus was a refugee from Syria during the Arab conquests, the creation of Greek fire appears to have been a direct response to Arab expansion and the Byzantium's inability to stop the Arabs. The recipe for it was one of the most closely guarded secrets in the empire; indeed, there does not seem to be any evidence that the recipe ever left Byzantine hands.

Its secret was so closely guarded that even today its exact composition is still uncertain. Nonetheless, scholars have determined that it was most likely a composition of naphtha, quicklime, and sulfur. Naphtha is a product derived from distilling oil. When combined in the correct recipe, these ingredients would ignite on contact and even burn in water. Because of its petroleum base,

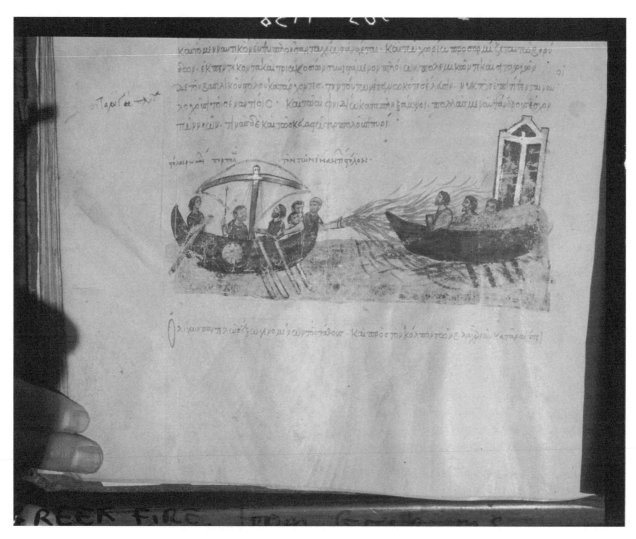

Depiction of Greek Fire.   © *Visual Arts Library (London)/Alamy*

Greek fire stuck to objects and was difficult to extinguish, much like its modern equivalent, napalm.

Greek Fire Against Wooden Ships Greek fire was primarily used as a naval weapon, but only the imperial fleet was equipped with it on a regular basis. The provincial navies were equipped in emergencies. In combat, Greek fire was spread through a nozzle that sprayed it with a high velocity. (Scholars are not in agreement on exactly how this spraying was done.) The person who manned the apparatus was known as the *siphonarios*. Protected by a large iron shield, the siphonarios stood in the bow of the ship and aimed it at enemy ships. Greek fire was also used in bombs made of pottery, which functioned like hand grenades. Once thrown, these bombs would shatter and spread the Greek fire, which ignited when exposed to oxygen.

Greek fire played a vital role throughout the history of the Byzantine Empire, particularly during the time of Arab conquests. During the Umayyad sieges of Constantinople in 674–678 and 717–718, it was a critical weapon not only in defending the walls, but especially in naval battles. Indeed, its appearance at the first siege may have been the debut of Greek fire in warfare, as it was invented around 673.

Arabs would not be the only enemy to face Greek fire, as the Byzantines fended off an attack by the Russians in 941 with it. Only on one occasion—the Fourth Crusade in 1204—did it fail to thwart an attack by an outside force. Still, considering the ups and downs of the efficacy of the Byzantine navy, there were periods where Greek fire does not seem to have constituted a primary weapon for the navy. The reason for this remains unknown.

Although it was a closely guarded secret that appears to have never been revealed to outsiders, eventually other powers did gain knowledge of its manufacture. How this was done is also not known. Nonetheless, several Islamic states did begin to use a variety of Greek fire in the Middle Ages. Indeed, it was used in a few naval encounters, and perhaps even sieges, during the Crusades.

⊕ Impact of the Expansion of Islam

The expansion of Islam has had a tremendous impact in world history. The most obvious being the rise of Islam from being a predominantly Arab religion into a universal world religion that has a broad appeal.

The Arab conquests and subsequent Turkic kingdoms that followed spread Islam, though not necessarily by the sword. Most converted to Islam because it was better economically, as Muslims did not have to pay a poll tax as did nonbelievers. Also, as it was the religion of the conquerors, many regional leaders thought it would be expedient and beneficial to convert. Of course, there were also many sincere conversions. While some zealous leaders attempted conversion at sword point, this was not very effective; most converts in this manner would resume their original religious practices as soon as the threat was removed.

However, the expansion of Islam also spread a civilization and culture that blended not only Arab tradition and Islamic principles, but also Roman, Hellenic, Persian, Indian, and Turkic practices into a single civilization. Someone from Cordoba, Spain, could travel to Ghazni in Afghanistan and not feel too out of place due to similar architecture, art, and practices.

Militarily, the expansion of Islam was profound. Two of the great empires of antiquity suffered greatly. The Sasanid Empire collapsed completely due to the Arab conquests. Meanwhile, the Byzantine Empire was greatly reduced, forever losing its Syrian and North African positions. After the Battle of Manzikert, most of Anatolia was also lost. In addition, the appearance of the Seljuks in the Byzantine Empire ultimately gave rise to the Crusades.

Ways of warfare also changed. The Arab threat to Constantinople directly led to the creation of the secret weapon known as Greek fire. With the arrival of the Turks, warfare in the region switched to an increasing reliance on Turkic horse archers throughout much of the Islamic Empire.

Although the Islamic world is often viewed in monolithic terms—one massive entity—in reality, it was too large and too divisive to exist as a single entity. Even the concept of a theocracy did not last long, which led to the diminished authority of the caliph. In addition to challenges to the religious authority of the caliph, the rise of the sultans challenged the temporal authority of the caliphs.

Although some territory was lost over time (such as in Spain), the lands brought under Muslim influence during the period when Islam expanded remain the core of the modern Islamic world.

BIBLIOGRAPHY

Books

Bosworth, Clifford E. *Later Ghaznavids: Splendour and Decay: The Dynasty in Afghanistan and Northern India, 1040–1186.* New York: Columbia University Press, 1977.

Kennedy, Hugh. *The Armies of the Caliphs: Military and Society in the Early Islamic State.* London: Routledge, 2001.

Kennedy, Hugh and Babir, Karl. *The Prophet and the Age of the Caliphates: The Islamic Near East from the Sixth to the Eleventh Century.* Harlow, UK: Longman, 2003.

Kennedy, Hugh. *The Great Arab Conquests: How the Spread of Islam Changed the World We Live In.* New York: Da Capo Press, 2007.

Morgan, David. *Medieval Persia, 1040–1797.* Harlow, UK: Routledge, 1988.

Robinson, Chase. *Empire and Elites after the Muslim Conquest: The Transformation of Northern Mesopotamia.* New York: Cambridge University Press, 2000.

Introduction to Viking Raids and Norman Conquests (Eighth to Eleventh centuries)

The Viking Age opened in the eighth century with unorganized but highly effective Viking attacks on unsuspecting villages bordering the rivers of Europe and the coast of England. It ended in the eleventh century with the descendent of a Viking launching one of the first major assaults on a kingdom across the water, a bold gamble that ended with a single battle (the Battle of Hastings) in 1066. Historians have called this battle the most important of British history because of the lasting and widespread influence the outcome had on governmental structure, language, and culture in that country. Yet the Vikings themselves—whose age ended with this decisive encounter and who had lost a major battle on English soil just weeks earlier—also altered the European landscape in ways that reverberate today.

The era began with the passage of the Frankish kingdom from the Merovingian dynasty to the Carolingians. The Carolingian line had plenty of trouble on their hands in the form of Viking invaders from Scandinavia. Their longships, later equipped with sails, drew so little water that these fearsome warriors could travel far inland along water routes, taking towns and monasteries by surprise. The Vikings soon found that European cathedrals and abbeys were undefended storehouses of treasure just waiting to be taken, and take them they did. They also made their way across the eastern part of the continent, from the Baltic to the Black Sea and Constantinople.

In an effort to forge a truce between Viking and Frank, Rollo the Viking received the duchy of Normandy from Charles the Simple in 911, a transfer that led to a melding of Frankish and Norse bloodlines and an almost complete assimilation of the Viking into Frankish culture. Rollo's remarkably stable patrimonial line led straight to William the Bastard, Duke of Normandy and Conqueror of England in 1066. Just three weeks before William (descendent of a settle Viking who married a Frankish princess) defeated Harold Godwinson (also descended from Vikings) at the Battle of Hastings, Harold Godwinson had defeated the last major Viking onslaught against England, taking down the Norwegian army of Harald of Norway at the battle of Stamford Bridge. This loss signaled the dusk of the Viking Age in Europe, and the Vikings themselves either returned to their increasingly stable kingdoms in what is known today collectively as Scandinavia, or faded into the European countryside, becoming British or Irish farmers, Frankish nobility or peasantry, or Russian traders.

Their legacy remains one of awe at their daring and cruelty. The Vikings also left the snowballing effects of their trade and raiding practices, a brutal and wholesale method of opening up routes between cultures, but one so effective that even after the Viking age came to a close, the opened exchange between cultures—sometimes peaceful, sometimes warlike—would never be sealed again.

Viking Raids and Norman Conquests (8th to 11th Centuries)

⊕ Major Figures

Charlemagne

Among the most famous and successful of the Frankish kings, Charlemagne (742–814) took what the previous line in power had accomplished and expanded it to cover the entirety of western Europe. In addition to this expanded kingdom, he established a historic alliance between king and pope that became the pattern for European leadership for centuries to come. He also oversaw what became the Carolingian Renaissance, a flowering of literacy, art, and scholarship in the name of Christian education and the fostering of learning through his empire.

Background and Early Life Charlemagne was a scion of one of the leading families of a nation called the Franks. (Franks were one of many tribes that invaded what were former Roman territories and eventually conquered what today lies roughly in the boundaries of France.) He was born in 742 under the rule of the Merovingians, a line established by Clovis three hundred years earlier. The Merovingians had allowed dilution of their power, placing it in the hands of palace officials called majordomos, and Charlemagne's grandfather, Charles Martel (known as "The Hammer"), was one of these "mayors of the palace."

Martel's son, Pepin III, obtained the pope's blessing to remove a Merovingian king from power. The pope was interested in the more material assistance Pepin could offer in the form of a defense of Italy against the Lombards. He gave Pepin the go-ahead, and Pepin III promptly took the throne and shifted the dynastic ruling house from the Merovingian line to the Carolingian line in 751. Charlemagne was his son.

As a boy, Charlemagne—who would become renowned for overseeing an intellectual enlightenment under his rule—was illiterate, and he may never have become completely literate, even as an adult. As a ruler in training, he did, however, learn to hunt and ride and fight in battle, all relevant attainments for a future Frankish king. He was nine when Pepin III took the throne, and Charlemagne and his brother Carloman were raised together as joint successors of the Frankish kingdom. Dividing the kingdom in this way followed Merovingian precedent.

Charlemagne Becomes Sole King Charlemagne was a giant among the men of his time at 6 feet 4 inches. He was known for his piercing blue eyes and his devout Christian piety. This prince stepped into his father's shoes at the age of 26 when Pepin died. At first, he shared those shoes with Carloman, but the younger brother died after three years, and Charlemagne was left as the sole ruler of the Franks.

Building an Empire Charlemagne's extensive training in war came in handy during the early part of his reign, which he spent fighting the Germanic tribe of the Saxons in the northern part of the kingdom and the Lombards in northern Italy. Although Charlemagne was known as a loving father—he had his son Pepin crowned king of Italy in 781—and a man interested in the welfare of his people, he also possessed the requisite brutality of a medieval ruler. In his continued campaign against the pagan Saxons, he quashed a rebellion in 781 and made an example of the rebel Germans by having five thousand of them beheaded. Having made his point with the Saxons, he went on to gain control over all of Italy by 786.

After conquering these lands and converting any pagans among the people to Christianity ("some under duress"), he turned to Muslim Spain. However, Charlemagne found defeat there in 778 in a campaign that eventually became immortalized in the "Song of Roland" in the twelfth century. The losses in Spain notwithstanding, Charlemagne usually won his battles, and he continued his military exploits through thirty years of his reign. At one point his empire stretched over much of Western Europe.

A skillful general, Charlemagne proved himself to be an elegant and masterful organizer of recruits and supplies as well. The people he conquered were converted

Bronze statue of the emperor Charlemagne on horseback. *Getty Images*

to Christianity as a means to assimilation into Frankish culture, and it was quite effective. He reinforced his defenses at the edges of his vast kingdom by creating military zones, known as marches, where armies garrisoned to defend the borders.

Establishing a Functional Bureaucracy Charlemagne's techniques of organizing the governance of his diverse and far-flung kingdom also proved quite successful. He had four hundred counties and two hundred dioceses to oversee, and to achieve appropriate supervision, he relied on institutions the Merovingians had put in place, just as his father had relied on their custom of heritable co-rulership. Using the existing framework of counts and bishops at the local level, Charlemagne governed as head of a central body of decision makers called the *palatium*. This entourage executed a variety of duties from their central position, including oversight of armies, managing royal resources, diplomacy, policy decision making, and, in an example of the joining of church and state under Charlemagne, ecclesiastical and religious responsibilities. The king kept everyone in line and communicating by using competent people chosen from the same small group of families, all aristocrats who wanted to hang on and maintain their powers under this powerful leader. Charlemagne

also relied heavily on vassalage, in which local leaders swore fealty to their overlord, promising faithfulness and loyalty in exchange for material benefits.

A Semi-Illiterate King with a Fascination for Scholarship This martial king also had a strong interest in the expansion of scholarship and the religious well being of his people. The Carolingian Renaissance took root in the 780s, just as the Frankish king was brutally slaughtering Saxons and taking over Italy, and it continued to flourish to its peak even after his death. Charlemagne made his court a kind of salon, bringing to it scholars from all over Europe. One of these was Alcuin, the commentator on the Viking invasion of Lindisfarne and a scholar convinced that the Vikings were the physical manifestation of God's wrath at the immorality of the times. In addition to his reactionary thinking, however, Alcuin also led the drive for a renewal of Latin studies and a revival of the kind of education applied at the peak of Greek and Roman civilization.

Counselors and scholars like Alcuin deliberately worked with the king to produce sweeping reforms in religious practices and institutions in his realm. They sought papal guidance in their quest to refine and define what was orthodox and what was not, and to establish a hierarchy of governance and better training for the clergy on the ground in villages and towns. These pursuits in their turn led to an explosion of Christian scholarship, all focused at Charlemagne's court and emphasizing his personal and deliberate conviction that a ruler should be both a king and a priest to his people, a king "by the grace of God." The use of the papal brain trust to achieve his reforms ensured a strong and continued foothold for Roman Catholicism in western Europe.

Charlemagne's palace became a school for the young men who would work in the king's government. It also became the site of a scriptorium, a place where monks copied (by hand) textbooks and other tomes of interest. This form of production was necessary in an age before the invention of the printing press, and thanks to these efforts, ninety percent of ancient Roman texts remain preserved in the form of copies from these Carolingian monks. In addition to this valuable contribution, the monks also used a form of text—Carolingian Miniscule, known today as Times New Roman—that was easily readable and included the novelties of italics and lowercase lettering.

Partnering with the Pope His interest in scholarship was admirable, but Charlemagne's place in history is as the prototype Holy Roman Emperor. He achieved his status by reaching out the hand of rulership to Pope Leo III. This pope had taken refuge in Charlemagne's court, where he hid from Roman mobs trying to kill him for being rather un-pope-like in his behavior. Charlemagne saw this as a good opportunity to unite the church and state, and after restoring Leo to power, he saw the favor returned when Leo III crowned him "Emperor of the Romans" on Christmas Day in 800, by the grace of God.

A Great Ruler Dies, an Empire Left Divided Charlemagne ruled for fourteen years following his coronation, living to see even the skeptical and threatened Byzantine emperors recognize his imperial crown in 813. Although he intended to divide his empire among his three sons, by the time of his death only one son, Louis the Pious, survived him and received the imperial crown. In January 814, Charlemagne took an ill-advised bath in a mineral spring. A fever overcame him, and he died a week later. His empire soon split among the sons of Louis the Pious, with his descendents ruling France only until 887.

Charles the Bald

Charles the Bald (823–877), also known as Charles II of France and the Holy Roman Emperor, was a grandson of Charlemagne and King of West Frankia. During his 54 years, he saw much of his grandfather's work destroyed, finding that the empire he ruled was too large and too diverse to manage. Even his efforts to unite the Franks against the Vikings failed, and at his death, part of the empire had fallen under the Moorish threat. His family embroilments reflected the culture clash within the empire, forming a confusing and shifting network of loyalties and betrayals.

The Treaty of Verdun Charles the Bald's best-known act is probably the signing of the Treaty of Verdun in 843. This treaty between Charles and his relatives established the rough boundaries of what would eventually become modern France and Germany. The treaty also had the unintended consequence of setting the stage for a territorial dispute that persisted for centuries. In actuality, the Treaty of Verdun was less a resolution of issues on a national scale than a way for relatives to settle a family dispute. The settlement was temporary, with the terms of the treaty being kept for only 26 years.

Family Complications Before Birth How Charles the Bald made it to the Treaty of Verdun is a story that begins with his father, Louis the Pious, son of Charlemagne. Louis the Pious succeeded his father as king of the Franks and Holy Roman Emperor, and when he ascended to the Frankish throne in 814, he had three sons, Lothair, Pepin (also known as Pippin), and Louis (later to be Louis the German). In what could have been a prototype of the King Lear story, Louis the Pious attempted to satisfy his sons by conferring Bavaria on Lothair and Aquitaine on Pepin. Louis the German received nothing in this initial partitioning of the empire's lands.

Then, in 817, a change of heart or agenda led Louis the Pious to make Lothair a co-emperor. Louis the German earned his sobriquet by becoming King of Bavaria in Lothair's place, and Pepin added Gascony, Toulouse, and some of Burgundy to his already resource-rich lands

of Aquitaine. Louis the Pious attempted to arrange the relationships so that Lothair would inherit the empire and his brothers would be as vassals, leading their own kingdoms but consulting with their brother about all major decisions, such as waging war or getting married.

A Nephew Punished One would expect the two brothers to rebel against such a construct, but oddly, the rebellion came from another quarter. Their cousin and the nephew of Louis the Pious, Bernard, King of Italy, found this distribution of land threatening; he tried to revolt against his uncle in 833, crossing the Alps in his failed effort. Louis the Pious punished his errant nephew by having him blinded, but Bernard died days later, leaving Louis so repentant that he felt compelled to undergo public penance and confession, an ill-advised display of weakness. This public humiliation put the emperor in the power of church officials who supported Bernard. These ecclesiastics had their eyes open for any opportunity and shifted the sands of their loyalty to whichever of Louis the Pious's sons appeared to have the upper hand.

Charles the Bald is Born to Judith As though these arrangements were not complex enough, Louis the Pious took a second wife after his first wife died and sired another son, Charles the Bald. This wife, Judith, gave birth to Charles in 823. By 829, Louis the Pious had designated part of Lothair's inheritance to this new son and had dispatched the unhappy Lothair to Italy. From this time, the charters ceased to refer to Lothair as co-emperor, and the stage was set for a struggle among the factions supporting the oldest three sons and those who supported Judith and Charles. A civil war ensued that lasted until Louis the Pious breathed his last in 840.

The Strasbourg Oaths Finally, in 843, sick of war, the feuding family achieved some peace with the Treaty of Verdun. In a clear reminder of the deep cultural differences of the empire that extended even into the family, Louis the German and Charles the Bald each swore their oaths, known as the Strasbourg Oaths, in the language of the other, a sampling of emergent German and French, respectively.

Vikings Invade His internecine feuds with his family settled for the time being, Charles the Bald had no time to relax. By 850, Vikings were making their way up the Meuse, Seine, and Loire rivers, and no one was safe from their raids. They focused particularly on towns and villages along the Seine from 856 to 862, seizing Paris and pillaging Bayeux. Charles the Bald attempted to halt this onslaught by gathering his forces to build fortified bridges along the river, but to accomplish even this, he had to hire hundreds of laborers from elsewhere in the kingdom and the project was not even completed until 873. This effort at national unity and defense was a failure, and any successful defense against the Vikings in Frankish territories happened more at the grassroots level.

The Vikings focused particularly on religious houses, which they knew were essentially undefended repositories of treasure. Monks fled with sacred relics, and communities, in an effort to stop the onslaught, ransomed themselves in payments known as *danegeld*. Yet even these heavy fees were only a temporary respite; the Vikings would simply move on to a neighboring village and eventually return to the ransomed community, presumably concluding that the time they had bought had run out.

Charles the Bald paid ransoms in this way, forking over four thousand pounds of silver and some wine to Viking raiders in 866 to end a siege at Melun. As was usual, this payment sent the Vikings away from the Seine temporarily, but they eventually returned to besiege Paris itself in 886 until yet another payment of danegeld shifted their focus to Burgundy.

Vikings on One Hand, a Recalcitrant Nephew on the Other Charles the Bald also had to deal with his misbehaving nephew Pepin II in Aquitaine, who did not sufficiently attend to his fealty duties to his uncle. Charles tried to take Aquitaine from Pepin II, attempting to imprison his nephew in 855. This gambit failed utterly and left an opening for Louis the German to send his sons into Aquitaine and take it for themselves. Charles the Bald captured Pepin II a second time, the nephew meeting some unknown end, but the Frankish king never had the satisfaction of controlling Aquitaine as he wished.

Disloyal Nobles, a Scholarly Court His family and Norse raiders were not his only plagues. Charles also had to attend to the multitude of nobles whose loyalty shifted variously from him to one of the many factions that rose around his fractured family relations. His problems handling the Viking raids did nothing to boost his popularity, but nevertheless, Charles the Bald also presided over a court that was a center of scholarship and culture, attracting some of the Western world's most distinguished scholars.

Finally, Holy Roman Emperor Charles the Bald did not officially receive the imperial crown until 75 years to the day after the coronation of his grandfather Charlemagne. Charles was crowned on Christmas Day in 875 in Italy, but lived only just over a year as Holy Roman Emperor. As if the Viking raids, family feuds, civil war, and disloyal nobles were not crosses enough for Charles the Bald to bear, during his time in Italy he also had to contend with the threat of attack from Muslims. Not surprisingly, he opted to leave Italy in 877, traveling dispiritedly to his own kingdom, which was at the time under attack by Germans. On his way, he died, to be succeeded by his son, the unpromisingly named Louis the Stammerer.

Charles the Bald and his brother Louis the German form the treaty at Strasbourg in 842. *© Classic Image/Alamy*

Ragnar

When it comes to figures of legend, scholars have a difficult time sorting fact from fiction, especially when chroniclers with agendas are doing the writing. Ragnar, or Ragnar Lodbrok, has been described as a Scandinavian king, variously of Sweden or Denmark, who battled Charlemagne. He may have been a pirate who dropped dead at the feet of the king of Denmark after mocking French courage, or he may have been a man who died in a pit of vipers, paralyzed by their venom. Bits and pieces of the lives of men who may have been named Ragnar surface at various times from the seventh to the ninth centuries, and these pieces, conflated with the several famous literary sagas built around a Ragnar figure, make describing the real man—or even identifying his real name—a mystery remaining to be solved.

The Ragnar Literary Tradition Ragnar is the focus of several sagas, including the twelfth-century *Gesta Danorum*, penned by Saxo Grammaticus. The author describes Ragnar's capture by the Anglo-Saxons, who allegedly tossed the Viking warrior into a snake pit to die. The legend continues that Ragnar had three sons who invaded with their Vikings in East Anglia in 865 in revenge for Ragnar's murder.

The exploits of Ragnar are widely celebrated in many other Scandinavian verse and prose stories. A kind of Viking or Scandinavian King Arthur, Ragnar was probably a real man whose life grew into legend enhanced with the standard trappings of the epic hero. Some of the embroidery includes tales that a second wife, Aslaug, was the offspring of a dragonslayer and Brunhilde, one of the Valkyries. One of his sons, Ivar the Boneless, is a prominent figure of terror in Irish and English storytelling, not least because Ivar (also Inwaer) led terror raids in Britain, allegedly in revenge for his father's death at Anglo-Saxon hands.

Ragnar at Paris There also is a genuine historic figure named Ragnar who was a Viking captain. This Ragnar sailed at the head of a fleet of 120 longships that traveled up the Seine River to Paris. Encountering Charles the Bald's troops mustered on both sides of the river, the brutal Ragnar apparently was unimpressed and expressed his feeling by hanging more than 100 Frankish soldiers on one bank while their comrades watched from across the water, horrified. The result was an en masse desertion from the Frankish army, and Charles the Bald had to pay several thousand pounds in *danegeld* (ransom money) to rid himself of Ragnar's flotilla. Before Ragnar and his men departed, however, they sacked the Abbey of Saint-Germain.

This piratical Ragnar took his tale of success back to Denmark in 845 to report to King Horik that he had discovered the Franks to be rich and cowardly. Legend has it that just as Ragnar derided the Franks for lacking bravery, he dropped to the ground, swelled up, burst,

and died. Some others of the Ragnar contingent also fell ill, and Horik was so disturbed by this evidence of the wrath of the Christian God that he actually returned the looted treasures to St-Germain and had the troops who had accompanied Ragnar killed.

Ragnar and the Anglo Saxons That tale of Ragnar the Viking's explosive death conflicts with stories of a Ragnar of the same period who terrorized the Anglo Saxons until he was put to death by his archenemy, Aelle, ruler of York. As paralysis from the snake venom gradually overcame him, this Ragnar is supposed to have said, "How the little pigs will grunt when they hear how the old boar has died." This final utterance refers to his sons (the little pigs), who later are credited with attacking the British in revenge for their father's death. The revenge was horrific. Ivar and his brothers captured Aelle and killed him by their rite of the blood eagle. This torturous death involved creating an image of an eagle by slicing open the victim's backbone, breaking open the ribcage, and throwing the victim's lungs over his shoulders. The resulting macabre, bloody image was supposed to resemble an eagle in flight and recall the sacred bird of Odin, chief of the Viking gods.

Historical Disagreement Most historical sources consider much of the story of Ragnar to be legend. The *Anglo-Saxon Chronicle* describes him as father of Half-dan, Ivar the Boneless, and Hubba (Ubbe). The *Gesta Danorum* makes him a Danish king who battled the Holy Roman Emperor. Some historians and literary critics assert that the hero Ragnar is a melding of two actual historical figures: Reginheri, the Viking leader who sacked Paris in 845, and Lodrok, who first appears in eleventh century chronicles and about whom little is known. At least one scholar has suggested that the two names did not even occur together until twelfth century sources. Yet other scholars believe that Lodbrok is simply a nickname for Ragnar, meaning "Shaggy Breeches." Some believe that the men considered to be sons of Ragnar may have been born to a mother named Lodbroka. Other scholars are skeptical of these associations, and no one has been able to establish for a fact that the Viking known as Reginheri did indeed sire the men thought to have been Ragnar's sons.

The Hero and the Dragon The *Gesta Danorum* contains entertaining, if suspect, information about Ragnar the legend, including a tale of a worm belonging to one Thora, daughter of Count Herothus. Thora raises the worm from an egg that she places in a box on top of some gold. The worm grows bigger than its box, and the amount of gold increases, too. Eventually, the worm becomes a dragon, eating an ox a day. Herothus promises his daughter and the gold to anyone who can kill the beast; Ragnar takes on the task, succeeds, and wins Thora and the wealth. Thus, Ragnar not only fought Charlemagne, burst to death in Denmark, and died in a snake pit, he also killed a dragon, as any good European figure of myth should.

Chroniclers with Agendas

There has even been some conflation of English and Scandinavian elements of Ragnar's story. For example, things that King Aelle of Northumbria did have been attributed to Ragnar, the man whom Aelle murdered by snake pit. A story of the rape of a neighboring nobleman's wife, once attributed to King Aelle, was added to Ragnar's biography in English versions. With these conflicting agendas of chroniclers and poets playing fast and loose with the facts about who did what and who was who, it's no wonder that pinning down who Ragnar actually was is difficult. Even tales that Ragnar's sons attacked England out of vengeance for their father's death may have been manufactured after the fact by Anglo-Scandinavian chroniclers anxious to lessen the impression of Viking bloodthirstiness.

Alfred the Great

An Anglo-Saxon king, Alfred (848/849–899) became the only English monarch to receive the appellation "the Great." His greatness was not that of size or impressive intellect, but of foresight and charisma that brought together his people into the first unified kingdom of Great Britain.

Alfred's Early Life

Alfred was born in Berkshire, Wessex (in the west of England) to Ethelwulf, the king of Wessex. He was one of five brothers, and as an Anglo-Saxon prince he made his pilgrimage to Rome in 853 for his baptism by Pope Leo IV in 853. While he was in Rome, on this visit and another in 855, he left impressed with the culture and learnedness of its courts. Even though Alfred did not learn to read until he was a teenager and did not read Latin until later life, he emphasized learning and knowledge for his people, efforts that helped position Great Britain as an important player on the European stage.

This great king suffered illness throughout his life, but his afflictions did not stop him from becoming the wily challenger to the marauding Danes that invaded his kingdom after conquering all of the other English monarchies. Britain, in Alfred's minority, was what some historians have called a heptarchy, a loosely organized grouping of the kingdoms of Mercia, Northumbria, East Anglia, Essex, Sussex, Wessex, and Kent. The Angles, Jutes, and Saxons had crossed the sea to Britain after the Romans departed the isles in the fifth century. They conquered the native peoples, dividing up the kingdoms with the Saxons ruling Wessex, Essex, and Sussex in the south, the Jutes settling in Kent and the Isle of Wight, and the Angles taking the rest. Anglo-Saxon came to be the catchall word to describe all of these tribes of England.

Vikings Harass the Kingdom

Three of Ethelwulf's sons—Ethelbald, Ethelbert, and Ethelred (not the Unready of fame)—all died trying to protect their kingdom from Viking raids. The Vikings—or Danes, as the Anglo-Saxons called them—had already captured almost all of the other Anglo-Saxon kingdoms, and Wessex was the only surviving holdout. Ivar the Boneless, the Viking terror of the British Isles, and his brother Halfdan crushed every attempt of the Saxon armies to challenge them. East Anglia saw Danes wintering in their countryside in 865, and by 867, Northumbria, weakened by civil war, fell. Mercia was their next target, and the Mercians turned to Wessex for help. Brothers Alfred and Ethelred (who was now King) attempted to help but could not penetrate the walls of the Mercian city of Nottingham, where the Danes had taken up position. Unable to help, the West Saxons returned home, and the Mercian king gave up Nottingham to the Vikings. Ivar murdered East Anglian's king, Edmund, in 870 in the terrible blood eagle ritual, and that same year, Halfdan made his move on Wessex.

The Battle of Ashdown

Following a valiant but failed effort to defeat the Vikings at Reading, Ethelred and Alfred found themselves with a weakened army battling the Danes at Ashdown on January 8, 871. Attempting to match the Danish army's split into two divisions, Ethelred also split his forces into two units. But when January 8 dawned and the Vikings mustered for battle and bellowed for blood, Ethelred was sitting in his tent, unaware and praying. Alfred, seeing that the Danes were not in the mood to wait for the somewhat-unready Ethelred, got his men together and charged the powerful and larger Viking army. In spite of the imbalance between the forces and the fact that Ethelred only belatedly hurried from his tent and called for his sword, the Saxon forces finally pushed the Danes into retreat.

Bribes for a Temporary Peace

After distinguishing himself at Ashdown, however, Alfred suffered a series of losses, both in battle and in his personal life. His brother King Ethelred died in 871, leaving his throne to the twenty-one-year-old Alfred, who was understandably conflicted about taking over a kingdom whose Christianity was threatened, whose monastic centers of learning had been destroyed, and whose lands were under constant bloody threat from a relentless and merciless invading force. The Wessex army lost a series of battles to the Danes, who had received reinforcements from Europe, and Alfred finally offered the Danes a large payoff to turn their eyes away from his lands. The Danes obliged, promptly setting sword to Mercia, but as Alfred knew and experience had shown, the Vikings would be back.

Alfred quietly began gathering forces and rebuilding his towns, but before he could finish, some Danes began stealing into Wessex, followed by fresh reinforcements. Alfred was forced again to pay them off, this time in

Statue of King Alfred. © *Bettmann/Corbis*

exchange for their oaths that they would never return. The Vikings kept their promise for about a year and then, under the command of a new Danish leader, Guthrum, they were back in Alfred's lands by 878. Guthrum chased Alfred and his forces around Wessex, basing his Danish army at Chippenham and forcing Alfred eventually to hide himself and his few remaining men in the marshes of Somerset.

Alfred at Edington Hunkered down in the marshes and for the moment out of sight and out of mind of the Danes, Alfred again quietly began contacting and uniting his supporters throughout the region, occasionally leading quick raids on the Danish forces. Finally, gathering his fighters together, Alfred and his army converged in 878 at Edington. There, Alfred and his men fought a fierce battle and turned the Danes fleeing to Chippenham, where Alfred besieged them for two weeks. Finally, Guthrum gave up, converted to Christianity, and struck a treaty with Alfred leaving the Danes in charge of the Danelaw, a large part of north and east England that would remain essentially Scandinavian for the next two centuries.

A King with Foresight and a Belief in the Importance of Knowledge Although Alfred the Great had to contend with more Viking troubles (including resistance

from an Anglo-Saxon puppet king who did not want to give up London to him), he managed to turn his thoughts to other issues of importance to his country. One of the things that made Alfred great was his recognition that infrastructure needed boosting. He began a systematic fortification of towns and bridges, simultaneously expanding his rule until his kingdom roughly matched the modern-day borders of Great Britain. His fortified towns made it safe for traders to travel again, which encouraged commerce, and his work in London of creating new streets, markets, and wharves brought renewed life to the beleaguered city. Alfred also addressed his concerns that Christianity was fading among his people, a disturbing trend for this pious king who was baptized by the pope himself.

The Vikings, through their destruction of the monasteries, had also destroyed much of what Christians relied on to educate themselves and support their religion. As priests died and relics disappeared, Christianity faded with them. Alfred sought to remedy this loss through more rebuilding projects and through supporting monasteries again as centers of learning. He is even rumored, or mythologized, as having established Britain's first university at Oxford.

A Great Medieval Ruler Part of the truth of Alfred's life is that he, like any other successful monarch in the Middle Ages, could be a brutal and unpredictable man. No medieval king could have survived and ruled as successfully as Alfred did without these traits. However, his wiliness in defeating the Danes, his statesmanship in holding out the hand of peace and allowing the establishment of the Danelaw, and his lasting contributions to Britain's rebuilding, unification, and laws, are the qualities that made him truly great. Alfred the Great died in 899, having ruled his united people for almost thirty years.

Count Odo

Odo (860–898), also called Eudes, was born to Robert the Strong, a count of Anjou. Odo's military victories against the Vikings eventually earned him a kingship, but he was never able to fully unite the fractured domain he had inherited.

Odo, Count of Paris, vs. the Vikings He was one of the highest-ranking noblemen in West Francia when the Vikings attacked Paris with a flotilla of boats and thousands of men in 885. The Viking fleet Odo faced was the largest ever to make its way up the Seine, with up to forty thousand warriors bent on death and destruction. They found Odo garrisoned on the Ile de la Cite, the island that lies in the heart of the Seine, the river that runs through what is now the metropolis of Paris. In Odo's time, the Ile was Paris, and he and his men guarded the two bridges that linked the island to the mainland on each bank of the river.

An Offer Refused When they arrived, the Vikings demanded payment in exchange for leaving the Franks alone, but Odo declined. Incensed, the Vikings hauled out literally every weapon they had; they even invented some new tactics, including piling up the corpses of animals and people in the river to try to fill in the moat that kept them from Odo's men. The siege dragged on for a year, with sporadic Viking attempts to breach the Frankish defenses. Nothing worked until a flood raised the water high enough to wash out the wooden bridge on one of the river's banks. The Vikings, relieved at being able to leave the site of the siege and travel upriver to continue their depredations, headed off, leaving some of their number behind to maintain the siege.

Joscelin, Bishop of Paris and Comrade in Arms Odo spent the time with several of the Frankish nobility and well born at his side. Among them was Joscelin (also given as Goslin or Gauzlinus), abbot of Saint-Germain and ultimately Bishop of Paris. It was common in this age for men of the cloth also to be men of war and take up arms in defense against the Nordic invaders. Joscelin was no exception, and for many of Odo's men, he was a source of morale-boosting faith and drive. He led an expansion of a bridge tower in the dead of night that left the Viking force surprised at dawn at the dramatic increase in the Frankish defense. Joscelin himself had already survived one Viking kidnapping, being released only after a ransom was paid for him and his brother Louis. He also had the high-profile position of chancellor to Charles the Bald, the king of the Franks who preceded his considerably less-successful heir, Charles the Fat.

As the count and bishop of Paris, respectively, Odo and Joscelin fought and defended their city and kingdom side by side. Thus, it must have been a moment of despair for Odo when Joscelin, the moral support of his army, succumbed to a disease that swept the ranks during the siege. Odo was left alone to continue his attempts to get the attention of their king, Charles the Fat.

A King Arrives and Offers a Bribe Even after he succeeded in smuggling a message of desperation to Charles the Fat, Odo did not benefit from the response of the king of the Franks. Charles the Fat had his own agenda, which involved using the Vikings as a hit squad on Burgundians who were rebelling against him. Thus, rather than crush the Viking forces when he arrived with his own substantial army, Charles the Fat elected to offer them seven hundred pounds of silver to handle the rebels. The Vikings agreed to do so and promptly went elsewhere, ravaging the northern countryside and failing to do anything with the Burgundians. Charles the Fat paid them anyway.

Odo is Made King Frankish contemporaries with a dark sense of humor were undoubtedly bemused by Charles the Fat's short-sightedness in dealing with the Northmen, who were known for returning for more

bribe money once they had exhausted pillaging opportunities elsewhere. Frankish nobles, weary of Charles the Fat's mismanagement of their kingdom, deposed him in 887, selecting Count Odo as their new king.

Odo, having survived the siege of Paris although losing Joscelin, his comrade in arms, now had another struggle on his hands. West Francia was a house divided, with two kingdoms in conflict. Odo found himself sovereign of Neustria, which included his ancestral lands and lay between the Seine and the Loire rivers. Ruling over Aquitaine was Charles the Simple, grandson of Charles the Bald and future participant in a land deal with the Viking Rollo that would mark the beginning of established Viking settlement in Francia.

Struggles with His Rival, Charles the Simple In addition to his struggle against Charles the Simple (whose epithet indicates directness, rather than simple-mindedness), Odo still had Viking incursions to repel, blocking one attack on Paris in 889. He experienced some successes, but always in the midst of his wins were his troubles with Charles the Simple (Charles III).

Odo turned to the king of East Francia, Arnulf, for help and even paid homage to him, but Arnulf rebuffed his hand of peace and threw his support behind Charles. Ultimately, Odo was forced to turn over part of his lands north of the Seine to Charles.

Nature Aids in the Struggle Against the Vikings In his continuing quest to keep the Vikings at bay, Odo finally got help from the one factor that had been missing in the formula for success against the Vikings: famine. The Vikings were not fond of starvation, and rather than ride out the famine, they elected instead to turn their minds and boats back to England. Some historians believe that the Franks provided the Vikings with the ships necessary to hasten their departure.

Successes and Odo's Death While battling Vikings and rivals to his throne, Odo managed to add to the fortifications of his lands, enhancing the Frankish defense against the invaders. After a life of one warlike engagement after another, this king of the Franks died without an heir, and his kingdom went to his rival from Aquitaine,

Charles the Simple, on Odo's death in 898. It would be Charles the Simple who would strike a deal with Rollo to bring in an age of more peaceful Viking settlement and mark the decline of the Viking ravages of Western Europe.

Rollo

Possibly more than any other personage, Rollo, Duke of Normandy and sometime "pirate chief" embodied the Viking influence in Western Europe during the Viking Age and the influence of Western Europe on the Vikings. He lived from 860 to 932.

Melding the Viking and the West Rollo emerged from his homeland, either Denmark or Norway, to terrorize unsuspecting villagers up and down the Seine River, also possibly turning his sights on Ireland, before striking an "our affair" style bargain with a Frankish king to convert to Christianity and protect the king's homeland in exchange for what would become the duchy of Normandy. A Norman duke and descendent of Rollo, William the Conqueror, brought this Norman culture and language to a permanent place in British history in what became known as the Norman Conquest.

Normandy's position on the shores of the English channel and as home to the mouth of the Seine River made it both a perfect offensive launching pad and a vulnerable target for seafaring marauders. Through the Middle Ages, this province had a high profile in the shifting sands of power and culture in Western Europe. Rollo, in exile from his home and estranged from his family, took full advantage of this vulnerability, coming to France and planning to stay.

The Seine: An Invitation to Invasion The mouth of the Seine was an irresistible invitation to the Vikings from 820 onward to move up the river in their stealthy longships, attacking and pillaging as they went. They spent their first Frankish winter in the lower Seine, in what would become Normandy, in 851. Rouen and Paris were favorite targets, and the Vikings attacked Paris so often that its weary leaders would sometimes pay the marauders the Viking bribe known as danegeld for a few years of respite from the harassment. The Frankish leaders were simply unable to muster an organized defense, although Charles the Bald had tried in the mid-ninth century. Rollo, known as a huge man whose horse could not even carry him because of his girth, was probably a member of these raiding parties in the early tenth century. In Icelandic sagas, his name is Hrolf the Walker, possibly because he could not find a horse that could support him and had to walk instead.

Even though Rollo was a raider, the tenth century saw the beginning of a period when Vikings coming into Frankish territory were sometimes more interested in settling down than in taking and destroying. Their attempts to establish Viking settlements in the Loire valley, however, were understandably unwelcome, and

even though the Franks recognized their reign in the 920s, a less-amenable Breton named Alan Crooked-Beard drove the Vikings out in 937. Their efforts to settle in Normandy were more successful, primarily because of Rollo.

A Viking Becomes a Frankish Count In 911, Charles III (Charles the Simple, meaning "straightforward" or "blunt"), King of the Franks, made a not-so-simple decision to give Rollo rule over Normandy in exchange for Rollo's conversion to Christianity and protection of the Frankish seat in Paris. Charles' tactic, one used previously for protection along the Rhine, cleared away the threat of Viking raids and opened for France a new period of reasonably peaceful Viking-Frankish relations.

In spite of his sobriquet, Charles was rather cunning in the timing of his offer, as well as in its nature: He offered Rollo this hand of peace just as Rollo had lost a battle with Charles near Chartres. Although there appears to have been an official treaty, no written document confirming the terms has survived. There is a tale that at the time of Rollo's investiture, he was to kneel and kiss Charles the Simple's foot. Rollo, possibly too fat and definitely too proud to engage in such an activity, had one of his men stand in for him. This hapless fellow grasped and raised the monarch's foot so abruptly that Charles fell over backwards, much to the amusement of the onlookers.

Viking and Frankish Lineages Merge Rollo's new land lay to the southwest of Paris, closer to the mouth of the Seine than the future French capital, and thus strategically a good place to have a giant Viking leader stationed to protect cities from other Vikings. This détente, sealed by the reinstatement of the Bishop of Rouen, led to Rollo's being recognized as a Christian ruler by 913. It is likely that no one believed that Rollo's conversion was anything more than a means to achieving his agenda, but he sired a long line of Norman dukes who were undoubtedly Christian. His son married a Frankish princess, as did his grandson. Rollo himself, in a gesture of goodwill from both men, married Charles's daughter, Giselle. Thus, the blood of Charlemagne the Carolingian and Rollo the Viking flowed in the veins of their descendent, William the Conqueror, who took England for his own.

The Viking Culture Fades In many ways, this melding of the Viking and the Frankish culminated in the complete effacement of Viking culture in the region, additionally catalyzed by the Celtic influences many of the Viking settlers had brought with them from Ireland. By the time Rollo's grandson, Richard I (942–996), was of age, he had to travel from Rouen to a Viking settlement in Bayeux to learn Viking ways that he could no longer acquire in his birthplace.

Just as he and his men had converted to the Christian faith, Rollo and his descendants were required to tolerate the practice of Christianity among their people. However, Rollo's line did retain one aspect of Viking military authority—they had the power to banish the disobedient from their realm, a power that lasted beyond the time of William the Conqueror. This power may be one reason Rollo's lineage maintained a stability that was extraordinary for a European ruling family.

A Stable Lineage Rollo, who initially was a Carolingian count (the Count of Rouen) rather than a duke, sired an unusually long and stable line of Norman dukes. While western European history is littered with the bodies of aspirants to kingship, dukedoms, and earldoms, Rollo's immediate descendants, Richard I and Richard II, enjoyed long reigns and were apparently competent rulers. This stability and competence lasted to the time of William the Conqueror and beyond. There were some missteps and aggressions along the way, including the assassination of Rollo's son and heir to his throne, William Longsword, who stepped up as Duke of Normandy when Rollo abdicated in 927.

A Successful Frankish Strategy Charles the Simple's strategy of welcoming a Viking raider as a brother and protector in arms paid off significantly for the Frankish kings. Rollo was the leader of the last major Viking raid against France but also became a major ruling presence in an essentially Frankish duchy. As for Rollo and his Viking culture, while Norman aristocrats were often of Viking descent, the peasantry were consistently Frankish, leading to a Scandinavian aristocracy governing a French people. In spite of this imbalance, the people of Normandy all became known as Normans, while much of their original culture, including Frankish law, persisted for generations.

Harold Godwinson, Harold II of England

Born in 1022, Harold II became King of England in 1066. Also in that year, he decisively defeated a Viking force at the Battle of Stamford Bridge, but then lost the Battle of Hastings—and his life—to the Norman ruler known as William the Conqueror. Harold's defeat led to the Norman conquest of Great Britain.

Connected to a King Harold I of England was the son of Canute (Cnut), the Danish king who married Emma (widow of Ethelred the Unready) and who ruled all of Britain. When Harold succeeded to Canute's throne, the two sons of Ethelred, Alfred and Edward, returned from exile in Normandy to lay their own claim to the throne. Alfred was killed, however, and Edward fled back to Normandy. The reigns of two Danish kings, Harold I and Hardicanute, would have to end before Edward would return once again to receive his crown. At his death, Edward named Harold Godwinson, son of Godwin, Earl of Wessex, his successor to the throne.

A Leader Forged in the Welsh Borderlands During the eleventh century border wars with the Welsh in the west of England, Harold Godwinson proved himself repeatedly as a warrior and a leader. Harold had inherited his earldom in 1053, and the new earl served Edward the Confessor as an ever-present advisor, wielding great influence. In 1053, Harold's first military nemesis, the Welsh leader Gruffydd ap Llewelyn, began attacking the Saxons, defeating the English army on several occasions in a bitter battle over the Welsh Marches. That same year, an earl whom Edward had exiled for treason brought Viking mercenaries to join forces with ap Llewellyn to fight the English. Harold and his men went to meet the attack, but they moved so slowly that the offending forces had vanished by the time they arrived at the Welsh border. This experience may provide one explanation for Harold's almost reflexive emphasis on speed in the events leading up to the Battle of Hastings in 1066.

When Harold did finally catch up with the Welsh leader and the treacherous earl, he tried diplomacy, with an agenda of breaking up the alliance between the two. His gambit ultimately failed, and for the next several years, Harold found himself chasing the elusive Welsh leader over the countryside, unable either to capture or defeat him. The earl died in 1062, leaving ap Llewellyn on his own. Harold had apparently had enough of the slippery Welsh prince, and in spring 1063, he put into action a careful plan. His brother, Earl Tostig, crossed the Welsh border with a mounted army while Harold sailed up the coast with his men and his group of housecarls, the British medieval equivalent of special forces, feared and fearless warriors who could kill a horse and its rider with one well-placed swing of a two-handed Viking ax. They dressed like Normans in mail and pointed helmets, but Harold's plan was to increase their mobility by having them wear leather. In addition, he changed their weapon of choice to match that of the Welsh army: the javelin.

Relying on these men, who moved fast and light through Welsh territory, Harold made his way into North Wales, wreaking havoc up the coast and taking hostages as he went. With his brother's army, he and his men took their destruction into the heart of the Welsh king's lands, razing villages and transforming ap Llewellyn from a slippery eel into a hunted animal.

Harold did not end up killing the Welsh king, however, as the weary Godwinson was apparently not the only person tired of constantly moving to track his quarry. In 1063, ap Llewellyn's own men turned on him and murdered him in the mountains of Snowdonia, apparently for persisting in fighting the English forces. Harold, no doubt relieved to be rid of this thorn in his side, sent the man's head and the prow of his ship to Edward as proof that the Welsh war was finally over. In a sort of posthumously inflicted coup de grâce, Harold then took for his wife the Welsh king's widow, Ealdgth, whose other claim to fame was her grandmother, Lady Godiva.

An Involuntary and Fatal Oath Harold's constant activity on behalf of Edward strengthened his position as an advisor to the king, for whom he also served as ambassador. It may have been in this latter role that Harold actually met his future nemesis, William the Bastard, duke of Normandy. Harold made a trip to the Norman duchy in 1064, which he began by first blowing off course while crossing the English Channel, washing up on the shores of William's enemy, the Count of Ponthieu. The count held Harold and his retinue until convinced under William's threats to let them go. Harold now, however, owed William a huge debt. No one knows exactly why Harold was on the seas in the first place, but the prevailing theory is that his mission was diplomatic.

The two future rivals were very different, as their response to a certain incident illustrates. Harold accompanied William on a march during which the army crossed an area of quicksand. One of William's soldiers fell and became stuck. The Duke of Normandy kept going, ignoring the man's mortal predicament. Harold, however, immediately leapt from his horse and pulled the man from the sucking sands, putting his own life at risk. Harold's spontaneity early on would eventually be tempered by experience, but William exhibited a calculating character from the beginning. The most famous example of his manipulation involving Harold was his ambush of the diplomat at a state dinner. William suddenly called Harold before all the company to lay his hands on sacred relics and swear loyalty to William. Harold, torn between insulting his diplomatically powerful host before all of the guests or swearing an oath he could not keep, pledged his loyalty. Unable to support an oath given under duress and potentially under threat to his life, Harold then made haste to England.

A Bad Year for a King Harold stepped into the kingship at a bad time, immediately becoming embroiled in a deadly dispute with a duke, a king, and his own brother over the throne. When Edward died, he had no heirs, leaving open the question of his succession. The *witan*, or royal council, was responsible for making that decision, although their track record of selection was perhaps not exemplary, given the split decision of Canute versus Edmund Ironside in a previous century. This council of 1066 had a lot to worry about, as there were claims from three sides: Harald III (Hardraade or Hardrada) of Norway, Duke William of Normandy (a claimant despite his illegitimacy), and Harold Godwinson, right-hand man to Edward himself. Harold was no royal, but he was Earl of Wessex, the most powerful earldom in England and producer of a previous great Saxon king, Alfred.

Thus, Harold received the crown, although there is some dispute over whether or not he took it for himself or was given it. The witan, at any rate, had no interest in having William the Bastard become their king. They still held the view that Normans, as descendents of the marauding and pillaging Vikings, were thieves and pirates. William himself attempted to bolster his claim by asserting that Harold had promised to support Norman succession to the English throne, probably a reference to Harold's controversial pledge of loyalty in 1064. In fact, William used this claim to gain papal support for his claim to kingship. Regardless, the crown was placed on Harold's head in Westminster Abbey in January 1066. Within a month, William, Duke of Normandy and bastard son of Robert the Magnificent, was readying for battle.

A Brother's Treachery Harold knew the attack from the south was coming and began readying his own troops. What he ignored, however, was the growing threat from the North as Hardraade and Tostig, Harold's own brother, decided to take England for their own. To them, as well as to William of Normandy, Edward's death looked like an excellent excuse to invade the country. Hardraade laid his tenuous claim based on the assertion that one of his wives was related to Canute, a previous, Danish-born king of England. His claim was enough to attract warriors from all over the continent to his side, including Tostig.

Tostig's treachery to his brother fit with his past behavior. As earl of Northumbria, he had been so cruel that his vassals revolted against him in 1065, and his king, Edward the Confessor, exiled him. Edward seemed incapable of simple, summary execution of traitors, instead relying, however unsuccessfully, on exile as punishment. As happened with the repeated banishments of the treacherous earl who allied with the Welsh, this punishment simply incited the perpetrator to revenge, especially when Tostig saw one of the revolutionaries made earl in his place. Tostig was not successful in his effort to take the country, however, and ended up fleeing ignominiously to shelter in the Scottish court of King Malcolm III.

Firedrake and the Death of Kings A portent known to contemporary astronomers as "Firedrake" and to people now as Halley's Comet flashed across the sky in 1066, foretelling, it was said, the death of kings. Harold thought it signaled the time for him to head south with his forces, including his housecarls. While he marched in the wrong direction, a huge fleet of Viking warriors made their way to his kingdom in the north, arriving in September 1066 and meeting up with the defeated Tostig. They immediately set to raiding their way south, navigating their longships along the rivers and plundering as they went. They finally arrived at their intended seat of York, where their banner sporting Odin's Raven flew alongside the Golden Lion of Tostig's flag.

Convinced that the Norman invasion was nigh, the earls Morcar and Edwin decided to attack the daunting Norseman force, in spite of the fact that their forces numbered only one-sixth of the Viking army. Not surprisingly, they suffered a heavy defeat, losing half their force along with one hundred local monks. York surrendered and promised to deliver one hundred hostages to Hardraade at a nearby location called Stamford Bridge.

Victory in the North Harold, meanwhile, still awaited the Norman invasion, even though the north-blowing winds might have tipped off a savvy warrior to a threat from the north. By the time the beacon fires informed him of the northern peril, the crops lay rotting in fields and Harold had sent many of his men home, optimistic that the Normans would not invade after all. He gathered his troops together again, knowing that marching them north to engage the Vikings would weaken them significantly just as they would have to march south again to take on the Normans. Even so, he had no choice. Given the task, Harold executed it with vigor, perhaps driven by memories of losing the Welsh king too many times because of delay. He marched his six-thousand-man force 185 miles over four days, adding recruits as he went. By the time he arrived within attacking distance of York, he had a fighting force of nine thousand men.

This large army took the ten-thousand-man combined forces of Hardraade and Tostig completely by surprise on a hot September 25, 1066. Some of the Vikings, feeling secure in their victory and sure that Harold would be unable to arrive so quickly, had wandered off for supplies or returned to guard their ships. Hardraade was caught with only part of his army at his side. He quickly deployed a small phalanx to the west bank of the Derwent River, where they were encamped, and took the remainder with him to the east bank. Harold's men promptly crushed the small group on the west bank and then paused only long enough to dispatch a berserker—the Viking answer to a special forces fighter—who was guarding the bridge and may have single-handedly killed a dozen English soldiers before one pierced him from beneath the bridge and the housecarls cut him to pieces.

The Battle of Stamford Bridge The two armies engaged with axes swinging. Tostig recommended retreat, but Hardraade ignored his advice. His decision was fatal. The English forces organized into a formation of seven separate phalanxes, probably with the housecarls in the vanguard. The onslaught was relentless, and chroniclers relate that Hardraade himself fell early on, slain by an arrow. Despite the loss of their leader and Tostig, who also died during the battle, the Vikings refused to give, and the wearying march across their country began to tell on the British soldiers. Harold, seeing this, pulled them back in a fake retreat. His maneuver tricked the Vikings into breaking up their densely layered lines of defense as they rushed to follow the "retreating" army. As the broken ranks closed in on the English, Harold's housecarls suddenly turned and attacked, their energy renewed. The Viking leaders, however, stood by their standards, falling one by one,

choosing death over dishonor. The victorious English spent the remainder of that blistering, bloody day hunting down every Viking man they could find and killing him. Harold followed up on his victory by then taking the Viking fleet. He did have his brother's bloodied corpse borne to the cathedral of York Minster for a proper interment.

Death at the Battle of Hastings Harold's victory, however, was short-lived, and it played right into William's hands by eliminating two rival claimants to the English throne. By September 27, the wind shifted to the south, allowing William the Bastard to point his ships across the English channel, landing the very next morning to start building forts and pillaging villages. Strangely enough, the tactic of false retreat that served Harold so well in the destruction of the Viking age in Britain would, in a matter of weeks, contribute to his devastating defeat at Hastings.

England had left behind Viking rule only to end up in the hands of the French, who were actually led by a man descended from Vikings. Harold Godwinson, Harold II of England, died on October 14, 1066, in the battle that left his kingdom under the rule of William the Bastard of Normandy, also known to history as William the Conqueror.

William the Conqueror

Leaving his stronghold in Normandy, William (1027–1087) crossed the English Channel and defeated the English king Harold II at the Battle of Hastings, establishing Norman rule in that kingdom and changing the course of British history irrevocably.

Bastard Son of a Magnificent Devil The father of William the Conqueror, Robert, became duke when he was only twenty. As with many prominent men of his time, Robert earned sobriquets that concisely conveyed his personality. In his case, he had two. He was occasionally known as "Robert the Devil," earning this moniker because of his devilish sadism. Robert once defeated a man who had insulted his son; following the victory, he had the man (a great lord) swear fealty to him barefoot and with a saddle on his back. After humiliating the landowner, Robert then generously gave the man his lands back. His other sobriquet was "Robert the Magnificent," possibly because of his generosity to religious orders in the region. It was his dedication to his religion that led to his death.

William was born the bastard son of Robert and Herleve (also Arlette, Herleva, or Harlette), the daughter of a tanner known as Fulbert. The story goes that she was washing clothes near a stream or dancing in the road when Robert encountered her and sired one of Europe's most influential and famous rulers, a man who would himself warrant more than one nickname. William, although illegitimate, was born in his father's castle keep, and he was known to contemporaries as William

This detail from the Bayeux Tapestry shows William the Conqueror and his army attacking Dinan.   © *Gianni Dagli Orti/Corbis*

the Bastard. His illegitimacy, however, did not stand in his way. Robert ultimately recognized William as his son just before departing on a pilgrimage to Jerusalem in the Holy Land, and he convinced his nobles to recognize the child's legitimacy, as well.

William was only seven when his father left on this final journey: Robert the Magnificent made it to the Holy Land but perished on the return trip, and the fatherless young boy was left to fend off barons desperate to seize power. Robert had tried to leave the child well guarded in his absence, with the king of the Franks, Henry I, protecting him. In addition, Robert left his cousin, Alan, Count of Brittany, as regent, and a friend, Gilbert of Brionne, as guardian.

Young William Defends his Duchy
Unfortunately, the people guarding William began dying one by one—his guardian, steward, and even his tutor were murdered—until the boy was forced to take shelter in the forests, protected by a maternal uncle and hiding in peasant cottages. (Henry, king of the Franks, was a dilatory protector

at best.) By the time William reached the age of thirteen, however, he was personally fighting the treacherous usurpers, winning his first battle. By age fifteen, he was knighted, and he defeated his enemies once and for all at age twenty after successfully quelling a rebellion at age nineteen. Thus, even before reaching adulthood, William had successfully defended his own duchy against rivals to his place.

Personal Life
In 1053, William married his twenty-two-year-old cousin, Matilda, daughter of the Count of Flanders. The marriage was, according to accounts, a happy one. The pope did not give approval for the union, but William made the match anyway and had at least nine children (four sons and five or six daughters). By 1065, he was Duke of Normandy in name and reality. The duke was a bit taller than average for a man of his time, with striking grey eyes, red hair, thin lips, and a strong jaw. Chroniclers remarked on his voice, describing it as harsh and guttural. Certainly, in addition to this voice, he had a harsh pragmatism that drove him to successes so notable

that the world would cease to call him "Bastard" and come instead to know him as "Conqueror."

This future conqueror, when he first settled into his dukedom, still had to fend off outside challenges to his position, including a southern confrontation with Count Geoffrey, the Hammer of Anjou and ancestor of the redoubtable Henry II of England. William spent a great deal of time fending off Geoffrey's incursions into Norman territory, which had the sporadic support of Henry I, the erstwhile protector of the young duke William. Obviously, Henry had decided that the duke no longer required his services, and in fact, he was deeply concerned about the brutal power of the young Norman. To deal with the constant threats to his leadership, William instituted a policy of forming new counties and placing known loyal family members and associates in positions of power under his sole rule. These family members included his half brothers Odo and Robert.

A Controversial Oath A turning point in William's career came when Harold Godwinson, the future Harold II of England, washed up on the shores of France and eventually ended up in William's court. What happened at that court is a matter of some dispute. The gist of the story is that at a state dinner one evening, William suddenly turned to Harold and demanded that his visitor swear fealty to him. According to persistent legend, Harold did so. However, what remains in dispute is whether or not there was an implicit, or even explicit, threat to Harold's life at that moment and whether or not Harold made the promise under duress. Regardless, William latched onto the incident as his strongest argument for moving against England after Edward the Confessor, king of England, died in January 1066, leaving Harold the throne. William's argument was convincing enough at least for the pope, who gave his blessing to William.

Although the oath from Harold provided an excuse to take revenge, no one knows exactly why William decided in the first place that he was the true heir to the English throne. Some historians argue that Edward, perhaps during his time in exile in Normandy, decided to make a Norman his successor. Edward's mother, Emma, was the daughter of a Norman duke and wife of Ethelred the Unready; she also was William's great aunt. It may be that the Normans viewed her status as queen consort of England as an entrée into the line of succession after Edward the Confessor died.

William's Victory at the Battle of Hastings The Battle of Hastings, the upshot of William's effort, has been called the most significant event in British history. Certainly, it and the events surrounding it had a number of unusual features and strange coincidences. Halley's Comet blazed across the skies that year, as depicted in the Norman-woven Bayeaux Tapestry. To many, it was an ill omen, meaning no good to Harold. However, William saw it as permission from an authority higher

SENSITIVE TO HIS ORIGINS

William remained sensitive to his illegitimate origins, even after he had his duchy firmly in hand. He was not above atrocity to achieve his ends and enact revenge. In one besieged stronghold, the people of the town beat skins hanging from the walls, calling jeeringly, "Plenty of work for the tanner's son!" mocking William's maternal heritage. William was so incensed that he took many prisoners and had their eyes put out. He also had their hands and feet cut off and tossed over the walls into the city, leaving the maimed to crawl home if they could. The horrified townspeople surrendered at once.

than the pope to move ahead with his attack. Accordingly, he assembled a huge fleet of about 1,400 craft, ready to cross the English Channel. His intention was a lightning-fast assault that would end in defeat of Harold's forces in a single crushing battle, leaving William king of England. There on the shores of Normandy, William and his men waited for the winds to change and favor their departure.

And they waited. After several weeks, the south wind finally gave the signal to sail, and in a matter of a day, William had landed his fleet in England, at Pevensey. Harold, who had in his turn waited impatiently for William, was forced north to battle a Viking onslaught, only to turn his army immediately on a 250-mile march south to meet William's troops. With his seven-thousand-man, exhausted force, Harold hoped to surprise the Norman invaders, but a scout espied his encampment and reported it to William. Even after the lost element of surprise, the battle between the weary British troops and the invigorated Norman army was a fairly even match through much of the day. William's forces eventually prevailed; Harold died by nightfall that October 14, 1066; the Normans took the victory; and William was crowned King of England on Christmas Day that same year. He was only thirty-nine.

Norman Rule in Saxon England Not surprisingly, quite a few English nobles were not pleased with William's victory, and the new king spent several years working to take and maintain control of the whole kingdom. Many of the English nobles were so desperate not to have a Norman king that they threw their support behind the Danish king, Sven Estridsson, who arrived in 1070 but retreated before William's powerful defense. The Danes tried again five years later when Sven's son, Cnut (Canute, Knut), tried to launch a fleet to attack the Conqueror. The ill-fated attempt faltered when the fleet was destroyed before it even landed. Again in 1085, the hapless Cnut pulled together a fleet, this time with the full intention of conquering England for himself. However, this fleet never even sailed, although William had intelligence of it and took the threat seriously. With these failures, the Viking age was over, and William was the Conqueror.

William did not just take England for his own and turn it from a Viking/Saxon nation into something decidedly more French in language and architecture. He also remade England into a Norman nation, bringing with him a powerful central bureaucracy born of his need to control. The Domesday Book, a census and a database of English wealth and landholders started in 1085, is a standing monument to this detailed and widespread bureaucratic interest and interference. Naturally, his interference, which was far more than clerical and often cruel and unyielding, bred the kind of response chronicled in the tales of Robin Hood. The Robin Hood of legend is a Saxon noble who takes arms against the oppressive Norman leaders, embodied in villains like the Sheriff of Nottingham and the ultimate Norman incarnation of evil, Sir Guy of Gisbourne.

Ignominy in Death Ultimately, as the subsequent melding of the Saxon and the Norman attest, William prevailed. He continued his warlike pursuits, even as his body, "great" but "not ungainly" in youth, bloated into gross obesity. It was during one of these warlike endeavors that William severely injured himself on the pommel of his saddle, an injury probably exacerbated by his large size. His greatness of body had bloated into grossness of body, and after he died on September 9, 1087, the final scene of his life bookended the ignominy of his beginnings. As his pallbearers struggled to force William's oversized coffin into his tomb, the huge, bloated corpse inside burst from the jostling. The fluid issuing from the sarcophagus emitted a stench so overwhelming that it drove the people from the church.

At his death, his servants rushed to steal his treasures or to secure their own estates, not pausing to mourn his passing. His ruthless material pragmatism stands in sharp contrast to the obvious intellectual and scholarly interests of the great kings who preceded him, Charlemagne and Alfred the Great. The immediate legacy of rapacity at the moment of his death may reflect this emphasis on material acquisition under his leadership.

The Long-Term Legacy of William the Conqueror William, the Conqueror and the Bastard, had a reputation as a relentless and relentlessly practical man. His accession to power was the harbinger of a new age and marked the end of Viking dominance and terror in Europe. His role at the close of the Viking age is ironic yet fitting because he himself was descended from Vikings, but he was also a Frankish duke. Even though his direct descendents did not rule England after 1135, all English rulers who followed him can trace their ancestry to this man whose ambition triggered the most important event in British history.

⊕ Major Battles

Sacking of Lindisfarne, 793

The Holiest Place in Britain Lindisfarne, also known as the Holy Island, was the site of the Vikings' first major assault on the English coastline. The scholar-monks who lived in the monastery at Lindisfarne enjoyed a life of intellectual pursuits, producing one of Europe's most famous illuminated manuscripts, the *Lindisfarne Gospels*. It was, without doubt, the holiest place in Britain for ecclesiastics and pilgrims alike.

The Idyll Comes To an End The monk's contemplative idyll on the sometime-island—Lindisfarne becomes a peninsula at low tide—came to an abrupt end on June 8, 793 (the date is sometimes given as January 8, 793). Looking up from their work at the windows of the monastery or even perhaps from a stroll along the coastline, the monks would have seen something new to their eyes: Viking longships. As they watched the ships approach, each carrying one hundred men, the monks could not have known that they were watching their doom come near, although even the appearance of a Viking longship and its warlike crew probably augured nothing but ill to these servants of God.

Before the day was done, the Vikings had slaughtered some monks as they tried to flee, capturing and selling others into slavery. The marauders from the North took jewels from the monk's jewelry workshop and any relics that seemed valuable, wantonly destroying what remained. Even though some monks escaped and returned to try to reestablish Lindisfarne, that fateful day marked the end of their quiet, scholarly time on the Holy Island.

The doom was not Lindisfarne's alone. This invasion of the Vikings was only the beginning of a three-hundred-year reign of pillage, terror, and slaughter. Even though the Viking Age finally ended through defeat and assimilation, their initial assault on Lindisfarne reverberates through the centuries to today.

Lindisfarne Before the Vikings Established in 635, Lindisfarne was the work of Saint Aidan, a monk of Scottish-Celtic origins. The Holy Island, lying off the coast of northern England on the North Sea, became a peninsula at low tide, providing a link to the larger island mass of Britain. The monks of Lindisfarne used their outpost as the incubator for missionaries, who crossed over the low-tide flats to spread their message of Christianity to the interior. As a result of their missionary activities and the fine illuminated manuscripts they produced, Lindisfarne became an important ecclesiastical center during the Dark Ages.

This center of Christian missionary and intellectual zeal attracted Saint Cuthbert, the "Fire of the North" and the man responsible for establishing Roman Catholicism in England, to Lindisfarne's shores in 685. This healer and

The monastery of Lindisfarne was founded by Irish born Saint Aidan, sent to Northumbria by King Oswald around 635. © *Patrick Ward/ Corbis*

miracle worker was laid to rest at the monastery, where his tomb became a site of pilgrimage, the devout biding their time to low tide before picking their way across the soggy tidal flats to the monastery.

The subsequent decades were a time of peace, prosperity, and broad influence for the inhabitants of the monastery, with the comings and goings of pilgrims, missionaries, and ecclesiastical intellectuals. Thus, the Vikings arrived when Lindisfarne was at its peak. No one knows how many of the people who watched the Viking boats push inexorably closer to shore were monks or pilgrims. What is known is that once the bottoms of those boats scraped sand and the Vikings left their first footprints on Lindisfarne's shores, the age of Lindisfarne's prosperity ended. The island ceased to be an intellectual and religious center and instead became a starting point for many subsequent Viking raids to nearby English territories.

Portents and the Vikings as God's Wrath In those boats sat oarsmen and warriors, each warrior wearing a metal helmet and wielding an axe or a sword. As they leapt from their crafts, their intentions were clear. The helpless monks and pilgrims could only watch or try to hide as these huge, remorseless men slaughtered them

recklessly and plundered the monastery for its treasure. The Vikings had quickly learned that European religious houses were not only repositories of the faithful and their books, but that they also housed a large portion of the people's treasure in gold and fine works. Add to that the fact that the monasteries were completely defenseless when the Vikings began their raids, and there may be some understanding of why the gold-hungry Northmen found such targets irresistible.

Some chroniclers reported that the monks knew from "heavenly portents,"—which included lightning storms, famine, a rain of blood, and "fiery dragons,"—of the terror coming to them across the sea. After the slaughter, Charlemagne heard from Alcuin, his English adviser, that "never before has there been such a terror appeared in Britain and never was such a landing from the sea thought possible." Alcuin averred that the Vikings were agents of God's wrath, visited on the Northumbrians for their moral turpitude.

In more worldly terms, the Vikings saw an opportunity and took it. The monks thought they needed no defenses because the sea was their defense. They had not counted on the Viking longboats, which made it possible for the Northmen to gain passage across seas and navigate inland rivers alike.

VARANGIAN AND RUS

Varangians was a general term used to describe Swedish traders on these Russian rivers, but it came to describe any Viking living in Russia. *Rus*, which in histories and biographies is sometimes conflated with Varangian, specifically refers to Vikings who followed a leader named Rurik. Rurik eventually brought his people to settle on the banks of the River Volkhov in Novgorod, which became known as *Rusland*, today's Russia.

After the initial raid and slaughter, the Vikings returned for repeated attacks on Lindisfarne. Weary of what must have become a life of continual anticipation of terror, the monks relocated their monastery (including St. Cuthbert's miraculously preserved remains) to the mainland, where it eventually returned to its importance as an ecclesiastic focal point for England.

The Lindisfarne Gospels When St. Cuthbert died, the monks at Lindisfarne produced their most famous work, the *Lindisfarne Gospels*, to commemorate his passing. Such a work, an illuminated text of the four New Testament gospels, was suited to the mystical feel of Lindisfarne, with its eerie castle teetering on a rocky promontory. The work would still be at Lindisfarne were it not for the Vikings; in an effort to preserve it, the fleeing monks took it with them to Durham, where they had relocated. In a conflict between the Church and Henry VIII centuries later, the king's lackeys demonstrated Henry's disdain for the Mother Church by seizing the Gospels and taking them to London. There they reside, in the British Library, the subject of a movement to have them returned to their original birthplace.

Constantinople, June 860

The Great City In the eighth century, as their brethren plundered Western Europe, some Vikings made their way south across Slavic territory from the Baltic to the Black Sea, aiming for Constantinople (today, Istanbul), which they called *Miklagard* (the "great city"). This capital of Byzantium was the Paris or New York of its age, a Mecca for the ambitious and the learned alike—or, in the case of Vikings, for the acquisitive.

As the Vikings established their trade routes, they built towns along the route to Constantinople. One of the major settlements in the eighth century was the Finnish trading post of Staraja Lagoda, lying on the River Volkhov, a major artery for traders making their way between the Baltic and Slavic territories. This trading post eventually grew into more than a place for traders to take a rest—the inhabitants began to produce goods of their own to sell to the constant stream of travelers. In addition to

offering luxury items for sale, they specialized in refitting ships and loading boats.

Arab Silver, Viking Greed Swedish Vikings hanging out at Staraja Lagoda were the first Northmen to lay greedy eyes on Arab silver and hear of the bright Miklagard, the crown jewel of the Greek Empire. At that time, in the early ninth century, the population of Constantinople was a bustling one million people, not counting the endless movement of travelers and traders. Drawn by the glint of precious metal, the Vikings pointed their longships southward on the Dniester, Dvina, Lovat, Dnieper, and Volga rivers, traveling across the Slavic regions to the Great City in Byzantium.

By 830, Swedish Rus had landed on the southern shores of the Black Sea, where the Byzantine emperor had an escort conduct a party of the Vikings over the Mediterranean Sea to Francia. Oddly, these particular Vikings had apparently undergone such a harrowing experience crossing through Slavic territory that they feared returning by the same route and took a chance on the benevolence of the Byzantine emperor. In fact, the impression of terror was so great that for the next few decades, no more Rus Vikings are recorded as having ventured through Slavic lands to visit Constantinople.

That next visit in 860, however, did not involve asking the emperor for mercy or even requesting a safe escort to Francia. Instead, it left the people of Constantinople stunned, unsure of how to handle the scourge that had just descended on them from the north.

The Attack on Constantinople The Rus Vikings made Novgorod, one hundred miles south of Staraja Lagoda, their home base. Strategically, this location suited the boatsmen, who could travel three miles to Lake Ilmen, cross it to the River Lovat, and travel to the River Dnieper, which flowed to the Black Sea. With a few portages at rough spots, the Vikings could essentially traverse the entirety of the Slavic territories by water, which is exactly what they did in 860, snaking their way along watery routes to the Black Sea.

Along the river, five hundred miles south of Novgorod, the Viking captains Askold and Dir had set their base in the town of Kiev. In 860, they gathered a fleet of two hundred longships and pointed their bows southward, coming to the walls of Constantinople on June 18, 860.

When they arrived, the emperor was out, attending to wars against the Arabs. The Vikings found the wall effective at barring their entry into the Great City and turned instead to what Vikings all over Europe had become best at doing: plundering surrounding monasteries and killing every man, woman, and child in their path.

When Photius, patriarch of Byzantium, finally managed to get word to the Emperor Michael of the Vikings' depredations, the ruler dropped his Moorish concerns and quickly hurried back to his capital. Yet, even though he managed to get into his city, he could not get rid of the

Vikings, who waved their swords in derision as they slipped past Constantinople's walls in their longships, bent on further destruction of holy sites beyond the Great City.

Byzantium in Disbelief No one knows exactly why Askold and Dir even decided to leave their attempted attack on Constantinople. Maybe their boats were full of looted treasures, although their pillaging further south suggests they had some space left. At any rate, they left behind a city of one million shocked, horrified inhabitants still trying to process what had just happened. Photius's comments on the occasion reflect their struggle to understand. In obvious disbelief, he sermonized about the "obscure nation . . . of no account . . . " that was once unknown but now had become famous, people from a place far away from the cultured elegance of Byzantium, come to them "armed with arrogance," and "in the twinkling of an eye, like a wave of the sea poured over our frontiers."

It is difficult to tell whether Photius was more horrified by the destruction and death or by the fact that the people who had done it were not quite the right sort. It was as though the aristocrats were trying to grapple with the fact that the peasants had mustered the temerity to come within striking distance.

Oleg, "Elder Statesman" Askold and Dir became famous for the wealth they had accumulated during their bloody sojourn, their names making the rounds from Kiev to Novgorod. As with any tale of wealth in the context of Viking greed, the reports of their newfound treasures sparked factionalism and discord, with various Rus groups attempting to control the rivers and thus the spoils of raiding and trading. Oleg, successor to Rurik in Novgorod, lured Askold and Dir to a meeting, ostensibly to determine who would control what. When the two captains arrived, however, Oleg summarily killed them and took over, and Kiev became the center of Rus power. Although Oleg achieved his place through treachery, he still managed to persuade the Byzantine emperor to accept his people as a trading partner, and ended his days in 914 viewed as a kind of elder statesman, "at peace with all nations."

Edington, May 878

A Turning Point for England's Future The Battle of Edington was decisive for England, determining the future culture and language of what would become Great Britain. The victor, Alfred the Great (king of Saxon Wessex), did not lead his army to a rout, but the battle and a subsequent siege were decisive enough to bring the Vikings to the negotiation table in an agreement that echoed Charles the Bald's treaty with Rollo the Viking in Normandy.

King Alfred the Great Alfred stepped up to the Wessex throne after the death of his brother, Ethelred, who went to the halls of his fathers just as a second, fresh

THE VARANGIAN GUARD IN BYZANTIUM

The Viking ferocity, however, did not go completely unappreciated or unexploited. In later times of greater amity between the Rus Vikings and Byzantine leaders, the Byzantine emperors took mercenaries from among the Rus into their service. These bands of strongmen at the side of the emperor became known as the Varangian Guard.

Danish army was arriving to finish off the kingdom of Wessex. The new king was only twenty-one years old and inherited a land enduring a wave of Viking attacks that had already brought the surrounding kingdoms to their knees. He and his brother had managed to ward off the Vikings, and Alfred continued successfully keeping Wessex out of Viking hands, through either armed resistance or large payoffs of *danegeld*, the bribes universally doled out to Vikings to keep them away for at least a few years.

Alfred Takes Refuge His bribes, like those of other European leaders, were only temporarily effective, and in 876, the Vikings were back in force and crossing the borders of Wessex, having decided to take over Alfred's kingdom once and for all. In the interim, Alfred had attempted to refortify his kingdom, rebuilding towns and forts and attempting to recruit a united army. Alfred and his army put up a spirited defense against this new Danish incursion, but years of battle with little time for rebuilding had undermined men and resources. A surprise Viking attack in January 878 sent Alfred and his few remaining loyalists into hiding in the marshes of Somerset; many people of Wessex fled to Europe.

From the marshes, Alfred led raiding forays on the Viking forces, quick attack-and-retreat ventures that always ended in withdrawal back to Athelney, the island location of Alfred's marsh hideout. At one point in spring of 878, the waters rose so high that Alfred was forced to stay on his island for refuge, and the Danes decided that they had officially conquered all of Anglo-Saxon Britain. They did not realize that Alfred was still king, and that the swamps were really a perfect place to keep him inaccessible while he made further plans.

Alfred Unites His People Local farmers knew exactly where to find him, however, and they brought him food and information, while Alfred's men hunted in the nearby forests and conducted lightning raids on the Danish troops. While conducting these raids and staying generally beneath the Viking radar, Alfred was also quietly recruiting leaders from the surrounding countryside for a united effort against the Vikings when the time was right. He concluded that time had come in spring of 878. The Danes had settled their army nearby at a place called Edington, a village watched over by a white horse carved into the chalky stone by an ancient hand, and Alfred believed that the Anglo-Saxon moment had arrived. The horse may have provided inspiration—it was the counterpart of a similar figure carved into the hillside of Ashdown, where Alfred and his brother Ethelred had enjoyed a decisive victory over the Viking horde. Under the watchful profile of the white horse, Alfred gathered his newly united forces from Somerset, Wiltshire, and Hampshire and attacked the Danish army, which was led by King Guthrum.

The Battle is Engaged Bishop Asser, who chronicled Alfred's military success against the Vikings, wrote that the West Saxon king "closed his ranks, shield locked with shield, and fought fiercely against the entire heathen host in long and stubborn stand." Alfred eventually had the satisfaction of watching the Danish army flee and followed up his victory by having any remaining wounded or straggling Danes killed. The Anglo-Saxon army rounded up everything they could that belonged to the Danes (including their horses, cattle, and supplies) and then chased them fifteen miles to their stronghold at Chippenham.

Siege at Chippenham, Then Relative Peace Alfred stood at the gates of the fortress, calling for Guthrum to surrender, which Guthrum not surprisingly refused to do. In response, Alfred held siege against the Danes for two weeks. Finally, weary of the ensuing starvation and forced inactivity—a probable torture to these Viking men of action—Guthrum took the hand of peace from Alfred and negotiated the Peace of Chippenham. Their treaty included a promise from Guthrum to leave Wessex and stay out and to convert to Christianity.

Guthrum kept both promises and was baptized three days later. Alfred, for his part, gave Guthrum and the Danes self-rule of the Danelaw, the central eastern part of England that was largely settled by Scandinavians. As of 886, Alfred had expanded his kingdom to include Mercia and other Anglo-Saxon territories that had fallen into Viking hands. When his rule ended, the boundaries of the Britain he had united reflected in large part those of the Britain that exists today.

Although the Battle of Edington was not a rout, it was a decisive victory for the Anglo-Saxons and ensured that this last bastion of Saxon rule did not fall irrevocably into the hands of the raiding Danes. Had the battle victory gone to the Vikings, England today might well have been a Scandinavian country with Scandinavian culture and languages, and the English in which this story is written would never have come into existence.

The Siege of Paris, Late Ninth Century

A Tale of Two Bridges In 885, Count Odo of Paris, his comrade Bishop Joscelin, and two hundred of their men were garrisoned on the Ile de la Cite, the site of the Paris of the time. This small force was in charge of protecting lands further up the river from marauders making their way via the Seine. At the Ile de la Cite, the Seine was forced to split into a fork that encircled the island on each side and merged again at its eastern point to continue its flow. A stone bridge connected one riverbank to the island, while a wooden bridge linked it to the opposite bank. The passage under these bridges was so low that no craft, not even the low and long Viking longships, could move beneath them. They made an effective blockade against progress, at least forcing invading forces to portage around.

The Viking force that arrived at the Ile de la Cite in 885 would have been hard pressed to complete an efficient portage. Estimates vary, with many asserting that there were forty thousand Viking warriors, which would require at least four hundred ships. (Some counts go as high as seven hundred ships.) This daunting flotilla arrived at the bridges connecting the Ile to the mainland, and their leader, the Danish Sigfrid, issued an ultimatum. Sigfrid had received 2,400 pounds of precious metal from Charles the Fat, king of the Franks, to decamp from the River Meuse, and the Danish leader informed Odo that he and his fleet would depart Paris as well, for an appropriate sum.

Odo Defies the Viking Force Odo defiantly declined this offer, incensing the Viking leader. Sigfrid responded by pulling out every offensive weapon he had. His Danes attacked the quartered Frankish troops with all manner of missiles, using catapults and arrows and stones. When these proved ineffective, the Vikings turned to fire, sending flaming boats toward the impassable bridges in an attempt to set them on fire. The fire did not take, although it did significant damage to one of the bridges.

Frustrated and thwarted, the Vikings prepared to make siege. As though to mock their ineffective offense, the Frankish men managed to add an entire tower to one of the bridges in a single night, fired by the passion of Joscelin, Bishop of Paris, who fought side-by-side with Count Odo, reportedly engaging the Vikings with bow and axe.

New Tactics in Medieval Warfare In a macabre and inventive effort to cross the watery barrier surrounding the Ile de la Cite, a few weeks into the siege the Vikings began filling in the shallow water with the corpses of people and animals, as well as anything else they could find. However, this gambit also failed to break the siege and place the Ile in Viking hands. Finally, nature interfered on the Northmen's behalf, sending cold, heavy rains in February 886 that overflowed the Seine, which carried away the weakened, burned bridge in its current.

Finally able to pass on, many of the Viking force headed further upriver to maraud and destroy villages at the confluence of the Loire and Seine. The force that remained behind maintained the siege against the Franks.

A King Lets His People Down During this time, the king of the Franks—Charles the Fat, a man focused on his personal agenda—was in Italy. Odo finally managed to smuggle a message to the king, desperate for him to bring reinforcements to break the siege. Charles the Fat did arrive with a substantial force, but rather than crush the remnant of the Viking army that remained, he instead offered Sigfrid a paltry sixty pounds of silver to move on. Sigfrid, surprisingly, agreed to the sum, even though he had obtained forty times that amount to leave the River Meuse. His men were certainly surprised and not happy, and they refused to budge.

Ultimately, Charles the Fat promised the Vikings seven hundred pounds of silver if they would leave, but he wanted them to complete a mission before receiving payment. The Vikings were charged with dealing with some rebellious Burgundians who had been plaguing the king, and when they succeeded, he would pay them their money. They did leave, but ignored their hit-squad orders and instead went north to pillage and destroy the countryside. In spite of the fact that they dropped their part of the bargain, Charles the Fat gave them their money anyway.

The End of the Siege and a New King Meanwhile, disease had overtaken the besieged Frankish force, decimating their ranks and killing Joscelin, their passionate bishop and co-leader. Nevertheless, they had enough manpower to force the Vikings to portage their remaining fleet overland rather than making their way via the river.

The Frankish sense of betrayal at Charles the Fat's failure to break the siege by crushing the Viking forces in battle eventually led to the deposition of the king. Charles the Fat died soon after he was deposed, under mysterious circumstances. The nobles installed Count Odo in Charles' place as king of Neustria, part of West Francia, where he led a successful defense against a Viking attack in 889.

Odo was, however, forced to contend with challenges to his throne, including from the rule of the other part of West Francia, Charles the Simple, ruler of Aquitaine. Charles the Fat's failure to retain his throne and keep the Carolingian empire intact left these kingdoms divided, and the empire that Charlemagne built was never again united. Odo died in 989, at which time Charles the Simple became ruler of both Neustria and Aquitaine.

Maldon, 991

Poetry and War Maldon, in the historical sense, is both a poem and a battle. The poem is a partial manuscript, an epic told from the Anglo-Saxon point of view, and historians believe it was written not long after the

battle. It provides almost literally a blow-by-blow account of the British defense against the Danish Viking raiders at Maldon, where the English army was annihilated but their bravery recorded for history as poetry.

Ethelred the Unready Ethelred the Unready, descendent of Alfred the Great, became king on May 4, 978. He stepped to the throne of a rich, well-organized kingdom thanks to efforts initiated by Alfred, and when his turn to rule came, there were no bitter rivals waiting in the wings to try to assassinate him. For the age, it was a smooth transition to what could have been an easy rule, except for a few disadvantages, such as the fact that no one was quite sure what constituted Ethelred's kingdom. Wessex was a certainty, and most of southern England, but as for the Danelaw in the east and the north of England, whether or not that belonged to the Saxon kingdom was settled on a ruler-by-ruler basis.

Another disadvantage was that Ethelred was barely a teenager when he inherited his throne. The throne itself had become vacant only because of the murder of Ethelred's half brother, Edward, in 978 or 979. Ethelred himself was not responsible, but rumor blamed his mother and loyal members of his retinue. Whether or not the rumors had a kernel of truth is unknown, and Edward himself was apparently not a congenial ruler. In spite of his unpopularity, however, his murder ensured his status as a saint.

Thus, when Ethelred the Unready stepped up to the throne and did nothing about his brother's murder, the cloud of fratricide hung over his rule from the beginning. One chronicler reported that Ethelred shed tears over his brother's death, only to have his mother beat him with candles in her wrath.

Counsel Out of Balance The "unready" part of Ethelred's name does not arise from his unpreparedness for leadership, but rather is an Anglo-Saxon pun. His given name, Ethelred, means "wise counsel." *Un-raed* in Anglo-Saxon translates as "bad counsel" or "no counsel." Thus, the joke was that the man of wise counsel had poor counsel. Yet, in the beginning of his reign, he appeared to suffer from an overdose of counsel, from his mother to bishops to aldermen. There was not enough counsel in the kingdom, however, to tell him what to do when the next wave of Viking attacks hit Britain from over the sea. England had weathered the first wave in the ninth century, with Alfred the Great achieving a separated peace with the invaders, establishing himself as King of England, and leaving the Danelaw to the Danes.

The Vikings Return: The Second Wave In the 980s, the Danes returned. They had drained the silver mines of the Arabs and lost Ireland in the Battle of Tara in 980. Francia was off limits thanks to agreements between the Franks and Vikings that started with Charles the Bald and Rollo, a Viking and progenitor of the dukes of

In this modern reenactment, soldiers from the Norman Army march to fight in the Battle of Hastings.   © *Travelshots.com/Alamy*

Normandy. The Vikings, casting about for some new way to acquire wealth rapidly and in large quantity, turned their eyes back to the shores of Britain.

In the first wave of Viking attacks in the ninth century, Ethelred's ancestor Alfred the Great had gained the upper hand through a combination of wile, charisma, bravery, and luck. At the least, Ethelred lacked the wile and the luck. When the Vikings began raiding along the coastline of southern England in their second wave of attacks, predators looking for a breach in the defense, they realized that England had regrouped and restocked; the treasures of the nation were once again available for the taking, given a large enough force.

Their first big hit, in 991, began on Northey Island, which lay off the southeast coast just a hundred yards from the town of Maldon in Essex. To the shock and terror of the inhabitants of Maldon, a fleet of ninety-three longships, which might have held one hundred men each, landed on Northey Island to await low tide, which would open up the causeway between them and the mainland.

Byrhtnoth, Ealdorman of Essex   The ealdorman of Essex, Byrhtnoth (also given as Birthnot), gathered his forces to defend the causeway. The poem, "The Battle of Maldon," although incomplete, gives the reader the details of what happened next. The Anglo-Saxon men take up battle positions along the banks of the river that fed into the sea at Maldon. The Vikings hail the Anglo-Saxon leader, Byrhtnoth, who is riding his horse among his troops to rally them, and offer their usual retreat in exchange for a large payout. Byrhtnoth haughtily rejects this proposal, and the Vikings respond that they cannot engage in battle with the armies on opposite sides of the river. Oddly, and for reasons not chronicled, Byrhtnoth has his men stand down so that the Vikings can cross the causeway and engage in the battle.

The Wolves of War Prevail   Perhaps Byrhtnoth had not had much experience with these "wolves of war." In response to his gentlemanly gesture, the Vikings elected to completely obliterate the Maldon forces. The poem relates that some of the Anglo-Saxon soldiers fled from the onslaught, including one Godric, who escaped on

Byrhtnoth's horse, leaving the impression that Byrhtnoth himself had decamped. The closing lines of the poem are lost to history, leaving a blank at the close of the battle, but what is known is that the Vikings won in a rout.

The Viking Leaders and Danegeld The Viking captain in this epic battle was Olaf Tryggvason, who had the greater ambition of becoming king of Norway. Also possibly present at the Battle of Maldon was the King of Denmark, Svein Forkbeard. King Ethelred, now confronted with the fact that Vikings had overrun part of his kingdom, turned to bribery to get rid of them. This time-honored and completely temporary solution to the Viking problem was just one example of Ethelred's lack of wise counsel. His huge payment of the so-called *danegeld* to the Danes had the predictable effect of bringing more Vikings to threaten his lands in the hope of a big payout. In all, Ethelred paid six large tributes to the invaders, one of them sixteen thousand pounds of silver to Olaf.

Anglo-Saxons Lose the Throne, Again Ethelred also blundered by calling for the deaths of all Danes in his kingdom, which resulted in the death of Svein Forkbeard's sister. The Vikings now had double the reason to attack, and Svein Forkbeard went for the kingdom in an all-out war that lasted twelve years. Ethelred ended up making a total of 110,000 pounds of payouts in silver, to no avail. After the hapless and unready king fled the country, the Vikings took and held the English throne for several decades. Soon after it fell back into Anglo-Saxon hands, William the Conqueror, Duke of Normandy, showed up to take it from them again.

Ashingdon, October 18, 1016

An Unsteady Peace Ends The separate peace achieved between Alfred the Great and the Danes, which gave Vikings the Danelaw and left Alfred as ruler of a united Britain lasted for about a century. They lived side-by-side, the Danes in their northeastern stronghold and the English everywhere else. There was even some intermarrying between the cultures, but the peace itself was unsteady, and greedy eyes on both sides watched warily for an opening to acquire more land.

After this period of relative calm, problems churned again. Alfred's descendent Ethelred the Unready had ignominiously decamped to the European continent in 1013, unable to bribe newly aggressive Vikings out of his lands or defeat them in battle. He took shelter in Normandy with his brother-in-law, using it as a base for his plans to try to take back his country. Ethelred had lost much of England to Sweyn Haraldson, king of Denmark, and Haraldson's son Canute, who went with his father to raid England when he was only about nineteen years old.

Danish Army Proclaims Canute King While Ethelred sheltered in the pleasant countryside of Normandy, Sweyn died, leaving the Danish throne to his oldest son, Harold.

The Danish army in England, however, loudly proclaimed Canute their leader in Britain. Unsurprisingly, Ethelred still considered himself king of England, and to emphasize his position he returned to his native land in 1014 with a large army that managed to force the Danes into retreat. Canute drew back all the way to Denmark, and the Danes even lost control of the Danelaw for the first time in a century.

Edmund Ironside Canute, now only twenty years old, did not languish in Denmark for long. By fall of 1015, he had returned to England, intent on taking the country back. With dispatch, his forces took control of Wessex and Northumbria, and turned their eyes to London. As they made their plans to attack the town, Ethelred died unexpectedly on April 23, 1016. A worthier man, his son Edmund, stepped up to the throne and took over the fight for England. Edmund, known as Ironside, had more than the Danes to battle, however. He also had to deal with the treachery of the ealdorman of Mercia, Edric, who time and again falsely treated Edmund and the English army, the last time to devastating and lasting effect.

The Treacherous Ealdorman While Ethelred was still alive, Edric had joined forces with Canute to compromise Mercia and place it in Danish hands. Edmund, struggling to put together a decent army, spent this time attempting to breach the defenses of Northumbria, but found his efforts rebuffed when Canute showed up and sent Edmund and his army packing back to London. When Ethelred died, the *witan*, or council of nobles, were supposed to choose the king's successor. The members of the witan in London, and the London citizens themselves, selected Edmund; however, the remainder of the witan met in Southampton and chose Canute as their leader.

Edmund's struggle to maintain a strong and united force against his rival faltered in the face of this split decision. Every battle seemed to scatter his men and leave his defenses in tatters. Canute besieged London, but its citizens held off the Danish forces as Edmund took Wessex back for the English side. Canute then led Edmund all over the countryside, pulling him from battle to battle at Pen in Somersetshire, Sherston in Wiltshire, through another attack on London, and in a handful of subsequent battles. Edmund, in spite of his straggling army, managed to maintain the upper hand in these engagements, and it appeared that the English were making progress, having been able to maintain their hold on London in the face of siege and to take back Wessex.

Treachery at Ashingdon The treacherous Edric reentered the picture as Edmund made the fateful decision on October 18, 1016, to attack the Danes at their base in Essex at a place called Ashingdon (also Ashdon or Assandun). The fighting was fierce, and Edric once again proved himself a traitor by falsely leading a flank of Edmund's forces into retreat in a successful gambit apparently designed to reduce English numbers. The slaughter was horrific, and the *Anglo Saxon Chronicle* reported mournfully that "All the nobility of England was there destroyed."

The Throne in Danish Hands A beaten and badly injured Edmund retreated to Gloucestershire where Canute trailed him. Edmund still wanted to fight, but the weary witan counseled him otherwise, led by the traitorous Edric. Canute and Edmund reached an agreement at Olney, called the "Compact of Olney," that gave Edmund the southern part of the kingdom, which included Wessex, leaving the rest to Canute. Edmund did not live long to enjoy even this minor return for his efforts; he died, possibly from his injuries, on November 30, 1016, leaving Canute in control of all of Britain. The battle of Ashingdon decisively left the kingdom in the hands of the Danes. Canute made a good-faith effort not to crush English culture and even married the widow of the late Ethelred in a gesture of solidarity with his subjects. Danish rule of Britain, however, was transient and ended in 1042 when Edward the Confessor, Ethelred's son, laid claim to the English throne.

Death of a Traitor Unlike some well-known false friends in history—such as Richard Rich, the perjurer and liar whose testimony led Sir Thomas More to his doom and who died peacefully of old age in his bed—Edric met with a less pleasant fate. Canute at first rewarded him for his assistance in defeating the English by restoring to him his earldom. The king, however, must have had second thoughts about this obviously untrustworthy and mercenary fellow, because he eventually had Edric killed for his falseness. In addition to his infamy as a traitor to his king and country, Edric also has been faulted by some historians as being Edmund's murderer, although the accusation remains unproven.

Civitate, June 18, 1053

The Hautevilles, a Warlike Clan The buildup to the Battle of Civitate, a town in southern Italy, begins with the story of five brothers. These brothers were Normans, descendents of Vikings who settled in the duchy of Normandy. The sons of Tancred of Hauteville, acting together the brothers William, Drogo, Humphrey, Robert, and Roger created a principality for themselves and soundly defeated a pope while defending their territory.

Norman Interest in Southern Italy The Normans made first footfall in Italy as mercenaries fighting the Arab incursion into southern parts of the region. Once arrived in the Mediterranean paradise, however, the paid fighting men were quite pleased with the abundant riches of the land around them. In the Norman way, these mercenaries decided to take parts of Italy for their

own, and in 1042, a settlement of former Vikings in the southern Italian area of Apulia—which forms the northern peninsula of Italy's familiar "boot,"—selected one of the Hauteville brothers, William "Iron Arm," to be the Count of Apulia. William's home base was located at Melfi, which lies on the southern slopes of the Apennines, the mountain range that trails along the center of the Italian peninsula.

Robert Guiscard, the Terror of the World Soon after, William's brothers Drogo and Humphrey took his place, and by 1047, Robert, the most fearsome of the Hauteville clan, had made himself known. Robert had a terrible reputation as a crafty and resourceful man; his nickname, Guiscard, means "crafty" and his tombstone immortalized him as "the terror of the world." Before stepping into the forefront in Apulia, he had spent his time pillaging his way through Calabria, the province that makes up the southern peninsula of the Italian "boot." He also engaged in a kind of proto-Mafia racketeering, using threats to obtain money in exchange for offering protection.

Pope Leo IX Loses at Civitate Given Robert's reputation, it comes as no surprise that some people on the European chessboard were not pleased with his growing dominance. Among these was Pope Leo IX, whose primary concerns centered on church reform, but who also was a close ally of Emperor Henry III of France, a ruler unhappy with the unstable conditions in the Italian peninsula.

It was not unusual for churchmen of the day also to be warlike, and in 1053, Leo IX led a coalition army of Swabians (a Germanic tribe), other Italians, and Lombards against the Normans, only to lose in a complete rout at the town of Civitate (also known as Civitella, or the battle of Civitella del Fortore) on June 18. He suffered defeat at the hands of three thousand mounted Norman soldiers, significantly fewer in number than his own forces. Their leaders included Count Humphrey, one of the Hauteville brothers, and Robert, who commanded a fighting wing.

The Pope a Prisoner The pope ended up prisoner of the brothers; whether by his own surrender or turned over by the people of the town is unknown. He was kept captive for nine months in relatively high style and by all accounts with great respect until Humphrey escorted him north to Capua and released him. The pope, however, did not long survive the ignominy of defeat and capture, and he died within a month of his release.

Although those involved did not realize it at the time, the battle of Civitate proved to be the moment the Normans founded their southern empire. It also was the trigger for the formation of what would become known as the kingdom of the Two Sicilies. Given Robert's propensity for racketeering, it is perhaps only to be expected that the kingdoms birthed by his success in battle would eventually in turn produce the mythologized and romanticized Cosa Nostra of later times.

A New Pope, a New Tactic

Humphrey died in 1057, and Robert took his place, stepping over Humphrey's own sons and the traditions of patrimony in his haste to take the helm. Pope Nicholas II, the third pope following Leo IX, decided on a different approach to the Hauteville menace. In analyzing the situation, Pope Nicholas had a choice between what he perceived to be two evils. On the one hand, there were the underhanded and strong-arm tactics of Robert the terror. On the other hand, Sicily was in the hands of the Arabs (infidels to the Pope), and Nicholas desperately wanted Sicily out of the hands of Islam. The Arabs had spent many years attacking southern Italy with relative impunity, unimpeded by the Byzantine rulers who were supposed to be allies of the papal regime and who had oversight of the area. The pope had a strong enemy close by and a weak ally far away. A pragmatic man, he turned to the strong enemy and called him friend.

Sicily in European Hands

His decision turned out well for his religion and his more materialistic goals. In spite of their less-desirable qualities and their contrary behavior, the Hautevilles were staunch and zealous Christians, and the pope selected them as the lesser of two evils and as a way to achieve his goal for the island of Sicily. He promoted Robert the Crafty to Duke of Apulia and Calabria and also appointed him future lord of Sicily. This latter carrot had the desired effect, and although it took them thirty years, Robert and his brother Roger did eventually manage to wrest Sicily out of Arab hands. While he was at it, Robert also conquered the rest of Southern Italy, taking the last stronghold of the Byzantine empire, Bari, in 1071. In his hubris and acquisitiveness, he even turned to the empire itself, hoping to see himself as Robert the Emperor, but he died in 1085 on the island of Cephalonia, and this dream went unfulfilled.

Hastings, October 14, 1066

A Decisive Victory

The Battle of Hastings was a bold, one-shot win for William the Bastard, Duke of Normandy, and a perfect storm of flawed judgments for Harold II, also known as Harold Godwinson, King of England.

Harold knew that William was coming. Indeed, the English king had expected William since the death of Edward the Confessor on January 4, 1066, and Harold's own accession to the throne. The English king had spent the summer of that year watching the waters off of his southern coast, languishing with his army of thousands, anxiously awaiting the arrival of William and his forces. It would be an unusual attack in the annals of European history, a huge assault from across the sea, mounted with the intent to take a kingdom.

The Attack That Came Too Late

Yet as Harold and his men waited and waited, the attack never came. The winds were to blame, persistently from the north and not the warm southerlies the Norman duke needed to launch his invasion. Then, in September 1066, Harold received word of an attack on his country's north flank, launched by his treacherous and cruel brother Tostig in collusion with the king of Norway, Harald III, also known as Hardraade. These two had taken advantage of the northerly winds to sail their fleet to Harold's lands and launch an attack that was stoutly defended by the earls of Mercia and Northumbria. The earls were hard pressed, however, and eventually lost to the Viking onslaught. The signal fires telling the tale of the attack made it to Harold Godwinson in the south only days later, where he had just decided to send his troops home because food and supplies were dwindling and crops were rotting in the fields.

A Northern Distraction

When Harold received word of the assault to the north, he hastily gathered his men together and made tracks for the Viking encampment, covering an astonishing number of miles (almost two hundred) in a handful of days. His progress with his thousands of men—whose numbers grew as he traveled—was so rapid that he caught the Norwegian king and his own brother completely by surprise. The Northmen had even dispersed, on missions for food and to guard the harbored fleet.

In spite of their scattered defense, however, Hardraade managed to pull them together enough to produce an impenetrable wall of shielded fighters against the English king and his much feared housecarls. The tide turned only when Harold's men faked a retreat, leading the Viking phalanx to break ranks in the chase. The weakened wall fell quickly before the renewed attacks from the British troops, and Tostig and Hardraade both died at this melee, known as the Battle of Stamford Bridge.

William Lands in England

Breathless and with his men exhausted and wounded, Harold then received word that William of Normandy had taken advantage of suddenly favorable winds to sail the channel and land at Pevensey in the south. Weary and probably dazed from the seemingly endless series of travails, Harold nevertheless gathered his forces around him and hastened again with almost superhuman rapidity across 250 miles to reach William.

What Harold did not stop to think about and realize at the time was that waiting might have been the better strategy. Tactics of the time often involved more siege than slaughter, often because it was difficult for armies to maintain supplies for troops on the move. William had taken a tremendous chance in bringing his large army to a new land without a plan to besiege. He intended, instead, to risk all on a single battle, hoping not to have to spend too much time burning through his limited supplies before engaging with Harold. Had Harold simply stopped at Stamford Bridge and outwaited the Normans, William's men probably would have suffered significantly from the resulting diminution of his resources.

Harold's First Tactical Error Harold did not, however, wait. Three weeks after the Norwegians had landed in the North, he found himself heading south to face his most bitter rival. The two men had a murky history: William claimed that Harold had sworn fealty to him during a visit to his duchy a couple of years earlier. Certainly, the pope believed William enough to sanction the attack. Harold, whose general behavior suggested him to be a man of honor, apparently did not agree with William's interpretation of events. Some historians suggest that Harold may have made such a promise, but under duress, possibly even under tacit threat to his life. To Norman apologists, however, Harold was a man who had broken an oath and who therefore deserved to lose his kingdom.

Regardless of the defensibility of his stance, William was in England. Harold, possibly hoping to use speed as a surprise tactic after it had worked so well against the Norwegians, made it to battle, near Hastings, in record time with his exhausted troops. His army, all foot soldiers bearing battle axes and other hand weapons, consisted of his commando-like housecarls and armed peasantry. The Norman forces, on the other hand, had mounted cavalry and archers on their side.

Harold lost all hope of surprise when a scout espied his bedraggled retinue encamped at Hastings and reported their presence to William. William, seeing an excellent chance and realizing that Harold had also just done him the favor of removing his other two rivals to the English throne (Hardraade and Tostig), decided immediately to attack.

According to the chronicler William of Malmesbury, the Normans spent the evening before the attack praying, culminating in a campwide participation in communion. The British troops, on the other hand, wrote the chronicler, spent their night in the usual fashion of Anglo-Saxons before a battle: drinking and singing and staying awake until dawn.

The English Withstand the Norman Onslaught Just as their pre-battle rituals were strikingly different, so were their methods in battle. The Battle of Hastings, which took place on October 14, 1066, was surprisingly evenly balanced through much of the day. The English troops formed a line of shields several football fields long and a dozen men deep. Their swinging battle axes felled any mounted cavalryman who came near, while their shields successfully deflected enough of the archers' arrows to maintain the shield wall. Much as the Franks had stymied every Viking effort to destroy their stronghold during the Siege of Paris, the English proved an impenetrable line of Anglo-Saxon strength, every man in the wall of shields

defending his little spot of land, not giving an inch. William tried every weapon in his arsenal, from sword to arrow to javelin, to no avail. In spite of their exhaustion, the English held the line.

The Second Tactical Error of the English Army William then turned to a different tactic, possibly inspired by an event that occurred early in the day. At some point during the fighting, a rumor that William himself had fallen spread through the Norman ranks. Immediately demoralized, the Norman troops began a scattered retreat, which had the effect of breaking up the English ranks as Harold's soldiers began to follow. It was an exact repeat of the very strategy Harold himself had tried with great success against the Viking forces three weeks earlier.

A few hours later, the Norman troops appeared to be again in retreat. Historians disagree about whether this was truly a clever tactic of William's or a cover-up for an actual, ignominious retreat. Regardless, the effect was to break up the English forces again as they straggled away from the shield wall in pursuit of the Norman enemy. With the wall broken, William's men could turn back to the British and the archers could launch arrows that met their now-solitary targets. Still, the English fought valiantly until, with a breach to the rear guard, an archer's arrow felled Harold Godwinson, and William the Bastard became William the Conqueror of England.

William, Conqueror Having met his goal of taking the kingdom in a single decisive battle, William was crowned king on Christmas Day, 1066. He spent the next seven years trying to quell resistance to his rule among the 1,500,000 inhabitants of his new land, but he also built England into a unified kingdom long before France could make that claim. There would not be another cross-Channel invasion for almost one thousand years, in 1944, when Allied forces stormed the beaches of Normandy during World War II.

⊕ Key Elements of Warcraft

Viking Longships

Multipurpose Craft Possibly the only thing that conjures the image of a Viking faster than a helmet with two horns is the characteristic two-prowed longship that made their transcontinental and transoceanic exploits possible. Just about every success the Vikings experienced in battle and exploration during their golden age from the eighth to the eleventh century was attributable to their innovations in boat design. These versatile ships served them well for all of their purposes: war, exploration, and the toting of treasures back home.

River Travel and the Element of Surprise The Vikings took their boats over sea and up rivers. They had the advantage of not having to use overland routes,

A large Viking Longship in the Viking Ship Museum, Oslo, Norway. *Photograph by Susan D. Rock. Reproduced by permission*

which made the previously inaccessible shores of places like England available for plundering. In addition, their ability to move swiftly and quietly along rivers gave them the advantage of surprise in their attacks on unsuspecting villages and towns. Some villages endured Viking raids in the double digits during the three hundred years the Northmen dominated Europe.

Some of the rivers they navigated include the Seine, the Rhine, and the Loire. These legendary waterways turned into highways of slaughter as the Vikings trammeled over the Eurasian continent, from the British Isles to the Near East. The Vikings did not, however, rely on river navigation to make their way deep into the British mainland; instead, they relied on ancient Roman roads, horses, and Anglo-Saxon trackways to penetrate beyond the island nation's shores.

Building a Viking Ship   The first modern peek into the Viking way of ship building came through discoveries of Viking graves and digs uncovering reused ship parts in excavated Viking villages. These sites have helped provide the pieces of the story of how the Vikings made the crafts that enabled them to cast a wide net of invasion and exploration that extended from Constantinople to the coastline of Canada. An understanding of how they designed and built their boats contributes to

an understanding of how they managed to influence trade and interactions among cultures during their centuries of dominance.

Viking ships were built using an approach called the "clinker technique." This technique is a way of placing the planks that form the base of the vessel. In the clinker technique, the planks overlap, rather than being placed flush side by side, as they are in the carvel technique. The boats had a central keel (the large beam around which the ship is built). The ends of the keel of a Viking ship were identical, providing the anchoring point for the identical prows.

With the clinker technique, the planking overlaps, and each layer of planking upwards from the keel is shaped in order to create the outward curve of the ship's sides. On top of these shaped planks, the shipwrights added floor planks, attached either with rope, or in later models, with treenails. Timbers provided the side supports.

A Viking shipmaker focused especially on the hull of the boat, which had to be strong, but light and resilient for its manifold duties. On the starboard side was the steering rudder; a single sail, squared and pendant, hung from the central mast of sailing ships. The ship materials were oak or pine for the hulls, while the sails were made from sheep's wool. Vikings rode in open boats, with no cabins or weather decks to escape threatening weather or the vicissitudes of travel on the open ocean. If water got into the boat (which had to be a frequent occurrence during severe storms), the only way to get it out was by bailing.

Ships for War, Ships for Exploration Viking longships served many purposes, and some were specifically modified either for war or for carrying cargo. Others were multifunctional, prepared to carry troops for battle or bear a heavy load of plundered treasures back to the homeland. One of the standout modifications the Vikings made to their ships was the combination of oar power with sail power. A longship could be propelled equally swiftly by oar or by wind, as necessary. An 1893 test of a well-known archaeological treasure, the longship Gokstad, demonstrated that the boat could maintain an average speed of 9.3 knots, equivalent to the power of the cargo steamers of the late nineteenth century. Strong winds could push along a Viking ship with a sail as fast as seventeen miles an hour.

Unlike a hulking cargo steamer, however, a Viking longship was a thing of elegantly designed craftsmanship. The prows curved fore and aft; some were highly decorated with the archetypal dragon, while others remained unadorned except for gilding. The characteristic long, slender bodies of the crafts reflected the Vikings' expansion of their boats to hold more oarsmen and their decision to make the boats narrower, adding swiftness. On the heels of these modifications came the addition of the sail in the late eighth century, which gave them a combination of oar and wind power that opened up the coastlines and rivers to them.

The long, narrow ships did not draw a lot of water. The Gokstad, built of oak in the mid-ninth century, weighed eighteen tons but drew only three feet. This feature gave the Vikings the ability to navigate shallow waters and take their fleets directly to the shores, as they did in their first major attack on British lands at Lindisfarne in 793. The Gokstad was 76.5 feet long and 17.5 feet wide amidships, but some ships may have been as long as 110 feet.

Ships of these lengths could easily hold at least thirty oarsmen. A warship had holes in the sides into which the oars were fitted, with a place along the rail to hang shields. The boats that landed at Lindisfarne, for example, held one hundred Vikings, both oarsmen and the warriors in battle gear. The low and long personnel carriers were swift when rowed and perfect for transporting troops and were generally used for military ventures, while deeper and shorter boats served commercial purposes, such as hauling cargo, using their square rigging for the sail to get them home. A ship with higher sides might also have been intended for exploration across the open ocean, the oars mounted on the rails. A large-capacity Viking cargo ship could hold as much as sixty tons.

The Vikings and Navigation Riding in a Viking longship was no ferryboat trip. There is little evidence to suggest that the Vikings used any kind of material cover on their boats, even as they took them long distances for raiding, trading, or exploration. And in spite of their well-earned reputation for excellent seamanship, their claim to fame truly lies in their ship engineering. Like other mariners of their time, they navigated using landmarks, such as what they observed along the coastline. Their abilities in this regard were excellent: Leif Erickson, following only descriptions of coastal landmarks left by Bjarni Herjolfsson in 985, was able to retrace Bjarni's path a few years later and identify the three places along the North American coastline that Bjarni had described.

Burial Ships In addition to their multipurpose use in life, longships also served the Vikings in death. Many Viking burial ships have been found, including one associated with a high-ranking woman. This boat may have been her personal vessel, and it accompanied her in death along with an abundance of elaborately decorated belongings.

Battle Axes

Weapons Advantage: None One might think that the Vikings had a major weapons advantage over the people they attacked and whose towns they destroyed. After all, a relatively small Viking contingent could arrive at a major city like Paris and terrorize the inhabitants to the point that the king was compelled to pay off the invaders to make them go away. However, the truth is that Viking weapons were not particularly special, and they were by no means superior to the swords and siege weapons in common use in western Europe. The real edge for the Vikings was their stealthy use of the longship and possibly their utter fearlessness and aggression in battle.

An Era of Close-Quarter Combat Any battle during the Viking Age involved close-quarter combat, and the weapons used on both sides were the standard sword and spear. Most men carried shields. A Viking shield was about three feet across, formed from wood with a trim of metal or iron. In the center of the shield was a cone of raised metal, or "boss," used to deflect blows and protect the hand gripping the shield on the other side. Although the archetypal Viking image includes a metal helmet with two horns, the average infantryman may have worn a simple leather cap.

Swords Swords were at a premium, and swords fashioned from steel were even more precious and rare. A Viking lucky enough to have a sword to wield probably had one made of iron, which blunted easily. Swordplay during the Viking Age was not the en garde, swishy fencing of a swashbuckling Errol Flynn movie, but instead brute-force swinging of the heavy blade, aiming for the vulnerable legs. Legs were a good target because a warrior usually wore only a leather, apron-like protective garment

Lithograph of Leif Eriksson, holding various Viking weapons. *The Library of Congress*

that reached just to the knees. Even though swords were scarce, some examples of Viking swords with intricately traced, silver-inlaid hilts have been discovered in grave fields.

With only the leather apron for protection, Vikings lacked body armor, and the Europeans, used to seeing mail-clad warriors, often described the raiders from the North as "naked." Seeing shiploads of "naked," gigantic warriors disembarking with a war cry from a fleet of stealthy longships on a fine day must have struck many of the Northmen's victims cold with terror. And each raider would have wielded, in addition to his shield and possibly a sword, his battle axe.

Fighting Men and Their Axes The battle axe is associated closely with the Vikings. An axe could be made of iron, lightweight enough to wield with one hand, or crafted with a heavier, broad blade for two-handed swinging. Since swords were not plentiful, the battle axe was the weapon of the Viking infantryman, and they could be highly prized and personal, some of them beautifully decorated. Others were obviously simply basic fighting tools, such as some examples unearthed in a Viking hoard found along the Thames, made of metal blades mounted on sturdy sticks without ornamentation.

Wielding a battle axe effectively required tremendous brute strength and an accurate aim. A weak blow was worthless and left the axeman vulnerable, while a missed blow could throw the offender off balance, leaving him open to a death blow from an opponent.

The Battle Axe in Literature The Icelandic *Saga of Burnt Njal*, written in the thirteenth century, describes the kind of use a Viking could make of an axe in battle. In the story, Skarp-Hedin takes his vengeance on his enemy, Thrain. As Thrain and his retinue pause on a clump of ice in a river, Skarp-Hedin makes for them, skidding across the frozen surface. Skarp-Hedin reaches his enemy just as Thrain is reaching to put on his helmet. Wielding his battle axe as he skates by, Skarp-Hedin cleaves Thrain's head in two and continues sliding past the astonished men accompanying their now-dead leader.

This is not the only Viking story, fact or fiction, to feature axes. King Guthrum, the Viking defeated by the Anglo-Saxon King Alfred at Edington, is described in one tale as a "brute beast in man's shape ... who with sword and axe" felled the men around him. Then there was Brodir, chief of the Manx Vikings in Ireland in the tenth century. A vicious fighter with black hair so long that he tucked it into his belt, this Viking chief brutally slew the elderly Brian Boru, High King of Ireland, by "burying his axe deep into Brian's skull," then calling out, "Now, let man tell man that Brodir felled Brian!"

Axes in the "New World" The Vikings took their axes with them on exploring adventures as well as for marauding. When they landed in what would become Canada in the eleventh century and attempted to install a settlement there, they left the Native Americans—Skraelings to the Vikings—rather unimpressed with their weaponry. One story related that the Skraelings came across a dead Viking with his axe lying beside him. They shattered the axe with a rock and then threw the pieces away, concluding that the axe was worthless because it could not resist stone. Indeed, the axes were not that helpful to the Vikings in what came to be known to them as "Vinland." When they battled the Skraelings, their axes were no better than the handheld weapons and missiles that the Native Americans used, although the "Skraelings" were somewhat impressed with the fact that the Vikings had weapons made of metal.

Regardless of the effectiveness of the Viking battle axe compared to other weapons of the time, the Vikings themselves were effective enough to trigger a few changes in European warfare and defense. Their tactic of sudden, surprise attacks led the European nobility to build the first castles to withstand the onslaught while they gathered their people for battle.

⊕ Impact on World History

The Viking Age ended in the mid-eleventh century. These men from the North had been the prevailing force of change for almost three centuries, warrior-seamen who descended on the weakened or divided kingdoms of the Franks, the British Isles, and the Low Countries (Frisia). They set up communities in Iceland and Greenland and raided all of Europe from Britain down to Constantinople, yet Iceland is their only surviving settlement. In spite of their widespread travels for pillaging and exploration, they and their culture disappeared from many of the places they invaded and even settled. They thieved and they killed for their own gain, but they drove the unification of England and rearranged the Frankish landscape, themselves eventually becoming Scots or French or British, armed with plows instead of battle axes.

During their age, however, the Vikings were the dominant sea power in Europe. They explored the coastlines of the continent, the British Isles, and North Africa, touching shore from Canada to Constantinople. Their influence and their bloody ways came with them to Russia; they affected the Byzantine Empire and left their mark in North America. Viking raiding parties profoundly affected medieval Europe, and trade routes that they established as their presence became more perma-

nent allowed the flow of coins, silver, and goods from the Middle East to Northern Europe.

Their presence in Europe tested European rulers, forging from this crucible some of the best leaders in medieval history, men forced to lead or fail and required to raise the armies they needed to succeed. In some places, such as Normandy and Britain, Vikings took over ruling, but in others, especially early in the age, they plundered and moved on. Their actions, in addition to forcing strong leadership, also were the impetus for fortification and infrastructure projects throughout Europe, from Alfred the Great's efforts in England to those of Count Odo in Paris. Although much of their culture vanished or was assimilated, their laws (Norse law) is found in the earliest legal codes of some modern European nations.

No one really knows why the Vikings decided to head south from their native strongholds of modern-day Sweden, Denmark, and Norway. Many reasons have been suggested, from overpopulation to curiosity to essential acquisitiveness. The Danish Vikings focused their efforts on England, France, and Frisia (today, the Netherlands). The Swedes of that time went to the Baltic and through Russia, establishing what would become known as the "Rus Vikings" and fostering trade relations with the Near East. Norwegians took on the northern British Isles.

Although their reasons for emerging from their homelands to terrorize Europe and explore widely remain mysterious, their reasons for ending their raiding are less cryptic. Things at home began to improve because of stabilized domestic politics. Around this time, the boundaries of the countries we know collectively as "Scandinavia" began to emerge, united but having separate monarchies. Populations ceased to be known as "Viking" and either assimilated into cultures or became their own cultures (e.g., Danish). By 1000, most Vikings had made the conversion to Christianity, giving them a bridge to understanding and better relations with Western European countries and possibly a theological counterbalance to their bloody pursuits guided by their paganism.

In addition to establishing trade routes that lasted through much of the Middle Ages, the Norseman also revolutionized warfare through their use of longships. These boats, with their curved prows and long slender bodies, made their raiding and exploration possible and helped to rewrite the cultural and geographic connections of the medieval world.

After the almost complete assimilation of the Northmen into the cultures they joined, however, historians must search to create a short list of the more tangible legacies these invaders and explorers left behind. Their efforts at colonization of the "New World" failed, leaving behind only artifacts. They assimilated so completely into British and French culture that only a few linguistic reminders exist of their historic dominance—words that end in -*tot* in France, for example, and some of the linguistic peculiarities of Cornwall and Yorkshire. They did, however, spread gold and silver money throughout Europe and left behind, codified into laws, some of their ideas about property ownership and testifying under oath.

Any written record of Viking origin is rare, primarily confined to carved writings (runes) on stones that do not even date from the time of their peak dominance. They or the people who fought them are celebrated in numerous epic poems and tales, and certainly their exploits permeate even some of our modern literature, such as the writings of *Beowulf* scholar, J.R.R. Tolkien.

Their arrival and presence in Western Europe changed the course of history, of warfare, of kingship, and of infrastructure and defense. Alcuin, the famed scholar in Charlemagne's court, believed the Vikings were a scourge sent from God to punish the people for falling away from divine guidance. However, hindsight shows a more complex influence of these raiders from the north. Without them, there would have been no Battle of Hastings, no William the Conqueror, no trading with the Near East, and no castles, which the nobility began to build to defend themselves from these lightning-strike marauders. In other words, without the influence of these persistent and bloodthirsty invaders, there would be no Europe as it is known today.

Introduction to the Crusades (1096–1291)

Between the late eleventh and late thirteenth centuries, the Middle East was subject to waves of invasion known as the Crusades. Thousands of western European Christians came to Palestine, Egypt, and Syria with the idea of placing these areas in Christian hands. The primary motivation was genuine piety; they believed that God willed them to do it. However, other motivations also inspired individuals, ranging from greed or desire for land, to simple adventure.

Pope Urban II made the first call for Crusade. In 1095, Emperor Alexius of the Byzantine Empire requested aid to help regain territory in modern Turkey overrun by the Muslim Seljuk Turks. What he received was unexpected. Rather than recruiting a few hundred knights as Alexius desired, Urban called for a holy war against the Muslims, urging all to take the cross and fight to restore the lands of Jesus to the Christian world. Although not known as a Crusade at the time, the term gained ground, coming from the Latin word *crux*, or cross, the symbol of Christianity. As an enticement to leave their homes and take on the enormous financial burden of the trip, Pope Urban promised salvation to those who marched to Jerusalem or died in the cause. Thousands of people from all walks of life answered the call, sewed red crosses on their clothing, and marched east.

Despite the dangers of the trips, over one hundred thousand Crusaders marched east between 1096 and 1101. During the course of this period, they established four states: Edessa, Antioch, Jerusalem (the largest, eventually stretching from Gaza to Beirut), and the County of Tripoli.

Although the original idea was to restore conquered territory to the Byzantines, the knights secured the territories for themselves, as they mistrusted the Orthodox Byzantine emperors. Secured with castles, they eventually adopted many of the customs of the indigenous population. Although the bulk of the Crusaders, regardless of which Crusade, would return to Europe, those who stayed learned the reality of the situation. In order to survive they made alliances with Muslim rulers and occasionally fought each other.

In 1144, Edessa fell to Zengi of Mosul, triggering another Crusade. The Second Crusade (1147–1149) failed and never even attempted to regain Edessa. Lack of unity—a constant problem for the Crusaders— undermined it from the start. Meanwhile, the foreign presence helped Middle East leaders like Zengi, his son Nur ed-Din, and the leader Saladin unify resistance against the "Franks."

Saladin captured Jerusalem in 1187, and the Third Crusade (1189–1192) sailed to the Holy Land to capture it back. This is the most famous Crusade as Saladin faced Richard the Lionheart, King of England. While Richard triumphed over Saladin on several occasions, he could not capture Jerusalem.

Afterwards, other Crusades took place. Many of them were disorganized and often did more harm than good for those who dwelt in the Crusader states. The term had lost its luster, but even so, the significance and impact of the Crusades remains relevant in the Middle East of the twenty-first century.

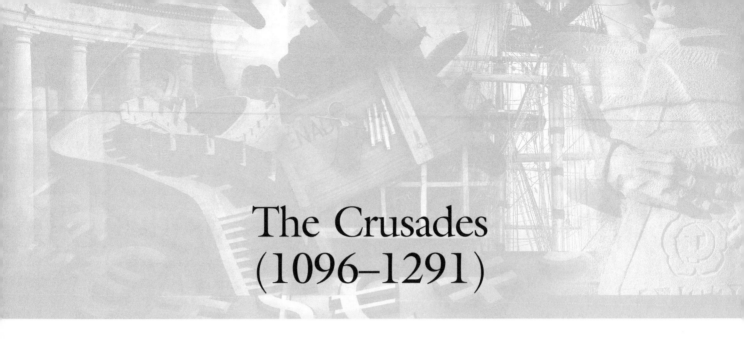

The Crusades
(1096–1291)

🌐 Major Figures

Pope Urban II

Pope Urban II (ca. 1040–1099) was the catalyst for the First Crusade. It is doubtful that the Crusades would have ever been launched without his guidance. Although Pope Urban II became the pope in 1088, he was unable to occupy the Vatican until 1094 due to a conflict with Henry IV (1056–1106), the Holy Roman Emperor. However, once he became the undisputed head of the Church, Urban's actions revived the influence of the Pope and the Church during the Middle Ages.

Before the Crusade The conflict between Henry IV and Urban II was tied to the Investiture Controversy (1057–1122) that dominated relationships between the papacy and the Holy Roman Empire throughout the early Middle Ages. The issue was whether the emperor or the pope could appoint bishops within the empire. Henry IV had submitted to the authority of Pope Gregory VII (1073–1085), Urban's predecessor, but he would not recognize Urban. Instead, he backed and recognized another candidate, Clement II. Urban's successful conclusion of this affair, along with his support of the archbishop of Canterbury against the English King and the excommunication of King Philip of France for repudiating his wife, gave Urban unparalleled prestige.

The Call for Crusade In 1095, Urban II received a message from the Byzantine Emperor, Alexius Comnenus (1081–1118), requesting a few hundred knights to aid in his effort to retake territory from the Turks. All Alexius sought was a mercenary force to augment his army; what Urban recruited for him would be quite beyond his expectations or needs.

The arrival of the Byzantine envoy coincided with reforms that Urban had spent much of his early years creating. With his earlier achievements against Henry IV and Philip of France, Urban had the authority to take a greater step. At the Council of Clermont, where a large number of archbishops, bishops, and priests, as well as many of the nobility of southern France had gathered, Urban made a call for Crusade in 1095. It was an unexpected announcement, but it made a significant impression.

At Clermont and a number of meetings afterwards, Urban greatly exaggerated the plight of the Byzantines as well as the atrocities inflicted upon Christian pilgrims going to Jerusalem, artfully spinning tales of cruelty and mayhem. Whereas Alexius wanted troops for the Byzantine Empire, Urban called for an expedition to liberate Jerusalem.

For Europe, Urban's call to Crusade was the first of its kind. Urban justified his actions through the idea of pilgrimage, which European Christians had undertaken for years. It was a form of penance. If one completed it, his sins would be wiped away. Yet this time, it would be an armed pilgrimage. It was a trip of great hardship and expense, often requiring a knight to spend three times or more of his annual income. To encourage participants, he also granted Papal Indulgences, which gave the person who held one complete remission of their sins, even if they died before reaching Jerusalem.

Others soon took up the preaching of the Crusade. Urban had originally sought only knights and soldiers; even priests and monks had to gain special permission to go with the expedition. However, the message was so powerful that many non-warriors, ranging from peasant farmers to old women, would abandon their fields and homes to accompany the Crusade. Eventually these groups coalesced round the leadership of individuals such as Peter the Hermit and Walter Sansavoir. This became known as the Peasant's Crusade and was crushed in 1097 by the Turks near Nicea.

The main body of Crusaders, consisting mainly of nobles and their armies, set forth from multiple locations in August of 1096. It is not known exactly how many began the journey, but estimates run from sixty thousand people to well over a hundred thousand. To observers in the east, it was not so much an army on the march but a migration.

Legacy and Impact of Urban II Few popes would have the impact and prestige that Urban II gained. His call for Crusade unleashed a force that Urban did not fully comprehend. The vast majority of the participants in the Crusades were religiously motivated. Before the Crusade, not even Urban fully understood how influential the papacy could be. Afterwards, it gave the papacy more power than ever before.

The First Crusade was a success; indeed, it was the only successful Crusade. Urban, however, did not live to enjoy the fruits of his labors. He died before learning that the Crusaders captured Jerusalem.

Raymond of Toulouse

Raymond of Toulouse (1040–1105) was the ruler of thirteen counties in southern France. He was at Clermont when Pope Urban II made the original call for Crusade. One of the principal leaders of the First Crusade, Raymond often clashed with others and although he was the most powerful leader, he lost twice in political battles for leadership positions. He played a crucial role throughout the campaign, but his lasting achievement was the founding of the County of Tripoli in modern Lebanon.

The First Crusade Raymond was fifty-five when he took the cross. Much of his early life was spent extending his power over a large portion of southern France. Indeed, his wealth, army, and even the amount of territory he directly controlled was greater than what Philip, the King of France, controlled. Once he took the cross, Raymond committed himself to the venture completely. He gave his lands to his son, gathered a sizeable force of fifteen to twenty thousand men, and began his march to Constantinople in October, 1096.

Arriving at Constantinople on April 21, 1097, Raymond heard of Emperor Alexius Comnenus (1048–1118) extracting oaths of loyalty. Raymond deftly avoided this by explaining that he had come to serve God and would not serve anyone else. Although Alexius was annoyed, he and Raymond eventually developed a mutual respect and understanding.

After Constantinople, Raymond emerged as one of the major leaders of the Crusade, rivaled only by Bohemund of Taranto. Their rivalry came to the fore at Antioch, when Raymond did not agree with Bohemund's claim to the city. Their disagreement led to Raymond's refusal to participate in the battle against Kerbogha, an Arab leader who came to Antioch's aid. Bohemund's victory further strengthened his claim to the city.

The root of the disagreement was that Bohemund, unlike Raymond, had sworn an oath to Alexius. Therefore, regardless of the circumstances of the siege, the city belonged to Alexius and not Bohemund. Raymond may have also felt slighted, since Bohemund had tricked the other barons into agreeing to circumstances that Bohemund had already arranged. Also, as Raymond was the most powerful in terms of wealth and army size,

he may have naturally felt that it was his right to claim the city.

Their bickering continued well after the city was secured. Raymond eventually accompanied the army to Jerusalem after the rank and file almost mutinied after months of waiting. At Jerusalem, Raymond again lost an opportunity to rule. After capturing Jerusalem, he was offered the title of King of Jerusalem by the barons. Raymond was a devout Christian, but also a political animal. When offered the title, he refused on the grounds that Christ alone reigned in Jerusalem.

Raymond, always concerned about image, felt that if he accepted the title too readily, he would be viewed as an opportunist. Therefore, he refused, believing that the barons would insist that he take the title. However, this did not happen, as they then asked the popular northern French leader, Godfrey of Bouillon, to be King of Jerusalem. Godfrey also refused the title of King, but he accepted the position of ruler under the title of Advocate of the Holy Sepulchre.

After the Crusade Godfrey's acceptance of the top spot in Jerusalem naturally annoyed Raymond. Godfrey also forced Raymond from the Tower of David, where Raymond had quartered. Eventually, Raymond abandoned Jerusalem altogether and returned to the Byzantine Empire, where he encountered new waves of Crusaders in 1100. He then accompanied them on a disastrous journey across Anatolia where Turks destroyed most of the army. However, Raymond used the survivors to create a kingdom for himself in the Holy Land.

THE CRUSADES THROUGH ARAB EYES

In the West, the term *Crusade* has become synonymous with undertaking a good cause. Indeed, the word has lost much of its meaning and has been applied to fighting disease, poverty, and even to the superhero Batman (the "Caped Crusader"). Because of this overuse, many people who applied the term often have little understanding of what it actually means or its historic implications. This was most notable when in 2001, after 9/11, American President George W. Bush said he compared the war on terrorism to a crusade. He meant something that would be the benefit for all; however, in the Islamic and European world, people cringed.

During the Crusading era, the Muslim world looked at the Crusades in a variety of ways. The First Crusade was seen initially as a Byzantine invasion or a barbarian invasion. They had little understanding that it was religiously motivated war. Gradually, this perception changed. Eventually, the action of the Crusades revived the Muslim concept of *jihad* as a holy war, which had more or less become a thing of the past. In other words, one religious war created another.

Pilgrims arriving in the Holy Land during the First Crusade.
© *Bettmann/Corbis*

Raymond set his eyes on the city of Tripoli, a rich trading city in modern Lebanon that also served as the port for Damascus. As it was on the coastal route between Antioch and Edessa in the north and Jerusalem in the south, it severed communications between the two Crusader states. Thus Tripoli had significant strategic importance. Raymond built a fortress on Mount Pilgrim, as he called it, outside of the city to begin the siege in 1103.

The siege was long and Raymond had to fend off sorties from the city as well as relief armies. In all cases he was successful, even when outnumbered. Even though he had not captured the city, Raymond was already known as the Count of Tripoli. However, he did not live to see the fall of the city, as he died in 1105, and the city fell in 1109. Nonetheless, Raymond was truly responsible for the creation of the last Crusader state.

Bohemund of Antioch

Bohemund (1057–1111) was the first ruler of the Crusader state of Antioch. As the eldest son of Robert Guiscard, the Norman conqueror of Sicily and Southern Italy, he received a sizeable inheritance. He and his brother Roger divided it, with Bohemund receiving the eastern portion. Unfortunately, much of that territory had been seized by the Byzantines under Emperor Alex-

ius Comnenus (1048–1118). This left Bohemund with a rather small inheritance based in the Italian city of Taranto.

The First Crusade In hopes of increasing his realm, Bohemund joined the First Crusade in 1096. He proved to be one of the best military leaders on the expedition. Despite his hostility towards the Byzantines for most of his life, Bohemund did swear an oath of allegiance to Emperor Alexius when the Crusaders passed through Constantinople.

Bohemund, however, found reason to break that oath after the capture of Antioch, in which he played a large part not only in capturing the city, but also in defending it against a relief army in 1098. In Bohemund's eyes, when Alexius did not come to Antioch to assist him, the conditions of the oath had been nullified. However, Alexius had been informed by deserters that the Crusaders had been destroyed. This misunderstanding would become a major point of contention between the two.

After the capture of Antioch, Bohemund remained in the city and did not accompany the rest of the Crusaders to Jerusalem. Whereas most of the Crusaders had joined primarily out of religious devotion, Bohemund had accompanied the Crusade for personal gain. At Antioch, he created a principality, although Raymond of Toulouse objected, as he felt that the territory should be returned to the Byzantines. Nonetheless, Bohemund remained at Antioch.

Prince of Antioch Bohemund then continued to expand his territory, seizing territory from nearby Muslim lords. During one of his raids, Bohemund was captured in Anatolia and imprisoned in 1100. In the meantime, his nephew Tancred ruled Antioch as regent. Bohemund was released in 1103 after a ransom was paid.

Upon his release, Bohemund looked at his neighbors and determined that Aleppo was his greatest threat. Bohemund and Baldwin of Bourcq, the ruler of Edessa, made an alliance and marched on Aleppo in 1104. The campaign, however, proved disastrous. Their army was routed at Harran and Baldwin was captured. Bohemund barely escaped.

War with the Byzantine Empire A new and greater threat emerged from the West. When he first passed through Constantinople, Bohemund swore an oath to turn over any conquered lands to Emperor Alexius. Bohemund reneged on that oath with the conquest of Antioch. After Bohemund's defeat at Harran, the emperor now sought to make good on that oath. He seized Cilicia, which Tancred had conquered while Bohemund was imprisoned. Then the Byzantines seized the important port of Lattikieh. It would not be long before Alexius would march on Antioch.

Bohemund did not stay in Antioch. Instead, he returned to Europe. He went to France and Rome to gather support for the war against the Byzantines, and he was successful in recruiting an army of Normans to open a western front against the Byzantines. Meanwhile, he left Tancred to serve as a regent. Bohemund crossed the Adriatic Sea from Italy, landing at Durazzo. Bohemund, however, miscalculated the abilities of the Byzantines. Alexius had restored the Byzantine army and navy to a formidable force, and he defeated Bohemund.

As part of the Treaty of Devol (1108), Bohemund was to remain the ruler of Antioch, but he would rule it as the vassal of Alexius. Thus, Antioch would return to the Byzantine Empire. It would be reduced in territory, as Cilicia and Lattikieh would remain in Byzantine hands. Alexius, however, did allow Bohemund the opportunity to increase his territory by conquering the lands of Aleppo.

Bohemund was humiliated, but he found the loophole in the truce. As long as he did not return to Antioch, it remained independent. Thus Bohemund remained in Italy and left Tancred as the ruler of Antioch.

Bohemund was the most ruthless and ambitious of the leaders of the First Crusade. He died in 1111, far from the principality he created, yet even in defeat he found a means to ensure it remained independent. Meanwhile, his successors would rule Antioch until it fell to the Mamluk Sultanate (1250–1517) in 1275.

Yagi Siyan

Yagi Siyan (d. 1098) was the ruler of Antioch and an official of the empire of the Seljuk Turks. Yagi Siyan was the first Syrian ruler to face the First Crusade when the European knights descended into the Orontes River valley where Antioch is located.

The Siege Begins As an army of over thirty thousand attempted to surround Antioch, Yagi Siyan had to defend the city with a garrison of approximately six thousand men. Throughout the siege, Yagi Siyan attempted to get assistance from his neighbors. This was not an easy task as the nearest and most powerful neighbors, Ridwan of Aleppo and Duqaq of Damascus, were brothers and mortal enemies.

Yagi Siyan feared to form an alliance with Ridwan (who was also his son-in-law) because Yagi Siyan had learned that Ridwan desired to incorporate Antioch into his own realm. Duqaq was preferable, but in order to reach Antioch, the army of Damascus would have to march through the territory of Aleppo.

Upon the approach of the Crusaders, Yagi Siyan expelled the Christians of the city. It was due not to fears of religious solidarity, but rather to the fact that the Seljuks had captured Antioch from the Byzantines in 1087. It was rumored that the Crusaders were in alliance with the Byzantines, so there was too much at risk to allow former Byzantine citizenry to remain in the city. Yagi Siyan, however, did allow their wives and children to remain in the city under his protection.

Betrayal and Death Yagi Siyan's own actions as a ruler ultimately undermined the city. As the siege wore on, prices for food skyrocketed. Those who profited through black market practices were fined. One such person was Firuz, a captain of a one of the towers on the walls. Firuz, annoyed by the fine (and a possibility that Yagi Siyan had seduced his wife), negotiated with Bohemund of Taranto, a Crusader leader, and allowed his men entry to the city.

As the Crusaders stormed the city, the defense of Antioch collapsed. Yagi Siyan attempted to flee, but his horse tripped, causing Yagi Siyan to fall from the saddle. He was killed by the mob.

Godfrey of Bouillon

Godfrey of Bouillon (1061–1100) was one of the major leaders of the First Crusade and was the first ruler of the Kingdom of Jerusalem. Godfrey abandoned his realm in Europe and established a new state in a turbulent region, a polity that lasted almost two hundred years.

Early Life Before ruling Jerusalem, Godfrey was the duke of Lotharinga or Lower Lorraine, with his capital at Bouillon. He had gained his position in 1087. Before the Crusade, Godfrey spent considerable time and effort in consolidating his lands and expanding them. However, when he heard the preaching of the First Crusade, Godfrey was swept up in the enthusiasm for the First Crusade and joined it with his brother, Baldwin I (d. 1118), the first ruler of Edessa and then the second king of Jerusalem.

After taking the cross, he abandoned his efforts to expand his territory and instead began to accumulate wealth to finance his expedition. Godfrey sold many of his lands and also settled other disputes, often to his disadvantage. Although he planned to go on Crusade, he had every intention to return to Lorraine as he never relinquished his title to Lower Lorraine.

At Constantinople Although the march east was long, Godfrey kept his troops in good order and passed into Byzantine territory with little trouble. He and Baldwin arrived at Constantinople in 1096 and received an invitation from Emperor Alexius Comnenus to come to his palace. Godfrey also learned from other Crusader leaders (who had arrived before him) that Alexius expected an oath of allegiance from Godfrey and Baldwin, and that the emperor would most likely not release them until they did so.

Godfrey did not oblige the emperor's request. Emperor Alexius countered by refusing to allow Godfrey's army to cross the Bosporus Straits into Asia until Godfrey met with him. Furthermore, he cut off provisions to Godfrey's army. Alexius eventually reopened the markets after Godfrey's troops pillaged the suburbs and outlying villages. Nonetheless, Godfrey still waited three months for Alexius to allow his troops to cross. Alexius proved to be equally obstinate, and so Godfrey ordered an attack on Constantinople. This attack was quickly quelled as well-disciplined Byzantine troops sorted out of the city. After this, Godfrey realized that attacking the best defended city in the world was probably not in his best interests; he agreed to swear the oath of allegiance on January 20, 1097. Alexius then allowed Godfrey to cross into Asia.

On Crusade Once the Crusader army was united, Godfrey did not emerge as a dominant figure in the Crusade until after the siege of Antioch, as Bohemund of Taranto and Raymond of Toulouse dominated most of the decisions. Nonetheless, he performed well at Dorylaeum and at Antioch.

At Jerusalem in 1099, Godfrey and Raymond shared in the responsibilities of directing the siege. He and Raymond both launched attacks with siege towers. Godfrey's was the first to breach the wall and storm the city.

Raymond was offered the title of King of Jerusalem first, but he refused, believing that it would be pressed upon him. However, because of Godfrey's performance during the siege, the rest of the barons turned to him. Godfrey was generally viewed by the barons, as well as the rank and file, as a great warrior and leader. Consequently, he was chosen by the others as the ruler of Jerusalem. Godfrey refused the title of King and instead used the title of Advocate of the Holy Sepulchre.

This move angered Raymond, who refused to give up the Tower of David, the strongest location in the fortifications of Jerusalem. His refusal to do so almost led to violence between Raymond and Godfrey. However, cooler heads prevailed and reminded them that a Fatimid army was approaching from Egypt.

Advocate of the Holy Sepulchre Godfrey led the Crusaders towards Ascalon, along the coast, where the Fatimid forces were located. The Fatimid forces had assumed that the outnumbered Crusaders would remain behind the walls of Jerusalem. Yet on August 11, 1099, Godfrey's small force of a few hundred knights surprised the sleeping Fatimid army and crushed it.

Afterwards, most of the Crusaders returned home to Europe, having completed their vows of liberating Jerusalem from the Muslims. Godfrey, however, remained. Those who returned to Europe increased his legend and he was idealized as the perfect example of a Christian knight. Godfrey died on July 18, 1100. He created a state that stretched from the Sinai to Beirut and would last—albeit in a much reduced form—until 1291. After his death, his brother Baldwin was summoned from Edessa to serve as his successor.

Zengi

Imad ad-Din Zengi (d. 1146) was the *atabeg* (ruler) of Mosul who conquered Edessa, the first Crusader state. Although much of his focus was on restoring Mosul's authority over Syria, he revived the idea of *jihad* ("holy struggle") among the Muslims in the Holy Land, despite not being very religious himself.

Rise to Power Previously, Zengi had served as a Seljuk governor of Basra. His major achievement was crushing a revolt by Caliph al-Mustarshid Billah against the Seljuks when he came to power. Zengi decisively defeated the Caliph's army in a single battle. As a reward for his efforts, Zengi was appointed the atabeg of Mosul in 1127.

Historically, the atabeg of Mosul had wielded authority over the Syrian possessions of the Seljuk sultans. In reality, the Syrian polities generally ignored the atabeg of Mosul as much as they could. This was vividly demonstrated during the siege of Antioch in 1098 when Kerbogha, the atabeg of Mosul at the time, was defeated by Bohemund as his Syrian allies deserted him. Zengi was determined to make sure that did not happen to him.

Expansion Zengi was able to expand his authority over Aleppo in 1128 partially because of the lack of unity among the Crusader states. When the ruler of Aleppo (Balak) died in 1124, Bohemund II of Antioch did not take advantage of the situation. Instead, he committed himself to continue Antioch's occasional war with Edessa. Zengi went to Aleppo with little opposition and took the reins of power. This allowed Zengi to quickly unite two of the most powerful polities in the region, virtually without any resistance by the Crusaders.

During the Third Crusade, Richard led the crusaders against the great Muslim leader Saladin. © *Michael Nicholson/Corbis*

Fortunately for the Crusaders, Zengi seemed more interested in fighting his fellow Muslims. He spent much time and effort attempting to capture or coerce Damascus into joining his camp. While he could not break the city's defenses, the constant threat began to wear down the defenders. Eventually, Damascus formed an alliance with the Kingdom of Jerusalem to counter Zengi's power in 1139. King Fulk of Jerusalem, who ruled from 1131 to 1143, was only too happy to oblige. Although he would have preferred to own Damascus himself, Fulk appreciated the benefits of forming an alliance with Damascus.

Thwarted by the Jerusalem-Damascus alliance, Zengi focused his attention elsewhere. The majority of his efforts concerned consolidating his power in northern Iraq as Seljuk authority began to crumble in that region. However, he eventually began to turn his attention to the west.

Zengi the Mujahid

Zengi's attention was attracted by two events. In 1143, King Fulk died in a hunting incident, placing his wife Melisende (1131–1152) in charge, as his thirteen-year-old son, Baldwin III (1143–1163), was too young to rule. In addition, Antioch and Edessa continued to clash. For Zengi, this was the moment to strike.

Taking advantage of the fact that the bulk of the army was out of the city (near the border with the Seljuk Turks in Anatolia), Zengi besieged Edessa in November 1144. Despite having few defenders, Zengi could not immediately take the city due to its strong fortifications. However, he maintained pressure on it and dug a series of mines underneath the wall. On December 24, 1144, Zengi collapsed the wall and sacked the city.

After his conquest of Edessa, Zengi's prestige and popularity soared. Titles were bestowed upon him; instead of atabeg, he was called Sultan and Defender of the Faith, and *Mujahid*, or Holy Warrior. The irony of the situation was that Zengi had little time for religion or any member of the clergy. Indeed, his leadership was based more on fear than piety or devotion. His troops marched in close ranks and an orderly formation, as those who fell out of rank and trampled the crops of the villages were crucified. Ultimately, he was killed on September 14, 1146, by a slave who Zengi had chastised earlier for drinking.

Although Zengi died, his actions set several events in motion, as the fall of Edessa initiated the Second Crusade. Zengi's success also revived the spirit and idea of *jihad*. For the Muslims, it now seemed possible to find unity and to drive the Crusaders out of the region. Zengi's son Nur ed-Din (1117–1174) was truly motivated by religion and would carry out this religious and militaristic ideal.

Conrad III

Conrad III (1093–1152) ruled Germany from 1138 to 1152. Although Pope Eugenius III attempted to pre-

vent him from going on Crusade, Conrad led the German knights on the Second Crusade.

Rise to Power

Conrad became the king of Germany in 1138, not long after the investiture conflict—a long-running dispute between secular and religious leaders concerning which group would control the appointment of bishops, among other issues—came to an end. Even with this dispute behind him, Conrad's reign was not without crises. The king of Germany was elected by the leading lords of Germany, but he quickly alienated them by forbidding them to hold more than one duchy. It was a reasonable demand; if a baron held more than one duchy, their power could rival that of the king. Reasonable or not, the rebellion did not end until 1142.

The Second Crusade

When Pope Eugenius III called for a Crusade to regain Edessa in 1145, he had no desire for Conrad to partake in the venture. Eugenius hoped to persuade only the French to go. Because of the threat of the expanding Norman state in Sicily and southern Italy, the pope needed Conrad's military might to shield Rome.

Despite his best efforts to prevent the Crusade from being preached in the German lands, he could not control every individual. One such person was the monk Radulf, who not only preached the Crusade, but also laced it with anti-Semitism. Bernard of Clairvaux (1090—1153), who Eugenius placed in charge of preaching the Crusade, remembered the havoc caused by Crusaders in Germany during the First Crusade. Jewish populations in the cities of the Rhine were massacred during the religious hysteria.

Bernard entered Germany to stop Radulf. However, even after he sent Radulf back to his monastery in France, Bernard could not stop himself from preaching the Crusade in Germany, despite knowing Eugenius' desires. Initially, Conrad III was not interested, but the eloquent Bernard finally persuaded him to take the cross in 1146 on Christmas.

Conrad III and the German knights departed in May 1147 and arrived at Constantinople in September. The Byzantine Emperor, Manuel Comnenus (1143–1180), was displeased to see the Germans. It was a large force with poor discipline; as they marched through Byzantine territory, they clashed with townspeople and troops on several occasions. Although Manuel wanted to keep a civil relationship with Conrad, Manuel also needed to get rid of the Germans, so he had the German army ferried over to Asia.

From Constantinople, Conrad marched into the territory of the Seljuk Turks. He had heard that Louis VII of France was only days behind him, but Conrad pushed on rather than waiting to march in a united force. After deciding that the route of the First Crusade was good luck, he followed it. Like the First Crusade, Conrad encountered the Seljuk Turks at Dorylaeum. Unfortunately, he did not fair as well as the First Crusaders did.

KING OR CRUSADER?

Louis VII had considered an expedition to the Holy Land prior to Eugenius's call. With the success of the First Crusade, the act of going to the Holy Land—particularly to Jerusalem—and serving militarily would erase one's sins. Unsurprisingly, this act of redemption appealed to the monastery-raised ruler. However, Suger and other advisors had successfully dissuaded him from the idea.

His army was surrounded and annihilated, and few made it back to Byzantine territory.

Despite the massive loss, Conrad continued on to Jerusalem, but via ship. At Jerusalem, he joined the forces of Louis VII. The two European kings then called an assembly of the barons of Jerusalem to determine the goal of the Crusade. After much debate, they targeted Damascus, an ally of Jerusalem. The siege was a disaster and the army retreated after only four days on July 28, 1148.

After the Crusade In September, Conrad left Palestine in disgust. He sailed back to Constantinople where he stayed as a guest of Emperor Manuel. There the two found a mutual interest in their animosity of the Normans of Sicily. Their plans never materialized, as a rebellion prevented Conrad from taking action against the Normans.

The king of Germany typically became the Holy Roman Emperor. Because of rivalries within the Empire, however, Conrad had never built the support to claim the crown of the emperor. Even so, in 1152 Pope Eugenius III urged him to come to Rome for the title. Conrad III died on February 15, 1152, before he could make the journey.

King Louis VII

Born in 1120, King Louis VII ruled France from the age of seventeen to his death in 1180. Although he defended France from the aggressions of King Henry II of England (who was not only his enemy but the husband of Louis VII's former wife, Eleanor of Aquitaine), Louis VII is best known as one of the leaders of the Second Crusade.

Rise to Power Louis came to power after his father, Louis VI, died in 1137. Louis VI had ensured that his son inherited a strong and much enlarged state by arranging a marriage with Eleanor of Aquitaine, who came from a large and rich region in southern France. Intensely religious, Louis VII spent the previous ten years before he became king cloistered in a monastery.

Thus Louis came to power with little political experience, with a fiery and much worldlier queen at his side. Despite his inexperience, the kingdom of France was kept in good order, with Louis VII earning a particular reputation for the maintenance of justice. However, as both king and queen came to the throne as teenagers, their political and administrative experience was lacking. Therefore they relied heavily on Suger, the Abbot of St. Denis, who acted as the king's key advisor.

The Second Crusade In 1145, a year after the fall of Edessa to the Arab leader Zengi, Pope Eugenius III (1143–1153) made a call for Crusade. To preach the Crusade, Eugenius called upon Bernard of Clairvaux, (later Saint Bernard). Bernard was perhaps the most eloquent and persuasive speaker in all of Europe, although it is probable that Louis would have answered the call even without Bernard's formidable skills.

Louis received his cross from Bernard himself and left France on June 11, 1147. Near Constantinople he met the German king Conrad III (1093–1153), whose armies had been crushed by the Seljuk Turks. Now united, the two leaders took ships to Antioch. However a sizeable portion of the army had to march overland where they were subjected to constant attacks by the Turks. Most were killed.

Raymond, Antioch's ruler and uncle to Eleanor, attempted to persuade Louis to attack Aleppo. Louis objected. In his view, before any campaign could be undertaken, he and the Crusaders must fulfill their pilgrimage vow by going to Jerusalem first. This idea was probably due to his piety rather than the rumors of an affair between Raymond and Eleanor. Nonetheless, the rumors played a role. Eleanor threatened to have the marriage annulled if Louis did not adhere to Raymond's plan. Louis ignored her and marched the army to Jerusalem. Eleanor made good on her promise in 1152.

On June 24, 1148, Louis and Conrad met with the nobles and clergy of the Kingdom of Jerusalem to discuss the direction of the Crusade. Bolstered by reinforcements, it was determined that they would attack Damascus. The knights of Jerusalem were divided, as Damascus was their ally. Louis, however, could not understand how they could make treaties with infidels.

The brief and disastrous siege of Damascus began on July 24, 1148. After four days, dissension among the Crusaders from Europe and those from Jerusalem led the army to retreat. Despite the defeat, Louis remained in the Holy Land until Easter in 1149, trying to benefit the kingdom in some way, mainly by repairing fortresses.

After the Crusade Reconciliation with Eleanor proved impossible once they returned home. In 1152, the marriage was ended based on consanguinity, or being too closely related. To make matters worse, she married Henry II (1154–1189) of England. Henry and Louis VII engaged in war, not over Eleanor, but over territory. Nonetheless, one cannot doubt that it was in the back of their minds.

Engravings of the tombs of King Henry II of England and Eleanor of Aquitaine at Fontebrault.   © *Bettmann/Corbis*

Now, however, Louis was a wiser ruler even without Suger. He waged a cautious war and gained allies as well as the support of the Church in the conflict. His religious devotion may have cost him the Crusade and his wife, but it assisted him in keeping his kingdom. Louis died as an invalid, possibly due to a stroke that left him partially paralyzed.

Eleanor of Aquitaine

Eleanor of Aquitaine (1122–1204) was not a warrior queen. Although she went on the Second Crusade, she did not fight. Nevertheless, as Queen of France and the wife of King Louis VII (1120–1180), and then as Queen of England and the wife of Henry II (1154–1189), she had a profound impact on the era of the Crusades.

Early Life and Queen of France   In twelfth-century France, although many regions nominally recognized the Capetian monarchy based in Paris, many vassals were independent and more powerful than the king. The duchy of Aquitaine in southern France was the richest and most powerful of these regions. Eleanor inherited Aquitaine at the age of fifteen when her father, William X, died in 1137 without a male heir.

Louis VI, seeing this as an opportunity to bring more of France under his control, married her to his son Louis VII. The two were married in 1137 and ascended their thrones not long after their wedding

with the death of Louis VI in the same year. The two teenaged regents were almost polar opposites. Having spent ten years in a monastery, Louis VII was serious and very pious. Eleanor, on the other hand, was beautiful, intelligent, and cultured. Louis could not help but be impressed with her and may have even truly loved her, despite the arranged marriage.

The Second Crusade   Shortly after the fall of Edessa in 1144, Pope Eugenius II (1145–1153) called for a new Crusade to restore it to Christian hands. Louis responded eagerly and Eleanor took the cross as well, not willing to be left behind, and her presence altered the nature of the venture. While wives had accompanied their husbands before, Eleanor also took numerous ladies-in-waiting with her. They traveled east in 1147.

The French army arrived in Antioch, which was ruled by Eleanor's uncle, Raymond of Poitiers, in 1148. Raymond was handsome, charismatic, and of a much more similar nature to Eleanor than her pious husband. As a result of their kinship and kindred spirits, Eleanor spent considerable time with him; rumors soon spread that their relationship was more than familial. It remains unknown if there was any substance to the rumors, but the fact remains that tension rose between Raymond and Louis.

Raymond sought to direct the Crusade against Nur ed-Din by either recapturing Edessa, or, as Raymond hoped, Aleppo (Nur ed-Din's capital). Louis was reluctant to do so, as he felt the Crusade should continue to march to Jerusalem first. Raymond, seeing the issue as life or death for his state, persuaded Eleanor of his cause. Eleanor then went to Louis and stated that if Louis did not assent to Raymond's plan, she would annul their marriage based on consanguinity, or being too closely related, and remove Aquitaine from Capetian control.

Beyond the rumors and this threat (which may have convinced Louis that Eleanor was having an affair with her uncle), Louis VII and Eleanor's marriage was strained. Despite almost eleven years of marriage, they still had only one child, a daughter. On top of this, their temperaments were too different. Eleanor was passionate; Louis was pious. In any case, Louis placed Eleanor under guard and led his army to Jerusalem.

After reaching Jerusalem, the Second Crusade attempted to take Damascus. This gambit ended in failure, and the marriage of Eleanor and Louis ended as well. They left the Holy Land in 1149 on separate ships. Although reconciliation was attempted, the papacy granted the annulment in 1152, as Louis and Eleanor were fourth cousins.

Queen of England   Now independent of Louis, Eleanor ruled Aquitaine. To protect her realm from possible attacks from France, she secured the realm in 1152 by marrying Henry Plantagenet, the heir to the throne of England. Henry II came to the throne in 1154, making their kingdom extremely powerful. Unfortunately for

MASSACRE AT EDESSA

Joscelin II, the ruler of Edessa before Zengi captured the city, regained Edessa in 1146. Nur ed-Din quickly marched to Edessa before Joscelin could establish himself there. Joscelin fled, leaving Edessa to its fate. To ensure that it could never fall into the hands of the Crusaders again, Nur ed-Din massacred the Christian population.

Eleanor, she could not control him as she did Louis, although she was twelve years his senior. Furthermore, Eleanor was the one who became jealous in the new marriage, as Henry openly had an affair. As a result, Eleanor established her own court at Poitiers.

Unlike with Louis, as Henry's wife, Eleanor gave birth to eight children—three daughters and five sons. Angry at her husband's affair, Eleanor encouraged her sons to revolt against the king, and to the chagrin of their father these dutiful sons obeyed their mother. Although the revolt (1173–1174) was quelled, it was significant. For instigating the revolt, Eleanor was imprisoned for sixteen years in Touraine. She was only released with the ascension of her son, Richard I, to the throne.

Richard, of course, became known as Richard the Lionheart and commanded the Third Crusade. Eleanor served as Richard's regent and defended the realm against the machinations of Prince John. It was a difficult task, as John was aided by the king of France, Philip II Augustus. While in the Holy Land, Philip was the ally of Richard. However, he returned before Richard and took the opportunity to attack Richard's territory in the south of France. After Richard died in 1199, Eleanor also influenced John's reign. She secured his ascension to the throne and served as his advisor until her death in 1204.

Legacy In addition to perhaps inadvertently causing the Second Crusade to be diverted from Edessa and Aleppo, Eleanor gave birth to perhaps the most famous of Crusaders, Richard the Lionheart. Although she did not participate in the Third Crusade, her capacity as regent played a major role in organizing the funding and support of it in Richard's territory.

Furthermore, Eleanor was a patron of the arts. Her court at Poitiers was a center for the popular poets and musicians known as troubadours and a place where the idea of courtly love developed. Both the troubadour songs and the idea of courtly love held Middle Eastern influences due to Eleanor's stay in the Middle East during the Second Crusade.

Nur ed-Din

Nur ed-Din (1117–1174) created a sizeable empire in Syria and Egypt that brought a unified resistance to the Crusader kingdoms. He was a devout Muslim and was instrumental in bringing the concept of *jihad*, or a holy struggle against the Crusades. Before this period, that concept had diminished in use.

Political Actions Before the Second Crusade Nur ed-Din became the ruler of Aleppo in 1146 with the death of his father Zengi. After his father died, Nur ed-Din took his father's ring and assumed control of Aleppo. His brother, Sayf al-Din, ruled Mosul.

Unlike his father, Nur ed-Din was very religious. He believed that religious purity was essential to driving the Crusaders out of the region. Like his father, he believed that there must be union among the Muslim leaders in order to achieve this goal. However, unlike his father, Nur ed-Din did not attempt to conquer other Muslim polities; instead, he sought to bring them under his control through more subtle measures.

Nur ed-Din had writers send letters to the leaders and local notables of the Muslim states. All of the letters extolled Nur ed-Din's virtues. Indeed, it was expedient for the region's rulers to support Nur ed-Din on campaigns against the Crusaders, for if they did not, the religious leaders in their respective cities would curse them in public.

The Second Crusade and Damascus Nur ed-Din's biggest threat was the Second Crusade, especially as Raymond of Antioch (1136–1149) tried to persuade them to either regain Edessa or attack Aleppo. However, the divided leadership of the Crusade instead focused on Damascus, a city that was not only allied to the Kingdom of Jerusalem, but also in opposition to union with Nur ed-Din. The Franks who lived in the Holy Land tried to persuade the Second Crusaders to choose some other target, but to no avail.

This gave Nur ed-Din an opportunity to insert himself into Damascene politics. He led his army to relieve the besieged city in 1148. For Muin al-Din Unar, the ruler of Damascus, this was the worst possible scenario. If the Crusaders won, he lost his city. If Nur ed-Din defeated them, then it would be impossible to deny Nur ed-Din's supremacy. To counter both situations, Unar sent letters to the Crusaders to persuade them to abandon the siege. The plan succeeded and Nur ed-Din failed to capture Damascus.

Nonetheless, Nur ed-Din did not give up on Damascus. When Unar died in 1149, Nur ed-Din marched on Damascus. However, he did not lay waste to the countryside. Indeed, he took great pains to not burden the people; he avoided fighting with the army of Damascus; and he retreated when Jerusalem's army approached. His efforts paid off, as Nur ed-Din appeared as the model Muslim ruler while the leaders of Damascus were in league with the enemy. A coup occurred in 1154, and citizenry proclaimed Nur ed-Din as the ruler.

An illness left Nur ed-Din incapacitated for almost two years. It was not until 1162 that he could risk advancing his efforts against the Kingdom of Jerusalem. However, rather than invading Jerusalem, his efforts were focused in Egypt.

Land of the Ancient Pharaohs Both Nur ed-Din and King Almaric (1163–1174) of Jerusalem desired to rule Egypt. As the Fatimid Caliphate—a Shi'a Muslim state—waned, it sought support. Eventually the Fatimids decided that Amalric, despite having made several raids into Egypt, was a lesser threat. It would be possible to make an alliance with King Amalric, but Nur ed-Din, an ardent Sunni, viewed the Shi'a as heretics.

A number of clashes occurred, but in 1171, Nur ed-Din's top general, a Kurd named Shirkuh, took over Egypt. One of Shirkuh's lieutenants was his unassuming and rather unimpressive nephew, Saladin. Saladin was made governor after Shirkuh died two months later.

With the capture of Egypt, Nur ed-Din had the Crusaders states surrounded and the resources to annihilate them. However, events did not go well. Although he and Saladin attacked the Kingdom of Jerusalem, tension began to arise. Saladin was not always obedient and began acting increasingly independent. It was evident that conflict was coming, but Nur ed-Din died from illness in 1174 before fighting occurred. Nonetheless, Nur ed-Din had resurrected the idea of *jihad* and demonstrated the importance of unity in fighting the Crusaders.

Saladin

Saladin (1138–1193) was the name that the Crusaders gave Salah al-Din Yusuf, the ruler of the Ayyubid Empire. Saladin united this region—which stretched from Mosul in Iraq to Egypt and included all of Syria—after the death of Nur ed-Din. After stabilizing his realm, Saladin made a concentrated push against the Crusaders, crushing them at Hattin and then capturing Jerusalem. Although he pushed the Crusaders to a string of castles on the coast, Saladin's efforts were thwarted by the English king Richard the Lionheart. Throughout his career, Saladin was the embodiment of chivalry.

Early Life and Egypt Saladin was a Kurd from the town of Tikrit, located in modern day Iraq. In his youth he was an unassuming man. He entered the service of Nur ed-Din in 1152 due to family connections. (His uncle, Shirkuh, was a leading general of Nur ed-Din.) The uncle took him to Egypt in 1164 almost as an afterthought, but the Crusaders drove them out of Cairo shortly thereafter. Five years later, in 1169, Shirkuh and Saladin had greater success.

The uncle/nephew celebration was brief as Shirkuh died two months after their victory. After Shirkuh died, Nur ed-Din appointed Saladin as his governor in Egypt, primarily because Saladin was deemed the least ambitious and threatening. Once in power, he carried out Nur

Saladin commanded Muslim forces against Christians in the Third Crusade. © *Bettmann/UPI/Corbis*

ed-Din's orders, but he also began to show an independent streak as well as military and administrative talent.

While he served as Nur ed-Din's governor, he was also the vizier of the Fatimid Caliphate. In this capacity he improved the economy and also returned Sunni Muslim practices to the Shi'a Muslim state. In 1171 he overthrew the Fatimid Caliphate and ruled Egypt directly. A rebellion among the African infantry led to Saladin crushing their regiments.

A United Front, A Common Foe Saladin's growing independence created tension with Nur ed-Din, but the death of Nur ed-Din in 1174 prevented a collision between the two. Saladin then promptly moved against Nur ed-Din's successor and captured Damascus. His next move was to conquer Aleppo and Mosul in an effort to unite the Muslim world against the Crusaders.

The unification of these cities gave Saladin the resources needed to conduct a long term campaign against the Crusaders. Just as the Crusaders carried out a Holy War to conquer Jerusalem, Saladin planned to use that emotional appeal and message to drive the Crusaders out of Jerusalem. Thus he began a *jihad* against the Kingdom of Jerusalem.

In 1187, he invaded the Kingdom of Jerusalem with nearly thirty thousand troops. King Guy de Lusignan, the ruler of Jerusalem, met Saladin at Hattin (near Lake Tiberias in modern day Israel) with more than twenty thousand men. It was the largest army the Kingdom of Jerusalem ever assembled, as the Crusaders stripped most of their garrisons for this battle. All the added troop strength counted for naught, however, for Saladin lured them into a waterless plain and carefully sapped their strength through thirst and well-timed attacks.

After defeating and capturing King Guy, Saladin immediately moved on to other various cities, capturing them one by one. With the army destroyed at Hattin, most cities surrendered without a fight. Saladin then laid siege to an isolated Jerusalem. The garrison fought bravely, but ultimately surrendered after negotiating a peace treaty. As part of the conditions of the surrender, the population had to pay a ransom to leave the city and have passage to the coast. Saldin's generosity and kindness even in war was immediately noted by the defeated, as he personally paid the ransom of many to keep mothers and children together.

The Third Wave of Franks Saladin continued to pressure the Crusader states. In 1189, the Third Crusade arrived and defeated Saladin's forces at Acre. Despite Saladin's brilliance, he met his equal in Richard the Lionheart. Although Richard defeated Saladin at Acre, Arsuf, and Jaffa, he could not take Jerusalem. At the same time, Saladin could not risk further battle with Richard, as the defeats had eroded his reputation of invincibility. Thus in 1192, they agreed to a truce.

Saladin did not live long afterwards. He died in Damascus in 1193. Although he united the Muslim states, his heirs and relatives quickly fragmented it into a loosely bound confederacy rather than the unified empire it once was.

Saladin's legend only grew after his death. Although he was a Kurd, in the modern era Saladin became the symbol of independence and Arab and Muslim greatness in the face of Western dominance.

Richard the Lionheart

Richard I (1157–1199) is one of the best known leaders of the Crusading era. His prowess in battle earned him the sobriquet of "Coeur de Lion" or the Lionheart. Richard left his kingdom of England and spent several years campaigning and often besting Saladin during the Third Crusade. Despite his successes, he made many enemies among his erstwhile allies, and this ultimately led to his abandonment of the Crusade and his imprisonment in Austria.

Before the Crusade Although Richard was the king of England, he only visited England twice in his life. Richard spent the majority of his time in his territories in France. As the son of Eleanor of Aquitaine and Henry

II, Richard ascended the throne of England in 1189, when his father Henry II died.

As Jerusalem had fallen to Saladin in 1187, a new call for Crusade had swept through Europe. Even before ascending the throne, Richard planned to participate in the campaign. Now as king, he would have even more influence.

On Crusade While going to the Holy Land, a few of his ships—including one of his treasure ships and one carrying his sister, Joan, and fiancée Berengeria—wrecked on the island of Cyprus. Isaac Comnenus, the ruler, did not treat them well. As a consequence, Richard stormed the island in May 1191 and took it. Thereafter, it served as an important base of operations for the Crusades.

Once in the Holy Land, Richard made an immediate impact. His troops and fleet turned the tide and gave the Crusaders the city of Acre in June 1191. It was here that he overshadowed King Philip Augustus of France, who returned to France after securing Acre.

After winning at Acre, Richard marched south towards Jaffa, the port of Jerusalem. Along the way, Saladin's forces shadowed them and harassed his army. Richard kept his troops in good order until he found a desirable location at Arsuf. Saladin and Richard met in battle on September 7, 1191. Richard kept his knights behind a line of crossbowmen and spearmen. These kept Saladin's horse archers from getting too close. Richard planned to unleash his knights at the appropriate moment. When the time came, the charge split the Muslim army and inflicted heavy casualties. For the Muslims, it was an important reminder of how devastating a well-conducted charge could be.

Before marching to Jaffa, Richard massacred nearly three thousand Muslim prisoners in front of Saladin's army. They were to be ransomed, but as Saladin was late in making the first installment, Richard had them all killed.

After Arsuf, Saladin would not challenge Richard in open combat again. Richard continued on to Jaffa and captured it. He then turned on to Jerusalem. The march was slow as Richard insisted on repairing fortifications along the route from Jaffa to Jerusalem. He realized that without secure communication and supply routes, the Crusaders would not be able to hold Jerusalem even if they conquered it. Facing such difficult logistics, Richard ultimately abandoned the march in January, 1192. The army withdrew to Acre.

While there, he received news that Saladin was attacking Jaffa. While his army began the march, Richard and a small force set sail. Richard landed with a crossbow in one hand and a battle axe in the other. He quickly cleared the beach of attackers, due to his bravado as much as the actual attack. He then secured Jaffa, again defeating Saladin.

Richard and Saladin eventually agreed to a truce. Saladin could not continue the war against Richard due to his losses. Meanwhile Richard realized that he needed to return to Europe. Furthermore, he realized that the conquest of Jerusalem was not to be. Even with this setback, Richard had restored much of the Kingdom of Jerusalem to the Crusaders and also won the right for Christian pilgrims to visit Jerusalem. Richard set sail from the Holy Land on October 9, 1192.

Imprisonment Unfortunately, due to a shipwreck, Richard passed through the territory of Duke Leopold V, the ruler of Austria, and was taken prisoner. At the siege of Acre, Richard had offended him by tearing down his banner and replacing it with his own.

A ransom was paid, although Prince John (of Robin Hood fame), Richard's brother and regent, did his best to prevent Richard's release. He and King Philip II Augustus of France conspired to keep Richard from returning. Nonetheless, Richard returned to his lands in France, which Philip had invaded. The two former allies were at war. During the course of this conflict, Richard was wounded by a crossbow bolt; he died from complications from the wound in 1199.

Frederick Barbarossa

In 1152, Frederick Barbarossa (1122–1190) succeeded Conrad III as king of Germany, and he became the Holy Roman Emperor in 1155. After the fall of Jerusalem in 1187, Frederick took the cross and led a large army into the East, only to die while on Crusade.

Rise to Power Frederick's election to the German throne in 1152 was an effort to promote peace in Germany. As Frederick was related to both of the warring factions (the Hohenstaufens and the Welfs), it was hoped that the country would unite under his leadership.

Frederick formed an alliance with Pope Eugenius III against rival claimants to the papacy. As a result, Frederick was crowned the Holy Roman Emperor in 1155. Eventually, he abandoned the alliance with the pope in order to deal with politics within the Empire. Over the next few years, Frederick increased his personal domains as well as the authority of the Holy Roman Emperor. His most difficult efforts were trying to quell rebellions in Italy beginning in 1158. Papal intrigues fueled further tensions in northern Italy.

Frederick was constantly on campaign, dealing with Italian cities or rebellious German princes who resisted his efforts to centralize his authority within the Holy Roman Empire. Frederick's focus shifted in 1188 when he received news of the fall of Jerusalem to Saladin. Frederick took the cross at the age of sixty-six years old. The Third Crusade would not be his first Crusade, as he had also participated in the disastrous Second Crusade.

The Third Crusade Frederick led a large army—perhaps the largest German army ever assembled up to that time—in May 1189. They marched down the Danube to Constantinople. Having learned from Conrad's mistakes, Frederick sent envoys ahead of the army to secure markets and a peaceful route. Even so, Byzantine Emperor Isaac II did not trust the Germans. Isaac was also on peaceful terms with Saladin (both viewed the Seljuks as enemies), and he did not welcome the massive German army.

Unfortunately for Isaac, Frederick learned of the treaty; tensions between Isaac and Frederick arose almost immediately. The markets and supplies that had been promised to the envoys did not materialize. In addition to the fact that Frederick was leading the large army of Europe in his territory, Isaac also resented Frederick's use of the title of Emperor. In Isaac's eyes, the only Emperor was that of the Byzantine Empire and not some half-barbarous polity in Central Europe.

Negotiations between the two deteriorated quickly. Frederick, however, did not hesitate to use force. He preferred peaceful relations, but his ultimate goal was to reach Jerusalem. Thus he conquered Adrianople, a provincial capital, an action which gained Isaac' attention. Aware that an assault on Constantinople was not out of the question, Isaac offered to transport the Germans to Asia.

Frederick led his forces into Seljuk territory on April 25, 1190. Originally he had secured a treaty with the Turks in order to pass through their lands peacefully. However, the temptation of looting Frederick's camps and wagons was too great for the Turks, who launched an attack on May 18, 1190. The Germans crushed them in a resounding victory.

Some harassing attacks followed, but a major attack did not occur on the Germans. The march across Anatolia went well, and it appeared that unlike the Second Crusade, the German army on the Third Crusade would arrive in the Holy Land intact. However, as they entered Cilicia and crossed the river Saleph on June 10, 1190, Frederick suffered a heart attack.

Afterwards, most of the army dissolved and returned to Europe. A sizeable contingent continued under the command of the Austrian ruler, Duke Frederick. This unit, however, was paltry compared to the force that Frederick had led. Although the Third Crusade enjoyed some success, one can only speculate what it could have achieved had Frederick's complete army arrived under his leadership.

Philip Augustus

Philip Augustus (1165–1223), also known as Philip II, was one of the most powerful medieval kings of France. Despite increasing the size of the royal domains and regaining territory from England, he is best known for his role in the Third Crusade. Even then, however, he often is portrayed in a negative light compared to the swashbuckling Richard the Lionheart.

Frederick I, Barbarossa. *Archive Photos, Inc./Getty Images*

Rise to Power Philip Augustus inherited the throne when Louis VII died in 1180. The new king was quite unlike his pious father, who focused so much on justice. Cynical, shrewd, and calculating, Philip would not hesitate to manipulate a situation to his benefit. His mind was his greatest asset, as throughout his life Philip had a frail constitution and was often sick.

In addition to inheriting the throne, Philip also inherited his father's wars with England. Although Henry II was the ruler of England, by virtue of marrying Eleanor of Aquitaine and by right of conquest, that kingdom also included much of western and southern France. Indeed, Henry ruled more of France than Philip did.

Philip defended his kingdom as best he could. At the same time, he wisely manipulated Henry's sons, Richard and John. In this manner, Philip gained important allies against Henry. He also became the feudal lord of Henry's English territory in France. Thus Henry was not only the King of England, but also a vassal of Philip by 1189.

The fall of Jerusalem in 1187 momentarily ended this conflict. As the call for the Third Crusade made its way through Europe, Philip reluctantly took the cross. His concerns had little to do with the Holy Land and more to do with stabilizing his realm.

The Third Crusade Richard, now King of England, and Philip agreed to join the endeavor together and to split whatever booty they accumulated. They left on July 4, 1190, and traveled to Sicily. There Richard sacked the city of Messina over a slight to his sister. Philip did not take part, but he insisted on his share of the plunder due to their agreement. His real agenda was that Richard had taken another woman as his wife, despite being engaged to Philip's sister, Alice.

Philip left Sicily on March 30, 1191, ahead of Richard who still awaited his own ships. Philip arrived at Acre where Guy de Lusignan and Conrad of Montferrat had laid siege to the city. Both claimed the crown of Jerusalem. Philip supported Conrad's claim to the throne, as did most of the barons of the much reduced Kingdom of Jerusalem.

Even with the siege weapons that Philip had brought, the Crusaders had little success in taking the city. Added to this frustration was the annoyance that Richard was late and most of the army anticipated victory with his arrival. In addition, Philip was chronically sick while at Acre. Although Richard's arrival on June 7 did lead to the capture of Acre, it took over a month to capture the city.

Afterwards, Philip decided to return to France despite the pleas not only from his own army but from the leaders of other forces, including Richard. Philip, however, had had enough of the Holy Land. Overshadowed by Richard and suffering from illnesses that he could only attribute to Palestine, he simply wished to return home. In addition, his wife had died in 1190 and Prince Louis (the future Louis IX) had barely survived a severe illness. He was needed at home.

When the Lion's Away, Philip Makes a Play Once he was back in France, Philip took advantage of Richard's absence. He and John, the younger brother of Richard, began to attack Richard's holdings in France, successfully conquering Normandy. Philip and Richard's rivalry continued until Richard was killed in 1199. Then John, as the new king of England, became the enemy of Philip. John, however, was not the equal of his brother (or Philip) on the battlefield or in politics. Philip simply used feudal law to acquire the French territories of John north of the Loire River.

The conflict with England ended in 1214 at the battle of Bouvines. John tried to reconquer his territories while aligning himself with Otto IV of Germany. Philip sent one army to southwestern France to deal with John; John fled rather than risk battle. Meanwhile, Philip engaged Otto IV at Bouvines and crushed the combined Anglo-German army on July 27, 1214.

With this victory, the war was over. Philip Augustus had secured peace for France against foreign aggression until his death in 1223.

Louis IX

Louis IX (1214–1270) came to the throne of France in 1226 while still a minor. His mother, Blanche of Castile, served as his regent during this period, and also later when he served on the Crusades. Louis IX was largely responsible for maintaining the Crusades during the thirteenth century. Although both Crusades that he led were failures, he later became a saint for his devotion to the church.

Early Life It is not surprising that Louis led two crusading expeditions; he was devout and believed that true Christians should not tolerate nonbelievers of any sort. Indeed, in 1240 he held a trial for the *Talmud*, the book of Jewish law, accusing it of heresy. Not surprisingly, the *Talmud* was found guilty and all Talmudic works that the government acquired were burned.

By all accounts (including his detractor's), the pious Louis was a man of integrity and a just ruler. Although Louis was descended from Crusaders as the grandson of Louis VII, and had considered going on Crusade for several years, he had not. His mother, Blanche, successfully discouraged it until 1244. While stricken with illness, Louis took the cross; however, his mother had the vow commuted, as the oath was made while Louis was delirious. Nonetheless, Louis persisted in fulfilling that vow.

The Seventh Crusade In 1248, the king led what is known as the Seventh Crusade. Although a few contingents arrived from other European countries, it was largely a French venture. The Crusaders wintered at Cyprus and then sailed to Egypt. Initially, the invasion was tremendously successful, capturing Damietta on June 4, 1249. However, at Mansurah, his brother (Robert of Artois) led a disastrous attack on the city. This turned the tide of battle.

As Louis IX withdrew from the battle, his armies were harassed. The enemy cut off their escape route, and to make matters worse, disease became rampant in his camp. Louis did not escape this either and was stricken with dysentery. The Muslim forces forced the French to surrender, and Louis was released on a ransom of four hundred thousand bezants. To his credit, he did not desert his forces, but generated funds to ransom the rest of his army from captivity.

Although the Seventh Crusade ended in disaster, Louis did not return to France. Instead, he remained in the Middle East and spent considerable time repairing fortresses. He returned to France in 1254, but funded a regiment of one hundred knights to supplement the army of the Kingdom of Jerusalem. Even after he returned to France, King Louis IX sent significant funds to assist the kingdom.

During this period, Louis IX also established contact with the Mongols. He hoped to develop an alliance with them against the Muslims as he had received news that several of the Mongol leaders were Christians. While on Cyprus, he sent emissaries to Baiju, the Mongol commander stationed in the Middle East. This ended in disaster as Louis had sent sumptuous gifts which were interpreted by the Mongols as tribute. Thus in their eyes, Louis IX had submitted to their authority.

Louis also had other contacts with the Mongols through his envoy, William of Rubruck, who met with Mongke Khan in Mongolia. Even after the Mongol Empire broke apart, some contact continued between the Mongols and Louis. However, an alliance never developed from this.

The Final Crusade of Louis IX After spending several years tending to the affairs of his kingdom, Louis IX planned another Crusade. News of this alarmed the Mamluk Sultanate, which now dominated Egypt and Syria as a result of Louis' invasion in 1250. However, Louis IX instead invaded Tunis. He thought, wrongly, that capturing Tunis would deprive Egypt of revenue. However, it is also clear that Tunis was just a stepping stone to the Holy Land.

Despite his best intentions, the Crusade ended at Tunis. They landed on July 18, 1270, and seized a fortress by the ancient city of Carthage. While waiting for reinforcements, disease broke out in Louis' camp. No one was exempt from the disease, and Louis died on August 25, 1270. With his death, the campaign collapsed.

In 1297, the papacy canonized Louis IX as Saint Louis for his devoted works to the Church, despite the fact that he failed in both efforts for which he is most remembered.

⊕ Major Battles

Dorylaeum, June 1097

This was the first significant field battle between Crusader and Muslim armies. After the members of the First Crusade (1095–1099) captured Nicea from the Seljuk Turks of Rum, they pressed on for the Holy Land. The route they traveled required them to pass through the valley of Dorylaeum. There the Seljuk sultan, Kilij Arslan, awaited them.

Crusaders defeating Muslim forces of Sultan Kilij Arsian at Dorylaeum, 1097. © *North Wind Picture Archives/Alamy*

Not Like the Previous Pilgrims Prior to the arrival of the nobles such as Bohemund of Taranto, Godfrey of Bouillon, and Raymond of Toulouse, Kilij Arslan's army had encountered Europeans. These were the first Crusaders who had passed into Anatolia, led by Peter the Hermit in October 21, 1096. These had been mainly peasants and only a handful of knights. In contrast, the new army that entered Anatolia was primarily a military force of knights and professional men at arms. Furthermore, it was much larger than the ten to fifteen thousand led by Peter the Hermit, and these troops had already bloodied the forces of Kilij Arslan (1092–1107) at Nicea. There, the Seljuk sultan did not take them too seriously and found, much to his chagrin, that they were indeed a most formidable force.

After Nicea fell, the Crusaders continued east. Their progress in 1097 alarmed Kilij Arslan, forcing him to form an alliance with his rivals, the Danishmend Turks. The Turks, primarily being light horse-archers, felt confident that in open battle, they would defeat the Crusaders.

The Battle Begins Meanwhile, the Crusaders marched in two sections. The first section, under Bohemund of Taranto, camped in a field not far from Dorylaeum (near present day Eskisehir, Turkey). At sunrise the following day (June 29, 1097), the Seljuk forces charged from the hills. Under a barrage of arrows, the European knights charged. The Turks, wheeling on their horses, avoided the charge and maintained the attack.

The Crusaders were forced back to their camp. Under the direction of Bohemund, the knights dismounted and formed a protective barrier with the noncombatants in the middle where springs of water existed. Bohemund also sent a courier to the second section.

The Turks, however, maintained a steady hail of arrows upon the Crusaders. Surrounded, the Crusaders faced destruction or slavery. Despite the constant barrage, they held against the onslaught.

The Second Section Turns the Tide Fortunately, the main body of the Crusaders arrived under the command of Raymond of Toulouse. This second force surprised the Turks. As the Crusader armies merged, they began to counterattack; the Turks struggled to withstand them. Their initial surprise turned to panic as the papal legate, Bishop Adhemar of Le Puy, successfully executed an outflanking maneuver.

Although the Turks wore armor and could deliver charges, their primary attack was with their powerful composite bows, which had a greater range than the bows of the Europeans. Furthermore, they were a very mobile force, able to lure the Crusaders into a charge and then avoid contact. When the Crusader knights charged and made contact, few could resist them. The Turks quickly realized this and avoided them. However, the successful attacks by Raymond and Adhemar crushed the Turks and threw the army of Kilij Arslan into disorder. The Turks were routed and the camp of Kilij Arslan fell to the Crusaders.

The victory served the Crusaders well. They learned early that warfare in the east was much different from that of Western Europe. Although mounted archers continued to be troublesome, the Crusaders on the First Crusade mastered tactics and formations that allowed them to counter the continuous harassment that could occur.

After Dorylaeum, the Crusaders easily dispersed other Seljuk forces they encountered in Anatolia, and were able to continue to the Holy Land with minimum trouble. Until they reached Antioch, their greatest enemy would be the harsh environment and starvation.

Siege of Antioch, 1097–1098

Antioch was the first major city the Crusaders captured outside of Anatolia. The city carried importance not only as a former possession of the Byzantine Empire but also for its importance in Christianity. Located in the fertile Orontes River valley, it was protected by natural defenses (such as the river and its location atop high ridges) as well as a citadel and a high wall with four hundred towers. The Battle of Antioch occurred in two stages. The first part consisted of the Crusaders siege of Antioch, while the second consisted of their defense of the city.

First Stage Before Bohemund of Taranto and Raymond of Toulouse laid siege to Antioch on October 20, 1097, Yagi Siyan (ruler of Antioch) had expelled all of the Christians from the city for fear of treason. Nonetheless, Bohemund hoped to win the city through subterfuge and keep it for himself. Raymond, however, generally opposed the idea.

Although the Crusaders attempted to isolate the city and built fortresses—such as Malregard—around the city, they could not completely surround it. The city continued to receive supplies from the countryside for months. At the same time that they conducted the siege, the Crusaders repeatedly fended off sorties from the garrisons, made foraging raids, and fought relief armies.

Before a large relief army arrived, Bohemund had successfully negotiated with a renegade Armenian within the city named Firuz. He was the captain of one of the towers and had a grievance against Yagi Siyan.

Since it was well known that the relief army led by Kerbogha of Mosul was approaching, Bohemund led the army east, as if to meet him. Then, at night on June 3, 1098, sixty knights climbed a ladder to Firuz's tower. They promptly seized two other towers and opened the gates to the returning Crusader army. The city quickly fell, although the citadel remained in the hands of the Turkic garrison. Yagi Siyan, however, perished while fleeing the city.

Second Stage Despite their victory, the approach of Kerbogha loomed over their heads. On June 4, 1098, Kerbogha's army entered the vicinity of Antioch. Kerbogha had brought the armies of Damascus and Homs in addition to his own, so his army outnumbered the Crusader forces.

As the citadel was still in the hands of the original garrison, Kerbogha hoped to use it as an entrance to the city. However, while the Crusaders had destroyed their old fortifications that they used during the siege, they erected new ones to isolate the citadel from the rest of the city.

As Kerbogha's army arrived, the Crusaders in Antioch faced a dire situation. Not only were they now trapped between the garrison and the relief army, but having captured a city that had endured eight months of siege, their food stores were dangerously low. Bohemund had to bar and lock the gates to prevent a general exodus.

Some of the Crusaders, such as Stephen of Blois, did flee. He eventually met a relief army led by the Byzantine Emperor Alexius. Stephen, who had viewed the size of the enemy army, convinced the emperor that by the time they reached Antioch, the Crusaders would have been destroyed. This unintentional abandonment ended all loyalty the Crusaders had toward the Byzantines.

NON-RELIGIOUS GAINS

At Dorylaeum, a massive amount of loot fell into the Crusaders' hands. They received very little at Nicea, as the city surrendered to the Byzantines who accompanied the Crusaders. This prevented the Franks from plundering the city. At Dorylaeum, however, their morale—and financial situation—improved with the plunder from Kilij-Arlsan's camp.

After failed negotiations, the Crusaders marshaled their army before Antioch on June 28, 1098. Inspired by the Holy Lance, the knights advanced through a hail of arrows from the Turkic horse archers. When the archery fire failed to stop the knights, panic seized the Muslim army. Kerbogha attempted to turn a flank, but Bohemund countered it with his reserves. Kerbogha's forces, many of whom were there against their will, began to desert. The Crusaders pressed home their advantage and completely routed the Muslims. With Kerbogha's defeat, the garrison quickly surrendered. Bohemund claimed the city as his own.

The capture of the city, however, had important repercussions for the history of the Crusades. The First Crusade's victory at Antioch established a Latin state in the Middle East, and Bohemund became the first ruler of the Principality of Antioch.

Siege of Jerusalem, 1099

Its religious importance unparalleled, Jerusalem had always been the goal of the First Crusade. Even before the Crusades, many Christian pilgrims from Europe believed that if they traveled to the city, their sins would be cleansed. In fact, alleged mistreatment towards the pilgrims was one of the reasons that the Crusades began. That had been a brief aberration when the Seljuk Turks conquered Palestine. Once the Shi'a Muslim Fatimid Caliphate (909–1171) regained control of Jerusalem, the persecution had ended.

This, however, did not matter to the Crusaders, as the differences in Islam were unknown to them. Furthermore, in their eyes, it was God's will that Jerusalem should be in Christian hands.

The Franks Arrive On June 7, 1099, the members of the First Crusade encamped before the walls of Jerusalem. After years of hardship, they had reached their goal, although to enter the city they faced considerable difficulties. The city was defended by strong walls and a moat on the northern side of the city. Furthermore, the Fatimids had poisoned local wells to deprive the Crusaders of their use, and virtually all materials useful for

PIERRE L'HERMITE
1096

LOUIS VI DIT LE GROS
de 1108 à 1137

Imp. Lemercier, Paris

PRISE DE JÉRUSALEM.

This print depicts the conquering and looting of Jerusalem during the First Crusade. © Leonard de Selva/Corbis

construction had been destroyed or removed. This meant the Crusaders had to send foraging parties often a day's outside the city.

Over the years, the Crusader army had declined. Much of this was due to death, but many had remained in Antioch with Bohemund as well as in Edessa with Tancred. With only fifteen thousand men, the Crusaders could not completely encircle the city. Fortunately for them, even though the Fatimid garrison was numerous and well armed, it could not man the entire wall. Not willing to risk a battle with the Crusaders, they waited behind their walls in hope of the arrival of a relief army from Egypt.

The First Attempt Led by Godfrey of Bouillon and Raymond of Tolouse, the Crusaders began their attack on June 13, 1099, assaulting the walls with siege ladders. They gained access on the outer walls, but because they lacked sufficient ladders and siege engines to support the attack, they were forced to withdraw.

To remedy the situation (as well as to procure water), the Crusaders endured skirmishes while securing lumber from as far away as Lebanon in order to build siege engines. Luck also came on their side as six ships from Europe, filled with lumber, sailed into the port of Jaffa.

Despite this break, morale declined as news of the approach of a Fatimid army circulated in their camp. Nonetheless, the Crusaders' resilience paid off, and soon they had two siege towers and allegedly forty catapults.

The City Is Gained With the relief army approaching rapidly, Raymond and Godfrey realized that time was short. Nonetheless, prior to attacking, the entire army fasted and made a procession up Mount of Olives, where they held mass on July 8. The garrison of Jerusalem was shocked and baffled by these pious actions prior to attack.

The Crusaders launched their attack on July 13, 1099. Raymond led the assault on one tower against the southern wall and Godfrey attacked another tower on the northeastern wall. It was not until July 15, 1099, that they successfully seized a portion of a wall. With this breach, the Crusaders stormed the city. Iftikhar al-Dawla realized he'd lost Jerusalem and surrendered to Raymond. However, this did not save the city.

Filled with religious zeal and bloodlust, the Crusaders rampaged through the city, massacring all they encountered. Muslims, even those who took refuge in mosques, were cut down regardless of age or gender. The Jewish population also was given no quarter. While the reports of the massacre are often exaggerated to the point where the blood flowed up to the knees of a horse, it nevertheless was an enormous orgy of destruction.

Despite petty jealousies throughout the leadership of the Crusade, the capture of Jerusalem culminated in the establishment of the Kingdom of Jerusalem, which lasted as a Latin presence in the Holy Land for almost two hundred years.

Harran, May 1104

Although it is one of the most important battles of the Crusades, this battle's significance is often overshadowed by later events. The Crusader defeat at Harran undermined the security of Edessa and Antioch for years due to the capture of many leaders and the destruction of a sizeable army.

Crusader Territorial Gains In late 1103 and early 1104, the states of Antioch and Edessa aggressively expanded their domains. Bohemund of Antioch captured territory from Aleppo. Meanwhile, the expansion of Edessa and Antioch eastward cut off Syria from Mosul. This made the ruler of Mosul, Jokermish, nervous, as he was at least the nominal overlord of the region. The town of Harran was also in a precarious situation due to raids by the Crusaders. It would only be a matter of time before it would be forced to submit to Edessa if the raids continued.

Jokermish gathered an army together from Mosul and other cities and marched towards Edessa in May 1104. Baldwin II of Edessa, who ruled that polity from 1100 to 1118, informed Bohemund of their approach. They decided to intercept the Muslim army.

Baldwin left Edessa with a small garrison and set out with his knights and a sizeable force of Armenian infantry. Near Harran, Joscelin de Courtenay (who would later rule Edessa from 1119 to 1131) joined him. Joscelin was Baldwin's most important vassal. Bohemund also came with his army. With the combined forces of Edessa and Antioch, the army numbered three thousand knights and almost ten thousand infantry—virtually all of the soldiers in their kingdoms excluding the garrisons.

A Clash of Egos, then Swords Although the army of Mosul was still some distance away, the Crusaders did

---

A TRUE(?) RELIC TO RAISE HOPES

The Crusaders' morale, however, was improved by the discovery of the Holy Lance of Antioch. This spear was, according to legend, the lance that had pierced the side of Jesus. Many people, including the Papal Legate, Bishop Adhemar of Le Puy, doubted that this relic was real. While its authenticty was questionable, its power to rasie morale was undeniable. In light of the ongoing crisis, this led most doubters to remain silent.

---

not attempt to storm Harran. It is thought that they hoped that it would surrender peacefully and they would not have to destroy its fortifications. Indeed, their hopes appeared to come true as the city negotiated.

However, as happened so often among the Crusaders, egos intervened. Baldwin and Bohemund quarreled over whose banner would be raised first, signaling who claimed the city and would be awarded the greatest share of plunder. This delay while bickering would cost them, as it gave the army from Mosul time to arrive before the Crusaders invested the city. Naturally, with the arrival of help, the citizenry of Harran ended their negotiations and waited to see who won.

The battle took place near the Balikh river, very close to the ancient battleground of Carrhae. Knowing that Jokermish was approaching, the Crusaders planned their strategy carefully. Baldwin's army would engage the enemy, while Bohemund's Antiochene forces would stay hidden in the nearby hills to deliver the killing blow.

It was a good plan, but the Muslims had a similar idea. A sizeable force of cavalry advanced and engaged Baldwin's army. After some fighting, they turned and fled. The Edessans, believing they had routed the Muslims, pursued, leaving the Antiochenes behind. Their pursuit took them across the Balikh River where they rode into an ambush. The feigned flight of the Muslims successfully lured the Crusaders to the rest of the Muslim army, who had also hidden in the hills to deliver a killing blow.

The majority of the Edessan force was annihilated. Bohemund and the Antioch troops did catch up and engage some of the Muslims, but seeing the destruction of Baldwin's army and the flight of those who could, he also retreated. However, as the Crusaders attempted to cross the river, bands of Turkic horse archers shot them. The retreat continued to their camp before the walls of Harran. The garrison, seeing the plight of the Crusaders, then sallied forth and attacked. However, in the confusion and due to the lateness of the day, they also killed many of the Muslim army.

The Aftermath Bohemund's army escaped with heavy losses. Bohemund himself had to hide to avoid capture. Meanwhile, the Edessan army simply was no more. Realizing the vulnerability of Antioch and Edessa, Bohemund rallied his remaining troops to defend them both. He sent his talented cousin Tancred to defend Edessa.

Jokermish did not advance on either city immediately, and his army disintegrated. Much like Kerbogha at Antioch, his arrogance alienated the other leaders. Indeed, his troops even attacked Soqman of Mardin's camp in order to secure Baldwin, who had been captured. (Often both sides took opposing leaders prisoner, as they fetched a handsome ransom.) Soqman eventually returned to Mardin while Jokermish pressed on to Edessa. However, the delay gave Tancred time to organize the city's defenses, and a sortie in the middle of the night routed Jokermish.

Harran was an important defeat, for the loss of manpower would keep Antioch and Edessa weak for decades. It also exposed the vulnerabilities of the Crusaders. Bohemund's reputation suffered, as his martial prowess had previously been feared by all. Aleppo was able to regain recently lost territory from Antioch with little opposition.

In addition, there was a vacuum of leadership as both Joscelin and Baldwin were captured. Tancred was reluctant to pay the ransom, as he enjoyed ruling Edessa. This would lead to later troubles after Baldwin secured his release in 1108.

Edessa, 1144

Edessa was the first state established by the Crusaders in the Middle East in 1098. It had long been an economic center in the region, and its inhabitants welcomed the Crusaders as a counter to the growing Turkish presence in the region. Despite these advantages, Edessa was also the first state to fall in 1144.

Problems Start at the Top Prior to its fall, Edessa suffered from a series of poor rulers. They were often at odds with the Principality of Antioch (another Crusader state to the south), and the state was constantly threatened by neighboring Muslim states. The only true stability it ever had was when John II Komnenos, the Byzantine Emperor, forced Joscelin II (the Count of Edessa) to submit to him. This deterred attacks by the Turks, but that protection disappeared with the death of John in 1143.

Although Zengi had not been willing to risk war with the Byzantines, he was more than happy to engage the state of Edessa. Zengi chose his time wisely. Joscelin II was away from Edessa when he attacked. He had gone to defend his borders and had the bulk of his troops near Turbessel.

With Joscelin engaged elsewhere, Zengi began his siege of the city in November 1144. Joscelin did not have sufficient troops to launch an attack on Zengi, so he requested troops from Raymond of Antioch. However, the two were rivals and had cooperated in previous years only due to Byzantine influence.

Crusader Spurns Crusader Despite the dire need, Raymond preferred to see Joscelin stripped of his city than to aid him against Zengi. Joscelin also sent an appeal to the Kingdom of Jerusalem; a relief force was sent, but it was much farther away than Antioch.

The relief army from Jerusalem did not arrive in time. With most of the Crusaders with Joscelin, the city's garrison consisted primarily of Syrian and Armenian Christians. These were town militia, not professional soldiers, and they had neither the skill nor the ability to hold off a determined army indefinitely.

After a four week siege, the city fell. On December 24, 1144, Zengi's troops opened a breach in the wall. Muslim sappers had spent weeks digging tunnels towards the wall. Once they reached it, they set fire to its supports, causing that section of the wall to collapse. Zengi's army stormed the city. The Franks—as the Muslims referred to the Crusaders—were massacred, but Eastern Christians were spared (along with their churches). Zengi then went on to conquer most of the county. All the while, Joscelin held at Turbessel.

The City is Taken Again and Again After the murder of Zengi in 1146, Joscelin quickly seized the city, but he did not hold it for long. Nur ed-Din, Zengi'son approached it, and Joscelin fled. Nur ed-Din massacred all of the Christian population to ensure that the Crusaders could never seize the city through treachery, and thus ended the County of Edessa. Although its fall triggered the Second Crusade, the Crusaders never made another attempt to regain Edessa.

Siege of Ascalon, 1153

The Siege of Ascalon took place from January 1153 until August of the same year. King Baldwin III (1143–1163) employed all of the Kingdom of Jerusalem's resources into conquering the port city. Since the Crusaders first arrived, Ascalon had been used by the Fatimid Caliphate as a launching point for raids into the Kingdom. Until it was captured, Jerusalem would never be truly secured from a Fatimid attack.

A Lingering Thorn in the Frankish Side Over the years, raiding had been nullified as the Crusaders had erected a series of castles around Ascalon. Nonetheless, the heavily fortified city continued to be a nuisance as the Fatimid fleet could disrupt shipping and still attack ships bearing pilgrims. Even with the fortifications, it remained possible that the Muslims could invade the Kingdom of Jerusalem from Ascalon. Thus, Baldwin was determined to capture the city and secure Palestine from any Fatimid attacks.

The siege began on January 25, 1153. Carrying the relic of the True Cross with them, the Crusaders were confident of victory. Nonetheless, the siege went on for months. Although the Crusaders could blockade it, they could not penetrate the walls. A constant stream of pilgrims from the West added to their forces, but the Fatimid navy kept the city supplied as a fleet of seventy ships intimidated the small Crusader fleet of twenty galleys. Yet for some reason, the Egyptian fleet did not remain at the siege and returned to Egypt after unloading their cargo.

Meanwhile, the Crusaders bombarded the city with their siege engines. The most intimidating device was a massive siege tower that was taller than the city walls. From this structure, the Crusaders launched stones and flaming material into the streets of the city. This tower almost led to the capture of the city in an unexpected way.

Because of its threat, a commando attack was made by the garrison of Ascalon to destroy it. They successfully set it on fire. However, the wind shifted and the tower and flames crashed against the city wall. The inferno caused the masonry of that section of the wall to crack and disintegrate, and a breach opened. What happened next is a perfect illustration of the general lack of unity of command among the Crusaders.

The Ever-Bickering Leaders
Although Baldwin was the commander of the army, most units were commanded by their own lords with their own agendas. The army functioned by forming a consensus, often after much debate. The military order known as the Templars commanded the section of the breach. They stormed the opening. As the elite force of the Crusaders, they easily overcame any opposition. However, they had also decided to keep the glory (and plunder) for themselves. Therefore, they also posted men to keep other Crusaders from entering the breach. Seeing how few men actually entered the city, the garrison rallied, annihilated the Templars, and then repaired the wall.

Thus, the siege continued. After the Templars debacle, the Crusaders almost abandoned the whole venture. However, the King was persuaded them to continue the siege, so the bombardment of the city continued. Without sustained support from Egypt, the city could not continue. Thus, on August 19, 1153, the garrison surrendered. As part of the negotiations, the citizenry were guaranteed safe passage. The greater part of the population left the city under the protection of Baldwin III, Ascalon became the property of the Kingdom of Jerusalem.

Beginning of the End
Despite the victory, Ascalon came with a price. It was the last great conquest by the kings of Jerusalem. Also, while the kings focused on Ascalon, Nur ed-Din took advantage of the situation and secured Damascus. This meant the Crusaders lost an ally while Nur ed-Din's power increased.

Perhaps most importantly, with Ascalon in their possession, the road to Egypt was now open for the Jerusalem Franks. Known since time immemorial for its wealth, Egypt became a temptation for the rulers of Jerusalem, and it often distracted them from other concerns.

Hattin, 1187
The battle of Hattin (or more correctly, Hittin) was a turning point in the history of the Crusades. Not only did Saladin annihilate the army of the Kingdom of Jerusalem, but he also conquered most of the kingdom, leaving only a scant handful of cities in Crusader hands.

Saladin Isolates the Franks
Since his rise to power, Saladin had focused most of his efforts not on the Crusaders but on uniting Egypt, Syria, and much of modern northern Iraq. This formed a crescent around the Crusader states. Saladin did want to drive the Crusaders from Palestine, but he was patient and waited for the right moment.

That moment arrived in 1187. Reynald de Chatillon, the ruler of Transjordan (consisting of the Castles of Kerak and Montreal [or Shawbak]), broke the peace and pillaged a Muslim caravan.

Saladin had endured previous raids by Reynald; however, under the leadership of the leper king, Baldwin IV (1174–1185), a détente had been achieved. The current king, Guy de Lusignan (1186–1190), did not command the same respect from Saladin. Therefore Saladin mobilized his army, drawing units from throughout his empire. As he crossed the Jordan River from Syria into Palestine with thirty thousand men, the Crusaders mobilized.

While Saladin's army marched on the city of Tiberias, in the district of Galilee, King Guy marched with an army of almost twenty thousand men. It included over one thousand knights, sizeable contingents from the military orders of the Templars and Hospitallers (the elite troops of the Crusaders), and thousands of infantry. In order to mobilize such a force to meet Saladin's army, Guy swept up almost all available troops in the Kingdom of Jerusalem.

The Franks Argue (Again)
As usual, the Crusaders were not in agreement on what course of action to take. Count Raymond of Tripoli, who also was the ruler of Tiberias, argued to wait Saladin out as they had in previous years. If they did so, his feudal army would eventually dissolve. If they marched near Tiberias and kept a defensive position, it would prevent Saladin from taking the city. Others argued that it was a cowardly move and that they must attack immediately to save Tiberias. Guy, convinced by this rhetoric, led the army forward.

On July 3, 1187, the army marched from Jerusalem as quickly as they could. The army had not heeded Raymond's advice to stay near water. Their approach to Tiberias took them across a waterless plain between two hills known as the Horns of Hattin, only a few miles from water. On this plain they camped, for they did not wish to advance too close to Saladin after their long march.

Saladin, however, was well aware of the Crusaders' approach. His troops surrounded their camp to prevent them from reaching water. As the bulk of Saladin's army consisted of horse archers, they held the advantage of mobility and could harass the Crusaders constantly with arrows. (Indeed, Saladin had camel-loads of arrows waiting to supply any who ran out of them.)

A Bad Situation Gets Worse The Crusaders, under constant harassing fire and already suffering from the summer heat and thirst, were then subjected to billowing smoke as Saladin set fire to the dry bushes and grass surrounding the Crusader camp. Guy ordered Raymond of Tripoli to lead a charge. The charge of the knights could be a devastating and unstoppable attack, and the charge did break a hole in the enemy. However, it was also Saladin's plan to allow that charge to break through. Its overall effect on the battle was minimal.

Realizing the futility of trying to salvage a victory, Raymond retreated to try and save the rest of the kingdom. The battle continued with the Muslims tightening their noose. Suffocating in the heat and smoke, many of the Crusader army surrendered. Other fought on, rallying around the tent of King Guy. Although they repulsed numerous attacks and even launched a few counterattacks, it was not enough and they were overwhelmed.

Saladin was victorious and the Crusader army annihilated. There were some prisoners, but all of the Templars and Hospitallers were beheaded. King Guy and Reynald were taken to Saladin's tent. There Guy was treated honorably and Reynald—who was not invited, but simply accompanied the king—was executed.

Consequences of the Battle Afterwards, Saladin overran most of the Kingdom of Jerusalem. Stripped of their defenders, cities and castles surrendered or gave little defense. Even the fortifications of Jerusalem could not save it from Saladin's attack. On October 2, 1187, Jerusalem fell. Only the timely arrival of a fleet from Europe saved Tyre.

After Hattin, the Kingdom of Jerusalem consisted of only a few towns on the coast. Even so, Saladin's failure to eliminate Tyre allowed the Kingdom to live another hundred years.

Siege of Acre, August 1189–July 1191

The siege of Acre was the opening battle of the Third Crusade. Although Richard the Lionheart and Philip Augustus participated and ultimately won the battle, it was initiated by Guy de Lusignan, whom Saladin had defeated at Hattin in 1187. The significance of Acre is that it was the first major defeat for Saladin and gave hope to the Kingdom of Jerusalem.

Down but Not Yet Out After defeating and humiliating King Guy at Hattin, Saladin swept through Palestine and captured most of the cities and fortresses. He almost captured the port city of Tyre, but the timely arrival of Conrad of Montferrat revived the resistance. Saladin had to give up the siege.

Saladin released his prisoners (including King Guy) from Hattin in June 1188 after securing an oath that they never take up arms against him again. The Christian clergy gave the freed knights absolution from the vow. In their eyes, an oath sworn to an infidel could not be upheld in the eyes of God. Thus King Guy was ruler of a much reduced kingdom again. However, not everyone wanted him to be king. Indeed, Conrad would not even allow him into the city.

When a Pisan fleet arrived, Guy took advantage of the situation and the reinforcements by marching to Acre in August 1189. A large part of this move, which seemed suicidal considering the paucity of Guy's army, was to resuscitate Guy's reputation as a leader.

Guy's plan worked. In the eyes of the newcomers, Guy appeared as an active Crusader, whereas Conrad sat in Tyre and did nothing. Conrad's position was strategic, but one must remember that the recently arrived Crusaders were there to liberate the Holy Land, and this required action. Furthermore, with Tyre denied to him, Guy needed a base, and Acre was the best option. Eventually, Conrad had no option but to go to Acre in September 1189 and make a tentative peace with Guy in the spring of 1190.

The Siege Gains Strength With a steady flow of Crusaders coming ahead of Richard and Philip (along with the Germans who continued after Frederick Barbarossa's death), the army steadily grew. As the Pisan fleet blockaded the port, the Crusader army launched numerous—but ultimately unsuccessful—attacks. The boldness (or foolishness) of the attacks caught Saladin by surprise; since the Muslims could trap the Crusaders between the city and Saladin's army, it did not seem a wise course of action for an army to take. Even so, the Crusaders had high hopes.

In the early part of 1190, the Crusaders assaulted the city. The Pisan fleet won a sea battle, but an attempt to storm the city failed on May 5. The Muslims used Greek fire to destroy their siege towers. Meanwhile, Saladin launched attacks on the Crusader camp, but these were repulsed. On July 25, the infantry unwisely tried to launch an attack on Saladin's camp and was defeated.

Both sides were at an impasse. The Crusaders could neither take Acre nor drive off Saladin, nor could Saladin crush them. The Crusader's dominance of the sea allowed supplies and men to arrive unimpeded and their camp had good fortifications.

Despite driving Saladin from his hilltop camp on November 12, 1190, the Crusaders' camp was not

This engraving shows members of the Knights Templars.   © *Bettmann/Corbis*

jubilant. A food shortage made life in the camp miserable. Fortunately, Philip Augustus arrived in the spring of 1191, restoring hope to the siege. Despite the reinforcements and French siege engines—including a great catapult known as "Bad Neighbor"—the siege was still a stalemate, as Philip, although methodical, was too cautious. When a breach was made, the Crusaders attacked, but then Saladin attacked their camp, forcing the Crusaders to withdraw from the city.

The Besiegers Outlast the Besieged   Richard arrived in June and re-invigorated the Franks. His fleet defeated an Egyptian fleet that tried to supply the city, but illness prevented both Philip and Richard from taking advantage of the situation. Skirmishing continued through all of June. Finally in July 1191, the Crusaders learned that the garrison was on the verge of collapse. The city offered to surrender and pay a ransom. A deal was made, and the Crusaders claimed the city.

Despite the victory, all was not well in the Crusader camp. Philip returned to Europe as soon as he could, as he tired of being in Richard's shadow. The rivalry between Guy and Conrad continued, and Richard massacred close to three thousand prisoners when Saladin failed to pay their ransom at the designated time. This was primarily because Richard grew impatient, as he wanted to move to the next conquest and had no desire to be bogged down with prisoners. It also clearly demonstrated the difference between Richard and Saladin,

who had allowed many from Jerusalem to leave rather than to become slaves.

Constantinople, April 1204

The siege of Constantinople was a turning point for the Crusading era. Previously the Byzantine Empire was an active participant in the affairs of the Crusader states on a variety of levels that ranged from ally to enemy and all points in between. Nonetheless, it was a Christian state, albeit Orthodox rather than Catholic. The sacking of Constantinople during the Fourth Crusade was the virtual death knell for the Byzantine state. It continued for another two hundred fifty years, but the Byzantines never fully recovered.

As for the Crusaders, the sacking of Constantinople—perhaps more so than any other instance—tainted the image of the Crusades in the eyes of not only historians, but also contemporary observers. Nonetheless, it was an impressive feat considering that no foreign power had ever successfully attacked the city.

Once More into the Holy Land   In 1198, Pope Innocent III called for a new Crusade shortly after he assumed his papal duties. He was determined to restore all of Palestine to Christian control. Unfortunately, Europe was a little too busy fighting itself to leave off and go fight infidels. The kings of France and England were at war, and a civil war wracked the Holy Roman Emperor. Nonetheless, many younger and less experienced nobles stepped forward. Command was ultimately given to Boniface of Montferrat (1155–1207), a seasoned leader in his fifties.

The largest obstacle for any Crusader traveling to the Holy Land was finding a way to actually get there. As none of the barons possessed ships, envoys were sent to Venice to negotiate passage. In return for eighty-five thousand silver marks, Doge Dandolo (Doge was a title) agreed to transport 33,500 men, their horses, and supplies, as well as to provide naval support for a year. Although blind and old, the Doge was a savvy negotiator. He also made sure the Venetians would receive half of any booty gained through the Crusade. It was also revealed that they planned to attack Egypt and then go on to Jerusalem. The two sides agreed that the fleet would sail on June 29, 1202.

The Crusade leaders soon began to encounter other problems. Being young and inexperienced in organizing large expeditions, they seriously overestimated how many troops they could raise. By the agreed-upon date in late June, the Crusaders were well short of the men they had expected. Only eleven thousand men arrived. The Venetians were also concerned about the payment.

Regardless of the number of men the Crusaders would provide, the Venetians had put all of their effort into building a fleet of five hundred ships. They had even suspended much of their mercantile shipping to ensure that enough ships and sailors would be present to transport the Crusaders.

The Crusade Goes Off Topic Dandolo was in a bind. Although he was the ruler, he also had to answer to his people. So he suggested that the Crusaders could work off the debt by helping the Venetians recapture the city of Zara across the Adriatic Sea.

Boniface agreed to the terms, but many of the leaders were uneasy about the deal as it meant attacking a city controlled by other Christians. They had agreed to take part in a Crusade, not to attack a Christian city. However, they had little choice. The fleet left Venice in November 1202 and sacked Zara shortly thereafter. Shocked, Innocent III excommunicated the entire expedition.

While at Zara, the Crusaders also received a Byzantine prince, Alexis IV, son of the deposed Eastern Emperor Isaac II (who ruled from 1185–1195 and 1203–1204). He revealed that his uncle, Alexis III (ruler from 1195–1203), had usurped the throne, and Alexis IV sought aid to overthrow the usurper. If the Crusaders would help him, Alexis IV promised to pay them handsomely and provide ten thousand soldiers for the Crusade. In 1203, the Crusaders agreed, although some again protested, as it distracted them from the true intent of the Crusade.

Siege or Folly? The Crusaders arrived at Constantinople in July 1203. On July 5, 1203, a Crusader army of less than twenty thousand men attacked a city of a half million. Fortunately for the Crusaders, the Byzantine army declined an engagement and did not possess a navy.

Initially it was a two-pronged attack. The Crusaders attacked the land walls while the Venetians attacked via the sea. The Venetians broke through, but they were forced to retreat.

Although the Byzantines were winning, they began to question their ruler. He had not led the army out to fight the Crusaders, and the Venetians had done considerable damage when they penetrated the city. Sensing the mood of the populace, Alexis III fled the city.

The following morning, the Crusaders awoke to find emissaries from Isaac II welcoming them to the city. This caused an awkward situation for Alexis IV as he now had to fulfill his promises to the Crusaders. It is not clear how he had planned to achieve this from the start. Indeed, Emperor Isaac II was shocked when he learned the terms, but now he had no choice but to accept the conditions.

A Debt is Paid, But None Too Gently The Crusaders waited at Constantinople for months as Alexius IV tried to gather the required sum of two hundred thousand silver marks. Alexius IV doled out money slowly, often with funds confiscated from the Byzantine nobles. Naturally, tensions arose in Constantinople not only over Alexius IV's actions, but also over the presence of the less sophisticated Crusaders. Meanwhile the rank and file among the Crusaders were becoming uneasy about the long diversion from the true Crusade. In addition, the knights began to extract their payment by raiding villages.

Alexius IV tried to oppose these attacks, but with little luck. Early in 1204, Alexius IV was deposed by his lieutenant Murzuphlos, who then ascended the throne as Alexius V. This revitalized Byzantine resistance. However, the Crusaders now had a better understanding of the city as well as access to it. They attacked Constantinople in April 1204; it fell quickly, and the Crusaders pillaged for three days.

After the sack, the Crusaders selected Baldwin IX of Flanders as leader and divided the territory between the Crusaders and the Venetians. Thus, the majority of Greece, the Aegean islands, and a part of Western Anatolia came under their control. This new Latin Empire would last until 1261.

Mansurah, 1249–1250

This engagement proved to be the pivotal battle of the Seventh Crusade, which was led by France's King Louis IX (who later became more commonly known as Saint Louis). Louis's defeat at Mansurah became an impetus to the rise of the Mamluk sultanate.

The Seventh Follows the Fifth King Louis of France departed from Aigues Mortes in August 1248, and wintered in Cyprus. Then in May 1249, he and an army of approximately twenty thousand men sailed for Egypt.

During the Fifth Crusade (1218–1221), the Crusaders had landed near the city of Damietta in the Nile delta. Louis intended to do the same. Sultan al-Salih, the ruler of Egypt, was not surprised. He had already increased the garrison there and established his own camp nearby. Yet despite attempts by the army of Sultan al-Salih to prevent a landing, the Crusader army charged ashore and secured the beach. To their surprise, the Muslim army not only retreated from the beach, but also abandoned Damietta, which had resisted the Fifth Crusade for eighteen months.

After securing Damietta, King Louis IX and the other leading figures held a council of war to determine their goal. Many argued that only by conquering Egypt could they make the Crusader states secure. Others argued they should simply hold onto Damietta and take Alexandria. Both were port cities, and since the Crusaders dominated the sea, they would be able to hold them. Furthermore, they could also use the cities as bargaining chips to regain territory in Palestine.

Being deeply religious, Louis saw the victory at Damietta as a sign of God's favor that they would conquer Egypt. Thus, on November 20, 1249, King Louis led his army towards Mansurah, marching southward along the Nile.

Down the Great River The Crusaders arrived before Mansurah in December 1249 and found their army between the Nile and a tributary. Mansurah sat across the tributary along with the camp of Fakhr al-Din, the commander in charge of the Muslim army. (Sultan al-Salih had died on the retreat from Damietta, and the heir to the throne was still in Syria.) Fakhr al-Din's troops were sufficient to prevent any landing via ship. Therefore, the Crusaders began to build a causeway. The Muslim's catapults bombed it with stones and Greek fire. Even under this barrage, slowly but surely the Crusaders made progress.

In the meantime, Louis also learned of a ford further down. Louis intended to use the ford and strike Mansurah from the rear, so he sent the vanguard, which was commanded by his brother, Robert of Artois. Robert was to cross the ford and secure a foothold to allow the rest of the army to cross. The entire army would then sweep down on Mansurah and Fakhr al-Din's camp, which would still be distracted by a force building the causeway.

Robert crossed the ford with the Templars; however, he did not wait for Louis. Instead, he moved forward and attacked the Egyptian camp. The Muslims were taken completely by surprise and were routed. Fakhr al-Din was cut down before he was armed. Emboldened by this, Robert advanced into the city of Mansurah rather than waiting for reinforcements.

The Tide of Battle Turns This overextension proved to be a disastrous mistake. The narrow streets of Mansurah became a gauntlet for the knights as arrows,

stones, and tiles hailed down from the rooftops. The Egyptian counterattack, led by the Mamluks (elite Turkic slave troops), annihilated the vanguard, including Robert.

Louis had successfully crossed the ford but, of course, he did not find his brother. The victorious Mamluks now descended upon Louis. The Crusaders could not retreat and had to fight their way along the river until they were opposite their camp, which could provide archery support. With this, the Crusaders were able to take possession of the enemy camp, but they now lacked sufficient numbers to take the city. Sure that God would grant him victory, Louis refused to retreat.

Instead of getting better, the situation became much worse for the Crusaders. Muslim forces harried the Crusaders' supply lines on land and on the river. Furthermore, disease struck their camp, leaving King Louis himself with dysentery. On April 5, 1250, the Crusaders began their retreat back to Damietta, subject to constant attack the entire time.

Halfway to Damietta, the starving and sick army could go no further. Thus on April 6, 1250, King Louis surrendered and offered himself as a hostage. The invasion of Egypt ended with the exchange of King Louis for the city of Damietta and the ransoming of his army.

Fall of Acre, 1291

Although it was known as the Kingdom of Jerusalem, by 1291 the kingdom consisted of the port city of Acre and a few other towns on the coast. Since the end of the Third Crusade in 1192, the Kingdom of Jerusalem slowly lost the territory that Richard the Lionheart had regained. Saladin's victory at Hattin and then Jerusalem had destroyed the foundation and security of the state. The fall of Acre signaled not only the end of the Kingdom of Jerusalem, but—in the eyes of some historians—the end of the Crusades as well.

The Mamluks Come Prepared It is uncertain how large the Muslim army that attacked Acre was. Sultan al-Ashraf al-Khalil (the ruler of the Mamluk Sultanate that replaced the empire that Saladin built) began the siege on April 6, 1291. Some sources list the Muslim army as well over one hundred thousand. This, however, is extremely doubtful. Nonetheless, the exaggerated numbers indicate that the attackers vastly outnumbered the defenders. More importantly, Ashraf al-Khalil also brought large numbers of siege weapons, for he was determined to destroy the Crusaders once and for all.

The Crusaders were led by Amalric, the brother of King Henry II, the ruler of Jerusalem and Cyprus. Henry was not present due to an incapacitating illness. The Military Orders who had so long provided the backbone of the defense of the Holy Land were also present. The Templars, Hospitallers, and the German Teutonic Knights had requested all available aid from their brethren in Europe. Notwithstanding the troops, the

RE-ARMING THE COUNTERWEIGHT TREBUCHET

With a counterweight trebuchet, men would sometimes pull the weight with ropes in order to reset it. However, another method to reset the counterweight employed a large wheel with men inside it; this method operated on the same principles as a waterwheel. To modern eyes, such a contraption would look like an enormous hamster wheel, but it did allow one or two men to pull a much greater weight much faster than could be done using ropes. An example of these counterweight trebuchets can be seen in the movie *The Kingdom of Heaven*.

fortifications of Acre were superb; twin walls surrounded the city, and towers were evenly spaced along these walls.

The Crusaders had one more key advantage, thanks to the support of the Italian city-states; they held the sea, and thus could not be threatened by a naval attack. However, one section of the wall was vulnerable. A salient point protruded from the walls, allowing it to be attacked on two sides. Naturally, Ashraf al-Khalil focused his attack there, but it was defended by one of the most intimidating Crusader units—the Teutonic Knights.

Both Sides Maneuver From the beginning, Sultan Ashraf al-Khalil ordered a continuous bombardment from his siege engines. Stones and fire hailed down on the city while Muslim engineers dug tunnels in hope of collapsing the walls of Acre. The Crusaders attempted to counter the bombardment with two sorties, including one night attack by the Knights Templar and another by the Hospitallers. They were unsuccessful in breaking the siege.

Although the Crusaders's numbers diminished throughout the siege, the fortifications held. Reinforcements arrived on May 4 as King Henry arrived with forty ships. King Henry's arrival raised morale, but the reinforcements were too paltry in number to launch a significant counterattack. Negotiations by the king also failed to make a difference, as Sultan Ashraf al-Khalil was determined to capture the city.

Their best hope was to continue to hold the city and hope that the Muslim army disbanded due to the logistics of feeding thirty to forty thousand troops. Also, some of his vassals would tire of sitting before the city and desire to retire to their homes.

The Walls Crumble Fortunately for the sultan, after a month of digging, his sappers finally collapsed a section

of the wall on May 15. Now the sultan could finally take advantage of his superior numbers.

After taking the outer wall, the Muslims were quick to take the inner wall. After this breach, King Henry's troops could not withstand the onslaught despite the aid of the military orders. From there, the battle devolved into house-to-house fighting.

Soon only the Templars headquarters remained in Christian hands. Henry and Amalric were forced to their ships and escaped. The Templars negotiated free passage, but Muslim troops attempted to seize some of the women in the building, and the Templars retaliated. They then barred the doors and endured a siege. Again, the sappers undermined the foundations and collapsed a wall. Muslim warriors streamed in, but soon thereafter the entire building collapsed, killing all inside on May 28, 1291.

Henry and Amalric returned to Cyprus. Those not fortunate enough to escape on the ships were sold into slavery or massacred, with almost thirty thousand being killed. The remaining cities of Tyre and Sidon and the few remaining castles surrendered afterwards. The two-hundred-year-old Kingdom of Jerusalem was no more.

⊕ Key Elements of Warcraft

Military Orders (Hospitallers, Templars)

The Military Orders were among the most important institutions and fighting forces during the Crusades. They combined the discipline of monks with the martial skills of the knights. From their rather modest beginnings, the Military Orders increased not only in importance as military units but in land holdings. As time went on, the Crusaders increasingly depended on their manpower to garrison the fortresses of the Holy Land.

Origin of the Templars The Templars were the first and most famous Military Order. Hugh of Payns and eight companions established the order in 1119 in order to protect pilgrims on the road from Jaffa to Jerusalem. The group was granted use of the Al-Aqsa mosque on the Temple Mount (where the Temple of Solomon was once located) for their headquarters. From this location, their name evolved into the Templars.

The Templars were granted a formal rule by Bernard of Clairvaux in 1129. With Bernard's support and a general enthusiasm for their work, the order grew quickly. Temples, as their monasteries were often called in Europe, were established in Europe, and these served as recruiting offices. In the 1130s, with their expanded manpower, the Templars received several castles to defend.

Most of the Templars came from noble families as most knights did, but the majority of the Templars were sergeants. Sergeants were the backbone of all European armies. They were professional soldiers who served as infantry or as cavalry, but were of common background.

Although they could never be knights, they often fought in the same manner.

In addition, regular priests could join in order to provide religious services. Because of increased garrisoning duties, the Templars also hired mercenaries to serve with them. The Templars were easily recognizable as they wore white tunics emblazoned with a red cross.

Like monks, they took an oath of poverty, chastity, and obedience. The Templars—and for that matter, all of the military orders—had to maintain daily liturgical hours, even while in the field. They were governed by a Grand Master located in Jerusalem. All of their properties were divided and governed by commanders who answered to the Grand Master; proceeds were sent to the east.

Creation of the Hospitallers The second most important Military Order were the Knights of St. John, also known as the Hospitallers. Originally founded by Italian merchants in Jerusalem, they were a monastic order that offered hospital services. The hospital was attached to a monastery dedicated to St. John the Baptist. The papacy recognized it as a monastic order in 1113, but it did not acquire a military component until the 1130s. Although the military wing became more dominant, it never abandoned its hospital work, which provided services to pilgrims to the Holy Land regardless of wealth or social status.

Its organization and membership was similar to that of the Templars. Originally, the military wing of the Hospitallers was probably created to protect the hospitals that the order established in various towns in the Kingdom of Jerusalem. As the Crusader states were chronically short of manpower, they often called upon the Hospitallers for assistance.

Like the Templars, they were disciplined fighters. Initially they wore black tunics with a white cross, but after 1259 they wore red surcoats with a white cross. Soon, they also acquired many castles to garrison, the most important being Krak des Chevaliers in Syria. This mammoth structure served as their headquarters.

Like the Templars, the Hospitallers also had offices throughout Europe and were subject only to the pope's authority. There was a rivalry between the two orders that was not very conducive to the well being of the Crusader states. However, they could also cooperate. On campaigns, due to their discipline and prowess, the Templars served as the vanguard of the army, while the Hospitallers served as the rear guard.

After the fall of Acre in 1291, the Hospitallers moved to Cyprus and then Rhodes, which became their headquarters in 1309. Forced to become a naval power by this relocation, they acted essentially as pirates on Muslim shipping. Eventually, the Ottomans forced them from Rhodes in 1523. Homeless for seven years, they were granted the island of Malta, where they stayed until their destruction by Napoleon in 1798.

WEALTH OF THE TEMPLARS

The Templars initiated an early form of banking. Travelers discovered they could leave money safely with a Temple in Europe, and then show the receipt in Jerusalem and recover it, minus a service charge. Later, this led to rumors of tremendous wealth, and these rumors were the primary reason behind the attack on the Templars by Philip the Fair in 1307. Looking for their money, Philip accused them of heresy and sodomy, among other crimes, in an inquisition.

Although many were arrested, tortured, and burned at the stake, others escaped and disappeared into secular society, although many myths arose that still influence the modern era as demonstrated in the novel and film *The Da Vinci Code* and also the movie *National Treasure*.

In the twenty-first century, the Hospitallers live on as a monastic order in Rome.

Siege Engines

Although the Crusades were known for knights in armor and famous warriors such as Bohemund, Saladin, and Richard the Lionheart, the vast majority of battles took place in the form of sieges rather than field battles. Part of this was due to a chronic lack of manpower on the part of the Crusaders. It was easier to control territory with castles than large armies. For both sides, a disastrous encounter in the field could leave an entire region exposed to conquest, so most decided to stay in their fortresses and wait out marauding armies.

Because of the emphasis on siege warfare, both fortification and siege engines advanced significantly. Many of the castle designs and weaponry used in the Crusades spread into Europe and even into China.

Ladders, battering rams, and sapping (digging tunnels to undermine the foundations of a wall) had been standard parts of siege warfare for centuries. However, none of these tactics were successful unless they were used in conjunction with siege engines such as towers, catapults, and trebuchets.

Design of a Siege Tower Siege towers were critical at Jerusalem and Ascalon, and it is doubtful if the sieges would have been successful without them. This construct was essentially a wooden tower on wheels that could be pushed up to the wall. Typically, it was designed to be higher than the wall, since this allowed archers or catapults to dominate their sector.

As they were made from wood, towers were susceptible to fire (particularly Greek fire which could only be extinguished with vinegar). To help shield it, animal hides covered a tower, as the hides tended to resist the

Reproduction of a trebuchet at Caerlaverock Castle, Scotland.
© Gary Cook/Alamy

fire, or if set aflame, could be cut away before the fire ignited the entire structure.

Towers often had one or more openings. Battering rams could be used to open a breach, or a bridge could be lowered to allow troops to cross over to the enemy's walls.

Machines of Destruction Catapults had been standard siege engines since the ancient period. Those used in the Middle Ages were based on torsion and tension. One such device was the mangonel, which was powered by twisted rope. A bowl-shaped holder held a projectile and was attached to an arm. When fired, the energy stored in the ropes released the arm, which hit a crossbeam, sending the projectile forward. It was not accurate, but it could be effective.

Another weapon was a trebuchet. This was simply a long beam with a sling attached to it. The arm was attached to a framework and powered by men pulling ropes attached to the other end of the arm. The longer end with the sling would move forward and release the missile. These were known as traction trebuchets. Their range and power was based on the number of people pulling the ropes.

The most destructive weapon was the counterweight trebuchet. Rather than having men pulling ropes, a box filled with heavy weights would power it. When released, the weights would swing down with more force, giving the missile greater range and velocity, and consequently causing more damage. Many of these engines were given colorful nicknames, such as "Bad Neighbor." A European invention, the first recorded use of them was around 1187 by Saladin.

Another weapon in common use was the ballista. This was an oversized crossbow. Although oversized bolts could be used, it was more common to use stones. As trebuchets became more common, the ballista gradually declined in use.

⊕ Impact of the Crusades

The impact of the Crusades on World History is undeniable. The contact that the Crusaders had in the Middle East resulted in a transfusion and dissemination of ideas, technology, and culture between that region, Europe, and beyond.

The use of the papal indulgence, or the remission of sins and the guarantee of salvation for participating in the Crusades, increased from Pope Urban II's first use of the indulgence. Soon it was used not only for those going to the Holy Land, but for those who fought against infidels in Spain, the Baltic region, or against heretics in Christendom. The indulgence was then extended to those who donated money to the effort. Eventually, the indulgence was simply sold as a way for the church to raise money. This abuse became one of the principle complaints of Martin Luther, which led to the Reformation (1517–1689).

The Inquisition also came out of the Crusades. This program of rooting out heresy came out during the Albigensian Crusade (a crusade in southern France against a heretical group in 1208–1229). After the Crusade, to ensure that heresy had been stamped out, the Inquisitors interrogated and tortured anyone suspected of not adhering to the doctrine of the Church. Best known as the Spanish Inquisition, the Inquisition became a standard tool of the Church in the later Middle Ages and throughout the Reformation.

The Crusades also served as an opportunity for centralization, not only in Europe but also in the Middle East. The Crusades made long-range planning and organization absolutely necessary. For a king to go on Crusade meant a massive mobilization of men and resources. Furthermore, he had to ensure the state ran smoothly in his absence, a requirement that often demanded better organization within a state. It should be remembered that states also expanded by taking advantage of the absence of various rulers, such as Philip Augustus's opportunism against the domains of Richard I.

This was also seen in the Muslim world. Before the Crusades, Syria was a hodgepodge of small polities and city-states. The need for unity forced leaders to consider consolidating the region to mobilize more resources against the Crusaders, a unification that was carried on until completed with Saladin. Even after Saladin's successors were overthrown by the Mamluks after the battle of Mansurah, the Mamluks maintained that unity, forever transforming the politics of the region.

The Crusades continued to live in the minds of politicians and writers in the nineteenth century. In the age of Imperialism, Europeans (especially the French) viewed the Crusades as a glorious period that justified their own expansion. Others would use it as a way of explaining Western expansion and dominance during the modern period. The adventurism and drive of the Crusaders demonstrated Europe's dominance over other countries.

While the interpretation was inaccurate—considering that when they started the Crusaders were viewed by Byzantines and Muslims alike as rude, crude, and socially unacceptable—there is an element of truth in it. The Reconquista of Spain was a territorial war which transformed into a holy war to drive the Muslims from Spain. The Spanish victory in 1492 allowed Spain to fund Christopher Columbus's journey. Furthermore, it instilled a religious zeal among the Spanish and Portuguese that carried over as part of their empires. They expanded not only for empire, but to spread the glory of Christianity to the infidels.

In addition, ideas about fortification expanded. As they traveled back to Europe, the Crusaders brought with them Byzantine and Islamic ideas about architecture and other matters. Meanwhile, European siege weapons (such as the counterweight trebuchet) entered the Middle East, eventually making their way to China in the late thirteenth century.

Trade networks were also extended. The Italian city-states benefited greatly from the Crusades. Although they participated in them, they also traded with Muslim states. Even after the Crusaders were expelled, many Italians remained active in trading in the Middle East.

BIBLIOGRAPHY

Books

Madden, Thomas F. *The New Concise History of the Crusades.* Oxford: Rowman and Littlefield, 2006.

Marshall, Christopher. *Warfare in the Latin East, 1192–1291.* Cambridge: Cambridge University Press, 1992.

Richard, Jean. *The Crusades.* Cambridge: Cambridge University Press, 1999.

Tyerman, Christopher. *God's War: A New History of the Crusades.* Cambridge, Mass.: Belknap Press, 2006.

Introduction to the Mongol Conquests (1200–1400)

In the early thirteenth century, an empire arose on the steppes of Mongolia that forever changed the map of Eurasia as well as the nature of warfare itself. The Mongol Empire stretched from the Sea of Japan to the Carpathian Mountains at its height, making it the largest contiguous empire in history.

The Mongol empire began with the unification of the nomadic tribes of Mongolia by Genghis Khan (1165–1227) in a series of wars from 1180 to 1206. These twenty-six years were the most difficult in the career of the great Mongol leader, but he succeeded and created a single nation—known as the Yeke Mongol Ulus, or Great Mongol Nation—from the warring tribes.

The Mongols expanded south in 1209, conquering Xi Xia (the modern Chinese provinces of Ningxia and Gansu). Then, in 1211, Genghis Khan invaded the Jin Empire of northern China. Although he had conquered most of the Jin Empire by 1216, the Jin continued to resist the Mongols for almost two more decades.

While the war raged in China, the Mongols expanded into Central Asia, pursuing tribal leaders who opposed Genghis Khan's rise to power. Eventually, the Mongols bordered the empire of Khwarazm, a vast state whose territory included Central Asia, Afghanistan, Iran, and part of modern Iraq.

A trade dispute in 1218 initiated a war between the two empires. In one of the most brilliant campaigns in history, Genghis Khan divided his army and struck Khwarazm at several points, overrunning the nation by 1224. Immediately afterwards, Genghis Khan returned east to deal with a rebellion in Xi Xia, keeping only the territory north of the Amu Darya. In the course of crushing the rebellion, Genghis Khan died in 1227.

Ogodei (1185–1241), Genghis Khan's second son, ascended to the throne in 1230 and finished the conquest of the Jin in 1234. Meanwhile Mongol forces invaded Iran, Armenia, and Georgia, bringing those regions under their control. An immense force marched west in 1238 and conquered the Russian principalities before invading Hungary and Poland in 1240. Although they devastated both regions, they withdrew in 1241 upon hearing of Ogodei's death.

Guyuk, the son of Ogodei, came to the throne in 1246, after a lengthy regency by his mother, Toregene, but he died after a two-year reign. His wife, Oghul Qaimish, served as regent until a coup brought Mongke (1208–1259), the son of Genghis Khan's fourth son, to power. After ten years of inaction, with Mongke the Mongol armies were once again on the march. His brother Kublai invaded the Song empire in south China while another brother, Hulegu, marched into the Middle East.

The Mongol Empire unraveled with the death of Mongke in 1259 and the eruption of civil war. Kublai prevailed in 1265, but the damage was done. While the other khanates grudgingly accepted Kublai as the ruler, his influence outside of East Asia was limited. The empire split into four distinct states consisting of the Great Khanate in East Asia, the Il-Khanate in the Middle East, the Chaghatayid Khanate in Central Asia, and the Golden Horde, which stretched from Russia to modern Kazakhstan.

Mongol Conquests (1200–1400)

✪ Major Figures

Genghis Khan

Late in the twelfth century, an individual emerged from among several warring tribal confederations in the steppes of Mongolia to not only unite his people, but also to establish the largest contiguous empire in history. Born in 1165 to the name of Temujin (1165–1227), he received the title of Genghis Khan first as the Khan or leader of his own tribe, the Mongols, and then as the Emperor of all the tribes of Mongolia. Earning these titles took twenty years of conflict, but in the process Genghis Khan forged a new identity for the nomads by organizing them into one supra-tribe known as the Yeke Mongol Ulus (Great Mongol Nation). Genghis Khan led his unified tribesmen into northern China and then into Central Asia and Iran, conquering more territory than even Alexander the Great. His successors continued the conquests until the Mongol empire stretched from the Pacific Ocean to the Carpathian Mountains and Mediterranean Sea.

Early Life Genghis Khan, also known as Chinggis Khan or Temujin in his youth, assumed the mantle of leadership early in his life. After the murder of his father—Yesugei, who was also a tribal leader—in 1175, Yesugei's family was deserted by his tribe. At the time, Temujin was only ten years old. Temujin had two half-brothers from Yesugei's second wife, Ko'agchin; these brothers may have been older or equivalent in age, so it is unclear whether Temujin was the logical successor. However, none of Yesugei's children were old enough to lead the Borgijin clan of the Mongols. A power struggle ensued between the sons of Ho'elun, the mother of Temujin, and those of Ko'agchin. The end result of the struggle in 1180 was that Temujin and his brother Jochi Qasar murdered the eldest of Ko'agchin's sons Bekhtar but spared Belgutei, the younger son.

In 1180, Temujin reached the age of fifteen, essentially attaining his majority (typically males aged fifteen to sixty fought in warfare, so a fifteen-year-old would be considered a man and not a boy). Temujin (now Genghis Khan) served as the leader of his small following, enduring a period of captivity among the Tayichi'ud, a tribe that once served his father, and other hardships including the kidnapping of his wife Borte by the Merkits, another tribe. In spite of this, Temujin gradually won the loyalty of others and gradually increased his following. In addition, he became the vassal of Toghril Ong-Khan, the ruler of the powerful Kereit tribal confederation. Through this alliance, Genghis Khan rescued his wife and steadily rose through the ranks of Toghril's followers. He gained a reputation for respecting merit over heredity and status, as well as rewarding loyalty.

Unification of Mongolia Genghis Khan gained supporters from other tribes. Since he divided the plunder acquired in warfare among all of those who participated, he attracted many followers. He also ordered that anyone who stopped to gather booty during a raid would be punished. Genghis Khan insisted that all should continue fighting until the battle was won, because if they plundered the enemy's camp before complete victory, the enemy could counterattack. Traditionally, plunder tended to be divided amongst the leaders who then distributed amongst their men. As a consequence, everyone had an incentive to take what one could on a raid to increase his share. Genghis Khan had a new, and superior, system.

Genghis Khan remained loyal to Toghril for several years, but tensions built as Genghis Khan's influence and power increased. In 1203, the two former allies clashed; Genghis Khan emerged victorious. With his defeat of the Kereit, the Mongols now controlled Eastern and Central Mongolia. The only significant force that remained in Mongolia was that of the Naiman, another tribal confederation. Initially, the Naiman planned to attack the Mongols by invading their territory, but Genghis Khan learned of their intentions and attacked them instead.

Mongol warrior and ruler Genghis Khan.   *Public Domain*

He led his army into Western Mongolia and defeated the Naiman in 1204.

The victory over the Naiman gave Genghis Khan complete control over Mongolia. In 1206, Genghis Khan was officially declared the supreme ruler of the steppes. At this time, he organized his newly won empire in a more formal manner. He assigned commanders to the mingans, the units of a thousand or ten thousand men. He also organized his society. As the wars to unify Mongolia involved fighting numerous tribal groups, in order to maintain unity a new entity had to be born. Thus Genghis Khan created the Yeke Mongol Ulus, the Great Mongol Nation. Tribes that had been loyal to him through the years maintained their integrity. Those that he had defeated, however, were divided up and integrated into the new units.

The World Conqueror   After uniting Mongolia, Genghis Khan went on to conquer much of northern China and Central Asia. His wars were as often occasioned by his desire for retaliation for perceived wrongs as for

territory or riches. In 1207 the Mongols began operations against the kingdom of Xi Xia, which comprised much of northwestern China and parts of Tibet. This campaign lasted until 1210, when the Xi Xia ruler submitted to Genghis Khan.

In 1211 he led his armies against the Jin dynasty, which ruled northern China. War continued against the Jin until 1234, well after Genghis Khan's death. Meanwhile, in 1219, during the war in China, a caravan under the protection of Genghis Khan was massacred in Otrar, a city of the empire of Khwarazm, which consisted of much of modern Uzbekistan, Turkmenistan, Iran, Afghanistan, and Tajikistan.

With his armies engaged in China, Genghis Khan attempted to find a peaceful solution, but his diplomacy failed. Genghis Khan left a trusted general, Muqali, to continue to fight the Jin while he led an army into Central Asia. The war lasted from 1219 to 1222, and the Mongols destroyed Khwarazm. Striking from several directions, Genghis Khan's armies carried out a campaign that is still considered strategically remarkable. Yet despite having conquered Khwarazm, Genghis Khan kept only the territories north of the Amu Darya River so as not to overextend his armies.

In 1226 his armies invaded Xi Xia once again to quell an uprising there. During the campaign, Genghis Khan fell from his horse and later died from internal injuries suffered in the fall. His followers completed the reconquest of Xi Xia and then buried Genghis Khan in a secret location that remains a mystery, although several modern expeditions have attempted to find it.

Achievements and Legacy   Genghis Khan's achievements as a leader went far beyond his conquests. While these certainly gained him recognition among historians as a military genius, perhaps his greatest achievements were not in the field of military conquest. Indeed, he played a major role in five significant areas in the development of Mongolian society. The first was that he united the tribes of Mongolia into one nation that remained unified through his might and charisma. Second, he introduced a writing system into Mongolian society and forced the Mongolian nobility to become literate, although he himself remained illiterate.

The last three cultural achievements were institutions he imposed on the Mongols that lasted well beyond his death. The first of these three was the Yasa, or law code, which he imposed over the empire. He also created an army with absolute discipline out of the unruly tribes. With this army he was able to forge an empire that stretched from the coasts of China to the shores of the Caspian Sea in his lifetime. It continued to grow after his death, a phenomenal achievement in nomadic empires. The last institution that Genghis Khan developed—or rather foresaw the advantages of—was an organized system of administration to govern his empire.

ARTS AND LITERATURE— *THE SECRET HISTORY OF THE MONGOLS*

The Secret History of the Mongols is one of the very few documents concerning the Mongols that comes from the Mongols themselves. It is said that the victors write the history, but in the case of the Mongols, it was usually written by the conquered. Most of the primary sources on the Mongols were written by Persians, Chinese, Russians, Arabs, Armenians, Europeans, and others. While some of the documents were written by people employed by the Mongols, their history was almost always written from the viewpoint of an outsider.

This is why *The Secret History of the Mongols* is such an important source. Although it only goes up to the reign of Ogodei, it tells the reader much about the Mongols. While it is an important historical source, it is also in the form of epic literature, often blending history with myth, particularly concerning the origins of the Mongols.

The title comes from the idea that it was something meant only for the eyes of the Mongols. While this is true, it is not something that is used solely for the glorification of the Mongol rulers. Instead it gives a rather intimate portrayal of the rise of Genghis Khan from his youth to become the ruler of a vast empire. It does not attempt to conceal embarrassing facts or weaknesses. In the *Secret History*, readers learn that Genghis Khan killed his half-brother, was afraid of dogs, and fled when his wife was kidnapped.

What is also remarkable about this work is that it also provides the reader with insight into the Mongol mind. Since it was written for Mongols, many things are omitted or just barely referred to. A Mongol would automatically understand certain statements or comprehend what was implied. To the modern reader it can be somewhat difficult to understand, and many of its deeper meanings are coded in simple statements, yet it is still a rich source of information particularly on the early stages of the Mongol Empire.

Subedei

Subedei (1176–1248) was one of Khan's most capable military officers. He entered Genghis Khan's service as a young man. Subedei had a long, distinguished career leading Mongol troops all across Europe and Asia.

Early Life Subedei's elder brother, Jelme, had been a companion and servant of Genghis Khan since his youth and rose to be one of his most trusted aides. Jelme and Subedei were of the Uriangkhai, a forest-dwelling people to the north of Mongolia. Subedei followed in his brother's footsteps. Like Jelme, Subedei began his career as a servant, earning the trust of his lord by performing menial tasks such as tending his horses. At the same time, he learned leadership and military skills from Genghis Khan.

In time, Subedei amply proved his talent. He first served as a commander of one hundred men. By 1204 he was known as one of the "Four Hounds" of Genghis Khan, Genghis Khan's most trusted generals: Subedei, his brother Jelme, Jebe, and Khubilai (not to be confused with Genghis Khan's grandson, Kublai). As one of the Four Hounds, he was sent on the most urgent of missions and led an elite regiment of troops. After the unification of Mongolia in 1206, Subedei was appointed as commander of one thousand men, although it is very likely that he held this position before the official announcement took place at the crowning of Genghis Khan as ruler of Mongolia in 1206.

Military Successes Subedei's first military foray outside of Mongolia was conducted under the tutelage of Jebe. He pursued the renegade Naiman and Merkit tribes, tribes that refused to bow to Genghis Khan, into western Siberia in 1209. His success in this area also brought him into contact with the armies of the Khwarazmian Empire that were also in the region. Although the outcome of the war with the Khwarazmian Empire (1219–1223) was a draw, the ferocity of the outnumbered Mongols was such that it left Sultan Muhammad II, the Khwarazmian ruler, quite shaken.

After the Khwarazmian War, Subedei and Jebe set out through Transcaucasia (modern day Armenia, Azerbaijan, and Georgia) and across the Caucasus Mountains. There, they defeated a combined army of Russian princes and Kipchak Turks at the battle of the Kalka River in 1223. Jebe apparently died not long afterwards, but Subedei, now fully in charge, continued the mission and successfully joined forces with Jochi, son of Genghis Khan, in what is now Kazakhstan. This feat remains an unparalleled accomplishment: his forces rode approximately five thousand miles without the assistance of modern communications or reinforcements, and always in hostile territory.

Afterwards, Subedei had a few years of rest from campaigning. While stationed in Kazakhstan, he organized an army to protect the western flank of the empire. When Genghis Khan led his armies to deal with the recalcitrant Tanguts of Xi Xia in 1226–1227, Subedei led Mongol forces in the invasion. After Genghis Khan's death, Subedei had a brief falling-out with the new Mongol ruler Ogodei, but soon he was once again called upon to lead the Mongol armies. This time it was the all-out assault on the Jin Empire, and he was instrumental in that empire's ultimate destruction.

Later Campaigns In 1236, at the age of sixty, Subedei was ordered to lead the Mongols west towards the Volga River and into the Russian heartland. Batu, the son of Jochi, was the senior Mongol prince and held the nominal command of the campaign, but Subedei prepared the strategy and assumed overall operational command. In addition to an army of 150,000 men, they were accompanied by the dozens of grandsons of

An illustration of the camp of Genghis Khan from a book by Rashid al-Din, an official in the Ilkhanid court. *The Bridgeman Art Library/Getty Images*

Genghis Khan. Sudebei's most amazing achievement as a commander was not so much leading the army in this major campaign, but rather managing the egos of dozens of high-ranking Mongol princes. The fact that they accomplished anything despite constant princely rivalry is truly a testament to his abilities.

On this campaign, the Volga region fell quickly and by the end of 1237, the Mongols began their attack on Russian cities. Kiev, the grandest of the Russian cities, fell on December 6, 1240, but during the three years of campaigning, the Mongols had extended their empire by hundred of miles, from the Volga River to the Carpathian Mountains, conquering not only the Russian cities but also the Kipchak Turks of the steppes.

Subedei then planned his invasion of Central Europe with Mongol armies striking simultaneously at Hungary and Poland. The invasion of Poland was a diversion to keep Polish armies from potentially joining forces with the Hungarians. Subedei himself led the

assault on Hungary. The Mongols overpowered the mountain fortresses that guarded the passes. Subedei then encountered the Hungarian army at a spot called Mohi by the Sajo River. Here, Subedei demonstrated strategic and tactical genius by seizing the bridge over the river through the use of a rolling barrage from catapults. While one force did that, Subedei outflanked the Hungarians by building a pontoon bridge at another spot on the river. The two wings then proceeded to crush the Hungarians during a siege of their camp and the subsequent retreat.

Despite having free rein in Hungary, Subedei ordered his forces to withdraw in 1240 after receiving news of the death of Ogodei Khan. He and the princes in the army were needed for the selection process of the new ruler, which did not happen until 1246. Subedei's talents were still so respected that even after six years of inactivity (no fighting occurred until the election of a new khan) he was again asked to lead the army. Guyuk

Khan, the new ruler, asked the now seventy-year-old general to lead Mongol forces against the Song Empire. Subedei continued to demonstrate his talents, but after two years of inconclusive war, he was finally able to retire to the Tula River basin in Mongolia where he died in 1248.

Batu

One of the many sons of Jochi, the eldest son of Genghis Khan, Batu (1203–1255) became one of the most influential and powerful figures in the Mongol Empire. It had long been rumored that the father of Jochi was not really Genghis Khan but a Merkit prince who had kidnapped Borte, Genghis Khan's wife. Neither Batu nor anyone descended from Jochi had a legitimate chance of ruling the empire. Nonetheless, Batu became a powerful figure in his own right.

Batu's Patrimony   The territory of the Jochids, as the descendents of Jochi were known, was as far west as the Mongols had traveled. In the 1220s, a Mongol army led by Subedei (a trusted general of Genghis Khan) had reached the Black Sea. However, effective Mongol control only reached as far as the Aral Sea. The rest was in the hands of the Bulgars, who controlled much of the Volga River, the nomadic Kipchak Turks who controlled the steppe lands between the Caspian and Black Seas, and finally the Russian principalities.

In 1234, Ogodei Khan, the ruler of the Mongol empire after Genghis Khan, announced that it was time to claim the territory bequeathed to the sons of Jochi. Subedei, who had been recalled from the final stages of the war against the Jin Empire, was to lead the military campaign. Batu, as the leading prince, would be the nominal commander of an army of 150,000 men.

Bulgar and Russia   The army set out in February, 1236. The first target was the city of Bulgar, near modern Kazan, on the Volga River. Bulgar was an important commercial city in the region because its denizens procured furs from Siberia and sold them throughout Eurasia.

Batu led one part of the army against Bulgar, while the main body under Subedei marched against the Kipchaks. Bulgar fell in 1236 and most of the Kipchaks submitted to the Mongols later that year. This brought the present day Volga and Ural river basins under Mongol control.

In the winter of 1237, the Mongols invaded northeastern Russia. Ryazan fell in December. From there, the Mongols quickly overran Vladimir and other cities. An early spring thaw in March 1238 spared Novgorod from attack. Nonetheless, the Novgorodians saw the wisdom in submitting to the Mongols rather than risking an attack.

Batu's forces then overran southern Russia. Kiev refused to submit and was stormed in December 1240.

The Mongols then rested for the duration of the winter before invading Hungary and Poland.

Europe   The Mongols invaded Europe in 1241. Batu and Subedei led most of the Mongol army into Hungary while another force entered Poland. The Mongols won successive victories at Liegnitz and over the Hungarians at Mohi. The Mongols also raided deep into the Balkans and approached Vienna. All of Europe trembled before the impending attack, but then the Mongols suddenly retreated back behind the Carpathian Mountains.

Rivalry with Guyuk   The main reason for their retreat was the death of Ogodei in 1241. Guyuk, who was one of the sons of Ogodei and Batu's rival, was a contender for the throne. Batu led his forces back to the Volga River where he made his camp. Here the city of Sarai was built, which served as Batu's capital. Batu then watched and awaited the outcome of the Mongol election.

Unfortunately for Batu, Guyuk was chosen ruler in 1246. The two were enemies not only because Guyuk disparaged Batu's lineage, but also because Guyuk had been sent back to Ogodei due to insubordination during the Russian campaign. A livid Ogodei almost had his son executed; however, Ogodei died before any punishment could be meted out. Once in power, Guyuk intended to wage war against Batu.

Power of the Golden Horde   The war never occurred, however, since Guyuk died in 1248. Afterwards, Batu, now the most senior ranking prince in the empire, became engaged in politics. Knowing that he could never be khan, he instead engineered the election of Mongke, the son of Tolui (Genghis Khan's fourth son), in 1251. Mongke served on the Russian campaign and had proven his worth. In return for Batu's support, Mongke gave Batu almost complete autonomy in the west. Batu then spent the remainder of his life ruling his kingdom from Sarai and making the region a major power for the next two hundred years.

Yuri II

Yuri Vsevolodovich II (1189–1238) was the Grand Prince of the Russian principalities at the time of the Mongol invasion. His career reflects the complications of being the ruler (theoretically, at least) of medieval Russia. Although he was the Grand Prince, the subordinate princes carried out their own agendas, and unity was often ephemeral.

Rise to Power   Yuri was the third of the seven sons of Vsevolod III (d. 1212), the Grand Prince of Russia. His elder brothers Boris and Gleb had died in 1188 and 1189, respectively, making Yuri the eldest son. Yuri Vsevolodovich's family was from the province of Suzdal and although Kiev was the historic center of power and culture for the medieval Russians, Suzdal in the northeast of

Russia would remain the true base of his power. Yuri's rise to power was enhanced by a marriage to Agafia Vsevolodova arranged by Vsevolod a year before his death. Agafia was the daughter of Vsevolod Chermnyy, a long-time rival of Grand Prince Vsevolod. The marriage concluded a peace treaty on April 10, 1211.

After Vsevolod's death, Yuri was not guaranteed the throne. A considerable amount of infighting took place between all of the sons of Vsevolod before Yuri's claims were secure. In the meantime, those distractions allowed the dissolution of the unity that had been created by the marriage of Yuri and Agafia. Other wars between the princes throughout Russia became quite frequent as they all jockeyed for power.

Not until 1217 was Yuri secure in his position of Grand Prince, and then only in the northern cities was he completely accepted as ruler. Another three years went by before he was the undisputed Grand Prince of Russia. To aid in the process, Yuri placed his brothers as governors and princes in some cities when the opportunity arose.

Mongol Threat Although Yuri was Grand Prince, the decade of warfare that occurred after the death of his father ended the days of the all-powerful ruler. Although Yuri held the title, he could not assert himself in local matters even if he wanted to. He had become more of a first among equals. His power was respected, but whenever possible, the princes—particularly in southern Russia—ignored him.

Thus when the Mongols invaded southern Russia in 1223, Yuri's army was not involved in the crushing defeat at Kalka River. To Yuri, the Mongol invasion appeared to be just another incursion by steppe nomads, and the Bulgars on the Volga River were of greater concern. In the early 1220s, Yuri led a few campaigns against them, particularly when they took advantage of the disorder of the previous decade. Hostilities ended in 1229 as the Bulgars signed a peace treaty as a result of their own growing fears about the Mongols. After the peace treaty they had minimal contact until 1236, when the Bulgars appealed to Yuri for aid against the Mongols. Yuri declined.

The Mongol invasion began in 1237 at Ryazan, roughly 120 miles from Yuri's capital, Vladimir. Ryazan fell after a five-day siege on December 21, 1237. Yuri tried to lure the Mongols into open battle, but his attempt failed. The Mongols shadowed his moves, but meanwhile they continued to assault city after city. Yuri fell back to a sound defensive position on the Sit River, near the confluence of the Oka and Moskva rivers. The rivers, he hoped, would limit the mobility of the Mongols.

Unfortunately for Yuri, the Mongols took their time and did not rush to the attack. They surrounded him while they destroyed Vladimir. In the attack, Yuri's family, including his wife and daughters, were killed in February 1238. Yuri was helpless to prevent this, for although the Mongols did not attack him, they were always on the horizon, preventing him from moving his army.

Battle of Sit River On March 4, 1238, the Mongols launched their attack. Very little is known about it, primarily because on the Russian side there were few survivors and the Mongols merely listed it as a victory. The Mongol general Burundai crushed the Russian forces. Yuri was decapitated during the battle. Apparently, after Yuri's death the rest of the Russian army broke up and fled, only to be chased down and slaughtered by the Mongols.

After Yuri's death, his son Yaroslav ascended to the throne of the increasingly shrinking kingdom. He wisely submitted to the Mongols and ruled as a vassal over Suzdal until 1246, but with the Mongol presence, his authority was obviously limited.

Mongke

Mongke (1208–1259) was the last khan of a unified Mongol Empire. He was the eldest son of Tolui, the fourth son of Genghis Khan. Mongke resurrected the dynamism of the empire, sending it on another round of conquests after a decade of little fighting.

Mongke served with distinction in the great westward expansion of the Mongol Empire led by Batu and Subedei. He fought against the Kipchaks and then later in the Caucasus region (present day Chechnya) in 1238–1239. During these campaigns he formed a good relationship with his cousin, Batu. Whereas virtually all of the princes of the Mongol Empire were cousins to one degree or another, the bond between the families of Jochi and Tolui were especially close. The wives of Jochi and Tolui—Chaur and Sorqoqtani, respectively—were also sisters.

The Coup This close relationship was pivotal in the rise of Mongke. After the death of Guyuk Khan in 1248, the administration of the empire came to a halt as the regent, Oghul Qaimish (Guyuk's wife), showed no intention of selecting a new khan. Seeing an opportunity and tired of the governmental malaise, Sorqoqtani and Batu plotted to overthrow her. They agreed to place Mongke on the throne.

A *quriltai*, or meeting, was held in 1251. Although Batu did not attend, he provided thirty thousand troops for security. In the meantime, Sorqoqtani procured the support of some of the princes from outside the Toluid and Jochid families. Thus Mongke ascended the throne; he arrested Oghul Qaimish and accused her of a variety of crimes, ranging from negligence of state matters to witchcraft. Indeed, the Mongols brought in special shamans in case of any magical threats.

Purge Initially there was little opposition from the other branches of Genghis Khan's family. However, the dissenters soon made their discontent known. Shiremun, a son of Ogodei, believed that he should be the new khan. Indeed, he had been a candidate for the crown when Guyuk was elected. He and others plotted against Mongke. They pretended to come to Mongke's court to pay homage, but their wagons contained armed warriors rather than their families. Fortunately for Mongke, the plot was discovered. Accompanied by his own troops and those of Batu, he intercepted the plotters and arrested them.

The ringleaders were executed and a purge began. Mongke set up an investigative board, and all the princes and government officials were scrutinized to determine their loyalty. In the end, most of the descendents of Ogodei were executed along with many of those of Chaghatay, another son of Genghis Khan. Only those who were personally known and trusted by Mongke were spared.

Mongke also used the purges as an effective means of reconstructing the administration of the empire. During the time of Oghul Qaimish, government positions were easily bought and used to exploit the subjects of the empire. Mongke returned qualified administrators to their positions and restored the efficiency of the government. He then marshaled the resources of the empire in order to resume the expansion of the Mongol state.

China Mongke ordered two invasions. While his brother Hulegu invaded the Middle East, Mongke sought to complete the conquest of the Song Empire, which had begun in 1234 and made little progress since. His brother, Kublai, led the initial forces against the Song. Mongke set off to join him.

In 1258, Mongke crossed the Yellow River and divided his army into four corps, attacking the Song on multiple fronts. Mongke's personal army did quite well, capturing the cities of Chengdu and Tongchuan, along with multiple fortresses. He then moved against the important city of Hezhou in 1259. The siege began in typical fashion, as the Mongols surrounded the city with a palisade and began to bombard it with their siege engines. However, during the siege, Mongke died. It is not clear if he died from an arrow wound or from dysentery, since the sources disagree.

Mongke's death set the stage for the breakup of the Mongol Empire. Kublai and Ariq Boke—the youngest son of Tolui and brother to Mongke, Kublai, and Hulegu—both claimed the throne. A civil war erupted and the western portions of the empire began to act on their own and fight their own disputes, thus ending the unity of the empire.

Kublai Khan

Kublai Khan (1215–1294) was probably the most famous Mongol Khan after his grandfather, Genghis Khan (1165–1227). Kublai was one of the four sons of Sorqoqtani, a Mongolian queen who greatly influenced

Kublai Khan. *The Library of Congress*

the course of the empire, and Tolui. Although Kublai established himself as the titular ruler of the Mongol empire, his brothers were also significant personages in history. Mongke, his elder brother, ruled the empire from 1251 to 1259 while Hulegu established the Mongol Il-Khanate in the Middle East. After Mongke's death, Kublai fought a civil war with his brother Ariq Boke for control of the empire, which Kublai won in 1264.

The empire he won was not the entire Mongol Empire, which had stretched from the Sea of Japan to the Carpathian Mountains. Instead, this "Great Khanate" consisted only of Mongolia, Korea, and modern China, including Tibet. Meanwhile, the Chaghatayid Khanate in Central Asia alternated between fighting Kublai and recognizing him as its overlord, depending on who was currently in power. The Il-Khanate in the Middle East remained a steadfast ally and subordinate state, but the Golden Horde, as the Il-Khanate eventually became known in Russia, remained distant and only provided token recognition to Kublai Khan.

Conquest of the Song Empire Kublai's greatest military achievement was the conquest of southern China, the location of the Song Empire. The Mongols had been at war with the Song Empire since 1234, but had made little headway. Mongke died during the largest invasion, of which Kublai was the leader. After securing the state against Ariq Boke, Kublai redoubled his efforts. He steadily moved against the Song Empire's mountain fortresses and captured cities along the rivers with the use of a navy and increased use of Chinese infantry.

The use of the navy and infantry was pivotal because the mountainous terrain and numerous rice paddies hampered the traditional Mongol cavalry. Finally, in 1272 the Mongols captured the city of Xiangyang after a three-year siege. Although the conflict lasted another six years, Kublai conquered the Song empire in 1279 with a naval victory at Yaishan.

Failed Invasions When not embroiled with civil wars against his cousins, Kublai did attempt to expand his empire. Kublai sent ambassadors to Japan, requesting that they come to him and submit to his authority. Despite the Mongols' reputation, the Japanese believed that their samurai tradition and the isolation provided by being an island state would protect them from the Mongol onslaught. Therefore, they rebuffed the request.

In the eyes of the Mongols, who believed that heaven had decreed that they should rule the world, this was an act of rebellion. In 1274, Kublai sent an army of almost thirty thousand men and more than three hundred ships to Japan. After initial successes, the navy was destroyed by storms. The same thing would happen in 1281 when the Mongols sent two armies, numbering more than one hundred thousand men in total. Thus Japan was spared from Mongol conquest.

Kublai's overseas ventures did not end with Japan, though. In 1289, Kublai's envoys requested the submission of the kingdoms of Java. Initially, the Mongols had success, especially after fighting broke out among rival powers on Java. Some of the rulers submitted to the Mongols. After the Mongols won at the battle of Kediri, it appeared that the island was theirs. However, Prince Vijaya, who had submitted to the Mongols, betrayed them and drove the Mongols off the island.

Kublai's attempts at conquest outside of China continued to prove unsuccessful. Invasions of modern-day Vietnam and Burma failed, although many of the princes decided it was better to pay tribute than to face continual Mongol raids and invasions.

Although Kublai's military operations overseas and in southeast Asia were desultory, it is still amazing that he could even attempt them. During his entire reign, his armies were continuously active against other Mongol armies in Central Asia. In many ways, the invasions of Japan and Java were extravagant—Kublai's major concern was quelling the war with his rival Qaidu, a cousin, in Central Asia. This war, however, continued even after Kublai's death in 1295.

Kublai was known for the magnificence of his court, and his wisdom and accomplishments. Although his military record was not like his grandfather's, Kublai's

---

KAMIKAZE

The Japanese were "miraculously" saved from Mongol invasion not once, but twice, by typhoons that destroyed the Mongol fleets. The grateful Japanese named the storms *kamikaze*, or "divine wind." The word would later be applied to the Japanese pilots who carried out suicide missions against U.S. forces during World War II.

---

fame endured. Immortalized in *The Travels of Marco Polo* as well as Samuel Taylor Coleridge's poem "Kubla Khan," Kublai Khan and his legacy have only grown over time.

Hulegu

The early life of Hulegu (1217–1265) is a mystery, but it is known that he was the son of Genghis Khan's fourth son, Tolui, and his wife Sorqoqtani. Hulegu was the younger brother of Mongke, the fourth Khan of the empire, and Kublai Khan, Mongke's successor. Despite being in the shadows of his elder brothers, Hulegu carved his own impressive legacy in history by conquering much of the Middle East.

After Mongke became khan, he ordered Hulegu to invade the Middle East with an army of 150,000 men. The Mongols had been operating in the Middle East since 1230, but the region was not fully under Mongol control.

The Assassins Hulegu's first target was the sect of Shi'a Muslims called the Ismailis, more popularly known as the Assassins. They were known for being masters of disguise and for their assassinations of political leaders throughout the region. While much of their lethal reputation was based on fact, it was greatly enhanced by legend and rumor.

Although the Mongol Empire had bordered the Assassin territory for twenty-five years, they still had not conquered them. The Assassins had once been allies and perhaps even clients of the Mongols. However, since 1240 there had been sporadic skirmishes between the two powers. During Mongke's enthronement, it was rumored that four hundred Assassins were making their way to Karakorum, the Mongol capital, to kill him.

It is not known if this was the truth, but the rumor was enough evidence for Mongke. In 1256, Hulegu's army marched on the Assassin-held territories in the Alborz Mountains south of the Caspian Sea. Ket Buqa, the commander of Hulegu's vanguard, began the assault on the mountain castles. The Assassins made some guerilla attacks, but realizing that they did not have a chance against the Mongol army in the open, they opted

FROM "KUBLA KHAN," BY SAMUEL TAYLOR COLERIDGE

In Xanadu did Kubla Khan
A stately pleasure-dome decree:
Where Alph, the sacred river, ran
Through caverns measureless to man
Down to a sunless sea.
So twice five miles of fertile ground
With walls and towers were girdled round:
And there were gardens bright with sinuous rills,
Where blossomed many an incense-bearing tree;
And here were forests ancient as the hills,
Enfolding sunny spots of greenery.

to focus primarily on the defense of their mountain fortresses.

The Mongols quickly set large forces against the principal fortresses of Alamut and Maymun-Diaz. In the meantime, Hulegu demanded that the Assassin leader, Rukn al-Din, come before him and submit. As Rukn al-Din had taken refuge at Maymun-Diaz, Hulegu focused his efforts there; the castle fell with two weeks.

Afterwards, Hulegu used Rukn al-Din as a pawn to secure the surrender of other fortresses. Eventually, however, his usefulness diminished, and Rukn al-Din was sent to Karakorum. At some point, possibly on the return journey, he was kicked to death.

Baghdad After the destruction of the Assassins, Hulegu advanced against Baghdad. Although the titular head of the Islamic world, in reality the Caliph had very little power. The Caliph, an incompetent named Mustasim, tried to ignore the Mongol threat, but Hulegu's forces overwhelmed the defenses of Baghdad in 1258, and the Abbasid Caliph came to an end.

Syria After the destruction of Baghdad, Hulegu advanced on Syria. Many of the local princes in what is now northern Iraq, eastern Turkey, and northern Syria came and submitted to him. One such ruler was Bohemund VII of Antioch and Tripoli, a Crusader prince.

Afterwards, Hulegu marched on Aleppo and quickly took it. While Ket Buqa captured Damascus in 1260, Hulegu withdrew the bulk of the army to the Mughan plain in modern Azerbaijan, where there was sufficient pasture for his horses. He had also heard of the death of his brother Mongke and needed to determine what would happen next.

The Il-Khanate At the same time, the Mamluks of Egypt defeated Ket Buqa and the Mongol garrison at Ayn Jalut in 1260. Thus the Mongols were driven out of Syria, but Hulegu could do little about it. After

Mongke's death, the empire split into four realms. Hulegu ruled what became known as the Il-Khanate of Persia, consisting mostly of Iran and Persia.

Most of Hulegu's time, until his death in 1265, was consumed by a civil war with his cousin, Berke, son of Jochi, who was the eldest son of Genghis Khan. The war was ostensibly triggered by Hulegu's execution of the Caliph, which angered Berke, a Muslim convert. However it was actually fought over Berke's claims to the Mughan plain. The issue was never resolved as the Il-Khanate would fight the Golden Horde, as Berke's state became known, basically until the end of the Il-Khanate in 1335.

Hulegu successfully established his own kingdom; unfortunately, the chronic warfare that erupted after his death prevented it from ever becoming very stable.

Mustasim

Abu Ahmad Abd Allah ibn al-Mustansir al-Mustasim bi Allah, more commonly known as Mustasim (1212–1258), has the dubious honor of being the last Caliph from the Abbasid family. During his reign from 1242 to 1258, the Mongols destroyed the Abbasid Caliphate and sacked Baghdad, doing so while Mustasim demonstrated an alarming amount of incompetence.

As Caliph Like so many medieval figures, little is known about his early life. His father, the Caliph al-Mustansir, died in December 1242. Al-Mustansir had been a determined leader and had even thwarted a few small invasions by the Mongols. He had kept the army in a constant state of readiness. When al-Mustasim came to the throne, he quickly proved that he was not the same caliber of leader as his father.

The first decade and a half of his reign was rather unremarkable. During this period the Mongols rarely even raided the territory controlled by the Abbasid Caliphate, which extended roughly from Basra to the south to Tikrit in the north, in modern-day Iraq. However, this is not to say that this region was tranquil.

The large army his father created was supported by fiefs known as *iqtas*. Unlike medieval European knights who ruled their fiefs on behalf of their lord, in the Middle East the warriors did not rule their fiefs. They instead received a share of the proceeds from the land, markets, and orchards. Since this served as their pay, the warriors had incentive to protect and also not to plunder the land.

Mustasim, feeling that the army was a drain on government revenues, began to reduce the number of iqtas allotted to the army in 1250–1251. Because of this change, the number of troops was also significantly reduced. Furthermore, Mustasim ignored tensions between minority Shi'a Muslims and the more numerous Sunni Muslims. Thus, when violence between the two groups erupted in 1258 after the Caliph's son Abu

Bikr massacred the Shi'a Muslims at Karkha and Mashad, Mustasim lacked the authority to quell the violence.

Mustasim also neglected affairs of state, spending most of his time preoccupied with his collection of doves. While he raced them and engaged in other bird games, he left the major affairs of state to his wazir, or minister of state, Alqami.

The Plot Against Mustasim Alqami, a Shi'a Muslim himself, was competent in his job, but there were also rivalries within the government. The *dawatdar*, or chief secretary, Sultan Mujahid al-Din-i-bak (a Sunni), challenged his every move. Alqami was also enraged by the actions of Mustasim's son and sought an alliance with the Mongols. Although the Mongols had just destroyed the Shi'a Assassin sect, Alqami saw the Mongols as a good alternative to the Sunnis. The Mongols were known for their policy of religious tolerance, something out of the norm for the age.

Alqami successfully contacted the Mongols, but some of the messages were intercepted and given to the dawatdar, Sultan Mujahid. The dawatdar knew of the wazir's hostility towards the Caliph's son and informed the Caliph of the plot. Alqami was not easily removed from office; he successfully turned the tables on Sultan Mujahid and said that Sultan Mujahid plotted to raise Abu Bikr to the throne. The confused Caliph did not know who to believe, so he ignored them both.

Meanwhile, Alqami continued his undermining of Baghdad. He dismissed Kurdish regiments under the pretence that it was part of maintaining peaceful relations with the Mongols. When Hulegu advanced on Baghdad, its defenses were dismal compared to when Mustasim's father was the Caliph. In addition, despite his own role in reducing the size and effectiveness of the army, Mustasim apparently did not think that anyone would dare attack the Caliph's city.

The Mongol Threat When the Mongol envoys arrived requesting tribute, Mustasim sent them back to Hulegu with a threatening letter. This only angered the Mongol prince, and the war began. Afterwards Mustasim had second thoughts and tried to appease the Mongols with an annual tribute, but Hulegu refused it.

The siege of Baghdad began in January and was completed by February 10, 1258. Hulegu allowed his men to plunder the city for several days. Ten days later he met with Mustasim and chastised him for hoarding his wealth instead of using it to pay his soldiers and improve the defenses of the city. He then had Mustasim honorably executed: so that his blood would not be spilt on to the ground, he was rolled in a carpet and trampled by horses. Thus ended the last of the Abbasid Caliphs.

Saif al-Din Qutuz

Saif al-Din Qutuz (?–1260) was a Mamluk amir (commander) of Egypt who faced the threat of the Mongol juggernaut. Within a span of five years, the Mongols had eliminated the menace of the Assassins, destroyed the former center of the Muslim world by sacking Baghdad, and almost casually swept over Syria. Rather than fleeing, as so many had, Qutuz instead took the battle to the Mongols and drove them out of Syria.

Becoming a Mamluk No one was born a Mamluk. The Mamluks, who were military slaves, were selected from the boys brought in by slave traders. Turks were usually preferred because most of them already had experience at riding horses and in archery. Saif al-Din Qutuz came to the slave market in Damascus during the Mongol invasion of the Middle East in the 1220s and 1230s, but the exact year is not known.

Qutuz was the nephew of Jalal al-Din Khwarazm-shah, the last ruler of the Khwarazmian Empire, which had been destroyed by the Mongols. Qutuz, taken captive by the Mongols, was then sold to a slave trader from Damascus who in turn sold him to a Mamluk amir in Cairo named Mu'izz Aybak al-Turkumani (1250–1257).

As their masters fed and clothed them quite well, Mamluks often developed an intense loyalty to their owners. Mamluks trained every day in the arts of archery, fencing, lancing, and horsemanship. With this intense training, the Mamluks became renowned for their abilities and were probably, man-for-man, the best soldiers in the world. Unfortunately, because of the expense in training and arming them, like most elite forces they were relatively few in number.

Rise to Power Prior to Qutuz, Egypt was ruled by Shajar al-Durr and Qutuz's master Aybak. Qutuz served as his viceroy. Aybak was assassinated in 1257 by his wife because he intended to take another wife, the daughter of the Sultan of Mosul in northern Iraq. In turn, Aybak's slaves murdered her. Aybak's son, al-Mansur Ali, was then proclaimed sultan while Qutuz continued to serve as viceroy.

From 1257 to 1258, Qutuz was very active, fighting other Mamluks and their Syrian allies who together sought to overthrow Aybak's young son. As this child was only ten, Qutuz was the real power behind the throne, but he remained loyal to the child out of respect for his former master. However, in 1259, Qutuz replaced al-Mansur as the Sultan of Egypt. He did promise that after defeating the Mongols, he would relinquish the throne to Aybak's son.

With the Mongols invading Syria in 1259, the sultanate could no longer be ruled by a child—a man of action was needed. In this time of danger, Qutuz's heritage did not hurt his reputation either, as his uncle, Jalal al-Din, had been one of the few leaders who had defeated the Mongols.

To better face the Mongols, Qutuz and the other Mamluk leaders—including Baybars, who was one of his most ardent opponents—came to terms. Not only did Qutuz accept Baybars's services, but he awarded him territory and a high rank. Thus, Qutuz was able to recruit a strong army.

War with the Mongols Mongol envoys arrived in Cairo, demanding that Egypt submit or face destruction. Qutuz's response was to execute them, a clear declaration of war. Furthermore, he decided to lead the Mamluk army against the Mongols in Syria.

Qutuz chose his time perfectly. He struck while the Mongol prince Hulegu was occupied in Azerbaijan waiting for information concerning the death of Mongke, his brother and the ruler of the Mongol Empire. Hulegu had left a small but suitable garrison to maintain order in Syria. This was a sufficient force to ensure order, but only so long as no other destabilizing factors entered the country.

Qutuz's army overran the Mongol border guard at Gaza and made their way to Ayn Jalut, in modern Israel. Here Qutuz met the Mongol forces led by Kit Buqa and defeated the Mongols.

Qutuz could not savor his victory though. After securing Syria from further Mongol attacks, he marched back to Cairo. One day when they stopped to rest, Qutuz was assassinated by Baybars and other commanders. Baybars then assumed the throne. It was rumored that enmity between Qutuz and Baybars arose again after Qutuz refused to award Baybars the governorship of Aleppo for his role at Ayn Jalut. Qutuz did not trust Baybars, quite rightly as it turned out, and did not want him so far away. Unfortunately, having Baybars close to him was even deadlier.

Timur

Timur (1336–1405) was a Tatar ruler who conquered central Eurasia and much of the Near and Middle East. He was born near Kesh, near Samarkand (in modern day Uzbekistan). Timur was the son of Taragai of the Barlas Tribe, a tribe with Mongolian origins but thoroughly Turkic in ethnicity by Timur's lifetime. During his youth, Timur's right arm and leg were paralyzed from arrow wounds received during a raid. Later his detractors called him *Timur-i Leng*, Persian for "Timur the Lame," which became "Tamerlane" in the West. Timur began his career as a minor leader and occasional bandit during the unrest that marked much of Central Asia during the mid-fourteenth century. He eventually carved out a sizable empire in the region, doing so by means that were typically quite brutal.

Early Career With the collapse of the Chaghatayid Khanate (a successor state of the Mongol Empire that covered most of Central Asia), new opportunities arose in the region. Timur worked a chaotic situation to his advantage and became the lieutenant of his brother-in-law Emir Husain. The two gained control of Mawarannahr—Arabic for "Land Across the River," (i.e., the Amu Darya), also called Transoxiana—before a falling-

Tamerlane (Timur the Lame), an Islamic Turkic conqueror, set out to reestablish the great Asian empire of Genghis Khan and the Mongols. *Hulton Archive/Getty Images*

out pitted Timur and Husain against each other in 1370. After a heated contest, Timur emerged as the victor.

After defeating Husain, Timur spent the next ten years consolidating his control in the region and defending it from raids by the remnants of the Chaghatayid Khanate in Moghulistan (modern Kazakhstan and Xinjiang in modern China). Beginning in 1380, Timur became embroiled in external affairs when he began lending support to Toqtamysh, a prince in the Golden Horde. (Located in modern Russia and Ukraine, the Golden Horde was another remnant of the Mongol Empire.) Toqtamysh was embroiled in a civil war. Timur saw this as a valuable opportunity to not only secure a border, but also to have influence in the Golden Horde, a powerful neighbor.

Building an Empire Not until 1383 did Timur expand his realm beyond Mawarannahr. In that year, his forces crossed the Amu Darya River into Persia and conquered the area known as Khurasan (parts of modern Iran and Afghanistan and eastern Iran). By 1394, the regions of Fars, Iraq, Azerbaijan, Armenia, and Georgia succumbed to his armies as well. It is questionable if Timur actually sought to create a true stable empire, as he seems to have preferred to plunder these areas rather than to collect taxes and tribute.

Meanwhile, Timur's protégé and new ruler of the Golden Horde, Toqtamysh, challenged Timur's authority. As a descendent of Genghis Khan, Toqtamysh viewed himself as the rightful leader of the post-Mongol Empire. Toqtamysh invaded Timur's empire in 1385 and 1388, defeating Timur's generals twice. In retaliation, Timur invaded the Golden Horde in 1391 and defeated Toqtamysh. Although beaten, Toqtamysh regained power and invaded Timur's empire again in 1395.

Timur decided to finish the rivalry once and for all. He pursued Toqtamysh and finally caught him in a battle on the Kur River. Timur defeated him and then proceeded to break the power of the Golden Horde by inciting and supporting various contenders for the throne, but making sure none could be a threat to his own power. Although Timur effectively conquered the Golden Horde, he did not seek to incorporate it into his empire, perhaps realizing that as a non-Chinggisid prince, he would never be accepted as the ruler in that region. Thus he settled for its continued existence, in a weakened form.

With one border secure, Timur turned his attention to India, invading the Sultanate of Delhi in 1398. As he did for many campaigns, Timur justified his actions on religious grounds. His armies sacked and burned Delhi in a wanton display of destruction, but Timur—a Muslim—legitimized his invasion on the grounds of Sultan Mahmud Tughlak's excessive toleration of his Hindu subjects. As always after a campaign, wealth from the plunder poured into his capital at Samarkand.

Western Campaigns Despite the massive haul of plunder, Timur did not remain at his capital. In 1399, he marched west against the Mamluk Sultanate in Egypt and Syria and the Ottoman Empire in Anatolia (modern Turkey). Both states had supported rebellions against Timur or threatened his vassals. After putting down a rebellion in Azerbaijan, Timur invaded Syria in 1401 and defeated the Mamluks, sacking Aleppo and Damascus in the process. At Damascus, he ransomed it once, and then decided to plunder it after deeming the ransom insufficient. He then invaded Anatolia and defeated the Ottoman army at Ankara in 1402. Here he also captured Sultan Bayezid, formerly known as the terror of Europe, leaving the Ottoman Empire in turmoil for the next fifty years.

The Last Campaign of Timur With his western frontier now secure from the threat of attack, Timur returned to Samarkand in 1404. Despite being carried in a litter for most of his later campaigns, Timur did not plan a life of ease yet. Instead, he planned for an invasion of China, ruled by the Ming Dynasty. The invasion

ended prematurely as Timur died on January 19, 1405, at the city of Otrar. Although he had designated a successor, his empire, held together primarily through the force of his will, quickly disintegrated into smaller states ruled by his sons and grandsons.

Legend and Legacy Timur continues to be most often remembered for his conquests and cruelty. Massacres accompanied all of his victories, and he left reminders of his deeds in the form of towers of skulls. These served both as monuments to his achievements and warnings to those who opposed him. Yet Timur was not a crude, unsophisticated barbarian. Even his enemies noted that he was an expert chess player, very intelligent, fluent in several languages, and well-versed in the art of debate. Indeed, he would debate Muslim theologians from either the Sunni or Shi'a perspective.

Although his own empire was ephemeral, Timur dramatically impacted five states. His defeat of the Ottomans spared the Byzantine Empire for another fifty years, as Bayezid had planned to attack Constantinople before his defeat at Ankara. Although he did not destroy them, Timur's defeat of the Mamluks exposed the slow decay of their once grand military might. With his defeat of Toqtamysh, Timur eroded the strength of the Golden Horde and accelerated the end of nomadic dominance over the principalities of Russia. Although he sacked Moscow (then a small town), Timur's defeat of Toqtamysh also contributed to the rise of Moscow. His destruction of Delhi was the death knell for the Sultanate of Delhi. Indeed, although his empire disintegrated after his death, Timur's descendents established the Moghul Empire in India, supplanting the Sultanate of Delhi.

Bayezid I

Bayezid (1354–1403) was one of the most dynamic sultans in the history of the Ottoman Empire. His military feats earned him the name of Yildirim ("Thunderbolt"). The rapidity of his conquest, particularly in the Balkans, also made him the "Terror of Europe." However, much to his regret, he eventually discovered that there was a conqueror even more powerful than he.

Rise to Power Bayezid accompanied his father, Sultan Murad I, on his campaigns in the Balkans. It was on one such campaign that Bayezid became the ruler of the Ottoman Empire. Murad suffered a mortal wound on the Field of Kosovo (June 15, 1389), and on that battlefield Bayezid became sultan.

He immediately had to secure his power against rivals and rebels. First he formed a marriage alliance with his Serbian vassals, then he returned to Anatolia to deal with rebellious subjects there. Afterwards, the Ottoman Empire in Anatolia stretched to the Karaman state in eastern Anatolia.

BAJAZET I.

Bayezid I was defeated by the Mongols under Timur in 1402.
© The Print Collector/Alamy

The Terror of Europe In Europe, Bulgaria and Serbia had rebelled and Greece was restless as well. Although the Ottoman garrisons located in Europe did their best to quell the rebellions, the magnitude of the uprisings required Sultan Bayezid's presence.

In 1393, Bayezid's forces invaded Bulgaria and quickly overran Trnovo, the Bulgarian capital city. Meanwhile, he sent troops to establish a blockade of Constantinople. The Byzantine Empire was at this point less an empire than just a city, but it remained influential because it still represented the legacy of the Roman Empire. Its prestige was greater than its power. In 1394, Bayezid began what became a seven-year blockade.

As the blockade continued, Bayezid led his main forces deeper into Europe. With continued Ottoman successes, the call for a Crusade spread throughout Europe, sponsored by the Venetians and Hungarians. This Crusade ended at Nicopolis in 1396 as a complete disaster. Despite the warnings of the Hungarians, French knights fell for the feigned retreat of the Ottoman cav-alry and were mowed down by the Janissary archers. The rest of the Crusader army was also annihilated.

Ottoman Military Power Bayezid is often credited for implementing or strengthening new military innovations in the Ottoman army. It is during his reign that the *devshirme* system, or tribute paid in children, increased. The children were then the slaves of the Sultan, and fed, clothed, and trained by him. This gave the Sultan a loyal counter to the traditional cavalry forces of the Turkic aristocracy. Some of the children were trained to serve in the administration of the Ottoman Empire, but the majority entered the Janissary corps, the Yeni Cheri ("New Army" in Turkish). They served as infantry, first as archers but later as musketeers. Their loyalty and effectiveness made them the most feared fighting force in Europe and western Asia.

Demise of the Thunderbolt In addition to securing and expanding Ottoman territory in Europe, Bayezid also sought to consolidate and expand his territory in Asia. His reputation as a *ghazi*, or warrior of the faith, was undisputed after his victories over the Christian armies of Europe. However, in Anatolia, he faced his fellow Muslims, who were also Turks. This led to some complications, and Bayezid had to find ways of justifying his wars against them. Also, his Turkic troops were less enthusiastic about fighting their co-religionists, thus forcing Bayezid to rely more on his Janissaries and European vassals.

Ultimately, this ambitious endeavor to conquer Europe and the Middle East led him into conflict with another powerful leader: Timur of Central Asia. In the early 1390s, Bayezid had expanded his Anatolian holdings to the borders of the small state of Karaman in eastern Anatolia. In 1397, Bayezid choose to annex the territory. This is what brought him into conflict with Timur, who had claims on the territory as well.

The two rulers, with equally large egos, could not resolve the issue diplomatically. In addition, Bayezid was known to have assisted Timur's rival Toqtamysh, further drawing his ire. Eventually the two collided in battle at Ankara in July 1402. In the end, Bayezid was defeated. Timur took him captive and hauled the Ottoman ruler back to Samarkand in an iron cage. Bayezid eventually died in captivity.

Timur did not attempt to conquer the Ottoman state. Instead, Timur left Bayezid's sons to fight amongst themselves, leaving it too weak to be a threat to him.

⊕ Major Battles

Zhongdu, 1210s

Zhongdu was the capital of the Jin Empire (1125–1234) in northern China. Located near modern Beijing, it was an impressive city, boasting a population nearly one million people. Zhongdu was well-protected by strong walls and outlying fortresses. Furthermore, the Jin had an army that consisted of over 500,000 cavalry and even more infantry. At the time of the Mongol invasions, they were one of the most advanced civilizations in the world in terms of technology.

Early Attacks Mongol attacks on the Jin Empire began in 1211. Although the Jin possessed much larger armies, they had no one who could match Genghis Khan's brilliance or the talent of his generals. The Mongols had burst through mountain passes and even raided the environs of Zhongdu by January 1212. As the surrounding towns surrendered or were pillaged, Zhongdu became an island in a sea of Mongol attacks. The Mongols then withdrew, content with the plunder they gained. However, this peace was brief, for later that year the Mongols attacked again.

The 1212–1214 War Beginning in 1212, Mongol armies invaded and spread across the Jin Empire like a plague of locusts. The Jin attempted to counter their attacks. At the end of November 1213, the Jin army defeated two Mongol forces north of Zhongdu. A third Mongol attack annihilated the Jin troops, leading the Jin to extend the olive branch in December 1213. The Mongols rejected the peace terms.

Rather than tying down his army with a siege, Genghis Khan left five thousand men to patrol and blockade Zhongdu. Meanwhile he divided the main army into three forces and attacked the rest of the empire. As the three-pronged attack devastated the rest of the empire, it was difficult for the Jin armies to coordinate their efforts, and so they remained on the defensive.

Meanwhile, the garrison of Zhongdu discovered they could not attempt an attack on the Mongols outside the city. As the Mongol armies moved quickly (both in retreat and advance), the unnerved garrison became paralyzed by the fact that Genghis Khan might suddenly descend upon them.

Then in late February or March of 1214, Genghis Khan launched two unsuccessful attacks on Zhongdu, which convinced the Jin to attempt peace negotiations. Weary of war, the Jin negotiated a peace treaty that gave Genghis Khan the daughter of the previous emperor, five hundred boys and girls for the daughter's retinue, three thousand horses, and several carts loaded with gold and silk. Content with the loot, the Mongols withdrew north.

The Final Destruction The lull in hostilities between the Mongols and the Jin was brief. As a result of the looming Mongol threat and the devastation around Zhongdu, the Jin Emperor moved south. Genghis Khan viewed this movement as a violation of the treaty. The Mongols sent an army of fifty thousand to Zhongdu and surrounded it in September 1214. Rather than attacking directly, the Mongols blockaded it in hopes of starving it into submission. As the siege continued, some Jin

commanders attempted to relieve the city. In April 1215, two such armies were defeated. After that, no other attempts were made.

The plight of the Jin worsened after these defeats as the Jin saw other cities fall to the Mongols throughout the month of May, leaving Zhongdu increasingly isolated and desperate. As the blockade of Zhongdu continued, there were incidents of cannibalism, and the commanders of the defense squabbled over the best course of action.

Finally, Zhongdu surrendered to the Mongols in June 1215. Genghis Khan returned north while his armies looted the city. Khwarazmian merchants who visited the city months after the siege ended noted the slaughter: there were bodies piled as high as hills.

Implications for the Jin The fall of Zhongdu was not only a great military defeat for the Jin, but it also undermined their defense of other territories. Many areas simply surrendered rather than trying to resist the Mongol onslaught any longer. Rebellions broke out and spread across the dwindling Jin Empire. Some of the rebels submitted to the Mongols while others attempted to create their own kingdoms. The Mongols dealt with the latter harshly. At the same time, forces from the Song Empire and the Tangut Kingdom to the west invaded the Empire as well. The Jin could hold off the Tangut and the Song, but not the Mongols. Nonetheless, the Jin Empire struggled on until 1234, partially because Genghis Khan became distracted by events in Central Asia that led him and most of the army west.

Kalka, 1224

The first encounter between the Mongols and the Russians occurred in 1224 at the Kalka River. The battle was an unforeseen result of a reconnaissance expedition by the Mongol generals Subedei and Jebe. After the Mongols invaded the Khwarazmian Empire in Central Asia in 1219, Genghis Khan granted permission to these generals to continue west and explore the region.

After leaving Persia, the Mongols continued north and crossed the Caucasus Mountains and into the Kipchak steppes, which were the grasslands around the Black and Caspian seas. Here they defeated an army of Kipchak Turks, the dominant tribe in the region. The defeated nomads under Kotian Khan turned to Russian princes of Kiev for help, as Kotian's tribe had several marriage alliances with them. (Indeed, Kotian's brother-in-law was Prince Mstislav Mstislavich of Galicia.) The Russians joined the Kipchaks after the nomads convinced them that if they did not form an alliance now, the Mongols would advance upon them after defeating the Kipchaks. Furthermore, the Russians realized that if defeated, the Kipchaks would most likely be incorporated into the Mongol forces.

In the meantime, the Mongols denied any interest in the Russians and informed them that their grudge

Mongol invaders are victorious at the Kalka River.   © *Mary Evans Picture Library/Alamy*

was solely with the Kipchaks. By way of a reply, the Russians killed the Mongol envoy and prepared for war. The Russian force included Grand Prince Mstislav Romanovich of Kiev, Prince Mikhail of Chernigov, Mstislav Mstislavich of Galicia, Daniilo Romanovich, the grandson of Mstislav of Kiev, and others. As they set out against the Mongols, they met another Mongolian emissary who warned them that since they had killed the previous envoy, war was guaranteed. The murder of the envoy had been a bold move, for despite the fact that the Russians did not know much about the Mongols, they had heard rumors that the Mongols defeated everyone they encountered.

The Russian armies joined the Kipchaks at the Dnieper River. Not long after crossing the Dnieper, scouts reported that the Mongols were in sight and surveying the Russian boats. This prompted Daniilo Romanovich to ride ahead and scout out the enemy. A sizable number of troops accompanied him. Having verified the report, he and Prince Mstislav Mstislavich decided to attack. They defeated a Mongol force and pursued the survivors.

Other princes advanced after Mstislav Mstislavich's success and joined the pursuit. Although the Mongols

fled before the Russians, they always remained in view but out of reach. Thus the Russian-Kipchak forces chased the Mongols for eight days before reaching the Kalka River. On the ninth day, Prince Mstislav Mstislavich ordered Prince Daniilo Romanovich to cross the Kalka River and continue the pursuit while he established a camp along the banks.

Lightly armed Kipchaks served as a vanguard and scouts for the pursuit force, and these units frequently skirmished with the Mongols. This delayed the Mongols enough so that the Russians caught up with their vanguard. Once again the Mongols took flight. As the Russian cavalry charged after them for the kill, other Mongol forces emerged from concealed positions among the rolling hills of the steppe. The Russians and Kipchaks began to realize that the whole retreat had been a trap; Mongol forces surrounded the Russians and raked them with volleys of arrows.

The Kipchaks broke and fled, pursued by Mongol troops. Prince Vasil'ko Gavrilovich and Prince Daniilo Romanovich and their men were cut down by the Mongol assault. (The two princes were struck by lances.) Meanwhile the terrified Kipchaks continued to flee to the Russian camp on the Kalka River. However, they did not halt at the camp but continued their flight, stampeding through the camp and throwing it in turmoil.

Unfortunately for the Russians, the Mongols had pursued the Kipchaks closely and attacked the camp. A massacre ensued as the Russians could barely organize a defense. Many of the Russians attempted to flee, only to be cut down. Prince Aleksandr Dubrovich and Prince Mstislav Romanovich of Kiev and his son-in-law, Prince Andrei, and rallied a force at a better defensive position along the river. They fortified a rocky area on the banks of the Kalka and resisted Mongol attacks. Meanwhile some of the Mongols pursued the rest of the Kipchaks and remaining Russian forces to the banks of the Dnieper.

After three days of siege, Prince Mstislav Romanovich and the others finally surrendered after negotiations with a man only known as Ploskinia. He was a member of the Brodniki, predecessors to the Cossacks. Whether the Brodniki had joined the Mongols of their free will is unknown, but they served as translators for the Mongols since they knew the Kipchak and Russian languages. Ploskinia secured Mstislav's surrender and the Mongols took the fort.

After their victory, the Mongols celebrated with a feast. They constructed a platform where they ate, drank, probably sang songs raucously, stomped their feet, and perhaps even danced. The captive Russian princes, however, did not enjoy the banquet, for the Mongols used them in the construction of the platform as support for the planks. The princes were crushed under the platform boards during the feast.

Of the major Russian leaders, only Prince Mstislav Mstislavich survived, having safely crossed the Dnieper. Only one in ten soldiers returned home. After the victory, the Mongols simply turned east and disappeared. The Russians never learned who the Mongols really were and instead explained away the defeat as a punishment from God for their sins.

As for the Mongols, at the time they were not interested in conquest. This force was one of reconnaissance. They did not attempt to seize any territory, but made sure that neither the Russians nor the Kipchaks could interfere with their return to the region. Nonetheless, the Mongols gained valuable information from the experience: approximate troop strengths, tactics of their opponents, knowledge of the terrain, and the fact that the Kipchaks and the Russians were allies. Amazingly, the Russians simply resumed their civil wars and daily life, evidently not worried that the Mongols might return. Unfortunately for them, fourteen years later the Mongols did return—in unprecedented numbers and intent on conquest.

Kaifeng, 1233

The southern capital of the Jin Empire (1125–1234), Kaifeng was the city that the Jin court fled to in 1214 in the face of the Mongol invasion led by Genghis Khan. The flight triggered the destruction of Zhongdu, which had a population of over one million people. Although Genghis Khan died in 1227, the war against the Jin continued. Ogodei, the next Mongol ruler, continued the war and eventually brought it to Kaifeng.

Ogodei's Invasion In 1219, Genghis Khan left his most trusted general, Muqali, in charge of the campaign against the Jin, while he moved west to deal with the Khwarazmian Empire. Although Muqali made gains, he died in 1223. During the period between Muqali's death and when Ogodei came to the Mongol throne, the Jin had regained some territory. When Ogodei invaded in January 1230, he planned on destroying the Jin once and for all.

As with most Mongol invasions, the Mongols divided their forces after they entered enemy territory in order to cause the most destruction possible. By the year 1231, the Jin Empire had been reduced to the province of Honan and the city of Kaifeng.

The situation of the Jin worsened in 1233 when Ogodei formed an alliance with the Song Empire. Although the Song provided the Mongols with twenty thousand men, the alliance was primarily made so that the Song could supply the Mongols with food. Although the Mongols were very good at conquest, often their destruction limited the food resources in the region since most farmers fled.

Ogodei sent the best general in the Mongol army, Subedei, to deal with Kaifeng. In 1233, Subedei led his army against the city. His opening maneuvers successfully lured the Jin army from its defensive positions. This allowed Subedei to cross the Yellow River while other Mongol forces dealt with the Jin field army.

The Jin tried to delay him by bursting the dams that held the yearly flooding of the Yellow River in check. However, Subedei—who campaigned against the Jin during the lifetime of Genghis Khan—had anticipated this. Thus when the Jin sent troops to the dikes, they found them already in the possession of the Mongols. Subedei then began a slow but steady encirclement of the city, beginning miles away. This was part of a hunting technique used by the Mongols known as the *nerge*. Gradually the circle tightened, herding everything into the center. Those that did not flee fast enough were cut down by the Mongols.

The influx of refugees broke the will of the city. Food and water stores were exhausted, and the newcomers spread stories of terror. The city fell after a relatively brief siege in May 1233.

The Mongols did not subject Kaifeng to destruction or excessive pillaging. Yelu Qu Cai, the primary advisor to Ogodei, had convinced the Mongols that in the long term the city would be more beneficial if it was spared the celebratory sacking that usually accompanied a Mongol victory.

Although Kaifeng fell, the Jin Emperor was not in Mongol hands. Even so, it was a forgone conclusion that the demise of the Jin Empire had arrived. Subedei was recalled to help plan for the invasion of the western steppes and the Russian principalities, while a lower-ranking general finished off the Jin Empire at Caizhou, where the Jin court had taken refuge. Caizhou fell in 1234, thus ending the Jin Empire.

Isfahan, 1230s

An important city in Persia for centuries, Isfahan in the thirteenth century became a center of resistance to the Mongols. During the initial invasions of the 1220s, Isfahan was largely spared from the depredation of the Mongols. Naturally, refugees fled to Isfahan because of this and because the eastern portion of Persia had been devastated.

Isfahan's importance as a center of resistance to the Mongols intensified with the arrival of Jalal al-Din (d. 1231), the last ruler of the Khwarazmian Empire. While the core of this empire was now firmly under Mongol control north of the Amu Darya River, in the 1220s the Mongols largely withdrew from Persia and the area south of the Amu Darya.

Jalal al-Din had fled to India after Genghis Khan defeated him in 1221. After the Mongols withdrew, Jalal al-Din returned from India to regain control of what remained of his father's empire. Because of the looming Mongol threat, he focused most of his efforts in trying to conquer territories in the west, such as Azerbaijan, Georgia, and Armenia. Meanwhile, he made Isfahan his capital.

While Genghis Khan was invading Xi Xia (northwestern China and parts of Tibet) again in 1227, he received reports of Jalal al-Din's activities and ordered Chin-Temur, the Mongol governor in the region, to deal with him. Chin-Temur sent a small army of four thousand into Persia where it met Jalal al-Din at Damghan. Here, Jalal al-Din defeated the Mongols.

It is unclear if Jalal al-Din defeated the main force or just the vanguard, because the Mongols later captured Damghan and defeated other Khwarazmian troops. Then, in August 1228, they fought Jalal al-Din near Isfahan and defeated him. However, they could not eliminate the resistance, perhaps due to heavy losses incurred in battle. Furthermore, the Mongols did not attempt to occupy the territory.

In 1230, the Mongols decided to conquer all of Persia. An army of thirty thousand led by the Mongol general Chormaqan (d.1240) crossed the Amu Darya River. Despite the relative ease at which Chormaqan conquered Persia, Isfahan still did not fall. However, it became increasingly isolated. Chormaqan made his headquarters to the north, while other territories around Isfahan were secured.

The Mongols pursued Jalal al-Din, who fled upon Chormaqan's approach, into Azerbaijan. Meanwhile, the rest of Persia submitted to the Mongols. Isfahan was surrounded, with only a narrow corridor open to the Abbasid Caliphate on the Tigris River. Its isolation became complete when Jalal al-Din was killed while fleeing from the Mongols in 1231. His army dispersed; some of them escaped to Isfahan through the corridor, but not even this was safe as the Mongols made several probing attacks on Baghdad and its protectorates.

The Mongols made several attacks on Isfahan, but it did not fall until 1237. As the Mongols encircled the city, they made contact—as they often did—with dissatisfied groups within the city. At this time, the city was divided between Hanafis and Shafi'is, two rival schools of interpretation of Islamic law. Even before the Mongols, their factionalism could become quite violent and clashes were frequent. The Shafi'is went to the Mongols and established contact, promising the Mongols that they would submit to them if in return the Shafi'i interpretation of Islamic law would be accepted over the Hanafi. The Mongols agreed and approached the city.

As the Mongols attacked Isfahan, the Shafi'is attacked and killed the Hanafi *qadi*, or judge, who had been a vociferous opponent of the Mongols for years and who directed the city's defenses. They then attacked the Hanafis and opened the gates for the Mongols. The Mongols stormed the city and cut down all they encountered, including Shafi'is. The citizens were massacred and the city plundered before being set on fire.

Vladimir, 1238

In 1224 the Mongols destroyed a sizeable Russian army at the Kalka River and razed the Muslim city of Bulgar on the Volga River, just east of the Russian cities. However, the princes of Russia were too immersed in their own quarrels to realize the significance of the Mongol threat. A little over a decade later, this oversight would lead to their demise.

The invasion of Russia began at Ryazan on December 16, 1237. The city fell shortly before Christmas, five days after the invasion began. Grand Prince Yuri II sent a relief force to Ryazan, but it did not arrive in time. The Mongol forces destroyed his army near the city of Kolomna, located where the Oka and Moskva rivers join. Afterwards, the Mongols sacked Kolomna. The next major city targeted by the Mongols was Vladimir.

Vladimir was the capital of Suzdalia, the province of Grand Prince Yuri II, who was the titular ruler of the Russians. Although Yuri had done little to prepare his city after the fall of Bulgar, once he heard the news of the Mongol approach on Ryazan, Yuri quickly readied the defenses of Vladimir. His efforts were aided by the stout, but doomed, resistance of Moscow.

In the thirteenth century, Moscow was little more than a fortified outpost for the city of Vladimir.

Nonetheless, it lay in the path of the Mongols. Although the Mongols captured Moscow quickly in January 1238, its resistance slowed them and allowed Yuri to continue his preparations. Meanwhile, the Mongol general Subedei ordered the Mongol army to break into smaller units and spread out. In doing so, Subedei now outflanked Vladimir and threatened all of northern Russia, rather than simply proceeding from one city to the next.

As the Mongols marched towards Vladimir, Grand Prince Yuri retreated to the Sit River, twenty miles west of the city, in hopes of meeting the Mongols in battle and luring them away from Vladimir. Yuri had chosen his position wisely' as the Volga, Mologa, and Sit rivers would form natural defenses and help limit the Mongols' mobility.

Initially, Mongol scouts simply reconnoitered the surrounding territory while Subedei and Prince Batu, son of Jochi and the nominal commander of the expedition, established their headquarters. (Jochi was the eldest of Genghis Khan's sons.) Although Mongol scouts followed and observed the Russians, Subedei did not comply with Yuri's wishes and would not engage. Instead, he led the main army against the city of Vladimir and began the siege on February 3, 1238.

Yuri had left his wife and sons, Vsevolod and Mstislav, in command of Vladimir. They were aided by Petr Oslyadyukovich, the commander of the Vladimir garrison, but the city's fate rested largely in the hands of the Grand Prince's family.

The Mongols asked for the city's submission and were met with a hail of arrows. The Mongols then produced a prisoner, Prince Vladimir, Yuri's son who had led the relief army that was defeated at Kolomna. They again requested the city's surrender in exchange for Prince Vladimir's life. It was an exchange of one Vladimir for another. Although Yuri had left in an attempt to lure the Mongols away from the city, Vsevolod and Mstislav also knew that other troops from the cities of Suzdalia were joining their father's army. Despite knowing their brother's fate if they refused, they hoped that the city could resist until their father returned with the entire armed might of Suzdalia. Thus they rejected the offer and watched the Mongols execute their brother.

Then the Mongols moved on to the next stage of the siege. The officers rode out around the city walls, out of arrow range, to inspect the defenses. Then to the surprise of the inhabitants, the Mongols' siege engineers constructed a palisade around the city, completely surrounding them and cutting off any chance of escape. Meanwhile, Subedei sent a portion of his army to attack the city of Suzdal to the north, thus ensuring that no aid would come for the city of Vladimir. Scouts monitored and shadowed Yuri's camp so that he could not surprise the Mongols. Furthermore, their activities made Yuri believe that their attack on his camp was imminent, but it was all a bluff.

Suzdal fell quickly under the first assault, but unlike at Ryazan, the Mongols did not massacre the populace. Thousands of prisoners (clergy were spared) were then marched to Vladimir. They then served as manpower for the building of the palisade that surrounded the city, as well as manpower for the catapults, which functioned by several people pulling ropes to fling the stones through the air. Unfortunately for Vladimir, as catapults were not used by the Russians, they had no weapons that could return fire. The prisoners of Suzdal would also man the battering rams when the time came. Naturally, the defenders of Vladimir had no choice but to shoot their countrymen; from the Mongol perspective, the prisoners were nothing more than arrow-fodder.

Unfortunately, the preparations begun by Yuri were insufficient against the Mongol attack. From their fortified positions, the Mongols then proceeded to bombard the city with catapult fire day and night. The Mongols also built scaffolding to assist in storming the walls and to give shelter for those manning the battering rams. On the morning of February 7, 1238, the Mongols launched their assault, storming all four city gates at once and using ladders to ascend the walls.

Fear swept through the city, undermining the efforts of the defenders. Despite a valiant effort, the defenders could not hold back the Mongol onslaught, which broke through the western defenses. By the afternoon, the majority of the fighting was over. The city bishop, Mitrofan, took Yuri's wife, daughters, and grandchildren, as well as hundreds of other citizens, to the Cathedral of Assumption for refuge, believing that the Mongols would spare those who took sanctuary. The Mongols then attempted to seize the church, but resistance was tenacious. Rather than fighting their way through the church, the Mongols burned it to the ground, killing all of those who took shelter there. By the morning of February 8, 1238, all resistance in Vladimir had ended.

Afterwards, the Mongol army divided. One force led by Batu marched northeast, while Subedei sent troops under a lieutenant, Burundai, to finish off Grand Prince Yuri II. After Vladimir was taken, the rest of northern Russian fell quickly, with the exception of Novgorod, which was only spared because of an early thaw turned the ground into a morass, preventing the Mongols from riding. Whereas modern armies have floundered in the Russian winter, the Mongols took advantage of the frozen rivers and ground to move swiftly and were seemingly unaffected by the cold.

Liegnitz, 1241

When the Mongols invaded Europe in 1241, the main blow struck Hungary. Batu (the grandson of Genghis Khan) and the veteran general Subedei pursued fleeing

Mongols storming and capturing Baghdad. © *Visual Arts Library (London)/Alamy*

Kipchak tribes who sought refuge there, while an additional Mongol force of approximately twenty thousand men rode north into Poland. The commanders of the invasion of Poland—Baidar, son of Chaghatay (the second son of Genghis Khan), and Kadan, Batu's brother—had one directive: to prevent the armies of Bohemia, Poland, and Prussia from aiding the Hungarians. Poland was a fragmented state, but the Hungarian king, Bela IV, had relatives among the Polish dukes, such as his son-in-law Boleslaw V of Cracow and Sandomir, and Henry II of Silesia, Bela's cousin.

As the main Mongol army under Batu prepared to invade Hungary, the forces of Baidar and Kadan struck Poland, raiding the possessions of Boleslaw around Sandomir in February 1241 and burning the cities of Lublin and Zawichost. Next, using the frozen Vistula River as a bridge, they sacked the lightly defended Sandomir. Baidar and Kadan then divided their forces to terrorize a wider area.

Baidar continued to march towards Cracow. Boleslaw's forces marched against them and routed the Mongol vanguard. Baidar, however, was unconcerned; the

Mongols always tried to determine when and where they fought, and now that garrison of Cracow had been drawn out, he slowly retreated, luring them further out before ambushing them on March 18, 1241. Baidar's army defeated Boleslaw, who was forced to flee to Hungary. Unfortunately for him, his haven there was soon overrun by Batu's army. Meanwhile, Baidar burned Cracow.

Although the Mongols numbered only twenty thousand, their small numbers were compensated for by sudden strikes that left the Poles convinced a much larger force had invaded. As the Mongols advanced west across into the Oder valley, most of the nobles there withdrew rather than risk facing the Mongols. After sacking Cracow and several other cities, the Mongols received word that Henry II of Silesia (1238–1241) was forming an army of the northern princes near Liegnitz. A powerful army led by King Vaclav I (1230–1253)—the Good King Wencelas of Christmas-carol fame—of Bohemia was also on the march to join them. The Mongols then rode to Liegnitz to meet the Christian army before Vaclav could arrive.

The combined forces of Kadan and Baidar faced Henry's forces, comprised of the Silesian dukes, Duke Mieszko of Oppeln (a margrave from Bohemia), Boleslas (son of another margrave), and units from the military orders. These included a small force of Knights Templar, and a more sizeable force of Teutonic Knights led by Poppo von Osterna. There was also a contingent of several hundred German gold miners who volunteered to fight the Mongols, probably to protect their mines. Nonetheless, the combined force was only slightly larger than that of the Mongols, approximately twenty-five thousand men, and a large percentage of them were peasants and townspeople conscripted for the battle.

Battle was joined in April 1241. Unbeknownst to Henry, Vaclav's army was only a day's march away. Henry divided his army into four battles, as the Europeans called their military formations. One consisted of the miners under Boleslas and his men. The second consisted of the remnants of Boleslaw of Cracow's forces that had joined Henry, along with the peasant conscripts. Duke Mieszko commanded his own forces and was augmented by the powerful Teutonic Knights. In the center, the largest division was that of Henry with the combined forces of Silesia and the Templars.

As the Mongol vanguard advanced, Henry's Silesian knights rode to meet them, but were rebuffed by the Mongols archery. Henry ordered the rest of the cavalry, including the Teutonic Knights, to advance. As they charged, the Mongol vanguard fled, pulling the knights after them. As the knights pursued, more Mongol light cavalry began to appear on the flanks of the charging knights, raking them with arrows. The fleeing Mongol vanguard also continued to fire as they retreated, turning backwards in their saddles to shoot. Once the knights were sufficiently far from the rest of the army, riders from the flanks of the Mongol army rode behind the charging knights and set off smoke bombs, which screened them from the onlooking infantry. As the knights pursued the Mongols, their formation began to break apart as horses tired and the Mongol archery cut down riders.

Before the knights could reform their ranks, the Mongol light cavalry opened up, allowing the Mongol heavy cavalry to descend upon the Europeans. The momentum of the Mongol charge decimated the knights. Many were killed by the Mongol lances, many by being pulled from their horses (the Mongol lances also had a hook specifically for that purpose). The knights were destroyed as a fighting force.

Meanwhile, the European infantry waited, unsure of what occurred behind the wall of smoke. A hail of arrows hit them through the smoke as the Mongols suddenly appeared. Other Mongol forces flanked them and cut off their retreat, riding around them and firing into the massed ranks. The result was devastating.

Although Poppo von Osterna, the leader of the Teutonic knights, escaped, few others did. The Teutonic knights and the Templars were both annihilated. The Mongols kept track of how many they killed by cutting off the left ear of each of the slain. They later presented Batu with nine large sacks of ears. Not even Duke Henry escaped, although he tried. The Mongols pursued him, killing his guards and then finally him. He was beheaded, and the Mongols placed his head on a spear to display to the citizens of the city of Liegnitz before they burned the city.

In one battle, the army of Poland and the Teutonic Knights had been destroyed, although the Mongols also had taken heavy casualties. Vaclav would be the next to face Baidar and Kadan, but his army was too strong to be easily defeated. The Mongols merely had to keep him from Hungary. After a wild goose chase which drew the Bohemian King farther from Hungary, the Mongols again broke into smaller units and pillaged along the way as they rode to join Batu in Hungary.

Battle of Mohi or Sajo River, 1241

After conquering Russian principalities, the Mongol armies led by Subedei and Batu invaded Eastern Europe in February 1241. Twenty thousand men attacked Poland while forty thousand men invaded Hungary. At this time, Hungary possessed perhaps the finest army in Europe and was quite aware that the Mongols intended to invade.

During the conquest of Russian principalities, the Mongols had also subdued most of the Kipchak Turks that lived in the steppes north of the Black and Caspian Seas. Some of the Kipchaks resisted and were defeated, others simply submitted, and some fled. Led by Koten Khan, forty thousand Kipchaks escaped and took refuge in Hungary. King Bela IV, who ruled from 1235 to 1270, welcomed their arrival and accepted them into his kingdom on the condition that their leaders accepted Christianity and underwent the rite of baptism.

Bela had ulterior motives for accepting such a large population of steppe nomads, for they would serve as a useful counterweight to his own feudal vassals. Tensions between the crown and the vassals were high as Bela sought to increase the authority of the king throughout the kingdom. The vassals, naturally, were reluctant to lose some of their own power and influence. The arrival of the Kipchaks did nothing to ease these tensions.

Conflict between nomads and populations that primarily farm has existed since the two came into contact. During the medieval period, this was still the case. The Kipchaks not only came with forty thousand families, but also flocks of sheep and herds of goats, cattle, and horses. These animals required pasture to graze; the nomads did little to distinguish between a wild pasture and a farmer's field and this led to violence between the peasants and the nomads. Taking advantage of this and their own concerns about the Kipchaks, the Hungarian nobility seized Koten and hanged him. Koten's death made it clear to the Kipchaks that things would only get worse for them. Now caught between the threat of the Mongols and the Hungarian populace, the nomads headed south into the Balkans, pillaging and raiding as they went. The nomads would eventually be dispersed by other forces, enter the service of other kings as mercenaries, or be recaptured by the Mongols. Nonetheless, the Kipchaks remained in the region until the fourteenth century.

During this time, the Mongols also sent envoys to King Bela IV, requesting that he return the Kipchaks to them. The Mongols held that all nomads from the steppe were their subjects by command of Heaven. Any nomads who did not obey this order were renegades, and therefore, anyone who aided the renegades also violated the wishes of Heaven. Bela refused the order, and of course after the Kipchaks fled Hungary, he was in no position to comply. Thus, from the Mongol point of view, they had no option but to invade Hungary.

Although King Bela IV of Hungary fortified the passes of the Carpathian Mountains, the Mongol armies soon broke through by March 14, 1241. Despite their feud with Bela, the nobility recognized the threat of the Mongols and formed a formidable army. On April 9, 1241, King Bela advanced with an army of seventy thousand men. As the Hungarians moved against them, for several days the Mongol vanguard withdrew until they arrived at the plain of Mohi, located between the Sajo and Tisza rivers. The Hungarians camped in the plain, unaware that the Mongols specifically chose this site as the battlefield. The Mongols then crossed the Sajo River.

As was standard practice for the Hungarians, Bela formed his wagons into a circle, thus fortifying his camp against a sudden cavalry charge and a serving as a rallying point and headquarters for his army. He then stationed a thousand men at the only bridge for the Sajo River to hold it against the Mongols.

Around dawn, Batu attacked the bridge with archers and a rolling barrage of catapults firing naphtha (a flammable, petroleum-based pitch). The use of catapults in a field battle was a rare site in medieval warfare and most likely stunned the Hungarians. The Hungarians retreated from the bridge before the Mongols. Both sides suffered heavy casualties.

While Batu attacked the bridge, Subedei had marched several miles to find another location to cross the river. This enabled him to appear behind the Hungarians, forcing them to fall back to their camp rather than face a two-front attack. The Mongols then surrounded the camp. They began to bombard the fortified camp with catapult missiles and arrows.

Eventually, the Hungarians detected what appeared to be an accidental gap in the western portion of the Mongol ranks. Seeing an opening to freedom, a few Hungarians made a run from the imperiled camp. Soon, men poured from the Hungarian camp in that direction. Many dropped their weapons and armies in order to hasten their flight. Unfortunately, the Hungarians did not realize that the Mongols had intentionally left a hole in their lines, realizing that if trapped, the Hungarians would most likely give a more determined resistance, and possibly fight to the last man. As the unarmed Hungarians fled, the Mongols now wheeled upon them and slaughtered the fleeing Hungarians, cutting them down with their sabers or shooting them as they would do in a hunt.

The pursuit lasted for three days. With the army destroyed, the Mongols also ravaged Hungary unopposed. Neither the nobility nor the common people were spared from the wrath of the Mongols. Indeed, Bela IV barely escaped, fleeing to the coast of the Adriatic Sea. According to some reports, Mongol arrows rained down around his boat as it rowed from the shore.

The Mongols did not remain in Hungary for long, although fears arose in Italy and the Holy Roman Empire that the Mongols were preparing to invade. However, Batu ordered his armies to withdraw back into the steppes, probably because of the death of the Mongol ruler, Ogodei Khan. Nonetheless, Hungary remained a shadow of its former might for decades, and the rest of Europe lived in fear of future invasions.

Fall of Baghdad, 1258

The Abbasid Caliphate, centered in Baghdad, withstood several years of Mongol attacks in the 1230s and remained defiant. Baghdad had a sizeable army as well as strong city defenses. However, after ruling seventeen years, Caliph al-Mustansir died at the age of fifty-two in 1242. The collapse of Baghdad was hastened with the ascension of Mustasim ibn al-Mustansir in to the throne in 1242. Unlike his father, the new caliph did not take the Mongol threat seriously, focusing instead on personal amusements such as games and birds.

Mustasim reduced military pay, thus weakening the forces. In addition, in 1258, religious strife broke out between Shi'a Muslims and Sunni Muslims. These events led the Shi'a wazir Alqami, who ran the day-to-day affairs of the government, to hatch a plot to overthrow the Caliph. Alqami continued to disband military units under the pretence that it would create peace with the Mongols. Caliph Mustasim, preoccupied with less-serious matters, remained so oblivious of his actions that even when Mongol messengers fell into the hands of the Abbasid government, the Caliph failed to perceive that the Mongols planned to attack. Thus, Baghdad remained unprepared for the coming onslaught.

In 1257, Mongke (the fourth Mongol Khan) and Hulegu (his younger brother) marched from Persia (modern Iran) towards Baghdad. When Hulegu reached the border, he gathered his vassals; these included Muslim rulers such as Badr-al-Din-i Lu'lu' of Mosul and the Atabak Abu Bikr ibn Sa'd of Fars. While this was occurring, Ket Buqa, the commander of Hulegu's vanguard, captured the surrounding areas by December 1257. Then in 1258 Hulegu marched on Baghdad with an army that included Georgians, Armenians, and the garrison of Mosul. When Hulegu was twenty miles away, Abbasid military leaders (Sulaiman Shah and Malik Izz al-Din) urged the Caliph to take action, but the Caliph left the preparations in the hands of the wazir, who did nothing.

As Hulegu approached the city from the east, Baiju, a Mongol general, moved towards Baghdad from the northwest. Caliphate forces intercepted the vanguard of Baiju near the city of Tikrit. Initially, this forced the Mongols back, but Baiju arrived and secured a Mongol victory.

After constructing a boat bridge, Baiju's army (composed of Armenians and Georgians) crossed the Tigris River. The Caliphate forces stationed at Tikrit attempted to burn the bridge and prevent the crossing, but the Mongols rebuilt it and proceeded to capture the strongholds of Kufa, Hillah, and Karkh.

The Abbasid commanders Malik Izz al-Din and Mujahid al-Din led twenty thousand horsemen across the Tigris River to meet the main army of Hulegu. In the ensuing battle, the Mongols initiated the attack, but the Muslims defeated them. Malik Izz al-Din wanted to pursue the Mongols, but Mujahid al-Din held back, perhaps afraid that the Mongols feigned their retreat, a common tactic. The Abbasid forces made their camp near the stream Nahr-i-sher, a branch of the Euphrates. At night, the wazir Alqami had his agents sabotage the dikes, thus flooding the plain and the Abbasid camp. The Mongols then returned at dawn and defeated the Baghdad army.

Afterwards, the Muslims withdrew to Baghdad and stopped at fortifications named Sanjari Masjid and Kasr Sulaiman Shah. After the defeat of the Baghdad army, Baiju moved to the west side of the city on January 22, 1258, while Ket Buqa arrived from Najasiyya and Sarsar. A few days later, Hulegu arrived from the east and began the siege in earnest on January 29, 1258. Leading citizens of Baghdad attempted to open negotiations to surrender, but Hulegu simply kept the envoys in his camp and continued the siege. The Mongols focused their catapults on a single tower. While the siege engines pounded the walls, Hulegu conducted negotiations in order to undermine the resistance of the city. In return for the city's surrender, he offered to spare the clergy and noncombatants. Then on February 1, 1258, the Mongols pierced the walls of the city. While they were unable to achieve victory that first day, on the second day the city fell.

LOOKING TO THE STARS

Hulegu asked an astrologer when he should launch his attack. The astrologer informed Hulegu that the attack would cause a series of catastrophes to befall the Mongols: all of their horses would die, the soldiers would sicken, the sun would not rise, and there would be drought followed by cold destructive winds and earthquakes. Plants would cease to grow and the land would turn into desert. Finally, a great ruler would die with in a year. Opposing the astrologer were all the Mongol generals, who advised Hulegu to invade. To resolve the issue, Hulegu referred to Nasir al Din Tusi, a scholar and advisor. Nasir al-Din Tusi informed Hulegu to proceed with the invasion, as Caliphs had been killed before without any ill effects.

Izz al-Din and Mujahid al-Din tried to convince the Caliph to flee the Baghdad and escape to Basra. Alqami, however, convinced the Caliph that he would negotiate peace terms with the Mongols. Hulegu's terms consisted of taking Mustasim's daughter as a wife and the Caliph becoming a vassal. If these were accepted, the attack would cease. With little choice, the Caliph and the local leaders exited the city to conclude the treaty. The army of Baghdad surrendered and was divided and killed. Hulegu then executed most of the officials and eventually ordered the execution of the Caliph. The Caliph was rolled in a carpet and trampled, after Hulegu berated him for hoarding his wealth rather than spending it on the defense of Baghdad.

Thus in 1258 the Abbasid Caliphate came to an end and Baghdad, after a sporadic conflict that ranged for roughly twenty years, was now in Mongol hands. Hulegu gave his consent for a general pillaging of the town, which lasted thirty-four days beginning on February 13, 1258. Each general received a section of the city to pillage. Alqami's service to the Mongols did not go unnoticed. Hulegu asked the wazir what had been the source of his former prosperity. The wazir naturally said it was the Caliph. At that, Hulegu ordered his execution, telling Alqami that since he did not show gratitude to the Caliph, he was not worthy of serving the Mongol prince.

Aleppo, 1260

Aleppo had long been a powerful city-state in northern Syria. Its proximity to the Mediterranean made it an important trade city, and it was a formidable military power within Syria, although not as powerful as Damascus. Aleppo's ruler was at times a rival, and sometimes a vassal, of Damascus. Aleppo was also situated perfectly to be a menace to the Crusader states of Antioch and Tripoli. With its imposing citadel and fortifications, Aleppo was also a difficult target for attackers. Despite

Citadel at Aleppo, Syria. © *Brian Hamilton/Alamy*

this, Aleppo proved to be only a small obstacle to the Mongol armies of Hulegu.

After the sack of Baghdad in 1258, the Mongol leader Hulegu retired to Azerbaijan and received his vassals. Among those who came to his camp was King Hethum of Cilicia, who brought twelve thousand cavalry and several thousand infantry. Prince Bohemund of the Crusader state of Antioch also came to pay homage. At this time, the Mongols planned for the invasion of Syria. Hethum, who had gained considerable favor among the Mongols for his willingness to support their campaigns with troops and provisions, recommended that the conquest of Syria begin with Aleppo.

After sending detachments to quell a rebellion in Georgia, the invasion of Syria began. Before entering Syria, the Mongols—along with contingents from Cilicia and Antioch—marched on Harran and Edessa, both of which submitted without a fight. The Mongols also captured a number of fortresses in the region, including the important fortress of Aklat. The Mongol general Ket Buqa served as the vanguard commander and led the invasion.

Refugees from Harran and Edessa, and from Baghdad, had fled before the invading Mongols to seek refuge in Aleppo. When news of the Mongols' approach arrived, the refugees once again fled, this time to Dam-

ascus. Many died in the cold of winter, while others were robbed of all their goods.

By January 19, 1260, Aleppo was under siege as Ket Buqa's vanguard arrived. The garrison and a corps of volunteers immediately sallied forth to deal with it, but upon discovering that the Mongol force was larger than they realized, the Aleppans quickly retreated. The next day the Mongols approached closer to the walls. Despite the protestations of Muazzam Turanshah, the city's ruler, another attempt was made against the Mongols. This time the Mongols fled before the attack. The Aleppans followed, but it was a feigned retreat, and they lured the Aleppans into an ambush. Few made it back inside the city.

Meanwhile, Hulegu offered terms to Aleppo, but Muazzam Turanshah refused them. The next day the citizenry woke up to find that the Mongols built a wall to surround the city. Hulegu then ordered twenty mangonels to attack the Bab al-Iraq, the gate facing Iraq. After six days of concentrated fire by the Mongols' siege artillery, they broke through at that sector. The Mongols swept through the city, cutting down any who opposed them. Only a few buildings were spared, including a school and a synagogue where refugees took shelter. The city was then turned over to the soldiers for five days for pillaging.

Only the great citadel of Aleppo still held out. With a massive ditch and a narrow causeway, it continued to resist the Mongols. However, after a month even the citadel could resist no more. Within the citadel the Mongols found the treasury and put the skilled artisans to work in their camps. In addition, Muazzam Turanshah was captured during the seizure of the citadel. The Mongols spared him, as they admired his defense of the citadel.

With Aleppo in the hands of the Mongols, Hulegu withdrew back to the pastures. Meanwhile, Ket Buqa led his army towards Damascus. News of the fall of Aleppo spread quickly. Afterwards the city of Damascus surrendered rather than face the Mongol onslaught, leaving the rest of Syria open to the Mongols.

Ayn Jalut, 1260

After the Mongols conquered Syria, it appeared that Egypt would fall next. Indeed, envoys came to the Mamluks (a caste of Turkic military slaves that ruled the region) with the same demand the Mongols always made: surrender or die. Qutuz, the Mamluk leader at the time, gave his answer by cutting off the heads of the Mongol envoys—an automatic declaration of war.

The Mamluk invasion of Mongol-held Syria began at Gaza, where Qutuz defeated the Mongol advance guard. This victory was very helpful, for in addition to worrying about the Mongols, Qutuz also had to consider the Crusader states in the region. He was aware that not all of the Franks, as the Muslims called the

European Crusaders, were favorable to the Mongols. Although Antioch was a vassal of the Mongols, many of the barons of the Kingdom of Jerusalem were opposed to the idea of an alliance with the Mongols. If the Mongols won without the aid of a crusading army from Europe, the Latin East would surely fall into Mongol hands in due time. If the Mamluks won, they were less intimidating than the Mongols. Thus when Qutuz took Gaza, he was soon met by envoys from the Franks, who promised they would be neutral in the coming fight.

The coming struggle for control over Syria took place at Ayn Jalut, or the "Springs of Goliath," in the Jezreel valley on September 3, 1260. The Mamluks were to meet the Mongols on equal terms, which did not bode well for the Mamluks. In previous encounters throughout their conquests, the Mongols were able to defeat larger armies, such as at Liegnitz in 1241 where they defeated a combined European army of Germans and Poles.

The Mongols in Syria numbered around twenty thousand. One *tumen*, or group of ten thousand soldiers, under Kitbugha was of Mongols, while another was recruited from the local Ayyubid population. The reliability of this Ayyubid tumen was questionable, and it may have been useful only for garrison duty. As long as the Mongols were not challenged it is doubtful if the Ayyubids would have rebelled, as all previous Ayyubid attempts to rebel or defeat the Mongols had been fiascoes. They could, though, be an important factor if another Muslim force invaded Syria. Therefore, when Kitbugha marched to Ayn Jalut it was unlikely that he took more than a small contingent of the auxiliary Ayyubids with him for fear of treachery.

The battle itself was not one of great tactical maneuvering. The Mamluk leader Baybars, in charge of the vanguard, lured the Mongols into an ambush. The Mongols attacked Baybars's smaller force, which retreated into the hills. From the hills, the rest of the Mamluk army poured out and surrounded the Mongols, preventing their escape.

The Mamluks were aided by treachery; the local troops from Hims (that reinforced the Mongols) switched sides, and the Mamluks also received information given by a traitor named Sarim. The troops from Hims were positioned on the Mongol's left wing. Once the battle began, the unit from Hims fled, thus weakening the Mongol left wing. The Mongol right wing now faced a strengthened Mamluk left. The Mamluk flanks could now sweep in and crush the Mongol center in a pincer. Despite this act of treachery, the Mongols still almost defeated the Mamluks. The Mongols did break one of the wings of the Mamluks, after which Qutuz reportedly rallied his forces by crying, "O Islam." The troops of the Hims abandoned the Mongols probably when the Mamluks rallied, for the Mongols took the initiative at the onset.

Immediately after Ayn Jalut, the Mongols did attempt to reestablish their supremacy in Syria. In December 1260, a large force of Mongols entered Syria near Aleppo. The Aleppan amirs were not willing to face the Mongols alone, so the Aleppan army retreated south to avoid the Mongols. After raiding Aleppo, the Mongols followed them. At Hims the army of Aleppo joined the armies of Hamah and Hims. Battle was joined on December 11, 1260. The Mongols numbered around six thousand while the Syrian army numbered less than fifteen hundred. Details of the battle are not available, but in the end the Mongols were defeated, despite outnumbering the Muslims. This battle was extremely significant as local forces—not the elite Mamluks of Egypt—had defeated a larger Mongol army

The battle of Ayn Jalut was not won because of superior numbers but due to other factors. For one thing, the Mamluks took advantage of the terrain. They hid their troops in the hills surrounding the valley so that the Mongols could not estimate the strength of their army. The Mamluks also positioned themselves so that the Mongols faced the sun in the morning, thus hampering the Mongol view of the Mamluks proceeding down out of the hills. This may have also affected the Mongols' ability to fire their arrows as the sun would have also impaired their aim.

The Mongols, on the other hand, failed to acquire proper intelligence of the Mamluk force or leave a more appropriate force to garrison Palestine and Syria. This second factor forced them to rely on untrustworthy and recently conquered Syrian troops. The Mongols also failed to safeguard the route to Syria by either removing the Crusaders or coming to terms with them. By allowing the Crusaders to exist, they created a party that could decide the balance of power in the region even if they remained neutral.

The battle of Ayn Jalut indicated who the dominant power in Syria was to be. The events that occurred after the battle ultimately decided the fate of Syria and Palestine, but the Mamluk victory at Ayn Jalut was the pivotal factor because it showed that the Mongols could be defeated. This encouraged rebellion, and the Mongols were soon driven out of Syria. The victory at Ayn Jalut also gave confidence to the local amirs. As demonstrated at Hims in 1260, the amirs discovered that they could defend themselves without the aid of the Mamluks of Egypt. Thus, in order for the Mongols to reestablish themselves in Syria, they would, in effect, be forced to conquer the country again instead of only having to defeat the Mamluks.

Xiangyang, 1268–1272

Xiangyang was located in the modern province of Hubei, China, on the banks of the Han River. As the key to the Yangtze River basin, the city was of great strategic importance; its seizure would open the rest of the Song Empire to Mongol attacks. However, taking Xiangyang would not be easy: it was strongly fortified with a citadel, surrounding walls, and a deep moat, in addition to the river that protected one side of the city.

The siege began in 1268. The Mongols assaulted it not only with siege weapons, but also with their new navy. The siege was an excellent example of the polyglot nature of the Mongol attacks: It was led by two Chinese generals, an Uighur Turk, and a Mongol. In addition, two Middle Easterners (Ismail and Ala al-Din) commanded the artillery. The siege progressed in a deliberate manner as Korean-made ships blockaded Xiangyang while the Mongol army captured outlying villages and towns. A fleet of five hundred ships was assembled for the blockade, and fortifications were built south of Xiangyang along the river to cut off attempts to relieve or supply it via the river. The garrison of Xiangyang attempted to break through the Mongol lines, but they were repulsed. There were repeated attempts in 1270, but all failed with heavy casualties. One attempt included a sortie of ten thousand men.

The Song also attempted to relieve the city and at times were successful. In August 1269, a Song fleet of three thousand ships approached, but the Mongol fleet fended it off and captured several of the Song boats. Meanwhile, the Mongols built a series of ramparts around Xiangyang. Nonetheless, it was impossible to prevent some blockade-runners and messengers from getting through the Mongol flotilla and defenses. Although the Mongols did not expect the siege to be a quick victory, the fact that they could not completely isolate the city prolonged the attack for five years. Indeed, despite Mongol successes, in 1270 the Mongol commander Aju requested that Kublai Khan send him seventy thousand men and an additional five thousand ships. Even with the reinforcements, the Mongols did not take the city.

The obstinacy of the Song resistance is not surprising, since the Song saw this as a life-and-death struggle against the Mongols. In addition, Song generals on the outside gave rich rewards to men who could sneak through the Mongol lines with messages to the city and make it back alive. The Song continued to attempt to relieve the city by land as well as by sea, but most of the attacks failed. One attack did succeed in 1272, breaking through the Mongol lines and making it to the city. Yet even this victory was fleeting since most of the force, including several officers, were killed.

Ultimately, the siege gradually exhausted Xiangyang's defenders. The Mongols, however, did not make significant headway in actually ending the siege until the arrival of Muslim engineers from the Middle East. In 1272, these engineers brought with them a new technology: the trebuchet. As it had a superior range and

was also capable of launching heavier missiles, the trebuchet had an immediate impact.

Initially, the two trebuchets built by Ismail and Ala al-Din were used on towns across the river from Xiangyang. Then they turned them against Xiangyang. The noise and damage caused was terrifying, and no wall could resist it. General Lu, the commander of Xiangyang, attempted to hold out, but the Mongols stationed both machines on the southeast corner of the city in order to concentrate their firepower. After a few days of bombardment, General Lu finally conceded defeat and surrendered after resisting the Mongol attack for five years.

The siege of Xiangyang is a testament of the power of the Mongol Empire. A mixed army of Chinese, Mongols, and Turks fought the Song Empire of southern China for five years on land and on the water. When those efforts failed, they produced a new weapon from another region of the empire. The resources and innovations of the empire were simply too great for any other state to resist.

Attempted Invasions of Japan, 1274 and 1280

The Mongols were known to be an almost unstoppable army. Many contemporaries compared them with forces of nature. Since the Mongols believed that they were destined to rule the world, they traditionally sent emissaries to other states and requested their submission. Refusal to come to the throne of the Khan meant war.

In 1268 and 1271, Kublai Khan (1215–1294) sent emissaries to Japan to reestablish contact and to ask for submission. Both times, the Japanese court refused to meet with the Mongol ambassadors. In 1272, another ambassador arrived with an ultimatum—submit or be destroyed. He too was sent back without a meeting. Kublai was furious and determined to subdue Japan. Since the Mongols had recently captured Xiangyang, Kublai could now divert some of his army against the Japanese.

A fleet of seven hundred to eight hundred ships sailed from Korea in November of 1274. The ships carried almost forty thousand soldiers and sailors. They quickly captured the small islands of Tsushima and Iki. The Mongols then landed on Kyushu at Hakata. The Japanese had gathered an army to meet them. The Japanese attacked the Mongol forces and quickly found out why the Mongols had conquered Eurasia. For the samurai, battle was an individualized action, but for the Mongols it was a team sport.

The Japanese retreated at the end of the day on November 19 under the cover of night. Although the Mongol invasion force was relatively small, it had lived up to its reputation as a force of nature. Fortunately for the Japanese, another force of nature struck the Mongol fleet that same night: a typhoon hit the island. Although

HISTOIRE DU JAPON.
8. Destruction de la flotte mongole.
PRODUITS LIEBIG: DIMINUENT LA DEPENSE.
Reproduction interdite   Explication au verso.

The Mongols under Kublai Khan sought to conquer Japan, but their invasion fleet was devastated by storms called kamikaze, or "divine wind," by the Japanese. © *Mary Evans Picture Library/Alamy*

the Mongols attempted to get to open water before the winds destroyed their ships, the storm was faster. Hundreds of ships were destroyed and thirteen thousand troops died. The Mongol invaders had no choice but to return to Kublai Khan.

Kublai could not avenge his loss since he was tied down with finishing his conquest of the Song Empire and fighting wars in Central Asia. However, he did not forget the defeat. In the meantime, he wrote it off as simply bad luck. It was not until 1280, after the destruction of the Song Empire, that Kublai could attempt another invasion. His anger grew after the Japanese executed the Mongol ambassadors as spies in 1279.

In the interim, the Japanese put into practice what they had learned from the invasion. In 1275, they constructed a long wall along Hakata Bay on Kyushu. This was the most logical landing area on the island for an attack from Korea. Fortunately for the Japanese, they finished it before the next attack. Although the Mongols might land elsewhere, at least they would be diverted to less desirable landings.

Kublai placed Hong Tagu, a Korean admiral, in charge of the fleet of nine hundred vessels. Together, Fan Wan-hu (a former Song general) and Shintu (a Mongol) commanded an army of 140,000 men. The

invasion was a two-pronged attack on the island of Iki, which would then serve as the launching point for the Kyushu invasion.

The planned rendezvous did not take place. The force of forty thousand captured Iki in June 1280, and then waited two weeks for the arrival of the larger army. Hong Tagu finally could wait no longer. He directed his ships to the north of the wall, to Manakata. When the other army finally arrived, they landed south of the wall. The generals coordinated a plan to rendezvous in the middle. The samurai forces resisted fiercely, and the Mongols could not gain the upper hand. The bulk of the Mongol forces were former Song troops from southern China, more suited to defending fortresses and cities. In addition, the Japanese had learned from previous experience to fight the Mongols as a unit, not as individuals.

Inconclusive fighting lasted for two months, then disaster struck the Mongols again. A typhoon struck in mid-August, destroying the fleet and many of the troops. Few of the Mongol army escaped the weather. Those stranded on Kyushu were killed or made prisoner by the Japanese. When Kublai learned of the defeat, he ordered yet another invasion. Eventually, his advisors dissuaded him. To the Japanese, the victories over the

Mongols were not due to luck or military strategy, but rather divine intervention. The typhoons that wrecked the Mongol fleets were due to the *kamikaze*, or divine winds, and a sign of Heaven's favor for Japan.

Red Turban Revolt, mid-fourteenth century

Kublai Kahn conquered the Song Dynasty in 1279 and created a new state to rule China and the rest of East Asia. This was known as the Yuan Dynasty. Although his empire was vast and powerful, the quality of the empire's rulers and government were inferior to the talents of Kublai. Furthermore, although many regions had become accustomed to Mongol rule, it was always resented in southern China. Eventually this would lead to a rebellion that drove the Mongols out of China.

Problems of the Yuan Dynasty
Southern China never fully accepted Mongol rule. In the first decades resistance was crushed without hesitation, but as the Yuan rulers and government became ineffectual, rebels seized their opportunity. The last Yuan ruler, Togon-Temur, inherited a bad situation that only became worse as more Chinese rebelled, including members of the military.

Chinese resentment was understandable. Mongol appropriation of land brought starvation to much of China towards the end of their rule. In addition, the government failed to maintain the system of dikes and levees that prevented the Yellow River from flooding, leading to massive destruction and loss of life. Finally, ever-increasing taxes alienated nearly all Chinese citizens, ranging from peasants to the aristocracy. These grievances fueled the resentment towards foreign rule.

Rebellion
Several rebel states had formed by the 1360s. The Yuan generals could not effectively crush them partially because of the lack of leadership in the Yuan court. Also, the Mongol generals were often too busy with their own rivalries to pay attention to the rebels.

The Red Turbans emerged from the Buddhist White Lotus secret society. The White Lotus society believed that Buddha, in a messiah-like incarnation, would return and save the Chinese from Mongol oppression. The Red Turbans were a militant offshoot of this religious movement. Among the Red Turbans— so named for the red headbands they wore—was a monk named Zhu Yuanzhang. Born a peasant, his family had a distinguished background before Mongol rule. Zhu Yuanzhang became an important commander in the Red Turbans. With his background, he was able to cultivate ties with both the peasantry and the aristocracy.

Although he started out as just one of many commanders among the Red Turbans, Zhu Yuanzhang's military successes soon led him to dream of becoming emperor. In 1356, he captured Nanking in southern China and made it part of the kingdom formed by the Red Turbans. His successes continued as he conquered more territory from the Mongols. Soon Zhu Yuanzhang

considered his victories greater than those achieved by other leaders. He then split from the Red Turbans and established his own movement in 1368.

Rise of the Ming Empire
Whereas the Red Turban movement originally planned to drive the Mongols from southern China and restore the Song Empire, Zhu Yuanzhang had grander ideas. His new goal was to drive the Mongols from all of China, including northern China (which the Song had lost in the tenth century). His armies continued to have success against the Mongols. Finally in September 1368, Zhu Yuanzhang invaded the Mongol capital of Dadu (modern Beijing). The Mongols under Togon-Temur were forced to retreat to Mongolia. Here they continued to fight the Chinese, and also other Mongols who resented what they considered to be "Chinese" Mongols.

Although it would take thirty years before all of China was under his control, Zhu Yuanzhang established himself as the first emperor of the Ming dynasty in 1368. He took the title of Hongwu, or the "Vastly Martial." To prevent the return of the Mongols, Hongwu began building what became the Great Wall of China. Before the Mongol period a few border walls existed, but nothing like what Hongwu ordered. The dynasty Zhu Yuanzhang created would provide stability for China, although it was ultimately toppled in 1644.

Ankara, 1402

Although Ankara is the capital of modern Turkey, its importance only manifested when two major empires collided. The Ottoman Turks had steadily expanded in Europe as well as Asia under the leadership of Bayezid I (d. 1403). Meanwhile, to the east, the empire of Timur (1336–1405) extended from Central Asia into Anatolia. Eventually both leaders claimed the same territory, and this dispute led to war.

Bayezid's annexation of the Karamanid emirate in eastern Anatolia triggered the war with Timur. As Anatolia was the frontier of Timur's empire, the Karamanids had maintained a client relationship with the Central Asian ruler, if only to keep him from destroying them. This allowed the Karamanids to enjoy a level of autonomy and independence. With the outright annexation by the Ottomans, this independence vanished, so the Karamanids appealed to Timur for relief.

Timur had many faults as a leader (and as a human being), but he never backed down from a threat. Timur had developed a pattern of eliminating threats to his supremacy in Eurasia; in addition, it is quite likely that he held a grudge against Bayezid, since Bayezid had indirectly assisted one of Timur's rivals. For a host of reasons, Timur marched against the Ottomans.

The two forces met at Ankara in central Anatolia. Timur's army began to lay siege to the city, which was still a possession of the Ottoman Empire. This forced Bayezid to abandon his blockade of Constantinople and march his army across Anatolia. Bayezid's march was rapid but exhausting, since roughly a third of his troops were infantry (including the feared janissaries).

Both armies were large. Reports put the Ottomans at almost ninety thousand men, including Serbs, Tatars, and Turkmen, among others. Timur's army, mainly of cavalry, was anywhere between 100,000 to 150,000 men. The two generals sized each other up from strong defensive positions. Timur's camp, established during the siege, was protected by a palisade and a ditch. It blocked Bayezid from the city, which was still held by an Ottoman garrison.

On July 20, 1402, the battle began. Timur's right wing collided with the Ottoman cavalry. Timur's cavalry broke this wing as Timur's left wing outflanked the Ottoman right wing. This allowed Timur to then attack the Serbian troops without fear of the Ottoman cavalry. The Serbs, skilled mountain fighters, held against the Timurid cavalry and forced them to retreat. Unfortunately, it was a feigned retreat designed to draw the Serbs out of their position. The Timurid troops did not retreat quickly, but remained tantalizingly near. This enticed the Serbs to charge, and the Timurid cavalry drew them out so that the Serbian formations began to break rank. A Timurid charge forced them to abandon their attack.

Meanwhile, Tatars and Turkmen nomads—who served as light cavalry for the Ottomans—suddenly deserted. The Tatars then attacked the already wavering Ottoman left wing. Not even the Ottoman reserves could prevent the situation. Most of the auxiliaries were from regions that only recently came under Ottoman control and were resentful for the increased centralization of authority under Bayezid's rule. Timur had established contact with their leaders once he entered Anatolia. Given that Timur's capital of Samarkand was far removed from Anatolia, and that Timur's administrative apparatus was not nearly as onerous as the Ottomans, they gladly switched sides. This was the beginning of the end for Bayezid. Both Ottoman wings collapsed, leaving Bayezid's center exposed to Timur. Knowing the battle lost, Bayezid simply hoped to extract his army from the situation. He rallied his forces on a hilltop called Catal Tepe where the remnants of the cavalry had gathered.

Here they resisted several attacks by Timur. Once night fell, Bayezid attempted to retreat. However, during his escape (which involved leaving the bulk of his forces behind) his horse tripped, and Timur's troops captured him. Despite their steadfast resistance, the rest of the Serbs and janissaries were cut down. Bayezid was brought before Timur, who was in his tent playing chess. Ankara fell not long after.

The Ottoman defeat left the empire in a state of flux. Bayezid's sons spent the next decade fighting amongst themselves. Timur had no intent on conquer-

ing the Ottoman Empire, preferring to have it a weak neighbor on his flank. Bayezid was carried back to Samarkand in a litter with bars, either because he attempted to escape or due to illness. This would later give rise to a legend that Timur imprisoned him in a golden cage.

⊕ Key Elements of Warcraft

Mounted Archers

The mounted archer was the basis of the Mongol army. Since the nomads of the Eurasian steppes wielded the powerful composite bow from an early age, they were excellent archers. If the accounts of medieval travelers can be believed, Mongols often learned how to ride before they could walk. Mastering these essential military skills at an early age gave the Mongols a military force that could not be matched in terms of mobility and lethalness until the modern age. Genghis Khan then forged it into a highly disciplined army, a feat which enabled him to carve out the largest contiguous empire in history. Often their armies fought on several fronts at once, a difficult enough task in the modern period and practically unheard of during medieval times.

The keys to the Mongol army were not only their natural skills at archery and horsemanship, but also their training. All males between the ages of fifteen to around sixty were eligible for military service. The harsh climate of Mongolia gave the nomads an almost other-worldly endurance. Although nomadic horse archers had a long history of success in the ancient and medieval worlds, the army created by Genghis Khan perfected this form. He added the essential element that separated the Mongols from their peers: discipline. While other armies would disintegrate in order to loot the dead and baggage of an enemy in flight, Genghis Khan ordered his armies to wait until victory was complete before plundering. Anyone who disobeyed this command was executed.

Each trooper had a string of three to five horses. If one horse grew tired, the soldier simply switched horses. In non-nomadic armies, this was not possible. Horses were simply too expensive to maintain to allow each cavalryman to have more than one, especially the large horses necessary to carry an armored warrior.

In order to maintain their mobility, the Mongols were lightly armored. Their armor usually consisted of lacquered or boiled leather and a helmet. Some wore other types of armor, such as chain mail, but it was not as widespread among the Mongols due to its weight.

Weaponry The primary weapon of the Mongols was the composite bow, made of layers of sinew, horn, and wood. Each warrior carried one per horse, attached to their saddles, and quivers of arrows. The bow was incredibly powerful, often with a pull weight of over one hundred pounds. The Mongols also used a wide

Mongolian cavalry armed with spears and shields. © *Pauline Taylor/Alamy*

variety of arrows, such as armor piercing, blunt stun arrows, and even whistling arrows for signaling purposes. In addition, the soldiers carried sabers, maces, axes, and sometimes a short spear with a hook at the bottom of the blade. Other supplies (such as rope, rations, and files for sharpening arrows) were also carried. This made the soldiers of the Mongol army a self-sufficient unit, able to function independently of supply lines, thus allowing them to make rapid marches without being bogged down by supply wagons.

Organization The Mongol army was organized in decimal units, an old tradition of the steppe. The Mongol army was built upon a squad of ten (*arban*) and companies of a hundred (*jaghun*). The primary military unit was the regiment of a thousand (*mingghan*). Larger units of ten thousand (*tumen*) were also used. The Mongols also recruited defeated enemies into the Mongol army—especially other mounted archers. To prevent a mutiny, the Mongols divided the new recruits into existing units.

Before invading a territory, the Mongols held extensive meetings to decide not only how the upcoming war would be conducted, but which generals would participate in it. The Mongols also gathered intelligence on their opponents. Only after this was obtained would there be a declaration of hostilities.

While on the campaign, Mongol generals still held a high degree of independence. Thus they could complete their objectives on their terms. Even so, they still had to abide by a timetable. As a consequence of this, the Mongols could coordinate their movements and concentrate their forces at prearranged sites.

The Mongols also invaded in a set pattern. The Mongol army invaded in several columns, often a three-pronged attack consisting of a center army of the center with two flanking forces. All Mongol columns were covered by a screen of scouts who relayed information back to the generals. Because of their preplanned schedule and their scouts, the Mongols marched divided but were also able to fight united. Furthermore, because their forces often split up after the initial invasion, they marched in smaller concentrations and were not slowed by columns stretching for miles. With their spare horses, they moved fast and spread terror across the countryside. Thus, their opponents rarely prepared in time to face them as the Mongols appeared everywhere.

Tactics The Mongols preferred to destroy all field armies before attacking cities. Smaller fortresses, however, were taken as they came along. This had beneficial effects. First, it isolated the main cities. Second, refugees from these smaller cities fled to the main stronghold. The reports from the refugees helped reduce the morale of the inhabitants and garrison of the city. In addition, food and water reserves were taxed by the sudden influx of refugees.

The tactics by the Mongols in field battles or in sieges ultimately came back to being mounted archers: firepower and mobility. The Mongols had demonstrated on several occasions the advantages of concentrated firepower over any opponent. Not only did a withering hail of arrows break a charge of armored knights, but it also could pin units down. In sieges, concentrated bombardment by catapults broke through walls. Mobility was vital for the Mongols to carry out all of their tactics. By advancing, firing, wheeling, and retreating, the Mongol attack was in perpetual motion. Other tactics, such as encircling the enemy, could only be achieved with a high degree of mobility. Perhaps most importantly, mobility allowed the Mongols to withdraw and then reappear when they were least expected. This made it almost impossible for their opponents to accurately report on the movements of their armies.

The Mongols perfected the mounted archer art of war. With their armies of mounted archers, the Mongols conquered the steppes of Asia and Europe. It is no surprise that mounted archers from the steppes became the most coveted element in every sedentary army stretching from China to Egypt.

Gunpowder Weapons

The Mongol's first experience with gunpowder weapons was on the receiving end, but they quickly incorporated them into their arsenal and used them extensively in their wars against the Jin Empire in northern China and the Song Empire in southern China. The weapons came in two basic forms: explosive and incendiary. Although many consider gunpowder to be an explosive, it is also possible to concoct gunpowder recipes to create incendiaries. The Mongols may have used catapult-launched bombs in siege warfare outside of China. However, there is no conclusive evidence to determine if these bombs were explosive-based or filled with naphtha (a petroleum-based incendiary), or used with catapults and trebuchets.

The Mongols first encountered gunpowder-based weapons in their campaigns against the Jin Empire (1125–1234) in northern China. The weapons used by and against the Mongols in the thirteenth century were not cannons or firearms in the modern sense, as these weapons would not exist for approximately one hundred years. Instead, the Jin used explosives and fire lances. The explosives were called "thunder-crash bombs." Although they were primitive in form and function, they were effective. Thunder-crash bombs were made from metal containers and filled with gunpowder and a fuse. They were then launched against the enemy with a lit fuse through a variety of methods such as by hurling it from a catapult, or lowering it by chains against Mongol troops at the base of walls.

The explosives were very effective against wooden or skin-covered shelters, but has less impact against the thick base of city walls. Nonetheless, if they struck the top of the wall, defenders had little defense against them. In addition, the bombs could be used as landmines. When used as landmines, they were not very efficient because someone had to light a fuse. However, when properly placed in ambushes, the unexpected explosions created havoc and inflicted both physical and psychological damage on the Mongols and their horses.

Another gunpowder weapon widely used during the Mongol conquests was the fire lance. The fire lance was a spear with a short bamboo tube attached to the spear blade. When the fuse was lit, the fire lance functioned as a primitive flame thrower. A single warrior with this weapon was not terribly impressive, but often entire units among the Chinese were equipped with them, making them very formidable. In addition, the weapons could be a key component of a defensive network by placing the tubes—with or without the lance—on a rack. Thus a single person could light them and create a wall of flame.

Like the Jin, the Song Empire (1126–1279) also used gunpowder weapons such as thunder-crash bombs and fire lances. In addition, they used another primitive cannon that shot "fire arrows." Essentially, these were arrows shot from a vase-shaped vessel by a gunpowder explosion. As with most early gunpowder weapons, fire arrows were not very accurate. However, they had a greater range than the Mongols' composite bows (approximately 300–350 yards), and when used in large number, fire arrows could disrupt enemy formations before they could use their own weapons.

Defending against the thunder-crash bombs and fire lances proved to be a most difficult challenge for the Mongols. Indeed, they did not develop anything particularly effective against these weapons. Perhaps the only effective defense, if one could call it that, was perseverance in the sieges. Initially Mongol sieges consisted of blockading the enemy and thus forcing the city to surrender or face starvation while staying out of ranging of the bombs. In addition, the Mongols engaged the defenders by pummeling them with missiles from their own siege engines as well as their archers. Later, when deserters and Chinese engineers explained gunpowder technology to them, the Mongols adopted them in their arsenal and began using explosives against the Jin.

The Mongols were also instrumental in the spread of gunpowder weapons. However, it is not clear if the Mongols used thunder-crash bombs or other weapons in sieges west of China. The records of the Mongol conquests in Russia or the Middle East do not mention anything like an "earth-shattering kaboom!" One reason may be that the necessary resources required to manufacture gunpowder were easily available and properly stored in China. However, outside of China, even though Chinese engineers accompanied the Mongols it could be difficult to transport the weapons, keep the powder dry, or to find the proper materials to make more powder. The technology was previously unknown or only rumored outside of China.

Nonetheless, the Mongols were the primary transmitters of the knowledge of gunpowder. The technology spread either directly by witnessing its use in war, or by travelers (merchants, missionaries, adventurers) who went to the Mongol empire. This latter scenario seems more likely because most of the major trade routes ran through the empire, and the Mongols ensured the security of those routes. Therefore, while it is unlikely that Europe received gunpowder directly from the Mongols, it is known that it appeared there only after the Mongol invasions. Most likely, merchants like Marco Polo's family traveled through the Mongol Empire and carried the recipe back. Indeed, gunpowder appears in European arsenals as bombards, cannons, fire arrows, and fire lances—as well as in the form of celebratory fireworks in India, Central Asia, and the Middle East—after these regions encounter the Mongols.

⊕ Impact of the Mongol Conquests

In many ways, the Mongol conquests initiated the modern period, as the world became much more connected when the Mongols created the largest contiguous empire in history, one which stretched from the Sea of Japan to the Carpathian Mountains. Trade routes became more secure, and the Mongols further encouraged trade by willingly paying inflated prices to attract merchants to their capitals, thus developing the commercial hubs.

As a result, goods flowed throughout the empire and outside of it much more easily. Indeed, one of the reasons Christopher Columbus sought an oceanic trade route to the East is because by 1492, after the disintegration of the Mongol Empire, these land routes had collapsed due to war. Prices rose and security dropped.

During the Mongol period, however, ideas and technology flowed along with trade. Gunpowder weapons began to appear in Europe as did other forms of technology that had existed in China for centuries. Prior to the Mongol conquests, the wheelbarrow, for example, was unknown in the West. This is not to say that one fell off a Mongol cart, but rather that ideas began to spread and travelers, such as Marco Polo, reported what they saw in the East.

In terms of military world history, the Mongol impact was vast. Beyond just the spread of gunpowder, the Mongols impacted military history in many ways. The Japanese kamikaze pilots in World War II were inspired by the storms that wrecked Kublai Khan's invasion fleets. Vietnamese people throughout the twentieth century looked back to their fight against Kublai Khan's invading armies as inspiration to resist French imperialism, Chinese aggression, and American interference during the war in Vietnam.

During the rule of the Mongols, many of their subjects adopted Mongol military formations and methods of fighting. The Russians were the most notable group to do this. They realized that their old methods were ineffective as they served alongside the Mongols on campaigns. Indeed, even up to the period of Ivan the Terrible in the mid-sixteenth century, the primary enemies of the Russians were offshoots of the Golden Horde. To effectively combat them, one had to adopt the highly mobile form of warfare the Mongols used.

Once cannons and mass-manufactured firearms became commonplace, the dominance of the horse archer receded. While horse archers could still shoot faster than muskets, their discipline broke down, making them less effective as the primary body of troops. As firearms improved, the impact of horse archers disappeared for good in the nineteenth century.

After World War I and the staid offensive warfare of the period, military theoreticians began to reconsider the tactics and strategies of the Mongols. The military academies in Russia studied the tactics of the nomads beginning in the late nineteenth century. This continued during the period of the Soviet Union under the leadership of Marshal Tukhachevsky. By the 1930s, the Soviets created a mechanized force designed to emulate the Mongol art of war—high mobility, independence of command, and the capability of concentrating firepower and support. Unfortunately, Tukhachevsky and most of his subordinates perished in the Stalinist purges. This set back the Soviet military for more than a decade.

In the West, the primary advocate for using Mongol methods was B. H. Liddell Hart, a British theoretician. The British and American militaries used his strategies to remodel their tank and mechanized forces. At the time, tanks were seen primarily as support weapons for infantry and not organized into their own units. However, Hans Guderian, an officer in the German Wehrmacht, saw the potential of Liddell Hart's ideas. He incorporated these ideas and also some from the Soviets, laying the foundation for the German *blitzkrieg* (lightning warfare) that would make the Nazi armies feared throughout the world.

BIBLIOGRAPHY

Books

Buell, Paul. *Historical Dictionary of the Mongol World Empire.* Lanham, Md.: Scarecrow Press, 2003.

Jackson, Peter. *The Mongols and the West.* London and New York: Pearson, 2005.

May, Timothy. *The Mongol Art of War.* Yardly, Pa.: Westholme, 2007.

Morgan, David. *The Mongols.* Cambridge, Mass.: Basil Blackwell, 2007.

Rossabi, Morris. *Khubilai Khan.* Los Angeles: University of California Press, 1989.

Introduction to the Hundred Years' War (1337–1453)

Fought between England and France from 1337 to 1453 CE, the Hundred Years' War was essentially a series of raids, sieges, and diplomatic maneuvers punctuated by occasional pitched battles. What started as English attempts to win back lands lost to France in the thirteenth century evolved into a struggle for the future of the Kingdom of France itself, and very nearly saw the thrones of the two monarchies united under one crown.

Because of the length of the war as well as the military innovations that emerged over the course of the century, the Hundred Years' War is considered the most important of medieval conflicts. The English, with their deadly longbows, consistently proved the superiority of massed archery, while the French, whose armored knights were thought to be invincible, were defeated time and again in pitched battle.

Nonetheless, the English were unable to translate their victories on the battlefield into long-term gains, and in the end, inspired by the legendary Joan of Arc, the French rallied and drove the English almost entirely out of their country, giving birth in the process to a new sense of French nationalism and strengthening the monarchy.

Starting with William, Duke of Normandy's conquest in 1066, England amassed a continental empire, at one time controlling half the lands in France. From this zenith of power, England quickly ebbed, losing almost all of its French possessions by the mid-fourteenth century. The loss of all this territory, coupled with dynas-tic turmoil in France, prompted England's Edward III to make a case for war, which was formally declared in 1337.

The first phase of the war was dominated by the English under Edward III and his son Edward "The Black Prince." Winning stunning victories at Crécy and Poitiers, the English regained most of their lost territories and even managed to capture the French king in battle.

Despite these gains, the French were able to push the English back over the last half of the fourteenth century. Richard II of England was finally forced to sign a peace treaty in 1389, bringing a lull to the fighting for twenty-six years.

The peace was shattered by an English invasion in 1415 led by Henry V. Henry met the French in battle at Agincourt. Despite being vastly outnumbered, at the end of the day Henry held the field. Henry was determined to press his advantage and returned in 1417, taking first Normandy and then Paris itself. Henry arranged a treaty that guaranteed him the crown of France as soon as the ailing French king died. But it was not to be—Henry died first. By 1453, with the French victory at Castillon, the war was over.

This rapid decline in English fortunes is owed almost entirely to the inspirational figure of Joan of Arc, a teen-aged girl who personally led the effort to drive back the resurgent invaders at Orléans. She was later convicted of witchcraft and burned at the stake, but her death only made her a martyr to the cause that eventually resulted in total French victory.

The Hundred Years' War (1337–1453)

🌐 Major Figures

Edward III

Edward III (1312–1377) was one of the most remarkable monarchs of the Middle Ages and is ranked as one of England's greatest kings. His reign saw the beginning of the Hundred Years' War and the coming of the epidemic known as the "Black Death," as well as the rise of Parliament and the empowerment of the peasant classes and the decline of the armored knight as the dominant force on the battlefield, thanks in large part to tactics Edward developed himself.

Tumultuous Early Life Edward's birth came at a time when England's fortunes were at an all-time low. His father, Edward II (1284–1327), had proven himself a weak leader and incompetent general. The humiliating defeat at Bannockburn in 1314 had seen the English pushed out of Scotland, and the once massive "empire" of English holdings on the continent had been reduced to the region of Gascony in the southwest of France.

Edward's mother, Isabella (1292–1358), the daughter of the French king, would prove instrumental in putting her son on the throne. Edward II had long ignored his wife for a succession of court favorites, and Isabella had departed for France with her lover, Roger Mortimer (c. 1287–1330). There the pair drew much support from the many English nobles who wished to see their king deposed, and eventually Isabella returned to England with an army. Edward II abdicated, and his son was crowned Edward III on January 25, 1327, at the age of fourteen.

For the next four years, his mother and Roger Mortimer dominated Edward. Isabella had been named regent, or caretaker, of the kingdom, and she and Mortimer ruled the country independent of Edward. As he chafed under his mother's dominance, Edward married Philippa of Hainaut (c. 1314–1369) in 1328. The marriage was to last for forty-one years and produce seven sons and five daughters.

Shortly after turning eighteen, Edward led a coup, arresting Mortimer and sentencing him to hanging like a common criminal. Isabella was spared and lived out the rest of her life in a castle in Norfolk.

War with Scotland Edward III was eager to wield his kingly powers and soon began meddling in Scottish politics. He covertly backed the accession of the usurper Edward Baliol (c. 1282–1363) to the Scottish throne, then waged open war with his northern neighbors when Balliol was deposed in favor of the rightful king, David II (1324–1371).

At Halidon Hill in 1333, Edward personally led an outnumbered army to victory over the Scots employing massed ranks of archers in his army. This tactic, first used at Halidon Hill and refined in the Scottish wars, would prove the key to English success on the battlefield in the upcoming Hundred Years' War.

European Politics As he was fighting in Scotland, Edward was also dabbling in continental trade and politics. He instituted a policy of close cooperation with the wool trade in Flanders, an area mostly in modern-day Belgium, bringing Flemish weavers to London to teach the English their trade and forging alliances with the city-states of Bruges, Ypres, Ghent, and Cassel.

Edward's involvement in Flanders also saw the escalation of tensions with France, which viewed Flanders as belonging in its sphere of influence. Anglo-French tensions had been building since the death of King Charles IV of France in 1328. A French custom called the Salic law held that women could not inherit land; this law was extended to include female rulers inheriting the throne. Only male members of the royal family could inherit the crown of France, and furthermore, said interpreters of the Salic law, descent could only be traced through male heirs.

Thus, even though Edward III was the grandson of the king of France, since he traced his relationship through his mother, he could make no claim to the throne. The crown passed to Philip of Valois (Philip VI,

King Edward III wearing full armor. *Archive Photos, Inc./Getty Images*

1293–1350), a distant relation of Charles IV (1294–1328). Edward, however, had a different take on things and formally declared himself King of France in 1340, a claim that would be held by English monarchs until the reign of George III (1738–1820) in the late eighteenth century. It was this provocative move that would result in the Hundred Years' War.

French Defeat, English Glory Thanks to the new tactics he had developed, Edward III won one victory after another, beginning with the naval battle of Sluys, which simply employed the use of the longbow on the water in the same way it was used on land. Edward's initial military campaign saw the fall of the cities of Caen and Calais and the stunning defeat of the French army at Crécy in 1346.

The course of the war was interrupted by the arrival of the Black Death, a massive pandemic that swept across Europe, killing off a third of its total population. When the war resumed, Edward's son "the Black Prince" Edward (1330–1376) was leading the armies, still employing the tactics developed by his father.

The English won another major victory at Poitiers in 1356, capturing the French king, John II (1319–1364), in the process. The French soon sued for peace. The Treaty

of Brétigny restored the territory of Aquitaine to English rule, along with several other holdings throughout France. Edward now controlled about a third of French territory, leading the chronicler Jean le Bel to remark, "when the noble Edward gained England in his youth, nobody thought much of the English .... Now they are the finest and most daring warriors known to man."

The 1350s marked the high point of Edward's reign. He had the distinct honor of holding two sovereign kings captive: John II of France and David II of Scotland, who had been in 1346 at Neville's Cross. All of Europe hailed Edward as the greatest living monarch, and he himself could not resist drawing a comparison to the legendary King Arthur, founding the Order of the Garter in 1348 in emulation of the Round Table and its elite knights. He was even offered the title of Holy Roman Emperor, which he declined.

Years in Decline The last years of Edward's reign were marked by disappointment. On his fiftieth birthday in 1362, Edward turned the administration of his lands over to his sons, and much of England's gains in France, including Aquitaine, would soon fall back into French hands. The queen died in 1369, and Edward's favorite son and heir, the Black Prince, died in 1377, one year before his own death. Edward himself expired nearly alone, attended only by a priest and his mistress.

In many ways, Edward lived too long for his own good. The glorious victories of his early reign had brought massive debt and seen the rise of Parliament as a powerful force in English politics. But the victories had also created for the first time a sense of English nationalism, a common sense of purpose, and pride in simply being English. French, for example, was abandoned as the language of official court documents in 1362.

Edward III's fifty-year reign marked the beginning of the modern English state and a high point in English fortunes at home and abroad. Despite the setbacks of his later years, his reputation as one of England's greatest monarchs is well deserved.

Edward, the Black Prince

Edward, Prince of Wales, also known as "the Black Prince" (1330–1376), was perhaps the most famous English royal to never actually hold the throne. Renowned across Europe in his own lifetime as a paragon of chivalry and martial prowess, Edward personally led his troops to victory at the Battle of Poitiers and played a major role in many other events of the Hundred Years' War before dying prematurely, just a year shy of inheriting the crown.

The Prince Wins His Spurs The Black Prince's first brush with greatness came in 1346, when he was only sixteen years old. His father, Edward III, had invaded France in the opening offensive of the Hundred Years' War, and Edward had been brought along and put in charge of a third of the army.

THE BLACK DEATH

Most likely emerging from somewhere east of the Caspian Sea, the bubonic plague came to Europe via Genoan soldiers returning from wars on the Crimean Peninsula. Starting in 1347, the "Black Death," as it was known at the time, spread across Europe like wildfire, pausing only during the winters when the fleas that carried the disease went into hibernation.

The Italian writer Boccaccio wrote of the symptoms, as well as the fear and paranoia, spread by the scourge of the disease in his masterwork, the *Decameron*:

> In men and women alike it first betrayed itself by the emergence of certain tumors in the groin or the armpits, some of which grew as large as a common apple, others as an egg .... Tedious were it to recount, how citizen avoided citizen, how among neighbors was scarce found any that showed fellow-feeling for another, how kinsfolk held aloof, and never met, or but rarely; enough that this sore affliction entered so deep into the minds of men and women, that in the horror thereof brother was forsaken by brother, nephew by uncle, brother by sister, and oftentimes husband by wife; nay, what is more, and scarcely to be believed, fathers and mothers were found to abandon their own children, untended, unvisited, to their fate, as if they had been strangers.

By 1350, about one in three Europeans had died. The plague would continue to flare up in various regions around the continent for the remainder of the Middle Ages, and indeed well into the eighteenth century, but no outbreaks were as deadly as the first pandemic.

The effect of the Black Death on European society was profound. For example, the nature of the feudal system, which bound laborers to the land, was undermined as peasants suddenly found their skills in demand from depopulated regions in need of craftsmen and farmers. Edward III passed acts to regulate wages and prices, much to the displeasure of the suddenly enfranchised peasant class. This displeasure would eventually result in the Peasants' Revolt of 1381.

The Black Death brought a complete halt to the course of the Hundred Years' War for several years. In England, Parliament was dissolved in 1349, leaving the king unable to raise funds for war for the time being. With as many as half the country's potential soldiers dead, Edward was unable to raise an army, even if his attentions were not already given over to the death of his fifteen-year-old daughter Joanna, whose passing left him bereft.

The ravages of plague left few untouched by such loss. The long-term effects of the epidemic would revolutionize European society, but it could only halt the progress of war for a few short years. By 1355, war with France had resumed under the leadership of the Black Prince.

At the battle of Crécy, the English archers won the day, but there were moments when the French assault threatened the English lines. The Black Prince, commanding the right wing of the army, was personally engaged in heavy hand-to-hand combat with the French knights, and there were fears that the French would overwhelm the position. A runner was sent to the king with a request for reinforcements. The chronicler Jean Froissart records the king's response:

> Go back ... to those who have sent you and tell them not to send for me again today, as long as my son is alive. Give them my command to let the boy win his spurs, for if God has so ordained it, I wish the day to be his and the honour to go to him and to those in whose charge I have placed him.

The prince did indeed win his spurs that day, driving off the French assault in the end. At the end of the battle, Edward III pronounced his son worthy to be king. (Crécy may also be where the prince picked up his nickname, supposedly for the blackened breastplate he wore during the battle. Another possible source of the nickname is the amount of grief Prince Edward caused to his foes. In either case, the nickname only came into popular usage after Edward's death.)

Poitiers By 1356, the English were back in France. This time the Black Prince was in command of the whole army, which set off from the English-held territory of Gascony in the southwest of France on an extended raid through the French countryside.

Marching hundreds of miles, the English army found itself stranded in the middle of hostile territory, pinned between a river and a massive French army at Poitiers. Edward led his troops into battle personally, bolstering the wavering lines on multiple occasions. In a desperately fought battle, the outnumbered English once again prevailed, even capturing the French king in the process.

Prince of Aquitaine The Black Prince returned home to a frenzied welcome, hailed as a national hero. The victory at Poitiers forced the French to the negotiating table, and England walked away in possession of a third of France, including the rich territory of Aquitaine. Edward was named Prince of Aquitaine by his father in 1362, a year after he had caused a stir by marrying Joan of Kent (1328–1385), not for political gain but for love, a new concept in marriage and an apt demonstration of the prince's chivalrous ideals.

Now in command of an army of French knights, Edward became involved in military campaigns in the

Edward, The Black Prince of Wales. *Public Domain*

Spanish kingdom of Castile, which was being torn apart by dynastic struggles. The campaign would prove a disaster for the English prince. On a personal level, Edward contracted dysentery, an intestinal disease common among armies at the time, due to the filthy conditions they lived in while on the march. More broadly, the war had not brought the promised loot that any soldier of the day would expect as his just reward for fighting. The French knights serving under Edward, already unwilling subjects, now appealed to the king of France, Charles V (1338–1480), to revoke Edward's title as Prince of Aquitaine.

This touched on one of the underlying causes of the Hundred Years' War: Who had the authority in France? The kings of England and France both claimed sovereignty over the English-held lands, and the dispute could not be resolved peacefully. So it was again, with Charles claiming the right to revoke Edward's title and the Black Prince claiming that only his father, who had bestowed the title, could do such a thing.

Charles V invaded Aquitaine in 1369, inaugurating a turn in French fortunes. The Black Prince was too ill to personally command his armies—at the siege of Limoges in 1370, he supervised his troops from a stretcher. The French in turn had begun developing tactics to deal with

the feared English longbow. Aquitaine was soon back in French hands.

A Premature Death Edward never recovered from the dysentery he had contracted in Spain. He died in 1376 after securing the succession of his son Richard to the English throne. One year later, Edward III would die and the prince's son would become Richard II (1367–1400), who would go on to sign a temporary peace treaty with the resurgent French.

This legacy did not dampen the Black Prince's renown, which was so great that after he died, his body lay in state for four months as thousands of mourners from across England filed past, paying their last respects. He was finally laid to rest at Canterbury Cathedral.

Charles V

The reign of King Charles V of France (1338–1380) marked the end of the first phase of English dominance and the reconquest of nearly all the territories acquired by France's enemies up to that point.

Since the beginning of the Hundred Years' War in 1337, the French had suffered defeat after defeat at the hands of the English. These defeats had culminated in the Battle of Poitiers in 1356, in which Charles's father, King John II, was captured and the French army was nearly annihilated. Charles, as Dauphin (crown prince), acted as regent during his father's captivity and quickly proved himself an able leader.

France in Chaos The situation Charles inherited must have seemed extremely daunting. France was without an effective army and bankrupt, forced to literally pay a king's ransom to England. The Treaty of Brétigny, signed in the wake of Poitiers, had granted a third of French territory to England, mostly in the prosperous southwestern region known as Aquitaine. The remainder of the countryside was overrun with gangs of unemployed mercenaries, who were little more than bandits.

The situation was so bad that a mass peasant uprising—known as the Jacquerie—in northern France bloodily renounced allegiance to the French crown. Paris briefly fell to rioting mobs as nobles in the countryside were seized, tortured, and killed. The rebellion was brutally suppressed by Charles's brother-in-law King Charles II "The Bad" of Navarre, a small kingdom situated between France and Spain.

The relationship between the two Charleses would prove to be yet another difficulty for the Dauphin, who would find himself at war with Navarre soon after taking the crown. Charles V ascended to the throne in 1364 upon the death of his father, recently returned from captivity in England.

The Situation Stabilizes One thing Charles did have on his side was able advisors, particularly Bertrand du Guesclin (c. 1320–1380), France's answer to the "Black Prince" Edward of England. It was du Guesclin who would crush Charles the Bad's army the same year as Charles V's coronation, putting an end to the threat from Navarre. The king also managed to bring the semi-independent Dukedom of Brittany to heel, receiving homage from the previously pro-English duke.

Once king, Charles convened the Estates General, France's parliament, and instituted a strict system of taxation designed to fill the royal treasury once again. Appointing able men to governorships, Charles strengthened his infrastructure and administration, further increasing the income from the new taxes. With the fresh revenue, Charles started to put an army together again, finally quelling the rampaging hordes of unemployed soldiers that had terrorized the countryside for nearly a decade. With his internal situation stable, Charles turned his attention to foreign politics. Wars between Spanish kingdoms had attracted the interest of the English, who would have liked very much to have allied armies they could call upon in future battles with France.

Despite defeat at the Battle of Nájera, the French-backed faction in the Kingdom of Castile was soon on the throne, and the Black Prince, who had been named Prince of Aquitaine, was in serious debt for his part in the Spanish wars. Raising taxes on his French subjects to pay these debts only drove them to Charles with demands that the Prince be replaced. The Black Prince argued, however, that Charles did not have the authority to do such a thing, and the Hundred Years' War was back on.

Renewed War with England   Charles invaded Aquitaine in 1369. Learning from past defeats, he developed a strategy that was radically different from that of his predecessors: Instead of seeking a major battle, Charles and du Guesclin relied on hit-and-run tactics and quick sieges that won back town after town.

The English were further hindered by lack of leadership—the Black Prince was dying of dysentery and was unable to lead troops in battle—and naval defeat at the hands of French-allied Castile. By 1374, Charles had reconquered all of Aquitaine save for the traditional English enclave of Gascony. The Treaty of Brétigny had effectively been undone, and major English operations would not resume until Henry V's (1387–1422) invasion in 1415.

Charles, never in the best of health, died at the age of forty-two in 1380. His son and heir, Charles VI (1368–1422), signed a formal treaty with the English in 1396, completing his father's work.

Legacy   Charles V left behind a mixed legacy. In addition to his military victories, he is remembered as a patron of the arts and of learning, founding a royal library at the Louvre. His administrative reforms strengthened the French monarchy and rescued the government from its near-annihilation.

Nevertheless, his policies did not prove effective in the long-term. Combined with the mental defects of his successor, they pushed France back into a state of chaos and civil strife, leaving it ripe for English invasion. Charles's reign ultimately proved merely a check, rather than a reversal, of English fortunes.

John of Gaunt

John of Gaunt (1340–1399) played a key role in the Hundred Years' War, even though he never fought a major battle. His son, Henry of Bolingbroke (later Henry IV, 1367–1413), would take the English throne from Richard II, establishing a new dynasty, and his grandson, Henry V, would lead the English to perhaps their greatest victory of the war at Agincourt.

John forms a bridge between the first two major phases of the war. His father, Edward III, had started the war in a bid to win back the lands in France that had once belonged to England, which, during the reign of Henry II (1133–1189), had constituted nearly half the country.

Power Plays at Home and Abroad   John was the fourth son of Edward III, and never became king himself. Nevertheless, he wielded great power behind the scenes. Although constantly overshadowed by his dynamic and long-lived father, as well as his elder brother Edward, "the Black Prince," he was created Duke of Lancaster in 1362 and led a military expedition through France in 1370, marching an army from Calais on the English Channel to Bordeaux in the southwest. The expedition failed to win any significant victories, however, and John soon returned to England.

In Parliament he formed a power bloc to support the radical preacher John Wyclif and protect him from church reprisals. The Good Parliament of 1376 developed the impeachment process specifically to break this bloc.

With the accession of Richard II, John developed a reputation as an advisor to the king and as a top diplomat, brokering peace with Scotland in 1380. It was this Scottish mission that saved John's life: He was away from home when, in 1381, angry mobs participating in the Peasant's Revolt attacked his residence at the Savoy Palace.

John's Castilian Expedition   John spent the remainder of the decade pursuing a claim on the throne of the Spanish kingdom of Castile, as he was married to the daughter of the recently deceased Castilian king. He personally led a campaign in Castile from 1386–1388, but it came to nothing. Unsuccessful, he returned to England and married his daughter to the future King Henry of Castile.

Late in his life, John finally married his longtime mistress, Catherine Swynford, who had borne him four children. Interestingly, these children, known as the Beauforts, formed a branch of the English royal family through which Henry Tudor (later Henry VII, 1457–1509) would claim his right to the throne in the Wars of the Roses, nearly a century later.

Construction on Dunstanburgh Castle began under Thomas, Earl of Lancaster. © *David Gowans/Alamy*

Lancastrian Legacy John's main contribution to the course of the Hundred Years' War was through his son, Henry Bolingbroke. Although he had been careful to never appear to openly work against the king, John never gained Richard's full trust. So it was that when John died in 1399, Richard declared his estates forfeit and seized them in the name of the crown. Henry, who had been exiled the year before, returned, ostensibly to claim his inheritance. In actuality he raised an army upon landing in England and soon deposed Richard II, taking the crown for himself, becoming Henry IV, and founding the Lancastrian dynasty in the process.

Henry V

Henry V (1387–1422) reigned as king of England for a mere nine years, but in that time, enjoyed one of the most dynamic and successful reigns of any English monarch and very nearly united the crowns of England and France. One of the central figures of the Hundred Years'

War, his ambition and rise to power was stopped only by his premature death.

Early Life Henry was the son of an usurper, Henry IV, called Henry Bolingbroke before taking the throne, who established the Lancastrian dynasty when he deposed the unpopular Richard II in 1399. Young Henry grew up at court and even went with Richard II on campaign in Ireland, where he got his first taste of war.

Meanwhile, his father (Bolingbroke, the son of John of Gaunt) worked with a faction of Parliamentarians who opposed Richard II, an opposition that led to Bolingbroke's exile in 1398. The elder Henry returned the next year when Richard attempted to seize his inheritance and, after raising an army, forced the king to abdicate.

The kingdom did not pass quietly into Lancastrian hands, and Henry IV spent much of his reign working to legitimize his rule and put down rebellions, particularly in Wales.

Prince Henry's first experience as a war leader came at the age of just fourteen, when he led a campaign against Welsh rebel Owen Glendower. Ably advised by Harry "Hotspur" Percy (1366–1403), a knight of great renown, Henry quickly impressed his elders with his willingness to learn and attention to detail.

These qualities of leadership were further honed when Henry led an army to put down a rebellion by his former advisor, Hotspur. The Percys had joined with the Welsh in a bid to place Richard II's designated heir on the throne, but were defeated at Shrewsbury in 1403 by the teenage prince, who had quickly come into his own as a general and leader of men.

After Shrewsbury, Henry also demonstrated some of the stoic grit that would later come to dominate his reputation. During the battle, an arrow had struck the young prince in the face below his right eye socket. The arrowhead had lodged in his skull and was extracted with a drill-like instrument, the head of which was actually wider than the wound itself. The operation, like all procedures at the time, was administered without pain-killers. By all accounts, Henry weathered the ordeal with quiet resolve.

Henry IV died while only in his forties, beset by boils and fever. Henry V took the throne and immediately began planning a military expedition to France, the first such undertaking since Richard II had signed the Peace of Paris in 1389. The expedition was aimed at glorifying Lancastrian rule and drumming up popular support for the fledgling dynasty, which was facing plots against the king's life.

Furthermore, Henry was a very pious man and was quite convinced of the moral and spiritual rightness of his campaign. In his mind, the lands he was fighting to regain had been granted to England by God's divine will, and he was simply exercising his right as God's instrument on Earth to take back what rightfully belonged to him.

As the English army began to assemble, Henry sent a series of outrageous diplomatic demands to Paris. The French had no choice but to reject the English claims, giving Henry a legal justification for invasion.

Campaigning in France

His fleet landed at the port city of Harfleur in France in August of 1415. The city fell by September, but the English army had been beset by a terrible outbreak of dysentery. Although he had hoped to march on Paris, Henry, with the campaigning season growing late and his army weakened by disease, decided to finish things off with a march to the English-occupied city of Calais as a show of force. Although trying to avoid open battle, Henry had no choice but to engage the French army at Agincourt. Although desperately outnumbered, the king personally led his troops to victory. At one point, on hearing that his brother had fallen wounded, Henry led his personal bodyguard in cutting a bloody swathe through the opposition to reach his stricken brother and guarded him until he could be borne away.

Returning to a hero's welcome in England, Henry was able to raise funds for a second campaign in France, which he launched in 1417. His navy included the largest ships yet built in England, and the siege train that marched with him boasted the latest in massive cannons and trebuchets, giant rock hurling machines, both of which were a match for all but the thickest walls.

Henry took Caen and pressed his advantage, campaigning through the winter. The French were paralyzed, their leadership in tatters after the deaths at Agincourt and their armies too busy fighting each other. The English enlisted one of the two factions in the ongoing struggle, the Burgundians, who kept their rivals pinned down and unable to bring battle to the rampaging British.

In 1418, Henry took the key city of Rouen after a brutal siege that saw twelve thousand women and old men trapped between the city walls and the English lines, kicked out of the city to conserve food and water, yet not allowed safe passage by Henry, who argued their fate was bound to that of Rouen. By this time, Henry viewed himself as the "scourge of God," dispensing righteous justice to those who dared oppose his claims. When the city fell, the citizens of Rouen were treated like rebellious subjects who had defied Henry's rule. His army sacked and pillaged the town as Henry took mass in the grand cathedral.

The Treaty of Troyes

Working in concert with the Burgundians, who had formally allied with the English, Henry finally took Paris in 1420 and forced france's mad King Charles VI to the negotiating table.

The agreement that resulted, the Treaty of Troyes, was remarkable in its terms. Although it recognized Charles's right to the throne, it named Henry V as his heir, disinheriting the king's legitimate son. Upon Charles's death, which everyone expected to be quite soon, the English king Henry would also assume the throne of France, uniting the monarchies of the two countries. Henry's son was furthermore named as heir to the French crown after Henry's death.

Premature Death

That death came much sooner than any would have suspected. Henry was obliged to continue campaigning against the Dauphin, the original heir to the throne, and while besieging the city of Meaux contracted dysentery. By the end of August he was dead, a mere two months before Charles VI.

Henry's son, still an infant, was in no position to press for his rights as heir to Henry's claim on the French throne, and the Dauphin began a campaign that, with the help of Joan of Arc (1412–1431), would see him crowned Charles VII (1403–1461). Within a generation of Henry's death, the resurgent French would reclaim all their lost territory save the city of Calais and bring the Hundred Years' War to an end.

Sculpture depicting Joan of Arc. *The Library of Congress*

Joan of Arc

Joan of Arc (1412–1431) was arguably the most important French figure in the whole of the Hundred Years' War. Her inspirational leadership revitalized the French cause at a time when all seemed lost, igniting a new sense of national pride and unity—new concepts for the time, especially in such a traditionally factional and divided country as France. After her death, her story was largely marginalized until the nineteenth century, when she was rediscovered by artists, writers, and theologians, all of whom used her story to further their own needs for a hero from the past.

France in Crisis   Joan of Arc, also called "the Maid" (*la pucelle*), was born to a fairly well-off farming family in the eastern French territory of Domrémy. She came of age during the Hundred Years' War, a conflict that had been raging between England and France off and on since 1337.

By 1420, after a series of victories, the English king Henry V had secured a treaty with France's mad King Charles VI, promising Henry the crown upon Charles's death. Despite Henry's premature death, the French royalty found itself in a precarious position when Charles VI died not long after Henry.

The Dauphin, Charles (1403–1461), rightful heir to the French throne, was living in exile in the southern town of Bourges, paralyzed by petty politics and lack of money. The English occupied the north and south-west of the country and were allied with a powerful French faction known as the Burgundians, who controlled most of eastern France.

Joan's Mission   Back in Domrémy, Joan began hearing voices around the age of thirteen. According to Joan, they were Saints Michael, Catherine, and Margaret, and they were telling her to go aid the Dauphin in driving the English out of the country. By 1429, Joan decided the time had come to act. She set out for the Dauphin's court with a small escort provided by the local garrison.

Word of Joan's remarkable mission preceded her. By the time she arrived at Chinon in February, the Dauphin was expecting her. Yet he delayed meeting with her for two days, displaying the ambivalence that would characterize his relationship with Joan. When Charles did finally allow Joan to visit his court, he disguised himself, placing a double on the throne. Joan, despite having no idea what the Dauphin looked like, saw through the deception and picked Charles out of the crowd of courtiers. This display convinced many of those present that Joan was indeed on a divine mission, but the Dauphin was not so sure. Joan was interviewed and examined for three weeks by leading theologians. A panel of learned midwives confirmed Joan's virginity and, at the end of the process, the clerics gave Joan their highest endorsement.

During this time, the English had besieged the vital city of Orléans. Despite the small size of the English army, most people on both sides of the conflict believed it was only a matter of time until Orléans fell. Charles was seriously considering where to flee. With little left to lose, he decided to grant Joan what she asked.

The Maid of Orléans   Joan was given a horse, a suit of white steel armor, a sword, and a banner. With a small escort, she set out for Orléans, slipping into the besieged city in late April 1429. She immediately began pressing the city garrison to attack the English positions. She personally led several such attacks herself. Despite heavy resistance from the captains of the garrison, she rallied the citizens and troops of the town to her cause.

Some indication of the passion of Joan's convictions can be seen in the letter she wrote to the English commanders at Orléans shortly before her departure for the city:

> King of England, render account to the King of Heaven of your royal blood. Return the keys of all the good cities which you have seized, to the Maid ... if you do not do these things, I am the commander of the military; and in whatever place I shall find your men in France, I will make them flee the country, whether they wish to or not; and if they will not obey, the Maid will have them all killed. She comes sent by the King of Heaven, body for body, to take you out of France.

On May 7, despite an arrow wound received in battle, Joan led the French to victory at Les Tourelles, the fortress outside Orléans that the English had been using as a headquarters. The next day the English army withdrew.

Orléans was the turning point of the Hundred Years' War and the first major French victory of the conflict. The myth of English invincibility was shattered. More importantly, the French people had found an inspirational leader to rally around.

Coronation at Rheims

Joan continued leading the army, her white banner serving as a beacon of hope to the increasingly jubilant French troops. With the crown prince at her side, Joan reached the ancient capital of Rheims by July, where the Dauphin was crowned King Charles VII.

This event marked the high point of Joan's short-lived career. She became involved in court politics over the following months as various factions pressed Charles to open peace negotiations. For Joan, nothing short of total victory was acceptable. Impatient, she personally led an army in an assault on English-occupied Paris, but was seriously wounded. The French withdrew after only a day, and Charles opened negotiations with the Burgundy.

Capture and Trial

Although angered with and alienated from the man she had made king, Joan was determined to continue leading the fight against the English. She led an army to relieve the besieged town of Compiègne. In May 1430, during a skirmish outside the city, Joan, while covering the retreat of her troops, was captured by the Burgundians.

The traditional practice at the time whenever a military leader was captured was to offer a ransom. Joan's family did not have sufficient funds to provide a suitable sum, and Charles VII, displaying his characteristic ambivalence, failed to act. The English convinced their Burgundian allies to "buy out" Joan's captor, and the Maid of Orléans was turned over to her enemies.

Despite facing impossible odds in what amounted to a political show trial, Joan consistently demonstrated wit, eloquence, and piety during her interrogations. Nevertheless, her long months of captivity in a dank tower cell took their toll on her resolve, and she eventually capitulated, receiving a life sentence. This was soon after changed to a death sentence—the reasons why are unclear; one oft-cited reason is that she reportedly refused to cease wearing men's clothes—and she was burned at the stake in the marketplace at Rheims on May 30, 1431. Maintaining her innocence to the last, she asked that a cross be held high enough for her to see over the flames, and she died calling out Jesus' name.

Remarkable Legacy

Unfortunately for the English, Joan had left an indelible mark on her countrymen. Despite somewhat inconsistent leadership, the French, now armed with a cause and a new sense of nationalism, drove the English out of their country, save for the small enclave of Calais, by 1453, bringing an end to the longest and most destructive war of the Middle Ages.

Joan herself was exonerated at a trial ordered by Charles VII, at the behest of Joan's mother and the Inquisition, in 1456. Her status as a heretic was overturned and her name was cleared.

Despite her instrumental role in the French victory, Joan of Arc remained a relatively minor historical figure until the nineteenth century. She was "rediscovered" by writers such as George Bernard Shaw and Mark Twain, who wrote of her exploits, and by artists who depicted her as a romanticized savior. The Catholic Church, similarly in need of heroes, began the process of naming Joan a saint. This process received a huge boost during World War I when France, once again on the brink of defeat, looked to Joan's story for inspiration. She was declared Saint Joan of Arc in 1920, shortly after the war's end, cementing her status as France's national and religious hero.

Charles VII

King Charles VII of France (1403–1461) rose from living in exile, the discredited heir to the throne of France, to eventual triumph over the English in the Hundred Years' War, bringing to an end the longest and most destructive war of the Middle Ages.

Internal Strife and the Treaty of Troyes

Charles's father, Charles VI, had been unable to rule effectively due to repeated bouts of madness. The king's instability had led to civil strife between two factions: the Armagnacs, supporters of the royal family; and the Burgundians, supporters of John the Fearless (1371–1419), Duke of Burgundy.

The future Charles VII, as Dauphin of France, did not help matters when he banished his mother from court. The Queen fled to the court of John the Fearless and together they marched on Paris. The Parisians welcomed them with open arms and the Dauphin fled. John declared himself regent, or caretaker, of the mad king.

The English, meanwhile, had been taking advantage of this internal strife, launching an invasion that marked the first major hostilities in more than two decades. Under the leadership of Henry V, the English had taken most of northern France over the course of five years' campaigning.

With France facing such a grave foreign threat, the Dauphin and John the Fearless agreed to meet on a bridge at Montereau to work out a peace agreement. The meeting ended with John being murdered by Charles's supporters. Although Charles claimed that the assassination took place without his consent, the incident drove Philip, John's son and the new Duke of Burgundy, to ally with the English.

Once a Roman settlement, Tintagel Castle is also thought to have been a royal residence of Celtic kings in the fifth century and has been associated with the legend of King Aurthur. *© Tony Watson/ Alamy*

Charles VI, in one of his last periods of lucidity, recognized that the new alliance constituted a major threat to his rule and his life. He negotiated the Treaty of Troyes, which allowed him to keep his crown, but named Henry V as heir to the French throne. Furthermore, the Dauphin's estranged mother claimed her son was illegitimate. Even after Henry V's premature death, the throne passed to the infant King Henry VI (1421–1471). The Dauphin, shaken by these reversals of fortune, withdrew to the southern town of Bourges, where he still had a strong base of support.

King of Bourges Although the English cause had suffered greatly with the death of the dynamic Henry V, their eventual victory seemed virtually assured. England directly held nearly all of northern France, including Paris, as well as their traditional enclave of Gascony on the southwest coast. Their Burgundian allies controlled the east. Most of the subjects in these territories accepted the idea of foreign rule, for it promised an end to the wars that had ravaged the country since the 1340s.

Thoroughly dispirited, Charles "reigned" from Bourges, where he was derisively called the "King of Bourges," since that was effectively all he controlled. He was further paralyzed by petty court politics as various favorites jockeyed for his approval and spent what little money the treasury generated.

As the 1420s came to a close, the English prepared for a renewed campaign, directed at the remaining southern territories loyal to Charles. The initial objective was the vital city of Orléans.

A further blow to French morale was struck when Charles dispatched a force to raid an English supply column carrying salted fish and, in what was dubbed "The Day of the Herrings," was driven off by the outnumbered English guards. Seemingly incapable of defeating the English, Charles left Orléans to its fate.

Joan of Arc It was at this point that Joan of Arc arrived at Charles's court at Chinon in February 1429, claiming that she had been ordered by angels to come rescue the Dauphin and drive the English out of France. So desperate was the French position that Charles offered his support.

Joan proved a dynamic new force in the war, single-handedly rallying the beleaguered French, who soon forced the English to raise the siege, heralding a turning point in the war. She also personally inspired Charles, rousing him from his long period of inaction. With Joan at the head of the army, Charles marched north, clearing the English out of the Loire Valley. The campaign culminated with the crushing French victory at the Battle of Patay. On July 17, at the ancient capital of Rheims, Charles was crowned King of France.

Charles's coronation marked the beginning of a renewed sense of nationalism that would gain a martyr in the form of Joan of Arc, who was captured by the Burgundians in 1430. Charles has long earned condemnation for failing to provide a ransom for Joan after her capture. With no ransom forthcoming, the Burgundians turned Joan over to the English, who burned her at the stake in 1431.

The End of the War Charles, with his characteristic hesitancy, slowly built upon the momentum started by Joan. He made peace with Burgundy, who had grown dissatisfied with their English alliance, in 1435. Charles publicly apologized for John the Fearless's death and was able to finally re-enter Paris, still strongly pro-Burgundian, in 1436.

Charles once again hesitated, but at the urging of his long-time mistress, Agnes Sorel, he eventually invaded Normandy, wresting it from the English by 1445. Gascony, an English territory for three centuries, finally fell in 1453 after the Battle of Castillon. Castillon is considered the last battle of the Hundred Years' War—no peace treaty ever marked the end of hostilities, but Charles declared the war over and the English, torn internally by Henry VI's ineffectual reign, were in no position to object.

Domestic Reforms and Legacy As the war was entering its final phases, Charles began a series of internal reforms, perhaps his greatest legacy. By combining the most able advisors from his own court and his new Burgundian allies, Charles earned his nickname "The Well-Served." These advisors helped Charles devise a system of permanent taxation that swelled the royal coffers with unprecedented wealth. Charles used this newfound wealth to put together Europe's first standing army since the days of the Western Roman Empire. The foundation of French military dominance over the next two centuries was laid during Charles VII's reign. Although the last years of his reign were marked by feuds with his son and heir, Charles left France considerably stronger than he had found it. He even took steps to repudiate Joan of Arc's heresy trial—in 1456 her sentence was nullified and her name was cleared. Despite his somewhat questionable leadership at times, Charles VII truly earned his other nickname "The Victorious."

⊕ Major Battles

Sluys, 1340

Fought on June 24, 1340, the Battle of Sluys was the first major engagement of the Hundred Years' War. The clash between the French and English navies ended with the near annihilation of the French fleet and the establishment of English naval superiority for the remainder of the war.

French Naval Dominance Like most English victories in the early course of the conflict, the victory at Sluys came as a bit of a shock to both sides. Prior to the battle, the French boasted what was widely considered the most powerful navy in Europe. Furthermore, over the previous two years, the French had been conducting a series of raids on coastal English towns virtually unopposed. The towns of Portsmouth and Southampton had been burned and looted by French marines and their Italian allies. By 1340, Edward III of England had had enough and sent a large fleet into the English Channel to put a stop to the raids once and for all.

The French, meanwhile, had been assembling a large fleet of their own, comprised of ships from their own navy and allied vessels from Genoa, with an eye to invading England. A letter King Edward later wrote to his son puts the size of the French fleet at 190 ships. Edward's own fleet was around the same size, but was bolstered by fifty ships from his Flemish (Belgian) allies. He found the French fleet riding at anchor in an inlet outside the town of Sluys.

The Battle The French commanders, although advised by their Genoese ally to sail out to meet the English in open waters, remained at anchor, their ships lashed to each other in the standard medieval naval defensive formation.

Edward sailed his ships into the bay and engaged the French in close fighting. His ships were carrying units of archers armed with the longbow, a weapon soon to prove its effectiveness on the field of battle. At Sluys, which was essentially a land engagement fought on the water, it helped carry the day as well. Edward's letter speaks of the fighting lasting all day and into the night, but by the next morning, the French fleet was in ruins.

Aftermath Both commanders of the French fleet lost their lives, one during the battle, the other after capture. Many of the sailors in the French fleet were also killed, both in the fighting and by Edward's Flemish allies while attempting to flee. Medieval chronicles give the French casualties as thirty thousand men lost, but these numbers are unreliable.

It is likely the English suffered heavily as well, for they remained at anchor for several days, neglecting to give chase to the Genoese, who had slipped away towards the end of the battle. Nevertheless, it was a battle well won for Edward. Although the French would occasionally employ Spanish ships in the future, their own navy would never again harass the English Channel or manage the sort of raids that saw Portsmouth and Southampton reduced to ashes.

England would enjoy command of the seas for the remainder of the war, an important foundation for the island nation. For example, the far-flung English province of Gascony, in southwest France with no direct link to other English territories, would have proven almost impossible to hold on to if the French controlled the sea as well as the land surrounding it. This thorn in the side of France would prove instrumental in future campaigns and in the course of the war in general.

More importantly, control of the sea lanes meant England was free to invade France at will and maintain supply lines to its armies on the European continent. After an unsuccessful invasion following on the heels of his victory at Sluys, Edward III would launch an invasion in 1346 that would culminate in the victory at Crécy. The Hundred Years' War had begun in earnest.

Crécy, 1346

The Battle of Crécy, fought on August 26, 1346, was the first great land battle of the Hundred Years' War. More importantly, the shocking victory marked the beginning of the end for the age of the heavily armored knight as the preeminent force on the battlefield.

Edward's Invasion of Normandy The roots of the battle lie with a five-year truce King Edward III of England had signed with his French foes after failing to take the city of Tournai in Flanders—modern-day Belgium—in an attempt to follow up on his naval victory at Sluys.

The truce had given Edward a chance to devise a new strategy. Although Flanders was geographically closest to England, it lacked a safe base from which to wage a protracted war. Edward decided instead to invade Normandy, once the jewel of English holdings in France.

Launching a one-thousand-ship invasion fleet in 1346, Edward landed in France and immediately besieged the city of Caen, which fell by the end of June. Leaving a garrison at the city, Edward then set out across the hostile French countryside, aware that a large French army led by King Philip VI was paralleling his progress.

Stokesay Castle in Shropshire, England, was not built by a king, but by a wealthy thirteenth-century wool merchant. © *John James/Alamy*

The English March Cross-Country Although Edward had entertained ideas of marching on Paris, he decided instead to march northeast toward Flanders. The army that marched with him constituted a new kind of army, one that was made up primarily of archers armed with the mighty English longbow. Edward's wars in Scotland had allowed him a chance to refine the tactics of the bow and massed firepower, and he knew that if he was allowed to choose the time and location of battle, he could defeat an army much larger than his.

Several mighty rivers crisscross Northern France, and it was these rivers that posed the biggest threat to Edward's plans. A race was on to get his troops across the rivers before the French could block every bridge and ford. At Poissy, as a French regiment bore down on them, English engineers barely managed to construct a bridge—only one plank wide—in time to allow troops across the Seine to establish a beachhead, successfully driving off the French.

With the English across the Seine, Paris was now threatened and Philip redoubled his efforts to pin the English down. Every crossing point along the mighty Somme River was guarded, and the French army was hot on Edward's heels.

Acting on a tip from a local, Edward made a desperate midnight march to the ford of Blanchetaque, which he found guarded, albeit lightly. As the sun rose, the English bowmen laid down a hail of arrows, covering a desperate river crossing. Reaching the far bank, the English drove the French, disorganized and depleted by the arrow fire, back from the river. The English were across the Somme. The French army was right behind them.

The Battle Edward knew the time had come to give battle, and he chose the town of Crécy as his ground. Occupying the high ground outside of town, Edward deployed his archers, around six thousand in all, in the center and on either flank of his army, which also included up to one hundred primitive cannons. Commanding the right wing of the infantry was the king's own son, sixteen-year-old Edward, "the Black Prince." The English were ready for battle.

The French arrived from the south in huge numbers. The size of the French army has been given as anywhere from two times to six times the size of the English, but most likely numbered about forty thousand troops against Edward's ten thousand. What's more, a large percentage of the French army was comprised of mounted knights, thought at the time to be nearly unbeatable. As the French arrived on the battlefield, the English, who had been at rest near their battle stations, rose and took up arms. The battle opened with an archery duel as Philip deployed his unit of fifteen thousand Genoese crossbowmen. Things did not bode well from the start, as the medieval chronicler Jean Froissart records:

> [The crossbowmen] were quite fatigued, having marched on foot that day six leagues, completely armed, and with their crossbows. They told the constable that they were not in a fit condition to do any great things that day in battle. The earl of Alençon, hearing this, said, "This is what one gets by employing such scoundrels, who fail when there is any need for them."

It was no contest. The rate of fire of the crossbow was no match for the English longbow. Furthermore, in addition to their fatigue, the Genoese suffered from a lack of pavises, large shields which they could use to shelter behind while reloading. To make matters worse, a rainstorm the night before had soaked their weapons, rendering them even less effective. The English archers, meanwhile, had kept their bowstrings tucked up under their helmets during the storm, safe and dry, ready to be restrung in the morning.

The English arrows fell like rain and the cannons added their own thunder as well. Although these early cannons were not terribly deadly, the casualties they did inflict, along with the noise and smoke they generated, had a further demoralizing effect. As the Genoese faltered, the impetuous French knights, who were so sure of victory that they had predetermined who would capture which English lord, sounded the charge, galloping over their own crossbowmen. The rainstorm had made the ground muddy and the uphill charge soon bogged down. As they made their way up the hill, most of the French knights were unhorsed, their unarmored mounts taken down by the ceaseless arrow storm. Advancing into a barrage of up to thirty thousand arrows a minute, the French died in great numbers. Yet more waves pressed forward, eventually reaching the English lines, exhausted and decimated, only to be driven back by the dismounted English knights.

The English fended off a succession of such wave attacks and, as the sun set, Philip VI, who was himself wounded, sounded a general retreat. He left behind at least a quarter of his army, dead and wounded on the battlefield. Among the dead were eleven princes, including Philip's brother, as well as the blind King John of Bohemia (1296–1346), who had insisted on being led into battle. As darkness fell, the English peasant-soldiers made their way through the field of French dead, searching for captives who could be ransomed for large sums and killing those knights too wounded to take prisoner. It was a fitting end to a battle that saw the triumph of the lowly archer over the once invincible knight.

Siege of Calais, 1346–1347

The Siege of Calais, begun in 1346, was a direct result of the English victory at Crécy. The city's eventual fall to the English would give that country an important military and mercantile base on the Continent for the following two hundred years.

The Importance of Calais Edward III had launched his invasion of Normandy in 1346, taking the city of Caen, then marching on to defeat the French army decisively at Crécy. The French had retreated in complete disarray, shocked and broken after their loss. Edward had a pick of where to point his army and chose to make for the city of Calais on the coast of the English Channel.

Edward's choice was both strategically and tactically sound. Although he faced no opposition in the open field, his men were running short of supplies. Paris, as well fortified as it was, would be too tough a nut to crack for Edward's small army. Calais, on the other hand, would provide England with a fine beachhead from which to launch future operations. It was itself a well-defended city that enjoyed brisk trade with the city-states of Flanders, with which England already had an alliance. Lastly, Edward would be able to re-supply his men, even as they settled in for a siege, as Calais is separated from England by a mere twenty-one miles.

The Siege The siege began in September 1346 and dragged on through the winter. The defenses that made Calais a prime choice for Edward in turn made it difficult to take the city from the French. The English, who bombarded the city walls with primitive cannons and large catapults, ringed in the city but were unable to take it by direct assault. Edward decided to starve out the inhabitants, blockading the port with his navy.

By the summer of 1347, the English army was close to reaching its goal. Food and water supplies in the city were nearly gone. In desperation, the city ejected its children and elderly, but Edward refused to grant them passage through the English lines. They starved to death outside the city walls as the siege dragged on.

Finally, on August 1, the city sent a delegation of six town leaders, shaven headed and wearing nooses around their necks, to meet with Edward and offer surrender. Edward, enraged by the city's stubborn resistance, ordered the six men hanged, but his wife, Queen Philippa, tearfully begged him to spare the delegates. Edward consented and even granted the rest of the townsfolk safe passage out of the city, an unusually merciful act for the times. Calais was repopulated with English merchants and soldiers and their families.

Philip's Plot The French king Philip VI, who had been unable to muster an army during the course of the siege, did not give up on the city entirely. A plot was hatched to bribe the governor of Calais to sell the city out to the French. Word of this plot reached Edward in time, however, and he set out for Calais with a small army.

The French were caught off guard when Edward personally led a charge of his knights out of the town

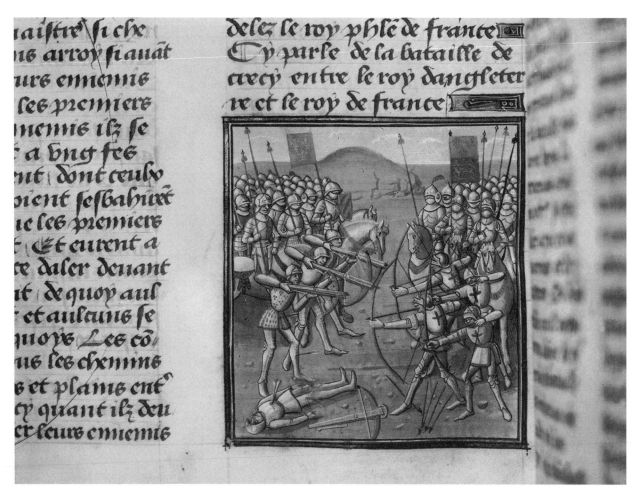

An illustration of war weaponry of the fourteenth century.   © *Visual Arts Library (London)/Alamy*

gates and directly into the heart of the attacking French. With the king rode his son, "the Black Prince," who in the course of fighting, saved Edward's life when he found himself surrounded by hostile troops—the young prince and his retinue hacked through the enemy lines to reach their king and lead him back to safety.

The French attack was repulsed and Calais remained in English hands. It was to stay that way well beyond the course of the Hundred Years' War, becoming as English as England itself, even sending representatives to Parliament. It would not return to France until the reign of Mary I (1516–1558) in the sixteenth century.

Poitiers, 1356

The Battle of Poitiers, fought on September 19, 1356, was the high point of English fortunes in the first phase of the Hundred Years' War and the victory that cemented the international reputation of Edward "the Black Prince."

Prince Edward's father, Edward III, had inaugurated the Hundred Years' War in 1337, winning a major victory at Crécy in 1346. The prince had "won his spurs" at that battle, meaning he had experienced battle and proven his valor.

English Raid in France Ten years after Crécy, Prince Edward was in command of a raiding force, setting out from the English-held territory of Gascony in the southwest of France. The army, which numbered about seven thousand men including one thousand archers was heading north to meet up with two other English armies, due to march in from the Channel coast.

Unfortunately for Edward, neither of the other two armies had set out as planned. Edward's men, after marching 260 miles in six weeks, realized they were in the middle of hostile territory with no hope of reinforcement. Worse still, the French army was finally coming after them.

Prince Edward Cornered Throughout the march, Edward had been trying to draw the French to battle. Despite the small size of his army, Edward was confident of victory, thanks to the tactics the English had perfected at Crécy. By using massed arrow fire supplied by the quick-firing and deadly longbow, the English army had proven that it could defeat a foe many times its size.

However, as Edward marched north towards the Loire River, he found himself less eager to join battle. His troops were low on supplies and tired. The Count of Poitiers had joined forces with his father, King John II of France, and now pursued Edward with a large army. As the French moved south of the English, making camp at the town of Poitiers, Edward found that all crossings over the Loire had been destroyed. He had two choices: surrender or fight. Edward chose to fight.

The French Battle Plan Although the French had felt the sting of defeat at the hands of English archery, John had reason to believe that would not be the case this time. He had assembled two special units of heavily armored knights riding armored horses, whose job was to charge the flanks of the English army, where the archers were normally deployed. The extra armor would allow the knights to close with the archers, who would then be ridden down, allowing the rest of the French to charge the English infantry and defeat it in close combat.

Edward—due to the small number of troops in his army—deployed his archers in the center, unintentionally foiling John's plan in the process. When the two French units advanced on the enemy's wings, they found no archers. Confused, they charged the main body of the English army instead.

The Battle Although the horses' heavy armor protected them from the front, English archers were able to pour their arrows into the flanks of the approaching French, breaking up the charge, but nearly running out of arrows in the process. Coming right on the heels of this first charge was a wave of dismounted French knights led by the Dauphin (crown prince) of France. At the sight of this massive army's approach, English morale faltered. It was a crucial moment. Prince Edward went before his assembled troops and exhorted them to fight—they were not beaten yet, he reminded them. In the desperate minutes before the French assault, archers darted out into the field to retrieve spent arrows from corpses of horses and knights alike. Edward meanwhile sent a small detachment of two hundred cavalry riding out around the French flank. Seeing these troops depart, and mistaking the move for retreat, the English once again despaired. His army on the brink of disintegration, Edward ordered a general charge.

With a cry of "St. George!" (England's patron saint), the entire English force rushed at the startled French, the archers firing the last of their arrows, then drawing their hand weapons and joining in. The sudden attack forced the French back, and general panic broke out when Edward's cavalry detachment appeared behind French lines, cutting off retreat. The French army fell into a general panic and routed off the field. King John II and his entourage were taken prisoner, and many more French nobles died. In total 7,500 Frenchmen were killed and two thousand were taken prisoner.

The Lasting Impact of Poitiers Poitiers marked the final defeat for the French in the first phase of the Hundred Years' War. Between Crécy and Poitiers, the French nobility had lost more members than were taken during the Black Death. The capture of John resulted in France paying a ruinous ransom equal to twice the country's yearly national income. In order to raise money for the ransom, many nobles raised taxes to outrageous levels. Leaderless, the French army would cease to be an effective fighting force for the next decade, turning instead to open banditry as the countryside descended into chaos. These factors directly provoked the peasantry to rise in a mass rebellion known as the *Jacquerie*.

In contrast to the instability quickly descending over France, news of the victory was welcomed in England with a national celebration. The prince was welcomed back to a London whose fountains had been made to flow with wine, as a unit of five hundred "Merry Men" dressed like Robin Hood escorted the captive French King John II. The English joked that the pope might have been French, but their king was the new Jesus. The "miracle" of Poitiers resulted in the English gaining a third of French territory, crippling the French war effort for years to come.

Nájera, 1367

The Battle of Nájera was perhaps the greatest tactical English victory of the Hundred Years' War. It was also England's greatest strategic mistake and led directly to a renewal of hostilities in France and the loss of most of the territories gained after the victories at Crécy and Poitiers. Finally, it was during the Nájera campaign that Edward, "the Black Prince," most likely contracted the disease that would eventually claim his life.

Sideshow Theaters The Hundred Years' War, like most major conflicts, could not be contained to a single theater. France's neighbors soon found themselves acting as puppets to both England and France, who threw their support behind opposing factions in hitherto local conflicts.

After the English victory at Poitiers, France had been forced to sue for peace, ceding nearly a third of its territory in the Treaty of Brétigny. The Treaty put thousands of soldiers "out of work." Organizing into so-called "free companies," these mercenary bands caused havoc as they looted and pillaged the countryside. Eventually, they were drawn south to a war between two Spanish kingdoms.

Castile's Pedro the Cruel (1334–1369) had been making war on Aragon for nearly a decade. With French and Aragonese backing, Pedro's half-brother Enrique led a mercenary army of free companies to victory, sending Pedro fleeing into neighboring Portugal, where he sent a desperate plea for aid to England's Prince Edward.

English Intervention Edward, as commander of all English territories in France, decided to march to Pedro's aid. The Black Prince sent out a call to arms that was immediately answered by the scattered English and allied-French companies. One English company that had served under Enrique literally had to fight its way out of Castile to meet up with Edward's army, gathering in the mountain kingdom of Navarre. Once assembled, Prince Edward's army invaded northern Castile. Edward's progress was stopped by Enrique's army, which held the mountainous high ground. The Castilian king's French advisors, only too aware of English battlefield superiority, advised Enrique to hold his ground.

Edward, unwilling to attack from such an unfavorable position, retreated back into Navarre, then swung south and marched into Castile through territory more suited to open battle. Enrique moved his army south as well, camping at the town of Nájera. Hungry for battle, and ignoring further French advice, he then marched his army across the Najerilla River to engage Edward.

The Battle The two armies met on April 3, 1367. Enrique's army was a patchwork of French veterans and Aragonese and Castilian troops. Commanding the center of the army was the Frenchman Bertrand du Guesclin, one of the most famous knights of his day. Both wings of the army were comprised of light cavalry and hordes of peasant levies. Enrique commanded the right flank, his brother Don Tello the left.

The peasant levies gave the Castilians the numerical edge, but the English force was still more than a match. Marching under the leadership of Prince Edward and his brother, John of Gaunt, Duke of Lancaster, as well as their ally, Pedro the Cruel, the army was, like all English armies of the day, amply supplied with the deadly longbow. Nájera marked the first use of the longbow in Spain, and it lived up to its reputation.

The hostilities opened with the centers of both armies locking in battle, a stalemate that would last all day. Victory would be determined by events on the wings of the battle. On the Spanish left, Don Tello fled from the field before the English had even reached his lines. As their flank dissolved, the Spanish center was hit on the side by the English right wing.

Meanwhile, on the English left, Enrique led his troops against a storm of English arrows. The Spanish levies, armed with javelins and slings, were no match, but the Spanish king rallied his troops and charged three times before finally turning away for good. Now the other wing of the English army crashed into the exposed Spanish flank. The French veterans held out as long as they could, but it was a losing fight. As the day came to a close, the English finally took the field.

As Enrique's center dissolved, the retreat turned into a rout. Many Spaniards, with the English bearing down on them, drowned in their attempts to get across the swift-flowing Najerilla.

A Hollow Victory After the battle, Enrique fled to Aragon, which promptly turned him over to the English. Pedro the Cruel was restored to the Castilian throne and

it appeared that Prince Edward could do no wrong. Nájera was the greatest tactical victory scored by the English in the course of the Hundred Years' War and notable as the first time in the war that the English had won a victory while attacking rather than defending.

Strategically, however, the English intervention in Spain would prove disastrous. Pedro, living up to his nickname, alienated himself from Edward with his unchivalrous behavior, killing several high-ranking prisoners of war. Furthermore, it soon became clear that he had no intention of repaying any of the war debt he had amassed at Edward's expense. The Black Prince soon marched back to France in disgust. Within two years of Nájera, Pedro the Cruel would be deposed, with French help, by Enrique, who would personally kill his half-brother and crown himself Henry II of Castile (1334–1379).

Meanwhile, Prince Edward had raised taxes on his French possessions to ruinous levels in an effort to pay off the debts that Pedro had shirked. This turn of events led his French subjects to petition Charles V, king of France, to depose Edward, thus leading to a renewal of hostilities in the Hundred Years' War to France's benefit.

Prince Edward himself would die while still relatively young, victim of a lingering disease, most likely dysentery picked up during his Nájera campaign. Thus, intervention in Castile, while resulting in a brilliant tactical victory, would indirectly cost the English nearly all their French gains as well as one of their most successful and beloved military leaders, losses that would not be offset until the rise of Henry V a generation later.

Agincourt, 1415

The Battle of Agincourt, fought on October 22, 1415, was one of the most remarkable victories of the Hundred Years' War and was the finest hour for the English in the whole of that long conflict. Vastly outnumbered, tired, and stricken with disease, the English managed to not only emerge victorious over the French army arrayed against them, but very nearly brought down the French aristocracy and monarchy in the process.

Invasion of France Upon taking the throne in 1413, Henry V grew anxious to renew the stalled war against France. Even as he was stamping out conspiracies against him at home, Henry began assembling an invasion army.

The English army of the Hundred Years' War had always been small and built around the country's legendary archers, armed with the deadly longbow. Although consistently outnumbered and lacking in heavy cavalry, the English outfought their French opponents time and again. The army Henry assembled followed the pattern. Numbering seven or eight thousand men total, the army was dominated by archers and lightly armored mounted infantry, with only about a quarter of the army consisting of heavily armored knights.

Illustration depicting the Battle of Agincourt.　© *Bettmann/Corbis*

The army landed at the French port city of Harfleur and immediately besieged it, a move that caught the French off guard. Nevertheless, Harfleur refused to surrender, and the English settled in for a long siege. The city was doomed from the start, as Henry's invasion coincided nicely with what amounted to a civil war between rival French noble factions. The Count of Orléans, whose followers were called the Armagnacs, was jockeying for power against his cousin, the Duke of Burgundy, as the mad French king Charles VI slipped further and further into ineffective irrelevancy. This squabbling, combined with the surprise of the English invasion, delayed French response and meant that Harfleur could not expect a relief force. Cut off, the inhabitants had no choice but to surrender.

The March to Calais　Although the English had taken the city, they were crippled by a massive outbreak of an intestinal disease, most likely dysentery. Fully one-third of the army was in no shape to march. Henry, abandoning plans for a march on Paris, decided instead to march his army through enemy territory, making for the English-occupied city of Calais. Henry told his men to set aside provisions for an eight-day march.

Unfortunately for the English, the French had finally managed to muster an army and were ready to engage the invaders in battle. Led by the cream of French nobility and made up almost entirely of Armagnacs, the army began paralleling Henry, trying to get between him and Calais and forcing the English further and further inland.

Agincourt　On October 22, short of provisions and still stricken with disease, the English came up against the French army near the town of Agincourt on the road to Calais, only sixty miles away.

The French took up a position between two woods, their multitudinous knights arrayed in three divisions. On either flank, they deployed their Italian crossbowmen. Then they waited. Henry, who had about six thousand men under his command, was outnumbered by as much as six to one. He was also working against time, as his army was close to disintegration due to fatigue, hunger, and disease. To make matters worse, conditions were miserable. Autumn rains had turned the area into a muddy quagmire. The mud was thick and deep, making walking a tiresome exercise. Five centuries later, British soldiers fighting in the region at the Battle of the Somme would encounter similar difficulties. But the muddy conditions at Agincourt worked against the French as well, all the more due to the preponderance of heavily armored knights in their army.

Henry realized it was up to him to make the first move. He ordered his army forward between the two woods and to within bowshot range of the French. The English archers, protected by a row of sharpened stakes that they drove into the ground, began laying a murderous volume of arrow fire into the French ranks. Braving the hail of arrows, the first wave of French knights charged on horseback and were cut down. The arrow fire from the longbows plucked knights from their saddles and drove wounded horses into a frenzy, causing chaos. The sharpened stakes of the archers turned back those that reached the English line. The retreating horsemen plowed through a second wave of knights who were advancing on foot, sowing even more chaos.

The French charge had managed to further churn up the mud of the battlefield, which made the going difficult for the dismounted knights. Sinking in mud that was sometimes knee-deep, the French presented an easy target for the English archers. Nevertheless, their heavy armor allowed most of the Frenchmen to reach the English lines and begin pushing back the thinly stretched army, nearly killing King Henry in the crush of melee.

However, the French numbers also worked against them. Constrained by the woods on either side that narrowed as they approached the English lines, the French were soon packed in shoulder to shoulder, slogging through the sucking mud. At this point the English archers, taking up daggers and hand axes, fell upon the helpless French knights, stabbing through vulnerable gaps in their armor. Many French knights were killed or taken prisoner.

Aftermath of the Battle   Henry sent the prisoners to the rear with the baggage and awaited another French attack that never materialized. However, late in the day, rumors spread of a French flanking force attacking the baggage train, and Henry, concerned that the French army before him would renew its attack and that the prisoners in the rear would join in, ordered the slaughter of all French prisoners. By the time Henry decided the French threat had passed, about two-thirds of the French prisoners had been killed.

Despite this slaughter, the English had much to celebrate. Henry and his nobles would go on to collect vast ransoms on the French knights captured that day. The English had only lost a few hundred men, with only two nobles among that number. The French had lost many more, perhaps as many as ten thousand, many of whom had suffocated in the mud of the battlefield, crushed by their compatriots, rather than from an English arrow.

Agincourt decimated the French nobility. Among the dead were the commanding general, the Constable of France, the Admiral of France, three dukes, seven counts, ninety lords, and over fifteen hundred knights. The sacred *oriflamme*, a French banner of victory that had been taken from the Abbey of St-Denis and brought to the battle, was lost, ground into the mud somewhere on the field.

The French very nearly lost their kingdom after Agincourt. Henry, after a second campaign, secured a promise to the throne of France but then died before he could make good on the claim. Only the emergence of Joan of Arc as a moral and military leader fifteen years after Agincourt saved the Kingdom of France in the end.

Orléans, 1428–1429

The Siege of Orléans, which lasted from October 1428 to May 1429, was the turning point of the last phase of the Hundred Years' War. The English suffered their first major reversal since Agincourt and the loss of a key ally. Most importantly, the end of the siege saw the French cause reignited under the leadership of Joan of Arc, who earned her nickname, "The Maid of Orléans," at this battle.

The Political Situation   By 1428, things looked quite grim for the French cause. Henry V had secured the promise of the French crown in 1422 but had died before that promise could be fulfilled. When the mad French King Charles VI soon followed Henry to the grave, the crown of France, by the terms of the Treaty of Troyes, was due to fall to Henry's infant son, Henry VI. There were many in France, however, who did not feel that a treaty signed with a mad king constituted a binding promise, and who instead pledged support to the Dauphin, or crown prince, of France.

The English directly controlled all of northern France, including Paris. Furthermore, they were allied with the Burgundians, one of two French factions that began vying for power during Charles VI's ineffectual reign. This left central France south of the Loire River in the hands of the Dauphin and his supporters. In 1428, the English decided to march south and secure the infant Henry's legacy. The future of France would hang on the outcome of this campaign.

Orléans   The immediate target for the English was Orléans, a city of forty thousand people, situated along the Loire River. Its capture would provide an ideal base of operations for further expeditions into the economically important provinces to the south. The English force that marched towards Orléans was ten thousand strong. Led by the popular Earl of Salisbury, it consisted mostly of troops from England and Normandy. After taking the towns surrounding the city and providing for their garrisons, there were only about four thousand Englishmen left to besiege Orléans itself.

The city sat on the north bank of the Loire, connected to the south bank by a quarter-mile long bridge. The garrison within Orléans was perhaps six hundred strong, made up of experienced veterans willing to sit out a long siege, bolstered by a large contingent of citizen militia.

The Siege Begins   The siege began with an assault on the southern end of the Loire bridge, which was guarded by a massive gatehouse/fortress known as Les Tourelles. The French defenders withdrew into the city, destroying

Les francops treffort reaillerut.

Soliders capture Joan of Arc. *Public Domain*

a portion of the bridge as they went. The Earl of Salisbury moved in, converting Les Tourelles into his headquarters. Lacking the men to surround the city, the English began constructing a series of small forts, concentrated to the south and west of the city, but also including the reinforced abbey of Saint Loup a mile east of the city. Using these forts as anchor points, the English set up a blockade, attempting to keep supplies from reaching the inhabitants behind the thick city walls. Meanwhile, those very walls were subjected to constant bombardment from English cannons. For example, on October 17 alone, 124 stone balls were fired at Orléans.

The English were not the only ones with cannons, though. In fact, it was a French cannonball that spelled doom for the Earl of Salisbury, who had half his face sheared off by flying debris kicked up by a ball that struck Les Tourelles in the last week of October. He died a week

later, much to the dismay of the entire English army, which ceased active operations for a month. Sir William Glasdale eventually took his place as commander, but the Earl could not be replaced in the hearts of his troops.

Despite the loss of Salisbury, the siege seemed to be going in England's favor as the year came to a close. Although some supplies were getting through the blockade—along with six hundred reinforcements in November—it was not enough, and the inhabitants of Orléans were beginning to feel the strain.

The Siege Turns in France's Favor The first real break for the French came when the Burgundians deserted their English allies. The citizens of Orléans had offered to surrender themselves to Burgundian control. The English overruled this, driving a major rift into their alliance in the process. The departure of the Burgundians further weakened the English blockade of the city. On April 29, 1429, one of the most remarkable personages of the Hundred Years' War slipped through this ineffectual perimeter, accompanied by a small unit of soldiers.

The teenaged girl was Joan of Arc, and she had come from a province on the eastern edge of France, guided by voices only she could hear. Appealing to the Dauphin to lift the siege, she was allowed to accompany a small relief force bearing supplies to the besieged city. Word of her approach emboldened those within the walls of Orléans, as for some years, stories had been circulating in the country that a maiden in armor would emerge as the savior of France. Her arrival in the city, dressed in a full suit of white steel armor and bearing a white banner, was met with cheers and adulation.

The Maid of Orléans   Joan did not lack for confidence. Believing herself to be acting on a divinely mandated mission, she sent a letter to the English before her departure for Orléans, warning them to raise the siege or suffer the consequences. Once in the city, she immediately began pressing for attacks on the English positions. She personally scouted out the enemy fortifications from the battlements of the city, at one point exchanging a shouted conversation with Glasdale himself.

Notified of a diversionary French attack on the English stronghold at Saint Loup, Joan led a unit of citizen militia into the fight, turning the skirmish into a full-blown battle that resulted in the English being routed from their positions. With the eastern approaches now open, more French troops began arriving at the city. Shortly thereafter, Joan and the French crossed the Loire and attacked the English positions outside Les Tourelles. By May 7, the French were ready to assault Les Tourelles itself. The fighting lasted all day. At one point, Joan was wounded when she was struck in the shoulder by an English arrow. After receiving treatment for the wound, she withdrew to the woods to pray. The French assault was nearly called off.

Returning from the woods, Joan argued to press the attack and made her way back into battle. The sight of her white banner advancing toward the fortress walls emboldened the French, who redoubled their efforts. By nightfall, the tower was in their hands, Sir William Glasdale drowned at the bottom of the Loire. The next day, the remaining English forces abandoned their fortifications and formed up for battle. The French also turned out in battle formation, but neither side advanced. Joan was for once reluctant to lead an attack, owing to the fact it was a Sunday. After an hour, the English withdrew to the north, leaving Orléans to the French.

The victory at Orléans was the beginning of the end of the Hundred Years' War. The French army cleared the rest of the Loire Valley of English opposition, then marched on Rouen, taking the city and crowning the Dauphin as Charles VII. Paris was next to fall. The English claim on the French throne was broken for good.

Castillon, 1453

The Battle of Castillon, fought on July 17, 1453, is considered the last battle of the Hundred Years' War. A French victory, it marked the death of England's great general John Talbot and the first use of massed artillery in battle.

The English, so long dominant in the Hundred Years' War, had been on the defensive ever since their defeat at the Siege of Orléans in 1429. Despite the capture and execution of Joan of Arc, hero of Orléans, the French had found their cause renewed, driving the English out of northern France.

Invasion of Gascony   In 1451, they turned their attentions to Gascony, a territory that had been in English hands for three centuries. The French army swept through quickly, taking most towns without a fight. When Bordeaux, the capital of the territory, fell to the French, a letter was sent to England's Henry VI asking for aid—most Gascons considered themselves more English than French.

In October 1452, an English army of three thousand men, led by the famous general John Talbot, landed near Bordeaux, which immediately opened its gates, ejecting the French garrison. Most of the other towns in Gascony did the same. In response to this renewed threat, the French King Charles VII raised three armies and marched them into Gascony in 1453. Talbot, meanwhile, received three thousand more reinforcements. When the main French army camped near the town of Castillon and prepared to lay siege to it, Talbot decided to march out from Bordeaux and meet them.

John Talbot was known for his rashness. In fact, it was his lighting attacks and recklessness in battle that had brought him most of his victories. This time, however, it would be his undoing.

The French Artillery Park   The French army consisted of about seven thousand men and three hundred guns. It is likely that most of these guns were large, two-man handguns, as opposed to massive siege cannon, but this concentration of firepower was still quite unusual at the time. The French had camped outside Castillon, fortifying their position when they heard of the English approach. Despite their recent victories, England's long history of battlefield dominance tended to dictate a cautious French approach. The fortified camp was situated between a river and a dry streambed. The wall of the camp followed the meandering course of the streambed, providing an ideal defensive setup.

Talbot, meanwhile, had personally led his mounted troops, about thirteen hundred strong, ahead of the main army on their approach to Castillon. Hoping to catch the French off-guard, the English cavalry marched through the night, arriving near the town before morning and scattering a unit of French archers. The English then took a well-deserved rest in the woods, waiting for the rest of the army to catch up.

Talbot's Rush to Battle As the sun rose on July 17, Talbot received word that the French were retreating. A large dust cloud rising up near the town seemed to confirm this. Eager to strike while the army was in disarray, Talbot ordered his men to mount up. The English cavalry arrived at the French camp to find it still in arms. The dust cloud and reports of retreat were both due to a column of camp followers who had been asked to leave in the face of the coming battle.

After his capture at the Battle of Patay in 1429, John Talbot had taken a solemn oath that he would never again personally don armor and stand in battle against France. True to his chivalric code, Talbot was unarmored and did not participate in the forthcoming battle. He ordered his men to dismount and assault the camp, despite the fact that the French clearly were not retreating.

In the first demonstration of the effectiveness of massed artillery in Western Europe, the English assault was torn to pieces by the French guns. The irregular line of the French palisade, constructed along the dry stream, only added to the effectiveness of the guns as the English drew closer to the wall—the cannons were able to shoot down the length of the English lines, a concept known as "enfilading fire." The remainder of the English army had begun to arrive on the field, but this only ensured that more units were shot up as they joined the assault one at a time. Despite some fierce fighting at the palisade, the English routed after an hour of battle when a unit of Breton cavalry charged into their flank.

During the rout, a cannonball killed Talbot's horse and the venerable English general was pinned under the carcass. A French archer, hot on the heels of the retreating English, recognized him and dispatched him with a hatchet blow to the head.

End of an Age Both sides mourned Talbot's death—he was considered the greatest general of his age, and a worthy foe for the French. Today, despite the battle's significance for the French cause, the sole monument at Castillon is a statue commemorating John Talbot.

Gascony fell under French rule for good. With the sole exception of the coastal city of Calais, all of France was under Charles VII's rule. Castillon marked the effective end of the Hundred Years' War. It also heralded the ascendancy of the gun, just as Crécy had heralded the age of the longbow. The age of modern warfare had begun.

⊕ Key Elements of Warcraft

Castles

There are few images more evocative of the Middle Ages than the mighty castle perched atop a hill, master of all it surveys. That is no accident of history. The castle played an integral role in medieval politics and warfare and dominated the European countryside for over six centuries.

Early Castles The evolution of the castle began with a need to combine a military fortress with a noble lord's residence. In the wake of the collapse of the empire of Charlemagne in the ninth century and the attendant invasions of Vikings, Magyars, and Arabs, early medieval rulers found castles the ideal location from which to control their holdings. On a practical level, the castle provided shelter from marauding armies for the local lords and their subjects. Just as importantly, the castle projected strength and authority, standing as a reassuring beacon and endorsement of its owner's importance.

The earliest castles were often made with timber, which was available in abundance and promised quick and cheap construction. These timber fastnesses most often took the form of the "motte and bailey"—an artificial mound, or motte, was raised fifteen to thirty feet high, upon which a tower surrounded by a wall was constructed. At the base of the motte was a separate walled bailey (a court inside a castle wall). The two were connected by a bridge or walkway. Although practical, these timber motte and bailey designs had many weaknesses, not the least of which was their wooden construction, which was obviously quite vulnerable to fire. Furthermore, the motte could be easily isolated from the bailey and vice-versa—they were not mutually supportive.

The next phase in castle evolution saw the appearance of the stone keep—a square or rectangular tower—a miniature castle in its own right usually encircled by a stone wall. As castle building increased through the twelfth century, France and England emerged as the primary castle-building countries. France in particular, as well as the neighboring region of Flanders, had the highest concentration of castles, a reflection of the lack of central authority in the region, as well as the many wars fought there, culminating in the anarchy and devastation of the Hundred Years' War.

Krak des Chevaliers: The Model Castle The art of castle building was actually perfected far from Europe. The Crusades brought Western armies into contact with the region that boasted the world's oldest fortified structures, and it was in the Near East that the Europeans built some of their greatest castles, learning lessons from the massive fortifications at cities such as Constantinople and Antioch, whose walls were so extensive that the besieging Crusaders could not totally surround the city.

Built by the military order of the Knights of St. John of the Hospital (or the Knights Hospitaler for short), Krak des Chevaliers stands as the purest expression of medieval fortification technology and served as a model for later castles built in Europe, especially during Edward I's conquest of Wales.

Situated on a great natural outcropping, Krak utilized the latest castle design, which eliminated the central keep and instead consisted of two great concentric rings of curtain walls. The inner wall was built higher than the outer wall, so that defenders on both walls could fire arrows and missiles at attackers. Krak boasted walls one hundred feet thick, which were studded with great round towers. The castle was surrounded by a great moat and was only accessible via a long exposed bridge that spanned the moat. The spaces between the curtain walls—called baileys—were filled with everything necessary for a garrison of two thousand soldiers to withstand a five-year siege, from great stables to a massive pantry and water supply. In the end, Krak fell to the Muslims, not through siege but through trickery.

Castles during Wartime Indeed, the greatest weakness of castles, especially by the time of the Hundred Years' War, was often their garrisons, or rather the lack thereof. Keeping castles full of soldiers year-round was a costly endeavor, and it was not unusual for castles to host only a skeleton crew except in times of war.

A fully garrisoned castle was a serious menace for the prospective medieval conqueror, and this explains why the vast majority of conflicts in the Middle Ages were not open battles but sieges. Henry V, despite his stunning victory at Agincourt in 1415, did not force the French to the negotiating table until he had managed to successfully besiege and take most of the important castle-towns in northern France over the course of a nearly five-year campaign. The medieval general who ignored such a strategy did so at his peril, as leaving a castle full of enemy combatants behind him was to invite disaster in the form of raids and severed supply lines.

The end of the Hundred Years' War was also the beginning of the end for the castle as fortress-residence. The coming of the cannon, which Henry V used to such great effect in his second French campaign, brought the towering walls of the castle tumbling down to be replaced by squat gun-fortresses. Lords and their retinues, meanwhile, moved their living quarters to less Spartan accommodations and left defense of their realm to professional armies. After six centuries of dominance, the castle's time had at last come to a close.

The Trebuchet

Siege technology in the Middle Ages was not much different from that of ages past with one important exception: the trebuchet. Representing the height of pre-gunpowder siege technology, capable of bringing down castle walls with its unique combination of sheer power and pinpoint accuracy, the trebuchet was so effective that it continued to find use in sieges well into the age of the cannon.

Construction and Use The trebuchet, seemingly a complex machine, has an elegant simplicity about it. In essence it acts as a giant slingshot. A long beam pivots on tall posts—at one end is a sling containing the object to be hurled, at the other end is the counter-weight to propel the beam forward. The motion of the beam, combined with the length of the sling harness, fires the trebuchet's payload in a high arc for a considerable distance.

The trebuchet's name derives from the Old French *trebucher*, "to throw over," and this indicates one of its original uses. Developed by the Arabs, the first trebuchets were man-powered, utilizing a team of anywhere from forty to 250 men to provide the "counter-weight" action. Thus, they could only throw relatively light objects, which, combined with the trebuchet's high arc of fire, could be lofted over tall city or castle walls. These light payloads would often take the form of flaming missiles (to start fires) or parts of dead animals or enemies (to sow terror and spread disease). It is thought that the Black Death came to Europe with the use of trebuchets as machines of germ warfare. The Genoese defenders of Kaffa, on the Crimean peninsula, were exposed to plague victims lofted into the city by their Mongolian besiegers. When the siege was lifted in 1347, the Genoese returned home, bringing the plague with them.

Western Innovations Thanks to the Crusades, the trebuchet was finding use in the West by the twelfth century. There they quickly developed in size and sophistication, acquiring a new application in the process as engines of destruction. The new trebuchets were powered not by a team of heaving men, but by a large weight, most often a bucket filled with up to fifteen tons of rocks or lead weights. These new generation trebuchets were thus necessarily huge—they had to be to accommodate the massive counterweights. The sling harnesses were also lengthened, resting in a channel beneath the machine itself.

The greater weight added speed and distance, the longer harness added accuracy. Additionally, the new trebuchets could handle much larger payloads. The Dauphin of France, for example, commissioned a trebuchet in 1421 that could fire four hundred-pound stones. The trebuchet came into its own as siege engine, capable of bringing down castle walls with concentrated fire.

An experienced trebuchet crew could manage an impressive rate of fire. At the siege of Kenilworth in 1266, in which both the besiegers and the besieged were firing stones at each other, it was said that so many missiles were in the air at once that it was not uncommon to see enemy stones colliding in mid-air.

The main disadvantage of the trebuchet lay in the resources it consumed, namely in wood. While on crusade in 1249, St. Louis of France captured twenty-four enemy engines. They provided enough wood to build a wooden stockade around his entire encampment. The other disadvantage of the trebuchet lay in its great size—they made excellent targets for enemy trebuchets and, later, cannons.

Decline of the Trebuchet The advent of the cannon did eventually doom the trebuchet. Smaller and more easily managed—not to mention portable—while still packing a comparable destructive impact, the cannon quickly became the late medieval siegemaster's weapon of choice.

Nevertheless, the trebuchet did not go quietly. Until nearly the sixteenth century, the trebuchet was still

A trebuchet in Les Baux de Provence, France. © *WoodyStock/Alamy*

unmatched for accuracy and rate of fire, and was used alongside cannons as late as the siege of Burgos in the late 1470s, long after cannons had become a common sight on the battlefield.

Chivalry

The concept of chivalry has its roots in the tales of minstrels from the south of France. The greatest of these storytellers Chrétien de Troyes is generally credited with codifying chivalry in his tales of King Arthur and the quest for the Holy Grail in the late twelfth century. The root of the word comes from the phrase *chevalerie et clergie*, a concept of justice, courage, and right conduct, as espoused by Chrétien and his many imitators.

Chivalry was also strongly influenced by the medieval knights' intense interest in the long-past glory of Rome and its military triumphs. Translations of ancient Roman military writers such as Vegetius, which also first

King Henry VIII jousts at Westminster in honor of Queen Katherine of Aragon. *Hulton Archive/Getty Images*

appeared in the twelfth century, were widely read and copied. Christine de Pizan, writing in the fifteenth century, strongly influenced Henry V with her combination of ancient Roman and contemporary chivalric ideals and their application to military endeavors.

Prior to the popularization of chivalry, knights were often little more than armored thugs, descendants of the barbarian hordes who had overrun the Western Roman Empire and ushered in the so-called "Dark Ages." Chivalry gave these warriors something higher to aspire to, and exerted a civilizing influence upon them by promoting a code that emphasized honor, justice, and reverence for God.

The chivalrous knight took his duties with the utmost seriousness. To him, the nobleman was obligated to protect those weaker than him, namely women and the lower classes. The ideals of chivalry included honesty at all times, even when it would harm the knight, kindness in peace, honor in war, respect for the gentler aspects of Christianity (such as mercy and charity for the poor), as well as valor and courage in every deed. Another concept chivalry helped usher in was the idea of romantic love.

The concept of "courtly love," which had evolved independently in southern France starting in the eleventh century, was soon integrated into the overall concept of chivalry. In its purest form, courtly love was a contradictory balance of lust and denial. The ideal scenario played out with the smitten knight committing acts in the name of a lady who might not even be aware of his existence.

On a more practical level, courtly love introduced the idea of romance into the hard-bitten knight's life. Reciting poems, singing songs, and other such romantic gestures were increasingly seen as proper chivalric behavior. When "the Black Prince" Edward, widely regarded at the time as one of the greatest paragons of chivalry, married for love rather than political gain, he caused a sensation across Europe.

Although most knights failed to live up to every ideal of chivalry, there were many who tried during the closing centuries of the Middle Ages. Those who were acclaimed as "right chivalrous knights," knights like Prince Edward and his implacable foe, Bertrand du Guesclin, earned international fame for their adherence to the strict code. It was not just lip service, either—battles and even whole wars were won and lost over considerations of proper chivalrous behavior as knights adhered to a code that virtually guaranteed occasional conflicts of interest.

For example, du Guesclin was captured in battle with the English several times but was always released upon payment of a ransom, free to return to France and continue leading armies. After the Black Prince captured him at Nájera in 1367, du Guesclin paid his ransom and was back in Castile within two years, where he successfully backed the future Henry II in deposing the English favorite, Pedro the Cruel, who had only won his crown after Prince Edward's victory at Nájera. Thus, proper observance of chivalric code helped negate one of the greatest English victories in the Hundred Years' War.

Longbows and Crossbows

The Hundred Years' War saw key developments in the technology of medieval warfare as different weapons

TOURNAMENTS

Initially started as a form of battle practice, tournaments soon became a ritualized facet of chivalry, as far removed from the realties of combat as modern sporting events.

The earliest tournaments were simply brawls between opposing knights hoping to stay in practice between actual wars. These *mêlées* (pronounced MAY-lays) were often nearly as fatal as real combat—two teams of knights would assemble, usually with the purpose of attempting to raid the other team's base. Real weapons would be used, and although the intention was not to strike to kill, deaths were not at all uncommon.

As chivalry became more ingrained in medieval culture, tournaments became a venue for knights to demonstrate their martial abilities in a ritualized, gentler manner. The joust, in which two mounted knights charged at each other with blunted lances seeking to unseat the other, joined the mêlée, which itself had become tamer, often making use of blunted or wooden weapons.

Tournaments could also prove quite lucrative—defeated knights were often required to offer a "ransom" to their victor, and it was not unusual for knights to tour the tournament circuit in a manner resembling professional boxers of today. William Marshal, the most renowned knight of his age, first gained notice riding the tournament circuit. He fought in five thousand tournaments and never lost a single match.

As the knightly class waned and warfare became focused on mass ranks of troops, tournaments died along with chivalry. An attempt was made to revive them in the sixteenth century, but that came to an abrupt end with the accidental death of France's King Henry II in a joust, pierced through the eye by the sliver of a shattered lance.

---

ditions, the bow would be protected with a leather sheath while the bowstring would be rolled up and stowed in a dry place, oftentimes under the archer's hat. The ability to keep both bow and string dry even in wet weather added to the tactical flexibility of the English archer in battle, as the crossbow, which could not be unstrung and was constructed of composite materials, any of which could warp or bend, was extremely susceptible to inclement weather.

In addition to its tactical flexibility, the longbow's great strength lay in its ability to send arrows farther faster and with more hitting power than any other bow in use at the time. Capable of sending its missile up to four hundred yards, the longbow was most effective out to about half that range. Within fifty yards, the longbow was capable of piercing even the sturdiest steel plate armor. These range brackets may seem slight, but keep in mind that the range of firearms was almost identical until about the mid-nineteenth century.

Because the power of the bow ultimately depended on the strength of the user, England put a premium on archery training, requiring every common man and boy in the kingdom by law to devote time to practice with the bow. One of the reasons the longbow never spread to the continent was due to the reluctance of French nobles to train their peasantry in the use of weapons for fear of armed insurrection.

A fully trained English longbowman could loft ten or twelve arrows per minute. Thus, a full unit of archers could easily create a veritable storm of arrows raining down from the sky, as at Crécy and Agincourt.

The Crossbow In contrast, the longbow's main competitor, the crossbow, boasted a paltry rate of fire of no more than two or three arrows (or "bolts" as they were called) per minute. However, the crossbow did not require a lifetime of training to use effectively and could send a missile at least as far as an arrow from a longbow. Additionally, the crossbow's penetrating power was second to none. As such, despite the dominance of the English longbow, continental armies continued to employ the crossbow in war in units both mounted and on foot. The crossbow was also a favorite among European nobility as a hunting weapon.

Archers in Battle Throughout the course of the Hundred Years' War, archers and crossbowmen were seen in the conventional military wisdom of the day as secondary to the glorious knights, who were thought to be unstoppable. The French use of crossbowmen over the course of the war betrays this prejudice, as at Crécy when the French knights rode over and through their own crossbow units in a rush to get to grips with the enemy, or at Agincourt where the crossbowmen were deployed so far off to the side and rear as to render their presence ineffectual.

The fact that the English understood and appreciated the value of the longbow in battle and afforded their archers primary place in battle was the secret to their repeated military success, despite operating in an often

---

systems met in battle and long-cherished assumptions were forced to change in the face of cold results.

Nowhere was this process more apparent than in the ascendancy of the English longbow and the archer who wielded it, especially when contrasted with the ubiquitous crossbow.

The Longbow Made famous by the Welsh, the longbow quickly made its way into the ranks of the English army. The weapon's use was unique to the region and gave the English a powerful advantage against their continental enemies.

The longbow was aptly named, measuring about six feet in length from end to end. The bow itself was deceptively simple in its design, being carved from a single piece of wood, preferably yew, although ash and elm could substitute. The bow had a "D shaped" cross-section with a flat back and curved front that provided both strength and flexibility.

As the bow could be strung in mere seconds, it was usually kept unstrung until just before battle. In wet con-

hostile land and almost always outnumbered. By the end of the Hundred Years' War, the primacy of the knight had waned. The humble archer had brought down the knight in the shining armor, who was never to rise again.

Full Steel-plate Armor

The Hundred Years' War witnessed major developments in the technology and methodology of warfare. The English longbow proved its deadly effectiveness on the battlefield, defeating the previously unstoppable armored knight. Armor technology responded in kind by reaching new heights of sophistication and protection, which, although unable to completely insulate its wearer against the threats of the fifteenth century battlefield, offered unprecedented protection. The full suit of steel plate armor represented the zenith of the medieval armorer's art.

For most of the Middle Ages, a suit of chain mail, armor made up of small interlocking metal rings, protected the knight in battle. By the start of the Hundred Years' War, armorers had begun to add steel plates over the extremities and torso. Although these innovations increased the protective qualities of the armor, they also increased the weight, which had been heavy and cumbersome to begin with.

By the beginning of the fifteenth century, the hybrid plate and chain design had been replaced by a sophisticated suit of armor, consisting almost entirely of steel plates. Called "white armor" due to its brilliant finish, the new full plate suits were custom fitted and fully articulated, granting their wearer a high degree of movement and flexibility. Their weight—sixty to eighty pounds—was comparable to the load carried by a modern infantryman, and the image of a fully armored knight struggling to mount his horse unaided is nothing more than a myth. In fact, many knights of the period would demonstrate their fitness and agility by vaulting into the saddle while fully armored.

The armor consisted of a fitted breast and back plate that hinged on the left side and buckled on the right. Arm and leg pieces were attached in a similar manner. It was actually impossible for a knight to don the armor himself. Helping his lord armor up before battle was one of a squire's main duties. Some chain mail remained, protecting flexion points where rigid plate would encumber its wearer too much, such as at the elbow, armpit, and groin. Additionally, the knight would wear a padded jerkin under his armor, both to prevent chafing against the metal and to help cushion the impact of blows.

So effective was the new armor that shields—which had been the knight's primary method of displaying his heraldic crests—soon became obsolete. As a result, knights would wear "coats of arms" displaying their crests that served as an identifier for the otherwise anonymous knight encased inside his metal shell. Prominent display of a knight's heraldry also signaled to a potential captor in battle that the knight was someone of impor-tance and would be better taken prisoner rather than killed outright.

Much of a knight's anonymity in battle was due to his helmet, which often completely concealed his face. In contrast to the rest of the suit of full plate armor, the helmet continued to prove problematic in design utility. The issue was as old as the concept: how to provide maximum protection to the head and face while still allowing full use of the senses, vital to survival on the battlefield.

As it was, two helmet designs predominated. First was the bascinet, a design so common that soldiers were often referred to as such. For example, a chronicler might make reference to "eight thousand bascinets marching under the king's banner." Close-fitting and boasting a pointed top—the better to deflect blows and arrows coming in from above—it came in both open- and closed-face designs. Much more encumbering, but offering a similar increase in protection, was the great helm, which, as the name implies, covered the entirety of the head in a secure metal sheath. At Agincourt in 1415, the English King Henry V was saved from a mortal blow by his great helm.

Tudor suit of armour displayed in the Tower of London. © *Chris George/Alamy*

It was at Agincourt that the advantages and drawbacks of the new armor were put to the test. The French knights, forced to dismount due to a muddy field, engaged the feared English longbowmen in a frontal assault. Their slow slog across the morass that separated them from the English allowed ample time for the longbows to unleash a deadly storm of arrows, yet most of the French knights were able to reach the English lines, protected by their superior armor. Yet it was also this armor that cost many knights their lives that day, as the mud—knee-deep in places—pulled knights down, exhausted and unable to rise again, thanks to their heavy kit. Untold hundreds, if not thousands of knights drowned in the mud at Agincourt.

⊕ Impact of the Hundred Years' War

Although it is easy to view the Hundred Years' War as a series of set-piece battles and peace treaties, it has much greater implications that continue to reverberate to this day. Politically, the Hundred Years' War marked the birth of nationalism on both sides of the conflict and the creation of centralized government in France. Militarily, the war corresponds to the decline of the knight and the dominance of the longbow, outlasting that much-feared weapon just long enough to see the beginning of modern warfare in the form of professional armies and massed ranks of guns.

Military Impact

The Hundred Years' War was the most devastating pre-industrial war by far. It spilled over to include conflicts in Spain and witnessed the death of untold numbers of combatants and civilians due to battle, disease, and famine. The course of the war saw not only bloody battles and disease-ridden sieges, but also the horrors of plague, the depredations of the Free Companies, and the bloody uprising of the *Jacquerie*.

The battles should not be overlooked, for the deaths tallied in the course of fighting were often to have the farthest-reaching effects. For example, one of the reasons that France was able to coalesce as a unified nation at war's end was due to the fact that so many of the country's semi-independent nobles had died in battle, particularly at Agincourt in 1415.

It was the great French defeats at Crécy, Poitiers, and Agincourt that spelled the end of the dominance of the mounted knight on the battlefield. The power of massed missile fire, first from the longbow and later from the handgun, trumped the once-invincible *chevalier* (member of the French Legion of Honor or a French knight) and raised the lowly infantryman up to the level he enjoys today. Never again would cavalry dominate the battlefield.

Political Impact

Nationalism has a rather negative connotation these days, but as it emerged in the fourteenth and fifteenth centuries, it was generally a positive force that encouraged the growth of English culture and gave the beleaguered French something to believe in.

The war forced the two countries, united in language and culture since the days of William the Conqueror, to forge their own identities. England, for example, stopped using French as its official court language during the course of the war. France, long a collection of semi-autonomous fiefdoms, became a unified nation, and the king, "first among equals" for much of the Middle Ages, began to take on greater and greater authority, culminating in the absolute monarchies of the seventeenth and eighteenth centuries, which in turn led to the French Revolution.

France, in responding to the crisis of the war, could only survive by forming an effective infrastructure. By the war's end, the country had developed an efficient and lucrative taxation system and fielded the first standing army in Europe since the days of the Roman Empire. This newfound nationalism, power, and military might propelled France to dominance in European wars and politics for the next four centuries.

England, meanwhile, by withdrawing from continental politics, began to form its contemporary identity, seeing itself as not wholly part of Europe. With a common language and homeland, a sense of what it meant to be "English" quickly developed. It is no accident that Shakespeare would later choose Henry V as his mouthpiece of English patriotism.

In fact, it was Henry's stirring words, as imagined by Shakespeare, that gave the English hope when they stood alone against Germany in World War II. As for the French, the emergence of Joan of Arc as national cult hero in the nineteenth century gave the nation a reason for hope during the dark days of the First World War and the even darker days of Nazi occupation from 1940–1944.

The heroes of the Hundred Years' War continue to inspire us to this day. The histories of England, France, and even Spain were inexorably changed by the crucible of the war. The countries that emerged from the conflict would go on to shape the course of civilizations around the world. For good and for ill, the Hundred Years' War has had a profound effect on global history.

BIBLIOGRAPHY

Books

Bennet, Matthew. *Agincourt 1415: Triumph Against the Odds.* Oxford, UK: Osprey Publishing, 1991.

Boccaccio, Giovanni. *The Decameron.* Translated by G. H. McWilliam. London: Penguin Books, 1972.

Froissart, Jean. *Chronicles.* Translated by G. Brereton. London: Penguin Books, 1968.

Gravett, Christopher. *Medieval Siege Warfare.* London: Osprey Publishing, 1990.

Sumption, Jonathan. *The Hundred Years War: Trial by Battle*. Philadelphia: University of Philadelphia Press, 1990.

Web Sites

"Joan of Arc's Letter to the English." Translated by Belle Tuten from *Chronique de la Pucelle, ou Chronique de Cousinot*. Paris: Adolphe Delahaye, 1859, pp. 281–83. <www.fordham.edu/halsall/source/joanofarc.html> (accessed May 22, 2007).

"Siege of Orléans and the Loire Valley Campaign (1428–1429)." *Xenophon Group Military History Database*. <xenophongroup.com/montjoie/orleans.htm> (accessed May 22, 2007).

Villalon, L. J. Andrew. "'Seeking Castles in Spain': Sir Hugh Calveley and the Free Companies Intervention in Iberian Warfare (1366–1369)." <www.geocities.com/Athens/Parthenon/9507/hc-article.htm> (accessed May 22, 2007).

Introduction to the Rise and Fall of the Ottoman Empire (Fourteenth to Seventeenth Centuries)

It is an immutable law of history: empires rise, and empires fall. In the Western world, the mighty Roman Empire collapsed around the fifth century CE; in the Eastern world, it faded into the Byzantine Empire. By the thirteenth century Byzantium, too, was in decline. Taking Byzantium's place was a robust new dynasty in Anatolia (present-day Turkey). Named for its founder, Osman, the Ottoman Empire burst onto the world scene. In the space of roughly 150 years (1299–1453), the Ottomans went from a band of nomadic raiders to the rulers of much of Anatolia, Greece, and the Balkans.

By 1520, the Ottoman sultans ruled one of the largest, richest, and most powerful empires in the world. At one point in time they held sway over all of the Arab nations, northern Africa, the Mediterranean Sea, and Europe up to the gates of Vienna. The court of Suleiman I "the Magnificent" drew scholars, scientists, and artists from around the world.

Having forcibly assimilated so many cultures, Constantinople (now Istanbul) was a cosmopolitan center in which many languages were spoken and many faiths practiced. Although the Ottomans were unswerving in their Muslim devotion, they showed far more religious tolerance than some of their Christian counterparts. Jews and Christians lived in Ottoman lands as *dhimmi* (second-class citizens) and were relatively unmolested.

For hundreds of years, Christian Europe lived in dread of "the Grand Turk," whose armies seemed nigh-invincible. Bitterly divided amongst themselves, the Europeans could offer only intermittent resistance to the Ottoman *ghazis* (holy warriors) who dedicated their lives to the spread of Islam. Only in 1571 did a concerted Christian effort achieve a large-scale victory against the Turks, decimating their fleet at Lepanto.

While the early sixteenth century showed the Ottomans at their best, by the end of that century the empire was beginning to stagnate. Though still externally strong, the Ottomans' internal institutions began to crumble. Like those of successful empires before and since, their early vigor was sapped by corruption, conservatism, and decadence.

In the meantime, the army waged a continual border war with Austria, only to be definitely beaten back at Vienna in 1683. Eugene of Savoy demolished their European army in 1697, and two years later the Ottomans ceded Hungary and Transylvania.

Throughout the eighteenth century, the Russians made constant incursions against the Turks. This culminated in the Crimean War of 1853–1856 in which Great Britain, Sardinia, and France joined the Ottomans to beat back the tsar. The coalition succeeded, but the war exposed the Turks' military and economic weaknesses. By the turn of the century, the Ottoman Empire was called "the Sick Man of Europe."

National groups in the Balkans capitalized on the Empire's ills, revolting in 1875 and 1877. However, the Ottoman Empire did not fully dissolve until 1922, after having fought on the losing side in World War II.

Rise and Fall of the Ottoman Empire (Fourteenth to Seventeenth Centuries)

⊕ Major Figures

Osman

In the early fourteenth century, as the great Eurasian empires declined, a nomadic Turkoman chieftain named Osman (c. 1258–1326) established the foundations for a new empire, giving birth to one of the longest-lasting dynasties in world history.

His Times As Genghis Khan ravaged the Middle East in the twelfth century, Islamic nomadic family groups migrated into central Asia. Many of these groups settled into Anatolia (a region roughly equivalent to modern-day Turkey). These restless Anatolia Turkoman *beyliks* (principalities) were kept in check by the Greek Byzantine Empire to the west and the Turkish Seljuk Empire to the east.

By the fourteenth century, those checks had begun to erode. The Byzantines, ruling a vast empire from Constantinople, often neglected their Anatolian provinces. The Seljuks also controlled far-flung lands, having conquered Persia, Syria, Iraq, and Palestine. However, they fell to the Mongols in 1243; this created a power vacuum and triggered a wave of Turkish refugees into Anatolia.

The northwest corner of Anatolia was dominated by a beylik, which came to be known as the Osmanli after its most famous chieftain, Osman. Very little of the early history of Osman's clan can be historically verified, though it is vividly remembered in folktale.

His Legends Turkish lore has it that Osman's grandfather, Suleyman Sah, escaped from the Mongol invasion of Iran around 1200. According to tradition, Suleyman (also spelled Suleiman) drowned crossing the Euphrates River.

Suleyman's son, Ertogul, is said to have led his men west. On the way, his Turkoman warriors happened across a battle in which a large army was destroying a much smaller force. Joining the small army for honor's sake, Ertogul's band helped defeat the larger army,

which turned out to be Mongols. The rescued army was led by none other than the Seljuk sultan, Alaeddin, who bestowed a fiefdom on Ertogul in gratitude.

Ertogul was apparently commissioned to guard Sogut, in the northwest of Anatolia, on the border between Byzantine and Seljuk territories. He died around 1288, passing the task down to his son, Osman.

Osman, more aggressive than his father, was not content to remain in Sogut. Legend has it that he received a heavenly vision of a vast tree growing from his chest, supported by the Caucasus, Atlas, Taurus, and Haemus mountains. On the strength of this prophetic dream, Osman married the woman that he loved, Malkhatun, believing that their descendents would rule a great empire.

His History History records that Osman also took more concrete steps towards his dream. Other Turkoman warlords had already begun to expand their power by absorbing smaller beyliks. In 1299, Osman stopped paying tribute to the Mongol Emperor, thus establishing an independent state. He and his followers, the Osmanli, began to launch raids against Byzantine territories.

Turkish tradition remembers the Osmanli as *ghazis* (holy warriors) who fought against the infidel Christian empire. Recently, some historians have challenged this view. They claim that Osman, a traditional nomadic warlord, simply took advantage of Byzantine weakness to assert his strength against settled farmland.

In 1301, Osman soundly defeated Byzantine forces near Nicea in a battle that established him as the strongest leader of the region. Whether motivated by *jihad* (holy war), by nomadic solidarity, or by the spoils of war, Turkoman ghazis from many different beyliks joined the Osmanli. In the face of a growing Islamic army, many Anatolian Greeks began to flee to Constantinople. Others, disgusted by Byzantine weakness and corruption, joined the Turkomans.

Gradually the fortified Christian cities in Anatolia fell before Osman's forces. He conquered Eskishehir,

The deathbed of Ataturk in Dolmabahce Palace in Istanbul, Turkey. © *Alex Segre/Alamy*

Inonu, Bilejik, and Yenishehir. Only the strongest Byzantine cities—Bursa, Nicea, and Nicomedia—managed to hold out against him.

His Legacy By 1308, Osman had surrounded the well-fortified city of Bursa, on the slopes of Mount Olympus. Bursa was sturdily built, well supplied, and stubbornly defended. The siege continued for eighteen long years, but Bursa finally gave in to the Ottomans in 1326.

By the end of the siege, Osman had grown old and sick, and he had placed his army under the command of his son Orhan. Osman died in 1326 and was buried in Bursa. As the new chieftain, Orhan pursued his father's ambitions, taking Nicea in 1331 and Nicomedia in 1337. Orhan's son and grandsons would continue these conquests, eventually creating one of the world's great empires.

Osman is said to have been a handsome and charismatic man, who inspired great devotion in his followers. Despite his reputation for ruthlessness, he ruled justly, generally treating all ethnicities and religions alike. He established an independent state, a standing army, and a legal system for his people. In Europe, his name was corrupted over time to become Othoman, which in turn eventually became Ottoman.

Thirty-five generations succeeded Osman as sultans of the Ottoman Empire; his dynasty was to last until the early twentieth century. The Republic of Turkey abolished the sultanate in 1922, and in 1924, the Ankara government sent all of the royal family into exile. Female members of the sultanate could return to Turkey after thirty years; males would have to wait fifty.

Lazar Hrebeljanovic

As Murad I consolidated his hold on Anatolia and began to push into Europe, he was opposed by Prince Lazar Hrebeljanovic of Serbia (1329–1389). Later made a saint of Serbia, this legendary figure reunified Serbia and rallied the Slavic Christians to oppose the Turks.

The Serbian Empire In 1341, civil war broke out in the Byzantine Empire, between the young heir to the throne, John V Palaeologus, and his regent John VI Cantacuzenus. To the east, Serbian king Stefan Uros IV Dusan took full advantage of the resulting chaos. Without fighting any major battle on the open field, Serbia absorbed Macedonia, Albania, and Thessaly from Byzantium. During Dusan's reign, the Serbian Empire more than doubled in size.

The victories came cheap, given Byzantium's state of decay, and did not last. After Dusan's sudden death in

1355, Serbia disintegrated into its own civil war as noblemen vied for the throne. Dusan's son and heir, Uros V "the Weak," was compelled to appoint Vukasin Mrnjavcevic as co-ruler.

In 1371, aware of the growing Ottoman threat, Vukasin joined forces with his brother Jovan Ugljesa and marched on Murad I's new capitol at Edirne. The sultan's army routed the Serbs at the Battle of the Maritsa River; both Vukasin and Jovan were killed. Later that year, Uros V also passed away.

The Prince Before his death, Uros V had bestowed the title of *knez* (prince) on Lazar Hrebeljanovic, a nobleman whose land was situated between the Morava and Ibar rivers. Lazar did not participate in Vukasin's attack on the Ottomans. Instead, he set up his court in the city of Krusevac, in northern Serbia. It was not long before Christian refugees began pouring into his principality, fleeing the oncoming Turks.

In the power vacuum left by the Serbian defeat, Lazar quickly gained territory and power. Allied with the rulers of Bosnia and Hungary, Lazar helped defeat Nikola Altomanovic of Hum. From this victory he gained the Hum territories, including the mines of Rudnik. (Lazar already possessed the mine of Novo Brdo.) From the silver brought up from these acquisitions, Lazar soon ruled the richest and the most powerful of the Serbian principalities.

Lazar worked diligently to restore good relations between the Serbian Orthodox Church and the Byzantine Orthodox Church, which had schismed in 1351. The Patriarch of Constantinople agreed to acknowledge the Serbian Church's autonomy. In return, Lazar relinquished the right of Serbian princes to call themselves emperors.

In 1378, the Church supported Lazar's claim to the throne of Serbia. They proclaimed him "Lord of the Serbs and the Danube, Stefan Prince Lazar, Autocrat of All Serbs." Stefan and Autocrat were semi-imperial titles, and Serbian epic poems usually describe Lazar as "tsar" or emperor. Nevertheless, true to his promise, Lazar never took any formal title other than knez.

The Saint As Islamic incursions in to Europe became more frequent, Lazar and other Christian Slavs found themselves on the defensive. Putting aside their traditional enmities, Balkan feudal lords came together in a coalition, led by Lazar, to stop the Ottoman advance.

In the summer of 1389, the Ottoman army launched an assault on the Kosovo region. On June 15 by the Julian Calendar (June 28 by the Gregorian), Sultan Murad I and his sons met Prince Lazar's forces in a monumental battle.

The death of Lazar is shrouded in highly emotional and wildly partisan legend. Some say he was killed in battle, while others recount that he was taken prisoner and executed.

What is certain is that the prince died on the "Plain of Blackbirds" where the 1389 Battle of Kosovo was fought. Serbs, viewing Lazar as a national hero and martyr, enshrined his legend in epic poetry and song. After time he came to represent the Serbian predicament, as both a symbol of national humiliation and of nationalistic pride.

A popular Serbian legend recounts that the prophet Elijah appeared to Lazar on the eve of the battle. The prince was given a choice between an empire in heaven and an empire on earth. If he wanted the heavenly empire, he would have to lose both his army and his life. To win the earthly empire, he would have to treat with the Turks. Choosing the everlasting over the ephemeral, Lazar chose to fight.

Lazar's contemporary, Patriarch Danilo III, wrote that the prince addressed his men before leading them into battle, saying, "It is better to die in battle than to live in shame."

During his lifetime, Lazar devoted much of his energy to support and spread Christianity in his realm. He ordered that many churches be built, including the magnificent Ravanica monastery where his remains are interred. The Serbian Orthodox Church declared him a saint and made his feast day June 28—the anniversary of the Battle of Kosovo (also the Feast of St. Vitus).

It was on this date (June 28), more than five hundred years later, that Serbian nationalists assassinated Archduke Ferdinand, plunging all of Europe into World War I.

Murad I

In the late fourteenth century, Murad I (c. 1326–1389) consolidated his rule over Anatolia and set about conquest of southeastern Europe. Under his rule, the Osmanli principality became the Ottoman Empire.

Family and Friends Murad was born around 1326 into a powerful clan. His grandfather, Osman, had established the Osmanli ghazi as the predominant fighting force of Anatolia. Osman's son Orhan had reinforced that position, pushing the boundaries of their principality all the way to Europe though he did so partially by invitation.

In 1341, Byzantine Emperor Andronikos III Palaeologus died, leaving the throne to his nine-year-old son, John V Palaeologus. However, the child's regent John VI Cantacuzenus had himself crowned emperor, setting off a ruinous six-year civil war.

In 1346, Cantacuzenus married his daughter Theodora to Orhan, thus securing an alliance with the Ottomans. Turkish military assistance helped to establish Cantacuzenus' rule. It also gave the Ottomans their first foothold in Europe. In 1353, the Turks occupied the Greek peninsula of Gallipoli.

The Reign of Murad I Upon Orhan's death in 1359, Murad immediately had his three brothers executed. This practice of clearing away potential rivals to the throne became the established tradition of the Ottoman Empire.

Murad continued to expand Ottoman territory into Europe, seizing Edirne (Adrianople) in 1361 and making it his new capitol. Thrace followed in 1364. Two years later, Filibe (Philippopolis) also became part of his emerging Islamic empire.

Alarmed by the rapid advance of Murad's armies, John V Palaeologus—who had taken back the Byzantine throne in 1354—turned to the Western world. He begged the papacy for help in 1369, converting to Catholicism himself and promising to heal the breach between the Latin and Eastern Orthodox Churches.

However, military intervention did not come from Rome, but from Byzantium's perennial enemy, Serbia. In 1371, King Vukasin led a coalition of Serbian and Bulgarian armies to try and defeat the encroaching Turks, only to meet a crushing defeat at the Maritsa River. Thereafter, Macedonia lay at Murad's mercy.

By 1373, John V was forced to acknowledge Murad as his suzerain, or overlord. To the dismay of Christendom, the Byzantine Empire had become a vassal state to the Ottomans.

Despite his success in Europe, the Ottomans still faced challenges at home. In 1371, Murad led a successful campaign against his family's longtime Turkish rivals, the Karamanlis. Murad also had to deal with a more personal attack. His son Savci allied with John V's son Andronicus in open rebellion against both fathers. The rebellion was crushed, and Murad had Savci killed and Andronicus blinded.

Murad then turned his attention to the Balkan states, which were in almost total disarray. Plagued by rival noblemen and peasant rebellions, the Serbian Empire folded before Murad's advance. In 1383, he invaded Serbian Macedonia, capturing Serres. By 1387, Murad had seized Sophia, Nish, and Salonika. The next year, he subjugated Tsar Ivan Sisman of Bulgaria.

The Battle of Kosovo Unwilling to accept vassalage under Islamic rule, Prince Lazar Hrebeljanovic of Serbia formed an alliance with Tvrtko I of Bosnia. Together the two assembled an army of Bosnians, Serbs, Bulgarians, Wallachians, and Albanians. This Pan-Slavic coalition launched a counterattack in 1388. With Murad distracted in the east, the Christian alliance was initially successful. They managed to stop the Ottoman advance at Plocnic, on the Serbian-Bosnian border.

Murad returned to the western front. The two armies met on June 28, 1389, in the Battle of Kosovo, which ended in an overwhelming Turkish victory. Lazar was killed in the fighting, along with a huge number of Serbian knights.

The Turks also suffered enormous losses. Faced with defeat, a Serbian officer pretended to yield to the Otto-

MURAD AND THE JANISSARIES

It is said that Murad was primarily responsible for the formation of the non-Turk Turkish army—the *Janissaries* (new soldiers). The Janissaries army quickly became the finest fighters in Europe. As the only standing army in Europe at the time (feudal lords conscripted soldiers in times of war), they were largely responsible for the spread of the Ottoman Empire.

Janissaries soldiers were initially young Christians captured in battle. Later, the Empire took a *devsirme* (tribute of children) from their subject provinces—one child in every forty families. Taken from their homes, the Greek and Slavic boys became *kapikulu* (slaves of the gate). They were converted to Islam, taught Turkish, and given first-rate military training. Forbidden to marry and alienated from their native cultures, the Janissaries' loyalties belonged only to the sultan and to each other.

Murad and his successors considered the devsirme to be very humane, saving the boys' souls and providing material benefits to the infidel provinces. Nevertheless, many non-Turk peoples, especially in the Balkans, deeply resented what they saw as the theft and indoctrination of their children. The practice continued into the seventeenth century.

mans. When he came close enough, the assassin fatally stabbed the sultan.

Murad was succeeded by his son Bayezid, who turned Serbia into a tributary state, conquered much of the remaining Balkans, and laid siege to Constantinople.

Bayezid I (c.1360–1403)

The Ottoman sultan Bayezid (c. 1360–1403) lived a colorful life. His people nicknamed him *Yildirim* ("Lightning Bolt") for his personal impetuosity and for his deadly, rapid attacks. Like his father (Murad I), Bayezid was a skilled and ruthless warrior, and he significantly expanded Islamic holdings. However, he lacked his father's political acumen; less adept at assimilating local populations, Bayezid's strength lay in capturing lands, not in keeping them.

Rise to Power in Asia Minor After Murad I fell on the plains of Kosovo in 1389, his eldest son Bayezid ascended to the sultanate. Bayezid immediately ordered his younger brother Yakud strangled with a bowstring, as was the usual ritual for succession in the Ottoman Empire.

As sultan, Bayezid first attempted to consolidate his empire in Anatolia. He waged a campaign against the Turkish principalities (such as the Karamanli) who had constantly challenged Ottoman rule. For this task, he employed Serbian and Byzantine soldiers supplied by his vassal states, since the ghazis did not much relish war against fellow Muslims.

Bran Castle in Romania.   © *Catherine Karnow/Corbis*

The Asia campaign proved largely successful. Making an alliance with Manuel, the son of Byzantine Emperor John V Palaeologus, Bayezid besieged the city of Konya and eventually occupied the Karamanli lands. He then defeated the emirs of Sarukhan and Mentese, pushing his domains to the Mediterranean Sea. Having formed a fledgling navy, the Ottomans overran Chios Island; however, the more experienced fleets of Venice and Genoa kept them from the other Greek islands.

Bayezid executed his brother-in-law Alaeddin, emir of the Karamanlis, and set up direct Ottoman rule through most of Anatolia. However, the sultan himself preferred to remain in his luxurious court, where he indulged in alcohol and a large harem.

Conflict with Constantinople
In 1391, John V Palaeologus of Byzantium died. His heir, Manuel, had been reduced to a servant (and not a very highly respected one) in the sultan's court. Hearing of his father's death, Manuel escaped to Constantinople and assumed the imperial crown.

Bayezid demanded that Manuel continue as an Ottoman vassal, that he pay a higher tribute, and that he install an Islamic judge in the city. To enforce his ultimatum, Ottoman troops marched on the city, killing or enslaving Christian Greeks along the way.

Constantinople lay under siege for seven years, despite Manuel's attempts at conciliation. The Byzantine Emperor agreed to establish a full Islamic tribunal and to set aside a quarter of the city to Muslim immigrants. The tribute was increased, and a tax levied on vineyards and vegetable gardens.

Fighting in The Balkans
In 1394, Turkish raiders crossed the Danube into Wallachia, invoking the wrath of Sigismund I, king of Hungary. As Bayezid's chief rival in the area, Sigismund's fight against the Turkish ambitions turned into a lifelong obsession.

The Hungarian king had ample reason for concern. Sisman of Bulgaria had been defeated by Murad in 1388, and had been permitted to rule as an Ottoman vassal. However, in 1395 Bayezid retook Nicopolis in Bulgaria. Worried that the Bulgarian king might ally himself with Sigismund, Bayezid executed Sisman and absorbed Bulgaria fully into the Ottoman Empire.

In 1396 Sigismund turned to Europe for help. Pope Boniface IX (1356–1404) echoed his call, preaching for an international crusade. Knights gathered from France, England, Scotland, Poland, Italy, and Spain, and many other nations. "If the sky fell on our army," Sigismund is said to have boasted, "we should have enough lances to uphold it."

Boasting aside, the Hungarian king was keenly aware of his enemy's strength, as the other crusaders were not. Careless and overconfident, the Christians captured Nish with much unnecessary bloodshed, then they continued on to Nicopolis.

Bayezid, true to his nickname, advanced swiftly. He burst upon the unprepared Europeans, who fought without a coherent battle plan. The Christians suffered enormous losses during this disastrous crusade and fled as they could. Bayezid ordered a general slaughter of all prisoners. Only the French Comte of Nevers and his entourage were spared, since they promised to bring in a fabulous ransom.

Bayezid and the Mongols
In 1399, Bayezid attempted to seize the city of Constantinople, but was driven back by a small French contingent and two Italian navies. Manuel left the city for a tour of the European courts, attempting in vain to drum up support for his beleaguered city.

Three years later, deliverance came from an unexpected quarter. Full-scale war broke out between Bayezid and the Tartar chieftain Tamerlane, also known as Timur the Lame. Timur's troops overran Anatolia, in part supported by Turkish lords who had never fully accepted the Ottoman reign. Bayezid himself was taken prisoner. It was widely told that the sultan was exposed to a variety of public humiliations before he died in captivity.

The Blue Mosque in Istanbul, Turkey. © *Rose Hartman/Corbis*

After the death of Tamerlane, the former Ottoman Empire fell into civil war as the various Turkish houses vied for supremacy. Eventually Bayezid's son Mehmed emerged victorious in 1413.

Murad II

After an Ottoman civil war, Sultan Murad II (1404–1451) took the reigns of power. Though personally a peace-loving, scholarly man, Murad's reign was marked with almost continual warfare both in Europe and in Asia.

Early Reign After Bayezid Yildirim was captured in 1402, the Ottoman Empire split as the sultan's many sons vied for the throne. After eleven years of civil war, in 1413 Bayezid's son Mehmed managed to consolidate his grasp of most (but not all) of the former empire. The new sultan died in an accident only eight years later.

Mehmed's son Murad II took over from his father in 1421 at the age of eighteen. Almost immediately upon his ascension, he faced an insurrection by Düsme "False" Mustafa, who claimed to be Murad's brother. Byzantine Emperor Manuel II Palaeologus supported Mustafa in the hope that, should he win the sultanate, he would release Byzantium from Ottoman vassalage.

Mustafa made rapid advances into Ottoman territory, but the young Murad rallied and showed his innate military skills. He drove the pretender's forces back to Gallipoli, laid siege to his stronghold, and stormed it. He then had Mustafa hanged as an imposter.

Triumphant, Murad swore revenge on Palaeologus. Using cannon for the first time, he laid siege to Constantinople. The city held out for months, largely because it could be supplied by sea. In the meantime, the sultan's thirteen-year-old brother "Little" Mustafa rose against Murad in Anatolia, threatening Bursa. Murad broke off the siege and returned home, where he defeated and beheaded Mustafa. (The people of Constantinople attributed their reprieve to a miraculous intervention of the Virgin Mary.)

Murad faced other challenges at home, especially among the Turkish emirs who had supported his rivals. After heavy campaigning, he put down the Menteshe, Aydin, Teke, and Germiyan principalities. By 1428, he had restored the Ottoman state to what it had been under Bayezid.

A Turkish rival, the Timurid Shah Rukh of the Karamanli, also rebelled in Anatolia in 1435. The revolt was put down two years later, but the Karaman province retained its independence and remained a nagging threat on Murad's eastern border.

The Balkan Crusade In 1437, the Turk's most stalwart European enemy, Hungarian king Sigismund, died.

Taking advantage of the dynastic struggle that followed, Murad moved north to the Danube and seized the fortress of Semendria. Defeated Serbian despot George Brankovic fled to Hungary, where he pleaded for help. The sultan then laid siege to Belgrade, but failed to take the city.

The *boyars* (aristocrats) of Hungary, worried by the renewed Turkish raids, decided to offer the crown to Ladislaus III, king of Poland. Together with Transylvanian leader Janos Hunyadi, Ladislaus launched a Hungarian-Polish crusade against Murad in 1443.

Initially the Christians made rapid progress, taking Nish and Sophia, restoring Brankovic to power. Hunyadi's troops then won a significant victory over the sultan's army on Christmas day, before harsh weather and short supplies forced them to retreat.

Murad found himself in difficult straits. Heartened by their string of victories, the crusaders were already regrouping. In the meantime, the Karamanli were again causing trouble in Anatolia.

With the help of his Serbian wife, Murad pursued diplomacy and managed to negotiate a truce in June 1444. He agreed to liberate Serbia and Wallachia from Ottoman rule; in exchange, the Hungarians promised to leave Bulgaria in peace.

Tired of war, Murad withdrew to his palace at Magnesia, hoping to lead a quiet life of study and prayer. He left his twelve-year-old son Mehmed to govern Edirne, under the tutelage of Grand Vizier Halil Candarli Pasha.

The Christian West, seeing a child on the sultan's throne, almost immediately broke the treaty and marched across the Danube. Murad rushed back to the battlefront and handed the crusaders a crushing defeat at Varna.

Late Reign Having killed Ladislaus and scattered the Slavic army, Murad felt that he had finally secured the peace. This time he formally abdicated his crown to his son, who became Mehmed II.

This retirement, too, was to be short-lived. The Janissaries, a powerful military corps, staged an uprising against the young sultan, and Vizier Halil pleaded with Murad to return to power. Once convinced of the gravity of the situation, Murad rode back to Edirne and sent his son into political exile.

Having once again taken up the crown, Murad also took up the sword. In Attica, he stopped the advance of Constantine, Despot of Morea. In 1448, he also met the irrepressible Hunyadi in the Second Battle of Kosovo. Turkish arms carried the day—the Hungarian and Wallachian troops broke and fled before them.

Then the sultan turned north in an attempt to stamp out the rebellion in Albania. This time, however, his forces met a stunning defeat in 1450. A former Ottoman general, George Castrioti, nicknamed Skanderbeg, led the Albanians. Taken into the sultan's court at the age of three and brought up a Muslim, Skanderbeg had reclaimed his Albanian identity and turned

against the Turks. Murad was shocked and furious at the defection.

Sultan Murad II died of apoplexy in 1451 and was succeeded by Mehmed II, known to history as Mehmed the Conqueror for his successful defeat of Constantinople.

Ladislaus III

In the mid-fifteenth century, Ladislaus III (1424–1444) ascended the thrones of Poland and Hungary. In 1444, he led a crusade into Bulgaria, which ended in disaster at the Battle of Varna.

The Double Kingdom In the Middle Ages, Eastern European countries did not follow a system of primogeniture to determine the crown's succession. Instead, the nobles of the land voted to decide the next king. In 1434, a ten-year-old Ladislaus, third of that name, was elected king of Poland. In 1440, hoping for military assistance against the Turks, Hungarian nobles offered him the vacant throne of Hungary.

Ladislaus's assumption to his second throne did not go unchallenged. The previous king, Albert II (1397–1439), had left behind a pregnant widow: Elizabeth, daughter of Sigismund. A few months after her husband's death she gave birth to a son, known as Ladislaus the Posthumous. Elizabeth claimed the crown for her child and thus launched a two-year civil war.

Despite her many partisans (including George Brankovic of Serbia), Elizabeth's bid for the crown did not succeed. Ladislaus III was backed by most of the Hungarian nobles, notably by the Ban of Macva, Nicholas Ujlaki, and the Ban of Severin, Janos Hunyadi. (The term "Ban" denotes a prince or ruler.) Ladislaus installed these two renowned generals along his borders, both to put down Elizabeth's supporters and to guard against the Turks.

The Long Campaign Ladislaus also received help from Rome. Pope Eugene IV (1383–1447) was painfully aware of Christendom's vulnerability to Islamic conquest. He continually—though mostly ineffectively—exhorted Catholic Europe to crusade. The ongoing instability of Hungary and Byzantium, however, frustrated his designs. To rectify the situation, Eugene sent Cardinal Giuliano Cesarini (1398–1444) as papal legate to Buda. Cesarini promised to support Ladislaus, provided that the young king would take up arms against the Turks.

To many Christians, the time seemed ripe to expel the Muslims from Europe. News of Hunyadi's surprising victories over Ottoman forces in Transylvania lent impetus to the movement.

In 1443, Ladislaus crossed the Danube in an expedition known as the "Long Campaign." His army consisted of Hungarians, Poles, Serbs and other Slavic people. In short order they captured Nish and Sofia and restored George Brankovic to his seat in Serbia. The Christians were driven back at the Zlatitsa Pass, but they managed to score some victories as they retreated.

The Truce The Long Campaign (which actually only lasted six months) did not cripple the Ottomans in Europe. However, it struck a strong psychological blow. Venice, Genoa, and Burgundy flooded Ladislaus with congratulations and with promises of future support. Inspired by the crusaders' apparent success, small uprisings cropped up in Ottoman-controlled lands.

Ottoman sultan Murad II found himself plagued by family connections. His brother-in-law, Mahmud Çelebi, had been captured by the Hungarians. Murad's wife Mara pleaded with him on behalf of her father, George Brankovic. Another brother-in-law, Ibrahim Bey of Karaman, had started trouble for the empire in the east.

Mara arranged to offer her father a peace settlement, and Brankovic, newly restored to a very shaky throne, accepted it eagerly. Brankovic passed the peace offer to Hunyadi, who took it to Buda. In April of 1444, Ladislaus sent an envoy to negotiate in Edirne.

By mid-June, a treaty had been concluded with representatives of Ladislaus, Brankovic, and Hunyadi. Murad swore to release Brankovic and the king of Wallachia, Vlad Dracul, from Turkish allegiance. Murad also promised to quit as sultan; his twelve-year-old son, Mehmed, would take his place. Hungary in turn promised to observe a truce for ten years.

King Ladislaus's behavior during this episode is neither creditable nor easily understood. On July 25, he met the ambassadors at Szeged (in present-day Hungary) to sign the sultan's treaty. Just a few days later, on August 4, he swore—by the Holy Trinity, by the Virgin Mary, by St. Stephen, and by St. Ladislas—to drive the Ottomans out of Europe.

Whether Ladislaus immediately regretted the truce or whether he never intended to honor it, historians may never know. He may have been overly influenced by Cardinal Cesarini, who declared that oaths made to the infidel were not binding.

Onward to Varna Ladislaus's forces pushed through Bulgaria, fighting bloody skirmishes with Ottoman troops along the way. Since Murad had retired to Asia, the Hungarians believed that they faced only Mehmed and the child's paltry army at Edirne. They were thus caught by surprise when they met Murad (who reluctantly returned) and a massive Ottoman army before Varna.

For a while, the Christians fared well against the larger Ottoman force. However, at a crucial moment Ladislaus made a fateful error. Ignoring Hunyadi's advice, he led a charge against the sultan himself. Murad's guard, composed of hardened Janissaries, killed the young king and put his head on a pike. Appalled, the crusading army broke and ran.

Christian Europe was stunned and horrified. Many saw the defeat as divine retribution for having reneged on a sacred oath. In Hungary, many nobles refused to believe that Ladislaus had died, and it was two years before they elected his successor—Ladislaus V (the Posthumous), the son of Elizabeth and Albert II.

Janos Hunyadi

As the seemingly invincible Ottoman armies pushed westward, Christian Europeans began to despair for their future. They found a hero in Janos Hunyadi (1407–1456), a brilliant Hungarian solider who spent his life in fierce opposition to the Turks.

Early career Janos (John) Hunyadi was born in Transylvania to a boyar family. As a teenager he served as a knight in the court of King Sigismund of Hungary, during which time Hunyadi participated in the Czech war against the Hussites. Later he spent two years in Milan, where he learned Italian military techniques from the famed *condottiero* (mercenary) Francesco Sforza.

In 1437, as a commander of Sigismund's army, Hunyadi came to the relief of the castle of Semendria, where he successfully beat back the Turkish army. His military services were rewarded with lands and titles: Sigismund's short-lived successor Albert II made Hunyadi Ban of Severin. Later, ruler Ladislaus III appointed him captain of Belgrade and *Voivode* (governor) of Transylvania.

By 1439, Ottoman leader Murad II had retaken Semendria and ousted Serbian Ban George Brankovic. Turkish raiders drove further and further north, causing panic throughout the region.

Increasingly, Hungarians saw themselves as the vanguard of the West, Europe's last defense in the war against Ottoman domination. As a vassal of the king of Hungary, Hunyadi was placed at the very forefront of that war. By 1442 he had defeated and killed Ottoman commander Mezid Bey, whose forces had invaded Transylvania. Shortly afterwards, he crushed the forces of Sihabeddin Pasha, who had come to avenge Mezid.

The Long Campaign Encouraged by these unprecedented victories, Ladislaus III (now king of Hungary and Poland) launched an offensive against the Turks. With papal blessing, Ladislaus crossed the Danube in 1443. Hunyadi led twelve thousand horsemen in the advance guard.

As the Ottomans pulled back, Hunyadi's troops made a madly daring advance through the icy passes of the Haemus Mountains. Fighting in deep snow with tenuous supply lines, the Christians were driven back by a counterattack. They rallied and won a victory against the pursuing Turks on Christmas Eve. On February 2, they successfully ambushed an Ottoman force. They took a great many prisoners, including the sultan's brother-in-law Mahmud Çelebi.

Impossibly low on supplies, the Christian army began the long march to Buda. They arrived skeletal and half-frozen, but were welcomed back to the Hungarian capitol as conquering heroes.

Varna and Vlad In 1444, the sultan negotiated a ten-year truce with the Christians, which the Christians almost immediately violated. Together with King Ladislaus, Hunyadi marched through Bulgaria, determined once and for all to drive the Turks out of Europe.

The crusaders made steady progress, though Ottoman resistance increased as they pushed closer to the capitol at Edirne. Then, on November 10, 1444, at the city of Varna on the banks of the Black Sea, they met the army of Murad himself.

Outnumbered four to one, the Christians were put to rout, and Ladislaus was killed on the field. Hunyadi barely escaped with his life. On the way home, he fell into the hands of the Wallachian ruler Vlad Dracul. There was apparently no love lost between the two men, and Vlad kept him prisoner for some time in Wallachia.

Upon reaching home, Hunyadi took his place in the interim government, a panel of noblemen. In 1446 they chose Albert's young son, Ladislaus V, as the new king. As Ladislaus was a six-year-old child (and, until 1452, a virtual hostage in Vienna), Hunyadi ruled Hungary as regent.

Collapse at Kosovo Hunyadi's loss at Varna evidently rankled him deeply. Once again, he started to gather allies to expel the Turks. However, the new Pope Nicholas V showed less martial fervor than had his predecessor, and the other European courts only offered vague promises. George Brankovic, Despot of Serbia and Murad's father-in-law, flatly refused.

In 1448, Hunyadi's army of around forty thousand men advanced through Serbia, which they treated as enemy territory. They pillaged every city in their path before reaching the Plain of Blackbirds in Kosovo. There the sultan met them with an army around 55,000 strong. Battle was joined on October 17 and continued for three days.

Though the Hungarians were outnumbered, they had superior firearms and inflicted heavy losses on the Ottomans. Nevertheless, the battle was already turning against Hunyadi when eight thousand Wallachian troops defected to the Turks. Hunyadi fled, only to be captured by Brankovic and forced into a humiliating treaty.

Stand at Belgrade In 1456 Mehmed II renewed his attacks on Hungary, falling on Belgrade with some 200,000 men. This time, Hunyadi managed to hold the defenses against overwhelming odds. It was a signal victory and slowed Ottoman expansion considerably. However, Hunyadi died of the plague shortly after the battle.

After his death, Hunyadi's widow managed to put their son on the throne. Matthias Hunyadi Corvinus (1443–1490) became one of Hungary's most capable

rulers, and, like his father, kept the Turks at bay. The monarchy collapsed after Matthias' death, however, and the Ottoman Empire absorbed Hungary by 1526.

Skanderbeg

After Janos Hunyadi's unexpected death in 1456, Europe found a new defender: George Castriota, popularly known as Skanderbeg (c. 1405–1468), who defended Albania against Turkish occupation for almost a quarter century.

Ottoman Traitor Contemporary accounts of Skanderbeg's life survive, but are so infused with hero-worship that historians doubt their accuracy. Some facts seem clear, however. He was probably born around 1405 into the Castriota family, one of the many Albanian warlord clans. His father John Castriota, willingly or not, became a vassal to the Ottoman sultan. To ensure his loyalty, Castriota was obliged to send his young son to Edirne as a hostage.

As was normal in those cases, George converted to Islam and took the Muslim name Iskander. He seems to have received military training and eventually earned a high rank in the Janissary army. His title thereafter was Iskander Bey, which was later corrupted to Skanderbeg.

Perhaps inspired by some of Janos Hunyadi's victories in 1443, Skanderbeg defected that year, taking three hundred soldiers with him. He recaptured his birthplace, the mountain castle of Krujë, reconverted to Catholicism, and declared war against the Turks. According to legend he told his countrymen, "I do not bring you freedom; I have found it here with you."

Skanderbeg seems to have possessed great political skills as well as military acumen. At the time, Albania had little national cohesion; as in Serbia and Bosnia, petty lords feuded endlessly among themselves. For a brief time at least, Skanderbeg managed to unite most of the factions into the League of Lezhe, a loose coalition dedicated to the repulsion of the Ottoman Empire.

He had less success rallying support from outside Albania, though not through lack of effort. He corresponded regularly with the papacy (Pope Callistus II called him "the athlete of Christ") and sent appeals for aid throughout the Catholic world. In return he received much praise and many promises, but little material benefit. Only Naples and Venice, directly threatened by Ottoman invasion, sent money or troops.

Freedom Fighter Nevertheless, Skanderbeg's army forced the Ottomans from Albania and kept them out until after their leader's death. Albania's inhospitable terrain helped the cause, and the Albanians under his leadership put up a skilled and courageous resistance. They avoided battle in open fields and instead attacked in the narrow mountain passes. Against overwhelming odds, they defeated the Turks in battle after battle.

In April 1450, Sultan Murad II set out for Albania personally. By May, he had laid siege to Krujë with over 100,000 troops and heavy artillery. Skanderbeg left the castle in the hands of a small garrison, around two thousand strong. He himself took around eight thousand men to a nearby mountain fortress. Against Krujë's stubborn defense and Skanderbeg's guerilla attacks, Murad's host labored in vain for months. Finally, having attempted both to bribe the garrison and to negotiate with Skanderbeg, the sultan had to retreat before the oncoming winter.

Throughout his struggles with the Turks, Skanderbeg had to contend with the normal feudal bickering of Albanian warlords. Venice, while using him as a shield against the Turks, did not want Albania to become too strong. To that end they conspired with local rivals to keep him in check. He also faced defection within his own family, which had old ties with the Ottomans. In 1456, Skanderbeg defeated his uncle, Musa Komninos Golem, who led a Turkish auxiliary force against him. Musa later approached Skanderbeg and begged for forgiveness, promising to fight against the Muslims.

The next year, Skanderbeg's nephew Hamza, who had converted to Islam, joined forces with Isa Bey and forced the Albanian army back. Skanderbeg fell on the enemy at rest in Tomorrit, killing anywhere from fifteen thousand to thirty thousand Turks and taking a camp full of spoil. He spared Hamza's life, but exiled him under guard to Naples.

In 1466, after years of intermittent warfare, Mehmed II launched another mass invasion of Albania, and once more assaulted Krujë. Once more the defenses held; after five months, the sultan withdrew in disgust. He left the siege to his commander Balaban, with orders not to withdraw until he starved the castle to its knees. Before long, Skanderbeg had ambushed and captured Balaban's brother and nephew, Balaban himself was wounded, and the Turkish army fled in disarray.

National Legend

Skanderbeg died of fever on January 17, 1468, in a castle above Alessio. He commended the care of his country to Venice and the care of his infant son to Naples. The Neapolitan court welcomed the child, and Venice garrisoned the fortress at Krujë, but otherwise the West abandoned Albania.

In 1478, the Ottomans invaded and occupied the country. On entering Alessio, the sultan had Skanderbeg's body exhumed and displayed on the streets. Legend has it that many Turkish soldiers took one of the great warrior's bones to make them brave in battle.

Skanderbeg's countrymen preserved his memory throughout the long Ottoman rule. Even today he is revered as a national hero; his standard, a double-headed eagle, flies on the Albanian flag.

Vlad III Dracula

The infamous Vlad III Dracula (c. 1431–1477), also known as Vlad "the Impaler," has been immortalized in fiction as Bram Stoker's famous vampire. Ruling Wallachia

Vlad the Impaler (Vlad VI of Wallachia) died in 1462. *Imagno/ Getty Images*

three times in the fifteenth century, Vlad's brutal tactics terrorized both his subjects and his enemies.

The Father, Vlad II Dracul

Born an illegitimate son of a princely Wallachian family, Vlad II (1390–1447) served as a young man in Sigismund's court. There he joined the Order of the Dragon, a society devoted to the fight against the Muslims. In 1431, King Sigismund of Hungary appointed Vlad as governor of Transylvania. Five years later, he made himself king of Wallachia, calling himself Vlad II Dracul (Vlad II, the Dragon).

In 1442, the Ottomans invaded Transylvania. King Ladislaus of Hungary, blaming Vlad for not having protected his borders, removed him from power. The self-styled Dragon then turned to the sworn enemy of his Order, Ottoman sultan Murad II. With Turkish assistance, Vlad returned to rule Wallachia. The throne did not come cheap, however. Vlad was compelled to send his two young sons, Vlad and Radu, to Edirne as hostages.

When the Hungarians launched a crusade in 1444, they called on Vlad for help. Vlad had no wish to anger the Hungarian king or to endanger his sons in the sultan's court. He compromised by sending his oldest son Mircea to participate in the campaign, which ended in disaster at Varna.

In December 1447, Hungarian noblemen assassinated both Vlad II and Mircea. (Evidence suggests Mircea was buried alive.) Janos Hunyadi, who despised Vlad for his collaboration with the Turks, appointed a puppet ruler in Wallachia.

Vlad III Dracula

Vlad Dracul's second son Vlad was thirteen years old when he went into exile in Turkey. In 1448, the Ottomans released him and supported him as their candidate in Wallachia. With the Ottoman's help, he took the throne as Vlad III Dracula (Son of the Dragon). Only a few months later, though, Hunyadi drove him out and installed Vladislov III in his place.

However, Vladislov unexpectedly sided with the Ottomans. Furious, Hunyadi allied himself with Vlad Dracula, in whom he discovered a kindred hatred for the Turks. Vlad took possession of his father's former Transylvanian landholdings. In 1456, with Hunyadi's support, he invaded Wallachia and reclaimed the throne.

Many tales exist of Dracula's reign. Most of these come from sensationalized foreign pamphlets, which were printed for propaganda purposes or as gruesome entertainment. Nonetheless, a clear portrait emerges from the various sources: if even a fraction of the stories are true, Vlad III Dracula was one of the most sadistic rulers of all time.

Dracula instituted an iron rule of law in Wallachia, enforced by brutal torture and casual killing. He is said to have virtually wiped out the established boyars in order to create a more loyal ruling class. Many sources also recount that he murdered the poor and homeless in his land, saying that they drained the country's strength.

Vlad Dracula's favorite method of execution earned him the nickname Vlad *Tepes* ("the Impaler"). He skewered his victims on a sharp wooden pole, then left them to suffer slow, agonizing deaths. As a warning for others, the bodies would hang rotting in the air for months. The sentence was carried out for the most minor offenses: theft, adultery, even dishonesty or laziness. It was said that Vlad could leave a golden cup in any village square, and no one would dare steal it.

Scourge of the Ottomans

Besides his mania for law and order, Vlad nursed an obsessive hatred for the Turks. Shortly after coming to power he stopped paying tribute to the sultan and entered into alliance with King Hungary Matthias Corvinus of Hungary (1443–1490). Around 1461, Vlad crossed the Danube and ravished the Ottoman countryside.

Informed of this, Ottoman sultan Mehmed II stormed into Wallachia with a huge army. He faced bitter resistance from Dracula, who burnt his own villages and poisoned his own wells to deprive the Turks of supplies.

The Ottoman army pressed to the capitol at Tirgoviste. There they found a huge plain covered with impaled corpses; Dracula had arranged a forest of some twenty thousand dead Turks and Bulgarians. At this gruesome sight, Mehmed's forces simply turned around and left Wallachia.

Their withdrawal was a temporary one. By the end of 1462, Islamic generals had overrun the country, and Vlad Dracula had once again fled to Transylvania. His brother Radu "the Handsome"—a faithful Ottoman vassal—took the throne.

Exile in Hungary

In 1462, Matthias Corvinus intercepted a letter, which indicated that Vlad was conspiring with the sultan against Hungary. Matthias immediately had him arrested and imprisoned in Buda.

Vlad remained in Hungary for the next fourteen years. During that time his captivity became lighter as his relations with the Hungarian court improved. By 1466 he had married one of the king's cousins.

In 1474, Vlad once again attacked and ousted the Ottoman puppet in Wallachia. He reigned there for the next two years. But the Wallachians had tired of his insane rule, and they largely abandoned him when the Turks attacked again. Vastly outnumbered, Vlad was killed. His head was sent back to Constantinople to prove that the Impaler Prince had finally fallen.

Mehmed II

As the Middle Ages drew to a close, Ottoman sultan Mehmed II (1432–1481) conquered Constantinople and ended the Byzantine Empire. He went on to overthrow Greece and much of the Balkans, establishing the Ottoman Empire as a major world power.

Early Life

Mehmed was the third son of Sultan Murad II. His father preferred Mehmed's two older brothers, in part because they had been born to respectable Muslim noblewomen. Mehmed's mother was a slave girl, probably a Christian Albanian.

At the age of two, Mehmed was sent to Amasya, a province of northern Anatolia where his older brother Ahmed was governor. Ahmed died suddenly, and Mehmed (then six) took his place.

A few years later, his second brother Ali (their father's favorite) was mysteriously strangled in his sleep. Now heir to the throne, Mehmed returned to Edirne to learn the art of statecraft.

In 1443, Murad II concluded a ten-year treaty with Ladislaus III of Poland. Thinking that the peace had finally been secured, the sultan retired to his Asian palaces, leaving his twelve-year-old son to govern the Ottoman Europe.

A Young Sultan Rules in Fits and Starts

A precocious and arrogant child, Mehmed soon alienated his father's advisors by encouraging an unorthodox Persian mystic. Religious authorities overruled the young governor and burned the Persian at the stake.

Mehmed also faced an uprising from the Janissaries, the military elite. They demanded—and eventually received—an increase in pay. (It was not the last time the Janissaries were to revolt. Although nominally slaves, they became a powerful force in Ottoman government over the centuries.)

When Ladislaus broke the peace treaty and attacked Bulgaria, Murad returned to the Western world to deal with the threat. After defeating the Christians at Varna, and re-establishing Ottoman rule south of the Danube, Murad formally abdicated to Mehmed.

Over the next two years, the situation at the Edirne court once again grew tense. Mehmed's aggressive militarism (specifically his determination to take Constantinople) led him to clash with Vizier Halil and with the Janissaries. Recalled by his ministers, Murad took back the reins of empire, and banished his son to Magnesia.

Against Constantinople After Murad's death in 1451, Mehmed returned to the throne, determined to follow his plans for conquest and glory. He immediately ordered his infant half-brother drowned, and he forced his widowed stepmother to marry again. Rebellious Janissaries were ousted, and the corps reorganized into a more loyalist army.

Despite his early promises to respect Byzantine territories, Mehmed quickly set about constructing a fortress on the European side of the Bosporus Straits. The work progressed at a fevered pace, and the castle—*Boghaz Kesen*, meaning "Strait Cutter" or "Throat Cutter"—was finished in less than five months. When Constantinople sent a delegation in protest, the sultan arrested and beheaded the ambassadors.

In the spring of 1453, Mehmed besieged and overthrew Constantinople. On entering the city, he immediately began the construction of a magnificent palace. Mehmed saw himself as the heir of Alexander the Great and of the Caesars, as well as the champion of Islam. Accordingly he made Constantinople, the ancient symbol of the Christian Roman Empire, his new capitol.

For the next year, Mehmed attempted to subdue the ever-rebellious Balkans. However, the Ottomans met fierce resistance by Janos Hunyadi at the siege of Belgrade and were driven back. Injured in the leg, Mehmed retired for some time to his palace.

War with the West After he had recovered, the sultan turned his attention to Greece. In 1458, his armies took Athens. The next year the fortress of Smederevo surrendered to him, finally giving the Ottomans complete control of Serbia. By 1463, the Turkish army had overrun Wallachia and Bosnia, while the navy took the island of Lesbos. Aware that he was closing in on their territories, Venice (with Hungary's support) declared war.

The war did not go well for the Christians. Mehmed was distracted in Turkey by a two-year struggle with his family's perennial rivals, the Karamanlis; even so, the Ottomans took Montenegro after a long and horrible siege in 1469. Then they brought the Genoese to their knees, subjugated Crimea, and overran Albania. In the end, Venice sued for peace in 1479, agreeing to pay an annual tribute.

Towards the end of his life, Mehmed suffered from illness and remained mostly in Constantinople. Ottoman generals oversaw the empire's continued campaigns against Italy, the Balkans, and Syria. In 1481, the sultan died suddenly of stomach pains. It was widely suspected that his heir, Bayezid II, had poisoned him.

Mehmed, known to history as "the Conquerer," ushered in the golden age of the Ottoman Empire. Despite his almost breathtaking personal cruelty, he continued his forebears' relative tolerance towards non-Muslim subjects. He also patronized the arts and formalized the national code of law.

Selim I

Sultan Selim I (1465–1520) was one of the most important rulers in Ottoman history. In his short reign, he defeated the Persian and Mamluk empires. Under his command, the Turks conquered Armenia, Egypt, Syria, and Palestine, and they established lordship over the Arabian peninsula.

Ascent to the Throne Mehmed II's son, Bayezid II (1447–1512), ruled for thirty-one years. Less aggressive than his father, Bayezid consolidated Ottoman rule rather than expanding it. A patron of the arts and sciences, he tended to delegate leadership to his officials.

More significantly, he distributed power among his five sons. Bayezid appointed each of them to governorships throughout the empire. Once trained in civic and military matters, however, each son felt himself most qualified for the throne. It was not long before they began to quarrel over the succession.

Known to be ruthless, Selim was the youngest and least popular of the princes. As his brothers contended for influence, however, the militant Selim gained the loyalty of the Janissaries and the Balkan governors. In addition, after he led raids on Persian territory and put down insurrections in the eastern provinces, the Khan of the Crimea backed his candidacy.

With this support, Selim moved against the capitol, forcing Bayezid II to step down in 1512. Shortly afterwards, the old sultan died in political exile. When his two remaining brothers continued to press their claims, Selim's army hunted them down and killed them. Selim also had many nephews killed in order to clear the path of succession for his son, Suleiman.

Persia and Armenia The most serious challenge to Bayezid's rule had came not from Europe but from Iran, where *Shah* (King) Ismail I had risen to power. Ismail's Safavid dynasty had roots in the Shi'a Islamic sect, and he proved zealous in promoting the faith. To the fury of Ottoman civic and religious authorities, Persian agents constantly agitated among the Shi'ites in eastern Anatolia, causing them to rise up against their Sunni (a different branch of Islam) masters.

Selim's supporters—especially the Janissaries—expected him to confront Persia, and he soon obliged them. In 1514, Ismail supported Murat, one of Selim's surviving nephews, in attacking the city of Sivas on the Ottoman border. Selim repulsed the invasion. Then, although the local people had not supported Murat, the sultan ordered a general massacre of Shi'ites in the region. His troops slaughtered some forty thousand people and forcibly relocated thousands of others to the Balkans. This helped to Islamicize the newly subjugated Christian lands and robbed the shah of his followers in Anatolia.

The Ottoman army proceeded into Persia, defeating Ismail at the Battle of Chaldiran. They then pressed forward to capture Tabriz two weeks later. Although local Sunnis welcomed him as a liberator from the Shi'ite Safavids, Selim faced a rebellion among his Janissaries. He withdrew, claiming only northwestern Armenia as the spoils of war.

By the next year, however, the restless sultan had once again marshaled his forces. In short order, the Ottoman army had driven through Kemakh, Chemishgezek, Chapakchur, and Arabkir. Seeing their apparently inexorable advance, regional Kurdish emirs swore allegiance to the sultan.

Selim then laid siege to the city of Mardin. Here he was less successful—the fortress withstood his forces for years. In the meantime, however, the sultan conquered all of northern Mesopotamia, making Kurdish princes and Arab chieftains his vassals.

Syria and Egypt Turning south, the Ottoman army marched into the Mamluk Empire, which had been founded by the great Muslim leader Saladin in the twelfth century. At the time, this empire ruled Egypt, Syria, and Palestine. The Mamluk state was wealthy but their army was antiquated; they stood no chance against Selim's military skill and his modern Janissaries.

Selim claimed (falsely) that pretenders to the Ottoman throne received protection from Mamluk sultan al-Ghawri. Thus justified, the Ottoman army advanced through Armenia into northern Syria, taking Dulkadir, Malatya, and Ayntab. On August 24, 1516, they met the Egyptians at Marj Dabik, and Al-Ghawri was killed. Aleppo, Hama, Homs, and Damascus likewise fell before the Turks.

Because of Selim's political skill (to say nothing of his unstoppable armies), Arab religious leaders, caliphs, and chieftains threw themselves at his feet. When the new Mamluk sultan Tuman Bey took power, Selim offered to make him the viceroy of Egypt if he, too, would submit. Tuman Bey sent a defiant refusal, whereupon Selim marched across the Sinai Peninsula, routed the Egyptians at Reydaniyya, and had Tuman Bey killed.

Egypt was then reorganized as the Ottoman province Missir, while Syria became the province of Sham. Learning of this, Sharif Barakat II (guardian of the Islamic holy cities of Mecca and Medina) sent the keys to those cities to Selim. In return for his submission, he continued to rule the Holy Places of Islam as a Turkish vassal. The Turkish sultans had formerly been ghazis;

Under Selim they became *caliphs* (guardians of the faithful), foremost rulers of the Islamic world.

Death and Legacy Having consolidated his hold on the former Mamluk empire, Selim returned to Constantinople. In 1520, he began a journey to Edirne, evidently planning to begin a campaign against Christian Europe. However, he took ill and died en route.

In just eight years, Sultan Selim, known to history as "Selim the Grim," doubled the size of the Ottoman Empire. When his son Suleiman took the throne, he did so without the usual dynastic chaos. Thanks to his father's conquests, he also took control of a strong army and a fabulously rich treasury.

Ismail I

From 1501 to 1514, Shah Ismail I (1487–1524) conquered much of modern-day Iran. Although the Ottomans checked his progress, Ismail founded the Safavid dynasty, which was to rule Shi'ite Persia for over two hundred years.

The Sufis Ismail, son of Haydar who was son of Junaid, was born into the rapidly spreading movement of Shi'a Islam. His father and grandfathers were leaders of the *Safaviyeh*, a Sufi religious order founded around 1400 by famed mystic Safi Al-Din. Over time, the Safaviyeh adopted the Twelver sect of Shi'a Islam—in other words, they professed the infallible *caliphate* (religious leadership) of the Twelve Imams—descendants of Mohammed through his son-in-law Ali.

To spread this doctrine, the zealous and charismatic Haydar gathered a band of religious warriors called the *Qizilbash* (the "Redhats"). Fanatically loyal to the Safaviyeh Grand Masters, these ghazis attached twelve insignia to their distinctive red headgear to represent the imams. When Haydar died in battle in 1488, it is said that the Qizilbash saved his infant son Ismail and took him into hiding.

The Child King In 1501, at the age of fourteen, Ismail re-emerged, conquered Tabriz, and made it his capitol. The same year he defeated the Aq Qoyunlus (the "White Sheep"), a Sunni tribe prominent in the region. His next few years saw an unbroken string of military victories, as he and the Qizilbash consolidated their hold over all of Azerbaijan. He put down the Uzbeks to the east, and by 1508 he had seized Shiraz, Baghdad, and Herat.

Equally significantly, Ismail proclaimed *Ithna Ashari* (Twelver Shi'a) to be the official religion of his kingdom. He decreed that Muslims should ritually curse the first three Sunni caliphs (seen as usurpers of the imams) during Friday prayers. Though this aroused the resentment of many Sunni Persians (who, though the majority, were violently repressed), Shi'ism would eventually bring a sense of national identity and unity to the Iranian people.

However, this religious practice also provoked the enmity of their western neighbors in Turkey. Many of the Ottomans' Anatolian subjects had converted to Shi'-ism, and they, too, flocked to the Safavid flag. Ismail exasperated the situation by sending missionaries and spies into Ottoman territory. During 1511–1512, these agents helped provoke a Shi'ite rebellion in the Takkalu province of eastern Anatolia.

Sultan Selim I "the Grim" (one of the less broad-minded Ottoman monarchs) brutally squelched the rebellion, executing around forty thousand people. In addition, he forced tens of thousands of survivors to relocate to the Balkans, where they could exert a Muslim influence among the restless Christian natives.

The Young Messiah By this time, Ismail's Shi'ite followers had come to look on their young *shah* as a holy man and possibly something much more. Central to *Ithna Ashari* is the belief that the twelfth imam, Muhammad al-Mahdi, never died, but would one day return as messiah and redeemer. Many Persians believed Ismail to be this "Hidden Imam."

Certainly the Qizilbash, undefeated for fourteen years, saw their leader in a divine light. "There is no god but God," they shouted when charging into battle, and "Ismail is the Friend of God." One Persian source wrote that the Qizilbash went into battle without armor, confident in their shah's invincibility.

Chaldiran Relations between Turkey and Persia continued to worsen: the Ottomans launched raids into Safavid territory, and the Safavids promoted pretenders to the Ottoman throne. In 1415, Selim had the *ulema* (religious elders) issue a *fatwa* (condemnation) against Ismail, declaring the latter to be a heretic and an infidel. Selim then marched towards Tabriz, sending a very insulting declaration of war before him.

The two armies met at Chaldiran on August 23, 1514, where the Ottomans' superior artillery soundly defeated the Qizilbash. Ismail barely managed to escape, but his army was decimated and his favorite wife captured.

Selim marched on into Tabriz, which surrendered without a fight. A mutiny among his Janissaries forced him to withdraw, so Selim contented himself with some holdings in southwest Iran. Then he turned his attention towards the Egyptian Mamluk Empire.

Reprieved, Ismail regained his capitol a month later. However, his divine illusions shattered, he never again led the Qizilbash into battle. Rather he retreated, depressed, to his palace. He died ten years later at the age of thirty-six, to be replaced by his nine-year old son Tahmasp.

Despite his disappointment, Ismail's house remained in power until 1722. Tahmasp proved a capable ruler and managed to hold the empire against numerous invasions. Over time, the Persian people came to genuinely accept Shi'ism, laying the foundations for the modern state of Iran.

POEM OF DIVINITY

Ismail seems to have believed himself that he was the "Hidden Imam." The Safavids had fabricated a family tree to link themselves to Musa al-Kazim, the seventh Imam—Ismail seems to have taken it a step further. In one of his many poems, he wrote:

I am God's mystery. I am the leader of all these *ghazis*. My mother is Fatima (Mohammed's daughter), my father is Ali; and I am *Pir* (spiritual master) of the Twelve Imams . . .

I am the living Khidr (a Muslim saint) and Jesus, son of Mary. I am the Alexander of [my] contemporaries.

Suleiman I

Suleiman I (1494–1566) is remembered as the greatest ruler in his long and distinguished dynasty. Called "the Lawgiver" by the Turks and "the Magnificent" by the Western world, Suleiman reigned over the golden age of the Ottoman Empire.

Early Battles Suleiman ascended to the sultanate after his father's death in 1520. As Selim's only surviving son, he did not have to murder any relatives (a common practice in Ottoman successions).

Suleiman pursued conquest, as had his ancestors; he was devoutly attached to jihad. He also understood that the Janissary army must keep busy outside the Ottoman border or cause mayhem inside it. In 1521, Suleiman succeeded where his grandfather Mehmed the Conqueror had failed; he surrounded Belgrade, bombarded the walls, and forced the fortress' surrender.

Suleiman then turned his attention to another of Mehmed's failures—the Knights of St. John, a crusading order who controlled the island of Rhodes. Just eleven miles off the coast of Turkey, Rhodes sheltered Christian pirates who had for years played havoc with Ottoman shipping.

Rhodes was touted as an impenetrable island fortress, though it held only five thousand fighting men and seven thousand civilians. To counter this, the Turkish besieging force numbered well over 100,000 troops and carried an enormous weight of artillery. After a five month brutal siege, the Knights were granted an honorable surrender and the city's population was spared.

Austria and Hungary In 1526, the Turks attacked and briefly held Buda, killing King Louis II at the Battle of Mohács. The young king's death left Hungary divided. Hapsburg Archduke Ferdinand of Austria claimed the throne through marriage, but Suleiman did not agree. "Hungary is mine," the sultan declared. He was determined to give the crown to his Transylvanian vassal, "his slave," King John Zapolya.

Engraving of Suleiman the Magnificent. *The Library of Congress*

Accordingly, in 1529 Suleiman besieged and very nearly took Vienna, but was forced back by logistical problems and bad weather. Three years later he tried again, but was forced to retreat before reaching the city.

Iraq and Greece Suleiman then turned east to check Shah Tahmasp I of the Persian Safavid dynasty. Initially he sent Grand Vizier Ibrahim Pasha, his Greek slave and childhood friend. In 1534, Ibrahim marched east and took Tabriz and Baghdad.

Later, the sultan joined Ibrahim and launched a series of campaigns in the region. These floundered, however, due to the Persian's guerilla tactics. Tahmasp avoided direct battle, drawing Suleiman's forces deep into harsh terrain. The conflict dragged on, stalemated, until a settlement was worked out in 1555.

The Turks fared better on the water. Suleiman appointed a privateer named Barbarossa Hayreddin (c. 1478–1546), known to the Europeans as Redbeard, as admiral of his fleets. Barbarossa modernized the Ottoman fleet and won a signal victory against the Austrian navy in 1538. Within a few years, the Turks completely dominated the Mediterranean Sea.

In the meantime, Ottoman Admiral Piri Reis (c. 1465–1555) battled the Portuguese for control of the Indian Ocean. Piri, who became famous as a cartographer, secured the Red Sea but failed in the Persian Gulf.

In 1541, the Ottoman armies once more marched on Europe. After six years, they conquered and occupied Hungary and forced Austria to pay annual tribute.

Intrigue at The Palace Suleiman's victories stemmed from his diplomatic acumen as well as from his military skill. He thoroughly understood and exploited Europe's divisions. He allied himself with French king Francis I (1494–1547) against their mutual enemy Hapsburg Emperor Charles V (1500–1558). When Germany exploded over Martin Luther's Reformation, Suleiman encouraged the conflict by funding the Protestants.

Ironically, politics at home would prove his undoing. His well-liked vizier, Ibrahim, was an efficient administrator, but he aroused resentment from the Turkish elite. Word reached the sultan that Ibrahim had set his ambitions higher than his station, so in 1436, Suleiman had the vizier strangled.

Suleiman's true favorite in the palace was a Slavic slave girl named Roxelana (c. 1510–1558), with whom he was clearly infatuated. Against all tradition, he married her and moved her into the palace.

Aware that Ottoman princes must succeed the sultan or die trying, Roxelana schemed for her children. She managed to turn the sultan against his eldest and most promising son, Mustafa; the sultan ordered the young man murdered before his own eyes. Mustafa's brother Jahangir killed himself, leaving only Roxelana's sons Selim and Bayezid in contention for the throne.

After their mother's death in 1558, the two brothers took up arms against each other. Suleiman sided with Selim (later known as "Selim the Drunk"). Bayezid was defeated, captured, and executed.

Final Battles In 1565, over seventy years old, Suleiman attempted once more to rout out the Knights of St. John at Malta. Defeated, the sultan led one last campaign against Hungary. His armies overran the last of the defiant Hungarian fortresses, but Suleiman died on the road.

Suleiman was a great patron of art and architecture, as well as a just and capable administrator. He established enduring codes of law, built beautiful mosques, wrote poetry, and established the Ottoman Empire as a world superpower.

Don Juan

Don Juan of Austria (1547–1578) was born in Bavaria, the illegitimate son of Hapsburg Emperor Charles V. Adopted by the court of Philip II of Spain, he later earned renown at the Battle of Lepanto.

Birth and Childhood Hapsburg Emperor Charles V reigned in troubled times. As king of both Austria and Spain, he had significant responsibilities both in Europe and the New World. As Holy Roman Emperor, it fell to him to protect Catholic Christendom from both the Muslim Ottoman Emperor and the emerging Protestant Reformation.

Worn down by his burdens, Charles abdicated in 1556, leaving the imperial crown of Austria to his brother Ferdinand I and the throne of Spain to his son Philip II. He retired to a monastery, where he died two years later.

In his will, Charles acknowledged that he had fathered an illegitimate son with an obscure German woman. He had given the child to Spanish foster parents, who called him Jerónimo. Charles asked Philip to recognize the boy and give him an annual allowance.

Accordingly, King Philip brought the twelve-year-old to court, where he was called Juan de Austria (John of Austria) in recognition of his Hapsburg heritage. Over the years he became very popular; in stark contrast with his grim half-brother Philip, Juan was charismatic, athletic, and outgoing. It seems that Charles had wanted Juan to enter the church, but the young man showed no inclination in that direction. Though a fervent Catholic, he evidently wished to defend the faith on the battlefield.

Early Life Don Juan was about the same age as Philip's son and heir Don Carlos (1545–1568). Though of very different temperaments, the two became close friends in their teenage years. Unexpectedly, in 1567, Don Carlos approached Juan with a plan to assassinate his father, the king. Horrified, Juan revealed the plot to Philip. Carlos was arrested and died in prison the next year.

As reward for his loyalty, Philip gave his half-brother a significant naval commission. With thirty-three galleys under his command, Juan was ordered to drive North African corsairs from the Strait of Gibraltar. In 1569, Philip ordered him to put down a Morisco revolt in the Alpujarras region of Spain. (The Moriscos were Muslims who had unwillingly converted to Christianity under threat of expulsion.)

Don Juan acquitted himself well in these operations, showing vigor, courage and military skill. Within a few years his zeal and ability—and, perhaps, his good looks and charming manners—had earned the young general an international reputation.

The Battle of Lepanto In 1571, Pope Pius V put out a call for a combined Catholic effort to check Muslim expansion. Spain, Venice, Tuscany, Savoy, Rome, and the Knights of Malta assembled their navies to form the Holy League, a fleet composed of over two hundred galleys. Pius asked that Don Juan, at the time barely twenty-four years old, be appointed commander of the entire undertaking.

The Holy League sailed to Lepanto (off of Greece) where they engaged the Muslim fleet on October 7, 1571. The forces were evenly matched numerically, but the Christians possessed more modern artillery and better gunners. The Turks, who had so recently seemed invincible, were routed and scattered.

The battle turned Don Juan into a folk hero overnight. Churches throughout Western Europe rang out with praise and celebration of the new champion of Christendom.

Later Career Though the Holy League withdrew and disbanded, Don Juan continued to fight the Ottomans. He captured Tunis from the Turks in 1573, but he received no support from Spain and lost it the next year.

Philip feared his half-brother's popularity, and tried to muzzle the young man as best he could. Nevertheless, in 1574 he appointed Don Juan as governor of the Spanish Netherlands. The Low Countries had recently turned to Protestantism and had rebelled under the leadership of William the Silent (1533–1584). Philip hoped that Juan, a beloved war hero, would be able to sway the people back to Catholicism and to Spain.

Don Juan had little taste for his new assignment. As his royal brother feared, his ambitions were of a more lofty nature. With a few others, he plotted to launch a daring attack against England and overthrow Protestant Queen Elizabeth I (1533–1603). He would then free Mary, Queen of Scots (1542–1587), marry her, and sit on the throne of England. Philip seems to have encouraged this deluded plan, if only to direct Juan's energies away from Spain.

Juan met with little success in the Netherlands. The very day he arrived, the Spanish army perpetrated a massive atrocity in Antwerp. Enraged, the Dutch forced the new governor to withdraw Spanish troops from the country.

For the next few years, Juan struggled futilely to retain control. Acting on his own initiative, he defeated the Dutch rebels at Gembloux. The resistance continued, however, and Juan's health deteriorated. In 1578 he died of typhus, and his body was smuggled back to Spain.

⊕ Major Battles

Kosovo, June 28, 1389

The Battle of Kosovo was a turning point in Serbian—and indeed, world—history. To this day, Serbs remember this defeat by the Ottomans as the defining moment of their nation.

Old cannon at the gate of the Castile Pallace, the official residence of the Prime Minister of Malta. © *Ianni Dimitrov/Alamy*

The Stage Throughout recorded history, the many Balkan peoples and principalities had never lived very peaceably together. However, by 1381, the Christian Slavs had put aside their differences against a common enemy: the encroaching armies of Murad I, sultan of the Ottoman Empire.

Fighting in the name of Islam, Murad had established almost total control over Anatolia (modern-day Turkey). He had also gradually conquered much of Greece and Macedonia. In 1388, Bulgaria too was forced into submission.

It should be noted that the Ottomans generally allowed their non-Turkish subject peoples a great deal of autonomy and religious freedom. They also brought order and stability to many an ill-governed, neglected fief. Some Christians, eager to throw off the yolk of the Byzantine or Serbian empires, actually welcomed the Muslims as liberators.

A great many Europeans took a different view, however. Unwilling to become Turkish vassals, Christians rallied behind the strongest of the Serbian feudal lords, Prince Lazar Hrebeljanovic. Through military and diplomatic means, Lazar unified the Serbian lords and managed to arrange an alliance with ruler Tvrtko I of Bosnia. Their combined forces won a few victories over Turkish raiding parties in the early 1380s.

The Battle In 1389, however, the matter came to a dramatic head. Murad I and his sons led an army westward to *Kosovo Polje* ("Plain of Blackbirds"). There he was met by Lazar and a pan-Slavic army composed of Bosnians, Serbs, Bulgarians, Wallachians, and Albanians.

Kosovo was a strategically important crossroads, sitting on a watershed between the Vardar and Morava rivers. Surrounded by mountains, Kosovo guards the shortest north-south route across the Balkans.

Very little can be accurately known about the battle, given the scarcity of contemporary witnesses and the total absence of objective reports. The relative size of the armies is unknown. Even the outcome is not entirely clear, though both sides suffered terrible losses.

The battle was later widely accepted as a devastating defeat for the Christians, but it may not have been at the time: the Muslims did not advance to Kosovo but retreated back to their Western capitol of Edirne. All through Europe, thanksgiving masses were said for the death of Murad.

The Dead It is certain that both Lazar and Murad died that day, but the stories vary in both cases. Some Serbian epic poems describe Lazar's glorious death in battle. Others lament that he was captured, tortured, and executed by the Turks.

Murad seems to have been assassinated. According to Serbian sources, a knight walked into the sultan's tent, pretending to surrender. When he got close enough, the assassin (later named as Milos Obilic) stabbed Murad in the stomach. Ottoman writers assert that the Serbian knight was lying on the battlefield, pretending to be dead.

Both Murad and Lazar were considered martyrs by their respective faiths. A later Turkish historian wrote that Murad, seeing that the Serbian army was twice the size of his own, spent the evening in prayer. He offered his own life for the lives of his soldiers, an offer that was apparently accepted.

Serbian legends recount that the Christians (who were vastly outnumbered by the Turks) received a message from the Turks—surrender or be destroyed. Thereupon the prophet Elijah appeared to Lazar in the form of a bird, and offered him a choice between an empire of heaven (to be claimed by battle and death) and an empire of earth (which could be accomplished by negotiating with the enemy). According to the poems, Lazar chose the kingdom of heaven and fought.

The Serbian Orthodox Church canonized Lazar shortly after the battle. Serbs revere his memory to this day. Muslims remember Murad I as a ghazi.

The Legacy Murad's son Bazeyid took his father's place as ruler of the Ottoman Empire. His brother Yakub was immediately executed according to the custom. Then the army fell back to Edirne to crown the new sultan.

Bayezid permitted Lazar's son Stefan to rule Serbia as a vassal state. Stefan gave an annual tribute to the Turks, as well as lending soldiers for Bayezid's Asian wars. Serbia had lost a large number of her best soldiers and leaders and would remain under foreign rule for the next five hundred years.

For many Serbs, the Battle of Kosovo came to symbolize the tragic loss of their national sovereignty. The fall of Lazar became a rallying cry for Serbian nationalists from Princip Gavrilo (whose assassination of Archduke Franz Ferdinand of Austria sparked World War I) to modern Serbian leader Slobodan Milosevic (who was indicted for crimes against humanity by the United Nations International Criminal Tribunal).

Nicopolis, September 25, 1396

Faced with the seemingly invincible Ottoman armies, King Sigismund of Hungary (1368–1437) called for an international European crusade. The crusaders met the Muslims at Nicopolis, in Bulgaria, where the Christians were soundly defeated.

Call to Crusade (Again)

In 1388, Sultan Murad I had overthrown the city of Nicopolis, forcing Bulgarian king Sisman to accept Turkish suzerainty. When Ottoman ruler Bayezid (Murad's heir) killed Sisman in 1395 and installed his own ministers in Bulgaria, Hungary found the Muslims at their very doorstep.

As Holy Roman Emperor, Sigismund felt himself responsible for safeguarding Christianity from Islam. As king of Hungary, he was keenly aware that his country stood on the border between the two faiths.

Sigismund's fears were not unfounded. Bayezid was profoundly anti-Christian, and he was not as diplomatic as his father had been. Early in his career, the young sultan had boasted that he would crush Hungary, then continue on to Rome and stable his horse in St. Peter's Cathedral.

Bayezid's confidence was not unfounded either. His Janissaries were trained, well-disciplined professional soldiers that had seldom seen defeat. By 1395, almost all the lords of Anatolia, Macedonia, Byzantium, Serbia, Wallachia, and Bulgaria paid him tribute.

Sigismund sent emissaries to all of the courts of Europe, begging for aid. Around the same time, Emperor Manuel II Palaeologus (1350–1425) of Byzantium also launched a desperate appeal to the lords of Christendom—Constantinople was under siege.

Their timing was fortuitous. The Hundred Years War had finally ended, leaving many French and English knights without an enemy to fight. These feudal noblemen had been brought up on glorious (if highly inaccurate) tales of the Crusades. When Pope Boniface IX issued a call for a crusade against the heathen Turks, Europe responded with fervor.

John of Nevers (1371–1419), son of the Duke of Burgundy, left amid great public fanfare with a large French force. Inspired by his example, knights from England, Scotland, Germany, Spain, Italy, Poland, and Bohemia all marched upon Hungary. By the summer of 1396, a few hundred thousand men had gathered at Buda, the largest crusading force ever collected.

It was also one of the least competent. Most of the Christian knights were amateur soldiers at best, living out a chivalric fantasy several hundred years old. They had no notion of modern warfare, which had been perfected by the professional and highly experienced Ottoman army. The crusaders still fought in heavy armor with broadswords. They stood little chance against the Turkish cavalry, who employed swift, lightly armored mounted archers. Worse, they were unaware of their inadequacies, and they spoke confidently of liberating Jerusalem later in the campaign.

The Crusaders Go Looking for Trouble

Sigismund, on the other hand, was painfully aware of the Turks' military prowess. He expected an Ottoman assault into Hungary and prepared for a defensive campaign. When the invasion did not come, the Europeans grew restless and went on the offensive. They marched south, capturing Orsova and Nish with much unnecessary bloodshed.

Arriving at the important fortification of Nicopolis, they could not take the stronghold—they had brought no siege engines. Instead they camped around the city and waited, indulging in wine and women.

Bayezid's army arrived sixteen days later, reputedly up to 200,000 men strong. The Europeans were elated and threw themselves into the fight. The battle opened with initial Christian victories. The French lord Enguerrand de Coucy led a reconnaissance force into the mountains, scattering a Turkish vanguard.

Jealous of de Coucy's victory, the other French lords entered the fray, ignoring the Hungarian king's pleas for a coordinated, defensive use of their numbers. Sigismund had proposed that the mounted knights should form a line behind the Hungarian and Wallachian foot soldiers, who were experienced in fighting the Turks.

The chevaliers refused this well-considered battle plan, accusing the Hungarians of trying to steal their honor. Instead they charged up the hill and fell on the Turkish front line, cutting them to pieces.

The Crusaders Find Trouble

Bayezid was as unworried by the crusaders' initial victory as the crusaders were exultant. As was his practice, he had put his untrained, worthless troops in front as fodder for the enemy. After the seven hundred French chevaliers reached the hilltop, they met some sixty thousand members of the famed Ottoman army.

The Christians were scattered and routed. When the knights were thrown from their horses, their heavy armor prevented them from rising again. Sigismund and a few other lords managed to escape via the Danube River.

Thousands of Europeans fled as they could, and many died in a hard retreat on foot through the mountains.

The next day Bayezid ordered a general execution of all of the prisoners. John of Nevers and his men, spared on account of their ransom potential, were forced to watch their fellow crusaders beheaded. The sultan gave a contemptuous speech, daring any Christian knight to return and fight him. Then, not even bothering to give chase, he turned back to resume his blockade of Constantinople.

The international army of 1396 ended in an overwhelming Christian defeat on Christian soil. From that point on, few Western European nations would help oppose the Ottoman Empire.

Varna, November 10, 1444

On the fields before Varna, King Ladislaus III of Hungary and Poland met Murad II of the Ottoman Empire. Although both sides took heavy losses, ultimately the Turks defeated and scattered the Christians.

Breaking the Peace In June 1444, Sultan Murad II concluded a treaty with the Christian powers. He freed Serbia and Wallachia from Ottoman vassalage in exchange for a ten-year cessation of hostilities between Hungary and the Ottoman Empire. Believing his western border to be secure, Murad then retired to his Asian provinces.

Ladislaus of Hungary almost immediately violated this treaty and launched a crusade. He was encouraged in this venture by papal legate Giuliano Cesarini and joined by his vassal Janos Hunyadi. However, the Ban of Serbia, George Brankovic, refused to participate. The king of Wallachia, Vlad II Dracul, did not come himself but sent his son and a contingent of soldiers.

In September 1444, Ladislaus crossed the Danube into Bulgaria and began to work his way towards Edirne, the Ottoman capitol. Murad's twelve-year-old son Mehmed ruled the city, guarded (it was believed) by no more than eight thousand men.

Papal, Venetian, and Genoese ships guarded the Bosporus Straits against any Turkish counterattack from Asia. Ladislaus' army planned to join with the fleet when they reached the Black Sea.

The land force (around twenty thousand troops in all) advanced through Bulgaria. On November 9, they stopped and camped at Varna, a city on the banks of the Black Sea. There they were astonished to find Murad's entire army waiting for them, 80,000 to 100,000 men strong.

Murad's Return After an initial attempt to remain an ex-sultan failed, Murad had ridden north with his large army, reaching the Dardanelles in October. Finding the passage locked by the Christian fleet, the sultan contrived to cross the Bosporus Straits at night. It is not certain how he managed the passage. It seems that some Christians helped him, perhaps selling him boats. (The pope would later send out a general excommunication of all those involved.)

What is more, the Papal fleet did not sail north in time to aid Ladislaus. Some sources blame the delay on a violent storm; others hint that Murad bribed the Venetians and Genoese.

Whatever the case may be, Murad's force hurried on to Varna. The Hungarian army found itself massively outnumbered, with no reinforcements in sight on the water. The Turks had cut off their line of retreat, trapping them against rugged hill country to the north and the Black Sea to the east.

The Hungarian leaders held a desperate war council. Some advised taking a defensive position and waiting for the arrival of the fleet. Hunyadi, on the other hand, told the Christian lords that their only hope lay in open battle.

The Battle Hunyadi was placed in command of the field. The next morning, on November 10, he deployed the Christian troops in a crescent shape. Behind their main line of battle stood a *Wagenburg*, a fortified ring of wagons and carts.

The Ottomans launched the first attack. Karaca Bey, governor of Anatolia, led his *sipahis* (feudal cavalry) in an attempt to flank and scatter the Hungarian right wing. Other sipahis then fell on the left wing.

Accounts differ as to the order of battle, but it appears that Hunyadi persuaded Ladislaus to hold the center while he rode out to help with their embattled left flank. Somehow Hunyadi managed to break the Ottomans' line in that direction. Then he turned back to the right. The Turks put up valiant resistance, but suffered heavy losses, and their leader, Karaca Bey, fell. At this loss, his men apparently broke and ran, leaving the sultan alone on the field with his Janissaries.

At this point, Ladislaus made a fatal error. The young king (Ladislaus was twenty years old), caught up in the excitement of imminent victory, disregarded Hunyadi's military advice. With five hundred of his men, he attacked the sultan's guards directly. At first the mad charge was successful, but the Janissaries far outnumbered the Polish knights. Eventually overwhelmed, the king fell from his horse. The Turks chopped off his head and mounted it on a pole.

At this sight, the crusaders panicked and ran to the hills. The Ottomans, having taken massive casualties, withdrew in an orderly fashion and did not pursue that day.

Cardinal Cesarini was among those who fled, and he was never seen again. Hunyadi also escaped, only to be captured by Vlad Dracul. The king of Wallachia harbored a grudge against Hunyadi and imprisoned him for months.

Casualty counts varied widely, but they were generally acknowledged to be enormous on both sides. Several sources indicate that ten thousand crusaders died.

The Ottomans lost around thirty thousand troops, about a third of their army.

Constantinople, May 29, 1453

When the city of Constantinople fell to the Ottoman leader Mehmed the Conqueror, it signaled the end of the ancient Byzantine Empire.

The Ottomans Throughout the winter of 1452, Sultan Mehmed II planned feverishly for the campaign against Constantinople, the conquest of which had been his dream since childhood. He equipped his army with the best and most modern weaponry money could buy. He paid Urban, a legendary Hungarian metalworker, to construct heavy cannons. One of these was a twenty-nine foot gun named Basilica, which could throw a 1,200-pound ball over a mile.

The sultan assembled an army of more than a hundred thousand men, including twelve thousand battle-hardened Janissaries. He also strengthened the Ottoman navy, constructing a fleet of over one hundred vessels. This meant the Turks were capable of blockading the city from the south for the first time. (Other sieges had failed when Constantinople was supplied by sea.)

Mehmed's forces went on the march in the spring of 1453, buoyed by their sultan's obsessive energy. After centuries of decay, the "Golden Apple" of Constantinople lay within their grasp.

The Last Gasp of Byzantium The entire population of Constantinople barely exceeded fifty thousand, of which only five thousand were soldiers. Some two thousand Italian volunteers joined them, answering the call for Christian solidarity. Among these came Giovanni Giustiniani, an expert in fortifications, who strengthened the long walls of the city as best he could.

Morale was low among the citizens of Constantinople. Western Christendom had failed to come to their rescue. This was not due to lack of pleading; Emperor Constantine XI Palaeologus had even agreed to reunite the Orthodox Church with the Roman Catholic branch. This concession had brought little material aid and had caused rioting among his people. Rumors of ominous supernatural portents ran through the city as Christians prayed desperately for deliverance. For many, it seemed that the hour of the Antichrist had come.

On April 2, 1453, the last of the Ottoman army arrived at the gates of Constantinople. Emperor Constantine ordered the gates of the city to be closed and the moats to be flooded with seawater. A floating wooden wall stretched across the entrance of the Golden Horn harbor, protecting the ships within.

Four days later, in accordance with Islamic law, the sultan sent envoys demanding the city's surrender. The emperor refused. Shortly thereafter, cannon fire began to bombard the city.

The Siege For the next two months, the people of Constantinople stubbornly defended their home. When the bombardment cut through the wall, the defenders hastened to repair the damage, using wood, stone, hay bales, and leather. They poured boiling pitch down on the attackers as they attempted to scale the walls. The Turks wheeled tall wooden towers up to the wall, which the Greeks burned.

The two armies fought before the gates, from the turrets, and under the ground, digging tunnels and counter-tunnels. The air was choked with smoke and noise; the sultan ordered a constant barrage of cymbals, trumpets, pipes, tambourines and war cries, while the emperor replied with the massive, tireless bells of the Byzantine churches.

On April 18, the Ottomans staged a massive assault on the walls. After four hours of intense fighting, the invaders were pushed back. Two days later, four Christian ships managed to fight their way through the naval blockade, bringing a few hundred reinforcements. The contribution was small, but it raised the Greek's morale.

The sultan was furious. He had ships dragged overland from the Bosporus into the Golden Horn. Once this was accomplished, the city's defenders could only watch helplessly as Greeks lost control of the water.

In mid-May, Mehmed sent one more messenger. He gave the citizens of Constantinople two choices: they could agree to pay an enormous yearly tribute, or they could evacuate the city. Constantine and his council knew that they could not possibly raise the money, and they refused to abandon the city.

The Conquest In the early morning May 29, the Turks began a massive assault. Wave after wave of men flung themselves on the city. A well-aimed cannonball shattered a wooden blockade that had patched up one section of the wall, and the Janissaries swarmed in. The Greeks, led by the emperor himself, held the breach for hours, but they were exhausted and hugely outnumbered.

Eventually Giustiniani was badly injured. His men managed to carry him through the city and put him on a Genoese ship. Believing the city lost, many of the Genoese troops fled with him.

The Turks swept through the city, looting and killing. Some of the civilians fought on the streets, or threw bricks down from windows. Others huddled in the churches. Before the end of the day almost all of them had been killed or taken into slavery.

Tradition has it that Constantine cried, "The city is lost, and I am still alive!" He then dismounted, took off the imperial purple, and fought alongside the common soldiers. Killed and buried in a common grave, he is revered in Greece as a martyr and a saint.

The next day, Mehmed entered the city and made straight for the great cathedral, the Hagia Sophia. Marveling at the beauty of the building and giving thanks to God for his victory, the sultan had it converted to a

Turkish ceramic arts, like this plate, are known worldwide for their beauty. They often feature stylized tulips, poppies and dianthus. © *Interfoto Pressebildagentur/Alamy*

mosque. Constantinople became Istanbul, and it serves as the capitol of the Turks to this day.

Chaldiran, August 23, 1514

Early in the sixteenth century, the imperial and religious rivalry between the Turkish Ottoman Empire and the Persian Safavid Empire came to a head. Sultan Selim I and Shah Ismail I met on the field of Chaldiran in Azerbaijan, where superior Turkish firepower decisively won the day.

Ismail At the end of the fifteenth century, central Asia lay in turmoil as various Turkish, Uzbek, Mongol, and Tartar warlords battled endlessly for supremacy. This changed in 1501, when Ismail I ascended to the throne of Tabriz at the age of fourteen. Displaying an extraordinary military talent, the young shah set about pacifying the region. Within ten years, he had driven all opposition out of Persia and had captured other important cities such as Baghdad and Khorasan.

From his grandfather, Ismail had inherited religious leadership of the *Safaviyeh*, a militant Muslim order. In that capacity, Ismail proclaimed the official state religion to be *Ithna Ashari*—the Twelve Imam's sect of Shi'a Islam. This faith was to be the foundation of Ismail's Safavid dynasty. All other forms of Islam were ruthlessly suppressed.

Drained by the violent chaos before his reign, many Iranian Turks were inclined to view Shah Ismail as the *Mahdi* (a savior), or possibly as a reincarnation of the Hidden Twelfth Imam. Ismail accepted and encouraged this belief—he wrote poetry in which he described himself in frankly divine terms.

Although both Shi'ism and Sunnism teach that such claims are blasphemous, Ismail's core warriors—the Qizilbash—fought with fanatical devotion under his banner. They were named for their distinctive red headgear, which sported twelve studs symbolizing their devotion to the Twelve Imams.

Selim the Grim Is Not Amused The Ottomans watched with some dismay at their new neighbors' advance; the sultan was not pleased when large numbers of his Anatolian subjects flocked to Ismail's court at Tabriz. This led to a wave of crackdowns against Shi'ites in the Ottoman Empire, which in turn left the border provinces resentful and rebellious.

Safaviyeh missionaries and Persian agents were quick to capitalize on this discontent, provoking open uprisings against the Empire. Relations between Persia and Turkey became poisonous, and cross-boundary raids became more common. Finally, Selim and Ismail exchanged a series of belligerent and insulting letters, after which Selim marched to the east with more than sixty thousand men, composed in part of Janissary infantry and sipahis cavalry.

The Battle Shah Ismail was outnumbered, but that fact alone does not adequately explain his failure against Selim. The Janissaries were a standing army of disciplined soldiers, equipped with muskets and cannon. The Qizilbash carried no gunpowder weapons; their fighters were nomadic horsemen pulled from feudal levies. They were enthusiastic but unprepared for modern warfare.

The two armies met at the field of Chaldiran, about eighty miles northwest of Tabriz. The Ottoman force entrenched behind wagons and set artillery pieces.

The Persians had never before lost a battle under Ismail. Fired by religious fervor, they charged directly at the Turkish line. Though both sides took heavy losses, the result was a complete rout of the Qizilbash. Their cavalry was mown down by gunfire, Ismail himself was wounded, and the army was forced to retreat.

Threatened by the harsh Azerbaijan winter, the Ottomans made no effort to chase down the defeated Persians. Instead they continued forward and took Tabriz, apparently without a fight. The local Sunni population welcomed Selim as a liberator and urged him to free all of Persia from Shi'ite rule. At the suggestion, Selim's troops, exhausted by a long trek and a hard battle, came close to mutiny. The sultan contented himself with the provinces of Kurdistan and Diyarbekr and returned to Istanbul.

The Aftermath The loss was a heavy psychological blow to Ismail, who had believed himself divinely appointed and therefore invincible. Though his government did not flounder, the shah never again appeared at the head of his army. The battle effectively halted the expansion of the Safavid Empire. Furthermore, Iran turned away from the heretical messianic teachings of the Qizilbash and adopted a more orthodox brand of Shi'a Islam.

Ismail's son and heir, Shah Tahmasp, also learned from his father's tactical mistakes. When Selim's son Suleiman marched into Persian territories, Tahmasp never confronted the Turks directly. Instead he followed a scorched earth policy, destroying his own country's food and supplies so that the invaders could not live off the land. The Turks followed the Persians deeper and deeper into the harsh Central Asian steppes until cold and starvation forced them back. This cat-and-mouse routine continued without significant gains on either side until a peace treaty was concluded in 1555.

Historians often cite the Battle of Chaldiran as the first decisive proof of the importance of firearms in modern warfare.

Rhodes, 1522

During the siege of this island, Suleiman the Magnificent besieged and conquered the Knights of Rhodes, the last of the crusading orders. The hard-won victory helped to give the Ottomans mastery of the Mediterranean Sea.

The Knights Hospitaller The Knights of the Hospital of St. John of Jerusalem were a Catholic monastic order whose origins are lost in the early crusades. Though their rule (charter) concerned itself chiefly with medical services and hospitality for pilgrims, the Knights eventually became a military order, dedicated to the crusading cause. Their ranks included both professed monks and affiliated lay knights.

In 1187, the Knights managed to escape Jerusalem when Saladin took the city. They retired to Tripoli until 1291, and then took refuge in the Kingdom of Cyprus. In 1309 they conquered the island of Rhodes and established a fortress there.

Situated just eleven miles off the coast of Turkey, the Knights of Rhodes harassed the Ottoman Empire for centuries. They fought the Barbary pirates (Turkish corsairs) who preyed on Christian shipping and who did a brisk business in Christian slaves. At the same time the Knights of St. John outfitted their own corsairs, who pillaged Turkish merchant ships wherever they could find them. For all practical purposes, they became pirates.

Mehmed Doesn't Quite Conquer When Constantinople fell to Mehmed II in 1453, the island of Rhodes found itself surrounded by Ottoman territory. Mehmed, who saw himself as heir to the Byzantine Empire, would not tolerate an enemy stronghold in the very heart of his domain. In 1480, he sent his Greek-born Grand Vizier Gedik Ahmed Pasha to take the island.

The Knights had long expected such an attack. Under their Grand Master Pierre d'Aubusson (1423–1503), they had considerably strengthened the already impressive fortifications and had hoarded enough supplies to last three years.

The Ottomans landed on the island with up to 100,000 men. Confident of victory, Gedik forbade his troops to pillage—all spoils, he said, belonged to the sultan. At the same time he raised the black flag, which declared that everyone in the city would be slaughtered or enslaved. In this way he sapped his men of incentive, while giving the defenders a fighting edge of desperation.

The siege lasted from the end of May until August. The Turks' heavy cannon broke the thick walls in several places, but the defenders managed to withdraw to inner fortifications or to hold the breaches. Finally, having lost almost nine thousand men, Gedik sailed away.

Suleiman Tries Again D'Aubusson immediately set about repairing and modernizing the fortifications. Walls were rebuilt and thickened, double moats installed, and other up-to-date defenses added to the ancient fortress. By the time the Ottomans attacked again in 1522, the knights at Rhodes could boast one of the greatest strongholds in the world.

The new Grand Master, Phillipe Villiers de l'Isle-Adam (1464–1534), called for Knights of the Order from all around Europe, bringing their number to around seven hundred. With mercenaries and militiamen, the defenders numbered around five thousand fighters and seven thousand civilians.

Suleiman sent a fleet of almost four hundred ships to surround the island. With over 115,000 men, armed with the most advanced artilleries in the world, the Turks encircled the walls and began bombardment in late July, 1522.

The siege would last a brutal five months. The sultan's forces launched 85,000 cannonballs at the fortress walls, to little avail. More effective were the underground trenches, which were painstakingly dug up to and under the walls, then mined. The defenders dug their own series of counter-tunnels and countermines. These operations, bloody masterpieces of engineering, slowly ate away at the defenses.

In late September the Turks launched a series of direct assaults, which culminated in a major offensive. However, after six hours of frenzied fighting, the Janissaries were driven back with heavy losses.

By the end of November, the Turks had suffered tens of thousands of casualties, winter was coming on, and disease was spreading through the camp. The Knights, too, had reached their limit. Ammunition was running low. While they had lost fewer than the Turks, they had lost enough, and they could no longer effectively man the breaches.

After another failed assault in early December, the sultan offered the city a way to surrender with honor. Suleiman promised to allow the knights to leave with all of their weapons and valuables. He would also allow full civil liberties, including freedom of religion, to any civilian who wished to stay. The island would be pardoned any tribute for five years.

At first, de l'Isle-Adam insisted on fighting to the death. Eventually, however, the other townspeople prevailed upon him to surrender. On January 1, the Knights of Rhodes marched out of the fortress, their standards flying. Europeans generally praised Suleiman for his generosity towards the city's defenders.

Rhodes remained in Turkish possession for the next four hundred years. The Order regrouped as the Knights of Malta. In 1565, the Ottomans laid siege to Malta, but could not penetrate the defenses.

Tunis, 1535

As Ottoman privateers took control of the Mediterranean, they clashed with the navies of Italy and Spain, fighting over key fortresses on the north coast of Africa. In 1535, a Christian fleet drove the Turks out of the strategically important city of Tunis.

Piracy in the Mediterranean Beginning in the sixteenth century, southern Europe lived in dread of the so-called Barbary pirates—Muslim corsairs who preyed on Western shipping and coastal towns. Over the next three hundred years, it is estimated that they carried well over a million Christians into slavery.

The first of these pirates were Moors who had escaped Spain when Ferdinand and Isabella conquered Granada in 1492. They settled in the Maghreb (northwestern Africa) and took up arms against the despised Spanish. Alongside the usual acts of pillage, kidnapping, and rape, the Barbary pirates helped Moriscos (Moors trapped in Spain and forced to convert to Catholicism) to escape the Inquisition or rebel against the Spanish crown. Therefore, the early Barbary pirates are better described as privateers—private ships using piratical methods to political ends.

The Barbarossa Brothers The most famous of the Barbary pirates were brothers, Barbaros Oruc (c. 1474–1518) and Barbaros Hizir (c.1478–1546). They were both red-haired, so the Italians called them the "Barbarossa" brothers ("Redbearded" brothers.) Greeks of Turkish extraction, they were first-rate seamen and ferocious enemies of Christian Europe. They pillaged the coasts of France, Spain, and North Africa, finally seizing Algiers in 1518. Oruc was killed in the fighting.

Hizir quickly proved himself a formidable privateer and a skilled leader. Selim I gave him the name "Heyreddin," meaning "Protector of the Faith," and appointed him as a *Beylerbey* (governor). Eager to check Spain's

power, Selim also sent him two thousand Janissaries, four thousand Turkish volunteers, and heavy artillery.

From his base at Algiers, Barbarossa continuously plagued Spanish outposts. In 1522 he took back Velez de la Gomera on the coast of Morocco, and in 1529 he drove the last of the Spanish from the Peñón of Algiers.

Tunis In 1530, alarmed by these developments, Holy Roman Emperor Charles V gave Malta and Tripoli to the Knights of St. John. He also procured the services of Genoese *condottiere* (mercenary) Andrea Doria (1466–1560), whose seamanship rivaled Barbarossa's.

Despite these rivals, the Turks continued their advances. In 1534, Barbarossa took Tunis, driving out the Hafsid sultan Muley Hassan. From Tunis, the privateer could easily strike at either Malta or Sicily. Charles could not allow a sworn enemy to hold such a strategic position.

In June 1535, three hundred ships sailed from Sardinia, carrying thirty thousand men. Led by Charles himself, they laid siege to La Goletta, a fortress on the mouth of the Tunis harbor. After twenty-four days of strong Turkish resistance, the Knights of St. John breached the walls with a gun from one of their massive galleons.

The Spaniards and Italians then pressed on to Tunis, and Barbarossa prepared to hold them off. He neglected to consider, however, that the city still held thousands of Christian slaves. The prisoners revolted, seized the armory, and attacked the Turks from inside the walls. Barbarossa fled, and Charles entered the city with minimal fighting.

Once inside, the emperor authorized his troops to sack the city. The Christian troops went on a three-day spree of atrocities, raping and murdering many thousands of people. They sold as many as ten thousand Moors into slavery. Tunis's mosques were desecrated and its treasures looted.

Charles manned La Goletta with a Christian garrison and restored Mulay Hassan as his vassal in Tunis.

Counterattack Most of Barbarossa's ships had been captured in the lake of Tunis, but he had set aside a reserve at Bone in Algeria. He instantly set sail, not to Tunis or Algiers but to the Spanish Balearic Islands, the last place he was expected. Flying Spanish and Italian colors, his ships were hailed as the triumphant Christian fleet. Having caught the city off-guard, Barbarossa proceeded to sack Minorca, carrying off much treasure and thousands of slaves.

The emperor had no leisure to retaliate. French king Francis I, having made an alliance with Barbarossa and Suleiman I, attacked Italy and set off the second Franco-Hapsburg war. Charles, mad with rage that Francis had negotiated with the Muslims, challenged the king of France to a personal duel. Francis, unsurprisingly, declined.

Barbarossa died in 1546, having scourged the Christian Mediterranean for over forty years. After his

Guard tower near Mnajdra, Malta. © Peter Oshkai/Alamy

death and the decline of Ottoman sea power, the Muslim corsairs began operating out of semi-autonomous North African city-states. The Barbary States, as they were known, inflicted such damage on Western shipping that most major powers paid them a "tribute" to protect their trade. This continued for hundreds of years, until the fledgling United States trounced the pirates in the Barbary Wars of 1801 and 1815.

Malta, 1565

In the mid-sixteenth century, determined once and for all to destroy the Knights of St. John, Suleiman I set his armies upon their fortress at Malta. The defenders managed to beat back the Ottomans in one of the most famous sieges in the history of warfare.

Causus Belli In 1551, Ottoman privateer Turgut Reis attacked the Knights of St. John, a Catholic order of privateers dedicated to fighting Islam. He did not penetrate their fortress on Malta, but he did enslave the entire population of the nearby island of Gozo. A Christian force hoping to chase down Turgut found Ottoman admiral Piyale Pasha instead, who surprised and decimated the Christians off the coast of Tunisia.

Despite this setback, the Knights of Malta continued to savage Muslim military and civilian shipping.

The knights never had more than seven ships, but those ships were impressively built and seldom lost. Their ranks also included some truly audacious seafarers, such as the dreaded Brother Romegas (c. 1525–1581). In 1654, this unusual monk captured a large Turkish merchantman, carrying eighty thousand ducats (gold coins) worth of merchandise. Romegas's prisoners included the governor of Cairo, the governor of Alexandria, and the sultan's favorite daughter's nurse. The court at Istanbul stridently demanded vengeance, and Ottoman ruler Suleiman decided that he had suffered the Knights of St. John to live long enough.

Preparations Disguised as fishermen, Ottoman spies slipped into Malta and made detailed drawings of the fortifications, which Suleiman converted into a three-dimensional model at the palace. However, the knights also kept an espionage network in Istanbul, and their spymaster Giovan Barelli managed to relay detailed information on the attack back to Malta.

The Grand Master of Malta was Jean de Valette (1494–1568), a veteran of Rhodes and an old pirate who had spent years chained to a Turkish oar. At the age of seventy-one, he was still a force to be reckoned with. He immediately began raising troops, hoarding supplies, and building up the defenses.

Malta held around seven thousand fighters altogether, 546 of which were knights. Three fortresses guarded the capitol, Birgu: St. Elmo, at the mouth of the harbor; the main castle of St. Angelo; and St. Michael on the peninsula of Seneglea.

The Turkish invasion force appeared on May 18, 1565, around thirty thousand strong. Command was divided between Mustafa Pasha, Piyale Pasha, and Turgut Reis. After some squabbling, they decided on a direct assault on the harbor, believing that small St. Elmo would capitulate after a few days.

The Siege However, the fortress proved tougher than expected. The massive Turkish guns soon destroyed its walls, but the Christian garrison—a few hundred men—held the defenses for more than three weeks. Under constant bombardment, exhausted, and massively outnumbered, they beat back wave after wave of manned assaults using flame weapons and grenades. When St. Elmo finally fell, the Turks had lost four thousand men, including Turgut Reis. The city of Birgu now came under steady bombardment, which would eventually kill thousands of civilians.

Furious at the costly delay, Mustafa massacred the defenders, disemboweled their officers, and floated the bodies towards St. Angelo. In response, de Valette killed his Turkish prisoners and shot their heads across the harbor.

On July 15, the Turks tackled Fort St. Michael. A hundred small boats approached over the harbor, while soldiers attacked by land. However, the knights had installed sea-level guns below St. Angelo, and these demolished the small fleet and drowned most of those aboard. Reinforced from Birgu, St. Michael drove back the attackers after a day of intense fighting.

On August 7, Mustafa staged another massive assault, breaching the walls and pouring into the city. Even the Grand Master left the fortress to fight in the streets. It seemed that Malta had fallen at last, but at that critical junction, a cavalry regiment charged from Mdina, a city in the center of the island. They fell on an Ottoman field hospital, butchering the sick and wounded within. The Turks believed that Italian reinforcements had arrived and so withdrew.

The Conflict Drags On Another direct assault failed, so the engineers went to work. The Turks set mines; the Knights set countermines. The Turks built a bridge and a siege tower, both of which the defenders managed to destroy. The siege had devolved into a weary stalemate.

By September, the Turks were thoroughly demoralized. Disease had run rampant in their camp through the punishing African summer, and the rains had begun, rendering their gunpowder arquebuses useless. Supply lines stretched thin across the sea, and the army was starving. They had lost over twenty thousand men; the Janissaries had mutinied. The Turks had already begun to withdraw when reinforcements finally arrived from

Sicily. However, after a brief rout at St. Paul's Bay on September 11, the remaining Ottomans fled.

The victory was much celebrated in Christendom. Money poured in to rebuild Malta, which had lost a third of its people. It was widely believed, then and now, that the knights' grim defense forestalled an Ottoman invasion of Europe.

Lepanto, October 7, 1571

In this naval engagement, a Christian fleet confronted the Ottoman navy at Lepanto off the Greek coast. In the pitched battle that followed, Western Europe temporarily decimated the sultan's sea power.

Provocation Sixteenth century Europe was a chaotic place, deeply divided both politically and religiously. Sultan Suleiman I, a masterful politician, took full advantage of the Christian disunity. By his death in 1566, he had conquered Hungary and had established the Ottoman Empire as masters of the Mediterranean Sea.

Though far less subtle than his father, Suleiman's son Selim II "the Drunk" pursued the same expansionist policies. To that end, he built up a huge fleet at Lepanto, on the Gulf of Patras. From there Turkish galleys launched raids against the coastal states of southern Italy, threatening Venice and Rome itself.

The Venetians had traditionally placated the sultan, preferring to trade with the Turks than to fight them. However, when the Ottomans seized Cyprus from them in 1570, Venice turned to their traditional enemies—Genoa, Spain, and the papacy—for help.

Responding to Venice's plea, Pope Pius V (1503–1572) sent out a general call to Catholic Europe to unite and defend the faith. Catholic Spain, Venice, Tuscany, Savoy, Rome, and the Knights of Malta answered with ships, forming the so-called Holy League. All told, the fleet contained more than two hundred galleys.

In October, news came that the Famagusta fortress on Cyprus had surrendered to the Turks. The Ottomans had promised safe conduct to the defenders, a promise they rescinded once inside. A general slaughter followed; the heads of the Venetian lords were displayed on the street, and the Christian commander was flayed alive.

Horrified, the Holy League decided to make directly for Lepanto, where the entire Ottoman fleet had gathered under the command of Ali Pasha. On October 7, 1571, the two forces met in a massive sea engagement.

Battle The exact numbers of galleys involved is not certain, though it seems that the Muslims slightly outnumbered the Christians. Both fleets arranged themselves in a crescent formation, and both held a small reserve force a distance behind.

The Holy League attacked first. In the front of the Christian line, commander Don Juan of Austria placed six giant *galleasses*. These ships were ungainly, but could each throw 326 pounds of ordnance in a broadside (an ordinary galley could typically fire ninety pounds).

The galleasses initially inflicted serious losses on the Muslim formation. Nonetheless, the Ottoman north wing managed to outflank their Christian counterparts, who took serious damage. The south wings also clashed violently, and initially the Turks had the best of it. Thereafter the battle devolved into a confused free-for-all. Savage hand-to-hand fighting erupted as galleys closed and boarded one another.

In the center, Don Juan's flagship the *Real* charged directly at Ali Pasha's flagship the *Sultana*. After a bloody struggle, Ali was killed and beheaded. The crucifix standard was hoisted on the Ottoman flagship, striking a serious blow to Muslim morale.

The battle raged for over six hours before the last surviving Ottoman admiral, Uluj Ali, salvaged what he could and sailed away. Before he withdrew, he set upon the flagship of the Knights of Malta, killing all but one of its crew.

Aftermath Uluj Ali bore no good news back to Constantinople. Only around forty of the Turks' galleys had escaped. The Christians seized over a hundred Ottoman ships; the rest were sunk or destroyed. Up to thirty thousand Muslims had been killed or captured. In his fury, the enraged sultan demanded a slaughter of all Venetians and Spaniards in Istanbul, but eventually his ministers managed to change his mind.

The Holy League had lost seventeen ships and around eight thousand men. Indeed, in terms of manpower they ended with more than they started, since they freed more than fifteen thousand Christian galley slaves.

When the news reached the Western world, Europe went wild with rejoicing. Don Juan was feted extravagantly as the defender of Christendom. The immoderate praise excited jealousy—accusations of vanity and ambition would haunt him for the rest of his life.

The victory at Lepanto greatly excited Western imagination and has inspired numerous painters and poets over the years. Novelist Miguel de Cervantes fought in the battle and described it as "the greatest day's work we have seen done in centuries."

The Holy League owed its victory to many factors, the most evident of these being superior gunnery. Not only did Western cannon have a longer range, but their guns could be pointed down to target enemy ships below the water line. At the same time, Western hulls were armored with brass and harder to penetrate.

The Ottoman navy began rebuilding at a frenzied pace, and they were soon menacing the North African shore once more. Nevertheless, Lepanto proved a decisive psychological victory for the West, whose technology was steadily advancing beyond the Turks'.

The famous Barbarossa Brothers, pirates who established Turkish rule in North Africa. © *Popperfoto/Alamy*

Vienna, 1683

In 1683, the Ottoman army once more bore down on Vienna, which the Ottoman sultan Suleiman had failed to take in 1529. A Christian coalition force rode to the city's defense and decisively turned back the Turks at the Battle of Kahlenberg on September 12.

The Koprulus After the reign of Suleiman the Magnificent, the Ottoman Empire underwent a long period of stagnation. Turkish government officials slowly became corrupt, perhaps taking their example from a string of weak, decadent, and mentally ill sultans. The Janissaries' power increased, while their allegiance to the throne waned—in 1622 they went so far as to assassinate Sultan Osman II.

The Ottomans underwent a brief resurgence during the reign of Mehmed IV (1642—1693). Mehmed himself had little to do with it—the sultan chiefly concerned himself with hunting—but his extraordinary grand viziers Mehmed Koprulu and Fazil Ahmed Koprulu once more pushed the boundaries of the Turkish Empire. In 1663, Ahmed led the army into Hungary, where he won a series of battles until he was pushed back at the Battle St. Gotthard. Despite the defeat, the campaign did not end in disaster; the harassed Austrians agreed to a twenty-year truce, upholding Ottoman rule in most of Hungary.

By the time the truce expired, Grand Vizier Kara "Black" Mustafa (1634–1683) had risen to power. What Kara lacked in military talent, he made up for in ambition and personal cruelty. Taking advantage of a Hungarian revolt against Austria, in 1682 Mustafa persuaded the sultan to declare war on Holy Roman Emperor Leopold I.

The Siege Begins

In April 1683, around 200,000 Ottomans cut a swath across Austria, taking the fortress at Győr and the villages of Heinburg and Perchtoldsdorf before reaching the walls of Vienna in mid-July. Kara had permitted indiscriminate slaughter of the Austrian citizenry; now he mounted prisoners' heads on pikes in view of the city.

To prepare for the upcoming assault, the Viennese demolished buildings outside their walls in order to better expose the Turks to the city's guns. The city's commander, Count Ernst Rüdiger von Starhemberg (1638–1701), defied Mustafa's demands for surrender. With a garrison of eleven thousand men, Starhemberg held the defenses for almost two months.

Given the Turks' numbers, even the most spirited defense could not have prevented them from sacking the city if they had attacked in force. However, Kara preferred a gradual approach. If his troops took the city, tradition demanded that they be allowed a three-day looting spree. In contrast, a negotiated surrender would give all of Vienna's riches to the sultan, a much better arrangement for Mustafa.

Because of the difficulty of transportation, the Ottoman army carried only light artillery, which could not penetrate Vienna's modern fortifications. Instead, the Turks employed sappers (engineers who dug trenches up to the city and laid mines under the walls). These succeeded in breaching the defenses several times, but in each case the Viennese threw up barricades and savagely defended them.

Nevertheless, by early September the garrison was desperate, starving, and exhausted. They were at the point of surrender when they saw smoke rising on the horizon, signaling that relief had come at last.

The Holy League

All the previous year, Leopold had tried to rally Christian Europe against the invasion. With the support of Pope Innocent XI, he had managed to persuade the German dukes of Bavaria, Saxony, and Lorraine to help him. Most significantly, he had entered into a defensive alliance with Jan III Sobieski (1629–1696), king of Poland. As Vienna labored under siege, the Christians assembled a multinational force of roughly sixty thousand to eighty thousand troops.

The Holy League, as they called themselves, crossed the Danube and took their places along Kahlenberg hill north of Vienna. In response, Kara redoubled his assaults on the city, determined to take the city before the newcomers were ready for a fight. An intense underground battle ensued between Turkish sappers and Austrian

counterminers. Finally, a massive bomb broke the walls on the morning of September 12, but it came too late; at five o'clock that morning, Jan Sobieki's troops had said mass and had begun to move.

Mustafa had failed to prepare for the relief force: the army had not entrenched, they were poorly deployed, and they had made no effort to prevent the enemy from reaching an advantageous position on the highlands. Once battle was joined, Mustafa compounded his error by splitting his forces. Unwilling to abandon the siege, he had his men fight on two sides at once.

The Austrians took the left wing by the river, the Germans formed the center, and the Polish cavalry swept down from the right. After hours of fighting, the Christians forced their way into the Ottoman camp, which scattered in panic. The Viennese garrison made a triumphant sortie; the Janissaries, caught between the two forces, were slaughtered in the trenches. By sunset the Turks were in full retreat. Startled by the quick victory and afraid of some trick, Sobieski did not order a pursuit until the next day.

Europe rejoiced, lionizing Sobieski, while Mehmed executed Mustafa for his failure. The battle marked the high tide of Ottoman expansion; never again would the Turks menace central Europe.

Zenta, September 11, 1697

In the late seventeenth century, an Austrian force led by Eugene of Savoy surprised and annihilated the Ottoman army at Zenta, effectively ending the Austro-Turkish War.

The Holy League

In 1683, a confederation of Christian powers rescued Vienna from an Ottoman siege. Catholic France abstained from this so-called Holy League; Paris had long allied itself with Constantinople against their mutual foe, Hapsburg Austria. The next year, however, the Treaty of Ratisbon temporarily ended hostilities between Louis XIV of France and the Holy Roman Empire. This allowed Holy Roman Emperor Leopold I to take offensive action against the Turks, which he did. The Holy League pushed the Turks out of Hungary and Transylvania, and in 1688 they retook Belgrade.

There the Christians' advance slowed, since in 1689 the Austrians joined the Great Alliance against France. The ensuing conflict (called the War of the Grand Alliance, War of the League of Augsburg, and the Nine Years War) diverted troops away from the Turkish front.

The Caged Sultans

In its middle years, the wealthy Ottoman Empire suffered from the decadence of its leaders. For example, Murad III (1546–1595) so indulged in his harem that he sired over one hundred children. As a result, his son Mehmed III (1566–1603), in accordance with a common Turkish practice, was obliged to murder nineteen brothers when he took power.

Horrified, Mehmed's successor Ahmed I (1590–1617) decided to change the policy of imperial fratricide. Thereafter, royal Ottoman males were locked in a *kafe* (cage), a secluded set of rooms in the Topkapi Palace. Only when—and if—they ascended to the throne could the princes experience the outside world.

As it turned out, this system did not produce particularly capable sultans. When Mehmed IV was deposed in 1687, he was replaced by his brother Suleiman II (1642–1691), who at the age of forty-five had spent thirty-nine years in the kafe. Thrust onto the throne with no training whatsoever, the poor confused man died four years later. A third brother, Ahmed II (1643–1695), had been caged forty-three years; he also survived only four years.

Ahmed's nephew, Mustafa II (1664–1703), proved of more vigorous stock. Determined to restore the sultanate to its former glory, he insisted on personally leading the army against the Austrians. Despite his total inexperience in military matters, Mustafa's enthusiasm met initial success: the Ottomans took several fortresses and drove the Austrians out of Temesvar (in Romania).

Turkey rejoiced at their sultan's victories, but they were not to last. Unfortunately, Mustafa's next campaign pitted him against one of the great military minds of their time, Eugene of Savoy (1663–1736).

Zenta Eugene was a younger son of French nobility. Snubbed by Louis XIV as a young man, he fled his homeland to enlist with the Austrians. Leopold I gave him a commission in the defense of Vienna in 1683, where he distinguished himself. Eugene quickly advanced in rank and notoriety, and Napoleon would later call him one of the greatest commanders of all time.

In 1697, when Eugene looked over his Hungarian troops—his first independent command—he was not pleased. His 55,000 soldiers were exhausted, hungry, and poorly equipped. They had not been paid for months, and they had orders to remain on the defensive and to avoid unnecessary risks.

Eugene cleaned up the Imperial army as best he could, then set about hunting the Turks. The Ottomans avoided him, however, and instead moved to take Szeged (in present-day Hungary). From there, Mustafa decided to build a pontoon bridge and cross the Tisca River into Transylvania.

Having learned of their plans from a prisoner, the Austrians rode to intercept them on September 11. They achieved total surprise at an opportune moment, for the Ottoman army was halfway across the river. The sultan had crossed first; he waited on the left bank with most of the cavalry, artillery, and baggage. This left the grand vizier on the right bank with only the infantry.

Eugene hastily formed his troops into a crescent formation and fell on the stranded vizier. As the Turks tried to flee, the Austrian right wing rode through the shallow part of the river and cut off access to the bridge. Then they proceeded to slaughter the Ottoman army while their sultan watched helplessly from the opposite

The first known standing army, the Janissaries of the Ottoman Empire, are shown in this engraving. © *Corbis*

bank. Around twenty thousand Turks were cut down; another ten thousand drowned.

To the general acclaim of Europe, Eugene sent a huge booty back to Vienna: three million piasters (Turkish money), thousands of carts and camels, and the grand vizier's seal of office. Then he went on to raid Bosnia and sack Sarajevo.

Mustafa returned despondent to Temesvar, his European army decimated. Luckily for him, the winter rains were beginning, and Leopold could not immediately press the victory. Nevertheless, the Treaty of Rijswijk was signed shortly afterwards, ending the war with France. Austria was now free to concentrate its efforts in the Balkans.

In 1699, the sultan agreed to the Peace of Karlowitz with Austria, Poland, Venice, and Russia. The Ottomans gave up control of almost all of Hungary and Transylvania, and ceded land to Poland and Venice.

⊕ Key Elements of Warcraft

Janissaries

No single factor contributed to the Ottomans' success so much as their elite military corps, the Janissaries, a standing army of formerly Christian slaves.

The word Janissary means "new soldier." It seems that they were first organized under Sultan Murad I in the fourteenth century. Initially the corps recruited European boys captured in battle. By 1383, however, the Empire instituted the devsirme; once every five years or so, the Janissaries collected boys from the age of eleven to eighteen from the Christian subject provinces. (At first the selection was made randomly, but later they took the best looking and the most promising.) It is estimated up to 300,000 children were abducted before 1676.

The boys were brought back to Istanbul and placed for some years with a family. After they had adopted Turkish culture, language, and religion, the brightest candidates were sent to serve in the palace. Others moved to the Janissary barracks, where they underwent strict military training. Cut off from family, forbidden to marry, and forbidden any other work, the Janissaries developed an intense *esprit de corps*, a samurai-like code of personal bravery and fanatic loyalty to the sultan.

Most of the Janissary soldiers came from the Balkans or from Greece. Islamic law forbade the enslavement of a Muslim, so native Turks could not join. Nor could the Janissaries' sons, since they were born Muslim—this system prevented the rise of a hereditary class.

Those collected by the devsirme were called "slaves of the gate," but their situation cannot be compared to other forms of slavery. The Janissaries held prestige and often power. Many grew rich from plunder, and some of them became high government officials.

Professional Soldiers   The Janissaries were a standing army, a rarity for the times. In the thirteenth century, most European states levied their peasants or hired swordsman in times of war. Conscriptions were of poor quality and mercenaries of questionable loyalty. Small wonder, then, that the Christians stood little chance. When it came to warfare, the Janissaries literally had nothing else to do.

For centuries, the Janissaries threw down fortresses and kingdoms, virtually undefeated. However, their very strength proved problematic for their masters. Their support was indispensable in the bloody business of succession; most sultans were thus in their debt. Nor did they hesitate to depose a ruler who stood in their way.

In this way, the Janissaries virtually controlled the sultanate by the sixteenth century. In 1566 they demanded the right to marry legally, and soon their sons were admitted. Native Turks, also, could buy commissions. All of this distracted the soldiers' attention from the battlefield, and before long the Ottomans' military prowess began to decline.

In 1622, Sultan Osman II tried to rectify the situation, proposing to create a more loyal native Turkish army. The Janissaries promptly revolted. They strangled the sultan and brought Mustafa I (1592–1639) back to the throne.

By the early nineteenth century, the Ottoman military had fallen behind Europe in terms of military power, and Sultan Selim III (1761–1808) made another desperate effort at reform. But the Janissaries, too deeply invested in their privileges, blocked the attempt. In 1807, Selim was deposed and killed one year later.

The Janissaries promoted Mustafa IV (1779–1808) to the throne. However, Selim's cousin Mahmud II (1785–1839) raised support and took power a year later. Mahmud was in no humor to tolerate the Janissaries' tantrums. He set to work forming a new army, and when the Janissaries inevitably rose in protest he had them slaughtered en masse by burning them alive in their barracks. The Turks, who by this time loathed the Janissaries, called the event "the Auspicious Day."

Cannons

Gunpowder weapons were first introduced to the West in the thirteenth century, resulting in a frenzied arms race throughout Europe and the Middle East. The cannons developed during this time completely changed the face of modern warfare.

The Black Powder   In 1249, English alchemist Roger Bacon recorded a recipe for a volatile combination of carbon, sulfur, and potassium nitrate (saltpeter). Mixed in the correct proportions and subjected to a flame, the powder exploded with dramatic effect. The discovery certainly did not originate with him—he writes of "a child's toy of sound and fire made in various parts of the world" that "can make such a noise that it seriously distresses the ears of men."

In fact, the Chinese had used gunpowder in fireworks since well before the eleventh century. The knowledge gradually spread across the Middle East before reaching the far West. While the Mongols probably used some forms of gunpowder weapons, it was the Europeans who would fully exploit the invention's potential for violence.

The earliest recorded use of cannon dates to 1324, at the siege of Metz in northern France. Shaped like a giant tilted vase, the cannon shot a bolt-like projectile. In 1326 the city of Florence commissioned some "cannons of metal" to defend the city walls.

From these simple beginnings, gunpowder weapons underwent a rapid evolution, as kingdoms everywhere scrambled to outdo each other. Initially, bell founders cast small cannon in lightweight bronze, but a burgeoning cannon industry soon developed iron models. Bolt projectiles were replaced by giant stones, and then by cheaper cast iron cannonballs.

The new technology completely revolutionized siege warfare. With cannon, fortresses previously thought to be nigh-impregnable could be taken within a month. Ancient castles and towns had to completely redesign their fortifications. It was not an easy task—cannon could not be effectively mounted on existing fortifications because the recoil would damage medieval walls. Engineers had to cut gun ports into the sides of the fortress to effectively target the besieging army.

On the attacking side, trebuchets and battering rams declined in importance. In their place, gargantuan cannons called bombards became popular among those who could afford them. Manned by teams of as many as twenty men, they hurled enormous stones a great distance, and it was said that their noise alone could demoralize the enemy.

Field Cannon Before long, the enormous cannons began to shrink again. Lighter, wagon-mounted guns were developed that could be carried onto the battlefield. These guns were dangerous even for their handlers; small imperfections in the barrel could cause them to explode with deadly consequence. Nevertheless, the Hussites used field cannon to great success in the fifteenth century. When deploying their troops, they would circle the gun carts into an impromptu armed fortress called a *Wagenburg*, which could be held against an enemy charge.

Cannon leveled the battlefield, just as it leveled castle walls. Previously, war casualties reflected the iniquities of the feudal class system. The nobility—mounted, trained in personal combat, and sporting heavy armor—stood a far better chance of survival than the levied peasant foot soldiers. In the gunpowder age, death was more democratic, and victory favored those who invested in technology.

The Ottoman Arsenal The most famous of the early bombards was cast for Mehmed II by one of the most renowned cannon-smiths of the age, a Hungarian engineer named Urban. When the beleaguered Byzantine Emperor could not afford his services, Urban applied to the Ottoman court. The sultan took a modern approach to warfare, poring over manuals on siege techniques and consulting with military experts from all around the world.

Urban's first task was to arm the sultan's new fortress at Boghaz Kesen guarding the straits of the Bosphorus. The gun was finished in three months and passed its first test with flying colors, sinking a Venetian ship that refused to pay the Ottoman toll.

Delighted, Mehmed asked for an even larger gun, to be used on the walls of Constantinople in 1453. This monster gun, nicknamed "Basilica" by the Turks, measured twenty-six feet long and eight inches across, and could throw a 12,000-pound stone over a mile.

Mehmed had to level the roads to carry Basilica into battle. Because of its great weight the barrel cooled slowly, and it could only be fired six times in a day. Nevertheless, it was this great gun, combined with the rest of the Ottomans' smaller artillery, which eventually broke through the city's defenses.

The Ottomans continued to acquire the most recent weaponry for their armies, and their armies' success meant that they could afford to do so. Advanced artillery ensured the sultan's victory over the Persians and the Mamluks in the sixteenth century.

However, with the exploitation of the New World, Europe's economy (and therefore its armaments) began to surpass the Turks. Superior batteries contributed to the Holy League's victory over the Turkish fleet at Lepanto in 1571 and at Vienna in 1683.

Small Firearms

After the introduction of gunpowder, medieval Europe and the Ottoman Empire quickly embraced cannons and field artillery. More slowly but just as inexorably, they also developed handheld gunpowder weapons. Just as cannons revolutionized siege warfare, small firearms changed the face of the battlefield.

The Arms Race The Chinese first invented firearms sometime in the thirteenth century. It is suspected that the weapons traveled through the Mongols and the Turks before reaching the European courts. For the most part, Asian and African nations did not much develop their own guns. Rather, they tended to copy the most recent firearm design from the West, where centuries of warfare constantly refined the process.

Weapon technology spread in a variety of ways. For instance, the victors in a battle usually captured some of the enemy's weapons. More commonly, the technology was bought or traded in exchange for help against a common foe. In order to keep the Turks busy, for example, renaissance Christians gave guns to the Persians. Later, the Ottomans armed the Uzbeks against the Russians.

Handheld firearms appeared in Europe in the fourteenth century (the first reference to a "hand gonne" is found in a 1388 English document), but for a long time they were not very popular, having neither the accuracy nor the range of a bow. A good archer could fire ten arrows a minute, while a gunner needed several minutes to reload a primitive gun. Furthermore, early guns were so heavy that the soldier had to carry a forked metal stand to hold the barrel up.

Nevertheless, handheld firearms gradually pushed their way into the renaissance arsenal. After all, it took years to produce a good archer—gunners could be rapidly trained, poorly paid, easily sacrificed, and quickly replaced.

Lock, Stock, and Barrel As demand grew, handheld firearms underwent a rapid and comprehensive evolution, gradually becoming more effective. Early gun butts were originally straight and held to the chest, as a result of which the recoil often knocked over the gunner. In Germany they began to manufacture bent stocks, which could be rested against the shoulder. Such a gun came to be known as an arquebus (derived from a French word for "hook.")

The name may equally have derived from the arquebus' curved firing mechanism, the matchlock. Previous to its invention, soldiers had fired their guns by touching a lit match into the flash pan to ignite the gunpowder. This process required holding the heavy weapon with one hand, which made it difficult to aim. A matchlock arquebus, on the other hand, sported an S-shaped lever with a burning match on one end. When the trigger was pulled, the lever snapped down on the flash pan and fired the shot. A gunner could hold an arquebus with both hands and sight his target along the barrel. On the other hand, the lever match had to burn constantly, so arquebusses could not function well in the rain.

These deficiencies were addressed by the wheel-lock, with an intricate clock-like mechanism, and then by the cheaper flintlock, which created a spark by striking a piece of flint. These weapons did not smoke, so the enemy could not find their location as easily.

Barrels grew lighter as metalworking techniques improved. Sometime in the fifteenth century, gun manufacturers learned to score a spiral on the insides of a barrel—a process called rifling. This gave the ball spin and greater accuracy. Snipers used rifles from a distance, while the average foot soldier carried the cheaper smoothbore musket.

The Gunpowder Battlefield

The flintlock musket, which could put a lead bullet through plate armor a hundred yards away, swept all earlier technologies from the battlefield. Swords, halberds, crossbows, and longbows all gradually gave way to the musketeer. Only the pike remained for a while, deployed in front of the gunmen to protect them against a charge. Later, even the pike would be combined into the firearm in the form of a bayonet.

By the seventeenth century, a musket could be fired once in two minutes. Given their range, this afforded only one volley against an oncoming cavalry charge. Nevertheless, a large enough artillery volley would usually beat back the horses. The age of cavalry had begun to decline, giving way to the infantry.

Given the slowness and inaccuracy of firearms, the size of the infantry was of vital importance. Before long, standing armies swelled in size throughout Europe. Arming and feeding so many soldiers could strain a kingdom's treasury, so from that point on, the nation with the strongest economy had an overwhelming advantage in war.

Privateers

Piracy, defined as robbery on the high seas, has existed ever since man first ventured onto those seas. The sixteenth century gave the old story a twist; governments decided to harness pirates as a branch of the military. Kings commissioned captains to plunder another country's merchant shipping and seaports. This "legitimized" pirate, now called a privateer, would (theoretically) leave his own countrymen in peace while he waged a kind of economic warfare against the enemy.

Motivations

Some privateers, like Britain's Sir Francis Drake (c. 1540–1596), were recognized as heroes and given official positions in their national navies. Others were opportunist adventurers, almost as despised at home as they were abroad. Some, most notably the Knights of St. John, fought for religious rather than for political ideals, as did the famed Ottoman admirals Heyreddin Barbarossa, Turgus Reis, and Uluj Ali.

For sovereigns, privateering was appealing in that it was effective and cheap. Privateers earned their living from the ships they captured—their prizes. As plunder from the New World began to flow back to Europe, a privateer stood to become very wealthy indeed.

Contrary to legend, privateers were not interested only in gold bullion or pieces of eight. They could usually sell the prize ship herself to the regular navy, as well as all of the cargo. A lucrative human trade also existed. Privateers demanded enormous ransoms for wealthy prisoners. Others were not so lucky. Any Christian could be sold in the Muslim slave markets, and blacks of any faith fetched a high price in the Christian Americas. Both sides took thousands of galley slaves.

The Barbary States

A booming industry needs a place to do business. Christian privateers repaired to various fortified cities: La Rochelle in western France, Leghorn in Italy, and Valetta, which was founded on the ruins of Birgu on Malta. The Muslims likewise had their ports of call. The most important of these were located on the coast of the Mahgreb, the thinly populated desert of Northern Africa. There, the cities of Tunis, Tripoli, and Algiers began as vassals of the Turkish sultan, and their privateers fought on the western front of his war against the Hapsburgs.

Algiers, in particular, became the quintessential buccaneer port, providing a thriving market in stolen goods, slaves, prostitutes, ships, and weapons. Not only Turks, but renegade Christians joined the city's *taife reisi* (corsair's guild).

Privateering was ultimately a business venture, and a big one. Between 1560 and 1565, Barbary corsairs all but shut down mercantile shipping to Italy and Greece. Having cleared those waters, they attacked the coast of France, despite that country's formal alliance with the Ottoman Empire.

The pattern of independence continued as time went on. In fact, after 1580 Constantinople exerted little actual control. When the Ottomans signed a truce with the Spanish in 1581, the Barbary States paid no attention whatsoever. After all, war against the infidel was the foundation of their economies.

Thus the Barbary privateers continued to ply their trade until the beginning of the nineteenth century. It is estimated that in their three hundred years of operation, they enslaved anywhere from one to two million Christians. In 1631, a Barbary raid carried away almost every person in the village of Baltimore in Ireland.

So successful were the Barbary States that European countries often found it easier to pay a "tribute" than to fight the corsairs. By 1700, the British, French, and Dutch had treaties in place to protect their maritime trade. These treaties actually gave them a significant advantage over the weaker nations, who did not have the muscle to enforce any agreements. In other words, the great Christian naval powers came to use the Barbary as privateers against their economic rivals.

One such rival was the fledgling United States, who paid tribute to Tripoli from 1799 to 1801. However, Thomas Jefferson refused to submit to the humiliation and refused the payment. In response, the ruler of Tripoli declared war. From 1801 to 1815, the United States, with their newly formed Marine Corps, fought and defeated the Barbary pirates on "the shores of Tripoli." Shortly afterwards, Europe would force Tunis, Morocco, and Algiers to abandon piracy as a way of life.

⊕ Impact of the Rise and Fall of the Ottoman Empire

No dynasty as long and powerful as the Ottoman Empire could fail to leave a mark on world history. Osman's legacy is varied and complex.

Arguably, the Turks made their greatest impact in the art of war. Their standing Janissary army inspired awe from all quarters, not only for their ferocity but for their iron discipline, professional leadership, and up-to-date technology. The Ottomans were also among the first to employ massive artillery in siege warfare. The early sultans invested in their military in payment, in training, in prestige, and in equipment. Europe, after enduring repeated drumming from their "barbarian" neighbors, learned this lesson the hard way.

From their earliest days, the Turks considered themselves the vanguard of Islam's holy war against the infidel. They were unapologetically aggressive, and for centuries, Christendom justly feared them. While it is true that the Janissaries cut a path of atrocities through Eastern Europe, they were no worse than Christian armies in that regard.

Culturally, the Ottomans were in many ways progressive. Compared to the excesses of the Inquisition, the Ottomans were fairly tolerant of different ethnicities, cultures, and religions within their borders. Their complex code of law was much admired. Rather perversely, their extensive slave system gave rise to a true meritocracy; positions were not granted out of nepotism, as in Europe, but often given to the best slave for the job.

At her zenith, Turkey was the virtual center of the civilized world, where emissaries from India and Persia rubbed elbows with envoys from Italy, Spain, and England. The genius of many nations flowed through Istanbul—Persian poetry, Arab philosophy and science, and Chinese technology. The Ottomans even preserved the dying echoes of ancient Rome and Byzantium. European culture also heavily influenced the Ottomans. This was in part due to their many Christian slaves, who occasionally became high officials in the sultan's court or favored wives in his harem.

Politically the Ottomans played their part in the tangled game that was European politics: installing puppet rulers in the Balkans, siding with the French against the Austrians, and financing the Protestants against the Catholics. Even the Barbary pirates, only nominally under the sultan's banner, participated in the ever-shifting web of alliances. The Christian nations may have misunderstood and maligned Turkey, but they respected her as a world power.

The West advanced in part because they learned from the Ottomans; the Ottomans declined largely because they failed to learn from the West. Their navy ruled the Mediterranean but did not venture far beyond it, so they missed out on the riches of the New World. Confident in their cultural superiority, the sultan's court paid little heed to rumblings of the Renaissance or the Enlightenment, and they soon found themselves scientifically and philosophically behind the times.

In the meantime, traditional Ottoman institutions crumbled. The military grew restless and corrupt, while nepotism and bribery ran rampant in the bureaucracy. The new sultans, freed from the Darwinian selection of compulsory fratricide, ranged from weak-willed incompetents to the mentally ill.

The implosion of the Ottoman Empire was to have long-lasting effects. Serbia and Bulgaria broke free of Turkish control in 1877, creating a power vacuum. This led to "the Eastern Question," as Austria, Russia, and Balkan nationalists strove to exert their influence in the region. Their bickering catalyzed the bloodbath of World War I.

Finally, old resentments still linger in the long memories of Eastern Europe and Central Asia. Serbians referenced the Ottoman oppression during the Kosovo Wars in the 1990s, and Muslims speak bitterly of ancient and present-day crusaders. Some people fear that the clash of civilizations between Christendom and Islam—fought for so long, and so hard, and to so little purpose—has yet to resolve itself.

BIBLIOGRAPHY

Books

Lord Kinross. *The Ottoman Centuries: The Rise and Fall of the Turkish Empire*. New York: Marrow Quill, 1977.

Newman, Andrew J. *Safavid Iran: Rebirth of a Persian Empire*. New York: I.B. Taurus and Co., 2006.

Web Site

De Re Militari: The Society for Medieval Military History "The Battle of Kosovo: Early Reports of Victory and Defeat" <http://www.deremilitari.org/resources/articles/emmert.htm> (Accessed July 2, 2007).

Introduction to the Mogul Conquest of India (1526–1707)

The Mogul Empire (1526–1857) was the most important of the Indian Islamic states and one of the greatest of the Indian empires. The state was founded during the years 1526–30 by Babur (1483–1530), a Turkish prince and military adventurer. Babur invaded India from his kingdom in Afghanistan at the invitation of regional rulers during the civil war that developed in the powerful Lodi Sultanate of Delhi on the accession of Sultan Ibrahim Lodi (?–1526) to his father's throne. Babur defeated Sultan Ibrahim at the battle of Panipat on April 20, 1526, declared himself emperor at Delhi, and proceeded to conquer a territory that extended across northern India from Afghanistan to the borders of Bengal.

Babur's empire was almost lost by his son, Humayan (1508–1556), who was driven into exile by a confederation of disaffected Afghani nobles led by Sher Shah Sur, the ruler of Bihar from 1540–45. Taking advantage of a succession struggle among the Afghani nobles, Humayan retook Delhi in 1555 and died shortly thereafter.

The empire passed to his son Akbar (1542–1606) who lived up to his European title, "The Great Mogul." During his long reign, Akbar expanded the boundaries of his empire across north and central India, from Afghanistan to the Deccan Plateau (southern India). His reign was characterized by the political, economic, and administrative unification of the empire and a policy of religious tolerance toward his non-Muslim subjects. Akbar was succeeded by Jahangir, who ruled from 1605–1627, and Shah Jahan, who ruled from 1627–1658.

The empire's last major ruler was Aurangzeb (1618–1707), who imprisoned his father and took the throne at the end of a fratricidal civil war in 1658. He ruled until 1707. Aurangzeb was the first emperor since Akbar to extend the empire's boundaries, conquering the Deccani sultanates in 1686 and 1687. By the end of his reign, Aurangzeb ruled more territory than any Indian monarch before or since. His military success was counter-balanced by a policy of returning to more stringent Islamic practices, which alienated his non-Muslim subjects and resulted in several rebellions, the most serious being the Sikh uprising in the 1670s. After peaking in the 1680s, Aurengzeb's power quickly declined. By 1700, the Marathas, Hindu warriors, ravaged the Deccan. The Rajputs—friends of the Moguls since Akbar's time—abandoned their old ties with the empire. The Sikhs and Jats of the Punjab, no longer content with vassal status, established independent regimes.

Following Aurangzeb's death, the empire was faced with challenges to its supremacy on all sides. The five states of the Maratha Confederacy controlled most of south India and had replaced the Moguls as the dominant power in the Gujarat region. Regional Muslim governors like the Nizam of Hyderabad paid token respect to the emperor at Delhi and claimed to rule in his name, but had effectively become independent states. European trading companies had created spheres of influence along the coast. In 1739, Nadir Shah, the ruler of Persia, invaded India and sacked Delhi. Thereafter, the Mogul emperor was no more than a puppet ruler. By the end of the eighteenth century, the Mogul emperor ruled at the pleasure of the British East India Company. The last emperor, Bahadur Shah, who ruled from 1837–1857, was deposed by the British and exiled to Yangon (Rangoon) after the violence of 1857, commonly referred to as the Indian Mutiny.

Mogul Conquest of India (1526–1707)

🌐 Major Figures

Babur

Zahir-ud-din Muhammad Babur (1483–1530) was the first Mogul ruler in India. He was originally a prince of the Timurid state of Ferghana in the area known as Transoxiana (modern day Uzbekistan and Tajikistan). He was descended from the two great Central Asian conquerors: Timur and, more distantly, Genghis Khan. Babur was both a talented soldier and an accomplished poet. His vividly written memoir, called the *Tuzuk-i-Baburi* or *Book of Babur*, gives a first-hand account of his conquest of India in prose and poetry.

Babur took the throne of Timur's fabled capital of Samarqand at the age of twelve, but soon lost his kingdom to yet another nomadic people from the steppes, the Uzbek tribes of Turkistan. In 1501, he deserted Samarqand for Tashkent, the first step on his flight toward Afghanistan, where he conquered a new state for himself, centered in Kabul. He re-captured Samarqand from the Uzbeks in 1511, but held it for less than a year. Unable to regain the throne of Transoxiana, he turned his attention south, to the fertile plains of northern India.

The riches of Hindustan were legendary among the Islamic states of Central Asia. The countryside was lush and the reputation of Indian manufactured goods was high. Drawn by rich crops, luxury fabrics, precious stones, and fine steel, Islamic armies had invaded northern India for generations, beginning with Muhammad of Ghazni, who raided India more than twenty times between 1000 and 1027, and ending with Timur's devastating attack on the Delhi sultanate in 1398. Some invaders had only pillaged; others had established flourishing Muslim states.

In January, 1519, Babur, driven by the relative poverty of Kabul, followed his great-grandfather Timur's example and led his first raid into the area now known as the Northwest Frontier province of Pakistan. The raid was successful. Babur reported in his memoirs "we took four hundred thousand shahrukhis [a gold coin weighing 4.72 grams] worth of cash and goods, distributed it to the army according to the number of liege men and returned to Kabul." Between 1519 and 1524, Babur led four such forays into Hindustan.

In 1524, the nature of Babur's raiding changed. The Lodi sultanate in Delhi had grown weak under the rule of Sultan Ibrahim. Ibrahim's rule was threatened by resistance in the Deccan Plateau region (in south central India), the formation of independent Hindu kingdoms, and revolts by his provincial governors. The governors of the Punjab and Sind invited Babur to help them overthrow the Sultan and re-establish their equality and independence within the sultanate. Rana Sanga, the leader of the powerful Rajput state of Mewar (now Udaipur in modern India), also allied himself with Babur against the Sultan.

Inviting Babur to attack the sultanate proved to be a mistake. Babur was only too willing to bring his armies into northern India. In his memoir, the first Mogul emperor wrote, "From the year 910 [1504–05 on the Western calendar] when Kabul was conquered, until this date, I craved Hindustan. Sometimes because my begs [high-ranking officers] had poor opinions, and sometimes because my brothers lacked cooperation, the Hindustan campaign had not been possible and the realm had not been conquered. Finally all such impediments had been removed."

Babur's first victory came in 1524, when he defended Lahore against Ibrahim's army. In 1525, Babur turned on his allies, captured Lahore, and annexed the Punjab. He went on to defeat Sultan Ibrahim Lodi at the battle of Panipat on April 20, 1526, and established himself as the ruler of Delhi. With the Lodi capital under his control, he swept on to capture the other great cities of the north: Gwalior, Kanauj and Jaunpur.

Foundation of the Mogul Empire The battle at Panipat is generally accepted as the official beginning of the Mogul empire, but Babur still faced opposition. Ibrahim's brother Mahmud escaped from the defeat at Panipat to raise an army in Bengal, and a coalition of Rajput chieftains and Muslim nobles gathered around Rana Sanga of Mewar, the principal chieftain of Rajputana.

Rana Sanga was a more serious opponent than Ibrahim. Sanga's much larger force had Babur's army surrounded at Khauna, a village less than forty miles west of Agra, but the Rajput leader waited too long. By the time the one-eyed, one-armed veteran was ready to attack, his confederacy had been undermined by caste rivalries and some of his allies had deserted him. On March 16, 1527, Babur broke through Sanga's line with a combination of artillery and mounted horsemen. Sanga was forced off the field. He was poisoned shortly after his defeat; Rajput's hopes for the restoration of Hindu power in North India died with him.

Babur then led his army east into Uttar Pradesh against Mahmud Lodi's Bengali and Afghan forces. With their defeat on May 6, 1529, the sultanate was dead and Babur was the master of northern India.

Babur was never comfortable in India. "Hindustan is a place of little charm," he complained. "There is no beauty in its people, no graceful social intercourse, no poetic talent or understanding, no etiquette, nobility, or manliness. The arts and crafts have no harmony or symmetry. There are no good horses, meat, grapes, melons, or other fruit. There is no ice, cold water, good food, or bread in the markets. There are no baths or madrasas [Islamic schools]. There are no candles, torches or candlesticks." In short, he concluded, "The one nice aspect of Hindustan is that it is a large country with lots of gold and money." He looked forward to returning to the mountains of Kabul once he had consolidated his control over his vast new empire.

Babur never returned to the mountains that he loved. He died on Agra on December 26, 1530, at the age of forty-seven after the sudden onset of an illness (exactly what type is unknown). According to chroniclers, he had called on Allah to take his life in exchange for that of his son, Humayan, who was seriously ill. He left Humayan a territory that stretched from the Oxus River to the border of Bengal and from the Himalayas to Gwalior.

Sultan Ibrahim Lodi

Sultan Ibrahim Lodi (?–1526) was the last ruler of the Lodi Sultanate of Delhi. His defeat by Babur at the battle of Panipat marked the end of the Delhi Sultanate and the beginning of the Mogul empire in India.

The Lodi dynasty was the last of a succession of five Turkish and Afghan dynasties collectively known as the Delhi Sultanate, founded when the Ghurid general Qutb-ud-din Aibak declared himself sultan in 1206. The first Lodi sultan, Buhlul Lodi, was a member of an Afghan family that had received control of the Sirhind district of the Punjab in return for their services in defending the sultanate's northwest frontiers. When

the last Sayyid sultan, Alam Shah, retired to the provincial city of Baduan in 1448, the nobles of Delhi invited Buhlul Lodi to defend the city against an attack by the ruler of Malwa. In 1451, unopposed by Alam Shah, Buhlul took the throne and became the first Afghan ruler of India. For the nearly forty years of his reign, Buhlul concentrated on re-establishing control over the independent Hindu and Muslim kingdoms that had broken away from the sultanate's control during the final years of the Sayyid dynasty. After Buhlul's death in 1489, his son, Sikander, continued his father's policy of re-building and consolidating the sultanate's power.

The Afghan nobles who followed Buhlul Lodi to Delhi were both the main prop of the Lodi dynasty and its most dangerous challenge. The first two Lodi sultans managed the inevitable disputes with the Afghan nobles by giving them large land grants, modifying the traditional autocracy of the sultanate to fit with Afghan ideas of independence, and appealing to Afghan loyalty.

Sultan Sikander died in 1517 and was succeeded by Ibrahim Lodi. Unlike his predecessors, Ibrahim asserted the absolute power of the sultan without regard to tribal feelings. Opposition to Ibrahim grew until it overwhelmed tribal rivalries. The problems with Afghan nobles that had simmered throughout the Lodi dynasty escalated into civil war. Ibrahim faced rebellion first in Bihar and then Lahore.

In 1523, Daulat Khan Lodi, the sultan's uncle and governor of the Punjab, learned that Ibrahim intended to remove him from office. Lacking the forces to defend himself, Daulat Khan asked Babur, the Turkish ruler of Kabul, to defend him against his nephew in exchange for recognizing Babur as his sovereign. In 1524, Babur successfully defended the Punjab capital of Lahore against Ibrahim's army. Over the course of the following year, he turned on his allies, captured Lahore, and annexed the Punjab to his own kingdom.

In 1526, with the Punjab thoroughly under his control and his northwestern borders secure, Babur directed his attention to Ibrahim Lodi and Delhi. He wrote in his memoirs, "[W]e placed our feet in the stirrup of resolve, grabbed the reins of trust in God, and directed ourselves against Sultan Ibrahim, son of Sultan Sikander son of Buhlul Lodi the Afghan, who controlled the city of Delhi and the realm of Hindustan at the time." Babur fought Sultan Ibrahim at Panipat, some miles northwest of Delhi, on April 20, 1526. The forces were unequally matched. Babur reported that Ibrahim had a standing army of 100,000 and nearly 1,000 elephants. Babur himself fielded only 12,000 men, including merchants and servants, but those 12,000 included experienced armed horsemen backed by Central Asian artillery. At day's end, the sultan and 15,000 of his men were dead. Babur went on to take the twin Lodi capitals of Delhi and Agra and declared himself the emperor of Muslim India.

Humayan

Humayan (1508–56), the second Mogul emperor, almost lost the north Indian empire that his father, Babur, had conquered.

Humayan was already an experienced commander when he inherited the Mogul empire in 1530 at the age of twenty-three. He had fought with his father against the Lodi dynasty and had led the campaign against Muhhamed Lodi, a member of the deposed dynasty who had captured Jaunpur. Despite his experience, Humayan was not as capable as is father. By all accounts, he was more interested in opium and astronomy than power.

Humayan's claim to the throne was immediately threatened. Jealous relatives, including his three younger brothers, contested his succession. The most concentrated of these attacks on his position came from his brother Kamran, who was the governor of Kabul; Humayan transferred the Punjab to Kamran in an unsuccessful effort to win his support. To the west, Bahadur Shah, the ruler of Gujarat and Malwa, which had been independent of Delhi for more than a century, provided shelter to Muhhamed Zaman Mirza, who had plotted against Humayan. To the east, his authority was challenged by the Afghan chieftains, who had never become reconciled to their loss of power after the fall of the Lodi dynasty, led by Sher Khan Sur.

Humayan led a series of successful campaigns against Bahadur Shah's territories. In 1535, he defeated the Gujarati ruler at Mandsaur. Bahadur Shah fled first to the capital of Malwa and then into Gujarat, where Humayan took Champaner, one of the strongest fortresses in Gujarat, after a four-month-long siege. The rising power of Sher Khan forced Humayan to abandon his gains in Gujarat to move against Sher Khan in Bihar.

Sher Khan was the son of a minor Afghan *jagadir* (landholder) in Bihar. Sultan Buhlul Lodi had invited his grandfather to India. When Babur invaded northern India, Sher Khan left the service of the governor of Bihar to join the Mogul army. When he heard rumors that Babur had threatened to arrest him because he looked ambitious and capable, he returned to his estates and entered the service of the Sultan of Bihar. Sher Khan took advantage of the disturbed conditions that followed Babur's death to assert his supremacy in Bihar. After 1536, he attempted to claim Bengal as well. Humayan managed to oust him from Bengal's capital in 1539.

Fraternal Squabbles and the Might of Sher Khan

The news that his brother, Hindal, had declared himself emperor in Agra drove Humayan to withdraw from Bengal during the rainy season. Hindal's rebellion was quelled by Kamran, who led troops against him from Kabul. Humayan's forces were caught by the monsoon on the way to Agra. He lost part of his army to extreme weather before being defeated by Sher Khan at Chausa. The two armies met for a final time at Kanauj in April,

1540. According to Mirza Haider, author of *The Tarikh-i-Rashidi* and a minor member of the Mogul dynasty, the remains of Humayan's army were so demoralized that they fled in panic as soon as Sher Khan's forces advanced.

Humayan fled to Rajputana and Sind, looking for aid against the Afghans. When he received no help there, the deposed emperor attempted to take Qandahar, which was ruled by his brother, Askari. Finally he took refuge with Shah Tahmasp of Persia. In 1544, at the head of a Persian force, Humayan defeated Askari at Qandahar. He turned the city over to the Persians as payment for their support. He went on to take Babur's old kingdom of Kabul from Kamran. He blinded Kamran and exiled both brothers to Mecca. Humayan now had a base from which to recover his lost empire.

Sher Khan had proclaimed himself the ruler of north India in 1539 after the battle of Chausa, taking the title of Sher Shah Adil. After defeating Humayan at Kanauj, he quickly conquered Malwa, Rajputana, and Sind. To guard against Mogul invasion, he built a line of forts in the northwest Punjab. Sher Shah ruled for only six years, but in that time established the administrative structure for an imperial state that lasted under the Moguls for almost two hundred years. He reformed the revenue system, built a network of roads across northern India, and equipped them with caravanserais (desert inns for traveling caravans) and wells for travelers.

Sher Shah was succeeded by his son, Islam Shah, in 1545. Islam Shah was a weak ruler and his disregard of the Afghan chieftains weakened the position of the Sur dynasty.

The succession struggles that followed Islam Shah's death in 1554 gave Humayan the opportunity for which he had been waiting. In 1555, Humayan led a Persian army into India and recaptured the Punjab, Agra, and Delhi.

Before he had a chance to consolidate his gains, Humayan fell to his death on the steps of his private observatory in Delhi in January 1556, leaving his newly regained empire to his thirteen-year-old son, Akbar.

Akbar

Akbar (1542–1606), known to his European contemporaries as "The Great Mogul," was the true architect of the Mogul Empire. The administrative systems and policies that he established were the basis of his dynasty and its successors for almost two hundred years.

Akbar was born in Sind on October 15, 1542, while his father, Humayan, was fleeing Sher Khan Sur. Akbar was raised at the fortress of Qandahar under the care of Bairam Khan, who was a trusted friend of his father. Raised in exile in Afghanistan, Akbar learned to hunt, ride, and fight, but did not learn to read or write, an anomaly in a dynasty noted for its devotion to the

Red Fort, Agra. Agra and Delhi were the twin capitals of Mogul India. *© Lindsay Hebberd/Corbis*

literary arts. Scholars have speculated that Akbar was dyslexic.

Early Years of Akbar's Reign

When Akbar inherited the throne in 1556 at the age of thirteen, the Mogul Empire was not much more than a disputed title and a foothold in northern India. Humayan had regained control of the Punjab, Delhi, and Agra less than a year before, but had not subdued members of the Sur family and their supporters. When the leaders of the Sur family recaptured Delhi and Agra, it seemed certain that Akbar's rule, and his life, would be short.

For the first four years of Akbar's reign, the real ruler of the empire was Bairam Khan, who served as his regent. Bairam Khan defeated the Sur armies at the second battle of Panipat on November 5, 1556, and recaptured Delhi and Agra. He then began to assert Mogul control over the rest of Hindustan. Having reduced the great fortress of Gwalior and annexed the province of Jaunpur, he was planning the conquest of Malwa when Akbar took the power into his own hands in 1560 at the age of 17. After a brief resistance, Bairam Khan left on a pilgrimage to Mecca. He never made it: he was killed by a band of Pathans in Gujarat in 1561.

Over the course of almost fifty years, Akbar expanded his empire to include all of northern India, largely at the expense of other Muslim dynasties in India, using a combination of warfare and statecraft. He annexed Malwa in 1560, Gondwana in 1564, and Mewar in 1567. He incorporated the powerful Muslim state of Gujarat into the empire in 1573, and he conquered the remaining Afghan strongholds in Bihar and Bengal in 1576.

Ruling Rajput

Akbar's treatment of the Rajput states is perhaps the best example of his ability to combine force with diplomacy. The Rajput chiefs had been the leaders of Hindu opposition to Muslim rule in India. Every ruler at Delhi had been constantly at war with them. Akbar recognized at the beginning of his reign that alliance with the Rajputs would be necessary if he was to successfully rule his empire. He took his first step toward such alliance in 1562 when he married the daughter of Raja Bharmal of Amber (now Jaipur) and recognized the Raja, his son, and grandson as members of the Mogul nobility.

Not every Rajput ruler was willing to become a vassal of the Moguls, however. Udai Singh, the Rana of Mewar and descendant of Rana Sanga, whom Babur had defeated at Khanauj in 1527, refused to recognize Akbar's authority. Akbar led his troops against the Rana's fort at Chitor in October 1567. Udai Singh fled to the Aravali hills before the siege began. When the city fell in February, 1568, Akbar ordered the massacre of its 30,000 defenders. Mewar's royal regalia were dragged back to Agra as symbols of the Mogul victory.

Further Rajput resistance was short-lived. Ranthambhor surrendered in March, 1569, and Kalinjar in August. By November, 1570, most of the Rajput states had sworn allegiance to Akbar; in many cases the allegiance was sealed by the voluntary marriage of Rajput daughters to members of the royal family. Only one Rajput ruler refused to submit. Udai Singh continued to hide in the Aravali hills until his death in 1572. He was succeeded by his son, Pratap Singh. Akbar's repeated attempts to capture Pratap Singh failed. The Rana (the title of the kings of Rajput were called) was still at large when he died in 1597. His son continued to resist Mogul dominance until 1614.

After the fall of Bengal and Bihar in 1576, Akbar did not leave his capital on a military expedition again until 1581, when his brother, Mirza Hakim, invaded the Punjab from his kingdom in Kabul. Akbar drove Mirza Hakim back to Kabul, but left him in control of the area until Mirza Hakim's death in 1585.

Expanding the Empire

Mirza Hakim's attack was the beginning of a long period of challenges from the outskirts of the empire. Some of the border tribes had risen against the Moguls. More importantly the Uzbeks, who had driven Babur out of Samarqand, had organized under the leadership of Abdullah Khan and threatened to invade the empire's northwest frontier. Akbar remained in the north until Abdullah Khan's death in 1598 removed the Uzbek threat. Using Lahore as a temporary capital, he extended his empire to the north, taking Orissa in 1592, Sind in 1593, Baluchistan in 1594, and Qandahar in 1595.

With most of northwest India firmly under his control, Akbar turned his attention to the independent Muslim kingdoms in the Deccan Plateau region of south central India. The sultanates of Ahmadnagar, Bidar, Bijapur, and Golconda had been founded in the fifteenth century following the disintegration of the Bahmani Sultanate. Beginning in 1591, Akbar had sent envoys to the sultanates four times, asking their rulers to recognize his suzerainty (control). They refused each time. In 1599, Akbar led troops into the Deccan and annexed the greater part of Ahmadnagar, though the province was never fully subjugated. The other sultanates retained their independence until they were conquered by Akbar's great grandson, Aurangzeb, in 1686 and 1687.

Akbar returned to Agra in May 1601. At the age of 59, his career of conquest was over. His last years were troubled by hostile relations with his only surviving son, Prince Salim, who declared himself emperor in Allahabad in 1601 while his father was still engaged in the Deccan.

Akbar fell ill in August 1605. Unable to diagnose his illness, the doctors suspected that he was being poisoned, possibly with diamond dust. He died on January 7, 1606, after almost fifty years on the throne. He was succeeded by Prince Salim, who reigned under the Persian name *Jahangir* (World Seizer) from 1605 to 1627. Jahangir was succeeded by Shah Jahan, who is best known for the construction of the Taj Mahal as a memorial to his wife.

Pratap Singh

Pratap Singh (1545–97), the fifty-second Rana (ruler) of Mewar, was the only major Rajput chieftain who refused alliance with the Mogul empire. His story, represented as a proto-nationalist fight against foreign invaders, was a source of inspiration for the nationalist movement in the twentieth century.

The Rajput state of Mewar, known today as Udaipur, had a long history of resisting Muslim rule in India. Rana Sanga, who came to the throne in 1509, battled successfully against the Muslim rulers of Gujarat and Malwa as well as the Lodi Sultanate. He led a confederacy of Rajput and Afghan nobility that seriously challenged Mogul ruler Babur's conquest of northern India until his defeat at Khanauj in 1527.

Rana Sanga's son, Udai Singh, not only refused to give a daughter in marriage to the Mogul dynasty and become a vassal of the Mogul empire, he also gave

refuge to Baz Bahadur, the fugitive sultan of Malwa. In retaliation, Mogul ruler Akbar marched on the Mewar fortress of Chitor in October 1567. Udai Singh fled to the Aravali Hills, leaving Chitor's defense in the hands of the commander of the garrison. Chitor stands on a high rock in the middle of a flat plain and was considered to be impregnable; however, the fortress fell in February 1568. Akbar ordered the massacre of 30,000 of its defenders, mostly non-combatants, and dragged Mewar's royal regalia back to Delhi as a symbol of victory. The fall of Chitor signaled the end of Rajput resistance. By 1570, Udai Singh was the only Rajput king who had not sworn alliance with the Mogul state.

Udai Singh built a new capital in the Girwar and made no effort to retake Mewar. The conflict with the Moguls was renewed after his death in 1572 by his son, Pratap Singh. (Pratap Singh's younger brother, Jagmal, joined Akbar's court after a failed bid for the throne of Mewar.)

Defeat at Haldighati Between 1572 and 1573, Akbar sent four missions to Pratap Singh to convince him to become a Mogul vassal. When diplomacy failed, Akbar sent an army against Mewar for a second time. Akbar's forces, led by the Rajput general Raja Man Singh of Amber, defeated the Rana and his allies at Haldighati Pass in 1576. Pratap Singh managed to escape the battlefield because the head of the Jhala clan, who had served the Ranas of Mewar for several generations, took the Rana's place under the royal insignia.

Pratap Singh learned from his failures at Haldighati. He abandoned direct battle with his enemy in favor of the guerrilla tactics that were better suited to both the landscape and his limited resources.

Reclaiming Lost Territories Akbar sent two more expeditions against the recalcitrant Rana in 1580 and 1584. Although both expeditions captured forts in Mewar, they failed at their primary objective. Both times Pratap Singh successfully evaded capture by retreating to the mountains. From 1585 on, preoccupation with the Punjab, unrest on the northwest frontier, and the threat of an Uzbek invasion prevented the Mogul emperor from devoting resources to an active campaign against an enemy who harassed and exhausted his forces with guerrilla tactics. Before his death from a hunting accident in 1597, the Rana had recovered all his territories except Chitor and Mandalgarh and founded a new capital at Chavand.

In 1600, Akbar sent troops led by Prince Salim (later the emperor Jahangir) and Raja Man Singh against Pratap's successor, Amar Singh. Salim defeated Amar Singh in early confrontations, but the Mogul forces once again failed to consolidate their victory into control over Mewar due to the Prince's subsequent revolt against his father. Amar continued the fight against the Moguls until 1614, when the Mogul army changed its tactics and began to take women and children prisoner. He surrendered to Jahangir and became a Mogul feudatory (one who holds land by feudal fee).

Rama Raya

Rama Raya (1542–1565) ruled the Hindu empire of Vijayanagar in the name of the emperor Sadashiva from 1543 to 1564. His defeat at the hands of the combined forces of the Deccani sultanates (sultanates located in the Deccan Plateau region of south central India) at the battle of Talikota ended the 200-year-old empire and opened the way for the Mogul conquest of the Deccan under Aurangzeb.

Vijayanagar, the "City of Victory," was the capital of a powerful Hindu kingdom of the same name that was founded in 1336. Vijayanagar's military strength closed the southern half of the Indian peninsula to Muslim control and dominated the politics of the Deccan for almost two centuries over the reign of three ruling dynasties. The empire reached its greatest extent during the reign of the poet-king Krishnadevaraya, who ruled from 1509 to 1529.

The vicious succession struggles that followed Krishnadevaraya's death convulsed Vijayanagar from 1530 to 1542. Not only the throne itself, but other powerful court positions changed hands over and over as a result of successive murders and military coups.

The power struggles came to a head in 1543. The young prince Venkata I had succeeded to his father's throne. His regent and maternal uncle, Salakaraju China Tirumala, began to plot to overthrow his nephew and make himself king. At the same time, Krishnadevaraya's son-in-law, Rama Raya, who had tried to seize the throne outright or as regent several times over the prior twelve years, made another bid for the throne in the name of Sadashiva, a young member of the ruling dynasty. He liberated the imprisoned Sadashiva, proclaimed him emperor, and sent an appeal to Ibrahim Adil Shah, the sultan of Bijapur, for help in establishing the young ruler on the throne.

Tirumala Takes the Throne In response, Adil Shah invaded Vijayanagar and advanced on the capital. Tirumala took advantage of the crisis to seize the throne. He defeated Adil Shah before the Muslim ruler reached Vijayanagar City and put the Muslim army to flight. He then attempted to consolidate his position by strangling his deposed nephew and massacring all the members of the royal family that he could lay hands on. With growing paranoia, he began to attack friend and foe alike.

Rama Raya gathered his forces to take action against Tirumala in the name of Sadashiva, proclaiming him to be Krishnadevaraya's lawful heir. Tirumala fought bitterly to keep the throne. He was finally defeated and put to death by Rama Raya at the battle of the Tungabhadra.

Regent and More Sadashiva took the throne in the middle of 1543. His succession was uncontested; Tirumala had destroyed all the other potential heirs. Until 1552, Rama Raya ruled the empire as regent. Not content with the power alone, he assumed royal titles as if he were the emperor. When Sadashiva came of age in 1552, he did not challenge Rama Raya but prudently recognized him as co-regent.

Under Rama Raya's rule, the relationship between Vijayanagar and the Muslim states of the Deccan began to change. The Hindu empire had been in continuous conflict with the Bahmani sultanate and its successors. Unlike his predecessors, Rama Raya involved himself in the conflicts between the five sultanates. More than once, he was invited by one of the sultanates to intervene in their affairs. His repeated armed assistance in deciding quarrels between the two dominant sultanates, Bijapur and Ahmadnagar, kept the balance of power between the sultanates stable. At the same time, Vijayanagar's power grew to such an extent that it seemed to threaten the safety of the Muslim kingdoms.

Although each of them had at one time been an ally of the Hindu ruler against the others, the Muslim rulers became alarmed at the threat posed by such a wealthy and powerful neighbor. They formed an alliance against Vijayanagar. The allied armies of the Deccan met and defeated the forces of Vijayanagar at the battle of Talikota, also known as the battle of Rakshasi-Tengadi, on January 23, 1565. Vijayanagar's army was practically annihilated. Rama Raya was captured on the battlefield and beheaded. The great city of Vijayanagar was plundered and destroyed. Although the last dynasty of Vijayanagar continued to rule smaller kingdoms in southern India for nearly a century, the "City of Victory" was no longer the dominant power in the Deccan.

Aurangzeb

The Mogul empire reached its greatest extent under Aurangzeb (1618–1707), who ruled from 1658 to 1707. His reign was marked by increasing religious intolerance and subsequent rebellions.

Aurangzeb gained the throne in July 1658 after leading a fratricidal civil war against his father, Shah Jahan, and the heir to the throne, his older brother, Dara Shikoh. Aurangzeb joined forces with his youngest brother, Murad, who was the governor of Gujarat. Together, they defeated Dara at Samugarh, several miles outside of Agra, on May 29. Dara fled to Lahore. Besieged by his sons, Shah Jahan surrendered on June 8 and was imprisoned by them.

Aurangzeb then moved against his brothers. He arrested Murad immediately after their father's surrender; three years later, Murad was decapitated on his brother's order. He drove a fourth brother, Shuja, the governor of Bengal, out of India and across the border into Burma. After Dara's final defeat, Aurangzeb delivered a box containing his brother's head to their father.

Dara Shikoh, the appointed successor of Shah Jahan, tried unsuccessfully to defend his right to the throne against his younger brother, Aurangzeb. *Werner Forman/Art Resource, NY*

With Shah Jahan still his captive, Aurangzeb had disposed of all possible rivals to the throne.

End of Religious Tolerance As soon as he was securely on the throne, Aurangzeb abandoned the policy of religious tolerance for Hindus that had been an element of Islamic Mogul rule from the time of Babur. He passed laws forbidding astrologers and alcohol and prohibited music at his court. More important from the standpoint of public opinion, he doubled the taxes on Hindu merchants and reduced the authority of his Hindu officers. Beginning in 1668, he ordered the destruction of Hindu temples and attempted to enforce all the penalties on Hindus called for under Shari'a law (law based on the Koran, the holy text of Islam), including the head tax on individual *dhimmi* (unbelievers). He even applied the dhimmi tax to Hindus serving in the Mogul army.

Religious Conflicts Aurangzeb's reign was marked by widespread revolt, brought about by a combination of religious reaction and significant increases in revenue demands. The destruction of a popular temple in 1669 triggered a major rebellion among Jat farmers in the Doab. Led by a *zamindar* (landholder) named Gokula,

peasants and minor landholders cooperated to throw out the Mogul tax collectors. Three years later, the Satnamis, a sect of Hindu peasants that revered the poet-saint Kabir, marched on Delhi, where they were massacred by Mogul artillery.

Aurangzeb inherited problems with the Sikhs, another religious group, who had supported Dara Sikoh's claim to the throne. Since the founding of the Sikh faith by Guru Nanak in the early sixteenth century, the community had flourished in the Punjab, drawing converts from both Hindu and Muslim peasant populations in the area. Mogul oppression and persecution converted the Sikhs from a peaceful sect into a militant order prepared to defend their faith with their lives.

For the first years of his reign, Aurangzeb kept the Sikh menace at bay by holding one of the Guru's sons hostage in Delhi. When the ninth Guru came to power, he was arrested and beheaded for refusing to convert to Islam. Guru Gobind Rai, the tenth and last Guru, vowed to avenge his father's death and to fight against Mogul tyranny. Gobind was said to have as many as twenty thousand supporters. Although the Mogul armies outnumbered the Sikhs, they were unable to subdue the militant sect.

An equally fierce opponent to Mogul rule emerged in Maharastra under the leadership of Shivaji Bhonsle. The Hindu mountaineers of the Maratha coastlands, who had served in both the armies and administrations of the Deccani sultanates (sultanates located in the Deccan Plateau region of south central India), were discontented with the new imperial regime. Led by Shivaji, the Marathas captured a chain of hill fortresses from which they raided both the Mogul territories in the Deccan and the sultanate of Bijapur. Malcontents from all over the Deccan, Hindu and Muslim alike, joined Shivaji's "mountain rats." They soon controlled a substantial portion of Maharastra.

In 1664, Shivaji sacked the port of Surat. Enraged, Aurangzeb sent a large army against the Maratha. Besieged in one of his mountain fortresses, Shivaji surrendered in 1665, giving up twenty-three of his twenty-five fortresses in exchange for a position in the imperial Mogul service. Once at Aurangzeb's court, Shivaji complained loudly that he had not been treated with sufficient respect and was arrested. He escaped in a laundry basket and made his way back to the Deccan, where he was greeted as a returning monarch. By 1670, he had recaptured most of his mountain fortresses. In 1674, he had himself crowned Chatrapati (Lord of the Universe). Shivaji ruled unmolested until his death in 1680.

The year Shivaji died, the Rajputs of Jodhpur and Mewar rebelled against Aurangzeb's rule after the emperor destroyed their temples and interfered with the royal succession in their states. Aurangzeb sent his son, Akbar, at the head of a large force to subdue the Rajput rebellion; Akbar decided instead to join forces with the rebels and declared himself emperor. Abandoned by his allies on the eve of battle, Akbar fled to the Deccan with a few of his followers and sought support from Shivaji's eldest son, Sambhaji.

Aurangzeb marched south to subdue the Deccan and capture the rebel prince. In March 1682, he established camp at Aurangabad, the Deccan capital he had built as a young prince, and began a series of campaigns against the Deccani sultanates and the Maratha guerrillas. The prince escaped his grasp. When Akbar saw Bijapur fall under his father's attack in 1686, he fled to Persia, where he lived in exile until his death.

In 1687, Golconda, the last of the Deccani sultanates, surrendered and was absorbed into the Mogul empire. Only the Marathas remained to oppose Aurangzeb's expansion south. At first, Sambhaji successfully used the same guerrilla tactics as his father to harass and hide from Aurangzeb's far superior forces. In 1689, Sambhaji was captured and tortured to death. His younger brother Raja Ram took the title of Chatrapati and continued the cause of Maratha independence until his own death in 1700. His widow, Tara Bai, continued the struggle.

When Aurangzeb died in 1707, his empire reached from Kashmir to Hyderabad, from Kabul to Assam, but it was ready to crumble, threatened by fraternal warfare, rebellious subjects, and the new European enclaves on the coast.

⊕ Major Battles

Panipat

The defeat of Sultan Ibrahim Lodi by Babur at the battle of Panipat on April 20, 1526, is often described as the beginning of the Mogul empire in India.

The Lodi sultanate in Delhi had grown weak under the rule of Sultan Ibrahim Lodi. In 1524, the governors who ruled the Punjab and Sind invited Babur to help defend them against the Sultan. Rana (ruler) Sanga, the leader of the powerful Rajput state of Mewar, also allied himself with Babur against the Sultan, agreeing to attack Delhi from the south and west while Babur attacked from the north.

Babur proved to be more dangerous to the Punjab and Sind than Sultan Ibrahim had been. In 1525, he turned on his allies, captured Lahore, and annexed the Punjab. With the northwest secured, he turned his attention to Sultan Ibrahim and Delhi.

The two armies met at Panipat on April 20, 1526. Their numbers were unequal. According to Babur's memoirs, the *Tuzuk-i-Baburi* or *Book of Babur*, Ibrahim fielded 100,00 men and 1,000 elephants. Babur had only 12,000 men, including non-combatants, but those 12,000 included experienced horsemen backed by good field artillery.

This miniature from a Persian manuscript shows the battle of Panipat between the armies of Babur and Sultan Ibrahim Lodi. *HIP/Art Resource, NY*

Babur placed his forces so that the town of Panipat sheltered his extreme right while his left was protected by a ditch and a barricade of felled trees. His center was strengthened by a line of about 700 carts tied together with rawhide ropes. Between every two carts were six to seven shields to protect his matchlock men and artillery. Space was left at regular intervals, the "distance of an arrow shot," wide enough for 100 to 150 cavalrymen to advance.

For eight days, the armies stood face to face. Small parties of Babur's men went on raiding parties as far as the enemy camp, but Ibrahim did not attack. On April 20, Babur sent out several thousand men on an abortive night raid. The next morning at dawn, the Afghan forces moved into battle array. Babur arranged his troops in the traditional formation used by Turco-Mongolian forces,

Panipat Revisited

Two other critical battles took place at Panipat under the Moguls. Bairam Khan, the regent who ruled India briefly following Humayan's death, defeated the Sur Dynasty armies there in 1556 and went on to re-capture Delhi and Agra in the name of Akbar. The Afghan ruler Ahmad Shah Abdali and a consortium of North Indian Muslim nobles defeated the Maratha Confederacy at Panipat in 1761, ending the Marathas' efforts to replace the Moguls on the throne of Delhi.

with his matchlock men and artillery along the front of the entire line, protected by the palisade of carts and breastworks, his infantry in front of the carts, and two flying columns at the extreme right and left of the line.

The Afghan army came straight on at a rapid march, then halted as they neared Babur's defenses, causing confusion in their own rear lines. Babur sent his flying columns to wheel around the Afghans and attack from the rear while his right and left wings charged straight on. After the artillery and matchlocks began to fire from the center, Ibrahim's center gave way. His right and left flanks were so hemmed in that they could neither advance nor retreat.

By noon, Sultan Ibrahim and 15,000 of his men were dead and the road was open to Delhi and Agra. Akbar lost no time in consolidating his victory. Prince Humayan was dispatched with a force to occupy Agra. Babur followed with the main body of the army and reached Delhi three days later, where he proclaimed himself emperor.

Talikota

The defeat of Rama Raya at the battle of Talikota, also known as the battle of Rakshasi-Tangedi, on January 23, 1565, meant the effective end of the powerful Hindu empire of Vijayanagar, which had stood as a bulwark against Muslim expansion to the south for two hundred years.

Under Rama Raya's leadership, Vijayanagar had become increasingly involved in the internecine quarrels of the Deccani sultanates (sultanates located in the Deccan Plateau of south central India). Vijayanagar's armed intervention in their disputes over successions and boundaries kept the balance of power between the Muslim states stable, ensuring that none of them could grow powerful enough to threaten their Hindu neighbor. Eventually, the leaders of the Deccani sultanates came to resent the growing influence of Vijayanagar. In 1564, the sultans of Ahmednagar, Bidar, Bijapur, and Golconda managed to put aside their differences for the first time and allied themselves against the growing threat of Vijayanagar.

The allied armies of the Deccani sultanates gathered on December 26, 1564, at the town of Talikota in Bijapur, about twenty-two miles north of the Krishna River, which served as a border between the sultanates and Vijayanagar. (The battle itself took place about twenty-five miles south of Talikota and sixty-two miles northwest of the Hindu capital.) Accounts from the Portuguese settlements at Goa estimated the size of the allied army to be 50,000 horse soldiers and 3,000 foot soldiers, led by generals from Ahmadnagar, Bijapur, and Golconda.

Rama Raya lost no time in making preparations to meet the united forces of the sultanate. Estimates of the size of the Hindu army differ from chronicle to chronicle, ranging from 70,000 to 100,000 horse soldiers and 90,000 to 600,000 infantry. Despite his age, variously reported as 70, 80, and 96, Rama Raya had himself carried to the battlefield in a litter to command Vijayanagar's forces in person, aided by his two younger brothers.

After an initial exchange of arrows between the vanguards of the two armies, both forces moved into battle array. Rama Raya put his brothers, Tirumala and Venkatadri, in charge of his right and left wings, while he himself commanded the center. Two thousand armed elephants and a thousand pieces of ordnance were placed at intervals along his line. Each of the three Muslim divisions was led by a general from a different sultanate. Ikhas Khan, an officer of Ahmadnagar, was posted with a force of mounted archers in front of the center division. Gun carriages holding 600 pieces of ordnance of different calibers were fastened together with strong chains and lined in three ranks behind the archers. The sultanates' elephants were placed at intervals in the main line of battle.

The losses on both sides were heavy, but the battle was short. The left wing of the Hindu army, commanded by Venkatadri, was the first to attack, driving back its Muslim counterpart under the leadership of Adi Adil Shah of Bijapur. After Venkatardri opened the attack, the action became general. Muslim forces retreated under the force of Vijayanagar's attack and then returned to battle. When several detachments of the Hindu army were sent against the Muslim center line, Ikhas Khan drew his company of archers together to conceal the Muslim artillery as the Hindus advanced. When Vijayanagar's forces were close to the heavy battery, the archers fell back and the artillery opened fire. Vijayanagar retreated in confusion, followed by 5,000 cavalry from Bijapur, who routed the center of the Hindu line.

At the height of the battle, two Muslim commanders deserted the Vijayanagar army, taking with them 70,000–80,000 men each. In the resulting confusion, Rama Raya was captured on the battlefield and beheaded. When his head was displayed on a lance, Vijayanagar's forces fled the field under the command of Rama Raya's brother, Tirumala. They retreated to Vijayanagar City, where they collected the puppet emperor Sadashiva, his throne, and the imperial treasure. Abandoning the capital, they fled further into Vijayanagar to the fort of Penukonda, 125 miles to the southeast.

The Muslim armies pursued the defeated army to the undefended capital. Vijayanagar City was plundered and destroyed. No eyewitness accounts of the sack of Vijayanagar exist, but the archaeological records speak for themselves. Fires were set in temples and gateways. Sculptures were smashed. Precious materials were looted. The city never recovered; its ruins, now known as Hampi, have stood vacant for more than 400 years.

About 100,000 men died in the battle and subsequent pursuit. The defeat at Talikota shattered the military strength of Vijayanagar. Although the last dynasty of Vijayanagar continued to rule smaller kingdoms in southern India for nearly a century, the "City of Victory" was no longer the dominant power in the Deccan.

The union of the Deccani sultanates did not survive. As soon as the threat of the great Hindu kingdom was gone, they resumed their territorial disputes and dynastic quarrels, leaving themselves open to the greater threat posed by the Mogul empire to the north.

Haldighati

The defeat of Pratap Singh, the Rana (ruler) of Mewar, at the Battle of Haldighati on June 21, 1576, was technically a Mogul victory. However, the Mogul general, Man Singh, was not able to establish control over the region or capture the Rana. Mewar did not become part of the Mogul Empire until 1617.

Although Pratap Singh's defiance of Mogul rule is often portrayed as an example of early Hindu nationalism, the reality is more complex. Pratap Singh's forces at the battle of Haldighati included Afghan nobles and Bhil tribesmen. The Mogul army was led by the Rajput general Raja Man Singh and included many Rajput soldiers.

Anticipating an attack by Mogul forces, Pratap Singh fortified strategic outposts throughout his stronghold in the Girwar and posted seasoned soldiers to defend the neck of the Haldighati. The Haldighati is a narrow mountain pass (*ghati*) in the hilly region of Mewar. Its rocks, when crushed, produce yellow sand that resembles the Indian spice turmeric, called *haldi* in Hindi. Before the construction of a modern highway, the mile and a half long pass was so narrow that two men could barely walk side by side through most of its length. It was here that Pratap Singh chose to force the inevitable battle with the army that Akbar had sent to defeat him.

According to an eyewitness account of the battle by the Muslim historian Badauni, the two generals marshaled their troops on June 18. The forces were well matched in numbers. Pratap Singh had about 3,000

The Impregnable Fortress of Vijayanagar City

Vijayanagar City survived almost two hundred years of constant conflict with the sultanates, although it was located on the edge of disputed territory. It was besieged a number of times, but it was only taken after the battle of Talikota when the undefended city was sacked and burned.

The landscape surrounding Vijayanagar provided a natural fortress for the city. The hills north of the Tungabhadra River provided protection from invaders. The river was almost impassable to the north and west.

According to the account of the Muslim writer Abdul Razzaq, the city was surrounded by seven stone walls. The remains of three concentric rings of stone can be seen at the ruins, more than six meters tall in some places. Their outer faces are made of gigantic blocks of granite fitted together without mortar. The inner faces are earth packed with rubble. There are rectangular bastions at regular intervals with lookout posts on top of the bastions to guard the approaches to the city.

horsemen, 2,000 Bhil bowmen on foot, 100 elephants, and 100 pike men, drummers, and trumpeters. Man Singh fielded 5,000 troops supported by elephants and the renowned Mogul artillery. The Mogul army was lined east to west along the neck of the ghati on a low, uneven plain called the Badshah Bagh, with Man Singh and his Rajput contingents at the center of the line and eighty skirmishers on the front line. Pratap Singh had arranged his forces just beyond the ghati's neck in the traditional Rajput formation of a three-part front line with a reserve behind the central division.

The Rana's troops quit their defensive position early on the morning of June 21. One wing charged the Mogul vanguard and dispersed it. This put the Rajputs in the Mogul army's left wing to flight. A second wave of Mewar horsemen, led by Pratap Singh himself, charged the Mogul troops at the entrance of the pass and forced them back, allowing Mewar's troops onto the Badshah Bagh.

Mogul forces in the vanguard, left, and center were forced to give up their positions. The Mogul right wing lured the Rana's troops out of the readily defended Haldighati and onto the wider plain of Raktalalai nearby. Mitar Khan, the commander of the Mogul rear guard, rallied his forces and sent the reserves to aid the vanguard.

Meanwhile, the center line of battle, under the commands of Man Singh and Pratap Singh, was in deadlock. Both sides deployed their elephant corps without affect. The confusion in the center lines was such that Badauni reports that he was unable to distinguish friendly Rajputs from hostile Rajputs and shot his arrows indiscriminately on the advice of the Muslim general Asaf Khan, who told him "on whatever side they may be killed, it will be a gain to Islam."

The battle lasted until mid-day, with only a few hundred casualties. Pratap Singh fled the field before the battle was over. His retreat was disguised by one of his captains, Jhala Bida, who held the Rana's regalia and was killed in his place. When Bida fell, the remnants of the Rana's regular forces retreated. Pratap Singh's Bhil allies harassed the Mogul camp throughout the night, plundering their provisions and setting fire to their store of fodder.

When Man Singh reached Gogonda, Pratap Singh's temporary capital, the day after the battle, the city was deserted. The Mogul troops occupied and fortified Gogonda, but found themselves trapped behind their own fortifications by the Rana's guerrilla tactics. Man Singh's forces were unable to occupy the region around Gogonda or capture Pratap Singh. With their supply lines cut, the Mogul troops were reduced to eating their own pack animals and the mangoes that grew abundantly in the town. The only tangible result of the Mogul victory was the capture of Ram Prasad, an elephant belonging to Pratap Singh that was renowned for its size and strength. Man Singh sent the captured elephant to Akbar as a trophy under the care of the historian Badauni and retreated to Ajmer in September 1576.

Akbar, suspecting a Rajput conspiracy, blamed Man Singh for the failure to capture the Rana and banished the general from the court for several years. Akbar occupied Gogonda himself in October 1576, determined to finish the job. Akbar stayed in Rajputana for six months but was no more successful at capturing Pratap Singh than his deputy had been.

Pratap Singh learned from his failures at Haldighati. He abandoned direct battle with his enemy in favor of the guerrilla tactics suited to both the landscape and his limited resources. Before his death in 1597, the Rana had recovered all his territories except Ajmer, Chitor and Mandalgarh.

⊕ Key Elements of Warcraft

Unique Indian Blades

The metal used in creating the famous blades of Damascus was imported from India. Indian steel was made by a special process that created a highly valued "watered" pattern on the blade. Hot crumbled iron was reheated in a crucible with charcoal heaped around it until the iron became partly recarbonized. When the iron was later drawn out on the anvil as steel, it showed a beautiful pattern of lines as a result of the crystallizing of the metal.

When the Mongol conqueror Timur captured Damascus in about 1400, he moved its skilled artisans to Samarqand. Damascus continued to be a distribution center for fine weapons, but Persia and India took the Syrian capital's place as the best manufacturers of fine

Sikh warriors wore up to six of the sharpened metal rings known as chakram on their conical turbans. *Victoria and Albert Museum, London/Art Resource, NY*

blades. Indian sword-making reached its height during the Mogul empire.

In addition to making fine swords, the swordsmiths of India created blades unique to the Indian sub-continent. Some of them include:

Baghnakh, or Tiger Claws Tiger claws were formed of five curved steel hooks connected to a flat bar of steel. The steel had rings on either end that fitted on the index and little fingers like brass knuckles. The baghnakh could be concealed by closing the hand over it. It was sometimes disguised by setting the steel rings with precious stones so that it looked like the wearer had on real rings. The weapon was used to tear open the victim's throat or belly, as a tiger might.

Bichwa, or Scorpion The bichwa was originally a Maratha weapon. It takes its name from its double-edged, double-curved blade, which is the shape of a scorpion's tail. The hilt is formed into a loop for the hand. Sometimes the bichwa was combined with tiger claws into a single weapon.

Bhuj, or Elephant Dagger The bhuj comes from the city of Bhuj in Kutch. Its blade is a little over an inch wide and about eight inches long, with an S-shaped edge. Its grip is a circular piece of steel more than twice as long as the blade. At the base of the blade is a stylized elephant's head. The bhuj was used for thrusting and piercing as well as for slashing and cutting. Its long grip made it well suited for two-handed use.

Chakra, or War Quoit Sometimes called sun and moon rings, chakras were thin, flat, steel rings sharpened on the outside edge. The sharpened edge could be either smooth or serrated. The warrior twirled the chakra around his forefinger, raised his hand above his head, and launched it. Chakras were a Sikh weapon. Sikh warriors carried as many as six at one time on the top of their high conical turbans or around their arms. Skilled users of the chakra could be accurate to a distance of about sixty yards.

Jamadhar, or Katar The jamadhar, sometimes called the katar, is a punch dagger. It was originally a Rajput blade, though the Moguls rapidly adopted it. It is a triangular blade with a cross bar grip and parallel side bars that extend up the forearms. The point is thickened. Most daggers are held perpendicular to the forearm and the thrust comes from the elbow or shoulder. The jamadhar is held by the cross grip, putting the blade in line with the forearm so that the thrust is a straight punch with the weight of the entire body behind it. When used properly, it can split open chain mail.

Kora and Kukhri The kora and kukhri are the famous blades carried by the Gurkhas of Nepal. The kora was the historical war weapon of the Gurkhas. It was, and still is, also used for the ritual decapitation of animals in religious ceremonies. It is a single edge blade that is narrow at the root, curves sharply forward, and widens abruptly at the tip. The kukhri is a short, heavy, forward-angled blade that broadens toward the tip. There is a small nick at the root of the blade with a projecting tooth at the bottom. It was used as a jungle and hunting knife as well as for war. The kukhri was carried in a belted sheath. A small sheath attached to the back of the larger sheath held two kukhri shaped implements: a blunt sharpening steel and a small skinning knife. According to Nepalese folklore, a Gurkha will never sheath his blade unless he draws blood with it. Both blades are heavier at the point, which gives force to a swung blow. There are documented cases of Gurkhas splitting through the head of a man and down into his chest with a single blow.

Maru The maru was a thrusting and parrying weapon used by the Marathas and the Bhil tribes. It was made of a pair of antelope horns fixed horizontally to a small parrying shield. The tips of the horns were covered with pointed steel caps. The shield acted as a handguard and was made of metal or leather.

Pata, or Gauntlet Sword The pata was a favorite sword of the Marathas. It was a long, double-edged, flexible blade with a metal gauntlet that covered the

Shivaji's Claws

The tiger claw is best known for its use by the Maratha leader, Shivaji. In 1659, the Bijapur sultanate sent an army of several thousand troops against the Maratha guerrillas under the leadership of Azfal Kahn. Azfal Khan trapped Shivaji in one of the Maratha's mountain forts. Shivaji agreed to an unarmed meeting with Azfal Khan to discuss the terms of a surrender. Shivaji came to the meeting wearing a cloak that covered his hands and carrying a scorpion tail dagger in one hand and a baghnakh on the other. Shivaji ripped out the Bijapur general's belly with his concealed baghnakh when they embraced. Shivaji's troops, lying in ambush, fell on the leaderless Bijapur army and defeated them.

arm almost to the elbow. The inside of the gauntlet was padded with velvet. Thin steel straps at the top of the gauntlet anchored it to the forearm. The swordsman would grip the sword by a crossbar inside the gauntlet so that the blade became an extension of the arm. The pata was useless for fencing, but was well-suited for an armed horseman who could use it as a lance as well as a sword.

Zafar Takiya, or Pillow Sword The zafar takiya was carried by Indian princes when they were giving audience. It was kept under the cushion in case of emergency. The hilt was crutch-shaped. Because they were used in a court setting, these blades were often elaborately decorated.

⊕ Impact on World History

The Mogul dynasty ruled northern India for 200 years. At its peak, the Mogul Empire covered more territory than any other Indian empire, recreating an ideal of India as a single political unity in that had not been realized since the Guptas ruled the sub-continent between 300 and 500.

Unlike the Safavid and Ottoman empires that developed in much the same period, the Moguls ruled over a population that was predominantly non-Muslim. Moreover, most of the Muslims in India were Hindu converts. The Mogul nobility were both a religious and ethnic minority within their own empire. Babur remained a Chagaty Turk who felt that "Hindustan is a place of little charm"; under his heirs, India and the Moguls alike were changed. The Mogul court and bureaucracy became a synthesis of Indian, Persian, and Turkish culture. Indian daughters were given in marriage to members of the Mogul dynasty. (At least two Mogul emperors had Rajput mothers.) Afghan nobles served in the Rajput armies and Rajput generals led Mogul troops. Hindu administrators worked in Persian language law courts. Persian miniature painters adapted motifs and techniques from the indigenous traditions. The Indian language of Urdu is a combination of Persian script and vocabulary with Hindi grammar and pronunciation. Law, administrative systems, literature, art, and architecture all benefited from this complex cultural blending.

But this cultural blending did not necessarily mean tolerance. Muslim rulers whipsawed between attraction and repugnance in their treatment of their non-Muslim subjects. Under some Mogul rulers, like Akbar, there was a large-scale assimilation of indigenous elements. Under others, most notably Aurangzeb, religious persecution divided the empire's population.

The Moguls' twin legacy of universalism and communalism fundamentally shaped the policies of their political successors, the British East India Company and, later, the British Empire. (The British even adapted the Indo-Islamic style of architecture for their own use.) Although they never conquered the Moguls' old power base, Afghanistan, the British ruled the sub-continent as a single imperial unit in the nineteenth and twentieth centuries. At the same time, they classified and divided different social groups within the Empire through the use of legal codes and ethnographic distinctions: Muslim and Hindu, military and non-military, urban and rural, westernized and non-westernized.

In the end, communalism proved to be the stronger force, leading to the partition of British India into the independent nations of India and Pakistan in 1947.

BIBLIOGRAPHY
Books

Babur, Emperor of Hindustan. *The Baburnama: Memoirs of Babur, Prince and Emperor*. Translated, edited and annotated by Wheeler M. Thackston. Oxford: Freer Gallery of Art and Oxford University Press, 1996.

Mathur, M.N., ed. *Battle of Haldighati*. Jodhpur: Rajasthani Granthagar, 1981.

Pant, G. N. *Catalogue of Edged Arms and Armor in the Salarjung Museum, Hyderabad*. Hyderabad: Salarjung Museum, 1989.

Paul, E. Jaiwant. *"By My Sword and Shield": Traditional Weapons of the Indian Warrior*. New Delhi: Roli Books, 1995.

Sharma, G.N. *Mewar and the Mughal Emperors (1526-1707 AD)*. Agra: Shiva Lala Agarwala & Co. Ltd., 1954.

Wolpert, Stanley. *A New History of India*. Third edition. Oxford: Oxford University Press, 1989.

Introduction to the Conquest of the Americas (Fifteenth and Sixteenth Centuries)

The Spanish conquest of the Americas began witlessly as a quest for a western route to Asia. What Christopher Columbus, sailing under the auspices of Queen Isabella of Castile, encountered in 1492 were not the Indies but islands off a continent later dubbed North America.

To gain the immeasurable wealth in gold, silver, and precious stones the region yielded, Spain took advantage of its superior weaponry and the deadliness of its diseases (the indigenous populations had no immunity to smallpox and other European illnesses carried to the Americas by the colonizers). In a short time, the Caribbean islands became Spanish colonies economically based on plantations and mines.

In 1518, an expedition sent by the governor of Cuba landed on mainland Mexico, even richer in gold than the islands. Inland lay the empire of the Aztecs, founded in the fourteenth century by three Aztec cities: Tenochtitlan, Texcoco, and Tlacopan. Tenochtitlan, a city on an island in Lake Texcoco, came to dominate this trio.

Hernán Cortés led the 1519 expedition that would defeat this empire. Through bloodshed and clever persuasion, he exploited the social fractures that existed in Mexico, gaining allies among the malcontent subjects of the Aztecs. The Aztec leader Moctezuma reluctantly greeted the strangers—whom he believed might possibly be gods—and, after much dithering, willingly if not happily surrendered himself into Spanish captivity.

By giving himself to the Spanish, Moctezuma surrendered the trust of his subjects. The Aztecs besieged the Spanish quartered in the city. In the summer of 1520, Moctezuma was killed and the Spanish escaped from Tenochtitlan in a bloody debacle known as *La Noche Triste* ("Sorrowful Night").

A short while later, the decisive victory achieved at the battle of Otumba boosted Spanish morale. Cortés returned to Tenochtitlan in 1521 and, after months of siege against which the new emperor Cuauhtémoc bravely held out, destroyed the city and its empire. Cortés thus founded Spanish Mexico.

The Aztecs were the first group to be vanquished, but they were by no means the last. Spanish forces conquered Guatemala, Honduras, Panama, and beyond. Francisco Pizarro (Cortés's cousin) and Pedro de Alvarado destroyed the Peruvian empire of the Incas.

Foundations for the imperial Inca period were laid centuries before, but the empire had been expanding aggressively for about a hundred years by the time the Spaniards arrived in 1531. After the battle of Cajamarca in 1532 and the execution of the Inca emperor Atahualpa, Pizarro and his men went on to reap the rewards of discord within the empire. They defeated the headless state and installed a brief succession of puppet emperors, native figureheads for the newly founded Spanish colony.

The second of these Peruvian emperors, Manco Inca, rebelled. Having founded a new kingdom called Vilcabamba, he and his successors harassed the Spaniards, who were also fighting among themselves. With the execution of the last Inca ruler, Tupac Amaru, Vilcabamba vanished in the jungle.

Events in Central and South America were paralleled by those in North America. The introduction of European agriculture and other technologies—and European diseases—allowed the English, French, and Dutch to gain toeholds, and then firm footing, among the indigenous cultures of the eastern seaboard. These regions became colonies, rich not in gold but in other resources such as timber. Harvesting these goods made the European nations and their colonies wealthy, even as it impoverished and all but destroyed the indigenous American populations. This combination of wealth and sacrifice laid the foundations from which would later rise such independent nations as Mexico, Guatemala, Peru, and Chile.

The Conquest of the Americas (Fifteenth and Sixteenth Centuries)

⊕ Major Figures

Hernán Cortés

Hernán Cortés (ca. 1484–1547) led the conquest of Mexico, which resulted in the defeat of the Aztec empire and the establishment of Spanish rule on the American mainland.

Before the Americas Cortés's parents were minor nobles named Martín Cortés de Monroy and Catalina Pizarro Altimarano (a relative of Francisco Pizarro, conqueror of Peru). The parents hoped that Cortés would choose law as his profession, but after only two years of study, he left the University of Salamanca. Cortés intended to assume a soldier's life in Italy, but an injury delayed his departure. When he finally did set sail in 1506, he went not to Italy but to the Americas.

Early Years in the New World After several years as a farmer, miner, and notary in Hispaniola, Cortés joined the 1511 Cuban campaign of Diego Velázquez. Here Cortés again worked as a notary, acquired land, and found gold, and he also married Catalina Suarez. Despite trouble between the two men, Velázquez appointed Cortés captain-general of the expedition to Yucatan in 1518. This required financial investment from Cortés, who set about making the arrangements. In early 1519, Velázquez changed his mind, but Cortés set sail anyway.

The Conquest of Mexico After a brief period at the island of Cozumel, the expedition proceeded to the mainland. Although vastly outnumbered, Cortés led his men, equipped with horses, guns, and Spanish military tactics, to victory against the Tabascans. The defeated Tabascans gave Cortés gold from a land they called "Mexico" and twenty slave girls, among them a young woman called La Malinche who served as interpreter and who later gave birth to Cortés's son.

Aware of the riches to be found inland, Cortés took his fleet up the coast to a site where he founded Villa Rica de la Vera Cruz. He then established a town

council to elect him chief justice and captain of the army. This was a crucial step, because by founding a colony Cortés removed himself from Velázquez's jurisdiction and put himself directly under that of the Spanish crown. Some members of his party considered this to be an act of rebellion, but in the end all threw their lots in with Cortés.

By the time he arrived at the Aztec capital, Tenochtitlan, in November 1519, Cortés had greatly increased the size of his forces. Through a series of bloody battles, he won the allegiance of the Totonacs, the Tlaxcala, and other groups who were willing to oppose the Aztecs. Lying to Moctezuma, Cortés claimed to be an emissary of Charles V, come to invite Moctezuma to become a vassal of a king who already ruled (as Cortés said) most of the world. The deaths of several Spaniards in a dispute with an Aztec vassal on the coast gave Cortés the opportunity to convince Moctezuma to surrender himself. Somewhat amazingly, Moctezuma complied, and so Cortés gained control of the emperor of the Aztecs.

But Velazquez had sent Pánfilo Narváez after him, forcing Cortés to leave the capital in May 1520, under the care of Pedro de Alvarado. After Cortés had dealt with Narváez, he returned to find Alvarado besieged by the Aztecs. The Spaniards escaped the city in a devastating retreat known as *La Noche Triste* ("Sorrowful Night"), but returned to besiege Tenochtitlan through the summer of 1571. After the siege was successful, Cortés razed the magnificent Aztec city and, upon its ruins, founded Mexico City.

Enterprises His victory won him appointment as governor in 1522, the same year La Malinche gave birth to his son Martín, and his wife Catalina died under questionable circumstances. (Cortés's possible guilt in the matter was debated by both his contemporaries and modern historians.) Cortés took advantage of his status to promote conversion of the local population to Christianity, which he had initiated even during the conquest. He encouraged the introduction of European crops and domestic animals. He also undertook the production of guns and artillery and authorized an expedition that sailed as far west as the Philippines.

The Campaign in Honduras Cortés dispatched Pedro de Alvarado to seize Guatemala and Cristóbal de Olid to take Honduras. Olid, under the influence of Cortés's old rival Velázquez, declared his independence from Spain, so Cortés, in the company of the new Aztec emperor Cuauhtémoc, went south to defeat him.

This brutal campaign lasted nearly two years. By the time Cortés caught up with the rebels, many of his soldiers were dead, Cuauhtémoc had been murdered, Cortés himself was wounded, and Olid had already been killed. Cortés returned to Mexico in 1526, to the surprise of many. They had thought him dead, and the government of Mexico was now in the control of others.

A Decline of Power A cloud of suspicion, generated by the purportedly suspicious deaths of two Spanish officials, fell over Cortés, whose enemies were generating rumors both in Mexico and in Spain. In spring of 1528, Cortés traveled to Spain hoping to convince Charles V to appoint him viceroy. The emperor granted him titles and what amounted to a huge land grant, but his bid for the viceroyship failed, and Cortés and his new wife, Juana de Zúñiga, returned to New Spain.

Even stripped of his formal high appointments, Cortés was wealthy and could send out expeditions. In 1534 he founded a pearl fishery in Baja California, but the new viceroy, Antonio de Mendoza, refused to let him seek out the "Seven Cities of Cíbola," now known to be pueblos in Arizona and New Mexico.

Frustrated, the conqueror of Mexico returned to Spain in 1540, only to discover that Charles V was away from the court. The following year Cortés joined a campaign to capture Algiers, a port in North Africa used as a base by a dangerous band of pirates. A shipwreck nearly cost him his life and did cost him five priceless carved Mexican emeralds. The undertaking also cost him a significant portion of his honor, when he was not invited to a war council at which it was decided to cancel the siege. Back in Spain, Cortés gave up on lawsuits he had pending and drafted his will. On December 2, 1547, he died. His remains were returned to Mexico.

Pedro de Alvarado

The Spanish conquistador Pedro de Alvarado (1485–1541) participated in the Spanish conquest of Mexico and led the conquest of Guatemala. During the former, his actions brought about a series of events culminating in the battle known as *La Noche Triste*.

Early Years in the West Indies Born in Badajoz, Spain, to a family of minor nobility, Pedro de Alvarado left to seek his fortune in the New World in 1510. Eight years later he joined Juan de Grijalva's expedition to the Yucatan, dispatched by Governor Diego Velázquez.

During this expedition, Alvarado disobeyed orders by navigating up a river when separated from the rest of the fleet. This was an early display of his typical brashness, a trait that would later cause great trouble for himself and his fellow Spaniards.

Grijalva discovered that the Yucatan was a peninsula of a mainland and that a gold-rich land called Mexico lay at the heart of it. Alvarado sailed back to Cuba with the news and the gold to prove it. In 1519, Velázquez arranged for another expedition, commanded by Hernán Cortés, with Alvarado as Cortés's lieutenant.

The Conquest of Mexico In the company of his four brothers, Alvarado sailed for Cozumel before the rest of the fleet, again without authorization. Cortés caught up the following day, and together the fleet set off for the mainland. The Spaniards penetrated Mexico quickly but not easily; by early November, using wits rather than weaponry, they occupied the Aztec island-capital Tenochtitlan and had the emperor Moctezuma as their privileged hostage.

The Aztecs seemed to like Alvarado, whose sense of humor they appreciated. When tallying Cortés's points in a game played between the Spaniard and the emperor, he would add to Cortés's score, an open bit of cheating that everyone found amusing because what Cortés won was given to the Aztec servants, and what Moctezuma won was given to the Spanish guards. However, this camaraderie would not last.

In late spring 1520, Alvarado found himself commanding a garrison of no more than 120 men in Tenochtitlan, while Cortés took the rest to fend off a rival party of conquistadors landed on the coast by Velázquez. The motivation for Alvarado's next display of unfortunate audacity will never be known for sure. Whether inspired by fear of an Aztec revolt or merely opportunism (humor aside, he was known for his brutality), Alvarado led a massacre of Aztec nobility during a religious celebration.

This precipitated a revolt that pinned the Spaniards in the city until Cortés returned with reinforcements. During La Noche Triste, the Spaniards escaped but only with a heavy loss of life. Alvarado brought up the rear and narrowly escaped death, but the story that he vaulted across a gap in the causeway by means of a pike is merely legend. By his own account, he crossed that gap on a beam.

After the siege and destruction of Tenochtitlan (in 1522), Alvarado was appointed *alcalde* (administrator) of Mexico City, a place founded upon the ruins of Tenochtitlan. Yet bureaucratic chains did not bind him to the city.

The Conquest of Guatemala Alvarado ventured farther south in 1522, at which time he subdued the Zapotecs and Mixtecs of the Oaxaca Valley. He went south again in 1523, taking an army into Guatemala for two years of campaigning. He made an alliance with the Cakchiquels, who helped him defeat their enemies (the

Engraving of Cortez attacking the city of Mexico.   © *Bettmann/Corbis*

Quiché), but the partnership disintegrated in the face of Alvarado's cruelty, and he spent several years putting down indigenous resistance. During this period he founded what became the colonial capital of Guatemala, Santiago de los Caballeros de Guatemala. In the course of his conquests, he was so badly wounded in one leg that it shortened, and he walked thereafter with a limp.

Last Years Alvarado sailed to Spain in 1526 and returned a married man bearing the titles of governor and captain-general of Guatemala. But he was widowed in 1528 before he and his new bride could reach Guatemala. By then, he had heard of the immense wealth to be had even farther south, in what is now Ecuador and Peru.

Although lacking royal sanction, Alvarado assembled a company of five hundred experienced Spaniards and thousands of Guatemalans and brought them toward the Inca city of Quito, a region already occupied by the forces of Francisco Pizarro and Diego de Almagro. Almagro hurried to the area and negotiated Alvarado's withdrawal. In return for a sizable sum of money (some sources put the amount at 120,000 gold coins), Alvarado surrendered most of his forces and returned home.

Word of this affair reached Charles V of Spain, who forgave Alvarado's indiscretion and granted him the title of governor of Honduras. While in Spain from 1537 to 1539, Alvarado also received papal permission to wed the sister of his late wife before sailing back to Guatemala. In 1541, the Viceroy of New Spain (as the Spanish colonies were called) sent him to aid the governor of Guadalajara, who was trying to suppress an uprising of the Cazcanes. While retreating from an unsuccessful attempt to take the peak of Nochixtlan, Alvarado's horse fell. Alvarado died of injuries sustained in this fall a week later.

His widow, Doña Beatriz de la Cueva, assumed her husband's title, becoming the only woman governor in the Spanish colonial Americas. Her reign lasted only a few days, cut short by the eruption of the volcano called De Agua, which destroyed the city of Guatemala and claimed many lives, including that of the new governor.

La Malinche

Also known as Malinali, Malintzin, and Doña Marina, La Malinche (c. 1505–1530 or 1551) served as an interpreter for the Spanish conquest of Mexico led by Hernán

Engraving of Pedro de Alvarado. © *Biblioteca Nacional, Madrid, Spain/The Bridgeman Art Library Duran Pedro de Alvarado, photograph.*

Cortés. After the defeat of the Aztecs, she became Cortés's lover and bore him a son.

Before the Spaniards Malinali, as she was originally named, was born into a Nahuatl-speaking family of high status. ("Malinche" derives from "Malintzin," a form of her name with an honorific suffix added.) Hernán Cortés related what La Malinche told him of her origins, an account recorded years later by his secretary, Francisco López de Gómara: La Malinche was stolen from her parents in a village near Coatzacoalcos by merchants during a war. By the account of Bernal Díaz (who was with Cortés in Mexico), her father was a chief who died. When her mother remarried, Malinali's stepfather (also a chief) sold her into slavery to prevent any possible problem with an inheritance when Malinali's mother bore him a son.

SLAVERY IN THE AMERICAS

At the time of the European discovery of the Americas, slavery was a well-established institution in both eastern and western hemispheres. The indigenous American populations derived slaves from military conquests, raids, or trading ventures. A man might even sell himself or his child into slavery for economic reasons.

Starting in the twelfth century, slavery became more important in Europe with the rise of labor-intensive sugar plantations in the Mediterranean area. Among Europe's slave population, one could also find Christian Eastern Europeans as well as Africans.

In the New World, Europeans initially found that local populations made convenient sources not only of slaves to ship back to Europe (Columbus returned from his voyages with enslaved "Indians") but to labor in New World mines and plantations. However, when introduced diseases decimated captured Native American populations, Europeans turned to sub-Saharan Africa.

The first license to ship African slaves to the Spanish colonies was authorized in 1501, and the shipment took place the following year. As the Americas were colonized and conquered by other nations, slavery followed and remained an economic mainstay into the nineteenth century.

The British abolished the institution in 1834. The American Civil War ended the practice in the United States, but it persisted in Cuba until 1886. The forced importation of African people into the Americas had profound effects on the New World cultures that arose during the colonial and post-colonial period.

Malinali's native language, Nahuatl, belongs to the Uto-Aztecan language group, one of several spoken in the region at the time of the Spanish conquest. Another language group from that time was Mayan; when the Spaniards encountered La Malinche, she was a slave of Mayan-speaking Tabascans, and she spoke not only her native Nahuatl but also the Tabascans' Mayan language.

Translator In 1519, Malinali found herself as one of twenty female slaves the Tabascans granted as a gesture of goodwill to the Spaniards who had come to explore and conquer the region. Hernán Cortés, leader of the expedition, had all twenty baptized and parceled out among his men. La Malinche, baptized "Marina," was given to Alonso Hernández de Puertocarrero. However, when Cortés saw her speaking to Nahuatl-speakers, whom none of the Spaniards understood, he realized her utility and reclaimed her from Puertocarrero.

Among Cortés's men was one man, Gerónimo de Aguilar, who had learned Mayan after being shipwrecked in the region in 1511. What the Aztecs spoke in Nahuatl, La Malinche translated into Mayan, which Aguilar then rendered into Spanish. Through the course

of her time with the Spaniards, she eventually learned enough Spanish to dispense with Aguilar.

In exchange for making the Aztecs friendly to the Spaniards by her speech, Cortés promised La Malinche "more than her liberty." Certainly such liberty as she enjoyed—traveling and moving among men and participating in privileged conversations of treaty—would have seemed exceptional, not only for the Spanish but for the Aztecs themselves.

La Malinche became Cortés's mouth and ears, relaying Cortés's lie that he was seeking to visit the Aztec emperor Moctezuma as an emissary from Charles V, emperor of (as Cortés claimed) most of the world. Her role in this Spanish subterfuge against Moctezuma and the other native peoples earned her a reputation as a traitor after Mexican nationalistic movements began in the nineteenth century. Díaz refers to her as a "a person of great importance," while Cortés in his letters and Gómara in his biography of Cortés downplayed her role. Whether traitor or saint, La Malinche was instrumental in the conquest.

Whatever inspiration lay behind her loyalty to Cortés, she served him faithfully throughout the campaign, accompanying him everywhere. More than just a translator, she provided Cortés with intelligence—noting, for example, that Moctezuma's capital city, Tenochtitlan, was situated on an island in a lake, and that the ruling Aztecs were newcomers in the region. When the Spanish were in the city of Cholula, a Cholulan woman offered La Malinche escape from a massacre about to occur. Although the woman also offered her son in marriage, La Malinche remained steadfast beside Cortés, whom she warned about the attack and who meted out a bloody punishment upon the Cholulans. Nor, does it seem, was La Malinche above taking some degree of initiative, as she exhorted the Aztecs to bring food and water to the tired Spaniards and advised Moctezuma to surrender himself into Spanish custody to spare his life.

After the Conquest In 1522, about ten months after the siege of Tenochtitlan, La Malinche gave birth to Cortés's son, named Martín after Cortés's father. He recognized the child as his own and sent him to Spain.

Cortés's lawful wife joined him in Mexico, and La Malinche came to the end of her usefulness. La Malinche was married off to a Spaniard named Juan Jaramillo, by whom she had a daughter named Marina. Scholars do not agree on the date of La Malinche's death. Some believe that she died in 1529 or 1530, while others suggest that she lived until 1551.

Moctezuma

Known popularly as Montezuma, Moctezuma II (c. 1467 or c. 1480–1520;) ruled the Aztec empire when the Spaniards discovered mainland Mexico and began their conquest. Moctezuma died in Spanish custody.

The murder of Francisco Pizarro, by a supporter of Diego de Almagro. *Bildarchiv Preussischer Kulturbesitz/Art Resource, NY*

Moctezuma's Road to Power Moctezuma's father was mostly likely the emperor (or "Speaker") Axayacatl. Upon Axayacatl's death in battle in 1481, Moctezuma's uncle Tizoc III was chosen emperor, and he was succeeded in 1486 by another uncle, Ahuitzotl. Ahuitzotl added to the great pyramid at Tenochtitlan and to obtain victims for sacrifice, Ahuitzotl pushed his reach as far south as Guatemala. Ahuitzotl died in 1502, either from a concussion sustained in an accident or from disease contracted on campaign.

Moctezuma (also known as Motechuzoma and Montezuma) was a practiced warrior as well as a priest; this experience, coupled with his noted eloquence, probably contributed to his election as emperor in 1502. He promoted a new social exclusivity, limiting access to temple colleges and official appointments to members of the highest social status, contrary to the policies of his predecessors.

Known for stubbornness and displaying a tendency for perfectionism and deep religious devotion, Moctezuma sought obedience through the promotion of fear. Although he was not as aggressive in campaigning as his predecessor, he was said to have remarked that not being in battle was the same as being idle. He was not popular with his vassals.

The Spaniards in Mexico Presented in 1518 with evidence of strange-looking foreigners on the coast (Spaniards, yet unknown to the Aztecs), Moctezuma's reactions were more ritual than tactical. He consulted with priests and considered erecting a new temple complex to the war-god Huitzilopochtli. He also killed his consultants if he did not care for their replies. Gifts of Spanish goods (beads and biscuits), did not particularly impress him, but these strange-looking foreigners who had characteristics of divine beings worried him.

In 1519, the next encounter between Moctezuma's vassals and the Spaniards—led by Hernán Cortés and accompanied by firearms, horses, and large dogs—frightened Moctezuma considerably more. This time the strangers had not just come and gone away, which is what Moctezuma himself contemplated doing. The year 1519 was noted in the Aztec calendar as one in which the wind-god Quetzalcoatl might strike at the emperor. This and many other troubling coincidences and omens (Quetzalcoatl was neither the only, nor the most dangerous, deity with whom the Spaniards might have been associated) were greatly alarming. It was perhaps not surprising for a devout man such as Moctezuma to seek a divine explanation for the Spaniards' appearance.

Yet even as the possibly divine Spaniards approached, Moctezuma vacillated between welcoming or murdering them. Moctezuma opted for the former, but he tried to minimize the effect of the Spaniards' approach by forbidding crowds from watching their approach to Tenochtitlan. This order was not strictly obeyed, and in the city great numbers of onlookers watched as the strangers crossed the causeway and entered the island-city. Moctezuma and his courtiers met Cortés in November. He housed his guests in a palace formerly occupied by his father, Axayacatl.

A Hostage Emperor

Even the Spanish eyewitnesses differ in their accounts of how Moctezuma received his dreaded guests, whether he recognized them as mortal or divine. Certainly their objection to Aztec religious practices, and their devotion to Christianity, insulted him.

News reached Cortés that one of Moctezuma's vassals had killed a number of Spaniards on the coast. The emperor denied having anything to do with the matter, but, frightened by threats of death, he allowed himself to be held hostage in Axayacatl's palace until the matter was resolved.

Whether for his own self-preservation or through an acceptance of his forecast fate, Moctezuma settled into his captivity. He continued to govern and take his leisure and even participate in human sacrifices, but he relied on the Spaniards, whom he rewarded with gifts of precious stones and girls, to protect him. He also revealed the sources of his gold.

This arrangement disturbed the Aztec nobility. Moctezuma remained a willing captive as the Spaniards burned to death a number of noblemen, and he later surrendered himself and his empire into the vassalage of Charles V, rendering any action against the Spanish an act of treason against Moctezuma. Food, water, and gold were supplied to the Spaniards, who installed Christian icons in place of the Aztec ones (which Aztec priests removed) in the Great Pyramid.

In March 1520, Moctezuma informed the Spaniards that his gods had decreed a war between the Aztecs and the Spaniards. The Aztecs were assembling an army. At about this same time, Cortés made preparations to leave and to take Moctezuma with him to Spain.

A rival party of conquistadors, whom Cortés had to defeat on the coast, cut this plan short. In his absence, Aztec hospitality was withdrawn, and tortured prisoners yielded rumors of rebellion. During Toxcatl, an important religious feast whose celebration had been approved by both Cortés and Pedro de Alvarado (who was left in command of the garrison), the Spaniards massacred the Aztec nobility. Moctezuma, present at the feast, was guarded and spared.

The End of His Reign

Moctezuma remained in Spanish custody, besieged in Axayacatl's palace. After Cortés returned and the Spaniards failed to escape the city that June, Moctezuma was forced onto the roof to talk to the Aztec lords among the attacking crowd, which included his brother Cuitlahuac and young cousin Cuauhtémoc.

Before a hail of stones was directed at him, Moctezuma learned that Cuitlahuac had been elected emperor. Moctezuma died several days later, either of the wounds received from the stones or by the hands of his captors. His body was cremated without the usual honors of a dead king, and bystanders berated his corpse as it burned.

Cuauhtémoc

Cuauhtémoc (c. 1494?–1525) was the last Aztec emperor. Ruler during the siege of Tenochtitlan, he was taken prisoner and later executed by the Spanish.

During the Reign of Moctezuma II

Cuauhtémoc was the son of the Aztec emperor Ahuitzotl (who was uncle of two other Aztec emperors, Moctezuma II and Cuitlahuac) and Ahuitzotl's wife Tiacapantzin. At the time Hernán Cortés brought his expedition into Mexico, Cuauhtémoc was a lord of Itzapalapa and a high level functionary at Tlatelolco. When the nobility secretly asked officials to assemble an army to oust the Spanish who were holding Moctezuma hostage, Cuauhtémoc was among those who responded. However, when Moctezuma presented himself to the population in June of 1520, one account claims that Cuauhtémoc disparaged him as womanish and rejected his authority. Moctezuma's brother, Cuitlahuac, was chosen emperor. The crowd then stoned Moctezuma to death, the fatal blow possibly coming from Cuauhtémoc himself, although an Aztec account of the story attributes his murder to the Spaniards.

The Aztecs inflicted heavy losses upon the Spanish when the invaders retreated from Tenochtitlan during *La Noche Triste.* Yet in 1521, the Spanish returned to besiege the city.

Emperor

By this time, Cuauhtémoc was emperor as Cuitlahuac had died of smallpox, a disease introduced to Mexico by the Spaniards. Cuauhtémoc seems to have killed Moctezuma's sons whom he thought might

A gold vessel, made by the Chimu, one of the people conquered by the Incas in the fifteenth century, not long before the Spanish conquest. *© Museo del Oro, Lima, Peru/Bildarchiv Steffens/Henri Stierlin/The Bridgeman Art Library*

oppose his opposition to the Spanish occupiers, but he was married to Moctezuma's daughter, Xuchimatzatzin.

No doubt Cuauhtémoc's resolve against the Spanish, in addition to his reputation for bravery, were factors in his election as Cuitlahuac's successor. Surrounding towns that had allied themselves with the Spanish were fiercely punished, and Cortés's offer of a pardon in exchange for surrender was rebuffed.

Like Moctezuma and Cuitlahuac before him, Cuauhtémoc summoned allies to gather forces for his cause, but the responses were unenthusiastic: the Aztecs had made too many enemies. Even bribes of gold and exemption from future tribute (including victims for human sacrifice) did not rouse much hostility against the Spaniards.

Following an Aztec victory in June 1521, numerous captive Spaniards were sacrificed very publicly. Word of this, and the realization that the Spaniards could be defeated, finally frightened away many of the Spaniard's indigenous allies, but Cuauhtémoc failed to mount a follow-up campaign on the heels of this victory. Hunger, thirst, and disease brought on by the protected siege had debilitated his forces. To inflate the appearance of his army, the emperor even dressed women as warriors.

After rejecting repeated calls for peace from Cortés, Cuauhtémoc performed a final series of human sacrifices and held a meeting of his officials, at which it was decided that there would be a retreat from Tenochtitlan rather than a surrender. Yet a priest divined that in four days victory would come to the Aztecs, so the war continued. In the next battle on the lake, however, Cuauhtémoc surrendered (or was captured) and was presented to Cortés. The war was finally over.

After the Fall of Tenochtitlan Hostilities between the two groups ended, but Cuauhtémoc's battle continued. He tried to kill himself before being tortured to reveal the location of gold the Spaniards believed to be missing. He confessed it had been dumped into the lake, but if this was true, the Spaniards recovered only a fraction of it.

Despite his mistreatment by Cortés, Cuauhtémoc provided support for later Spanish campaigns, giving some fifteen thousand men to help the Spaniards extend their conquests in the south. Even so, he remained a prisoner of the Spaniards. Cuauhtémoc was brought along on Cortés's expedition to put down a revolt led by Cortés's former officer, Cristóbal de Olid. He was hanged during the campaign (in February 1525) for allegedly fomenting a rebellion.

Cuauhtémoc became a symbolic figure for later Mexican nationalist movements, a historical representative of patriotism, in stark contrast to La Malinche, who facilitated the Spanish conquest.

Francisco Pizarro

An illiterate man of humble beginnings, Francisco Pizarro (c. 1471?–1541) led the conquest of Peru, which he governed until his assassination.

Pizarro's Family Sometime between 1471 and 1478, Francisco Pizarro was born in Extremadura, Spain. He was the illegitimate son of Gonzalo Pizarro, an infantry officer of minor prestige, and Francisca González, a servant in a convent. Never acknowledged by his father, Pizarro had several younger half-brothers: Gonzalo (junior), Juan, and the elder Gonzalo's legitimate son Hernando. Among his cousins was Hernán Cortés, who led the conquest of Mexico.

Early Expeditions Pizarro left for the Americas in 1501 and the next year participated in Alonzo de Ojeda's expedition to the coast of Columbia and Panama. He was left in command of a settlement called San Sebastian but abandoned it after an attack by the indigenous population. Accused of cowardice, he found sympathy from Vasco Núñez de Balboa, who convinced Ojeda to relocate the destroyed colony. Pizarro was with Balboa when Balboa discovered the Pacific Ocean in 1513, but after Pedro Arias de Ávila replaced the discredited Balboa as governor, Pizarro turned on his former commander, who was subsequently executed in 1519.

Although a grant of land and of forced local labor afforded Pizarro a far better living than he could possibly have achieved in Spain, he aspired to more. With Diego de Almagro and Hernando de Luque (a priest acting on behalf of Gaspar de Espinosa), Pizarro formed a company to undertake exploration along the southern Pacific coast, from which a previous expedition had returned with news of a wealthy kingdom. Pizarro departed Panama in November 1524, leaving Almagro behind to prepare a second vessel and more men.

Pizarro met great hardships, storms, disease, and shortage of supplies. He turned back, catching up with Almagro at Chicama, near Panama. Despite their failure, the attempt had yielded enough gold to warrant a second expedition.

The Second Expedition and a Visit to Spain On March 10, 1526, Pizarro, Almagro, and Luque entered into a formal agreement in which all the acquisitions of the enterprise, from conquest or royal grant, would be divided equally among them. They departed that year, sailing to the Rio de San Juan, where they looted a village. Pizarro dispatched Bartolomé Ruiz to explore

A portrait of Francisco Pizarro. *Public Domain Kulturbesitz/Art Resource, NY*

the coast to the south and Almagro to return to Panama for more men while he and some men remained behind.

They suffered again from privation, but Ruiz returned with gold, silver, and emeralds, as well as three interpreters. With Almagro, the expedition pushed south to Tacamez (in what is now southern Colombia), at which point the question of returning to Panama was again raised. They had encountered more formidable opposition than they had previously. Convinced by Almagro, Pizarro stayed behind while his partner sought reinforcements.

A ship sent by the new governor, Pedro de Los Rios, came to Pizarro, not to deliver reinforcements but to bring back the survivors. A letter from Almagro and Luque asked Pizarro not to return because reinforcements would soon arrive. Fourteen Spaniards, including Pizarro, put faith in the partners and refused passage to Panama.

Almagro returned seven months later, without reinforcements. Even so, Pizarro explored further to the south, finding more evidence of the wealth of the Inca Empire and cause for a third expedition. Yet de Los Rios denied future expeditions, which forced Pizarro to return to Spain to seek permission from Charles V, King of Spain and Holy Roman Emperor. Contrary to the

Francisco Pizarro receives permission from the Spanish King to occupy and administer Peru. *Bildarchiv Preussischer Kulturbesitz/Art Resource, NY*

March 1526 agreement, Pizarro accepted titles above those of his two partners, including governor and captain-general, which created ill will among the parties.

The Conquest of Peru The third expedition launched in 1531, with Almagro seeking more recruits in Panama while Pizarro sailed on. In 1532, word of the Spanish presence along the coast reached the Inca emperor, Atahualpa. Pizarro was invited to meet him, so the Spanish soldiers headed for Cajamarca.

Pizarro tricked and defeated Atahualpa at the brief battle of Cajamarca in November 1532. Despite receiving a vast ransom for the emperor's life, at the urging of Almagro and his new troops, Pizarro tried and executed the emperor. While this angered the Incas, it engendered support from those whom the Incas had lately conquered.

With these allies, the Spanish, who numbered only about 160, marched on the Inca capital of Cuzco. Pizarro took the city in 1533, installing a puppet emperor, Tupac

Hualpa, who died and was replaced by Manco Inca in 1535. That same year Pizarro founded a new capital, Lima.

Manco rebelled and besieged Pizarro's forces in Lima and Cuzco. Control of the latter city was a major point of contention between Pizarro and Almagro, whom Charles V of Spain had appointed governor of Chile. After Almagro returned from rather unsuccessful campaigns in Chile, Manco withdrew his siege, leaving the Spaniards to fight among themselves. Pizarro's brother Hernando defeated Almagro and executed him in 1538.

Governor Pizarro governed Peru until 1541, beleaguered not only by Manco Inca's forces and other local uprisings but also by supporters of Almagro. In June of that year, a party of Almagrists—including Almagro's son, called Diego Almagro "El Mozo" ("the Lad")—forced their way into the governor's palace in Lima and assassinated Pizarro.

Almagro was captured and executed by Hernando Pizarro. *Giraudon/Art Resource, NY*

Neither of Pizarro's surviving brothers (Juan had died during the siege of Cuzco) succeeded him as governor. Until 1560, Hernando was imprisoned for the execution of Almagro. Gonzalo led a rebellion against the new viceroy, Blasco Núñez Vela, who was appointed in 1544 and imposed new laws protecting the native populations. Vela's successor, Pedro de La Gasca, repealed these laws that offended the Spaniards. This undercut support for Gonzalo. After surrendering, Gonzalo was executed in 1548.

Diego de Almagro

Diego de Almagro, who died in 1538, accompanied Francisco Pizarro on his conquest of Peru. Although instrumental in the Spaniards' success, his strained relations with Pizarro and Pizarro's brothers led to conflicts between the Spanish conquistadors, resulting in the supremacy of Pizarro's faction.

Before the Expeditions An illegitimate child, Almagro adopted as his surname the name of the city in Spain where he was born, but the year of his birth is unknown. Sources refer to Almagro as blunt-speaking, hasty, and short of stature.

In 1514, Almagro sought his fortune in the New World with Pedro Arias de Ávila when Ávila went to forcibly replace Vasco Núñez de Balboa as governor of the Isthmus of Darien (modern Isthmus of Panama).

Almagro married an indigenous woman, who in about 1522 gave birth to a son named Diego (later called "El Mozo" or "the Lad"). Ten years after arriving in the Americas, Almagro entered into an agreement with Francisco Pizarro for an expedition that ultimately led to the discovery and conquest of Peru.

The First Expedition Almagro oversaw the purchase and provisioning of the expedition's two small vessels, with funding arranged by Hernando de Luque, a priest acting as an agent for Gaspar de Espinosa. Almagro was also assigned the task of assembling men for the expedition. In November 1524, Pizarro, the expedition commander, set sail with more than one hundred men. Almagro then spent several months outfitting and assembling a company for the second ship.

Setting sail in 1525, Almagro followed Pizarro's southward coastal route. At Pueblo Quemado, Almagro's party received a hostile greeting from the local people. In retaliation for what amounted to little more than a show of force, Almagro attacked and burned the village. In the encounter, he received a head wound that cost him an eye, but this injury did not deter his progress.

Almagro arrived at the Rio de San Juan (modern Buenaventura, Columbia), where again he saw inhabitants, but no sign of Pizarro. Here he turned back, meeting up with Pizarro at Chicamá, near Panama. Pizarro had abandoned his southward course because of a supply shortage, but both men had acquired gold on their voyages. Certain of the wealth that was to be gained, the two resolved to undertake a second expedition.

The Second Expedition Hernando de Luque had to convince Ávila to endorse the second expedition. To Pizarro's displeasure, Ávila appointed Almagro to be Pizarro's equal in the venture. In March 1526, Almagro, Pizarro, and Luque (still acting for Gaspar de Espinosa) agreed that the land and all other gains acquired during the expedition or by grants of the Spanish crown were to be divided into equal thirds.

In command of new vessels, Almagro and Pizarro sailed for the Rio de San Juan, where they looted the village. Rather than campaign any farther, Pizarro encamped at the river while one vessel scouted the coastline and Almagro sailed back to Panama for more men and supplies. Almagro returned to the Rio de San Juan with some eighty soldiers of fortune and provisions. There he found Pizarro's remaining men near starvation, with many others dead from an unsuccessful attempt to penetrate inland.

Bolstered by Almagro's men and supplies and aware of a rich civilization to the south, the expedition continued. They landed at Tacamez, a coastal city in a gold-rich territory now in the south of Columbia, only recently conquered by the Incas. The local forces, perhaps as many as ten thousand, dismayed some of the

Drinking vessel or kero depicting a warrior with a club and featherwork shield, Inca, 1532. *© British Museum, London, UK/The Bridgeman Art Library*

Spaniards; in an argument that nearly came to blows, Almagro insisted that the expedition must continue.

Leaving Pizarro behind again, Almagro returned again for more troops, but found his efforts complicated by the discovery of a letter of complaint that had been smuggled back with him. The new governor, Pedro de los Rios, refused to grant anything to Almagro and Luque, and instead sent a ship to fetch any remaining survivors.

Almagro and Luque sent Pizarro a letter, begging him to not return because Almagro would be bringing necessary supplies and men. Meanwhile, Almagro and Luque persuaded Rios to give Pizarro more time. Having rejoined Pizarro, they resumed exploration of the coast in the company of some Indians who had joined them. Traveling south brought further confirmation of the location and vast wealth of the Inca Empire. After a total of about eighteen months, the expedition turned back to Panama to arrange a third expedition.

The Third Expedition and Conquest of Peru When the governor proved unreceptive, Pizarro sailed to Spain to petition the Spanish court directly. He returned appointed governor, while Almagro was to be commander of the fortress at Tumbez. This unequal division, contrary to their agreement, angered Almagro. Luque, appointed Bishop of Tumbez and Protector of the Indians of Peru, had feared that something like this might happen, and the relationship between Pizarro and Almagro became especially strained. In 1531, Pizarro left for the south again with almost two hundred well-armed men.

Luque died before Almagro departed with his 150 men, fifty horses, and suitable arms the next year. After his arrival at Tumbez, others warned Almagro not to trust Pizarro, who had gone on to Cajamarca and captured Atahualpa, ruler of the Inca Empire. By mid-February 1533, Almagro was also at Cajamarca with his troops. Fortified by Almagro's recruits, Pizarro felt confident about claiming the empire, which he had been, in effect, only holding hostage with Atahualpa. A huge ransom was collected for the emperor, and this was divided among the parties, with lesser amounts for Almagro's men. Almagro and certain men who accompanied him now insisted that they were better off with Atahualpa dead, and they convinced Pizarro to execute the Inca ruler.

The Spaniards left Cajamarca to conquer the rest of Atahualpa's domains. Upon entering the Inca capital Cuzco (where Atahualpa's half-brother Manco Inca was installed as a puppet emperor), Almagro took up residence in the palace built for Huascar, Atahualpa's brother and rival. In January 1534 he and a party went north, where the Spaniards continued to meet with local resistance. Another Spaniard, Pedro de Alvarado, had entered the northern region of Quito with an army, intent on conquest, only to find it already occupied by Pizarro's forces. Almagro convinced some of Alvarado's men to join his own ranks, and Almagro negotiated the intruder's withdrawal from the region with an offer of payment in gold, which left Pizarro with seven additional ships, horses, ammunition, and men.

The Expedition to Chile Pizarro rewarded Almagro's success with Alvarado by appointing him governor of Cuzco, but this situation was complicated when the Spanish crown awarded Almagro the southern portion of the Inca empire. No one was sure yet whether or not that included Cuzco, which Pizarro's brothers wanted. Pizarro had to make peace between his brothers and Almagro.

In July 1535, accompanied by Manco's half-brother Paullu, Almagro went south into Chile on a well-armed and brutal expedition that did not yield the riches Almagro had anticipated. Upon returning to Cuzco, he found the city occupied by Pizarro's brothers but under siege by an army raised by Manco Inca, who had rebelled against his Spanish overlords. Believing Manco to be in the better position, he promised the emperor that he would see that those who had wronged him were punished. This anti-Pizarro alliance never solidified. Manco

withdrew, leaving the Spaniards to fight among themselves for Cuzco, a struggle won by Almagro. Almagro installed Paullu as Inca.

Civil War Almagro's forces continued a civil war with Pizarro's. At Las Salinas in April 1538, Hernando Pizarro defeated and captured Almagro, and, after a brief trial for extremely lengthy charges, had him strangled and beheaded. In the wake of this event, Paullu remained Inca but abandoned Almagro's supporters for Pizarro's. Almagro's supporters continued to struggle against Pizarro and assassinated him in 1541. Almagro's son Diego was among the Almagrists who murdered Pizarro in 1541. "El Mozo" was captured and executed the following year.

Huayna Capac

Huayna Capac (c. 1493–1527) ruled the Inca empire, centered in what is now Peru. His sons Huascar and Atahualpa fought a dynastic war resulting in such division that a small force of Spaniards, led by Francisco Pizarro, was able to conquer the empire.

After death, the Inca emperor was mummified and provided for by his kin for generations. *Nick Saunders/Barbara Heller Photo Library, London/Art Resource, NY*

Huayna Capac's Early Years Born as Titu Cusi Hualpa, Huayna Capac was a son of the emperor, Tupac Inca Yupanqui (1471–1493), and the emperor's sister-wife Mama Ocllo. Tupac Inca extended the Inca empire, known as Tahuantinsuyu, far south into Chile, expanded the eastern borders, and seized the highlands as far north as Quito in modern Ecuador.

Upon his death, one of his other widows advised her own kin that Tupac Inca had initially appointed Capac Huari as his successor, but on his deathbed had changed his mind and named his other young son, Titu Cusi Hualpa, instead. Capac Huari's supporters plotted to kill Titu Cusi Hualpa, but Tupac Inca's brother, Huaman Acachi, uncovered the plot, safely concealed Titu Cusi Hualpa, and slew the conspirators. The boy was declared "Huayna Capac," "youthful chief."

Being quite young when he was awarded the fringe of feathers that denoted his supreme rank, Huayna Capac required a regent. First appointed to this position was his uncle Hualpaya, but Hualpaya coveted the fringe for himself. His treason uncovered, Hualpaya and his supporters were put to death. Huaman Achachi served as his replacement, and Huayna Capac's mother, Mama Ocllo, remained influential until she fell ill and died.

Huayna Capac had numerous wives, including his sister Cusi Rimay. She may have given birth to the heir, Ninan Cuyuchi. His other sister, Rahua Ocllo, gave birth to Tupac Cusi Hualpa, better known as Huascar. Atahualpa's mother, known as Tocto Coca or Tupa Palla, is sometimes identified as a princess of Quito, a city conquered by Tupac Inca.

Inspection and Campaign
Following Mama Ocllo's death, Huayna Capac undertook an inspection of Tahuantinsuyu, during which he changed government appointments, formed alliances, and ordered various construction projects and foundations. These projects ranged from establishing immense farms to refurbishing fortresses.

In addition to civil work, Huayna Capac attempted to expand his empire, but these military exploits were unsuccessful. Expansion might have been a bit ambitious, given that Huayna Capac and his forces were constantly putting down revolts by conquered peoples and rebellions by other nobles in Cuzco. Tomebamba, where he had been born, became Huayna Capac's stronghold for these efforts.

The Fates Portend Darkly
Toward the end of his reign, ominous signs—including strange lightning, coastal floods, earthquakes, and a comet—deeply worried Huayna Capac. In Cuzco, a plague was raging; it was probably smallpox or measles, two diseases recently introduced into the Americas by Spaniards and other Europeans. A number of Huayna Capac's relatives perished in this epidemic.

BLOOD LAKE

For one campaign in the north, Huayna Capac had Atahualpa and Ninan Cuyuchi accompany him while several other sons (including Tupac Cusi Hualpa and Manco Inca, remained at Cuzco). Although Huayna Capac had gone to great lengths to properly prepare his army before departing Cuzco, his military efforts were not entirely successful; local terrain contributed to the defeat of otherwise superior Inca forces. During one battle, the enemy literally unseated Huayna Capac and would have killed him had his guards not successfully intervened.

Huayna Capac exacted revenge for this attempted regicide by tricking the enemy into emerging from its fortress with a feint. His men forced them into a lake where they were killed amid a clump of willow trees. This earned the lake the name *Yaguarcocha*, "Blood Lake."

While in Tomebamba, Huayna Capac received word of thirteen bearded, white-skinned strangers who came to the coast at Tumbez in floating houses. The "houses" left, but two of the wild-looking foreigners remained behind. Huayna Capac ordered them brought to Quito, where he was staying.

These men, two members of Francisco Pizarro's second expedition, never arrived at Huayna Capac's court, disappearing from the historical record instead. Plague, however, did arrive, and the emperor was stricken. Before dying, he declared Ninan Cuyuchi to be his heir, but only if the reading of the entrails of a llama, sacrificed for the purpose, augured good fortune. If it augured bad, some accounts relate that the empire would go to Huascar. The signs for Ninan Cuyuchi were unfavorable, but Ninan Cuyuchi died before word could be sent to him.

The emperor's corpse was mummified and sent back to Cuzco, where Huascar had survived the plague. Fearing trouble with the succession, the members of his court tried to disguise his death until Huascar had been confirmed as emperor. However, Huascar's mother, who had been with the emperor, returned to Cuzco with the news of her son's succession.

Meanwhile, Huascar's half-brother Atahualpa remained behind in the north. His failure to accompany their father's funeral procession to Cuzco no doubt stoked Huascar's suspicions as to his motives, and soon Tahuantinsuyu was plunged into a dynastic war that would weaken it enough that it would fall to Pizarro's third expedition, which arrived in 1532, only five years after Huayna Capac's death.

Atahualpa
At the time of Francisco Pizarro's third expedition in 1532, Atahualpa (c. 1502?–1533) had just defeated his

The Incas typically carried their emperor in a litter, including into battle. Here, Atahualpa and his warriors approach Cajamarca, where Pizarro and his Spaniards will defeat him.   *Nick Saunders/Barbara Heller Photo Library, London/Art Resource, NY.*

half-brother Huascar in a dynastic war for rule of Tahuantinsuyu, also called the Inca Empire. Atahualpa's defeat at Cajamarca opened the way for the Spanish conquest in Peru and Chile.

Atahualpa's Early Years Atahualpa was born in about 1502 to a woman called either Tocto Coca or Tupa Palla. Possibly she was the daughter of a chief of the city of Quito, although some chroniclers record that she was related to a former emperor, Pachacutec. Atahualpa was one of several sons of the ruler Inca Huayna Capac.

His father brought him and his half-brother, Ninan Cuyuchi, on his long campaigns to secure the northern regions of Tahuantinsuyu. Atahualpa's grandfather (Tupac Inca Yupanqui) had originally expanded the empire into this territory, which included Quito, but the local people resisted and continuously rebelled against Inca rule.

The Succession Both Huayna Capac and Ninan Cuyuchi died of smallpox or measles, Old World diseases introduced by European explorers to which the people of the New World had no resistance. Atahualpa remained in Quito while his father's mummified body was conveyed to Cuzco, the capital; his death was kept secret at this time. In some accounts, Huayna Capac named Huascar as successor if the augurs deemed Ninan Cuyuchi to be unsuitable, but it is possible that Huascar's succession was due, at least in part, to the influence of his mother. She too had been with the campaign and traveled to Cuzco with the news.

That Atahualpa remained in the north with some of Huayna Capac's generals angered Huascar. Each half-brother was particularly associated with one of the ten Inca royal kin groups, but Huascar disassociated himself with his own kin group and certain other groups (comprising what was known as Upper Cuzco) and aligned himself with the less illustrious kin groups (known as Lower Cuzco). Huascar then had members of Upper Cuzco tortured to reveal why Atahualpa had not accompanied the funeral procession to Cuzco. Some of the survivors ran to inform Atahualpa.

If Atahualpa coveted Huascar's position in the immediate wake of their father's death, he completely concealed his interest, and by most accounts he accepted his brother's rule without question. In Tomebamba, Atahualpa began to erect palaces for his brother, but the local governor (who disliked Atahualpa) sent word to Huascar of Atahualpa's activities, implying that they were for Atahualpa's own gain.

This confirmed Huascar's fears. He rebuffed Atahualpa's gifts and killed the messengers who brought them. In return, Huascar sent Atahualpa a present of women's garments and ornaments. This exchange marked the beginning of the dynastic war. Atahualpa and the generals knew that they could not submit to Huascar's rule without forfeiting their own lives.

The Dynastic War The Cañaris, a tribe that rebelled against Atahualpa, might have carried out the first encounter in the brothers' war. Atahualpa was wounded and captured in a skirmish with the group, but he escaped and retreated north with his forces to Quito. Having regrouped, Atahualpa led his men against Tomebamba, his father's northern stronghold, which he destroyed.

The next encounter occurred between Atahualpa and Atoc, one of Huascar's generals and possibly another son of Huayna Capac. Atoc prevailed, but the following engagement went to Atahualpa—Atoc and the governor of Tomebamba were killed. While Huascar raised an army, Atahualpa proceeded south, destroying a famous oracle that predicted an unfortunate end for him.

Huascar sent Huanca Auqui at the head of a powerful army against Atahualpa. Although oracles predicted success for Huanca Auqui, Atahualpa's forces (commanded by Quizquiz and Challcochima) continually defeated him, prompting later speculation of collaboration between the general and the rebel. After a battle against Quizquiz at Cajamarca, Huanca Auqui's forces broke and ran, and some defected to Atahualpa's cause. Atahualpa himself remained in the town of Cajamarca, perhaps because he did not wish to risk approaching Cuzco personally or because, like his father, he had heard news of Spaniards along the coast.

As Atahualpa's general led his enlarged army south, Huascar relieved Huanca Auqui of command. This change in leadership did not help Huascar, whose forces continued to accumulate losses at the hands of Quizquiz and Challcochima. Huascar himself joined the campaign, but was captured near Huanuco Pampa. His imprisonment marked the defeat of his forces, and Atahualpa's army entered Cuzco.

Cusi Yupanqui, a relative of Atahualpa, went to Cuzco and oversaw the massacre of most of Huascar's family before Huascar's eyes. He also burned the mummy of Huascar's kin-group ancestor, Thupa Inca. Huascar

was spared for the time being, to be brought to Atahualpa at Cajamarca. In the north, the Cañaris, who had supported Huascar, were punished with death or removal from their homeland.

The Arrival of the Spaniards Atahualpa was in Cajamarca awaiting delivery of Huascar when news arrived that a small party of strange foreigners (the third expedition of Francisco Pizarro) had landed on the coast. Having no reason to suspect the threat these men would ultimately pose, Atahualpa remained in Cajamarca while they approached. He sent a force of twenty thousand to meet them and received the Spaniards at a hot spring near the city. However, Atahualpa was soon tricked into entering the city (which the Spanish had occupied), and his forces were massacred.

Like his half-brother Huascar, Atahualpa found himself the captive of an enemy army. Not realizing the Spaniards' imperial ambitions, he offered a vast amount of gold and silver in ransom. It took time for this treasure to accumulate; in the interim, Atahualpa learned about his captors' ways (including the game of chess) and they learned of the dynastic war that had just concluded. His captivity precluded any direct attack on Cajamarca, even for a rescue, by his own forces. Once the ransom was paid, Diego de Almagro and his men persuaded Pizarro that Atahualpa's usefulness had come to an end. Atahualpa had expected this. Like his father Huayna Capac, he had witnessed omens forecasting an unfortunate end.

In a move that outraged Emperor Charles V of Spain (as Atahualpa was fellow royalty), Pizarro convicted Atahualpa on a false charge of ordering one of his commanders to revolt and—because Huascar had been killed en route to Cajamarca—of murder. The penalty would be death by burning at the stake unless he converted to Christianity.

Horrified by the prospect of bodily destruction, Atahualpa acquiesced. He took the Christian name Francisco, after the conqueror who had defeated him. Sometime in June or July 1533, Atahualpa/Francisco was strangled as a Christian. Given a church burial, his body was taken by his supporters to be mummified and hidden.

Atahualpa's successor was another half-brother, Tupac Huallpa, installed by the Spaniards for only a brief time before being replaced by yet another of Huayna Capac's sons, Manco Inca.

Manco Inca

Manco Inca (died 1544, date of birth unknown) succeeded Tupac Hualpa as ruler of Tahuantinsuyu (the Inca empire) during the period of the Spanish conquest of the region. He ruled with the cooperation of the Spaniards but abandoned them to set up a "Neo-Inca" state called Vilcabamba.

This is the fortress of Sacsahuaman, above Cuzco, where the forces of Manco Inca besieged the Spanish. *The Library of Congress*

Rise to Power Manco Inca was one of the many sons of Huayna Capac. During the dynastic war fought between his half-brothers, Atahualpa and Huascar, he was among those family members in the capital city of Cuzco who Atahualpa had marked for death. Atahualpa's kinsman, Cusi Yupanqui, carried out the slaying but Manco escaped.

After the Spaniards captured and killed Atahualpa at Cajamarca in 1533, they bestowed the royal fringe of the Inca on another half-brother, Tupac Hualpa. Tupac Hualpa was to be only a token figure, with Francisco Pizarro and his conquistadores being the real rulers of the empire. The Spaniards then moved south, finding alliances among local peoples who opposed Atahualpa.

Before reaching Cuzco, Tupac Hualpa died of illness. This left open the question of the succession, which was never a simple affair among the Incas. Manco Inca probably saw this opportunity as his chance to rule, and he made this offer to the Spaniards. Knowing that they could not conquer Tahuantinsuyu without having control of the emperor, the Spanish accepted this offer. Exactly one year after they had defeated Atahualpa at Cajamarca, the Spaniards took Cuzco with little difficulty.

The next month, December 1533, the Spaniards had Manco Inca formally appointed emperor. His appointment did not create peace within the empire, which even in the days of his predecessors faced rebellions and unrest, and not all of the empire acquiesced to Manco Inca's rule.

In the north, Atahualpa's commanders, Quizquiz and Rumiñawi, continued to resist the invaders until their deaths. Quizquiz was killed by his own army, while Rumiñawi was captured and executed by Spanish forces. To the south, Pizarro dispatched Diego de Almagro and Manco Inca's half-brother Paullu Inca in an attempted conquest of Chile in 1535.

The Rebellion By late 1535, Manco had had enough of the Spanish, who pestered him ceaselessly for gold and silver. His first attempt to escape failed, and the Spanish abused him in his subsequent captivity until he was freed in January 1536.

He made his second escape attempt in April, under the pretext of attending to ceremonies outside of Cuzco. Manco promised Hernando Pizarro that he would return with a large statue of his father, Huayna Capac. Pizarro let him go, to the great alarm of many of the noblemen who feared—rightly—that Manco Inca would return with an army to destroy them.

A silver representation of a maize plant. Thousands of such artifacts were given to the Spaniards for melting down, in a vain attempt to ransom Atahualpa. *Werner Forman/Art Resource, NY*

Since before his first escape, Manco Inca had been secretly dispatching word of his impending rebellion. Unknown to the Spaniards, forces were assembling for Manco Inca near Cuzco. Within days of Manco Inca's departure, Hernando Pizarro learned of the revolt.

Manco's army besieged Cuzco and other Peruvian cities. Almagro and Paullu returned from their expedition to Chile to find things in a disrupted state; Spanish forces commanded by Hernando Pizarro were pleased to learn of Almagro's approach, believing that he would be able to provide them with some relief. However, Almagro, who had quarrels against Pizarro and his brothers, attempted to form an alliance with Manco, promising to punish those who had offended the Inca and also promising that his rebellion would be forgiven. Unable to trust the Spaniards, Manco withdrew. The Spaniards then installed his brother, Paullu, as Inca.

The Foundation of Vilcabamba Manco Inca retreated to Vilcabamba, in the mountainous jungles west of Cuzco. Here, in 1539, he founded a new Inca state. That same year, Francisco Pizarro's brother Gonzalo sought him out through difficult terrain. He brought two full-brothers of Manco's sister-wife, Cura Ocllo, to try to convince Manco to surrender, but the Inca murdered them instead, to the immense grief of his wife.

Gonzalo forced Manco to flee into the jungle and, in sacking Vilcabamba, captured one of his half-brothers as well as Cura Ocllo. When Manco rebuffed gifts from the Spaniards by killing the messengers, Pizarro brutally murdered Cura Ocllo. Pizarro followed this up by killing chiefs whom he suspected of harboring sympathies for Manco or his wife.

The difficulty of the terrain in the region of Vilcabamba dissuaded the Spanish from further campaigns, although Manco continued to stir up trouble for them. In 1544 he took in several men who had sympathized with Diego de Almagro, whose forces had been defeated by Pizarro's. Unbeknownst to Manco, these men had been promised pardons if they assassinated the Inca, which they did as they played a game of horseshoes.

Manco's son Titu Cusi, who was about nine years old at the time of the assassination, became Inca, and the state of Vilcabamba held out against the Spanish until the reign of Tupac Amaru ended in 1572.

Tupac Amaru

Tupac Amaru (died 1572, date of birth unknown) was the last native ruler of the Inca people. He ruled the Inca state of Vilcabamba until he was captured and executed by the Spanish. His resistance made him a model for later Peruvian revolutionaries.

The Succession at Vilcabamba In 1536, Manco Inca, the puppet emperor installed by Francisco Pizarro, rebelled and founded a new Inca state at Vilcabamba. After Manco's assassination by the Spaniards, his young son Sayri Tupac Inca succeeded him. Sayri Tupac and his regents surrendered to the Spanish but remained for years at Vilcabamba after the current puppet ruler, Paullu, died of disease. Sayri Tupac was baptized and granted estates, but he died in 1561, leaving behind a widow and a daughter.

Following his death, the officials in Vilcabamba declared one of his older half-brothers, Titu Cusi, ruler. It is possible that this position should have gone to the young Tupac Amaru, who was, like Sayri Tupac, a son of Manco and Manco's chief wife.

The Spaniards tried to tempt Titu Cusi from Vilcabamba. Negotiations were successful, culminating in peace treaties in 1566 and 1567, in which Titu Cusi would be permitted to remain in Vilcabamba. Catholic missionaries entered Vilcabamba and baptized Titu Cusi's son, and later the Inca himself, but the old Inca practices persisted. Upon Tito Cusi's death (brought about by illness or poison), the Inca's men slew a group of visiting Spanish missionaries, and the succession passed to Tupac Amaru.

Failed Diplomacy In 1571, Francisco de Toledo—Viceroy of Peru, who did not yet know the fate of the first party or Titu Cusi—sent some ambassadors to meet with the Inca. The Inca's men killed this group too, though it is possible that they did so against Tupac

Amaru's wishes. While the Inca was told that the Spaniards had sent a party to kill him, the Spaniards were told that Tupac Amaru had ordered the would-be diplomats killed.

When word of the murders reached the Viceroy Toledo, he was furious. In 1572, he sent a military expedition to conquer Vilcabamba, a feat that had been tried during the reign of Manco Inca. The Spanish force met the Inca's at the Chuquichaqa bridge, where the last murders had occurred. By one account, four rounds of small artillery and some shots from the arquebuses were enough to put the Inca's men to flight, so quickly that they did not have time to burn the bridge.

The Spanish pursued, and the Incas abandoned Vilcabamba. Captives taken along the way revealed to the Spaniards which direction Tupac Amaru had taken, so a reduced force of no more than fifty soldiers, led by Captain Martín Garcia Oñez de Loyola, continued the chase. Loyola finally caught up with Tupac Amaru and captured him, his wife, and all of his men and their families.

Trials and Executions   Tupac Amaru's generals were given quick, defenseless trials and sentenced to death, though only two survived the proceedings to die by hanging. Tupac Amaru was also convicted of crimes for which he could not have been held legally responsible and sentenced to beheading.

In the course of three days, two monks who spoke the Quechua language converted Tupac Amaru to Christianity in prison. The execution took place in front of as many as fifteen thousand witnesses. Some four hundred Cañaris, whom Tupac Amaru's forefathers had fought, served as guards; one would serve as executioner. The respected Bishop of Popayan and other clergymen begged on their knees that the Inca be sent to Spain to serve or be judged by the king, but it was to no avail.

Tupac Amaru was beheaded. His body was interred in the cathedral in Cuzco, but his head was left on a pike until the people began to worship it, at which point it was deposited with the rest of the corpse.

Although Tupac Amaru's death ended Inca rule, it did not end the resistance movement against the Spanish. The late eighteenth century revolutionary José Gabriel Condorcanqui took his ancestor's name. Tupac Amaru's resistance also inspired late twentieth century revolts in Peru, including the Tupac Amaru Revolutionary Movement (1984–1997).

✦ Major Battles

La Noche Triste, July 1, 1520

La Noche Triste occurred when the Spaniards and Tlascalan allies of Hernán Cortés escaped from their besieged quarters in the Aztec city of Tenochtitlan with heavy loss of life.

The Journey to Tenochtitlan   In early 1519, Hernán Cortés led an expedition of about six hundred men—authorized by Diego Velázquez, governor of Cuba—to the Mexican mainland. After founding Villa Rica de la Vera Cruz (and thus removing himself legally from Velázquez's jurisdiction), Cortés began the inland trek to the Aztec capital of Tenochtitlan. Along the way, the Spaniards gained allies, notably the Tlascalans, who were hostile toward their Aztec overlords.

The Occupation of Tenochtitlan   After the Spaniards massacred the city of Cholula in November 1519, the Aztec emperor Moctezuma agreed to meet them in Tenochtitlan, a city situated on an island in Lake Texcoco. On one hand, the Spaniards were dazzled by the enormous city's engineering, its market place, royal menagerie, and treasury; they were also horrified by the evidence of human sacrifice, carried out here on a scale they had not previously encountered. The Spaniards and their allies were housed within the palace of Moctezuma's father, Axayactl, and treated as honored guests.

An incident on the coast gave Cortés an excuse to convince Moctezuma to deliver himself as hostage into Spanish custody. Although the emperor continued to rule, this situation deeply worried the Aztecs.

Cortés might have maintained control of the situation if not for the untimely arrival of an expedition sent by Velázquez to curtail him. Cortés departed the city in May 1520, leaving behind a garrison of fewer than a hundred men. Pedro de Alvarado was in charge of this force and the hostage emperor.

The Aztecs had secured permission from both Alvarado and Cortés to celebrate the festival of Toxcatl during the latter's absence. Whether inspired by genuine fear of an uprising or brash opportunism, Alvarado and his men slaughtered the celebrants. The remainder of the population rose up against the Spaniards, trapping them in the palace.

The Spaniards and Tlascalans Besieged   When Cortés returned in late June with more than a thousand men, several of Alvarado's soldiers had been killed and there was no more food or water. He was furious at both Alvarado (who had precipitated the uprising) and Moctezuma (who had allegedly conspired against the Spaniards and who had issued orders to deny the Spaniard's food). Cortés demanded provisions, but Aztec warriors had gathered in the city and killed more than a dozen Spaniards.

The Aztecs set the palace ablaze and attacked; the Spaniards battled the fire and beat back an onslaught fiercer than anything even their most experienced soldiers had ever seen. Intent on escape, they constructed siege towers made of timbers taken from the palace. These were able to conceal twenty-five arquebusiers and crossbowmen who would cover the other troops as

In Theodore de Bry's engraving of the event leading up to La Noche Triste, the Spanish massacre of the Aztec nobles is set in the countryside rather than within the temple patio. © *John Judkyn Memorial, Bath, Avon, UK/The Bridgeman Art Library*

they marched out of the city, while cavalry charges kept the enemy at bay.

With the aid of these towers, the Spaniards and their allies advanced with great difficulty to the temple of Huitzilopochtli. They tried to set the city afire, but conditions prevented the blazes from spreading. The horses were useless in the streets and damp pavement of the temples, as were the firearms and crossbows once four thousand additional Aztec soldiers assumed defensive positions to prevent the advance up the temple steps.

Although a single cannon shot took out a dozen or so Aztecs, the numbers seemed insurmountable. Finally the Spaniards and their allies took the great temple. Earlier the Spaniards had installed Christian icons here, but these were gone, so the Spaniards burned the sanctuaries. The Aztecs attacked once more, and the Spaniards and Tlascalans had to return to the palace.

The siege continued. Cortés had Moctezuma go onto a roof to calm his subjects, but the Aztecs rejected Moctezuma's speech. They had already replaced him as ruler with his brother, Cuitlahuac, and they assaulted the former emperor with stones. Whether Moctezuma died of these wounds or, as Aztec sources later claimed, by Spanish hands is not certain.

The Sorrowful Night Gunpowder, food, and water grew in short supply within the palace, although the Spaniards had amassed fortunes in gold, silver, and precious stones. Most of the gold and silver was melted down into ingots. Some was set aside for the royal taxation. The soldiers took what they liked.

By this time, the Aztecs had taken control of the bridges that made the causeways between the island and the mainland passable, so the Spaniards built a portable bridge. On a rainy July night (sources vary as to the exact date), one hundred fifty Spaniards and four hundred Tlascalans carried this bridge to a causeway. The cannons were also brought, and companies of soldiers were deployed. Some of the Tlascalans guarded the prisoners and women, including La Malinche, Cortés's translator.

The Spaniards placed the bridge across to the first section of the causeway leading to the town of Tacuba. Cortés and some others crossed but the Aztecs, alerted by a passerby, arrived on the scene through the streets and by boat. In the ensuing battle, the Spaniards and their allies tried frantically to escape, while the Aztecs tried desperately to destroy those who threatened their empire. Some of the Spaniards and Tlascalans escaped when the Aztecs began to concentrate their attack on the rearguard. The looting of the baggage train also caused the attack to lose focus.

The Price of Escape Cortés's forces sustained heavy losses, especially with men whose inexperience had led them to more heavily weigh themselves down with loot. Among the dead were no fewer than six hundred Spaniards, several thousand Tlascalans, some of Moctezuma's children, and other important prisoners. Firearms and most of the crossbows had been left behind, and most of the treasure was lost.

The survivors gathered at Tacuba but were attacked there, too. Their Tlascalan allies guided them north, where they would meet another massive Aztec army in the battle of Otumba.

The Battle of Otumba, July 1520

The Aztecs' failure to defeat the Spanish and Tlascalan forces led by Hernán Cortés at the battle of Otumba in July 1520 paved the way for the siege of Tenochtitlan that brought down the Aztec empire.

Leaving Tenochtitlan In 1519, Hernán Cortés led a small force of Spaniards and their Tlascalan allies in a successful occupation of the Aztec city of Tenochtitlan; in the course of events, they were also able to take the Aztec ruler Moctezuma hostage. On the night of July 1, 1520, Cortés and his supporters were forced to flee the island city in a bloody retreat called *La Noche Triste*.

The Spaniards and Tlascalans escaped to the western shore of Lake Texcoco. The Tlascalans led the Spaniards northward to go around the lake, then eastward toward Tlascala, where Cortés had stored gold on the approach to Tenochtitlan.

During the escape from Tenochtitlan, the Spanish had lost the majority of their men and, according to the account of Bernal Díaz (an eyewitness), all but twenty-three horses. They had also lost their gunpowder, firearms, and most of their crossbows. The wounded, Spaniard and Tlascalan alike, were placed in the middle of the company with the supplies, and those too ill to walk were placed on lame horses. Fit horsemen and their mounts were deployed ahead and on the flanks.

Skirmishes on the March Through the countryside and villages the Spanish were harried by arrows, darts, and stones. Hostile voices taunted that they were all headed toward the place where they would die.

At one village, a number of Aztec warriors gathered in an attempt to surround Cortés's force. They could then make a more concerted attack with not only projectiles but also *macuahuitl*, wooden swords with blades of obsidian expertly chipped to razor-sharpness.

The terrain was too rough for Cortés to make effective use of the horses, but with their own steel blades the Spanish managed to ward off the Aztecs, killing several but at the cost of the lives of two Spanish soldiers and a horse. The Spanish occupied the town, where the starving Spaniards spent the night eating the flesh, skin, and bones of the slain mount.

The Battle on the Plain Early the next morning, either July 7 or 14 (accounts vary), the Spanish resumed their march, sending some horsemen ahead. About three miles beyond this pass lay the plain of Otumba (also called Otampan), and here the scouts reported seeing a large number of Aztec warriors lying in wait.

Once the forces met, the Aztecs attempted to surround Cortés's men, who remained in close formation to guard the baggage, the wounded, and other noncombatants, including their translator La Malinche. As Cortés had ordered, the cavalry, in groups of five, charged. These cavalry squads broke the Aztec ranks so that the swordsmen and the large dogs the Spaniards had brought with them could attack. Cavalry charged and retired, only to charge again, lancing the enemy.

The fighting was extremely close. Badly wounded, Cortés and his men persisted in their attacks, targeting the ornately attired Aztec officers, hoping that disrupting the command would put the troops to flight. Cortés personally led a contingent toward the commanding general. Cortés's charge caused the general's banner to fall. By Cortés's own account he slew the officer with two strikes of his lance, but according to Díaz, credit for that death belonged to another soldier, Juan de Salamanca.

With the officers stricken, the Aztec attack became weaker; the battle finally ended in a rout, in which the Spaniards and Tlascalans pursued the retreating survivors. According to Díaz, Cortés lost seventy-two Spanish soldiers and five Spanish women, all late-coming recruits who had not campaigned against the Aztec subjects en route to Tenochtitlan. Aztec losses numbered in the hundreds.

After the Battle People from nearby towns had witnessed the battle. Cortés's force was still attacked by projectiles as it marched eastward toward the Tlascalans' territory, but it met with no more organized resistance. Cortés spent more than two months in Tlascala (where they found that their stashed gold had been stolen) before moving on to Tepeaca, which resisted the Spanish advance and was seized. There Cortés began to prepare for the siege of Tenochtitlan.

The Siege of Tenochtitlan, 1520–1521

Led by the Spanish conquistador Hernán Cortés, the final campaign against the Aztecs ended with the siege of Tenochtitlan. When the city fell to the devastating blows of warfare and smallpox, the Aztec empire came to an end.

Preparations for the Siege The Aztecs had driven Cortés's Spaniards and local Tlascalan allies from the island-city of Tenochtitlan in July 1520, yet Cortés's victory at the battle of Otumba gave the Spaniards hope. What he had previously attempted to achieve through guile he would now attempt through more conventional (in the European experience) tactics: namely, a siege.

Prompted by the Tlascalans, Cortés aimed his first attack against Tepeaca, one of the Aztec's subject cities. Unlike the Tlascalans, the Tepeacans refused to capitulate to the foreigners. Cortés took the city in early August, sold the inhabitants as slaves if they were not executed (or sacrificed by the Tlascalans), and founded a Spanish settlement, Segura de la Frontera. Other cities were treated similarly.

In preparation for the siege, Cortés had gunpowder, firearms, and horses brought from the coast. Vessels from Cuba—not actually intended for Cortés—provided the necessary supplies as well as men. Resources were also obtained from Hispaniola and Jamaica. To take advantage of the fact that Tenochtitlan was in the middle of a lake, Cortés ordered ship's carpenters to construct thirteen brigantines which could be broken down and transported overland. The Spanish soldiery numbered five hundred and fifty. The Tlascalans were probably about ten thousand in number, with many more available to fight.

Meanwhile, the Aztec emperor Cuitlahuac also made preparations, largely of a different sort. His attempts to rally allies had failed, so he repaired damage the Spaniards had done during the occupation of Tenochtitlan. Priests sacrificed prisoners to gain divine favor in their fight against the foreign invaders. New weapons, such as lances, were devised. Before the siege, Cuitlahuac fell victim to an assault against which the Aztecs could not defend themselves: smallpox.

Subduing the Surrounds Cortés began the campaign in late December 1520. He took some cities—such as Texcoco (an important Aztec city of some 25,000) and Tacuba (strategically joined to Tenochtitlan by a causeway)—by force. Others willingly aligned themselves with the foreigners. Cuitlahuac's successor, Cuauhtémoc, refused Cortés's offers of peace. While more swords, firearms, gunpowder arrived, fighting continued between the Spaniards and Aztec armies around the lake.

PLAYING INTO THE ENEMY'S HOOVES

In the upcoming battle on the plain, the Spanish had the upper hand in terms of understanding their enemies' tactics. Cortés knew that Aztec battle formations were open, to facilitate swings of the macuahuitl. The Aztecs had never faced cavalry before, and they did not realize that they could not have chosen a worse terrain in which to engage the Spaniards. Their previous encounters with the horses had been on Tenochtitlan's streets and causeways, and on hilly broken terrain, where only the animals' weaknesses were apparent. Fighting on an open plain would help the Aztec warriors swing their macuahuitl, but it would give an even greater advantage to a mounted Spanish warrior.

Tenochtitlan Besieged Cortés and his allies had taken all but Tenochtitlan and the neighboring city Tlatelolco. He denied the Aztecs fresh food and water by destroying crops and the aqueduct, adding to the general misery caused by the smallpox.

In April 1521, Cortés launched his thirteen brigantines into Lake Texcoco, but he did not put them into action until June. He arranged his forces into four divisions: one naval (commanded by himself) and three infantry and cavalry, commanded by Pedro de Alvarado, Cristóbal de Olid, and Gonzalo de Sandoval. Cuauhtémoc appropriately mirrored his own forces to engage the Spaniards, but even hundreds of Aztec watercraft (probably logboats) were no match for the brigantines, which bombarded the city and severed vital waterborne supply lines.

Each day the Spaniards crossed the causeways to attack from three directions simultaneously before vacating the city each nightfall. Under cover of darkness, the Aztecs would undo Spanish efforts to make the causeways passable. The Aztecs disabled two brigantines by luring them into a section of the lake where submerged stakes tore open the hulls. Both Alvarado and Cortés, on separate occasions, fell for an equivalent ruse on land in which the Aztecs retreated, drawing the Spaniards forward. The Spaniards then found themselves attacked from the flanks or rear. The Aztecs killed or captured a number of Spaniards, including very nearly Cortés. Those the Aztecs seized in these actions were sacrificed, while their comrades could only watch helplessly from a distance.

This obvious demonstration of Spanish mortality, coupled with the tenacity of the Aztec defenders, undermined the morale of some of the Spaniards' allies, who fled their positions. (Prior to the Spaniards, Aztec battles did not drag on in this manner.) Cuauhtémoc sent

The Spaniards battle the Incas outside Cuzco. *Bildarchiv Preussischer Kulturbesitz/Art Resources*

Spanish body parts to his former subjects to convince them to relinquish their loyalty to Cortés, and Cortés had to fight to keep them.

For the first half of July, Spanish victory seemed in doubt, but the Spanish and their allies rallied. Ferocious fighting continued until mid-August. Cuauhtémoc was finally ready to surrender but the priests were not, so there was a final assault against the Spanish. However, on August 13, when Alvarado led his troops into Tlatelolco, he did so without a fight. Amid piles of corpses, people desperate to escape met him. The Tlascalans, against Cortés's orders, showed no mercy and slew countless noncombatants.

A brigantine encountered several Aztec boats. Among the passengers was Cuauhtémoc, who either surrendered or was captured. The siege was finally over.

The City Destroyed In name, Cuauhtémoc remained emperor as a vassal of Charles V, Holy Roman Emperor and King of Spain. At Cuauhtémoc's request, Cortés allowed the survivors of the siege to return to the Aztec homeland, Aztlan.

The city itself did not survive. Cortés had so admired it when he arrived in 1519 that he once hoped to hand it intact to Charles V. Spanish attacks, however, had demolished so much of Tenochtitlan and Tlatelolco that what remained was burned. Upon these ruins, Cortés founded Mexico City.

Cajamarca, 1532

At the Inca highland city of Cajamarca, in the northern Peruvian highlands, Spanish and Inca forces met for the first time in battle. Here the Spanish conquistador Francisco Pizarro captured, and later killed, Atahualpa, ruler of the Incas, whose death facilitated the Spanish conquest of their empire.

Before the battle at Cajamarca, Hernando Pizarro and Hernando De Soto confronted Atahualpa at the nearby hot spring. *© Private Collection/Look and Learn/The Bridgeman Art Library*

The Early History of Cajamarca

Indications of settlement at Cajamarca date back to at least 1500 BCE. In the late fifteenth century CE, the semi-arid but productive Cajamarca Valley was incorporated into the Inca kingdom (also called Tahuantinsuyu). The city of Cajamarca was founded near hot springs.

During the dynastic war that followed the death of the emperor Huayna Capac, his son Atahualpa remained at Cajamarca while his generals pressed the army of his brother Huascar southward. Atahualpa's forces defeated Huascar, and Atahualpa was still at Cajamarca when Francisco Pizarro led his third expedition into the region.

The Spaniards at Cajamarca

In 1532, Pizarro and his forces began the trek into the highlands from San Miguel de Piura, a city Pizarro had founded. Atahualpa had learned of their arrival and dispatched messengers with threatening gifts. News of their previous activities—raiding coastal villages—had reached Atahualpa, and he was most displeased.

When the Spanish arrived at Cajamarca in November, they found only several hundred men in the town, while the women were making preparations for festivities. Atahualpa and his forces were encamped near the hot spring. A hailstorm struck, forcing most of the Spaniards under cover, but Hernando de Soto and Pizarro's brother Hernando went with horsemen and an interpreter to confront Atahualpa. They obtained a promise from the Inca to enter Cajamarca the next day. Atahualpa's offer of friendship was as false as the

Spaniards'. He intended to variously kill them or castrate them for use in the emperor's harem.

Pizarro concealed his men and horses within the buildings that surrounded the plaza. This meant that Atahualpa was met not by the Spanish soldiers he expected, but a single Dominican friar and his interpreter instead. When Atahualpa discarded a book of prayer the friar gave him, Pizarro signaled the Spanish to attack.

Bursting from their concealments on horseback and firing cannons, the Spaniards destroyed Atahualpa's forces in about two hours. The Spaniards suffered no fatalities, while the Incas might have lost seven thousand. Atahualpa was not among the dead, however. Pizarro knew that he and his force of less than two hundred Spaniards were now trapped in an empire with an army of tens of thousands, and he needed Atahualpa to stay alive.

The Ransom of Atahualpa

In exchange for his freedom, Atahualpa proposed that he could order a certain room in Cajamarca to be half filled with gold objects and then half filled twice again with silver. Over the course of the next eight months the treasure slowly amassed, as did information. Some came from Atahualpa himself, who divulged enough that the Spanish knew that they could turn the divisions of loyalty within the Inca realm to their own purposes. Men sent to investigate Cuzco, the Inca capital, and the coastal city Pachacamac came back with word of the wealth of resources of Tahuantinsuyu, and they brought one of Atahualpa's generals, Challcochima, back to Cajamarca.

Beginning in late spring of the next year, the artifacts sent to ransom Atahualpa were melted down. The appropriate royal taxation was set aside, and the remainder was divided among the Spaniards. Pizarro received more than six hundred pounds of gold, a horseman one-seventh of this amount, and newly arrived reinforcements from Panama much less.

Led by Diego de Almagro, the Spanish reinforcements were especially suspicious of Atahualpa, and there were rumors that he had secretly dispatched orders for his general to lead an assault on Cajamarca. Pizarro eventually gave in to these fears; he accused Atahualpa of insurrection and, because his half-brother Huascar had been killed en route to Cajamarca, of murder. Found guilty, Atahualpa allowed himself to be baptized in order to avoid being burned at the stake. Instead, he was killed by strangulation in June or July 1533.

The End of Tahuantinsuyu

News of Atahualpa's death brought sorrow to his supporters and his family, as well as the ire of King Charles V of Spain (who disliked the precedent of having rulers killed). To fill the leadership void, the Spaniards set Tupac Huallpa, Atahualpa's half-brother, as a token king of Tahuantinsuyu, but he succumbed to illness soon afterwards.

Atahualpa's own generals took advantage of his death to attempt a more vigorous repulsion of the invaders, which they previously had not dared to do because of the danger posed to their king. However, many local populations chose to side with the Spaniards against Atahualpa's forces, which had committed atrocities against them.

The remaining Inca resistance, led by Atahualpa's commander Quizquiz, attempted and then failed to defend Cuzco, the Inca capital. In November 1533, Pizarro's troops took the city. In December they installed yet another puppet king, Manco Inca, yet another half-brother of Atahualpa. His rule also did not last long, but only because he abandoned Cuzco in 1536 to set up a new state at Vilcabamba, which resisted and otherwise opposed the Spanish occupation until Vilcabamba was finally conquered in 1572.

⊕ Key Elements of Warcraft

Warhorses

Because of their speed, size, and ability to be trained, horses have had many uses for military operations throughout history. These tasks have included carrying supplies, pulling chariots, and providing mounted soldiers with a movable weapons platform.

Domestication of the Horse

Archaeology has not revealed a clear picture of the domestication of the horse. Certainly by about 2000 BCE, a fully domesticated breed had appeared in the steppes of western Asia. Domestic horses spread rapidly throughout Asia and Europe and into Egypt during the Bronze Age.

Horses in the Wars of Antiquity

Horses made their first significant contributions to warfare during the Bronze Age, the heyday of chariot warfare. Beginning in the seventeenth century BCE, horse-drawn chariots dominated many battlefields in the region of the Aegean Sea, the Near East, and Egypt. The Iron Age, however, saw the replacement of chariot warfare with that of infantry, although some cultures—including the Persians and the Celts—continued to field chariots in battle.

Riding on horseback is attested to unequivocally in the artistic and archaeological record beginning only a little before 1000 BCE. Cavalry had superior mobility compared to chariots and infantry, but it could not be used to full advantage until the invention of the stirrup.

Warhorses in Medieval and Renaissance Europe

The Huns swept into Europe on horseback in the fifth century CE. By the time the mounted archers of the Mongols followed eight centuries later, the dominant European cavalrymen were heavily armored knights. Large breeds were required to support the immense weight of the rider, and the horse itself also often wore armor. The style of riding typically associated with the knight was known in Spanish as *a la brida*. Subduing the horse and

The development of guns allowed cavalry to be armed with long-range weapons other than bows and crossbows. *Erich Lessing/Art Resource, NY*

controlling it forcibly by bit and bridle, the rider sat stiff, legs braced forward in the stirrups.

Monarchs and horse traders alike recognized the value of the many regional breeds available throughout Europe. Spanish and Frisian breeds were especially prized. To improve their own stocks, governments variously mandated or banned specific imports, and the trade in military horses tended to be tightly regulated. Even so, shortages of good warhorses, of both heavy breeds and light, sometimes occurred.

Although heavy breeds predominated, smaller horses and even ponies saw battle. As was demonstrated, for example, during the Crusades and the wars between the English king Edward II and Robert the Bruce, this sort of cavalry could defeat heavily armored opponents through greater swiftness and dexterity.

From the Moors who occupied the Iberian Peninsula until the Spanish Reconquista, the Spanish adopted new techniques for smaller, faster breeds that were better suited to mounted combat with swords. This sort of riding, with knees bent, was referred to as *a la jineta*. Control was achieved less by force upon the mouth with the bit and more by coercive pressure of the rider's legs upon the horse's sides.

In Europe, both styles of riding fell out of fashion in the mid-sixteenth century, when Federico Grisone published two highly influential books on horsemanship which combined features of brida and jineta techniques. Jineta riding persisted in the Americas, however.

The Horse in the Americas At the time the first Spaniards arrived, horses were unknown in the New World. Except for the llamas and alpacas of the Andes, the Americas lacked domesticable animals capable of carrying sizeable burdens, let alone a rider.

Thus, when the Spaniards did arrive with horses, the cavalry initially terrified people, who thought each mount and rider to be a single creature. A horse is a large, intimidating animal—still useful today for crowd control—and it was no less so at the time of the Spanish conquest.

At first, the indigenous tribes had no tactical defenses against nimble cavalry, whose repeated charges could break up their infantry formations. Yet the Aztecs and the Incas did capitalize on the weaknesses of horses, particularly during sieges, when they used pits, for example, to stop their advance, or devised long lances to unseat Spanish riders.

For a time, Spanish colonial law forbade the indigenous subjects from riding horses. Such rules could hardly be enforced on the plains of North America, where, in the late seventeenth century, the tribes acquired horses in revolts against the Spaniards. By the time the United States came into full conflict with the indigenous tribes, the horse was an integral part of tribal warfare and daily life.

Drawing of an arquebusier, sixteenth century. *Mansell/Time Life Pictures/Getty Images*

Horses in Modern Warfare

Horses in Modern Warfare Horses, as pack and draft animals and as cavalry mounts, were of vital importance during wars of the seventeenth through early twentieth centuries.

Ironically, military horses are most useful today in situations in which they would have been least useful during the days of chariot and cavalry warfare. From World War II to the twenty-first century conflict in Afghanistan, they played vital roles in the transport of men and supplies in mountainous terrains and other regions beyond the reach of mechanized transport.

Arquebuses and Other Matchlock Guns

The matchlock was the first ignition device to allow the shooter to use both hands to steady the gun. Prior to the invention of the matchlock, firearms were ignited by means of a match stick, which had to be held in one hand while the other steadied the gun.

Firearm Improvements Two innovations made the more convenient matchlock possible. One was the matchcord, or slow match. This was a long wick of cotton, hemp, or flax soaked in a solution of saltpeter. It burned at a rate of four to five inches per hour. The second innovation was the serpentine, an S-shaped lever that held the matchcord. Variations of this mechanism abounded; in its simplest form, pressing one end of the lever brought the lighted matchcord down to the flash-pan that held the priming powder beside the touchhole in the barrel of the gun. This led to the ignition of the gunpowder and discharged the weapon.

Also instrumental in the utility of the matchlock was the stock. The stock of the arquebus could be pressed against the chest to steady it, and the barrel of the gun provided a line of sight for purposes of aiming. The weight of the weapon required the use of a fork stick to support the barrel, hence the name "arquebus," from the German *Hakenbüchse* ("hook-gun").

Although the matchlock was a German invention of the fifteenth century, its technology underwent no single evolutionary line of development. Individual gunsmiths innovated at will. Improvements were made to the flash-pan (moved from the top of the barrel to the side, and often covered to protect the powder from dampness and the soldier from mishap) and the stock (given large butts and thumb notches). The introduction of a spring-loaded catch improved the triggering mechanism, and by the late sixteenth century the trigger itself had roughly assumed its modern form, operated by a pull of the index finger.

By 1475, the principle of rifling—in which grooves in the barrel improve the accuracy of a bullet's trajectory—was in deliberate use, though smoothbore barrels remained the norm. A good smoothbore arquebus had a range of a hundred yards. At sixty or seventy yards, a heavy arquebus could pierce most plate armor.

Gun Types During the period, terminology was often not well defined. "Arquebus" and its many variations (including Hakenbüchse, harquebus, hackbut, haca-buche, and archibuso) might refer to any of a number of matchlock weapon types that today fall under other terms. The caliver, originally called *une arquebuse du caliber*, was a hand-held gun up to forty-four inches long and up to about ten pounds in weight. It was developed in the middle of the sixteenth century.

At about twice the weight of the caliver, the mosquete or musket required the use of a rest. Some authorities believe that the great weight of the early musket led the musketeer to brace the gun against his shoulder, a practice that persisted even after the weight had been reduced to sixteen pounds in the seventeenth century.

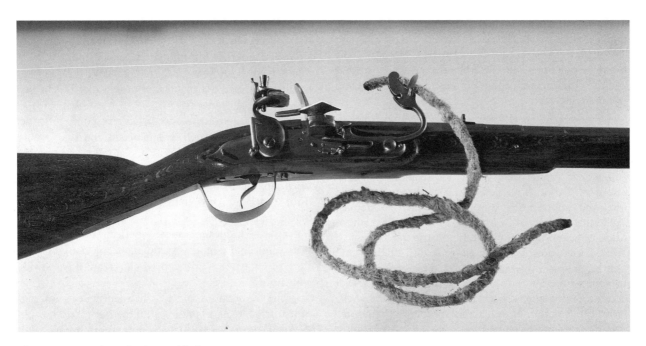

The serpentine and match of a matchlock gun.   *Erich Lessing/Art Resource, NY*

Use of the Arquebus   Between shots, the arquebusier or musketeer had to reload his weapon, a process that began with removing the burning match from the serpentine. He held the match (often kept lit at both ends) and the barrel with one hand while he opened and poured a charge of gunpowder. The arquebusier then inserted a ball and a wad of paper or tow (which then had to be rammed into the barrel). Using the other hand, he added priming powder to the pan. Then he aimed and fired. While this seems difficult, it was easier to train a man to perform these complicated and hazardous actions than it was to train a competent crossbowman.

The Arquebus in Asia and the Americas   The Spaniards and other Europeans were armed with crossbows and matchlocks when they came to the New World in the late fifteenth century and when they arrived in eastern Asia in the sixteenth century. The Japanese, with highly developed metallurgy, had the opportunity and ability to adopt and improve firearms provided by the Portuguese, but for cultural reasons they regulated the weapons and later rejected them for more than two hundred years.

The Aztecs in Mexico and Incas in Peru had only limited experience with metalworking and, unlike the Japanese, no experience with gunpowder. Although conditions were far from optimal for the operation of matchlocks, these and other guns (coupled with many other factors including disease and political instability) heavily contributed to the downfall of these two New World empires.

The End of the Arquebus   Its many weaknesses, from its slow rate of fire to the impracticality (in damp or windy conditions) and danger of the matchcord, ultimately doomed the matchlock. Yet its simplicity and economy of production sustained its use. It took the wheellock, first developed in about 1520, and other ignition devices about two centuries to supercede the matchlock in both the Americas and Europe.

⊕ The Impact of the Conquest of the Americas

Most immediately, the Spanish invasion resulted in the destruction of two major American empires, the Aztec and Inca, and it took a devastating toll on neighboring people. Warfare, disease, and forced acculturation and conversion exterminated or transformed indigenous cultures.

The sixteenth and seventeenth centuries witnessed a flood of immigration into the Americas, the Spanish and Portuguese being the first to arrive in significant numbers. That they were mostly men led to intermarriage with local women, and this resulted in a greater mingling of cultures than would be the case farther north among the English, Dutch, and French and their indigenous neighbors. This population of Europeans, natives, and *mestizos* (mixed-race) were joined by forced migrations of enslaved African men, women, and children sent in as substitutes for the native labor lost in epidemics of European diseases.

On these Iberian heels, late in the sixteenth century came other Europeans, notably the British and French.

These immigrants established their own colonies and trading outposts (such as Jamestown, Plymouth, and Tadoussac) in northern North America. Here too, the native populations suffered from the effects of disease and the introduction of European economic systems and technologies.

By their initial control of the American trade in precious metals and other commodities, Spain and Portugal usurped Italy's position as the premier luxury commodity agent of the Renaissance. However, enormous amounts of capital were required to exploit American resources. Labor, both slave and specialized, had to be imported either from Europe or Africa. Wilderness needed to be "tamed" with clear-cutting and the imposition of economic and political infrastructure.

By engaging in contraband trade, English and Dutch companies avoided certain overhead expenses. In time Spain lost possessions in the region to other nations. It was England and Holland that benefited the most from the transatlantic trade, turning imported raw materials (from the Americas, Asia, and Africa) into manufactured goods sold in Europe and the colonies.

What Spaniards and their laborers extracted at a high price benefited not only Spain but also the rest of Europe. Merchants from many nations prospered from the transatlantic trade. Besides using illegal trade to access the wealth of the Caribbean, the British also attacked the Spanish plate fleet. One consequence of this piracy and privateering was the launch of the Spanish Armada against England in 1588.

The influx of wealth also aided military operations. Spain was part of the Habsburg Empire; consequently, American silver especially helped to fund the Thirty Years War and campaigns that checked the advance of the Turkish Ottoman Empire into Europe. The influx of silver and gold also promoted the use of minted coins that served as internationally recognizable collateral for credit and helped to expand European trade. This helped foster a global economy.

More than just men and metals crossed the Atlantic. Old World crops, such as sugarcane and rice, would become staples of New World plantation economies. Domestic animals, such as pigs, and accidental introductions ranging from rats to nightcrawlers, would transform American ecosystems. American crops, notably maize and potatoes, as well as fish from its Atlantic waters, fed European nations. American tomatoes, chocolate, and chili peppers would refashion cuisines from Italy to China, and tobacco would create a worldwide addiction.

The foundations laid by the Spanish conquest and other early European presences in the New World would eventually bring forth independent nations, but not until such wars as the American Revolution and the European wars of empire of the nineteenth century.

BIBLIOGRAPHY

Books

Díaz, Bernal. *The Conquest of New Spain*, translated by J. M. Cohen. London: Penguin, 1963.

Gómara, Francisco Lopez de. *Cortés: The Life of the Conqueror by His Secretary*, translated and edited by Lesley Byrd Simpson. Berkeley: University of California Press, 1964.

Introduction to Religious Wars in Europe (1517–1648)

In the early sixteenth century, the Roman Catholic Church was still an influential organization. While its monarchical power had been somewhat diminished since the papal controversies surrounding the Avignonese captivity of the fourteenth century, the church held enormous sway over the realm of morality and social practices. Papal theorists equated universal Christianity with the Roman Church and the pope as the supreme head of all Christian believers. The pope therefore held a monopoly over doctrine, including the dispensation of grace, which operated through the sacraments of baptism, confirmation, the Eucharist, penance, ordination, marriage, and extreme unction. The clergy in turn administered the sacraments and, by so doing, served as conduits between individuals and their salvation.

Religious belief was largely monolithic. Revealed Christian truth was considered to be indivisible, and heresy was considered not only to be errant, but also a social ill that could incur the wrath of God upon the entire community if allowed to persist. Hence religious disputes occurred frequently and were often violent. At the same time, religious priorities were often inextricably bound to other interests. Nobles for instance, relied upon monarchs for their status, and hence wealth. Exclusion from royal favor could spell ruin for entire families of aristocrats. Therefore, the issue of a king's religious belief mattered enormously in political terms.

Once the passions of the Protestant Reformation were unleashed after 1517, nearly every war combined territorial and religious conflict. The Dutch Revolt, or Eighty Years War, fought from 1568 to 1648, saw the Seventeen Provinces of the Netherlands (Protestant) rise in opposition to Spanish (Catholic Habsburg) control. In the course of the revolt, the newly formed United Provinces of the Netherlands, or Dutch Republic, became a significant maritime trading power.

Frenchmen waged eight Wars of Religion between 1562 and 1598, a prolonged series of contests between Catholic and Protestant factions that were competing for the crown and the religious identity of France. The wars weakened the French state, and not until the last half of the seventeenth century would French influence be restored in Europe.

The major conflict of the early seventeenth century, the Thirty Years War (1618–1648) was the largest war waged during the period. It was an expansive and destructive conflict involving each of the major European states. Sparked largely by religious and territorial conflicts, the conflict gradually became a political contest. The wide-ranging fighting prompted a redistribution of military and political power. While the populace lay exhausted by the end of the war, with large parts of Germany laid waste, the centralized authority of state governments was permanently enhanced, and the foundation of a new state system emerged.

The pair of treaties signed in the Westphalian towns of Münster and Osnabrück in 1648 that ended the fighting became known as the "Peace of Westphalia." This general European agreement brought the Thirty Years War to a formal conclusion, as well as terminated conflict between the Netherlands and Spain, and while religious tension and violence did erupt in some states, the Westphalian settlement generally brought the era of religious wars to a close.

Although not universally applied, the Peace of Westphalia underscored the importance of state sovereignty and legal equality between states. Henceforward, religious disputes increasingly played a diminished role in international relations, as political and economic matters gained ascendancy.

Religious Wars in Europe (1517–1648)

⊕ Major Figures

Martin Luther

At the heart of the series of disputes in Europe during the early sixteenth century that eventually divided Christianity into Catholic and Protestant identities was the German monk and theologian, Martin Luther (1483–1546). The explicit shortcomings that Luther criticized in church practice and belief evolved into a comprehensive assault upon the foundations of Catholic identity and practice, ultimately creating alternative Protestant denominations and launching more than a century of political and religious strife in Europe.

Devout Beginnings Born in Eisleben, Germany, Luther came from the middle ranks of society, and he was characteristic of the hard-working and sober young men recruited to assume a monastic life in the service of the Catholic Church. His father, Hans, a younger son of a successful farming family, had entered the mining industry and married respectably in Saxony. Hans wanted Luther to receive an education and hoped that he would pursue a legal career. Hence in 1501, Luther entered the university at Erfurt.

Luther soon abandoned his law studies, later attributing his decision to an experience in which he was caught outdoors during a terrible thunderstorm in 1505. The impressionable Luther vowed to Saint Anne, the mother of the Virgin Mary, that he would enter the monastic life if he survived the tumult. When the storm passed, Luther kept his vow, entering an Augustinian monastery where he performed well, taking priestly orders in 1507. He began teaching at the University of Wittenberg soon thereafter.

From 1512 to 1516, Luther's knowledge of Scripture deepened as he lectured on Genesis, the Psalms, and Paul's Epistle to the Romans. Despite his use of humanist methods of teaching and writing, Luther gradually arrived at a pragmatic—if somewhat dark—view of the human condition, a philosophy that represented a rebel-lion against the formally scholastic approach that was a staple of northern Europe's intellectual climate.

A Call for Reform By 1517, Luther was frustrated with some church practices, notably the sale of indulgences. When a supplicant purchased an indulgence, a transfer of the merit accumulated by Christ and the saints to an individual was affected by the church to remit some or all of the penalties otherwise to be suffered in purgatory. Luther, because he denied the pope's authority over salvation, argued against this practice.

On October 31, Luther outlined his complaint in ninety-five statements, or theses, that he allegedly nailed to the Castle Church doors in Wittenberg. Whether he actually posted his theses or simply wrote to the Archbishop of Mainz, Luther's words soon circulated widely and ignited a firestorm of debate. Between 1517 and 1530, Luther found himself the unexpected leader of a comprehensive and radical program that directly challenged the foundations of Catholicism.

By returning a merciful God to the forefront of theology, Luther attacked the church's tight control over doctrine, morality, and social mores. Three formulas contain Luther's teaching: *sola fide* ("by faith alone"), *sola scriptura* ("by scripture alone"), and *sola gratia* ("by grace alone").

Sola fide emphasizes the magnificence of reason and the primacy of revelation by insisting that man is saved by faith alone. No man can earn salvation through works; rather, God mercifully chooses some few, and these, the elect, are predestined for salvation. *Sola fide*, or justification by faith, became a hallmark of later Protestantism.

Sola scriptura holds that the sole source of religious truth is the word of God as revealed in Scripture. The Bible is the authoritative record of God's revelation to man and the means through which God communicates to people. The role of priests and church officials as intermediaries was clearly and directly challenged by Luther.

Sola gratia means that man cannot know the truth of salvation or accomplish any good without the aid and free gift of God's grace. All virtue derives directly from grace and in no manner reflects any inherent abilities or works of individuals.

The Establishment Strikes Back Luther published three tracts in 1520 that outlined these radical thoughts. *An Open Letter to the Christian Nobility of the German Nation* , *The Babylonian Captivity of the Church*, and *On Christian Liberty* constituted a wide-ranging assault against papal prestige, and consequently Pope Leo X realized that he could no longer ignore the troublesome Luther. In 1520, the Pope issued a papal bull (a formal decree) accusing Luther of heresy and threatening him with excommunication if he did not retract many of his positions. When Luther stuck to his arguments, he was formally excommunicated in January 1521.

Luther fled to Saxon territory and was installed by supporters in the Wartburg castle above the city of Eisenach. In March, he was summonsed by Emperor Charles V to Worms to defend himself. During the Diet of Worms (a meeting of the various polities of the Holy Roman Empire), Luther refused to recant his position. Whether he actually said, "Here I stand, I can do no other" is uncertain. What is known is that he did refuse to recant, and on May 8 he was placed under Imperial Ban.

This placed Luther and his protectors in a dangerous position, as Luther was now a condemned and wanted man. Consequently he remained in hiding at the Wartburg castle until May 1522, when he returned to Wittenberg to resume teaching. In 1524 and 1525, the Peasants War raged in Germany. This uprising, which saw widespread destruction waged by peasants and commoners, was fueled by an assortment of legal, social, and economic tensions fueled by Luther's revolutionary prose that seemed to challenge the standing order. Luther disappointed the rebels, however, by arguing that they should adhere to temporal authorities.

Later Years In 1525, Luther married Katharina von Bora, definitively establishing the practice of clerical marriage for Protestants. He continued to study and advocate his positions. His translation of the New Testament in German appeared in 1522, followed by the Old Testament in 1534, yielding an entire German-language Bible. During the last years of his life, Luther served as the dean of the theology faculty at Wittenberg. He died in Eisleben on February 18, 1546.

The Reformation that Luther sparked was ultimately an argument about the conditions of salvation. Those who followed Luther and became known as Protestants believed that Catholic clergy did behave badly (as in the case of indulgences), but more profoundly maintained that the Catholic Church was wrong about God's plan for man's salvation. Luther and his adherents wished to restore Christianity to its biblical purity. It was a debate that led to social and political conflict for a century after Luther's death, and it is a theological debate that still resounds today.

Martin Luther. *Public Domain*

Philip II

King Philip II of Spain (1527–1598), the "Catholic King," was an ardent defender of his faith and a monarch admired at home and despised abroad. Among his many titles, he ruled as king of Spain from 1556 to 1598; as king of Naples and Sicily from 1554 to 1598; was king consort of England (husband of Mary) from 1554 to 1558; and was king of Portugal from 1580 until 1598. Philip's reign was characterized by both the expansion of Spanish military power and consolidation of imperial reach, but also by increasing debt and growing challenges to Spanish authority by other European states.

Born to Rule Philip's father was Charles V, Holy Roman Emperor, and his mother was Isabella of Portugal. Throughout his life, Philip was the emblem of Habsburg monarchy, and his personal life reflected his dynastic interests. His first marriage was to his cousin, the Princess Maria of Portugal, who bore him a son named Don Carlos. Don Carlos was unstable and sickly and died in 1568. Maria died in 1545, and Philip found a new wife in the English Catholic, Queen Mary. The match was not popular with the public in either England or Spain, but Mary, always insecure, grasped at the union.

St. Edward's Crown is the coronation crown of England.   © *Tim Graham/Alamy*

Philip spent little time with Mary, and when she died childless in 1558, he sought yet another wife. He next married Princess Elizabeth of Valois, daughter of Henry II of France. When Elizabeth passed in 1568, Philip married for the fourth time, this time to his niece, Anna of Austria, who bore him an heir, Philip III, in 1578.

Philip's reign as king was characterized by expansion and warfare. By the late 1580s, perhaps as many as 100,000 troops were in Spanish pay, and the defense of Spain's overseas colonies in the Americas demanded a large fleet. Likewise, Philip oversaw contests against both the Protestant forces of Western and Northern Europe as well as against Muslims in the Mediterranean.

Trouble in the Low Countries Beginning in the 1560s, the Netherlands rose in revolt against Habsburg rule. Protestant agitation and unwillingness to submit to Spanish administration prompted active resistance. Ruling from Madrid, Philip garrisoned thousands of Spanish troops in important Dutch cities and towns and sought funds from local citizens for their upkeep. The result was a war that simmered for decades and drained Spanish coffers while periodically inviting active military intervention from other powers, including England and France.

Queen Elizabeth of England, fearful of Spanish power and intervention in the Low Countries, had in the 1570s endorsed privateering as an effective and economic means to challenge Spain. By the mid-1580s, when it appeared that the longstanding tension would lead to war, she increased English support for Dutch rebels and launched more ambitious sea raids against Spanish maritime interests. In the fall of 1585, the English sea captain Sir Francis Drake plundered Spanish possessions and shipping in an expedition to the Spanish West Indies, inflicting significant damage to Spanish holdings and infuriating Philip.

Unwilling to allow Spain's reputation to be sullied, Philip initiated preparations for an invasion of England. After many difficulties, the famed Spanish Armada sailed during the late summer of 1588. A combination of unfavorable weather, English seamanship, and inadequate logistical support doomed the armada to defeat, inflicting upon Spain the greatest military loss of Philip's reign.

The event was the high point of Spanish influence in European and Atlantic waters. Thereafter, England's rise as a naval power continued unabated for two centuries, while Spanish influence, though not completely evident at the time, entered a period of long decline.

Conflicts with Other Nations From 1590 to 1598, Philip waged an unsuccessful war against Henry IV of France, allying with Duke Henry of Guise and the Catholic League. Henry IV was able to mobilize his subjects by characterizing Habsburg involvement in France's affairs as dangerous to the French nation, thereby stiffening resistance to Spain. The war gained nothing for Philip.

While fighting against the Protestant states of Europe, Philip also waged war in defense of Christianity. Philip's Spain, for many generations a battleground in the contest between Islam and Christianity, took religious war to the sea by confronting Turkish navies in the Mediterranean. During the late 1550s, Turkish warships raided the Spanish mainland. In 1560, Philip organized a Holy League by allying with Spain and the Republic of Venice, the Republic of Genoa, the Papal States, the Duchy of Savoy, and the Knights of Malta. The Christian fleet of some two hundred ships initially met defeat, but ultimately achieved a major victory at sea in the Battle of Lepanto in 1571. Thereafter, the Islamic threat was significantly reduced.

Years of war drained Spanish coffers. As early as 1565, debts absorbed more than 80 percent of Spanish revenues. By the end of Philip's reign, the total state debt ran eight times higher than annual income. While some of the debt could be relieved through bullion imported from the Americas, domestic taxes were also raised by more than 400 percent between the 1560s and 1590s. The result was an inflationary spiral that affected all segments of the Spanish economy.

When Philip died on September 13, 1598, Spain had reached new heights of influence, but it had also incurred debts that the state could not pay. His unyielding personality and ardent religiosity ensured the preservation of Catholicism at home but earned enemies in England, France, and the Netherlands. Nonetheless, by defeating the Ottoman navy, uniting the crowns of Portugal and Spain, and defending Catholicism across Western Europe, Philip demonstrated that he was one of the most important monarchs of his age.

Elizabeth I

Born at Greenwich Palace, Queen Elizabeth I (1533–1603) ruled England from 1558 until her death in 1603.

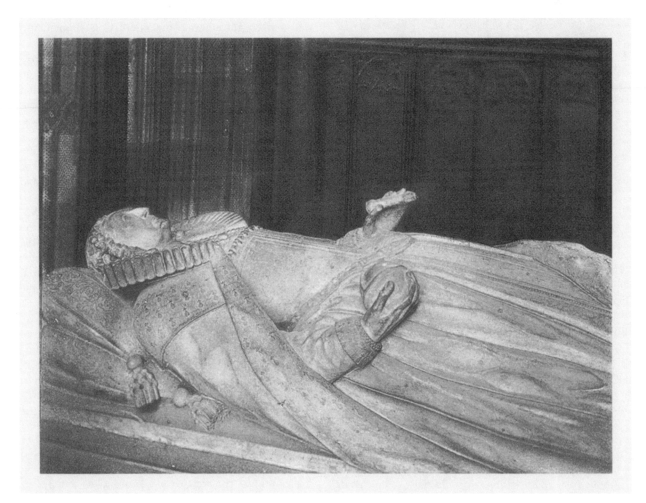

Tomb of Elizabeth I, in Westminster Abbey.   © *The Print Collector/Alamy*

GUY FAWKES AND THE GUNPOWDER PLOT

The Gunpowder Plot is the name given to the attempt to detonate barrels of gunpowder beneath the Houses of Parliament on November 5, 1605. That day was State Opening Day, when the King, the Lords, and the Commons would assemble to mark the initial session of Parliament.

Historians have long considered the goal of the conspiracy to be the restoration of Catholicism to England, although some revisionist scholars have investigated whether the plot was actually the work of Protestant agents who wished to discredit the Catholic cause.

Guy Fawkes—a Catholic, a mercenary, and a veteran of fighting in the Netherlands—is the conspirator most closely linked to the event in history, but he was not the leader of the small group of men preparing the explosion. The plot was revealed when Lord Monteagle received an anonymous letter warning him to stay away from the State Opening. A search on November 4, 1605, found both Fawkes and the gunpowder concealed in a cellar.

The conspirators were shortly rounded up, interrogated, tortured, and executed. As was the tradition, their bodies were placed on display around Westminster as a reminder to others who may consider rebellion.

Since the events of 1605, the fifth of November has been called, Fireworks Night, Bonfire Night, or most popularly, Guy Fawkes Day. Customs to mark the occasion include setting off fireworks and the construction—and destruction—of effigies of Fawkes. To keep alive the tradition of watchfulness that the holiday celebrates, the Yeomen of the Guard still conduct a ceremonious search of Parliament's chambers prior to their opening session.

died without issue, Elizabeth's accession was welcomed by both the general population and the noble order.

After the tumults raised by Mary's attempts to re-impose Catholicism upon a reluctant state, Elizabeth determined that a religious accommodation was one of her most important orders of business. The settlement she orchestrated in 1559 reflected her conviction that the era of reform instigated by her father in the late 1520s was now over; her institution of a revised prayer book and liturgical instructions was meant to be the final solution. To that end, and to the House of Commons' consternation, Elizabeth tolerated very little public discussion of the matter by government officials. Zealous Protestants were quieted, and adherents to the old faith were driven underground.

England Blossoms In 1569, the strength of Elizabeth's regime was tested when the northern Earls of Northumberland and Westmorland raised a revolt, calling for the restoration of Catholicism. The rapid collapse of the movement and the inability of the rebels to raise any sustained assistance from elsewhere in the kingdom was evidence that the 1559 settlement had become established. By the early 1570s, Elizabeth's popularity was marked throughout the country in spontaneous festivities to note Accession Day (November 17).

The two decades following 1570 were especially prosperous for England. Sufficient harvests and a respite from epidemic disease contributed to a growing population and domestic stability. Literature and the arts blossomed—this was the age of Francis Bacon, William Shakespeare, Christopher Marlowe, and Edmund Spenser.

Elizabeth was a decisive and strong leader, earning the confidence of her close advisors as well as that of the populace. Her style of command was highly personal and maximized her unique status as a female monarch. To her council and court she appeared tough and unyielding, demanding obedience to her orders. While always eager for flattery and often haughty, she did not easily succumb to the solicitations of supplicants. The aristocrats and servants Elizabeth maintained in her household were fiercely loyal to her, and her rule benefited from the continuity she oversaw.

Beyond her court, Elizabeth cultivated a much more feminine, pacific image. She made great display of attending to the needs and wishes of her subjects. During her annual summer progresses through the nation, she acted the role of a grateful, if distinguished, guest in country manors and great houses. Her propaganda relentlessly presented the queen as the defender of the realm against all threats.

A Quest for a Consort There were certainly threats to the security of her realm. One of her most vexing challenges was the search for a husband to solidify her succession and to perhaps forge an alliance with another European state. While Elizabeth had favorites—including

During her long rule, England prospered intellectually, economically, and politically.

Ascension Issues Elizabeth was the only surviving child of Henry VIII and Anne Boleyn. Elizabeth barely knew her mother, whom Henry executed when Elizabeth was only thirty-two months old. When Anne Boleyn's marriage to Henry was declared void, Elizabeth became illegitimate and was thus barred from inheriting the crown, as was Mary, Henry's daughter with Catherine of Aragon, before her. It was only later, when Henry was satisfied with the succession to his son Edward VI, that he recognized Mary and Elizabeth as potential successors if Edward's line failed.

Elizabeth received a thorough education and proved an intelligent child. She was supportive of Edward VI, but when he died young and Mary assumed the throne as a Catholic ruler, Elizabeth became a liability and a threat. She spent the years of Mary's reign keeping a low profile and avoiding suspicion as best she could. When Mary

Robert Dudley (earl of Leicester), Sir Christopher Hatton (the captain of her bodyguard), and Robert Devereux (earl of Essex)—these men were not sufficient matches in dynastic terms. Instead, she sought an alliance with another European monarchy.

Early in her reign she entered negotiations with Philip II of Spain, Mary's former husband, but these ended when Elizabeth confirmed her opposition to papal sovereignty. Another suitor was Charles, archduke of Austria, but negotiations in this direction also collapsed over religious disputes. Henri, duke of Anjou (the younger brother of Charles IX, king of France), presented himself as a candidate for a time, albeit unsuccessfully. Then Anjou's younger brother François, duke of Alençon, came to the forefront, and in November 1581 Elizabeth announced she would marry him, causing a sensation. Elizabeth may not have been sincere, especially given French persecution of the Protestant Huguenots, but in any case the matter concluded in 1584 when Alençon died.

Elizabeth's prospects for bearing a child were diminishing by now, and gradually she adopted the mantle of the "Virgin Queen," a status her publicity machine elevated to a position of unassailable virtue and dignity.

Suitors Wanting the Nation are Also Rebuffed In the realm of foreign affairs, Elizabeth maintained an on-and-off-again war with Spain. English sea captains such as Francis Drake, whom Elizabeth knighted in 1581, preyed upon Spanish merchant fleets sailing from the New World. England also supported the Netherlands in its struggles against Spain.

Philip believed that as the former husband of Mary (and as a devout Catholic king), he enjoyed a divine prerogative to invade heretical England. In 1587, Philip received approval from the pope to do just that, and the following year he launched his great armada against England. The armada was defeated by bad weather and English seamanship, but as hostilities between the two nations continued on, Elizabeth emerged the stalwart defender of England and the English Church.

Elizabeth died at Richmond Palace at the age of sixty-nine. Although she left behind no will, she had made it known that her cousin, James VI of Scotland, was her lawful successor. Thereafter, the crowns of England and Scotland would be united in the person of the monarch. While the final years of her reign lacked the vitality of her youth, her kingdom reached new levels of prosperity and influence under her rule. She remains as one of the United Kingdom's most important and effective monarchs.

Henry of Navarre

Henry IV, also known as Henry of Navarre (1553–1610), ruled as king of France from 1589 to 1610. Henry was

Castel Nuovo, built by Charles I of Anjou, begun in 1279 and completed three years later. © *Peter Horree/Alamy*

ST. BARTHOLOMEW'S DAY MASSACRE

The St. Bartholomew's Day Massacre was the murders of French Huguenots that began in Paris on August 24, 1572, and spread through many areas of France during the ensuing weeks. The massacre was symptomatic of the intense passions surrounding the question of France's religious—and hence, dynastic—identity.

The original scheme was probably conceived by Catherine de Medici, mother of France's king, Charles IX. A number of Huguenot nobles had gathered in Paris for the wedding of Henry of Navarre to Margaret of Valois. Seeing an opportunity to strike to advantage, Catherine plotted to eliminate some of the Catholic regime's most senior opponents.

The event that precipitated the massacre was the attempted assassination of the Protestant noble, Admiral Coligny, on August 22. Again Catherine and her advisors were involved, and when Charles was confronted with the failure of the murder, Catherine convinced him that to preserve his power he needed to act decisively. The new plan was to summon royal troops to murder the key Huguenot leaders lodged in Paris; Catholic mobs would be mobilized to threaten any local response from the Protestants.

Charles' minions assumed their positions in the middle of the night. Before dawn, Coligny had been slain, as had other targeted Huguenots. Yet once the murders began, the killing spread. House after house was pillaged until thousands of Protestants were dead. Most Catholics justified the mayhem by pointing to Huguenot conspiracies, and soon the murder spread to other French towns. Fearing that he had overreached, Charles tried to stem the bloodshed, but his call for calm was ineffective.

In the short term, thousands of Huguenots were forced to flee or to recant their faith. Thousands of others took flight, never to return to their homes. While the Protestant cause rallied and conflict persisted for decades more in France, the Protestant cause did suffer a severe blow from the massacre. The atrocities committed by the Catholic leadership horrified many observers, yet it was simply one of many excesses witnessed during the period.

Margaret, the sister of Charles IX, in August 1572, but was forced to abjure his faith as a consequence of the Catholic-led St. Bartholomew's Day Massacre that same month. Henry was initially held captive at the royal court, but when he escaped, he renounced his enforced Catholic allegiance.

Henry found himself in line for the throne of France when the Duke of Anjou died in 1584. However, he was formally excluded from the royal succession by the Treaty of Nemours, agreed upon by King Henry III of France and Duke Henry of Guise, leader of the Catholic League. Guise was adamant that a Protestant not ascend to become king, and another round of warfare ensued.

During the subsequent "War of Three Henrys," the Catholic League was allied with Spain against the Huguenots. The populace became polarized, forcing Henry III to flee Paris and join with Navarre. The way to the throne finally materialized in August 1589, when Henry III was assassinated.

Henry of Navarre demonstrated his military talent by fighting in numerous battles at the head of Protestant forces in the field, and he achieved a decisive victory while outnumbered at Arques in September 1589. Henry was repulsed from Paris later that year but returned to besiege the capital again in 1590. He operated against Rouen in 1591 and 1592.

Ascending the throne as King Henry IV, Henry was welcomed by many who were weary of the religious war and who had a desire for change from the vacillation of his predecessor. Nonetheless, the new monarch faced numerous challenges. Several years of poor harvests and rapid inflation had brought economic distress and heightened criminality to the countryside. Towns ran up debts as they increased their defenses and supplied the armies in their vicinity. Hardships suffered by the peasants sometimes led to open rebellion, like the uprising that began in 1593 and soon engulfed much of western France. Meanwhile, as Henry attempted to restore order within France, he also struggled to establish his own legitimacy.

Henry Decides Paris is Worth a Mass The Catholic League opposed Henry and had chosen the Cardinal de Bourbon to be monarch. The latter took the name Charles X, but he died in May 1590. This left the League without a suitable replacement, and some moderates suggested to Henry that he declare himself a Catholic to satisfy the League's demands. Henry had already included Catholic advisors in his court, and in July 1593, he formally abjured his Protestant faith. On February 27, 1594, he was crowned at Chartres, thus paving the way for his entrance into Paris.

Henry continued to confront challenges to his rule. In January 1595, he declared war on Spain for the purpose of eliminating foreign support for domestic Catholic agitation. Henry hoped to excite a sense of French nationalism and to isolate the Catholic League by uniting the French

popular in his day, and he earned a legacy of stability and reform for his kingdom, successfully drawing to a close the religious wars that had plagued the country for more than a generation.

Switching Religions Born at Pau in Béarn, Henry was the son of Antoine de Bourbon, Duke of Vendôme, and Jeanne d'Albret. Initially raised as a Catholic, young Henry was educated by his mother to be a Protestant when he joined her at the official court in 1564. As a teenager, he served under Admiral Gaspard de Coligny during the Third Huguenot War (1568–1570).

Upon his mother's death, Henry became king of Navarre (as Henry III) in June 1572. He married

Site of the Massacre of Glen Coe.   © *David Gowans/Alamy*

people in a common cause. In June of that year, Henry's forces won a battle over Spanish troops near Fontaine-Française during which the king demonstrated his courage by personally leading several cavalry charges.

He then led an army to the north, seizing Cambrai from Catholic loyalists and laying siege to La Fère, a key Spanish outpost. The war continued, but Henry had the upper hand. In the spring of 1597, he besieged Amiens and then later turned back a relieving Spanish army in mid-September, capturing the city.

Later Achievements   Having eliminated the Spanish threat, Henry spent the next decade consolidating his authority. In 1598, he issued the Edict of Nantes by which certain political and religious rights for Huguenots were guaranteed. Huguenots could not raise taxes, build fortifications, or levy troops, but they did enjoy a measure of civil independence. The immediate effect was to calm religious tension and preserve Protestant enclaves, but in the long term, the Protestant cause in France found itself circumscribed. Never again would the Huguenots challenge Catholic supremacy.

Assassinated by François Ravaillac in Paris on May 14, 1610, Henry IV was widely mourned.

By the time Henry became king, the wars of religion in France had damaged the reputation of the French monarchy. As the first Bourbon king, he did much to establish royal order and set in motion administrative reforms that would pay enormous dividends for French power and domestic security over the course of the eighteenth century. While he did not resolve religious tension, he did quell the violence and allowed a modicum of civil life to be restored in France.

⊕ Major Battles

Dreux, December 19, 1562

The Battle of Dreux was the first major battlefield engagement of the French religious wars. The Royalist (Catholic) army, led by Duke François of Guise, defeated Louis I de Bourbon, Prince of Condé's Huguenot (Protestant) force in a bloody but indecisive contest that settled nothing, but which was a harbinger of the decades of sectarian violence to come.

Forces Muster   As small-scale religious hostility and violence turned to outright war in France, each side mobilized forces. By mid-1562, the Royalists had

Sir Frances Drake. *The Library of Congress*

mustered nearly three hundred companies of all types, almost fifty thousand men. Approximately two-thirds were Frenchmen, with the remainder being foreigners and mercenaries. For the Huguenot cause, Condé gathered about six thousand infantry and two thousand cavalry from France. In the spring, roughly seven thousand additional troops (four thousand infantry and three thousand cavalry) from the Protestant principalities of Germany arrived to augment the Protestant army.

In July 1562, the main royal host departed Paris and marched south. It seized Blois from Huguenot forces and ordered separate columns under Marshal Saint-André and other Catholic commanders to retain the towns along the Loire and Poitou rivers. The Royalist troops next headed for Rouen, which the local Huguenots had seized. In late October, that city yielded and was subsequently sacked.

Discouraged but not defeated, Huguenot formations now marched from their garrisons around Orleans with vengeance in mind. Finding Chartres and Paris too strongly defended, they turned northeast and headed toward Normandy to subdue Catholic areas there and to link up with an English expedition marching from Le Havre.

After crossing the river Eure at Maintenon, the Huguenots encountered the Royal army (some nineteen

thousand men) south of Dreux. The Royalists formed a line of battle facing south, with their right anchored in the village of Epinay and with their left at a crossroads near Blainville. Catholic cavalry anchored each wing with infantry battalions and interposed some horse in the center of their position. The Huguenots arrayed themselves in two lines, with the cavalry to the front and the foot behind, and defended astride the Marville-Dreux road, facing north.

The Battle The Huguenot cavalry opened the fighting by charging the left wing of the Royalist line, striking the Swiss infantry posted there. The horsemen of Protestant commander Gaspard de Coligny, Admiral of France, sent the Catholic cavalry of Constable Montmorency to flight, capturing Montmorency in the process. Soon the Catholic left was in peril; the Swiss stood firm in the face of the Protestant battering, but the other Catholic troops nearby began to give way with the Huguenots in pursuit. On the other end of the line, the Catholic right under Guise and Saint-André held their ground as Condé's men pressed ahead.

Coligny's cavalry continued to charge the Swiss ranks, but made little progress. The Huguenot second line, composed mostly of German infantry, now joined the assault, but was repulsed as the Swiss fled behind temporary defenses within the village of Blainville. After several hours of sustained combat, the Protestants finally prevailed, sending the Swiss streaming back with the German cavalry in pursuit. Condé and Coligny then attempted to reassemble their cavalrymen, many who were now dispersed around the battlefield and were bent on looting the Catholic baggage train.

The rest of the Huguenot army, still standing in the middle of the field, was suddenly vulnerable, and a desperate attack by Guise and Saint-André met with unexpected success against the Protestant foot, who had little cavalry support. Condé himself was captured, and Guise led a contingent of his troops toward Blainville to compel the infantry holed up there to yield. However, at the last moment Coligny mounted one final countercharge with the horse he had gathered that blunted the Catholic advance. Confusion now reigned across the battlefield as each side withdrew to take account of the day's events.

Aftermath There was no clear winner to the fight. While the first and final cavalry charges of the day had been made by the Huguenot cavalry, the Catholic infantry had won the better part of the infantry contest. Casualties among the Swiss troops were especially high; probably more than one thousand died, including most of their officers. The Catholics lost about six thousand more, including many of their cavalry leaders. Saint-André was murdered by his Huguenot captors. Protestant losses were also heavy; probably about five thousand killed, wounded, and missing.

Battered and unwilling to continue the battle, the Huguenot army withdrew toward Orleans to garrison that city while reorganizing and refitting. The Catholic Regent Catherine de Medici made some preliminary peace overtures, but Admiral Coligny, who succeeded Condé, demurred. Therefore, the fighting continued until 1566, when a short period of peace was achieved, and the first war was brought to a close.

Brill, April 1572

The seizure of Brill by the Dutch Sea Beggars marked the opening of a second revolt against Habsburg occupation and consolidation of power in the Netherlands. While their attack did not seriously damage the long-term viability of Spanish administration, it did serve to open a new round of hostilities across the Netherlands and further drained Spanish coffers.

The Duke Honors Himself The Duke of Alva, Spanish King Philip II's governor general of the Netherlands, celebrated his military victories against the armies of William of Orange and his allies in 1568 by compelling the city of Antwerp to construct an enormous bronze statue in his honor. Alva had hoped that Philip would reward him with an offer of return to Spain, but instead his king ordered the duke to continue his pacification. Nor would the king make a visit; having recently lost his only son and then his wife in childbirth, Philip could not afford to leave Spain to travel. Alva would have to continue to enforce the rule of Spain until a replacement could be sent.

The military threat from William of Orange at bay for the moment, Alva pursued a series of domestic reforms. He installed the bishopric scheme that had been enacted a decade previously, standardized criminal legal procedures, and codified many customary laws. While these changes were rational in an administrative sense, his high-handed manner and use of force offended most Netherlanders who jealously guarded their local privileges.

Maintaining Spanish troops in the Netherlands was expensive, and Alva sought ways to add to the Spanish purse. In 1569 he convened the Estates of Netherland and petitioned for the collection of new taxes. One of these, the Tenth Penny tax, was a 10 percent levy on sales; a second, the Twentieth Penny tax, was a 5 percent levy on future sales of landed property; and the third, a Hundredth Penny tax, was a single occasion, 1 percent levy on all capital. The Estates rejected this scheme, but in 1571, with his treasury draining, Alva declared he would impose it anyway. Discontent and unrest reached new highs.

Anti-Spanish Sentiment Grows During these years, tens of thousands of Netherlanders fled Spanish persecution, mainly to Germany and England. These communities sustained anti-Spanish propaganda and agitated for other governments to act against Spanish interests. Some agitators met in councils at Emden, on the coast of the Dutch province of Friesland. There they developed a sense of shared purpose and published hundreds of pamphlets regarding Spanish atrocities. Alva had issued

an edict against such propaganda in November 1568, but to little effect.

While unrest against Alva and the Spanish persisted, a new open revolt was sparked by the Sea Beggars. The Dutch Sea Beggars were a loosely organized formation of brigands, patriots, pirates, soldiers, and sailors. Upset with Spanish trade and tax impositions, they were ostensibly anti-Spanish and pro-Orange, yet they frequently angered William and served no single master. They communicated only when convenient to themselves; they attacked seafaring vessels (both Spanish and neutral alike) for the purpose of securing treasure for their own ends; and they made a general nuisance wherever they gained control of a municipality.

Orange tried to impose discipline and direction to the Sea Beggars by clarifying rules by which they could employ military force, but he achieved only limited success. He frequently found himself responding to their actions, seeking to exploit them to success for his cause, rather than effectively coordinating their actions in advance.

Such was the case with the Sea Beggars' assault on Brill. Emboldened by the successful capture of the city, they next seized Flushing, thereby creating several lodgments from which they could move further inland into Holland and Zealand over the course of the summer of 1572. With Alva off balance, William of Orange had wanted to undertake his own offensives, yet the Sea Beggars moved before his forces could be made ready.

Although a small army under Louis of Nassau captured Mons in May, and another force led by Count van der Berg occupied Zutphen, Orange did not have time to secure French cooperation. Charles IX, king of France, was wary of war with Spain and wanted assurances that Orange and his troops could prevail before he risked open conflict with Philip II.

Orange, however, could no longer wait as the Sea Beggars continued their push. He convinced Charles to dispatch some six thousand men to join an invasion force. Yet Alva regrouped in time and ambushed the French, prompting Charles to withdraw immediately and leaving Orange to fight on without assistance. Hence the Sea Beggars, while harming the Spanish occupation in the short term, accomplished little in terms of the strategic situation, and the Eighty Years War continued.

Cadiz, April 1587

The raid by English Admiral Sir Francis Drake upon Spanish shipping in the port of Cadiz marked a personal victory for the great sea captain as well as a signal victory in England's maritime war with Spain. The raid disrupted Spanish preparations demanded by King Philip II for an armada to assemble and carry an invasion force, and it demonstrated the growing skill and lethality of the English navy.

Sir Francis Drake's defeat of the Spanish Armada in 1588. *HIP/Art Resource, NY*

Life of a Privateer Drake was born at Crowndale, near Tavistock, Devonshire, between the years of 1535 and 1543 (the exact year is unknown). His father was a tenant farmer who later became a Protestant preacher. In 1549, the Drake family fled Devon because of resurgent Catholicism. They traveled initially to Plymouth and then later to Kent.

The young Drake's first experience with the sea came as an apprentice on a small barque making trading voyages between England, France, and Holland. When the ship's captain died, Drake acquired the vessel and advanced his career as a sailor. In subsequent years, Drake participated in a number of sea voyages, culminating in his circumnavigation of the globe, an achievement for which Queen Elizabeth knighted him in 1581.

(Somewhat) Authorized Pirates Beginning in the 1570s, Queen Elizabeth I of England confronted an increasingly tense relationship with Philip. Spain was the great power of the age and conflict was a perilous proposition, but Spain's occupation of the Netherlands, growing confrontation regarding trade, and competition for overseas colonies prompted Elizabeth to seek ways to maintain an anti-Spanish coalition in northern Europe.

While England sent troops and funds to support the Dutch rebels on land, Elizabeth found it more expedient to support unofficial maritime opposition in the form of privateering. A semi-official form of warfare, privateering was dependent upon a combination of governmental sanction and private funding to mount naval expeditions to prey on Spanish shipping.

Since the English navy was relatively small, Queen Elizabeth promoted—and the parliament supported—privateering on a significant scale. Drake's voyage to the West Indies in 1585, during which he seized a number of Spanish prizes, was one such expedition that exposed the vulnerability of Spanish holdings to foreign depredation. The queen sponsored only two vessels from a fleet of more than thirty ships. While this reduced her government's span of direct control, it did provide scope for profit for the adventurers willing to equip and lead such

missions, and at the same time it provided England with an inexpensive maritime capability. As a result, each year during the late 1580s, between one hundred–two hundred vessels ranging from small barques of less than fifty tons to warships of three hundred tons roamed the seas searching for prizes on behalf of England.

Spanish Plans for Retaliation Philip was furious at such depredations; unwilling to allow such injuries to the Spanish Empire, he sought to punish England. After deliberation, Philip decided to launch an invasion of England. To do so, he would need a sizeable armada to carry infantry from the Netherlands across the English Channel. Although numerous logistical and organizational obstacles emerged, the Spanish began assembling the necessary fleet.

In the spring of 1587, Drake went to sea with four galleons of the English navy and seventeen other ships. His fleet included a squadron commanded by Captain Robert Flicke that had been making ready to cruise for Portuguese carracks returning from the East Indies. Drake sailed on April 2, meeting the London ships at sea, and pushed southward with a screen of pinnaces (small, fast ships), intercepting passing ships that could alert the Spanish to the English presence.

On April 19, Drake appeared off Cadiz and boldly entered the harbor. Cadiz was one of the home bases for the Spanish galleons that performed escort duties across the Atlantic. As the armada was gathering, a number of Spanish galleys were also present. The tactics of the day called for an English sea captain to maneuver with the wind at his back to employ his heaviest cannons against targets along or near the shore. The challenge for Drake at Cadiz was that galleys in shallow waters were at their strongest because they could more easily employ their own guns in defense.

However, when Drake appeared without warning, the astonished Spanish were completely unprepared for battle. The English warships fired upon the Spanish ships with impunity. When Drake ordered a withdrawal, two dozen Spanish ships had been destroyed.

Drake then sailed to Cape Sagres, a headland near Cape St. Vincent on the southwest coast of Spain. There, his fleet took position and preyed upon the inward-bound shipping arriving from the Indies, as well as coastal shipping between Lisbon and the Andalusian ports.

The psychological effect of Drake's raid on Cadiz was devastating. While the Spanish were shocked by the attack, the English rejoiced at the success of English arms. Elizabeth's reputation was enhanced, and although the raid did not prevent the armada from sailing against England, once more Spain's prestige had been hurt and her enemies encouraged.

The Spanish Armada, 1588

The defeat of the Spanish Armada, a key naval campaign waged between England and Spain, denoted the high-water mark of Spanish influence in European and Atlantic waters. Thereafter, England's rise as a naval power continued unabated for two centuries, while Spanish influence entered a period of stagnation and decline from which it never emerged.

European Rivalries By the mid-1580s, Queen Elizabeth I of England confronted an increasingly tense relationship with the most powerful monarch of the age, Philip II of Spain. Naval and trade competition, as well as English resistance to Spanish prosecution of Dutch rebels in the Netherlands, had created a situation in which open conflict became increasingly likely.

In 1584, Elizabeth decided that war was imminent, so she offered aid to the Dutch in the form of more than four thousand troops and funding to the city of Antwerp. By the end of the next year, twice that many English soldiers were fighting the Spanish in the Netherlands. She also turned to confrontation at sea through privateering. In the fall of 1585, the English sea captain Sir Francis Drake plundered Spanish possessions and shipping in an expedition to the Spanish West Indies, inflicting significant damage to Spanish holdings and pricking the aura of Spain's invincibility.

Philip was enraged; well aware of the importance of reputation among the courts of Europe, he knew that England must be punished. He immediately initiated plans for an invasion, but there was little either side could quickly accomplish since Spain and England did not share a border.

English privateers were sanctioned, and parliament increased funding for shipbuilding. Elizabeth possessed only a small fleet of galleons and some large merchantmen, perhaps forty sizeable ships total. While this force was small, its leaders were competent and English crews generally displayed high morale. While not capable of a large-scale offensive, the navy could pursue pre-emptive actions. Hence in 1587, Drake led a squadron off Cadiz that destroyed two dozen Spanish vessels. He then took position off Spain's southwestern coast at Cape St. Vincent, snapping up enemy ships.

Invasion Schemes Philip possessed several substantial fleets in Mediterranean waters and another in the Atlantic. However, he displayed little military leadership ability and did not like to receive bad news, so advisors often tempered the information they provided the monarch. After deliberation, Philip decided upon two ways to strike England. The first was to seize a port in England's west country or in Ireland and from there marshal forces for an invasion into the English countryside. The cost and time required for such an endeavor proved prohibitive, and while Philip maintained this option formally, he turned to his second course of action to achieve quicker results.

The Duke of Parma, commanding Spanish troops in Flanders, was Philip's nephew. Parma offered to prepare a landing force in secret and to be ready to embark it upon a Spanish fleet before the English could ready a defense. With Philip's approval, this plan was put into motion. However, difficulties soon arose.

The admiral in charge, the Marquis of Santa Cruz, struggled to assemble the needed supplies in Lisbon and other Spanish ports. By the end of 1587, the flow of provisions to the fleet was so inadequate that the crews were consuming their stores faster than they could be resupplied. To check desertion, crews were restricted onboard, but epidemics, especially typhus, took a heavy toll. A shortage of powder, shot, guns, and small arms also plagued the fleet.

The Armada Sails When Santa Cruz died in early 1588, the Duke of Medina Sidonia assumed command. Philip, exasperated with the delays, ordered the Spanish fleet to get underway. By the middle of May, over 140 ships with more than 7,600 seamen and 18,000 troops were at sea.

England maintained patrols and slowly readied its own fleet, but otherwise did little beyond wait for the Spanish attack. On the early afternoon of July 20, the two fleets sighted each another in thick weather. Medina Sidonia sailed with about 125 ships at this point, while the English commander Admiral Charles Howard (Lord Howard of Effingham) had with him about eighty ships of all sizes. Most were speedy, heavily armed galleons that carried twice the armament of the main Spanish warships.

As the armada sailed up the Channel in a standard line abreast formation with the main fighting strength in the center and wings trailing on each side, Howard beat up to windward on the seaward side of the Spanish flank. With this favorable position, he attacked the seaward wing, while England's second-in-command, Drake, led a small contingent against the other enemy wing.

The engagement was not decisive, but it established a pattern that would be repeated. Howard, fearful of becoming trapped near the coast or of becoming decisively engaged by Spanish musketeers, continued to

The Spanish Armada is defeated by the sailors of the English fleet in the English Channel.   *The Granger Collection, New York. Reproduced by permission*

assault the Spanish wings and let the longer-ranging English guns inflict damage.

While the two fleets sparred in the Channel, the Spanish situation grew more critical with the passage of time. Parma was late in preparing the landing force to sail, and in any case lacked the shallow draft ships necessary to protect the landing barges near the shore. When he finally promised to be ready in a week, Medina Sidonia anchored off Calais about thirty miles from Parma's men to wait.

Sensing an opportunity, the English launched eight small fireships against the stationary enemy vessels. The Spanish had foreseen such an attack and moved to sea to avoid the flaming hulks, but when dawn arrived, the individual Spanish ships had not reassembled. The English moved to attack, and again their artillery took a toll even though Medina Sedonia rallied his fleet; the armada was again intact by midday.

After dawn on July 30, a favorable wind allowed the Spanish to sail into the Channel, with the English following. Yet instead of linking up with Parma, Medina Sedonia continued northward, finally turning westward into the North Atlantic.

The Armada Sinks   During the long voyage around Ireland, the Spanish fleet suffered tremendous losses. Crews who sought water and shelter on the coast were virtually all lost, either drowned or killed by the Irish or English. Ultimately, only sixty-seven ships made it back to Spain, with a loss of about one-third of the armada's manpower.

The war between England and Spain would go on for another fifteen years, but never again did Spain launch such a large effort against any adversary. While the Spanish were stunned by the armada's defeat, the English rejoiced at their deliverance. Elizabeth's stature reached a new peak, and while little had been accomplished in terms of Spanish intervention in the Netherlands, England was for the time being satisfied with its preservation.

⊕ Key Elements of Warcraft

The Galleon

The galleon, the ship type that was the workhorse of the Spanish navy during the sixteenth and early seventeenth centuries, symbolized Spain's maritime empire and was the style of vessel that ensured that the tremendous wealth extracted from the American colonies reached European ports. Often associated with glamorous images of pirates, the galleon was actually a purpose-built and practical ship that reflected Spain's highly effective approach to naval strategy.

Ship Design   The galleon was an evolutionary design that emerged in the early sixteentth century from earlier oar and sail vessels that plied Mediterranean waters. Dispensing with the oars, galleons appeared as a distinct type by the 1530s. They featured high sides with a very tall sterncastle, which was useful for infantry fighting and was perhaps their most distinctive aspect. Galleons also had a lower forecastle, a flat stern, a protruding beak at the bow, and an unbroken gun deck. The hull sloped inward from bottom to top, providing a stable platform despite the ship's great height above the waterline. Beneath the gun deck was a hold for carrying cargo, passengers and troops. Most galleons used a bowsprit, a foremast, a mainmast, and a mizzen, with a largely square-rigged sail plan.

The most significant change in galleon design over time was an increase in their size. In the mid-sixteenth century, galleons listed in royal inventories had an average displacement of 334 *toneladas* (Spanish tons), or almost three times the weight of galleons of a decade previous. By 1570, galleons of five hundred tons were common, with some reaching one thousand tons when the armada sailed in 1588. After that point, a re-appraisal of Spanish tactics and convoy methods led to a general decrease in galleon size. Ships of about around five hundred *toneladas* became common, a typical size that lasted until the galleon era was surpassed in the mid-seventeenth century.

The Galleon's Purpose and Accomodations

Galleons performed essential duties for the government of Spain. By the time of King Philip II's ascension in 1556, Spain had been operating a convoy system to the New World for several decades. As the wealth carried by these convoys became apparent to other colonial powers, the fleets' vulnerability could no longer be tolerated. Galleons began to appear in increasing numbers as escort vessels. They usually sailed as part of a fleet. Gradually, they came to carry onboard an increasing proportion of the spices and specie, as Spanish officials wanted to directly supervise their precious cargo and could not do so as well with merchant vessels. Since 20 percent of all specie production in the Americas went to fill the coffers of the Spanish crown, the stakes were high.

Life aboard galleons was tightly circumscribed by routines and was rarely pleasant. A three-watch system regulated the daily routine, with each third of a ship's company standing a four-hour watch twice a day. Space onboard was very tight. Only the captain and his key officers enjoyed any sense of privacy and dedicated cabins; the rest of the crew and passengers lived and slept scattered about the decks. Temporary screens were erected at night to demarcate sleeping areas arranged by seniority.

Sanitation and diet were poor, leading to frequent outbreaks of disease. Rations of hard biscuit were a basic staple, augmented when possible with rice and beans, salted beef or fish, and perhaps cheese, beer, and a daily allotment of red wine. Protecting food stores from the ever-present rats and insects was an endless chore that usually met with limited success.

Manpower was assigned to a galleon according to an established quota. Although in practice manning varied considerably, the basic rule was that one man was allocated for every ton of the galleon's weight, although this was often increased to 1.5 men per ton in time of war.

Battle Tactics

Rosters indicated that an average five-hundred-ton galleon carried approximately fifteen officers, twenty-six seamen, nineteen apprentice seamen, ten pages, and twenty-one gunners. A company of 125 soldiers on board rounded out the complement. These troops were essential to the Spanish style of naval warfare. During battle, the infantry took positions throughout the ship. A squadron of the most experienced men was stationed in the forecastle, while other detachments were on the quarterdeck and on the poop deck. A reserve was often kept below decks. About one-half of the soldiers were armed with small arms, and these would fire their muskets and arquebuses in two rotating ranks from the gunwales before the remaining men boarded enemy vessels armed with knives, daggers, and swords suitable for close-in combat.

Since Spanish naval doctrine emphasized the use of infantry to seize enemy ships, galleons never realized the full potential of artillery. While galleons carried 24–50 cannons with bores 2.5–6 inches and a length of 7–12 feet, naval ordnance was for many decades hampered by inadequate carriages. Each Spanish gun was placed under the command of a ship's gunner, assisted by a crew of sailors and soldiers. Once the cannon was loaded, the crew dispersed to other action stations, leaving the gunner with his burning match, waiting for the order to fire.

Spanish tactics emphasized a broadside salvo by the guns immediately before boarding an enemy vessel. This was a successful technique until English ship captains countered by improving their long-range artillery so that they could stand off from the galleons and pound the Spanish ships at a distance.

As the main vessel type of the Spanish navy for more than a century, the galleon fulfilled a requirement to protect and later carry specie and valuable goods from the New World to Spain. Until surpassed by the ship-of-the-line, the galleon ruled European and American waters, and made Spain the richest of the colonial powers.

✣ Impact of the Religious Wars of Europe

The religious wars of Europe in the sixteenth and seventeenth centuries were a major feature of the period that transformed the political and ecclesiastical landscape of the continent. The fighting itself was not continuous and did not affect all parts of Europe equally. Some regions—like Normandy or Poitou in France, the United Provinces, and much of Germany—were the scenes of many campaigns, while others were spared the direct depredations of war. Nonetheless, nearly every aspect of human and cultural topography was touched by conflict.

Between 1517, the year of Martin Luther's criticism of Catholic practice, and 1648, when the Peace of Westphalia brought the Thirty Years War to a close, the ecclesiastical domination of the Catholic Church collapsed in Europe. The splintering of Christianity held enormous consequences for every European. The church, which during the Middle Ages had acted as a European-wide corporation, was broken into territorial churches whose reach was defined in many terms. Some churches were consistent with political boundaries of a state; others reached only as far as the prince who sponsored them; still others defined themselves provincially.

While the Catholic Church and the papacy attempted to reinvigorate their power and extend their reach after the mid-sixteenth century, the great doctrinal variety of the Protestant churches continued to blossom, serving as a seedbed for persistent agitation and resistance to authority. Secular rulers, whether aligned as Catholic or Protestant, all sought to claim jurisdiction over religious appointments, taxation, administration, and discipline. The progress of this contest between state and church played out differently in each country.

In Spain, the long struggle against Islamic occupation created a fervent, self-conscious Christian sensibility. Loyalty to the Catholic Church remained steadfast. Because of the personal devotion of the Spanish monarchs, as well as the widespread religious passion among the lowest reaches of society (a passion accompanied by deep-seated suspicion of differing beliefs), Protestantism could not establish a foothold.

England, in contrast, did convert to Protestantism in the sixteenth century, but gradually and without a civil war. King Henry VIII broke from Rome for dynastic and personal reasons, and when he did, his new Anglican Church remained largely Catholic in ideological terms. Nonetheless, the religious and the political were so intertwined that his rejection of papal supremacy meant that England would serve as a Protestant bulwark and the frequent military opponent of Catholic states.

The experience of France was more convoluted. Catholicism won the day in the 1590s with the Catholic conversion of Henry of Navarre as King Henry IV. Yet the French Church remained bound and subordinate to the French crown. By the Concordat of Bologna in 1516, King Francis I and his successors ensured that they would maintain supervision over ecclesiastical appointments in France as well as tight control of the property of the church. In return, the Pope received annates and some measure of security from the alliance. It was a typical compromise that melded political and religious interests, an accommodation that could lead to war when out of balance.

The largest of the religious wars was the Thirty Years War (1618–1648), a multifaceted, dynamically shifting, European-wide war that brought the many strands of inter-state conflict together. The contest began largely due to a religious dispute between German Roman Catholics and Protestants, but it quickly became ensnared in the dynastic competition for power within the Holy Roman Empire. The war also developed into a political conflict that pitted the ambitions of the Catholic Austrian rulers, and later Spanish Habsburg rulers, against the Protestant leaders of Denmark and Sweden, and then even against Catholic France. Throughout the struggle, the German states aligned themselves according to the fortunes of war and the calculations of their princes.

For generations, the horrors of the war's depredations haunted Europeans' collective memory. While not all of Europe suffered, and not all of Germany was plundered, the Holy Roman Empire was subject to almost continuous warfare between 1618 and 1648, causing terrible losses in life and property. Across the war zones, plague, famine, and failed harvest followed the armies.

Although the European social order composed of corporations, orders, and kinship and patronage ties proved resilient (long-lasting populist or peasant revolutions did not occur), European society was ultimately changed. The war banished the idea and ambition for a unified Christendom modeled after the glory of the long-vanished Roman Empire. The power of the papacy was permanently reduced; thereafter, government depended overwhelmingly upon its secular leaders for decisions and authority in all its forms. Fiscal, diplomatic, judicial, and military affairs increasingly became the province of a single, centralized, and secular authority.

The end of the major religious wars in 1648 pointed in the direction of the international state system still functioning today. New ways of war, the alignment of states according to balance of power and economic interests, and the growth of European political identities founded upon modern notions of statehood each sprang from the tumultuous years of religious conflict in Europe.

BIBLIOGRAPHY

Book

Bainton, Roland. *Here I Stand: A Life of Martin Luther.* New York: Abingdon Press, 1991.

Introduction to the Japanese Feudal Wars (Sixteenth Century)

The late feudal period in Japan, sometimes referred to as a period of unification, greatly transformed the country into a peaceful (and isolated) nation. This Tokugawa Era came after three determined and skilled samurai warriors took control of the central provinces on the main island of Honshu. During this time, the ancient capital of Kyoto was relocated to Edo (modern-day Tokyo).

A feudal system was common up through the Okugawa Era. Much like Medieval Europe, lords and vassals oversaw large tracts of lands and competed with one another for more power with loyal armies. In Japan, the shogun (the supreme military commander) received his title and authority from the hereditary emperor. Under the shogun, several *daimyos* (lords) oversaw their domains and directed large armies of samurai warriors. These lords also sought to gain greater wealth and prestige by taking rival daimyos' lands.

In 1560, one of the most aggressive warlords of the day, Oda Nobunaga, began his ascent to power. He took over several provinces in central Japan after defeating his opponent, Imagawa Yoshimoto, at the Battle of Okehazama. After taking his adversary, Oda also took in scores of Imagawa's samurai and foot soldiers, expanding his army. He also made good use of the musket, only recently introduced by the Portuguese.

Oda was murdered by one of his own vassals while in Kyoto in 1582. During his twenty-two year ascendancy, Oda had gained control of about two-thirds of Japan. He also had taken under his wing two faithful followers: Toyotomi Hideyoshi and Tokugawa Ieyasu. Toyotomi had served under Imagawa and swore his loyalties to the ruthless Oda after Okehazama. Toyotomi had risen from peasant, to simple messenger, to field commander; by the time of Oda's death, he had become heir apparent. He avenged Oda's death by delivering the head of his assassin to the temple where his fallen lord had burned. This act of loyalty solidified his right to Oda's realm.

During his reign, which lasted until his natural death in 1598, Toyotomi conducted a successful land survey. This made his subjects more accountable to the taxes he levied. Toyotomi died having expanded his empire, making faithful alliances over most of Japan and securing—he thought—his empire for his son.

Tokugawa Ieyasu had different plans. This soldier, who also began his military career under Imagawa, had been another follower of Oda. Tokugawa did not challenge Toyotomi when Oda fell, but instead waited patiently. After being appointed to a council to oversee Toyotomi's young son until he was of age, Tokugawa convinced other daimyo and their armies that he should rule the country instead.

After some fighting (like the Battle at Sekigahara), Tokugawa essentially took power by 1600. In 1603, he assumed the title of shogun from the emperor, a title neither Oda nor Toyotomi had enjoyed due to their lack of nobility. Tokugawa instituted a host of policies to ensure his control and to maintain a peace in Japan that lasted for over 250 years. The Tokugawa name, too, lasted as generations of his descendents maintained power until the mid-nineteenth century.

Tokugawa is often referred to as the Great Unifier, for he completed what his predecessors had started. Not until the Meiji Restoration began in 1868, which saw a degree of bloodshed and violent revolution, did Japan experience unrest that resulted in a modernizing and opening of the nation.

Japanese Feudal Wars (Sixteenth Century)

⊕ Major Figures

Imagawa Yoshimoto

Imagawa Yoshimoto (1519–1560) was a samurai warrior who ruled parts of central Japan during the waning days of the Warring States Period in the mid-sixteenth century. Attempting to expand his territory, Imagawa was defeated by Oda Nobunaga.

Rise to Power Since the Shiba family had fallen in 1467, Imagawa's family controlled the provinces of Suruga and Totomi. To Imagawa's west and south along the Pacific Coast were two adjacent provinces controlled by parallel daimyo. Immediately bordering Totomi was Mikawa, controlled by the Tokugawa family, and the next province was Owari, held by the Nobunaga family.

Early in life, Imagawa left his home to study religion. His father passed the vassalage onto his firstborn, but when this firstborn died, a controversy began among the surviving sons as to who would inherit the rule of Suruga and Totomi. Imagawa entered the competition for this right and eventually obtained it.

Imagawa was in a likely position to rule beyond these two provinces. He was married to the daughter of an Ashikaga court noble, a member of the family who ruled from Kyoto since 1338. The Ashikaga had turned the city into a cultural center. Imagawa followed suit with his castle town of Sumpu, giving it a beauty that echoed Kyoto's glamour. Imagawa and his court held flower-viewing parties, made the tea ceremony integral to daily life, and enjoyed paintings and poetry.

Desire to Expand Imagawa was a romantic first and a warrior second, but with the influence and assistance from his uncle (a samurai as well as a monk), Imagawa became an eager, power-hungry warlord who hoped to dominate additional provinces. After an encounter between two neighboring rivals (Tokugawa Hirotada and Oda Nobuhide), the damaged Tokugawa Hirotada asked Imagawa for military assistance. Imagawa responded positively to this request, as he saw this as an opportunity to take on the Oda clan and a chance to bring Tokugawa Hirotada into his service. Part of the agreement was that Tokugawa Hirotada give his son, Tokugawa Ieyasu, to Imagawa as a hostage. Reluctantly, Tokugawa Hirotada agreed. In transit, Oda Nobuhide kidnapped the young Tokugawa Ieyasu. Now Imagawa's collateral to control Tokugawa Hirotada was in the hands of his target; this only made their alliance stronger.

By 1549, Tokugawa Hirotada and Oda Nobuhide had died, but Imagawa still wanted to expand his lands and rescue Tokugawa Ieyasu from captivity. Supported by the Tokugawa military, Imagawa led his forces against Oda's sons, Oda Nobuhiro and Oda Nobunaga. The campaign against Oda Nobuhiro was successful, and by 1550 Imagawa had pinned him up in his castle. Oda Nobunaga agreed to terms, and a freed Tokugawa Ieyasu was taken back to "Little Kyoto."

An Eye for Art, Not Military Matters From 1555 the fortunes and military prowess of Imagawa began to decline. His samurai-monk uncle had died, leaving Imagawa with little military direction. The elegant lord now had to lead his army. He realized that Tokugawa Ieyasu had not only the lineage for greatness, but proved at an early age to show skills on the battlefield. So Imagawa named him a commander at age seventeen. By keeping the Tokugawa heir close under his influence, Imagawa was also able to control these lands and the military that remained after the elder Tokugawa died.

Imagawa and Tokugawa Ieyasu (referred to now as Tokugawa) returned to lead campaigns against Oda Nobunaga (referred to now as Oda), now clearly in charge of the Owari region and the greatest threat to Imagawa's plans. After a semi-successful raid on Oda's castle (burning and destroying its outer defenses), Imagawa awarded Tokugawa with a fine sword and the Tokugawa lands to which he was entitled. Not content, Imagawa kept Tokugawa by his side for bigger and better acquisitions.

IYEYASU (LAWGIVER AND FOUNDER OF THE TOKUGAWA DYNASTY OF SHOGUN).

Founder of the Tokugowa Dynasty, Tokugowa Ieyasu. © *Mary Evans Picture Library/Alamy*

Imagawa had his eye on Kyoto, something he had desired for most of his life. He planned on taking the Ashikaga capital, but he knew he must first eliminate Oda, the major obstacle between Imagawa and his destiny. In July 1560, Imagawa departed with a force of roughly 25,000 samurai warriors to crush Oda. The battle plan included a series of attacks on Oda's chain of forts.

Things began well. Imagawa and his detachment took the fort at Washizu, while Tokugawa brilliantly took the stronghold of Marune. Tokugawa had charged the fort and was repulsed with little surprise. Unconcerned at this initial setback, he had lined up archers on either side of the fortress entrance. As Tokugawa retreated, Oda's warriors charged out of the fortress gates; they were greeted by a downpour of flying arrows and the occasional bullet. Tokugawa took this garrison, and with Imagawa's defeat of the fort at Washizu, the road to Oda was open.

Defeated by a Superior Samurai Imagawa and Tokugawa were still in separate camps on their way to Oda.

This gave Oda the opportunity to defeat the forces in detail, before they could join up. Oda sent scouts to determine the location of his attackers. They reported that Imagawa and his forces were resting near the village of Okehazama. Feasting in preparation for later battle and with little guard on this camp, Oda saw the opportunity to end sixty years of local daimyo rivalry.

Outnumbered by at least twelve to one, Oda sent a decoy of his army with flags and banners to one side of Imagawa's camp. Then, with the vast majority of his two thousand warriors, Oda sneaked up behind Imagawa's distracted force. On that brutally hot day, a thunderstorm struck immediately before the two sides met, further hiding the sneak attack. Within minutes, Oda had defeated and killed Imagawa.

Tokugawa, stranded and with little choice, learned that his master was dead and that Oda was closing in. Imagawa had left his lands and empire to an ineffectual heir who knew the good points of a tea bowl rather than the skills of a field command. Tokugawa, now still only nineteen years old, considered his options and swore allegiance to Oda. Oda would prove a successful warrior who expanded his empire. In due course, he would be followed by Tokugawa, the great unifier of Japan.

Oda Nobunaga

Oda Nobunaga (1534–1582) rose to power in the late Warring States Period (1467–1590). In a time of warlords overthrowing warlords, Oda began to build an empire in central Japan with loyal daimyo under him, which led to the reunification of the nation. His pursuit of extended lands and securing samurai loyalties began the unification process, while his followers completed the job within twenty years of his death.

Inheriting the Domain Born in Nagoya in Owari Province, Oda's family ruled a small domain. His father, Oda Nobuhide, was a vassal to the Shiba house; Japanese folklore portrays him as a bold and romantic leader. By the time Oda Nobuhide died in 1551, he had secured for his son a modest following and a marriage to the daughter of Saito Dosan, a ruthless daimyo.

From an early age, Oda stood out as a unique figure. As a teenager he dressed in an eccentric fashion and soon earned the fitting nicknames, "Great Fool" and "Idiot." Disparaging remarks aside, it is likely that he played foolish so as to jump ahead of others who assumed he lacked fighting skills. After his father's death, Oda vied for control of Owari with his older brother, Oda Nobuhiro. Starting with an initial force of one thousand foot soldiers, Oda eventually ran his brother out of the province. Oda Nobuhiro later died, leaving Owari solely to Oda.

Expansion and Control Beginning in 1560, Oda rose to power like a phoenix. His first major victory was against Imagawa Yoshimoto, who held the adjacent provinces of Suguru and Totomi. On his way to take Kyoto, Imagawa first had to eliminate Oda. After taking two of Oda's fortresses, Imagawa was resting and feasting with his forces that numbered as many as 25,000. Oda preempted any possible attack against him and outsmarted Imagawa and his army at Okehazama. There, his forces soundly defeated the neighboring army, and Imagawa was killed. As a result of this victory, Oda gained an important ally: Tokugawa Ieyasu, Imagawa's former vassal and the future unifier of all Japan.

Defeating Imagawa was rather quick and decisive, and it gave Oda the provinces of Surugu, Totomi, and Mikawa. By 1567 he had defeated Saito Tatsuoki for control of Mino Province. He soon built a castle in the city of Gifu and established that as his capital. He chose as his motto, "The whole country under one military power."

Oda could not inherit the title of shogun himself, for he lacked the lineage. Therefore he developed a relationship with Ashikaga Yoshiaki, the last of the Ashi-

Oda Nobunaga. *© Asian Art & Archaeology, Inc./Corbis*

kaga shogun of Japan. This relationship became stormy, and by the early 1570s Oda overthrew the Ashikaga.

Why Oda Succeeded Where Others Failed Oda's many victories were the result of multiple factors. First, his geographic location was favorable. Stationed in central Honshu, he was able to divide competing warriors to the east and west of him, preventing dangerous enemy alliances. Secondly, Oda was one of the pioneers of European firearms. The Portuguese had introduced the musket in Japan in the 1540s, and Oda became fond of this weapon from an early age. He refused to keep to traditional weaponry as some of his adversaries did. His decision to rely upon infantrymen with a large arsenal of muskets in deference to the mounted warrior showed Oda's great foresight. At the Battle of Nagashino in 1575, Oda confronted the powerful Takeda daimyo, and Oda's musket wielding soldiers annihilated the enemy samurai cavalry that charged his defensive line.

In addition, Oda's long-term tactics and strategies proved brilliant. He developed faithful alliances and loyal vassals, and he chose his enemies wisely. Through lifelong friendships and arranged marriages, Oda forged loyal relationships with powerful assistants who might otherwise make possible adversaries.

In warring with other samurai, Oda did not face multifront battles, taking on only one neighboring warrior at a time. When he did acquire adjacent fiefs, he would offer lands and rank to his defeated enemy's vassals first, guaranteeing a mutual protection while dissuading them from leading attacks on him.

Death and Legacy

Oda's victories and reputation caused more and more daimyo to think twice about challenging him, but he was still occasionally opposed. His last confrontation occurred when Oda and his trusted ally Toyotomi Hideyoshi were trying to pacify an uprising in his western region. While taking shelter at a temple in Kyoto, Oda was attacked by thirteen thousand troops led by one of his own vassals, Akechi Mitsuhide. Whether Akechi or one of his underlings killed Oda directly or not remains a mystery. His body burned up inside the temple on June 21, 1582.

By the time of his death, Oda had gained fairly solid control of about one-third of Japan. Toyotomi would assume his realm and avenge his death by killing Akechi. One of his other followers, Tokugawa Ieyasu, would eventually take the empire that Toyotomi would expand. Within twenty years of Oda's death, Japan had become largely unified under one of his disciples.

Toyotomi Hideyoshi

Toyotomi Hideyoshi (1536–1598) rose from peasant to military ruler of Japan in 1582. His life is characterized by a unique case of social mobility and near unification of the nation.

Humble Beginnings Toyotomi was born into a peasant farming family so poor he did not even have a surname. He began his military career at age fifteen under the daimyo Imagawa Yoshimoto, his first job being that of a minor servant.

As Toyotomi learned the way of the warrior, Imagawa and the Oda clan competed for additional lands and greater power. His relationship with Oda Nobunaga, a ruthless warlord, began in 1558 when Toyotomi entered Oda's army as a common foot soldier. He soon worked his way up to become his master's most trusted vassal. All told, Toyotomi's roles ranged from basic messenger and attendant to field commander of over three thousand men. A relationship of trust and understanding between the two men lasted over twenty-four years.

Toyotomi became the leading samurai after Oda Nobunaga was killed by a rival vassal Akechi Mitsuhide in 1582. Toyotomi beheaded Akechi, an act that avenged his fallen leader and solidified Toyotomi's ascendancy to the top of the Japanese feudal ladder.

As leader, Toyotomi continued the reunification that his master had begun. Toyotomi's approach to guarantee

NOBUNAGA AND THE PRIESTS

Oda protected his gains shrewdly, but he was also a ruthless leader willing to commit atrocities if it suited his purpose. For example, Oda slaughtered Buddhist monks who threatened his rule. Many Buddhist temples had become centers for political, economic, and military activity; at the Heian school, Oda stormed this Buddhist stronghold and transformed it into a killing field of men, women, and children. This bloody act resulted in the deaths of between three thousand and four thousand priests.

After eliminating the threat of Heian, Oda turned to the Shinshu Buddhists, who were spread throughout the country. In July 1574, Oda attacked a Buddhist stronghold at Nagashima. The captive population tried to surrender, but Oda was not willing to accept. He had the fortress torched and had anyone trying to escape the fire shot on sight. The estimated slaughter reached twenty thousand lives.

the allegiance of his vassals was a bit gentler than his tyrannical predecessor. Toyotomi did indeed carry out military campaigns within the interior of central Japan, but he found it much more effective to simply convert a defeated enemy into a loyal ally. The lure of land rewards and his gentle hand with former foes, encouraged daimyo across central Japan to serve the new hegemony. By the time of his death, Toyotomi had amassed some two hundred faithful followers.

The World Beyond Japan Toyotomi established unique policies that included interaction and desired expansion beyond the Japanese islands. He encouraged foreign trade with European states, and Japanese commercial vessels traveled as far from Japan as Malaya and Siam. However, he did not accept the European package of trade with Christian missions. Portuguese and Spanish voyagers wanted to spread Christianity, and unlike his predecessor Oda, Toyotomi viewed the invasion of Christianity and European principles as a threat to Japanese culture and full unification. He was shocked to see the degree to which the Catholic Church had settled in Kyushi, especially in the port of Nagasaki. He issued a decree ordering the missionaries out of Japan, but did not spend much effort enforcing it.

Controlling Japan resulted not only from his earlier diplomatic appeals with potential rivals, but also from an extensive land survey that Oda had begun. When Toyotomi finished, for the first time in Japanese history, the government had a uniform system of measuring land and wealth, and an accurate plot-by-plot count of the nation's productive capacity. This allowed for more effective administration of taxing and enabled Hideyoshi to shift his lords around, properly rewarding or

Osaka Castle, built by Hideyoshi in the 1580s. © *Craig Lovell/Eagle Visions Photography/Alamy*

punishing his vassals. Toyotomi also ordered a mass confiscation of weapons from the peasantry. This eliminated any chance of an armed rebellion and further defined a class structure that he had once transcended.

The later days of Toyotomi's rule were characterized by an attempt to expand the Japanese Empire into Korea and China and to set up a familial line of inheritance. Neither succeeded. Toyotomi laid plans for his five-year-old son to take over his expanded empire, but these plans failed after his death when Tokugawa Ieyasu exerted his power to take Japan.

Tokugawa Ieyasu

A samurai warrior, Tokugawa Ieyasu (1542–1616) rose through the ranks in feudal Japan to become shogun. He is largely credited with unifying the Japanese nation at the beginning of the seventeenth century, which would go through a cultural, economic, and military transformation. The Tokugawa Era, also known as the Edo Period, lasted from Tokugawa's ascendancy in 1600 until the Meiji Restoration in the late 1860s.

Life in the Enemy's Camp Tokugawa was son of a minor daimyo who controlled the Mikawa Province (near the modern day Aichi Prefecture). From an early age, the young Tokugawa was exposed to the way in which feudal rivalries exploited each other, and the manner in which warring samurai battled to expand their holdings. His father's key rivals were the Oda and Imagawa families. As a child, Tokugawa was given to Imagawa as a hostage to guarantee his father's loyalty. While being transferred, Oda Nobuhide captured the boy. He became a lure for the senior Tokugawa's surrender. Eventually, Tokugawa Ieyasu was given to Imagawa, his intended captor, in a hostage swap. (Oda Nobunaga traded the boy for his own brother's release.) Now the young Tokugawa was under the control of the ambitious Imagawa.

For a total of thirteen years, Tokugawa remained a hostage to the Oda and Imagawa houses. At age seventeen, Tokugawa was given a ranking command of Imagawa's army, partly because of his own military skills and partly because of his master's lack thereof. In 1560, Oda soundly defeated the Imagawa house while his men killed Imagawa in the Battle of Okehazama. Now nineteen, Tokugawa took a realistic view of his future and offered his services to the strong and ruthless Oda Nobunaga.

Tokugawa became a faithful daimyo to Oda and maintained control over his province of Mikawa. Oda is credited with beginning the military unification of Japan during his reign, assisted by two of his most loyal daimyo, Tokugawa and Toyotomi. Toyotomi had risen from peasantry to one of Oda's most trusted samurai. After Oda was assassinated by one of his not-so-faithful warriors, Toyotomi became heir-apparent to his estates, roughly one-third of the lands in Japan.

A Waiting Game It was at this point that Tokugawa made the wise decision to yield to Toyotomi. Tales of how the two agreed upon a peaceful transition of Oda's lands make for good folklore, but one historian recounts their sporadic war that lasted eight months in 1584. At least twice their troops engaged in confrontation. However, by the end of 1584, they made peace. Toyotomi began to control Oda's holdings, and Tokugawa became one of his most reliable vassals.

Toyotomi defeated other lords and gained additional lands, continuing the unification process that Oda had begun. By 1590, he awarded Tokugawa the entire Kanto plain, the traditional area of conquest in feudal Japan and the area that surrounds modern-day Tokyo. This made Tokugawa the second strongest daimyo in Japan. Toyotomi, however, became sidetracked with conquering lands on the mainland in North Korea and China. These attempts were largely unsuccessful.

Toyotomi died in 1598, leaving his five-year-old son as heir. Toyotomi had appointed a council of five regents to administer the lands during his son's youth.

Geisha have been in existence since before the seventeenth century. These *maiko* (geisha apprentices) walk in the Higashiyama district of Kyoto, Japan. © *Ei Katsumata/Alamy*

Tokugawa, the most powerful member of this council, saw his opportunity. Another servant of Toyotomi, Ishida Mitsunari, formed a coalition against Tokugawa, but the experienced and powerful Tokugawa defeated this group in the Battle of Sekigahara in 1600. Tokugawa confiscated the lands of Ishida and the other daimyo conspirators. The empire assembled by Oda, Toyotomi, and Tokugawa had finally become his.

Shogun and Unifier

Now that Tokugawa had gained control of Japan, he began programs and policies to ensure his grip on the nation. These included a refined foreign policy, measures to ensure heightened loyalties, and an emphasis on the arts. These steps finalized unification and made strong the Tokugawa line until 1868.

Tokugawa decided quickly that the attempted exploits by his predecessor were impractical. Rather than seek out foreign lands across the sea, Tokugawa concentrated on securing adjacent lands on Honshu and the other Japanese Islands. His new foreign policy of isolationism would define Japan for the next 250 years.

Tokugawa did accept some traders that came into Japan in 1600, but he soon took steps to eliminate the invading Christian religion. Missionaries had gradually made their way into Japan since Oda ruled the central region. Tokugawa felt a growing political threat that accompanied the Christian religion, so he eventually ordered all foreign priests to leave the country.

Dividing Daimyo

Having waited a lifetime to secure absolute rule, Tokugawa was not going to risk losing it. He secured the title of shogun from the emperor in 1603 and soon began establishing policies to guarantee loyalty from his vassals. To guarantee that he would remain overlord of the new confederation of daimyo, Tokugawa divided these daimyo into three groups: *fudai*, or main vassals; *tozama*, or outside daimyo; and *shimpan*, or related daimyo. The fudai were rather loyal and served under Tokugawa at the Battle of Sekigahara. Some of these and others were rewarded with the title for their service on the battlefield.

Tokugawa was more wary of the tozama, for many of this group had already held the daimyo rank under the prior shoguns. These potential rivals worried him. The final group consisted of warriors and vassals who were of blood relation. The first of these being Tokugawa's two sons. He made a point to place them and other relatives close to him, as they would be heirs to the shogun office if the main Tokugawa line died out.

For all these vassals, Tokugawa required a direct oath of loyalty. Even samurai who had inherited lands prior to his rule still had to confirm their right to rule it through Tokugawa.

Keeping Friends and Enemies Close The shogun also relocated the capital to Edo, which was central to his established holdings in the Kanto plain. He required personal attendance at his court there. This practice was not born with Tokugawa, but expanded. His vassals, especially the more distant ones, were required to reside in Edo and build mansions.

At times when the vassals were away, their wives, heirs, and principal retainers remained in these mansions as collateral. Tokugawa was not the first lord to use this practice; perhaps it resulted from his early experiences as a hostage himself. At any rate, it prevented conspiracies and allowed him to keep an eye on his subordinates.

After establishing a strong control from Edo, Tokugawa handed his rule over to his son and controlled Japan to a degree from behind the scenes. By 1614, Tokugawa wanted to ensure against any lingering threats and make sure his family dynasty was set to begin. With his son, he led an assault on Toyotomi's son, Toyotomi Hideyori. Tokugawa offered him a peace agreement whereby he could keep his domains and castle if the outer works and moat systems were eliminated.

Later, it appeared to Tokugawa that these defense works were being strengthened. Worried about an uprising, the shogun moved against it with a strong force, causing Toyotomi Hideyori and his mother to commit suicide to avoid capture. To complete the elimination of any heirs to his former lord, Tokugawa sought out Toyotomi Hideyoshi's eight-year-old grandson and had him killed.

⊕ Major Battles

Okehazama, June 1560

The Battle of Okehazama was fought near a village by the same name in Owari Province, pitting Imagawa Yoshimoto against Oda Nobunaga. Imagawa was killed during the fighting. Just as important as the victory itself, Oda gained the future shogun Tokugawa Ieyasu—who was serving under Imagawa—as a vassal.

Thirst for Lands In the final years of the Warring States Period, Imagawa and Oda were competing to gain land on the island of Honshu. Imagawa had his eyes on the capital of Kyoto and planned to march on the ancient capital to take it. His rival Oda controlled Owari, the province between Imagawa's castle town of Sumpu and Kyoto and thus stood in his way. Imagawa decided to eliminate Oda on his march to Kyoto.

Imagawa had gathered an army of 25,000 warriors, and he had the allegiance of Tokugawa Ieyasu. The Tokugawa family controlled Mikawa Province, located between Oda's Owari and Imagawa's lands. Tokugawa Ieyasu had already gained the confidence of Imagawa, who had made him a ranking field commander, and the geographic position of the Tokugawa fief would make a comfortable buffer between Imagawa and Oda. In July 1560, the determined and well-equipped Imagawa set off to defeat Oda.

The first challenge was a series of forts that protected Oda. Imagawa took one column toward the fort in Washizu, while his trusty general Tokugawa Ieyasu headed toward the fort at Marune. With minimal losses, both strongholds were taken. The road into Nobunaga's province was cleared, giving Imagawa the upper hand.

Learning of his losses from his castle in Kiyosu, a confident Oda showed no genuine signs of concern. The next morning he rose at daylight, ate a full breakfast, and prepared for battle. Before departure, Oda stated, "Man's life is fifty years. In the Universe what is it but dream and illusion? Is there any who is born and does not die?"

With only six close companions and a few hundred men, Oda set off to meet Imagawa. Along the way, however, Oda picked up two thousand additional men ready to fight for him. Tokugawa Ieyasu and Imagawa were still separated when Oda received word from his advance scouts that Imagawa's men were resting and feasting in preparation for their attack. Imagawa was not the most skilled warrior, and he had left his camp unguarded. This gave Oda a chance to decisively end a daimyo rivalry that had existed for over sixty years.

Imagawa is Outmaneuvered Oda arrived and took a position opposite Imagawa's camp on the Tokaido Road. Here he set a dummy army as a decoy, complete with banners and flags so to make this small detachment look like his main army. As soon as the diversion was set, he rushed his remaining samurai—some reports say up to three thousand by this point—secretly behind the hill where Imagawa camped.

Oda knew these lands as a young boy, which helped him prepare his attack. On this very hot day, his men made a sneaky approach to Imagawa's rear as a rapid rain began to fall, which further concealed their movement. As the rain ceased, Oda and his samurai charged into Imagawa's camp.

One of Oda's samurai came face to face with Imagawa. The daimyo thought it was one of his own, and as soon as the attacker realized it was Oda's foe, he thrust his spear at him. Imagawa deflected the weapon, but before he could act further, another warrior charged and sliced off Imagawa's head. Within minutes, more than 2,500 of Imagawa's men became casualties.

Soon after the defeat at Okehazama, Imagawa's heir assumed his position as daimyo, and his field commander Tokugawa Ieyasu was faced with a difficult decision. The chosen daimyo, Ujizane, was not very savvy in the field or

Samurai combined the arts of war with appreciation for beauty and a number of social codes. © *Sakamoto Photo Research Laboratory/ Corbis*

as an administrator. Tokugawa Ieyasu weighed his options and decided to join Oda. The decision created an alliance that would begin the unification of the Japanese state.

Nagashino, June 1575

This battle was a decisive victory for Oda Nobunaga (and his vassals Tokugawa Ieyasu and Toyotomi Hideyoshi) against Takeda Katsuyori. This victory proved Oda's strength as the fasting rising daimyo in Japan and placed a stronger grip on his domain in his quest to gain control of the whole of Japan. The battle also proved that the musket—introduced into Japan only a generation before—was more than just a novel weapon for the battlefield.

Daimyo Dispute Control of Nagashino Castle As early as 1560, Oda had already defeated neighboring warlords and begun a fierce expansion of his vassalage. He had also gained the allegiance of Tokugawa and Toyotomi, and now controlled lands beyond his original Owari Province, including those of Mino, Mikawa, and others. Since 1571, Tokugawa held the Nagashino Castle, located in Mikawa.

One of Oda's rivals, the Takeda family, had shown interest in taking Nagashino, so Takeda Katsuyori (with roughly fifteen thousand troops) began a siege in early

May 1575. The siege was not quick for the castle was situated on a well-fortified hill at the confluence of two rivers. Some five hundred soldiers were garrisoned inside the castle, though neither Tokugawa nor Oda were in the vicinity. The men inside were capable defenders; in one of his first attempts, Takeda lost eight hundred of his own. As the days passed, Takeda realized that the best strategy was to starve those inside by cutting off supplies of food and ammunition to the castle.

Word was sent from Nagashino to Tokugawa and Oda that the castle needed reinforcements, but no help was immediately forthcoming. Some of Oda's counselors thought it too risky to try and defeat the penetrating Takeda. Eventually, Oda decided that if Takeda took the castle, Tokugawa might ally himself with the victor, making Oda susceptible if he had to face such a large, combined force later.

Tokugawa, too, got word of the danger his castle was in and went to lift the siege. Tokugawa and Oda arrived within days of each other, Tokugawa with a force of eight thousand and Oda with thirty thousand. They outnumbered Takeda, who would have been wise to retreat to his own province. Yet pride and his excellent, skilled cavalry convinced Takeda to stay and fight Oda.

Musket Beats Horse Though Takeda had one of the best mounted forces in Japan, he failed to realize the impact of Oda's muskets. Before heading to Nagashino, Oda had carefully selected three thousand marksmen for the mission. This made it the largest firing force ever mustered in Japan at that time.

Oda equipped his men with stakes and rope to create makeshift stockades. After constructing these fortresses in the short hills beyond the castle, he instructed his sharpshooters to hold their fire until the enemy was in close range. He also organized these musketeers into a system of alternate firing, rotating so that while one-third fired into their charging enemy, the other two groups would have a chance to reload.

When Takeda's cavalry charged, Oda's marksmen popped up behind their palisades and decimated them. Takeda's warriors went down in heaps. The fighting ended in the afternoon with only about three thousand of Takeda's force escaping.

The Battle of Nagashino proved that gun warfare, though a departure from traditional Japanese warfare, was a force to be reckoned with. The victory brought Oda a step closer to dominating the region and much of Japan, and it strengthened the relationship between Oda and Tokugawa that led to additional victories.

Yamazaki, 1582

The Battle of Yamazaki, and the events that followed, effectively placed rule of central Japan in the hands of Toyotomi Hideyoshi.

Daimyo Vie for Land and Power Since 1560, ruthless warlord Oda Nobunaga had controlled the lands

Samurai swords, made of folded, tempered steel, were feats of art, metallurgy, and engineering. This sword bears its maker's signature. © *Chris Willson/Alamy*

from the capital city of Kyoto to Suruga Province. Faithful vassals (such as Toyotomi Hideyoshi, Tokugawa Ieyasu, and others) maintained these lands and served their lord. Yet in the uncertain age of war in samurai Japan, a lord could rarely predict when one of his military servants might turn on him or ally with another vassal to overthrow their superior. This was the case for Oda in 1582.

The vassal Akechi Mitsuhide strategically attacked Oda at Honnoji Temple in Kyoto, and Akechi is credited with assassinating his lord Oda. Oda was either burned alive or he committed suicide in the ritual known as *seppuku*; whatever the cause, Akechi had murdered the most powerful daimyo in Japan.

By destroying Oda's guards as well, Akechi gave himself some additional time to continue his power play. He went on to plunder the nearby province of Omi to try and take control. Akechi also sought to create alliances with enemies of Oda. For eleven days Akechi went untouched.

When Toyotomi got word of his mentor's death, he vowed to remove Akechi from power. Toyotomi discovered the assassination of Oda through an emissary that Akechi had sent to advise his ally (the Mori clan) in the southwest of the island of Honshu. Toyotomi was already in a military campaign against the Mori house and nearing victory. After flooding one of their key castles and securing recognition of his power, Toyotomi shifted his focus from winning control of the Mori's Bitchu Province to killing the warrior who killed his lord and mentor, Oda.

Oda is Avenged Thirteen days after Oda's death, Toyotomi faced Akechi in the vicinity of Yamazaki in Yamashiro Province on his way toward Kyoto. Akechi's army was quickly and decisively destroyed. Toyotomi was able to defeat Akechi for a handful of reasons. His army, roughly twenty thousand, doubled that of his opponent, as he had been joined by Oda's son and other leading daimyo and their soldiers. In addition, Akechi's potential allies had refrained from assisting him. They saw the writing on the wall and gambled that their chances were best in not challenging Toyotomi.

Survivors, including Akechi, fled the battle. However, he was stopped to the north of the battle by a band of peasants, and then promptly executed. Toyotomi gathered the assassin's head and delivered it back to Honnoji to complete the task of avenging his master's spirit.

The battle eliminated the key challenger to Toyotomi's right to inherit Oda's lands, but it did not instantly make him overlord of the central provinces of Japan. A conference of daimyo was held at Kiyosu within a month to determine how the kingdom should be divided and governed. Most of Oda's men were present. Toyotomi used his performance at Yamazaki to argue that Oda's grandson should inherit his estate, effectively putting Toyotomi at the helm of the military and making him ruler of the Japanese lands that Oda had obtained. Toyotomi got his way at the conference, but soon had enforce his wishes in the Battle of Shizugatake.

Shizugatake, 1583

The Battle of Shizugatake in 1583 further solidified Toyotomi Hideyoshi's power over a partially unified Japan. His mentor and lord, Oda Nobunaga, had proven a ruthless, powerful, and respected warrior and had begun unifying Japan in a militant fashion with the help of his trusted vassal, Toyotomi. After one of his vassals attacked Oda while within the Honnoji Temple in Kyoto, Toyotomi became heir apparent to Oda's military empire. This ascendancy was not, however, instant; it took a series of negotiations, battles, and alliances. After the Battle of Shizugatake, it became clear that Toyotomi would inherit control of the provinces (about one-third of Japan) that he helped Oda secure over the prior twenty-four years.

Oda's Death Creates a Power Vacuum Toyotomi had proven a faithful servant to Oda Nobunaga and within thirteen days of his master's death, he defeated Oda's assassin Akechi Mitsuhide at the Battle of Yamazaki. Toyotomi returned to Honnoji with Akechi's decapitated head to lay it where Oda was killed. Toyotomi's master was avenged.

A conference of Oda daimyo followed at Kiyosu where Toyotomi, Shibata Katsuie (an elder conferee), and other daimyo determined who would inherit family leadership. Katsuie pushed for Oda's son, Nobutaka, as the recipient of this power, but Toyotomi argued for Oda's grandson, Samboshi.

Bolstered by his heroics at Yamazaki and his honoring Oda, Toyotomi had more than average clout at the Kiyosu conference. Even so, the conference ended with a degree of uncertainty. The daimyo simply reconfirmed their lands, and though Toyotomi (the leading daimyo at the time) was able to garner support for Oda's three-year-old grandson, other daimyo and Nobutaka departed the meeting with other plans in mind.

The Opposing Sides Coalesce By fall of 1582, the conflict between Toyotomi and Shibata grew. Nobutaka had wed his aunt to his supporter Shibata, which only strengthened their already tight alliance. Toyotomi then sent a well-crafted letter that reached Nobutaka, signaling that a diplomatic solution could be reached, while at the same time asserting that he meant business.

As Toyotomi pointed out in the letter, Nobutaka (Samboshi's guardian) had not installed Samboshi into Azuchi castle, even though he should have. Such delay, along with scheming between Shibata and Nobutaka, signaled their ulterior motives and disrespect to Toyotomi. The letter also reminded Nobutaka of Toyotomi's strong bond with the great Oda and asserted how his wishes, and the agreements ironed out at Kiyosu, should be honored.

The letter did nothing but infuriate Nobutaka and Shibata. In early 1583, Toyotomi began to prepare for a fight against these new opponents. He raised armies and announced his intentions to his other vassals.

Events did not begin well for Toyotomi. He soon learned of a defeat of one of his armies in Omi Province against Shibata. Toyotomi's response was swift and decisive, and some argue that his next moves were the most important in his military career.

Toyotomi's Bold Strike Again, Toyotomi set off for vengeance, covering over thirty miles from Mino to Shibata's camp in an amazing five hours. He brought nine of his most loyal vassals and a total of about thirty thousand soldiers. In a field outside a fortress at Shizugatake, the enemy scattered, including Shibata. The immediate victory showed Toyotomi's military might, but his key competitor, Shibata, escaped.

Toyotomi pursued his adversary to Shibata's castle in Echizen. Shibata climbed to the ninth floor of this structure where he realized his inevitable fate. Rather than let Toyotomi take his life, he took it himself. After uttering some words to his tearful followers there assembled, Shibata stabbed his wife, children, and other family members before committing seppuku.

Nobutaka had lost his most important ally, while Oda's other son, Nobukatsu, had joined forces with Toyotomi. Soon they together moved against Nobutaka at Gifu castle. Nobutaka, too, took his own life rather than allow his brother and Toyotomi to take it.

Toyotomi's attack at Shizugatake became a memorable imprint of his daring, speed, and resolve. He won congratulations from daimyo including Tokugawa Ieyasu, and others who were present at Kiyosu. His wishes from the conference realized, Toyotomi ruled Japan until his death in 1598.

Sekigahara, 1600

The Battle of Sekigahara took place in a valley along one of the ancient roads that connected Edo and Kyoto. In this bloody encounter in Mino Province, Tokugawa

Shitennojii Temple in Osaka. © *Jon Arnold Images/Alamy*

Ieyasu prevailed and soon became the undisputed leader and shogun of Japan.

Tokugawa Makes His Move Tokugawa had served in the armies of Oda Nobunaga and Toyotomi for decades. When Toyotomi died in 1598, a board of regents began to oversee his empire as his young son became the official heir. Tokugawa was the leading daimyo on this board and desired a greater share of the power. He began accepting oaths of allegiance from daimyo that had served Toyotomi. This proved his ambition and upset other warlords who served on this board. As their jealousy and tensions increased, all Tokugawa needed to finalize his quest was a chance to prove his military might, which came at Sekigahara.

By the middle of 1600, a key rival for Tokugawa, Ishida Mitsunari, formed a coalition against him. This coalition planned on forcing Tokugawa away from the Osaka and Kyoto regions, where he held great support, and into the north of Japan. They did so by leading a revolt in the Uesugi region. This tactic would bring their enemy away from the capital and allow them to take over. The mighty Tokugawa, however, had his suspicions. As he headed north, he gathered attritional troops from loyal provinces to enhance his already strong army. After handling the revolt, Tokugawa turned back to Kyoto.

The most strategic point in this affair was where two primary roads neared. The parallel roads—the Tokaido in the mountains and the Nakasendo along the east coast—came close to each other at the village and valley of Sekigahara. A series of castles and fortresses also dotted the region. Whoever controlled these structures would have the upper hand in controlling the region. When Tokugawa returned from Edo, he knew he needed to take these strongholds, and he did so.

The Path to Shogun is Swept Clear On his way from Osaka, Ishida marched his army up the Tokaido Road and met Tokugawa's soldiers at Sekigahara. A heavy fog from a prior rain had set in, muddying the terrain and obscuring the movements of both forces. When the fog lifted in the morning, the largest battle of samurai against samurai in Japanese feudal history began.

The basin of the valley, muddy from the earlier storms, made the heavy fighting treacherous. It was a fairly even bout until a host of Kobayakawa samurai, originally allied with Ishida, entered the fray on the side of Tokugawa. This was the deciding factor that forced Ishida to retreat.

Tokugawa thus became the undisputed heir to Toyotomi's military rule and began to unify Japan. His line would rule the nation from 1600 until 1868 during a rather peaceful era.

⊕ Key Elements of Warcraft

Samurai

In Feudal Japan, the samurai warlord and his band of soldiers relied on several unique tools in their arsenal and employed various techniques to overcome their enemy. These tools and tactics developed and changed over the long period, but a few are worth noting.

The Way of the Blade Among the Samurai's tools, perhaps the most identifiable weapon was the sword. It was what some, including Shogun Tokugawa Ieyasu, have called "the soul of the samurai." The time-consuming and artful process whereby the artisan forged the sword, an almost ritualistic procedure, made the swordsman appreciate it that much more.

The goal of the sword maker was to create a weapon that cut well and did not break in battle. While Japanese put great emphasis on ornate decoration in architecture and on tea bowls, the sword was functional first, decorative second. Samurai purchased swords knowing that this piece was to kill in order to protect.

A distinct sword etiquette developed during the peaceful, unified Japan of the Tokugawa Era. Bumping into a samurai's sword—even if by accident and while the sword was in its sheath—was a very serious offense. Carrying a sword into a fellow friend's house would violate the friendship. The visitor would typically leave the sword outside, but sometimes carry his smaller sword, the *wakizashi*, inside. Showing the blade was also a breach of etiquette, unless swordsmen were admiring each other's weapons.

As the samurai class began to fade in the late nineteenth century, so too did the sword. Samurai were put into retirement and in 1876, the wearing of swords by anyone other than those in the new armed forces was illegal.

Protection Armor for the samurai, while not so symbolic, was highly important. Initially, armor was much heavier, but the Mongol horses that the samurai had come to use required the horseman to be light. Since speed was his prime defense, lamellar armor became the standard. The lamellae were small scales of iron tied tightly together to make a horizontal strip, which was then lacquered. These strips were then laced together, overlapping one another to make a solid breastplate that would repel an arrow or deflect a sword.

Over the soldier's arms were long cloth socks, sewn with metal plates. On his head was a helmet, typically a heavy metal bowl made from a series of iron plates riveted together. There was much loyalty that came with armor. During the Warring States period, samurai wore a colorful *sashimono*, a little banner on the back of the armor, to acknowledge his loyalty to his lord.

Tactics These essential pieces of warcraft assisted and encouraged warlords throughout the land and throughout the times. The samurai's strategy in the field to protect or gain additional domains altered with technology. Initially, a samurai and his archers would launch a volley of arrows to commence a formal battle. Champion fighters from each side would engage each other; one might issue a challenge, typically picking a worthy opponent, and likely chant out his lineage of ancestors whom he honored in the fight.

Over time, military strategy moved from formal feats of swordsmanship and close combat to frontal assaults by large armies. Advances in weaponry largely caused this shift. For instance, the Portuguese introduced the gun in the 1540s; soon Japanese artisans began to mimic and mass produce weapons. The common model was the lightweight musket, fired by lighting a touch hole. The accuracy was not so great, but the availability of the gun encouraged many field commanders to send large volleys of ammunition into opposing forces. The musket eventually replaced the bow and arrow, a device that took more strength and skill.

When rival daimyo could not coordinate open battle in the field, or when an aggressive samurai lord wanted to press another into a fight, a siege proved useful. The primary skill necessary in siege success was patience. Samurai, with their archers, footsoldiers, and cavalry surrounding a castle, would wait out their victim. Eventually the inhabitants of the castle would run out of supplies or be starved out of the fortress. Some who staked out the castle would make large-scale attacks, sometimes using cannon that they had acquired from the Europeans.

Toyotomi Hideyoshi was known for his expertise with the siege. In the late sixteenth century, he carried out a series of attacks that brought several domains under his control. His practices included everything from bribery to flooding—he once diverted a river into a castle, flooding out his enemy.

These were the essential weapons and methods that Japan relied on throughout its feudal period, until a

Detail of a matchlock gun. © *The Print Collector/Alamy*

modernized, conscripted armed forces was created with the Meiji Restoration in the late nineteenth century.

⊕ Impact of the Japanese Feudal Wars

Japan came into its national character during the feudal era, especially during Tokugawa times. This created an insular nation that intrigued outsiders—outsiders who ultimately forced Japan to open foreign relations and to modernize.

For centuries, the way of the samurai, the feudal hierarchy, and Japan's isolation created both a sense of loyalty to the state and a rather ordered society. After the unifiers—especially Tokugawa Ieyasu—expanded centralized rule in Japan, a long peace followed. During the peace, Japan flourished. Now that samurai were not competing, the government could focus its efforts and resources on enhancing Japan. Internal improvements and government regulations on trade brought a strong Japanese economy. There was an emphasis on the arts, and samurai were now meant to be chivalrous, intellectual, Renaissance men.

As this thriving nation was coming into its own, it established a policy of seclusion that shut out foreigners who were interested in Japan and kept its native Japanese on the islands. In the early seventeenth century, Tokugawa Ieyasu had encouraged a degree of open trade and communication with Asian nations and some European powers. By the 1630s, Japan commonly traded as far away as Burma, and Japanese settlements could be found in Taiwan, the Philippines, Borneo, and other parts of Asia. Ieayasu's grandson Tokugawa Iemitsu, however, saw fit to stop such relations.

Tokugawa Iemitsu issued a series of edicts from 1633 to 1639 that restricted the people of Japan from interacting with those abroad. Several factors contributed to this ruling. Many Japanese believed that in trading thus far, the foreigners had only brought luxuries that their people did not need, and they took items that the Japanese could not spare. Additionally, the imperial court and the shogun felt the new isolationist policy was necessary for internal security. The more that daimyo traveled abroad acting as the shogun's vassals, the less control the *bakufu*, or military government, would have on them.

Iemitsu also did not want an influx of Western and other foreign ideas into Japan. He prohibited people from traveling overseas to the west of Korea, or south beyond Okinawa. Finally, he also wanted to stop Christianity, which was seen as a meddling infiltration of the West. No longer could those living in Japan teach Christianity, nor could any Catholics enter Japan. Iemitsu's bakufu suppressed an uprising against this policy in 1637–1638, killing some 37,000 people.

In 1633, a memorandum was issued to the provincial governors that emphasized three points: no vessel without a valid license could leave Japan; no Japanese subject could leave for a foreign country; and any Japanese who returned from abroad would be put to death. One year after the Portuguese were expelled, an illegal Portuguese mission arrived, only to have its members executed. At one point, coastal daimyo were ordered to shoot at any visiting vessels on sight.

Such drastic measures were enough to repel the foreign devils and to isolate Japan into a very unified and peaceful nation. Traders and foreign ambassadors lost interest in pursuing a friendly trade relationship with an unwilling partner. But after about two hundred years—enough time for a peaceful Tokugawa period to establish a handsome market for foreign traders—the West began looking at Japan with more and more interest.

Russia, Britain, the United States, and others encroached on Japan, hoping to open her shores. These industrializing nations felt that Japan should be part of the process. One Scottish newspaper editorialized that the seclusion of Japan was wrong not only to themselves, but to the outside world. Many believed that though Japan had a right to its lands, it should not bar all other nations of its riches and virtues. The British, Dutch, and Russians tried to penetrate Japan's coast during the early and mid-nineteenth century, but the Japanese government responded with unequivocal denials.

It would take two major events to change the course of isolated traditionalist Japan. Commodore Mathew Perry's arrival and opening of Japan, and a revolution in governance, industry, and thought in Japan known as the Meiji Restoration.

Mathew Perry, of the U.S. Navy, arrived with a strong message: agree to trade peacefully or suffer consequences. The United States had special interests in a relationship with Japan, as did the other countries that wanted the same ends. Whalers and other commercial ships had been traveling the Pacific Ocean and needed Japan as a possible stop. By this time, the United States had expanded to the Pacific Coast and had a new sense of military and imperial ambition. Furthermore, the U.S. Navy and Perry wanted the Japanese to sell the United States coal for its naval ships.

Perry appeared in Edo Bay (modern Tokyo) in 1853, with a show of military might and a promise to return the next year for negotiations. He did so with nine ships, and America won some rights in the 1854 Treaty of Kanagawa to allow some ships to stop over in remote Japanese ports. Other European powers soon benefited from Perry's negotiations and received these same rights. The treaty opened eight ports of trade and placed the administration of justice in courts operated by foreign judges applying foreign law.

At the time as Perry's visit, Japan's Tokugawa legacy was giving way to a modernizing of Japan. When major gunboats arrived from the West, the sword was still the common weapon in Japan's military. Outdated, the samurai had become as much a burden to the state as a benefit. No longer were military campaigns in Japan going to be civil wars with encounters between sword-wielding samurai on horseback. Many Japanese leaders realized that they had to start thinking like the other nations who were now at Japan's ports.

Understandably, a thirst for modern industry, education, and transportation came over the elite government class; Tokugawa hegemony and the samurai warriors gave way to the Meiji Restoration. In this movement, a conscripted national army replaced the traditional samurai warriors. National universities were established, and Japan began to study and emulate Western industry.

BIBLIOGRAPHY

Books

Sadler, A. L. *The Maker of Modern Japan: The Life of Tokugawa Ieyasu*. Rutland, VT: Charles E. Tuttle Company, 1937.

Turnbull, Stephen R. *The Book of the Samurai: The Warrior Class of Japan*. New York: Bison Books, 1982.

Introduction to the Thirty Years War (1618–1648)

The Thirty Years War was an expansive and destructive conflict involving the major European states. Sparked largely by religious and territorial conflicts, the war gradually became a political contest. Ultimately, the wide-ranging fighting prompted a redistribution of military and political power; while the populace lay exhausted by the end of the war (with large parts of Germany laid waste), the centralized authority of state governments was permanently enhanced, and the foundation of a new state system emerged.

The war's origins lay in a complex dynastic struggle between the Holy Roman Empire and the House of Habsburg, all buffeted by the strong currents of the Counter Reformation. The Peace of Augsburg of 1555, by which each German prince would have the right to determine the religion of his own state—the principle of *cuius regio, eius religio*—was unraveling by the early seventeenth century. In 1618, a rise in Catholic governance prompted Protestant resistance. Two Catholic officials were thrown from the palace windows in Prague; this "Defenestration of Prague" marked the war's opening spark.

Emperor Ferdinand II aligned himself with Maximilian, duke of Bavaria, head of the Catholic League, and defeated Frederick V, King of Bohemia, at the Battle of White Mountain in 1620. With this victory, Catholic power was ascendant. Military operations shifted north, where for the next several years imperial forces under Albrecht von Wallenstein defeated the armies of Denmark's Christian IV.

In 1630, Gustavus Adolphus of Sweden declared war on behalf of his fellow Protestants. After a decisive victory at the Battle of Breitenfeld in 1631, Adolphus was killed during the hard-won Battle of Lützen. Thereafter Swedish fortunes waned, and a stalemate resumed.

Catholic France, allied with the Protestant states, now changed military fortunes. At the Battle of Rocroi in 1643, French arms defeated a Habsburg Spanish-Imperial force, leading all sides to seek a conclusion.

The pair of treaties signed in the Westphalian towns of Münster and Osnabrück in 1648 became known as the Peace of Westphalia. This general European agreement brought the Thirty Years War to a formal conclusion. It also terminated conflict between Netherlands and Spain, resulting in independence for the United Provinces.

During the three decades of warfare, the size, cost, and professionalism of armies increased tremendously. In turn, the experience governments gained by organizing such extensive military efforts led to a growth in state power, which fed ever-larger armed forces. A so-called "Military Revolution" saw armies achieve rapid advances in technology, doctrine, and logistics, establishing a style of warfare that would endure until the twentieth century. Martial discipline; year-round service; standardized logistics, uniforms, and arms; the widespread use of field artillery; and the rise of trained infantrymen fighting in cohesive units all became trademarks of European warfare.

Although not universally applied, the Peace of Westphalia underscored the importance of state sovereignty and legal equality between states. Thereafter, religious disputes increasingly played a diminished role in European relations, as political and economic matters gained ascendancy.

Thirty Years War (1618–1648)

🌐 Major Figures

Albrecht von Wallenstein

Albrecht von Wallenstein (1583–1634) was an enigmatic and ambitious aristocrat who earned fame as an Imperial general during the Thirty Years War.

Early Years and Education Born in Bohemia, Wallenstein came from a protestant family that was nobility, but not wealthy nobility. He attended the Jesuit college at Olmütz, and after 1599 he pursued his education at the University of Altdorf and then at Bologna and Padua. Although he was not a distinguished student, astrology caught his attention, and it was a pursuit he followed throughout his life.

He toured Europe and joined the army of Emperor Rudolf II in Hungary, winning honors for his conduct at the siege of Gran in 1604. In 1606 he converted to Catholicism, although his conviction for authority remained stronger than his religious enthusiasm.

In 1609, Wallenstein returned to Bohemia and married a wealthy widow, inheriting her Moravian estates when she died in 1614. He deployed his wealth to earn favor, offering and commanding two hundred horses for Archduke Ferdinand of Styria at the siege of Gradisca during the Archduke's war with Venice in 1617.

The Conflict Begins Upon the outbreak of the Thirty Years War, Wallenstein rebuffed the propositions of the Bohemian rebels, instead leaving his estates there and moving with his funds to Vienna to raise a cuirassier (horse soldiers who wore a cuirass, which was a piece of armor protecting the chest and back) regiment. He won distinction fighting and in the wake of the Protestant defeat at White Mountain received large estates for his service from the emperor.

As was characteristic of his nature, Wallenstein exploited the uncertain political situation to his advantage. He regained his Bohemian estates, as well as confiscated Protestant lands. In 1622, further military success earned him rank as imperial count palatine, with

more titles to follow. In 1623, he married Isabella Katharina, daughter of Count Harrach, a confidential adviser of the emperor, and was made a prince. Having consolidated vast tracts, he was allowed to form them into a territory named Friedland. Soon thereafter, Albrecht von Wallenstein became Duke of Friedland.

When Ferdinand found few forces at hand to continue prosecuting the war, he turned to Wallenstein, who offered to raise an army in the emperor's service. Because of his popularity, recruiting proceeded quickly. In 1626, Wallenstein defeated Ernst von Manfeld at Dassau Bridge. Subsequently he campaigned to secure Silesia and to force Denmark from the war. As compensation for his contributions, he was made Duke (later Prince) of Sagan. In 1628 he was granted the duchy of Mecklenburg.

The Political Backlash Gains Strength Although he was unable to subdue Stralsund (a city on the Baltic whose port offered income from trade with the Scandinavian countries as well as the promise of developing naval power), Wallenstein's ambitious grasp was attracting resentment from higher-born nobility of the Empire. He frequently behaved independently and took efficient measures to extract plunder from his holdings.

Ferdinand listened to the complaints of his advisors, but he was hesitant to let go of someone who had provided so much to the Imperial cause. Nonetheless, Wallenstein's many centers of authority were too threatening to ignore. Ferdinand finally determined that Wallenstein's reach needed to be curtailed, so in September 1630 he sent envoys to announce his dismissal. Wallenstein yielded his army to General Tilly and retired to his duchy of Friedland.

The Swedes Arrive Wallenstein's retirement did not last very long. Swedish General Gustavus Adolphus invaded Germany, winning a decisive Swedish victory over Tilly at the Battle of Breitenfeld in 1631. The Swedish advance into southern Germany prompted the Emperor to recall Wallenstein in the spring of 1632. In response, Wallenstein rapidly raised a new army and opened an aggressive campaign. He expelled a Saxon force from Bohemia and in November fought the Swedes at the Battle of Lützen. In this contest Wallenstein was forced to withdraw, but Adolphus was killed.

During the next year, Wallenstein showed a reluctance to engage in decisive battle, instead entering into negotiations to abandon the Imperial cause and defect to his former enemies. Confident that his officers would remain loyal to him, Wallenstein retired to winter quarters in Bohemia. Meanwhile, the Emperor became aware of Wallenstein's treachery and engineered his removal by a patent of high treason published in Prague on February 18, 1634. Wallenstein fled, but was murdered on February 25, probably by an official loyal to the Emperor.

Wallenstein's career as a general, like his character, must be considered to be one of ambiguity. He was resourceful and effective with a penchant for grand projects, yet he was also personally harsh, fond of the pleasures of wealth, and secretive. He could inspire others to follow him and engendered lasting loyalty among his officers and subordinates.

While not a great strategist, he competently led his forces on campaign and did not shy from seeking battle when he believed it to his advantage. Wallenstein took as much pleasure in the administration of his extensive estates as he did with military affairs. He sought to improve the operation of his holdings and was willing to compromise religious convictions in the name of statecraft. He believed most of all in himself and in his ability to influence situations for his own benefit, a characteristic that ultimately led to his downfall.

Gustavus Adolphus

Gustavus Adolphus (1594–1632) was King of Sweden from 1611 to 1632. Known as the "Lion of the North," Gustavus Adolphus transformed military theory and practice. Although he did not bring about an end to the Thirty Years War, his modernized Swedish army changed the face of armed conflict in Europe.

The Prince Becomes King Adolphus began his career as a reformer and leader at an early age. He received a formal, rigorous academic education, studying Latin and Greek classics, history, theology, and law. He was bilingual in Swedish and German and eventually could converse in other European tongues as well.

While scholarly, Adolphus was no stranger to a battlefield. He saw military action in the Danish War at age sixteen, and he succeeded his father as king on October 30, 1611. This period was a time of trial for Sweden, for political dissension prevailed throughout the Baltic and within Sweden itself. Warfare with neighboring states seemed endemic; Sweden's small, inadequately trained and equipped army was poorly suited to engage its enemies.

TOTAL WAR

Albrecht von Wallenstein was a complex leader who combined religious zeal, political acumen, military ruthlessness, and strategic foresight in novel ways. He typified his age in that his innovations, while not systematic, nor consistent, nor rigorously applied in the armies he led, nonetheless utilized many of the improvements in military capability being developed most prominently in the Low Countries and by Swedish commander Gustavus Adolphus. Wallenstein's particular adaptation was to abandon the system of general plunder by which an invading army indiscriminately seized property along its route of march, irrespective as to whether the local inhabitants were friend or foe, and instead to target enemies for comprehensive plunder. He recognized that the destruction wrought by a marauding army was a terror tool that could be used to coerce an indifferent population and to penalize those who opposed him. By laying waste to enemies' lands and cities, he could effectively create battlefield victories without waging set-piece battles. The result, however, was ruinous for the peoples of central Europe.

The war's devastation, both in terms of the human cost as well as the toll on the infrastructure, has long been a source of investigation among historians. The traditional estimate that up to thirty percent of the population of Europe died as a result of the war, while a high percentage, probably was accurate for the most fought-over territories. Even though famine, pestilence, and disease were often byproducts of armies that carried illness with them wherever they marched, much of the destruction of civilian lives and property can be attributed to the deliberate devastation wrought by marauding soldiers. Wallenstein's forces were experts at extracting tolls, foodstuffs, supplies, and livestock from subject populations, leaving civilians with no means of support and making them completely vulnerable to all manner of misfortune. For hostile populations, especially in cities, the penalty for resisting Wallenstein's forces was frequently expulsion and often death. Military leaders such as Wallenstein brought total war to the lands and peoples of Europe on a scale not yet seen, and thereby established a way of war that would persist for centuries to come.

As king, Gustavus inherited no less than three wars with his neighbors (Denmark, Russia, and Poland). He first turned his attention to the nearest and most threatening opponent, Denmark. Competing sovereignty claims and Danish resentment of Swedish independence had prompted conflict that Gustavus now sought to conclude by initiating raids against Danish positions.

His attempts achieved little, and by summer he was forced to parry strong Danish offensive thrusts. Realizing that he could not prevail, he concluded a peace with Christian IV in 1614, a settlement more advantageous to Denmark than to Sweden.

From 1613 to 1617, Gustavus fought Russia, where a clash of territorial and economic interests led to

The arrest of Albrecht von Wallenstein at Eger by a force of Irish and Scottish officers under the command of General Butler. © *Visual Arts Library, London*

hostilities. Difficult campaigns under harsh conditions ensued, but by 1617 Gustavus's gains were sufficient to negotiate the Treaty of Stolbova. This ended favorably for Sweden, as they gained control of the Gulf of Finland and cut off Russia from the Baltic.

Competition with Poland prompted the King to lead an offensive in 1617 that he exploited in 1621 with the seizure of the important port and city of Riga. Further campaigns ensued but Gustavus had made his point that Sweden would not be denied. By 1629 Polish forces were largely defeated. With the Treaty of Altmark, Sweden gained further territory, Prussian ports, northern Livonia, and advantageous economic rights.

Battles Abroad, Reforms at Home Adolphus understood that a vigorous domestic political and economic foundation was necessary if Sweden was to become a major European power. He oversaw the increased development of natural resources, instituted novel manufacturing techniques, expanded trade, and reformed the government's fiscal structures.

Gustavus achieved his most significant reforms in terms of military affairs. During the sixteenth century in Europe, military practice languished. Dominating infantry combat was the Spanish *tercio* formation, which combined pikemen and arquebusiers in squares composed of fifteen hundred to three thousand men arranged in a primarily defensive formation. Cavalry formations lacked the offensive capability to attack. Horsemen largely restricted themselves to charging, firing their wheel-lock pistols, and then retiring (a tactic called the "caracole"). Artillery was heavy and difficult to position on the battlefield. Gustavus sought to change this static climate.

Gustavus returned a dynamic flexibility to warfare by building upon a number of the changes already set in motion by the great Dutch reformer Maurice of Nassau. For example, Adolphus restored the infantry's capacity for offensive action by emphasizing a linear brigade formation. Muskets were located on the flanks and were integrated in the center with pikes, allowing each arm to be

Illustration of the death of Gustavus Adolphus of Sweden in the Battle of Lutzen. © *Bettmann/Corbis*

more fully employed throughout an engagement. This also facilitated command and control, meaning leaders could more easily direct their units on the battlefield.

Gustavus's cavalry attacked in three ranks, firing their pistols once but then resorting to sabers for close combat. In terms of artillery, he lightened the weight and size so that cannons could be maneuvered in combat. Also, the use of barrage fires and rolling salvos meant that the artillery was again an active participant in the outcome of fighting. Finally, Gustavus imposed order to his camps and reformed logistical systems to ensure that pay, food, clothing, and training drastically improved.

The Improved Army Heads South After he had secured peace with Poland, Gustavus entered the Thirty Years War by invading Germany in July 1630. After a brief winter campaign, he assaulted Frankfurt an der Oder and skirmished with the Imperial General Tilly's forces. When Tilly's army sacked the city of Magdeburg, which had declared support for Gustavus, the King resolved to bring Tilly to battle.

On September 17, 1631, Gustavus decisively defeated Tilly at the Battle of Breitenfeld, showcasing the Swedish army's various reforms. Nonetheless, many of Tilly's men escaped, and the Imperial army soon regrouped. Gustavus next moved toward the Rhine, and in the spring of 1632 he turned eastward. Even though he crossed the Danube, he was unable to bring his Imperial adversaries to battle.

The Emperor now brought Wallenstein to oppose the Swedes, and moving northward, he parried with Gustavus. The Swedish King attacked on November 16 at the Battle of Lützen, and while forcing Wallenstein to retreat, Gustavus was killed.

Was the New Army Not So New? Revisionist historians assert that Gustavus's contributions are overstated. They point to the fact that native Swedes frequently constituted a minority of his army. Since the Swedish king could rarely fill his formations to strength, Swedish armies were similar to the mercenary forces fielded by other states. Critics also declare that because his battlefield victories did not bring an end to the Thirty Years War, his military reforms were not substantial; Gustavus was simply carrying through with earlier Spanish and Dutch advances.

Yet what cannot be denied is that Gustavus changed the face of warfare in his lifetime. At the time of his birth, the conduct of war appeared much as it had for a century prior: cumbersome infantry forces slugged it out while largely ineffective cavalry and artillery arms contributed little to the main engagements. By the time Gustavus was killed, all the major powers were emulating his reforms. His campaigns during the Thirty Years War restored mobility to land forces, demonstrated the effectiveness of combined arms, resurrected shock action for the cavalry, maximized the firepower of the artillery, and

MILITARY REVOLUTION

Gustavus Adolphus played a key role in the sweeping processes that transformed the nature of warfare and the organization of government during the seventeenth century in Europe. As Gustavus fashioned a new kind of army with greatly expanded materiel, financial, and technical demands, the dynamic relationship between society, government, and the armed forces underwent a transformation. Collectively, these changes are known as a "military revolution" and served as the foundation of the organization and function of modern, centralized state government.

As Swedish-style armies gained battlefield success and demonstrated their ability to overcome static fortifications and strike enemies at longer range, political rulers demanded even more such capabilities. This created a demand for even larger armies that—in turn—required additional support to train, organize, equip, and maintain on a permanent basis. Institutional standardization across the profession of arms through the general adoption of comprehensive drill, uniforms, weapons, and specialized military branches also necessitated supervisory governmental institutions to manage these requirements. Hence, governments found it necessary to expand their authority, develop more extensive formal administrative structures, and impose far heavier burdens (taxes) than ever before on society at large. In short, as armies expanded in capability and size, so did government, with profound consequences.

enabled generals to maneuver ever-larger armies on longer campaigns. For this, Gustavus still stands in the first rank of great leaders.

Lennart Torstensson

An extraordinary artillery officer, Lennart Torstensson (1603–1651) was a leading proponent for advances in early modern artillery doctrine and tactics. His work with the Swedish army helped transform that unit into Europe's most sophisticated fighting force.

A Soldier's Life Precocious as a youth, Torstensson became a page to Gustavus Adolphus as an adolescent. Showing potential as a soldier and leader, he was sent to the Netherlands from 1624 to 1626 to study military affairs under the leading theorist of the period, Maurice of Nassau. Upon his return, Torstensson served under Gustavus in the Prussian and Polish campaigns of 1627–1629. His abilities were rewarded with command of the six companies of the Swedish army's artillery regiment in 1629.

Torstensson immediately set about training his crews to emphasize mobility and firepower. He insisted that they be ready to deliver a striking blow in concert with the other arms in battle. Torstensson's artillery played a central role at the Battle of Breitenfeld on

September 17, 1631, Gustavus Adolphus's greatest victory. The Swedish batteries outmaneuvered and dominated the Imperialist cannon, providing the winning margin during the battle's final attacks. In honor of his achievements, Torstensson was promoted to the rank of general.

In April 1632, his artillery covered the Swedes' crossing of the Lech, confusing Tilly's forces and preventing an Imperial assault. Torstensson fought in the attack upon Wallenstein's encamped army at Alte Veste on September 3–4, 1632, but was captured and held prisoner for a year at Ingolstadt. When he was exchanged, he returned to Sweden and married Baroness Beata de la Gardie.

Once More Into the Thirty Years War Torstensson became chief of staff to the Swedish general Johan Banér, and between 1635 and 1641 he campaigned with Banér in eastern Germany, rendering important service at the Battle of Wittstock (October 4, 1636). Torstensson later assumed an independent command, although operating jointly with Banér. Torstensson's insistence that his field artillery be moved around the battlefield and kept firing in positions to aid his infantry became a hallmark of his offensives.

In the wake of the campaign of 1640, Torstensson fell ill and again returned to Sweden. There he was made a senator and promoted to field marshal on August 31, 1641. On his next campaign, he invaded Saxony and besieged Leipzig, assaulting and nearly annihilating the Imperial army during the Second Battle of Breitenfeld (November 2, 1642).

By now known for leading rapid, slashing marches against his opponents, in 1643 Torstensson invaded Moravia again, but he had to return north at the outbreak of war between Sweden and Denmark. He checked Danish advances and attacked as far as Holstein. However, a decade of constant war had robbed his army of many veterans, and his native Swedish regiments lacked their former swagger.

Torstensson soon set off once more for Germany at the head of his army. In early November 1644 he entered Bohemia, and when he scored a win at the Battle of Jankau (March 6, 1645), Vienna appeared to be vulnerable. Nonetheless, his army was exhausted and he was unable to capitalize on the moment. In the aftermath, the toll of many years in the saddle on campaign finally came due, and Torstensson resigned his command and returned to Sweden.

Life after the Military In 1647 he was made Count Torstensson of Ortola and became governor-general of the western provinces of Sweden. He died at Stockholm on April 7, 1651, and was buried with state honors at Riddarholm Church. Torstensson is remembered as a trusted lieutenant of Gustavus Adolphus; an aggressive artillery general who applied a rational, scientific approach to the employment of indirect fires; and a hero of Sweden.

Vicomte de Turenne

Henri de la Tour d'Auvergne, Vicomte de Turenne, (1611–1675) would earn fame as a brilliant operational and tactical leader. One of France's most popular and famous generals, his military actions helped bring the Thirty Years War to an end.

An Aristocratic Childhood Born into a noble protestant family, Turenne's father was a learned aristocrat who maintained close relationships with members of the French court. Turenne's mother was Elizabeth of Nassau, a capable and headstrong daughter of the Dutch royal line. Over the course of his life, Turenne would become involved in numerous dynastic, religious, and political intrigues among the leading families of France.

As a child, Turenne was sickly, and he fared poorly at his academic lessons. However, he was fond of classical military history and thus studied past martial glories. He became stronger as he grew older, and as an adolescent his mother sent him to her brother, Prince Maurice of Nassau, the greatest military theoretician and reformer of his age. Entering service as a soldier in the Prince's bodyguard, Turenne quickly demonstrated potential.

Early Military Action Turenne soon earned a captaincy and took an active role in the siege of Bois-le-Duc in 1629. He returned to French service the following year, where he took command of an infantry regiment and began a period of service in Piedmont and Lorraine. Turenne earned honors for his leadership during the assault at the siege of La Mothe in 1634. For his bravery he was promoted to *maréchal de camp*, equivalent to the rank of major-general.

In 1635 Turenne campaigned along the Rhine, lifting the siege of Mainz in August, but he was forced to retire due to logistical constraints. With France now having entered the Thirty Years War and fighting against the Habsburgs, Turenne's prowess as a commander in the field continued to mature, and he became an increasingly important French leader. In 1637 he took a leading role in the army's actions in Flanders. The next year, in concert with Bernhard of Saxe-Weimar, he coordinated the siege of the Rhine fortress of Breisach, compelling its capitulation in mid-December.

Under the Duke of Harcourt, Turenne next fought in the Italian campaign of 1639–1640 at Casale and Turin, where he suffered a serious wound. He was promoted to lieutenant general, and his fortune continued to ascend. Even though his elder brother was found to be involved in the conspiracy of Cinq-Mars in 1642, the French Minister Mazarin made Turenne Marshal of France in late 1643. Mazarin sent Turenne to Germany to reorganize and train Bernhard of Saxe-Weimar's troops who had been defeated at Tuttlingen in November 1643.

The Final Chapter of the Thirty Years War Begins Turenne crossed the Rhine with the advent of warm weather in the spring of 1644. Allied with the great Condé (Louis II de Bourbon, Prince de Condé), the two leaders waged a stiff fight against Bavarian General Franz von Mercy's forces in August 1644 at Freiburg. There, Turenne's promotion of a slashing, flanking attack provided the margin of victory.

In 1645, Turenne again opened a campaign across the Rhine, this time with a new army. He confronted Mercy in Franconia once more, but at Mergentheim on May 2 he was outmaneuvered and forced to retreat to Hesse. On August 3, Turenne exacted his revenge at Allerheim (near Nordlingen); the Bavarian host was defeated, and Mercy himself was killed.

In 1646, Turenne joined with Swedish forces under General Gustav Karl Wrangel near Giessen and opened a campaign in Bavaria. These actions resulted in the Truce of Ulm with the Bavarian Elector, Maximilian I, on March 14, 1647.

Facing a mutiny amongst the Weimar troops, Turenne turned his attention to suppressing this revolt with minimal loss of life before once again invading Bavaria, which had returned to active hostilities on behalf of the Habsburgs. The May 17 victory at Zusmarshausen brought an active end to the campaign.

Strife Within the Homeland The great families of France now became involved in the internal conflict of the *Fronde*, a rebellion against centralized royal authority. (This revolt was organized by some of France's leading aristocrats while the young French king, Louis XIV, was still a minor.) Initially, Turenne fled to Holland, where Condé's sister, Madame de Longueville, persuaded him to join the revolt.

The Treaty of Rueil in March 1649 put an end to the first war of the Fronde, and the second war began with the arrest of Condé and his associates in January 1650. Turenne escaped and engaged in minor actions, but conflict ended by negotiation with the royalist parties still in power and the arrested nobles released. Turenne reconciled himself to the royals and returned to Paris in May 1651. Soon thereafter, Condé again raised a revolt in the south of France. This time, Turenne would oppose his former colleague.

In the third (or Spanish) war of the Fronde, Turenne played a prominent role. He defeated Condé at Gien on April 7, 1652, and nearly ended the war at Porte de St. Antoine (St. Denis), in the Paris suburbs, in early July. In 1653 and 1654, Turenne was occupied with campaigns against the Spanish. He defeated the Spaniards at Arras in the summer of 1654 and continued to advance, capturing numerous towns through 1655, but he suffered a setback when Condé vanquished him at Valenciennes in July 1656. Final victory came on June 14, 1658 at the Battle of the Dunes near Dunkirk. The Treaty of the Pyrenees was signed on November 7, 1659.

Later Wars Upon consolidating his power, Louis XIV promoted Turenne to marshal-general, giving him authority over all other French marshals. Turenne campaigned

The Battle of White Mountain. © *Mary Evans Picture Library/Alamy*

actively in Flanders during the War of Devolution in 1667–1668, although Louis' personal attention to military operations often hindered the field marshal.

In the Dutch War of 1672, Turenne advanced with the king through the United Provinces but was thwarted when the dikes were opened. Turenne next led his army across the Rhine, outmaneuvering the army of the Italian Montecuccoli and Frederick William of Branderburg; this forced the latter out of the anti-French alliance.

Driven back across the Rhine in the fall of 1673, Turenne and his army recrossed in the spring, and in June 1674 he won the Battle of Sinsheim, opening the Palatinate to French arms and deprivations. Turenne next maneuvered to seize Strasbourg on September 24, 1674. Executing a daring winter campaign, he screened his forces with the Vosges range and surprised his enemies at Mulhouse on December 29, 1674, and again at Turckheim on January 5, 1675, thereby securing Alsace.

Turenne was struck and killed by a cannonball during the opening stage of a Battle at Sasbach on July 27, 1675. His remains were buried at St. Denis, the sacred burial grounds of French monarchs. Later, Napoleon would move them to the Invalides, in Paris.

At the Right Place and Time   Turenne's genius was uniquely suited for the style of warfare of the late sev-

enteenth century. Unafraid of battle, he demonstrated personal courage, tactical ferocity, and a willingness to strike boldly when the opportunity presented itself. Furthermore, he favored operational maneuver and sought to force his enemies into untenable positions from which their only choice was to yield or to surrender a key piece of terrain.

Given the increasingly expensive, technically trained and professional armies of the era, Turenne's sophisticated, economical approach to warfare was just what the monarchs he served wanted from their leaders in the field.

⊕ Major Battles

White Mountain, November 8, 1620

Won by the Catholic-Imperial side, the Battle of White Mountain was an early contest of the Thirty Years War that served to widen the conflict and firmly established Habsburg rule over the Czech people.

Religious Tolerance Goes out the Window   For years, a fragile balance existed between Protestant and Catholic princes and their subjects within the Holy Roman Empire. This delicate peace was undone in 1617, when Emperor Matthias designated Ferdinand of Styria as his successor. Ferdinand was an ardent Catholic, and although he outwardly promised to uphold the rights of the estates assemblies, the Protestant nobility fully expected him to pursue a strict Catholic ideology.

In May 1618, a group of Protestant nobles entered the palace in Prague and hurled several of Ferdinand's confidants from the windows into the ditch below. Although the ejected men survived, this "Defenestration of Prague" set in motion events that culminated in the outbreak of the Thirty Years War in Europe.

A general Protestant uprising in Bohemia and Hungary ensued, threatening Habsburg interests throughout the Empire. This unrest stretched even as far as the Low Countries, where allies might be attained with the restless Dutch who were actively fighting the Spanish Habsburgs.

In June 1619, a general assembly of the estates of the lands of the Bohemian Crown offered Frederick V of the Palatinate a crown to stand as rival king to Ferdinand. As a Calvinist married to the daughter of King James of England, Frederick came to the forefront as a leader with significant Protestant credentials, and he could be expected to draw substantial European support.

Start the Revolution Without Us Frederick arrived in Prague in October amidst much diplomatic activity, but he was disappointed to find little direct assistance proffered by fellow Protestant leaders. James, despite his daughter's direct involvement, faced a reluctant aristocracy in London that was tired of continental adventures and wary of Dutch plans. The Dutch offered a few thousand men and a modest subsidy only, as they already had their hands full contesting Imperial forces nearer to home. German Lutherans sensed that Frederick would be defeated and were unwilling to oppose the Emperor.

The Habsburgs moved to suppress the rebellion on several fronts. A Spanish fleet was dispatched to Flanders, and Spanish general Spinola captured Frederick's lands on the left bank of the Rhine in the summer of 1620. Fearful of Spanish ambitions, Maximilian of Bavaria offered his Catholic League forces to Ferdinand.

In July 1620, Maximilian's army—about thirty thousand strong and commanded by the experienced Count von Tilly—marched into Austria. This compelled the Austrian Estates to abandon their alliance with the Bohemian rebels. Frederick's commander, Christian Anhalt, was left to face the Imperialists alone.

The Battle of White Mountain Maneuvering in the vicinity of Prague in November, the opposing armies drew near and prepared for battle. Anhalt deployed his army along the crest of a hill, presumptuously named White Mountain (*Bílá Hora* in Czech), astride the road to Prague. His army's position was defensible, with one flank anchored near a hunting lodge that provided a degree of cover, while his other flank rested on a minor stream. Soft ground covered much of the low-lying areas at the bottom of the slopes.

THEY'VE DONE THIS BEFORE IN PRAGUE

Chucking out Ferdinand's supporters is the most well-known Defenestration of Prague, but it was not the first. Two hundred years before, a group of Hussites (a religious sect) came to Town Hall and demanded the release of some Hussite prisoners. The city council members refused this request, and events turned ugly when a rock was thrown at the Hussites. This prompted the Hussites to storm the Town Hall and hurl seven council members out the window.

The council members might have survived the fall if they had not landed on pikes carried by people in the crowd. As might be expected, this first defenestration helped pave the way to war just like the second defenestration did, with the Hussite Wars lasting for over a decade in the fifteenth century.

Nonetheless, Anhalt's men were poorly trained, lightly armed, and lacking a unifying élan. Tilly's army, on the other hand, contained more veterans and was organized for combat. After just a few hours fighting, Anhalt's men began streaming to the rear, with the center of his position broken.

Frederick V, thereafter known as the "Winter King," fled into an exile that lasted for the remainder of his life, dying in Mainz in 1632. His Bohemian rebels met a likewise harsh fate. Confident in the wake of his forces' victory, Ferdinand II exploited his advantage to political and personal gain. He mandated extensive transfers of property from rebel landholders, disrupting the broader economy and diminishing the value of Czech currency, but enriching his Catholic allies and solidifying their support for the Emperor's cause.

The Sands Do Not Question Authority Ferdinand also imposed a severe course of re-Catholicization, declaring, "Better to rule over a desert than a country full of heretics." Protestant ministers were ordered to depart Bohemia in 1624, and three years later all Bohemian subjects were compelled to choose between exile and Catholicism. Tens of thousands of subjects chose to depart their homeland. Many suffered even more harshly. In June 1621, more than two dozen rebel leaders were executed in Prague's town square.

While the course of the Thirty Years War would rage across Bohemia and central Europe until 1648, the Czech people would remain firmly within the orbit of Habsburg authority for the next three centuries.

Magdeburg, May 1631

The siege and sack of the Saxon city of Magdeburg by Imperial troops of the Holy Roman Empire under the command of Count Graf Johann Tserclaes von Tilly was one of the most notorious atrocities of the Thirty Years

---

The Minster of Magdeburg, where Martin Luther preached.
© Blickwinkel/Alamy

War. The destruction of the city served to galvanize Protestant resistance and symbolized the excesses of the war.

Catholic Ascendancy in the Early Years

In 1624, the Emperor Ferdinand II deposed the leading Protestant noble in Germany (the Elector Frederick V), giving the title to Maximilian of Bavaria. Frederick's expulsion and the consequent military disarray on the Protestant side left Tilly's army as the dominant force in northern Germany.

During the years 1625–1629, Protestant hopes were raised by the intervention of the Hague Alliance comprising England, the Netherlands, and Denmark. Once again, though, Catholic arms gained the upper hand, and it seemed the war might be winding down.

But in March 1629, the Emperor ignited Protestant resistance again by his declaration of the Edict of Restitution. Reaching back into the past, the Edict stated that the secularization of church lands was illegal, and that (in effect) only Lutheran Protestantism was permissible. Calvinism and other Protestant faiths were forbidden.

The restoration of Catholic properties and influence was clearly intended to effectively strangle Protestant believers within the Empire. Following the Edict, the Catholic electors reorganized Catholic military forces. In 1630, they compelled the removal of the mercenary general Albrecht von Wallenstein and named Count Tilly as commander of both the Imperial Army and the forces of the Catholic League, the latter numbering about twenty thousand men.

Sweden Enters the Fray

While Protestant fortunes waned during the 1620s, the Swedish commander Gustavus Adolphus was waging a lengthy war in Poland; hence, he did not contest the armies of the Emperor. Prompted in part by the Edict and partially by the desire to expand Swedish influence, Gustavus launched an invasion of central Europe in July, 1630.

The Swedish army soon occupied Stettin, capital of Pomerania. After securing his base, Gustavus planned an active campaign for the spring of 1631. However, before his army could make any substantial gains, Tilly besieged Magdeburg, which had declared allegiance to the Swedes and had resisted the re-Catholicization program mandated by the Edict.

Tilly was an experienced professional who had campaigned since the 1580s in the Low Countries. He had likewise been fighting since the opening years of the Thirty Years War. It was his army that confronted the Bohemian rebels under Frederick at the Battle of White Mountain, and he had inflicted the defeat that sent Frederick and the Protestant cause into retreat.

In March 1631, Tilly moved his army before the city's defenses and began a deliberate siege, reinforcing the troops of his field marshal Pappenheim who had started siege operations the previous November. Tilly counted slightly more than twenty thousand soldiers. This was not a large force, but it still overwhelmed the small Swedish force garrisoning the city, which was led by the Swedish colonel Diedrich von Falkenburg.

Realizing the seriousness of the situation at Magdeburg, Falkenburg appealed to Gustavus for relief. Recognizing that the appearance of Gustavus's army would force him to lift the siege and offer battle, Tilly ordered an assault on May 20. After a sharp fight lasting only a few hours and during which von Falkenburg was killed, Tilly's men seized the city.

A City Ravaged

While it was customary for occupants of a city that had resisted a siege to suffer at the hands of a victorious attacking force, the rampage of the Imperial troops at Magdeburg went far beyond contemporary conventions. In an orgy of destruction, Tilly's men proceeded to burn most of the dwellings and slaughter the city's men, women, and children. Only approximately five thousand of the city's thirty thousand inhabitants survived. Protestant broadsheets describing the terror of the pillage circulated widely throughout

Europe and served to galvanize Protestant determination to continue the war.

Following the sack, revenge became a new motivation for an already lengthy and bloody conflict. Gustavus took his measure when he inflicted a significant defeat upon Tilly's army at the Battle of Breitenfeld in September. Still fighting the Swedes, Tilly was mortally wounded and died in April 1632. Magdeburg did not recover for many years—by the mid-1630s, only a handful of families resided there.

First Breitenfeld, September 17, 1631

A critical contest of the Thirty Years War, the First Battle of Breitenfeld checked Habsburg momentum by turning back Imperial armies from northern Europe and reviving Protestant fortunes. The battle also marked the ascendancy of Gustavus Adolphus and his novel system of warfare that sought to provide commanders with the means to bring crushing firepower to bear on the battlefield.

The Swedes Modernize As the opening battles of the Thirty Years War raged across central Europe during the 1620s, Gustavus Adolphus was aggressively organizing, training, and equipping a new kind of army. His aim was to restore flexibility to land combat by capitalizing upon the reforms initiated by the great Dutch theoretician Maurice of Nassau. Under Gustavus's tutelage, Swedish infantry adopted a linear, brigade formation that maximized both firepower and maneuverability. The cavalry advanced in three ranks, firing their pistols when closing, but then resorting to sabers for close combat. The weight of Swedish artillery was lessened so that the guns could be repositioned during action, allowing commanders the ability to concentrate fires at the decisive time and place on the battlefield. And Gustavus built cohesive formations by ensuring that the soldiers were paid and fed, and that order was imposed in camp and on the march. This combination of efforts created an army that was fundamentally distinct from other fighting forces.

With a truce in hand with Poland, and seeking to check the Habsburgs on the continent, Gustavus invaded Germany in the summer of 1630 and spent much of the year consolidating his base and reinforcing his army. In the spring of 1631, the Swedes took to the field, but Gustavus could not bring the main Imperial host, under Count Tilly, to battle. In September, now augmented by the men brought by John George of Saxony, Gustavus pressed Tilly, who fell back upon Leipzig. Gustavus's army numbered about 42,000 while Tilly commanded approximately 35,000.

The Imperials Find the Swedes On September 16, Count Pappenheim, Tilly's cavalry commander, encountered a detachment of Swedes. Pappenheim sent word back to Tilly that he was engaged and requested support. Tilly marched from Leipzig, selecting advantageous terrain near the village of Breitenfeld. Aligning his army along a slight rise, he placed more than a dozen *tercios* in his army's center, with cavalry covering each wing and artillery at center front.

Shortly after dawn on September 17, Gustavus brought his army forward. Unbothered by Tilly's static formations, he assembled in a parallel line about a half mile distant. John George's Saxons claimed a spot to the Swedes' left, with their infantry in groups of one thousand men each, shaped into a pyramid-like formation. Gustavus's Swedes reflected their new, linear-style organization. Artillery covered the infantry in the center with cavalry on the flanks in the traditional manner. However, instead of a single line, the Swedish formations arranged themselves in depth, so that the brigades nearest the enemy were mutually supporting. Furthermore, several artillery pieces were located with each brigade, and cavalry appeared in small numbers amidst the infantry. Overall, Gustavus had achieved a combined-arms posture that would allow infantry, cavalry, and artillery to fight simultaneously.

About midday, the battle opened with a conventional barrage. Each side suffered, but the Swedes could fire faster than Tilly's cannoneers. Unwilling to bear any more casualties, Pappenheim charged the Swedish right. Musket fire and cannonades from the embedded infantry and guns shredded the Imperialists. Pappenheim would not be denied and ordered charge after charge, each with the same bloody result. When the Catholics had been repulsed seven times, Gustavus ordered a counterattack with his reserves, scattering Pappenheim's troopers.

Maneuvers During the Conflict On the Swedes' left flank, Imperial hopes were brighter. At the first assault by the Habsburg cavalry there, the Saxons had broken and fled. With one flank in desperate combat but the other victorious, Tilly sensed an opportunity. He ordered his *tercios* to march obliquely to the right, overlap the Swedish left, and then strike the open flank abandoned by the Saxons.

Yet Gustavus had organized and deployed his army to counter just such a maneuver. Instead of crumbling, the Swedes stiffened their defense. By shifting brigades and rearranging his cannon, Gustavus was able to pressure Tilly's greater numbers.

At the right moment, Gustavus ordered a counterattack. Tilly's *tercios* were by now smashed tightly together and could barely move or fight effectively, while the Imperial cannon remained immobile up the slope. The Swedes savagely assaulted across the front in an irresistible onslaught, destroying Tilly's army and chasing the remnants from the field.

Morning light revealed about 7,500 dead from Tilly's army on the field. Another several thousand were killed during the wild retreat, and nearly ten thousand were captured while thousands more deserted. In short, Tilly's army was grievously wounded and the Imperial cause suffered a severe blow. While he lost about five

King Gustavus Adolfus of Sweden fights the troops of Wallenstein at Lutzen. © *Visual Arts Library, London*

thousand men, Gustavus clearly demonstrated the superiority of his military reforms in action.

While the First Battle of Breitenfeld did not end the Thirty Years War, it changed the war's course in favor of the Protestant Alliance. Most importantly, it established Gustavus Adolphus and his Swedish reforms as the model for a European way of war that would dominate during the coming centuries.

Lützen, November 16, 1632

The Battle of Lützen, which pitted the Swedish army of the Great Captain Gustavus Adolphus against the army of the Imperial general Count Albrecht von Wallenstein, was a central event of the Thirty Years War. Although a tactical Swedish victory, Gustavus was killed, and Swedish ambitions never recovered from his demise and the battle's heavy loss of life.

The Swedes Move Through Germany In the wake of Gustavus's victory at the Battle of Breitenfeld in September 1631, fresh recruits arrived in number to the camps of his army. He also gained additional support from German

princes. Gustavus had a clearly devised strategy for subduing his opponents, and his objective was the destruction of the Emperor Ferdinand's armies in the field.

As part of this strategy, rather than march to occupy the Habsburg capital city of Vienna, Gustavus led his forces toward the Rhine and then down the Danube. This path served to deny Emperor Ferdinand support from Catholic Bavaria, while allowing Gustavus's men to gather provisions from the estates of their enemies.

By December 1631, Gustavus had occupied the Rhineland and forced the Spanish garrisons to retire back to the Netherlands. After wintering in the Main valley, Gustavus set off in the spring of 1632 with a host numbering more than 120,000 men (only a minority of this host were native Swedes). Adolphus crossed the Danube and brushed aside the Imperialist army gathered by Count von Tilly, his foe from Breitenfeld. When word reached the Swedish lines that Tilly himself had been killed, it seemed that the war might be soon over.

A Desperate Emperor Makes a Desperate Move
Worried about defeat, Ferdinand reached out to Count

von Wallenstein, the mercenary and ambitious general whom he had already removed due to Wallenstein's hunger for power. Wallenstein was wary of fighting Gustavus in a set-piece battle, so he first struck at the Swede's Protestant ally John George. In short order, Wallenstein attacked George and drove his Saxons back into Bohemia. Gustavus marched north to confront Wallenstein, but neither side wanted to risk battle on anything other than favorable terms. For weeks, stalemate persisted until, in early September, Gustavus feinted in the direction of Vienna.

Wallenstein, a wily military leader himself, did not take the bait, and instead headed farther north into Saxony. Gustavus returned on Wallenstein's heels, but by now it was November. Wallenstein therefore entered winter quarters, assuming the campaign season was concluded for the year. Wallenstein even sent his formidable cavalry general, Pappenheim, away on another mission.

Gustavus, however, wanted a battle and prepared a surprise attack. By chance, his assault was uncovered by a small detachment of Imperial cavalry. Hence, each army, now aware of the others' proximity, hastily prepared for battle.

Battle Formations The terrain near the village of Lützen was fairly level, with the most prominent feature being the ditched road running northeasterly to Leipzig. Wallenstein positioned his main line north of the road and placed musketeers at the road's edge. He tied his left flank into a shallow river, while his right rested on the edge of the village. In conventional fashion, four large *tercios* occupied the Imperial center, with artillery directly to their front on a slight rise. Cavalry guarded both flanks.

Gustavus deployed his army in two lines, thereby ensuring that his eight infantry brigades in the center were directly supported. The Swedish army continued to reflect the many reforms Gustavus had accomplished since the 1620s. Contingents of infantry were posted with the cavalry on each flank, and the Swedish artillery was lighter and hence more maneuverable than that of the Imperialist host. The Swedes' plan was to strike Wallenstein's left and then roll up the cumbersome *tercios* which would be unable to turn and meet the onrushing Swedish troops. Gustavus's force numbered about nineteen thousand, while Wallenstein totaled slightly less.

The Battle is Joined Led by Gustavus, the Swedish right successfully broke Wallenstein's army and began turning on the stiffening Imperial defenses. On his other flank and in the center, the Swedish army was making only slow progress. As Gustavus rode across the line to inspire his left, Pappenheim returned to the battlefield. Wallenstein immediately ordered him to attach the Swedish right, and when he did, the Swedes were completely surprised.

Confusion reigned as the battle became a swirling mass of horses and men, with smoke and fog obscuring the action. At that moment, Pappenheim was struck and killed by a cannonball, prompting the Imperial horse to panic. Wallenstein, who could not see this development, thought he had turned the tide and hence ordered a counterattack all along the line of the road. Gustavus, rallying his men, was then cut down, initially giving pause to the Swedish army. Then, in a fit of rage, the Swedes assaulted to avenge their leader, driving Wallenstein's men from the field.

Wallenstein withdrew to Leipzig, but the Swedish army was too devastated to offer effective pursuit. Each side lost between three thousand and five thousand dead and wounded, with several thousand more missing. More importantly, the Swedish army never fully recovered from the loss of so many veteran leaders, especially their king, Gustavus. This campaign would lead to French involvement and the expansion of the war.

Rocroi, May 19, 1643

The Battle of Rocroi opened the final chapter of the Thirty Years War. Most significantly, it marked the end of Spanish military domination in Western Europe. Subsequently, French arms and French military leaders would come to dominate European battlefields for the next century.

Combat Fatigue By the early 1640s, Europe had been at war for more than two decades and all parties were suffering from economic and social exhaustion. However, none of the major belligerents was yet willing to yield territory or make concessions without compensation for their protracted exertions.

France had stood on the sidelines as long as possible, but with the demise of Gustavus Adolphus and the subsequent defeat of the Swedish army at Nördlingen in 1634, French interests were now threatened. As Imperial armies gained the upper hand in Germany, and with Spanish forces occupying the western bank of the Rhine, Cardinal Richelieu (the French Prime Minister) considered the strategic situation too perilous to ignore. Hence, he led France into active conflict by opening another front against Spain in the Low Countries.

Leading French arms in the field was Condé, Louis II de Bourbon Duc d'Enghien, only twenty-two years old at the time of Rocroi. A noble by birth, Enghien received a Jesuit education before going to Paris in 1637 to study military affairs. Richelieu identified him as a young man of great promise; Enghien participated in the siege of the port of Fuentarrabia, and he volunteered to take part in the siege of Arras in 1640. Shortly before his death, Richelieu designated Enghien as commander of the northeastern armies.

The Spanish Enter France When a Spanish Imperial army more than 25,000 strong under Francisco de Melo advanced from the Netherlands through the Ardennes

Caricature of French and German soliders interacting. © *Interfoto Pressebildagentur/Alamy*

toward Paris, Enghien moved to confront the invader. He initially established a defensive position along the Meuse River, but fearful that the Spanish would be reinforced, he soon abandoned this line. After Melo halted to lay siege to the town of Rocroi, Enghien felt that he must attack at once with his 23,000 men.

Against the advice of his more experienced advisors, Enghien led his army on a difficult approach through heavily wooded defiles that Melo had failed to obstruct. Arriving near Rocroi late in the afternoon of May 18, the French army took up positions along a ridge south and east of the city. The Spanish responded by immediately moving from their works to confront Enghien's men. Both sides then spent the night in their positions.

Formations at Rocroi Melo deployed his infantry with the traditional *tercios* in the center of his line. Spanish troops comprised the first line nearest the French, and they were supported by less dependable Italian and German soldiers in a second line. Some three thousand cavalrymen protected the Spanish right, while another five thousand took their place on the left.

Enghien's army aligned itself in virtually the same formation: infantry in the center, guns forward, cavalry on each flank, and a cavalry reserve in the rear. However, the French army was organized into linear brigades that offered their commander a great deal of flexibility and increased the force's frontal firepower.

Rocroi Begins with Cavalry Shortly after sunrise, Enghien personally opened the battle by leading a successful cavalry charge that ruptured the Spanish left. Splitting his successful squadrons, he ordered some to pursue the fleeing enemy horsemen, while he turned into the waiting Spanish infantry with the remainder. Eager to enter the fight, Enghien's cavalry on his opposite flank also attacked, but these were thrown back and sent reeling in disarray. Only the French cavalry reserve was able to stop the surging Spanish horse.

Even with this setback, Enghien was an audacious commander, and he was determined to carry the day. When Enghien learned of the peril on his left, he led the cavalry still with him directly through the center rear of the Spanish tercios, cutting and slashing his way to assault the remaining Spanish cavalrymen. He finally scattered them and left the heavy Spanish infantry isolated on the field.

After two assaults by his brigades on the Spanish squares failed, Enghien concentrated all his artillery against the Spanish foot and opened a tremendous barrage. Isolated and losing hope that their cavalry would return, the Spanish infantry asked for quarter, a gesture Enghien accepted. However, as he advanced to receive the Spanish surrender, some of the infantry mistook his approach as the signal for yet another French attack and opened fire at his party. Infuriated by this apparent treachery, the French infantry assaulted the withered Spanish formations mercilessly, destroying them where they stood. More than eight thousand of Melo's men were killed and another seven thousand captured; Enghien's casualties numbered about four thousand.

Although the Thirty Years War would continue for another five years, Rocroi finally ended the Spanish tercio's domination of infantry combat in Europe. While Gustavus's Swedish brigades had demonstrated that they could defeat the tercios, it was not until Rocroi that the Spanish formation was finally shown to be outdated.

For France, the young Enghien would eventually earn the title of the "Great Condé" and enter the first rank of French military leaders.

Second Breitenfeld, November 2, 1643

The Second Battle of Breitenfeld was a Swedish victory in the later years of the Thirty Years War that marked a low point for Imperial prospects. Although the battle did not signal the end of the conflict, the fate of the Emperor was severely threatened by the loss; his forces were saved from further defeat only by the reprieve gained at the onset of war between Denmark and Sweden.

The War Drags On In the years following the death of the great Swedish field marshal Gustavus Adolphus, the generals he trained—including Johan Banér, Lennart Torstensson, and Karl Gustav Wrangel—continued to lead armies reflecting the Great Captain's reforms. Swedish forces, although their ranks were increasingly thinned by mercenary troops from other nations, deployed to battle in linear brigades that maximized infantry firepower. Swedish cavalry was aggressive and hard-hitting, charging with pistols and sabers to deliver shock to enemy formations. Importantly, mobile artillery was integrated with the other two arms to ensure that Swedish commanders could employ massed gunfire at the decisive time and place on the battlefield.

Nonetheless, Swedish arms had not brought the war to a conclusion, and though victories were won in many engagements, overall campaigns were not decisive. Over time, this endless cycle of war and encampment began to take a toll on all sides, including the Swedes. When Johan Banér died in May 1641, his army mutinied. Axel Oxenstierna, Chancellor of Sweden, appointed the aggressive Torstensson to restore order and achieve the victory Sweden needed.

In November 1641, Torstensson assumed command and added several thousand new recruits to his army's ranks. He quickly set about preparing for a fresh campaign. The year prior, a combined offensive by the armies of Sweden, France, and Brunswick had driven as far as the Danube at Regensburg but could advance no farther before being compelled to retire to winter quarters.

Torstensson opened his new campaign by marching into Silesia and defeating the Elector of Saxony's forces at Schweidnitz. Next he invaded Moravia and occupied its capital, Olmütz, in June 1642. Recognizing the threat posed by this Swedish host, an Imperial army led by Austrian General Octavio Piccolomini and Archduke Leopold-William moved to confront the Swedes. In the face of the Imperial advance, Torstensson retired to Saxony and laid siege to Leipzig.

Breitenfeld, Part II Outnumbered, Torstensson fell back near Breitenfeld and took up position for battle. His plan for his initial deployment was typical: long brigades of infantry in echelon occupying the center of his line, with cavalry squadrons on both flanks and a small reserve at the middle rear. While both sides were still moving into position, the Imperial artillery opened fire. Rather than assemble under the cannonade, Torstensson launched a hasty attack on his Imperial enemy's left flank, surprising his opponents and sending the Imperialist horse into headlong flight.

Alerted to the threat posed by the impetuous Swede commander, the Imperialist commanders were faring much better in the middle and on their own right flank. Although the Imperialist army had not adopted the kinds of reforms instituted by the Swedes, their leaders, as well as many of their foot soldiers, were veterans and not easily rattled.

Seeing that his center and left were now in peril, Torstensson led another charge, wheeling into the flank of the Imperialist infantry to provide enough space for his own struggling footmen to regain their formations and counterattack. Finally pressed hard by the Swedes, the Imperialist troops remaining on the field broke and ran or surrendered.

The Imperialists counted about five thousand killed and five thousand captured, while the Swedish losses amounted to approximately two thousand killed and two thousand seriously wounded. Torstensson completed his victory by capturing Leipzig the following month. He and his forces were diverted to attack Denmark thereafter, and the Thirty Years War continued.

Zusmarshausen, May 17, 1648

Fought near Augsburg, the Battle of Zusmarshausen was the final battle of the Thirty Years War. The defeat of the Imperial forces by a Swedish-led army and the siege of Prague finally compelled Emperor Ferdinand to enter into conclusive negotiations. This led to the Congress of Westphalia, which brought the war to an end.

The Long Stalemate The performance of each sides' armies leading up to Zusmarshausen gave little indication that the end of fighting was near, as neither side could gain a decisive advantage. Even the one significant diplomatic development, which held promise for a change of course in the war, ultimately proved barren. By the Treaty of Ulm (signed in March 1647), Maximilian of Bavaria turned away from his alliance with Ferdinand III and withdrew from the war. Although the peace would only last several months, during the interlude French and Swedish armies possessed an opportunity to press the Empire.

However, during the summer the Dutch war effort against Spain slackened, allowing the Spanish to move a larger number of forces southward to the borderlands of France. This repositioning successfully diverted French attention, as Mazarin ordered Turenne to move his forces into Luxembourg and northern France to repel the Spanish incursions. Compounding French problems, the Weimarian troops refused to advance beyond Germany, compelling Turenne to put down their revolt before moving on.

In the end, the Spanish offensives against France from the Low Countries turned into nothing more than another round of sieges and ineffectual maneuvering. The French proved they could do little better; they were repulsed in several places and had to withdraw upon the approach of Imperial forces.

Different Country, Same Outcome In the German lands, Swedish general Karl Gustav Wrangel attacked through Bohemia but was stopped in his tracks by the Imperial commander Peter Melander. As so often occurred at this late stage of the war, the need to find fresh sources of supply from the war-ravaged countryside

The Peace of Westphalia occurred with the signing of the Treaty of Münster and the Treaty of Osnabrück in 1648. © *Interfoto Pressebildagentur/Alamy*

effectively restricted the ability of commanders to maneuver their forces. Faced with limited logistical means that were always inadequate in any case, the Swedes gradually marched northward. The Imperialists, not seeking battle, were glad to see them go; instead of pursuing, they marched into Hesse to settle other disputes with the local nobility.

In the fall, the Treaty of Pilsen brought Bavaria back into the war on the side of Emperor Ferdinand III. The Bavarian army consequently marched into the Upper Palatinate to join Imperial troops in Bohemia. Wrangel retired through Saxony and Hesse as Turenne returned to Germany to again combine with the Swedes, although little more was achieved before the onset of another winter.

A New Year Brings a Change   Departing quarters in the spring of 1648, the French and Swedish forces of Turenne and Wrangel opened the new campaign by pushing back the Imperialists and Bavarians to the line of the Danube. After maneuvering independently for a period near Nördlingen, the French and Swedes pressed

forward, trapping the Imperialists at Zusmarshausen. The Imperial rearguard was routed, its commander Peter Melander becoming a casualty. While this sharp fight was not large, it was a defeat the Imperialists could ill afford.

The Imperial and Bavarian remnants fell back to the River Inn before general Octavio Piccolomini—called by the Emperor to restore order—was able to check Turenne and Wrangel's advance. Piccolomini hurriedly reorganized what remained of the Austro-Bavarian army, and checked his enemies from making any further progress.

While events in Bavaria were turning against the Empire, another Swedish army had entered Bohemia and was besieging Prague. This new threat prompted Ferdinand to demand the assistance of Piccolomini's army, thereby freeing Turenne and Wrangel to pressure Munich. Neither side could make much progress, however, and the campaign devolved into foraging and plundering.

Negotiation for a peace settlement had reached a critical stage, with all sides believing an end was near.

The Imperial defeat at Zusmarshausen and the persistence of Swedish and French armies in the heart of Germany was the final straw. Before Prague could be assaulted or any further offensives organized in Germany, word arrived to the armies that a peace accord had been reached. Finally, three decades of warfare came to a conclusion.

⊕ Key Elements of Warcraft

Standing Armies

The Thirty Years War (1618–1648) occurred during a centuries-long period of military transformation that witnessed a nearly ten-fold increase in the size of armies. Starting in the early sixteenth century, the manner in which officials raised, equipped, and deployed armies underwent significant change. Military and political leaders wrestled with emerging ideas of military organization, technology, and strategy as they waged war throughout Europe. During the three decades of the Thirty Years War, the identity and operation of government became increasingly tied to the ability to manage violence through permanently organized and increasingly large armed forces, resulting in changes to the administration of states as well as to broader military culture.

A European Arms Race In the late fifteenth century, the Spanish monarchy employed only about twenty thousand men in the army and navy; by the 1630s, Spain was funding 300,000. France supported perhaps forty thousand soldiers in 1500 but counted 400,000 two centuries later. Other nations followed a similar path. By the early eighteenth century, the Dutch and Swedes each boasted about 100,000 men in their armed forces, and England had nearly that many.

While most generals found it difficult to muster more than twenty thousand or thirty thousand fighting men for any single battle, the overall number of men in the field of all arms (infantry, cavalry, and artillery) was much greater. Even though the need to gather food for horses and men alike did limit the size of the force on campaign at any one time, military leaders learned to conduct rapid marches and soldiers were always adept at compelling residents to divulge their local stores.

As armies grew, so did the costs to sustain them. While states differed administratively, every monarchy found it necessary to dispatch commissioners to extract payments and subsidies to supplement income derived from hereditary lands and properties. Loans, either voluntary or under various degrees of duress, were also sought. The Imperial Armies alone may have cost as much as 250 million gulden during the war, the vast majority of this expense being borne by the Emperor.

Consequences of the Military Expansions The integration of military power with the development of states

GUNS FOR HIRE

In the German lands alone, there were several hundred entrepreneurs recruiting soldiers and organizing military units for profit. The minor gentry often raised small units, perhaps individual companies of infantry or cavalry squadrons. (Artillery was difficult for private, non-state promoters due to the cost and technical requirements.) The wealthier the noble, the greater profit could be made from providing larger units. The Imperial general Wallenstein, in the service of the Emperor, raised entire armies.

now appears to historians to have been so substantial in its effects that the concept of a military revolution has been thoroughly incorporated into the canon of early modern European history. The historiographical debate has turned to the precise nature and timing of military change in early modern Europe.

The military revolution that occurred in sixteenth- and seventeenth-century Europe sprang from the tactical reforms undertaken by Maurice of Nassau and Gustavus Adolphus—most notably a return to linear formations for short-armed infantry and limited, if aggressive, charges by cavalry. As the relative importance of cavalry declined, the significance of massed infantry, with their projectile-firing muskets, increased dramatically. Larger, infantry-centric armies thus became typical.

Weapons Bring Changes As Well Nonetheless, the initial surge in military manpower across Europe began before Maurice's reforms. Changes in siege warfare also prompted calls for larger armies. Castle and town walls designed to resist bombardment by medieval siege engines quickly succumbed to gunfire, so the masonry walls that had been the standard form of fortification throughout the Middle Ages no longer offered protection.

Improvements in gun-founding and the manufacture of gunpowder increased the effectiveness of cannons as instruments of destruction. The result was the erection of new fortifications consisting of earthworks faced with brick or stone. These were designed to achieve a low profile to offer the smallest possible target to an attacker's guns. The superb ability of this type of fortress, known as the *trace italienne,* to resist both bombardment and infantry assault tipped the strategic balance in favor of the defensive. Siege warfare, with its attendant entrenchments, artillery, and mining equipment, required manpower on an unprecedented scale. Hence, successful states were those that organized themselves by amassing military power.

Even as the Thirty Years War ravaged many areas within central Europe, the continent as a whole experienced economic and population expansion over the sixteenth and seventeenth centuries. The growing population and wealth of Europe are also key factors contributing to governments' willingness and ability to deploy larger standing armies.

What is clear is that the sustainment of armies was inextricably tied with the growing complexity of government. The centrally organized, bureaucratically governed nation-state—the paramount symbol of the modern era—that emerged from the simple beginning of late sixteenth-century tactical reforms matured on the battlefields of the Thirty Years War to play a key, even a pre-eminent, role in shaping the modern world.

⊕ Impact on World History

The Thirty Years War was a multifaceted, dynamically shifting, European-wide conflict. The war began largely due to a religious dispute between German Roman Catholics and Protestants, but the contest quickly became ensnared in the dynastic competition for power within the Holy Roman Empire. The war also developed into a political conflict that pitted the ambitions of the Catholic Austrian rulers, and later Spanish Habsburg rulers, against the Protestant leaders of Denmark and Sweden, and then even against Catholic France. Throughout the conflict, the German states aligned themselves according to the fortunes of war and the calculations of their princes.

Over the many years of fighting, the war developed a momentum of its own that became difficult to arrest. Ultimately the Thirty Years War was not decided by a single battle or even campaign. Even though exhaustion began to set in on all sides, no one power could bring the hostilities to an end. Governments had expended so much treasure and blood that leaders were reluctant to settle unless they could present specific advantages to their populaces and recoup their own investments in the war effort.

For generations, the horrors of the war's depredations haunted Europeans' collective memory. While not all of Europe suffered, and not all of Germany was plundered, the Holy Roman Empire was subject to almost continuous warfare between 1618 and 1648, causing terrible losses in life and property. A precise accounting is difficult, but German population increased over the last half of the sixteenth century but declined between 1600 (15 million) and 1650 (11 million). Tax records indicate that the number of "deserted places" grew significantly as villagers fled the approach of invading armies or simply could no longer earn an income from their devastated properties. Swedish forces alone destroyed about two thousand castles, over fifteen thousand villages, and more than a thousand towns. The most notable atrocity of the war occurred in the city of Magdeburg, which was sacked by the Imperial General Tilly in 1631. It was reduced from a population of more than twenty thousand people to only 394 households in

1635. Across the war zones, plague, famine, and failed harvest followed the armies.

Although the social order composed of corporations, orders, and kinship and patronage ties proved resilient—long-lasting populist or peasant revolutions did not occur—European society was transformed. The war banished the idea and ambition for a unified Christendom modeled after the glory of the long-vanished Roman Empire. The power of the papacy was permanently reduced; thereafter, governments depended overwhelmingly upon their secular leaders for decisions and authority in all its forms. Fiscal, diplomatic, judicial, and military power became increasingly the province of a single, centralized, and secular authority.

In addition, just as the armies of the Thirty Years War ignored their confessional loyalties to wage war alongside their ideological opponents, after 1648 confessional political alliances began fading. Mercantilist economic theory demanded that ideological uniformity be superseded by economic interests; lands and territories were viewed as sources of income for the central government, and this aspect was considered more important than religious identification.

The war also accelerated the complex transformation of government and a comprehensive change to the nature of warfare that was already underway in early modern Europe. In this "military revolution" which started in the late sixteenth century and into the first years of the war, military and political leaders wrestled with emerging ideas of military organization, technology, and strategy. Their solutions, which involved the adoption of massed, linear infantry formations and aggressive charges by cavalry supported by mobile artillery, characterized warfare for the next two centuries and required fundamental changes to how states organized, trained, and maintained armies. Likewise, soldiers adapted to new ideas of sustained, rigorous, and technical training that fundamentally changed how they prepared for battle.

Concurrent with the desire to avoid large-scale bloodshed and changes to military doctrine, new kinds of fortifications emerged that rendered Medieval-style castles and siege works obsolete. Earthworks were now faced with brick or stone and designed to achieve a low profile to offer the greatest possible resistance to an attacker's guns. States began to build complex series of fortresses to guard decisive points and to line frontiers. By the early eighteenth century, war became primarily an affair of sieges and the reduction of fixed fortifications. Siege warfare, with its attendant entrenchments, artillery, and mining equipment, required huge sums of money and manpower on an unprecedented scale, placing still further demands on governments that both reinforced central authority and stretched the capacity of state leaders to respond effectively.

The Peace of Westphalia was an incomplete settlement and did not achieve the general peace its promoters foretold. Within the German lands, social and political tensions, even if they were dampened by exhaustion, remained largely unaddressed. War continued between France and Spain until the Peace of the Pyrenees in 1659. Even then, French ascendance, sometimes attributed as a product of Westphalia, was not assured. It would take English assistance in the years soon after 1648 and then decades of campaigning by Louis XIV's generals before France finally emerged as triumphant over at least the Spanish Habsburgs.

Yet despite its short-term ambiguities, the Thirty Years War continues to matter to modern history. The settlements of 1648, while incomplete in many respects, marked a signpost to the future of Europe and ultimately the international state system still functioning today. New ways of war, the alignment of states according to balance of power and economic interests, and the growth of European political identities founded upon modern notions of statehood are each contained within the tumultuous years from 1618 to 1648.

BIBLIOGRAPHY

Book

Robinson, J.H., ed. *Readings in European History.* Boston: Ginn, 1906.

Further Reading

BOOKS

Abun-Nasr, Jamil Mir'i. *A History of the Maghrib in the Islamic Period*. Cambridge: Cambridge University Press, 1987.

Ahmed, Nazeer. *Islam in Global History*. Concord, Mass.: American Institute of Islamic History and Culture, 2000.

Allsen, Thomas T. *Culture and Conquest in Mongol Eurasia*. Cambridge and New York: Cambridge University Press, 2001.

———. *Mongol Imperialism*. Los Angeles: University of California Press, 1987.

Alston, Richard. *Aspects of Roman History, AD 14–117*. London: Routledge, 1998.

Alvarez, J. E. *The Betrothed of Death: The Spanish Foreign Legion during the Rif Rebellion, 1920–1927*. Westport, Conn.: Greenwood Press, 2001.

Ambrose, Stephen E. *Nothing Like It In The World: The Men Who Built the Transcontinental Railroad, 1863–1869*. New York: Simon & Schuster, 2000.

Amitai-Preiss, Reuven. *Mongols and Mamluks*. Cambridge and New York: Cambridge University Press, 1996.

Anderson, Fred. *Crucible of War*. New York: Alfred A. Knopf, 2000.

———. *The War That Made America*. New York: Viking, 2005.

Andrea, Alfred, editor and translator. *Contemporary Sources for the Fourth Crusade*. Leiden, The Netherlands: Brill, 2000.

Andrews, K. R. *Elizabethan Privateering*. Cambridge: Cambridge University Press, 1964.

Aperture Foundation. *City of Victory: Vijayanagara, The Medieval Hindu Capital of Southern India*. New York: Aperture. 1991.

Armstrong, Karen. *Muhammad: A Biography of the Prophet*. New York: HarperCollins, 1992.

Arnold, Guy. *Historical Dictionary of the Crimean War*. Lanham, Md.: Scarecrow Press, 2002.

Arnold, James. *Crisis on the Danube: Napoleon's Austrian Campaign of 1809*. St. Paul, Minn.: Paragon House, 1990.

Arnold, Martin. *Vikings: Wolves of War*. Lanham, Md.: Rowman & Littlefield Publishers, 2007.

Arrian. *The Campaigns of Alexander*, translated by Aubrey de Szlincourt. New York: Dorset Press, 1958.

Arthur, Charles B. *Remaking of the English Navy by Admiral St. Vincent—Key to the Victory over Napoleon: The Great Unclaimed Naval Revolution. 1795–1805*. Lanham, Md.: University Press of America, 1986.

Asprey, Robert. *The Reign of Napoleon Bonaparte*. New York: Basic Books, 2002.

———. *The Rise of Napoleon Bonaparte*. New York: Perseus Press, 2001.

Babinger, Franz. *Mehmed the Conqueror and His Time*. Princeton: Princeton University Press, 1978.

Babur, Emperor of Hindustan. *The Baburnama: Memoirs of Babur, Prince and Emperor*, translated, edited, and annotated by Wheeler M. Thackston. Washington D.C., New York, and Oxford: Freer Gallery of Art and Oxford University Press, 1996.

Bainton, Roland. *Here I Stand: A Life of Martin Luther*. Nashville, Tenn.: Abingdon Press, 1991.

Barber, Malcolm. *The New Knighthood: A History of the Order of the Temple*. Cambridge: Cambridge University Press, 1994.

Basler, Roy P., ed. *Collected Works. The Abraham Lincoln Association, Springfield, Illinois*. New Brunswick, N.J.: Rutgers University Press, 1953–1955.

Beasley, W. G. *The Modern History of Japan.* New York: Praeger, 1975.

Belloc, Hilaire. *Six British Battles.* Bristol, U.K.: Arrowsmith, 1931.

Bennett, Deb. *Conquerors: The Roots of New World Horsemanship.* Solvang, Calif.: Amigo, 1998.

Bennett, Matthew. *Agincourt 1415: Triumph Against the Odds.* Oxford: Osprey Publishing, 1991.

Bernier, Olivier. *Louis XIV.* New York: Doubleday, 1987.

Berry, Mary Elizabeth. *Hideyoshi.* Cambridge, Mass.: Harvard University Press, 1982.

Bertaud, Jean-Paul. *The Army of the French Revolution: From Citizen-Soldiers to Instrument of Power.* Princeton: Princeton University Press, 1988.

Bierman, Irene, ed. *Napoleon in Egypt.* Dryden, N.Y.: Ithaca Press, 2003.

Biran, Michal. *Qaidu and the Rise of the Independent Mongol State in Central Asia.* Richmond, U.K.: Curzon Press, 1997.

Birney, Hoffman. *Brothers of Doom: The Story of the Pizarros of Peru.* New York: G. P. Putnam's Sons, 1942.

Black, Jeremy. *European Warfare, 1660–1815.* New Haven, Conn.: Yale University, 1994.

Boardman, John. *Greek Art.* New York: Oxford University Press, 1973.

Boettcher, Thomas D. *Vietnam: The Valor and the Sorrow.* Boston: Little, Brown and Company, 1985.

Bonney, Richard. *The Thirty Years War, 1618–1648.* Oxford: Osprey Publishing, 2002.

Bosworth, A. B. *Conquest and Empire: The Reign of Alexander the Great.* Cambridge; New York: Cambridge University Press, 1988.

Bosworth, A. B., and E. J. Baynham, ed. *Alexander the Great in Fact and Fiction.* Cambridge; New York: Oxford University Press, 2002.

Botsford and Robinson's Hellenic History, revised by Donald Kagan. Fifth Edition. New York; London: MacMillan, 1969.

Bowden, Scott. *Armies on the Danube, 1809.* Chicago: Emperor's Press, 1989.

Braudel, Fernand. *The Mediterranean and the Mediterranean World in the Age of Philip II.* Los Angeles: University of California Press, 1966.

Brown, Dee. *Hear That Lonesome Whistle Blow: Railroads in the West.* New York: Holt, Rinehart and Winston, 1977.

Brown, M. L. *Firearms in Colonial America: The Impact on History and Technology, 1492–1792.* Washington, D.C.: Smithsonian Institution., 1981.

Brown, Peter. *The Rise of Western Christendom.* Malden, Mass.: Blackwell, 1997.

Browning, Reed. *The War of the Austrian Succession.* New York: St. Martin's, 1993.

Buell, Hal, ed. *World War II: A Complete Photographic History.* New York: Black Dog & Leventhal, 2002.

Buell, Paul. *Historical Dictionary of the Mongol World Empire.* Lanham, Md.: Scarecrow Press, 2003.

Buranelli, Vincent. *Louis XIV.* New York: Twayne, 1966.

Burns, Thomas S. *Barbarians Within the Gates of Rome.* Bloomington: Indiana University Press, 1994.

Bury, J. B. *History of the Later Roman Empire.* New York: Dover, 1931, rev. 1958.

Cadbury, Deborah. *Dreams of Iron and Steel.* New York: HarperCollins, 2003.

Cambridge Medieval History. Cambridge: The University Press, 1959.

Camon, G. *Le Maréchal de Luxembourg (1628–1695).* Paris: Éditions Berger-Levrault, 1936.

Canney, Donald L. *Lincoln's Navy: The Ships, Men and Organization, 1861–1865.* Annapolis, Md.: Naval Institute Press, 1998.

Canny, Nicholas, ed. *The Oxford History of the British Empire: The Origins of Empire.* Oxford: Oxford University Press, 1998.

Carlyle, Thomas. *History of Friedrich II of Prussia, Called Frederick the Great.* London: Chapman and Hall, 1864.

Carruthers, Bob. *The English Civil Wars.* London: Cassell, 2000.

Cartledge, Paul. *Alexander the Great.* Woodstock: Overlook Press, 2004.

Cary, George. *The Medieval Alexander.* Cambridge: Cambridge University Press, 1956.

Chandler, David. *The Art of Warfare in the Age of Marlborough.* New York: Hippocrene, 1976.

———. *The Campaigns of Napoleon.* London: Scribner, 1973.

———. *Marlborough as Military Commander.* New York: Charles Scribner's Sons, 1973.

Chase, Kenneth. *Firearms: A Global History to 1700.* Cambridge: Cambridge University Press, 2003.

Cima, Ronald J., ed. *Vietnam: A Country Study.* Washington, D.C.: GPO (Government Printing Office) for the Library of Congress, 1987.

Cleaves, F.W., translator and editor. *The Secret History of the Mongols.* Cambridge, Mass.: Harvard University Press, 1982.

Cleveland, William L. *A History of the Modern Middle East.* Boulder, Colo.: Westview Press, 1994.

Collins, Donald E. *The Death and Resurrection of Jefferson Davis.* Lanham, Md.: Rowman & Littlefield, 2005.

Collins, Roger. *Early Medieval Europe, 300–1000.* New York: St. Martin's Press, 1991.

Congressional Quarterly. *The Middle East,* tenth edition. Washington, D.C.: CQ Press, 2005.

Connolly, Peter. *The Legionary (The Roman World Series).* Oxford: Oxford University Press, 1989.

Coote, Stephen. *Royal Survivor.* New York: St. Martin's Press, 2000.

Cope, Kevin L. *John Locke Revisited.* New York: Twayne, 1999.

Corbett, Julian. *Principles of Maritime Strategy* Mineola, N.Y.: Dover Publications, 2004.

Cormack, William. *Revolution and Political Conflict in the French Navy, 1789–1794.* Cambridge: Cambridge University Press, 1995.

Corvisier, André, and John Childs. *A Dictionary of Military History and the Art of War.* Oxford: Blackwell Publishers, 1994.

Cowley, Robert, ed. *The Great War: Perspectives on the First World War.* New York: Random House, 2003.

Davis, Burke. *Sherman's March.* New York: Random House, 1980.

Davis, J. C. *Oliver Cromwell.* London: Arnold, 2001.

Davis, William. *Duel Between the First Ironclads.* Garden City, N.Y.: Doubleday, 1975.

Dent, Anthony. *The Horse Through Fifty Centuries of Civilization.* New York: Holt, Rinehart and Winston, 1974.

Dewy, John. *Thomas Hobbes in His Time,* edited by Ralph Ross, Herbert W. Schneider, Theodore Waldman. Minneapolis: University of Minnesota Press, 1974.

Diamond, Jared. *Guns, Germs, and Steel: The Fates of Human Society.* New York: W.W. Norton, 1998.

Díaz, Bernal. *The Conquest of New Spain,* translated by J. M. Cohen. London: Penguin, 1963.

Dictionary of the Middle Ages, 13 vols. American Council of Learned Societies. New York: Charles Scribner's Sons, 1989.

Diefendorf, Barbara. *Beneath the Cross: Catholics and Huguenots in Sixteenth-Century Paris.* Oxford: Oxford University Press, 1991.

Dillon, Matthew, and Lynda Garland. *Ancient Rome: From the Early Republic to the Assassination of Julius Caesar.* New York: Routledge, 2005.

Donner, Fred. *The Early Islamic Conquests.* Oxford: Rowman and Littlefield, 2006.

Dorland, Gil. *Legacy of Discord: Voices of the Vietnam War Era.* Washington, D.C.: Brassey's, 2001.

Dowdey, Clifford. *The Seven Days: The Emergence of Lee.* Boston: Little, Brown and Company, 1964.

Doyle, William. *The Oxford History of the French Revolution,* second edition. Oxford: Oxford University Press, 2003.

Drews, Robert. *The End of the Bronze Age.* Princeton: Princeton University Press, 1993.

Duffy, Christopher. *The Army of Frederick the Great.* New York: Hippocrene Books, 1974.

———. *Borodino.* London: Cassell, 1999.

———. *The Fortress in the Age of Vauban and Frederick the Great, 1660–1789.* London: Routledge and Kegan Paul, 1985.

———. *Siege Warfare: The Fortress in the Early Modern World, 1494–1660.* London: Routledge and Kegan Paul, 1979.

Duncan, Marcel, ed. *Larouse Encyclopedia of Ancient and Medieval History.* New York: Harper and Row, 1963.

Dupuy, Ernest. *World War II: A Compact History.* New York: Hawthorn Books, 1969.

Duus, Peter. *Feudalism in Japan.* New York: McGraw-Hill, 1993.

Dyer, Frederick H. *A Compendium of the War of the Rebellion, Compiled and Arranged from Official Records of the Federal and Confederate Armies, Reports of the Adjutant Generals of the Several States, the Army Registers and Other Reliable Documents and Sources.* Des Moines, Iowa: Dyer Publishing, 1908.

Early, Jubal A. *Memoir of the Last Year of the War For Independence in the Confederate States of America, Containing an Account of the Operations of His Commands in the Years 1864 and 1865.* New Orleans: Blelock, 1867.

Edwardes, Michael. *Plassey: The Founding of an Empire.* New York: Taplinger Publishing, 1969.

Edwardes, S. M., and H.L.O. Garrett. *Mughal Rule in India.* Delhi: S. Chand, 1956.

Edwards, Graham. *The Last Days of Charles I.* Stroud, Gloucestershire: Phoenix Mill, 1999.

Ehrman, John. *The Navy in the Wars of William III, 1689–1697.* Cambridge: Cambridge University Press, 1953.

Engl, Lieselotte, and Theo Engl. *Twilight of Ancient Peru: The Glory and Decline of the Inca Empire,* translated by Alisa Jaffe. New York: McGraw Hill, 1969.

Englund, Steven. *Napoleon: A Political Life.* London: Scribner, 2004.

Erickson, Carolly. *Bonnie Prince Charlie*. New York: William Morrow, 1989.

Evans, Martin. *Passchendale and the Battles of Ypres 1914–18*. London: Osprey Publishing, 1997.

Fage, John, and Anthony Roland. *The Cambridge History of Africa*. Cambridge: Cambridge University Press, 1986.

Fair, Charles. *From the Jaws of Victory*. New York: Simon & Schuster, 1971.

Faroqhi, Suraiya. *The Ottoman Empire and the World Around It*. London: I.B. Tauris, 2004.

Finkel, Caroline. *Osman's Dream: The History of the Ottoman Empire*. New York: Basic Books, 2005.

Finley, M. I., ed. *The Portable Greek Historians*. Middlesex; New York: Penguin, 1959.

Fleming, Thomas. *Liberty! The American Revolution*. New York: Viking, 1997.

Flood, Charles Bracelen. *Grant and Sherman: The Friendship That Won the Civil War*. New York: Farrar, Straus and Giroux, 2005.

Foote, Shelby. *The Civil War, A Narrative*. New York: Random House, 1958.

Forczyk, Robert. *Toulon, 1793: Napoleon's First Great Victory*. Oxford: Osprey, 2005.

Forster, Margaret. *The Rash Adventurer*. New York: Stein and Day, 1973.

Francis, David. *The First Peninsular War, 1702–1713*. New York: St. Martin's, 1975.

Fremont-Barnes, Gregory. *The French Revolutionary Wars*. Oxford: Osprey, 2001.

Fuller, J. F. C. *The Generalship of Alexander the Great*. New Brunswick, N.J.: Rutgers University Press, 1960.

Gabai, Rafael Varón. *Francisco Pizarro and His Brothers: The Illusion of Power in Sixteenth-Century Peru*. Norman, Okla.: University of Oklahoma, 1997.

Gabrieli, Francesco. *Arab Historians of the Crusades*. New York: Routledge, 1969.

Gallager, Gary W., ed. *The Third Day at Gettysburg & Beyond*. Chapel Hill, NC: The University of North Carolina Press, 1994.

Garthwaite, Gene Ralph. *The Persians*. Malden, Mass.: Blackwell Publishing, 2005.

Gates, David. *The Spanish Ulcer: A History of the Peninsular War*. London: W.W. Norton, 1986. (repr. 2001).

Gaunt, Peter. *Oliver Cromwell*. New York: New York University Press, 2004.

Gengles, Ian. *The New Model Army in England, Ireland and Scotland, 1645–1653*. Oxford: Blackwell, 1992.

Gilbert, Martin. *The Second World War: A Complete History*. New York: Henry Holt and Company, 1989.

Glete, Jan. *Warfare at Sea, 1500–1650: Maritime Conflicts and the Transformation of Europe*. London: Routledge Press, 2000.

Glubb, John Bagot. *The Great Arab Conquests*. New York: Barnes and Noble, 1995.

Godley, Eveline. *The Great Condé*. London: J. Murray, 1915.

Gómara, Francisco Lopez de. *Cortés: The Life of the Conqueror by His Secretary*, translated and edited by Lesley Byrd Simpson. Berkeley: University of California Press, 1964.

Gooch, G. P. *Political Thought in England: From Bacon to Halifax*. London: Thorton Butterworth, 1914.

Gordon, Andrew. *The Modern History of Japan: From Tokugawa Times to the Present*. New York: Oxford, 2003.

Grant, Michael. *From Alexander to Cleopatra: The Hellenistic World*. New York: Charles Scribner's Sons, 1982.

Grant, Ulysses S. *Personal Memoirs of U.S. Grant*. New York: C. L. Webster, 1885–1886.

Gravett, Christopher. *Medieval Siege Warfare*. Oxford: Osprey Publishing, 1990.

Greengrass, Mark. *France in the Age of Henry IV: The Struggle for Stability*. London; New York: Longman, 1995.

Griess, Thomas, ed. *The Dawn of Modern Warfare*. West Point Military History Series. New York: Avery Publishing, 1984.

———. *The Wars of Napoleon*. New York: Avery Publishing, 1985.

Griffith, Paddy, ed. *A History of the Peninsular War: Modern Studies of the War in Spain and Portugal, 1808–1814*. London: Greenhill Books, 1999.

Griffith, Paddy. *The Art of War of Revolutionary France 1789–1802*. London: Greenhill, 1998.

Guthrie, William P. *The Later Thirty Years War*. Westport, Conn.: Greenwood Press, 2003.

Guy, John. *Tudor England*. Oxford: Oxford University Press, 1990.

Hall, E. *The Fall of the Stuarts and Western Europe from 1678 to 1697*. New York: Scribner, Armstrong, 1876.

Halperin, Charles. *Russia and the Golden Horde*. Bloomington, Ind.: Indiana University Press, 1987.

Hancock, Anson Uriel. *A History of Chile*. Chicago: C. H. Sergel, 1893.

Hanson, V. D. *Western Way of War: Infantry Battle in Classical Greece.* New York: Alfred A. Knopf Publishing, 1989.

Hanson, V. D., editor. *Hoplites: The Classical Battle Experience.* New York: Routledge, 1991.

Hattaway, Herman, and Archer Jones. *How the North Won.* Urbana, Ill.: University of Illinois Press, 1981.

Hattendorf, John B., and Richard W. Unger, eds. *War at Sea in the Middle Ages and Renaissance.* Suffolk, U.K.: Boydell Press, 2002.

Haythornthwait, Philip. *The English Civil War, 1642–1651.* Poole, Dorset: Blandford, 1983.

———. *Napoleon's Campaigns in Italy.* Oxford: Osprey, 1993.

Held, Robert. *The Age of Firearms.* New York: Harper and Brothers, 1957.

Hemming, John. *The Conquest of the Incas.* New York: Harcourt Brace Jovanovich, 1970.

Henry, Chris. *English Civil War Artillery, 1642–1651.* Oxford: Osprey, 2005.

Heras, Henry. *The Aravidu Dynasty of Vijayanagara.* Madras: B. G. Paul, 1927.

Hibbert, Christopher. *Wellington: A Personal History.* New York: Da Capo Press, 2001.

Hiro, Dilip. *Iraq: In the Eye of the Storm.* New York: Thunder's Mouth Press/Nation Books, 2002.

Hofschröer, Peter. *1815, The Waterloo Campaign: The German Victory.* London: Greenhill, 1999.

Hollins, David. *Marengo 1800: Napoleon's Day of Fate.* Oxford: Osprey, 2000.

Holmes, Richard, ed. *The Oxford Companion to Military History.* Oxford: Oxford University Press, 2001.

Holmes, Richard. *Wellington: The Iron Duke.* New York: HarperCollins, 2005.

Holt, Mack. *French Wars of Religion, 1562–1629.* Cambridge: Cambridge University Press, 2005.

Holt, Peter, and Ann Lambton. *The Cambridge History of Islam.* Cambridge: Cambridge University Press, 1970.

Hooper, Frederick. *The Military Horse.* Cranbury, N.J.: Marshall Cavendish, 1976.

Howard, Michael. *War in European History.* Oxford: Oxford University Press, 1976.

Hyams, Edward, and George Ordish. *The Last of the Incas.* New York: Simon and Schuster, 1963.

Hyland, Ann. *The Warhorse 1250–1600.* Thrupp, Gloucestershire: Sutton, 1998.

Ikram, S. M. *Muslim Civilization in India.* New York: Columbia University Press, 1964.

Imber, Colin. *The Crusade of Varna, 1443–1445.* Hampshire, U.K.: Ashgate Publishing, 2006.

Isserman, Maurice. *The Vietnam War: America At War.* New York: Facts on File, 1992.

Jackson, Gabriel. *The Spanish Republic and the Civil War, 1931–1939.* Princeton, N.J.: Princeton University Press, 1965.

Jackson, Peter. *The Mongols and the West.* London and New York: Pearson, 2005.

Jacobs, Charles, ed. *Three Treatises.* Nashville, Tenn.: Abingdon Press, 1970.

James, Simon. *The World of the Celts.* London: Thames and Hudson, 1993.

Johnson, Curt. *Battles of the American Revolution.* New York: Bonanza Books, 1984.

Johnson, Robert Underwood, and Clarence Clough Buel, eds. *Battles and Leaders of the Civil War, in Four Volumes.* New York: Thomas Yoseloff, 1956.

Johnson, Rossiter. *Campfires and Battlefields: The Pictorial History of the Civil War.* New York: The Civil War Press, 1967.

Jones, Archer. *The Art of War in the Western World.* Oxford: Oxford University Press, 1987.

Julius Caesar. *The Civil War,* translated by John Carter. New York: Oxford University Press, 1997.

Julius Caesar. *The Gallic War,* translated by Carolyn Hammond. Oxford: Oxford University Press, 1996.

Kamen, Henry. *The Duke of Alba.* New Haven, Conn.: Yale University Press, 2004.

———. *Empire: How Spain Became a World Power, 1492–1763.* New York: HarperCollins Publishers, 2003.

———. *Philip II of Spain.* New Haven, Conn.: Yale University Press, 1997.

———. *Philip V of Spain.* New Haven, Conn.: Yale University Press, 2001.

Kaplan, Robert D. *Imperial Grunts: The American Military on the Ground.* New York: Random House, 2005.

Karnow, Stanley. *Vietnam: A History.* New York: Viking Press, 1983.

Karsten, Peter, ed. *Encyclopedia of War and American Society,* vol. 1. Thousand Oaks, Calif.: Sage Reference, 2005.

Katz, Solomon H., ed. *Encyclopedia of Food and Culture.* New York: Charles Scribner's Sons, 2003.

Kaufmann, Joseph E. *The Medieval Fortress: Castles, Forts and Walled Cities of the Middle Ages.* Conshohocken, PA: Combined Publishing, 2001.

Keegan, John. *A History of Warfare.* New York: Alfred A. Knopf, 1993.

———. *An Illustrated History of the First World War.* New York: Alfred A. Knopf, 2001.

———. *The Price of Admiralty: The Evolution of Naval Warfare.* New York: Penguin Group, 1990.

———. *The Second World War.* New York: Penguin Books, 1989.

Keen, Maurice Hugh. *Medieval Warfare: A History.* Oxford: Oxford University Press, 1999.

Kennedy, Hugh. *When Baghdad Ruled the Muslim World: The Rise and Fall of Islam's Greatest Dynasty* New York: Da Capo Press, 2005.

Kenyon, John *The Civil Wars of England.* New York: Alfred A. Knopf, 1988.

Kimball, Warren. *The Juggler: Franklin Roosevelt as Wartime Statesman.* Princeton, N.J.: Princeton University Press, 1991.

Kirchberger, Joe H. *The First World War: An Eyewitness History.* New York: Facts on File, 1992.

Kirkby, Michael Hasloch. *The Vikings.* New York: Dutton, 1977.

Kirsch, Peter. *The Galleon: Great Ships of the Armada Era.* Annapolis, Md.: Naval Institute Press, 1990.

Kistler, John M. *War Elephants.* Westport, Conn.: Praeger, 2006.

Knecht, R. J. *The French Civil Wars, 1562–1598.* London: Longman, 2000.

———. *The Rise and Fall of Renaissance France.* Oxford: Oxford University Press, 2001.

Knight, Roger. *Pursuit of Victory: The Life and Achievement of Horatio Nelson.* New York: Perseus Publishing, 2005.

Koch, Peter O. *The Aztecs, the Conquistadors, and the Making of Mexican Culture.* Jefferson, N.C.: McFarland, 2006.

Konstam, Angus. *Lepanto 1571: The Greatest Naval Battle of the Renaissance.* Oxford: Osprey Publishers, 2003.

Kulikowski, Michael. *Rome's Gothic Wars.* New York: Cambridge University Press, 2006.

Kutler, Stanley I., ed. *Dictionary of American History,* vol. 5, third edition. New York: Charles Scribner's Sons, 2003.

Landers, John. *The Field and the Forge: Population, Production, and Power in the Pre-Industrial West.* Oxford: Oxford University Press, 2003.

Lane Fox, Robin. *Alexander the Great.* New York: Dial Press, 1973.

Lanning, Michael Lee. *The Civil War 100: The Stories Behind the Most Influential Battles, People and Events in the War Between the States.* Naperville, Ill.: Sourcebooks, 2006.

Lapidus, Ira. *A History of Islamic Societies.* Cambridge: Cambridge University Press, 2004.

Laughton, John Knox, ed. *From Howard to Nelson: Twelve Sailors.* London: Lawrence and Bullen, 1899.

Leonard, Elizabeth D. *Lincoln's Avengers: Justice, Revenge, and Reunion after the Civil War.* New York: W. W. Norton, 2004.

Leon-Portilla, Miguel. *The Broken Spears: The Aztec Account of the Conquest of Mexico.* Expanded and updated edition. Boston: Beacon, 1992.

Lewis, Bernard W. *The Muslim Discovery of Europe.* New York: W.W. Norton, 2001.

Lewis, James. *The Louisiana Purchase: Jefferson's Noble Bargain?* Chapel Hill, NC: The University of North Carolina Press, 2003.

Limm, Peter. *The Thirty Years War.* London: Longman, 1984.

Locke, John. *Two Treatises of Government,* introduced by W. S. Carpenter. London: J. M. Dent and Sons, 1964.

Long, E. B., and Barbara Long. *The Civil War Day by Day: An Almanac 1861–1865.* New York: Da Capo Press, 1971.

Longford, Elizabeth. *Wellington: The Years of the Sword.* New York: Smithmark, 1996.

Lord Kinross. *The Ottoman Centuries: the Rise and Fall of the Turkish Empire.* New York: Marrow Quill, 1977.

Loughlin, James. *Saint Ambrose.* vol. 1 of *Catholic Encyclopedia.* New York: Robert Appleton, 1907.

Lynn, John. *The Bayonets of the Republic: Motivation and Tactics in the Army of Revolutionary France, 1791–1794.* Boulder, Colo.: Westview Press, 1996.

———. *The Wars of Louis XIV, 1667–1714.* London: Longman, 1999.

Lyons, Michael. *World War I: A Short History.* Upper Saddle River, N.J.: Prentice Hall, 2000.

Maalouf, Amin. *The Crusades Through Arab Eyes.* New York: Schocken Press, 1989.

MacCulloch, Diarmaid. *The Reformation.* New York: Viking Press, 2003.

Mackesy, Piers. *British Victory in Egypt, 1801: The End of Napoleon's Conquest.* London: Routledge, 1995.

Madden, Thomas F. *The New Concise History of the Crusades.* Oxford: Rowman and Littlefield, 2006.

Mahan, Alfred Thayer. *The Influence of Sea Power upon History, 1660–1783.* Boston: Little, Brown, 1918.

Majumdar, R.C., ed. *The History and Culture of the Indian People.* London: G. Allen & Unwin. 1951.

Maltby, William. *Alba: A Biography of Fernando Alvarez de Toledo, Third Duke of Alba, 1507–1582*. Berkeley, Calif.: University of California Press, 1983.

Mann, Golo. *Wallenstein, His Life Narrated*. New York: Holt, Rinehart and Winston, 1976.

Markham, Clements Robert. *A History of Peru*. Chicago: C.H. Sergel, 1892.

Marks, Richard Lee. *Cortés: The Great Adventurer and the Fate of Aztec Mexico*. New York: Knopf, 1993.

Marrin, Albert. *The War for Independence: The Story of the American Revolution*. New York: Atheneum, 1988.

Marshall, Christopher. *Warfare in the Latin East, 1192–1291*. Cambridge: Cambridge University Press, 1992.

Marsot, Afaf Lutfi Al-Sayyid. *A History of Egypt: From the Arab Conquest to the Present*. Cambridge: Cambridge University Press, 2007.

Martin, Colin, and Geoffrey Parker. *The Spanish Armada*. Manchester, U.K.: Manchester University Press, 2002.

Mathur, M.N., ed. *Battle of Haldighati*. Jodhpur: Rajasthani Granthagar. 1981.

Mattingly, Garrett. *The Armada*. New York: Houghton Mifflin, 2005.

May, Timothy. *The Mongol Art of War*. Yardly, PA: Westholme, 2007.

Mayer, Hans Eberhard. *The Crusades*. Oxford: Oxford University Press, 1988.

McCoy, Kathleen, and Judith A.V. Harlan. *English Literature to 1785*. New York: HarperCollins Publishers, 1992.

McGrail, Seán. *Boats of the World: From the Stone Age to Medieval Times*. Oxford: Oxford University Press, 2001.

McHenry, Robert, ed. *Webster's American Military Biographies*. Springfield, Mass.: G. & C. Merriam, 1978.

McKitterick, Rosamund, ed. *Medieval World*. London: Times Books, 2003.

Merriman, John, and Jay Winter, eds. *Encyclopedia of Modern Europe: Europe 1789–1914: Encyclopedia of the Age of Industry and Empire*, Volume 2. Detroit: Charles Scribner's Sons, 2006.

Métraux, Alfred. *The History of the Incas*. New York: Pantheon, 1969.

Miller, Donald. *The Story of World War II*. New York: Simon and Schuster, 1945.

Minks, Louise, and Benton Minks. *The Revolutionary War*. New York: Facts on File, 1992.

Mitchell, Joseph B. *Decisive Battles of the Civil War*. New York: G. P. Putnam's Sons, 1955.

Moore, Robin. *The Hunt For Bin Laden: Task Force Dagger*. New York: Random House, 2003.

Morgan, David. *The Mongols*. Cambridge, Mass.: Basil Blackwell, 2007.

Morgan, Edmund S. *The Birth of the Republic, 1763–1789*. Chicago: University of Chicago Press, 1956.

Morris, Donald R. *Washing of the Spears: The Rise and Fall of the Zulu Nation*. New York: Da Capo Press, 1998.

Murphey, Rhoads. *Ottoman Warfare, 1500–1700*. Oxford: Routledge, 1999.

Nafziger, George. *Napoleon's Invasion of Russia*. Novato, Calif.: Presidio Press, 1988.

Nevitt, Travor. *The Evolution of Weapons and Warfare*. New York: Da Capo Press, 1984.

Newman, Andrew J. *Safavid Iran: Rebirth of a Persian Empire*. New York: I.B. Tauris, 2006.

Nicasie, M. J. *Twilight of Empire*. Amsterdam: J.C. Gieben, 1998.

Nicholson, Helen. *The Knights Templar: A New History*. Stroud: Sutton, 2001.

Nicolle, David. *Armies of the Ottoman Turks, 1300–1744*. Oxford: Osprey Publishing, 1983.

Nicolson, Adam. *Seize the Fire: Heroism, Duty, and the Battle of Trafalgar*. New York: HarperCollins Publishers, 2005.

Norman, A. V. B., and Don Pottinger. *English Weapons and Warfare, 449–1660*. New York: Dorset, 1985.

Oberman, Heiko. *Luther: Man Between God and the Devil*. New Haven, Conn.: Yale University Press, 2006.

Ollard, Richard. *The Image of the King*. London: Phoenix, 1979.

Oman, Carola. *Nelson*. Annapolis, Md.: Naval Institute Press, 1996.

Oman, Sir Charles. *A History of the Peninsular War*, seven volumes. Oxford: Oxford University Press, 1902–1930. (repr. 1996).

Overy, Richard. *Why the Allies Won*. New York: W. W. Norton, 1995.

Palmer, Alan. *Napoleon in Russia: The 1812 Campaign*. New York: Simon and Schuster, 1967.

Pant, G. N. *Catalogue of Edged Arms and Armor in the Salarjung Museum, Hyderabad*. Hyderabad: Salarjung Museum, 1989.

Parker, Geoffrey, and Lesley M. Smith, eds. *The General Crisis of the Seventeenth Century*. London: Routledge, 1997.

Parker, Geoffrey. *The Army of Flanders and the Spanish Road, 1567–1659: The Logistics of Spanish Victory and Defeat in the Low Countries' Wars.* (Revised Edition.) Cambridge: Cambridge University Press, 2004.

———. *The Military Revolution: Military Innovation and the Rise of the West, 1500–1800.* Cambridge: Cambridge University Press, 1996.

———. *Philip II.* (reprint), Chicago: Open Court Publishing, 2002.

Patterson, B. R. *With the Heart of a King: Elizabeth I of England, Philip II of Spain, and the Fight for a Nation's Soul and Crown.* New York: St. Martin's Press, 2007.

Paul, E. Jaiwant. *By My Sword and Shield: Traditional Weapons of the Indian Warrior.* New Delhi: Roli Books, 1995.

Pauly, Roger. *Firearms: The Life Story of a Technology.* Westport, Conn.: Greenwood, 2004.

Perkins, James Breck. *France under Louis XV.* Boston: Houghton Mifflin, 1897.

Peters, Edward. *Europe and the Middle Ages.* Englewood Cliffs, N.J.: Prentice-Hall, 1983.

Peters, Francis E., *The Monotheists: Jews, Christians, and Muslims in Conflict and Competition.* Princeton, N.J.: Princeton University Press, 2003.

Peterson, Harold L. *Arms and Armor in Colonial America, 1526–1783.* Mineola, N.Y.: Dover, 2000.

Petre, F. Lorraine. *Napoleon and the Archduke Charles.* London: Greenhill Books, 1991.

Phillips, Jonathan. *The Fourth Crusade and the Sack of Constantinople.* New York: Viking, 2004.

Phipps, Ramsay. *The Armies of the First Republic,* five volumes. London: Oxford University Press, 1926–1939.

Pickles, Tim. *Malta 1565: Last Battle of the Crusades.* Oxford: Osprey Publishing, 1998.

Pinkham, Lucile. *William III and the Respectable Revolution.* Cambridge, Mass.: Harvard University Press, 1954.

Plutarch. *The Age of Alexander,* translated and annotated by Ian Scott-Kilvert. Middlesex, New York: Penguin, 1973.

Pohl, John, and Charles M. Robinson. *Aztecs and Conquistadors: The Spanish Invasion and the Collapse of the Aztec Empire.* Oxford: Osprey, 2005.

Polo, Marco. *The Travels of Marco Polo,* translated by Ronald Latham. London: Penguin Books, 1958.

Porter, Roy. *The Enlightenment (Studies in European History).* Hampshire, U.K.: Palgrave, 2001.

Prebble, John. *Culloden.* Harmondsworth, England: Penguin, 1967.

Prescott, William H. *History of the Conquest of Mexico.* Philadelphia: J. B. Lippincott, 1873.

Purdue, A. W. *The Second World War.* New York: St. Martin's Press, 1999.

Purkiss, Diane. *The English Civil War.* New York: Basic, 2006.

Rachewiltz, Igor de, translator and editor. *The Secret History of the Mongols.* Leiden, The Netherlands: Brill, 2004

Rady, Martyn. *The Netherlands: Revolt and Independence, 1550–1650.* London: Hodder and Staughton, 1987.

Ratchnevsky, Paul. *Genghis Khan: His Life and Legacy,* translated by Thomas Nivison Haining. Cambridge, Mass.: Blackwell, 1992.

Restall, Matthew. *Seven Myths of the Spanish Conquest.* Oxford: Oxford University Press, 2003.

Rice, Eugene, and Anthony Grafton. *The Foundations of Early Modern Europe, 1460–1559.* New York: W.W. Norton, 1994.

Richard, Jean. *The Crusades.* Cambridge: Cambridge University Press, 1999.

Riley-Smith, Jonathan. *The Crusades: A Short History.* New Haven: Yale University Press, 1987.

Robb, Nesca A. *William of Orange.* New York: St. Martin's, 1962.

Robert the Monk. *Robert the Monk's History of the First Crusade,* translated by Carol Sweetenham. Brookfield, Vt.: Ashgate, 2005.

Roberts, Michael. *Gustavus Adolphus: A History of Sweden, 1611–1632.* London: Longman, 1953.

Rodger, N. A. M. *The Command of the Ocean: A Naval History of Britain, 1649–1815.* New York: W. W. Norton, 2006.

———. *The Safeguard of the Sea; A Naval History of Britain, 660–1649.* New York: W. W. Norton, 1997.

Rogoziński, Jan. *Pirates!: Brigands, Buccaneers, and Privateers in Fact, Fiction, and Legend.* New York: Da Capo Press, 1995.

Rommel, Erwin. *Attacks.* Provo, Utah: Athena Press, 1979.

Roosevelt, Theodore. *The Rough Riders.* New York: Charles Scribner's Sons, 1923.

Rossabi, Morris. *Khubilai Khan.* Los Angeles: University of California Press, 1989.

Royle, Trevor. *The British Civil War.* New York: Palgrave Macmillan, 2004.

Runciman, Steven. *A History of the Crusades.* Cambridge: Cambridge University Press, 1950–1954.

Sadler, A. L. *The Maker of Modern Japan: the Life of Tokugawa Ieyasu.* Rutland, Vt.: Charles E. Tuttle Company, 1937.

Sandburg, Carl. *Abraham Lincoln*. New York: Charles Scribner's Sons, 1926.

Schama, Simon. *Citizens: A Chronicle of the French Revolution*. New York: Vintage Reprint Edition, 1990.

The Search for Alexander: An Exhibition. New York: New York Graphic Society, 1980.

Sears, Steven W. *Gettysburg*. New York: Houghton Mifflin, 2003.

Seligmann, Matthew S., and Roderick R. McLean. *Germany from Reich to Republic, 1871–1918*. New York: St. Martin's Press, 2000.

Sharma, G.N. *Mewar and the Mughal Emperors (1526–1707 AD)*. Agra, India: Shiva Lala Agarwala, 1954.

Sharma, G.N., and M. N. Mathur, eds. *Maharana Pratap and His Times*. Udaipur, India: Maharana Pratap Smarak Samiti. 1989.

Shennan, J. H. *International Relations in Europe, 1689–1789*. London: Routledge, 1995.

Sherman, General William T. *Memoirs of General William T. Sherman*. New York: D. Appleton and Company, 1889.

Smail, R. C. *Crusading Warfare, 1097–1193*. Cambridge: Cambridge University Press, 1995.

Smith, Digby. *1813 Leipzig: Napoleon and the Battle of Nations*. London: Greenhill Books, 2006.

Smith, Page. *A New Age Now Begins: A People's History of the American Revolution*. New York: McGraw Hill, 1976.

Snyder, Louis L. *Frederick the Great*. Englewood Cliffs, N.J.: Prentice-Hall, 1971.

Somerset, Anne. *The Affair of the Poisons*. New York: St. Martin's, 2004.

Soustelle, Jacques. *Daily Life of the Aztecs on the Eve of the Spanish Conquest*. Stanford, Calif.: Stanford University Press, 1970.

Spencer, Charles. *Battle for Europe*. Hoboken: John Wiley and Sons, 2004.

Spyeck, Jeff. *Becoming Charlemagne: Europe, Baghdad, and the Empires of A.D. 800*. New York: Ecco, 2006.

Steele, Brett D., and Tamera Dorland. *The Heirs of Archimedes: Science and the Art of War Through the Age of Enlightenment*. Cambridge, Mass.: MIT Press, 2005.

Stephen, Sir Leslie. *Hobbes*. Ann Arbor: University of Michigan, 1961.

Stephenson, Michael. *Battlegrounds: Geography and the History of Warfare*. Washington, D.C.: National Geographic, 2003.

Stone, George Cameron. *A Glossary of the Construction, Decoration and Use of Arms and Armor in All Countries and All Times, Together with Some Closely Related Subjects*. New York: Jack Russell, 1961.

Strachan, Hew. *The First World War*. New York: Viking Penguin: 2003.

Summers, Harry G., Jr. *Historical Atlas of the Vietnam War*. Boston: Houghton Mifflin, 1995.

Sumption, Jonathan. *The Hundred Years War: Trial by Battle*. University of Philadelphia Press, Philadelphia, PA, 1990.

Suskind, Ron. *The One Percent Doctrine: Deep Inside America's Pursuit of its Enemies Since 9/11*. New York: Simon & Schuster, 2006.

Taylor, Iain Cameron. *Culloden*. Edinburgh: The National Trust for Scotland, 1965.

Thackery, Frank W., and John E. Findling, eds. *Events That Changed the World in the Eighteenth Century*. Westport, Conn.: Greenwood, 1998.

Thapar, Romilla. *A History of India, I*. London: Penguin Books, 1966.

Thomas, Hugh. *Conquest: Montezuma, Cortés, and the Fall of Old Mexico*. New York: Simon and Schuster, 1993.

———. *The Spanish Civil War*. New York: Modern Library, 1989.

Thomson, Ann. *Barbary and Enlightenment: European Attitudes Towards the Maghreb in the 18th Century*. Leiden, The Netherlands: E.J. Brill, 1989.

Tolstoy, Leo. *War and Peace*. New York: Signet Classics Edition, 1993. (Original, 1869).

Townsend, Richard F. *The Aztecs*. Revised edition. London: Thames and Hudson, 2000.

Townshend, C. V. F. *The Military Life of Field-Marshal George First Marquess Townshend, 1724–1807*. London: John Murray, 1901.

Tracy, James Donald. *Emperor Charles V, Impresario of War*. Cambridge: Cambridge University Press, 2002.

Traill, H. D. *William the Third*. London; Macmillan, 1888.

Trevelyan, George Otto. *Selections from the Writings of Lord Macaulay*. New York: Longmans, Green, 1903.

Turnbull, Stephen R. *The Book of the Samurai: The Warrior Class of Japan*. New York: Bison Books, 1982.

Tyerman, Christopher. *God's War*. Cambridge, Mass.: Belknap Press, 2006.

U.S. War Department. *The War of the Rebellion: A Compilation of the Official Records of the Union* and *Confederate Armies.* Washington, D.C.: GPO (Government Printing Office), 1880–1901.

Unger, Richard W., ed. *Cogs, Caravels and Galleons: The Sailing Ship, 1000–1650.* London: Conway Maritime Press, 1994.

Van Creveld, M. *Supplying War: Logistics from Wallenstein to Patton.* Cambridge: Cambridge University Press, 1977.

Vietnam: A Television History. Boston: WGBH Video, 1983.

Viola, Herman J., and Carolyn Margolis. *Seeds of Change.* Washington, D.C.: Smithsonian Institution Press, 1991.

Warry, John Gibson. *Warfare in the Classical World.* Norman, Okla.: University of Oklahoma Press, 1995.

Watson, Bruce A. *Sieges: A Comparative Study.* Westport, Conn.: Praeger Publishers 1993.

Weapon: A Visual History of Arms and Armor. New York: DK Publishing, 2006.

Wedgewood, C. V. *The Thirty Years War.* New York: New York Review Books Classics, 2005.

Weygand, Max. *Turenne: Marshal of France.* New York: Houghton Mifflin, 1930.

Whitworth, Rex. *William Augustus, Duke of Cumberland.* London: Leo Cooper, 1992.

Wilkins, David E. *Uneven Ground: American Indian Sovereignty and Federal Law.* Norman, Okla.: University of Oklahoma Press, 2001.

Winter, Michael. *Egyptian Society Under Ottoman Rule, 1517–1798.* Oxford: Routledge, 1992.

Wolpert, Stanley. *A New History of India,* third edition. Oxford. Oxford University Press. 1989.

Wood, J. B. *The King's Army: Warfare, Soldiers and Society during the Wars of Religion in France, 1562–1576.* Cambridge: Cambridge University Press, 1996.

Woodward, Bob. *Plan of Attack.* New York: Simon & Schuster, 2004.

———. *State of Denial: Bush at War, Part III.* New York: Simon & Schuster, 2006.

Woolrych, Austin. *Battles of the English Civil War.* New York: Macmillan, 1961.

Worthington, Ian, ed. *Alexander the Great: A Reader.* Oxford: Routledge, 2003.

Wright, Lawrence. *The Looming Tower: Al-Qaeda and the Road to 9/11.* New York: Alfred A. Knopf, 2006.

Wyden, Peter. *The Passionate War: The Narrative History of the Spanish Civil War, 1936–1939.* New York: Simon and Schuster, 1983.

Zobel, Hillard B. *The Boston Massacre.* New York: W. W. Norton, 1970.

PERIODICALS

Bach, Caleb. "Historian with a Brush: Argentine Soldier-Painter Candido Lopez." *Americas* (English Edition) (November-December 1990).

Bádenas de la Peña, Pedro. "Del Báltico a Constantinopla. Los Vikingos en Bizancio. (Byzantina Graecia)." *Byzantion Nea Hellas* 83 (Annual 2002): 25.

Barratt, John. "Exiled King's Final Gamble." *Military History* 18.3 (August 2001).

Black, Jeremy. "Habsburgs and Ottomans: Between Vienna and Belgrade (1683–1739)." *Journal of European Studies* 26 (September 1996): 338.

"The Blackballers' Club; Turkey and Europe." *The Economist* (December 16, 2006): 13.

Brightwell, P. J. "Spain and Bohemia: the Decision to Intervene, 1619." *European Studies Review* (1982) vol. 12, p.117–134.

Brock, Darryl E. "Naval Technology from Dixie." *Americas* (English Edition) (July-August 1994).

Browning, Webster E. "The Liberation and the Liberators of Spanish America." *The Hispanic American Historical Review* (November 1921), pp. 690–714.

Buell, Paul D. "Kalmyk Tanggaci People: Thoughts on the Mechanics and Impact of Mongol Expansion." *Mongolian Studies* 6 (1980).

Cavendish, Richard. "The Battle of Civitate." *History Today* (June 2003): 53.

———. "The Relief of Mafeking." *History Today* (May 2000).

Chamberlain, Russell. "Charles V: Europe's Last Emperor?" *History Today.* (February 2000): 2.

Christensen, Peter G. "Johannes V. Jensen's 'Den Lange Rejse': A Blochian Approach. (Ernst Bloch)." *Scandinavian Studies* (Winter 1996): 51(25).

"Courageous Leadership Will Be Able to Eradicate Partition." *Irish Examiner* (October 2, 2006).

Daniel, Douglas A. "Tactical Factors in the Spanish Conquest of the Aztecs." *Anthropological Quarterly* 65.4 (October 1992).

Engelhardt, Armin. "The Battle of Caseros: The Dawn of Modern Argentina." *Military Affairs* (Winter 1948), pp. 217–225.

Ferrill, Arther. "Herodotus and the Strategy and Tactics of the Invasion of Xerxes." *The American Historical Review* 72 (October 1966): 102–115.

"The Foundation of Sinn Fein: November 28th, 1905." *History Today* (November 2005): vol. 55, p. 61.

Fournie, Daniel A. "Clash of Titans at Zama." *Military History* (February 2000).

Goodlad, Graham. "The Cromwellian Protectorate." *History Review* 57 (March): 1–5.

"Gunpowder: Bang, Bang. You're Dead." *The Economist.* (December 25, 1999): 98.

Gwin, Peter. "Kosovo: Overrun with Ghosts of Conflicts Past." *Europe.* (May 1999): 28.

Halperin, Charles. "The Kipchak Connection: The Ilkhans, the Mamluks, and Ayn Jalut." *Bulletin of the School of Oriental and African Studies 63* (2000).

Hergesell, Alexandra. "Echoes of World War I." *Europe* (October 2001).

Herrin, Judith. "The Fall of Constantinople." *History Today* 53 (June 2003): 12.

Hull, William. "The Scramble for Africa: White Man's Conquest of the Dark Continent from 1876–1912." *The Historian* 55 (Summer 1993): 80.

"In Harm's Way; The Sinking of the Lusitania." *The Economist* (April 20, 2002).

Isserlin, B. S. J., et al. "The Canal of Xerxes on the Mount Athos Peninsula." in *Annual of the British School at Athens* 89 (1994): 277–284.

Jochens, Jenny. "Um Haf Innan: Vestraenir Menn og Islenzk Menning a Midoldum (Review)." *The Journal of English and Germanic Philology* (April 1999): 278.

John, Eric. "The Battle of Maldon AD 991." *The Review of English Studies* (May 1993).

Jones, Lucy. "Austria 'Wants to Keep Muslim Countries Out of EU,' According to German Paper." *Washington Report on Middle East Affairs.* (December 2005): 40.

"Juan Modesto, 63, Spanish General." *The New York Times* (April 21, 1969): 47.

Knobler, Alfred. "Holy Wars, Empires, and the Portability of the Past: The Modern Uses of Medieval Crusades." *Comparative Studies in Society and History* 48: (2006).

Laband, John. "Rorke's Drift 1879: Anatomy of an Epic Zulu War Siege." *The Journal of African History* (July 2002).

Lee, C.D. "The Battle of Beachy Head: Lord Torrington's Conduct." *The Mariner's Mirror* 80.3 (August 1994).

Le Fevre, Peter. "'Mere Laziness;' or Incompetence: The Earl of Torrington and the Battle of Beachy Head." *The Mariner's Mirror* 80.3 (August 1994): 290–297.

Leitsch, Walter. "1683, the Siege of Vienna." *History Today.* (July 1983).

Low, D. A. "The Scramble for Africa: 1876–1912." *The English Historical Review* 109 (November 1994): 1319.

Markus-Takeshita, Kinga Ilona. "From Iranian Myth to Folk Narrative: The Legend of the Dragon-Slayer and the Spinning Maiden in the Persian Book of the Kings (Critical Essay)." *Asian Folklore Studies* (June 2001).

Mazzetti, Mark. "General Starwars." *U.S. News & World Report,* (September 3, 2001): 20.

McCarthy, Rory. "Taliban Under Siege." *The Guardian* (November 30, 2001).

McCarthy, Terry "A Volatile State Of Siege After a Taliban Ambush." *Time Magazine* (November 18, 2001).

Miklashevich, Elena. "Varangians to the East: Not Rain, Not Snow, Not Even Sand Could Stop These Traders." *Dig* Junior Edition. (November- December 2006).

Millen, Raymond. "The Hobbesian Notion of Self- Preservation Concerning Human Behavior During an Insurgency." *Parameters: U.S. Army War College Quarterly* 36.4 (Winter 2006–2007): 4–13.

Moniz, Dave. "Stakes in Iraq Rival Those in WWII, Gen. Myers Says." *USA Today* (September 27, 2005): 6A.

Moseley, Alexander. "John Locke's Morality of War." *Journal of Military Ethics* 4.2 (2005): 119–128.

Murphey, Rhoads. "An Economic and Social History of the Ottoman Empire, 1300–1914." *History Today* 47 (January 1997): 55.

———. "Ottoman Expansion Under Mehmed II." *History Review* (December 1999): 35.

Murray, William M. "The Athenian Trireme: The History and Reconstruction of an Ancient Greek Warship (Book Review)." *The Historian* (Spring-Summer 2002).

Norton, Graham Gendall. "Toussaint Louverture." *History Today* (April 2003).

O'Brien, Patrick. "Did Europe's Mercantilist Empires Pay?" *History Today* 46.3 (March 1996).

O'Donoghue, Heather. "Studies in Ragnar's Saga 'Lodhbrokar' and Its Major Scandinavian Analogues." *The Review of English Studies* (May 1994).

Otte, T. G. "'The Winston of Germany': The British Foreign Policy Elite and the Last German Emperor." *Canadian Journal of History* (December 2001): vol. 36, p. 471.

Pulsiano, Phillip. "Danish Men's Words are Worse than Murder: Viking Guile and The Battle of Maldon." *The Journal of English and Germanic Philology* (Jan 1997).

Reston, James, Jr. "'Be Christian or Die' (Viking History)." *Christian History* (August 1999).

Rexine, John E. "Mehmed the Conqueror and His Time." *Renaissance Quarterly* 47 (Summer 1994): 391.

Riley, Brent A. "William, from Bastard to Conqueror." *Military History* (April 2002).

"Safavid Persia." *The Middle East.* (December, 1996): 33.

Smith, John Masson. "Mongol Campaign Rations: Milk, Marmots, and Blood?" *Journal of Turkish Studies* 8 (1984).

———. "Mongol Manpower and Persian Population." *Journal of the Economic and Social History of the Orient 18/3* (1975).

Sowell, David. "The Mirror of Public Opinion: Bolívar, Republicanism and the United States Press, 1821–1831." *Revista de Historia de América* (January-June 2004).

Stafford, Pauline. "The Battle of Maldon." *The English Historical Review* (Sept 1994): 989(2).

Sued-Baudillo, Jalil. "Christopher Columbus and the Enslavement of the Amerindians in the Caribbean." *Monthly Review* 44 (July-August 1992).

"Swiss scholars want Hagia Sophia returned." *America* (September 26, 2005): 7.

Tennant, Anne W. "The Glorious Renunciation: Jose de San Martín Cedes the Field to Simon Bolívar." *Americas* (English Edition) (July-August 1997).

Thompson, Martyn P. "The Reception of Locke's Two Treatises of Government, 1690–1705." *Political Studies* 24.2 (1976): 184–191.

"The Turkish Empire: Goodbye to the Mamluks." *The Economist* (December 25, 1999).

Vesilind, Priit. "In Search of Vikings." *National Geographic* 197.5 (May 2000).

Werner, Louis. "Equine Allies in the New World." *Americas* 53.4 (July-August 2001).

Williams, John Hoyt. "'A Swamp of Blood': The Battle of Tuyutí." *Military History* (April 2000): 58.

Wilson, Peter H. "Latin America's Total War: Peter H. Wilson Revisits the War of the Triple Alliance, Latin America's Bloodiest Conflict." *History Today* (May 2004).

Woodward, Geoffrey. "The Ottomans in Europe." *History Review* (March 2001): 41.

Wright, John W. "Sieges and Customs of War at the Opening of the Eighteenth Century." *The American Historical Review* 39.4 (July 1934): 629–644.

WEB SITES

Air Force Magazine Online. "The Russians in MiG Alley." <http://www.afa.org/magazine/1991/0291russian.asp> (Accessed June 20, 2007).

All About Turkey. "The Ottomans and Their Dynasty." <http://www.allaboutturkey.com/ottoman.htm> (accessed July 2, 2007).

"The American Experience, MacArthur, Korean Maps." *PBS.* <www.pbs.org/wgbh/amex/ma carthur/maps/koreatxt.html> (accessed May 16, 2007).

Archaeology.com "Insight: Legacy of Medieval Serbia." <http://www.archaeology.org/9909/etc/insight.html> (accessed July 2, 2007).

Australian Korean Veterans "HISTORY OF THE KOREAN WAR AND AUSTRALIA'S ROLE." <http://www.austkoreavets.asn.au/content/history.html> (accessed June 20, 2007).

"The Austro-Hungarian Ultimatum to Serbia, English Translation (23 July 1914)." *World War I Document Library.* Brigham Young University Library. <http://net.lib.byu.edu/~rdh7/wwi/1914/austro-hungarian-ultimatum.html> (accessed April 22, 2007).

BBC.com "The Korean War: An Overview." <http://www.bbc.co.uk/history/worldwars/coldwar/korea_hickey_01.shtml> (accessed June 20,2007).

BBC News. "7 October: US launches air strikes against Taleban."<http://news.bbc.co.uk/onthisday/hi/dates/stories/october/7/newsid_2519000/2519353.stm> (accessed June 5, 2007).

Berman, Paul. "The Philosopher of Islamic Terror." *New York Times* March 23, 2003. <http://www.nytimes.com/2003/03/23/magazine/23GURU.html> (accessed March 17, 2007).

Boot, Max. "Special Forces and Horses." *Armed Forces Journal.* <http://www.armedforcesjournal.com/2006/11/2146103> (accessed June 9, 2007).

"Braddock's Grave." *Fort Necessity National Battlefield Website.* <http://www.nps.gov/archive/fone/braddock.htm> (accessed July 6, 2007).

Brainard, Rick. "The Divisions of 18th Century Armies and Their Weapons." *18th Century History; History 1700s.com.* <http://www.history1700s.com/articles/article1115.shtml> (accessed July 25, 2007).

BritishBattles.com. "The Battle of Alma." <http://www.britishbattles.com/crimean-war/alma.htm> (accessed April 18, 2007).

BritishBattles.com. "The Battle of Balaklava." <http://www.britishbattles.com/crimean-war/battle.htm> (accessed April 18, 2007).

BritishBattles.com. "The Battle of Inkerman." <http://www.britishbattles.com/crimean-war/inkerman.htm> (accessed April 18, 2007).

BritishBattles.com. "The Siege of Sevastopol." <http://www.britishbattles.com/crimean-war/sevastopol.htm> (accessed April 18, 2007).

Churchill, Winston S. "Iron Curtain Speech, March 5, 1946." *Internet Modern History Sourcebook.* <www.fordham.edu/halsall/mod/churchill-iron.html> (accessed May 11, 2007).

Coldstream Guards. "History of the Coldstream Guards." <http://www.army.mod.uk/coldstreamguards/index.htm> (accessed May 22, 2007).

"Colt Revolver: History of the Colt Revolver." <http://inventors.about.com/od/cstartinventions/a/colt_revolver.htm> (accessed July 30, 2007).

Crawford, Paul. "Crusades." <http://www.the-orb.net/encyclop/religion/crusades/crusade_intro.html> (accessed May 15, 2007).

Daily Life: Medieval History Net Links. <http://historymedren.about.com/education/history/historymedren/msubmenudaily.htm> (accessed June 3, 2007).

De Imperatoribus Romanis. "Manuel II PALAIOLOGOS (1391-1425 A.D.)." <http://www.romanemperors.org/manuel2.htm> (accessed July 4, 2007).

De Re Militari: The Society for Medieval Military History. "The Battle of Kosovo: Early Reports of Victory and Defeat."<http://www.deremilitari.org/resour ces/articles/emmert.htm> (accessed July 2, 2007).

Fonck, Bertrand. "François-Henri de Montmorency-Bouteville, maréchal de Luxembourg (1628–1695), Commander les armées pour Louis XIV. Thèse soutenue en 2003." <http://theses.enc.sorbonne.fr/document75.html> (accessed June 15, 2007).

Frahm, Jill. "SIGINT and the Pusan Perimeter." *National Security Agency.* <www.nsa.gov/publications/publi 00024.cfm#5> (accessed May 19, 2007).

Franklin, Benjamin. *The Autobiography of Benjamin Franklin.* Reprinted at Archiving Early America. <www.earlyamerica.com/lives/franklin> (acces sed March 10, 2007). Originally published in 1793.

Gaugamela.com. "Darius III." <http://www.gaugamela.com> (accessed March 7, 2007).

GlobalSecurity.org. "Ayman al-Zawahiri." <http://www.globalsecurity.org/military/world/para/zawahiri.htm> (accessed March 25, 2007).

Gordon, Michael R. "Shifting Fronts, Rising Danger: The Afghanistan War Evolves." *New York Times* (December 9, 2001). <http://www.pulitzer.org/year/2002/public-service/works/story3b.html> (accessed September 1, 2007.)

"Guernica." *Treasures of the World.* PBS Online, <http://www.pbs.org/treasuresoftheworld/a_nav/guernica_nav/main_guerfrm.html> (accessed May 2, 2007).

Hamilton, Alexander. *The Works of Alexander Hamilton, (Federal Edition),* Henry Cabot Lodge, editor. Reprinted at The Online Library of Liberty. <oll.libertyfund.org/Home3/HTML. php?recordID= 0249.07> (accessed March 27, 2007).

The Handbook of Texas Online. <http://www.tsha.utexas.edu/handbook/online/> (accessed July 30, 2007).

"Henry R. Luce and the Rise of the American News Media." *PBS.* <www.pbs.org/wnet/americanmasters/database/luce_h.html> (accessed May 9, 2007).

Hermansen, Max. "Inchon—Operation Chromite." *United States Military Logistics in the First Part of the Korean War.* University of Oslo. <http://vlib.iue.it/carrie/texts/carrie_books/hermansen/6.html> (accessed May 17, 2007).

"History of Korea, Part II." *Life In Korea.* <www.lifeinkorea.com/information/history2.cfm> (accessed May 15, 2007).

History of the Middle East Database. "The Mamluks." <http://www.nmhschool.org/tthornton/me historydatabase/mamluks.php> (accessed July 23, 2007).

History of War. "Crimean War, 1853–1856." <http://www.historyofwar.org/articles/wars_crimean.html> (accessed April 18, 2007).

Hobbes, Thomas. "Leviathan." <http://oregon state.edu/instruct/phl302/texts/hobbes/leviathan-a.html> (accessed May 3, 2007).

"INDEPENDENCE: The Birth of a New America." *Time* (July 4, 1976). Reprinted at <www.time.com/time/magazine/article/0,9171,712235-1,00.html> (accessed March 10, 2007).

"Interview with Lt. Col. Charles Bussy, U.S. Army." *CNN.* <www.cnn.com/interactive/specials/0005/korea.interviews/bussey.html> (accessed May 19, 2007).

Jarmul, David. "America's Fear of Communism in 1920 Becomes a Threat to Rights." *VOANews.com.* (May 17, 2006) <www.voanews.com/specialenglish/archive/2006-05/2006-05-17-voa2.cfm> (accessed May 2, 2007).

Jevtic, Borijove. "The Assassination of Archduke Franz Ferdinand (28 June 1914)." *World War I Document Library.* Brigham Young University Library. <http://net.lib.byu.edu/~rdh7/wwi/1914/ferddead.html> (accessed April 22, 2007).

Keller, Carol A., editor. "Explorations in Empire: Pre-Modern Imperialism Tutorial: The Mongol Empire." <http://www.accd.edu/sac/history/keller/Mongols/index.html> (accessed April 15, 2007).

"Kharg Oil Terminal Can Handle 5 m bpd." *Iran Daily.* December 27, 2004. <http://www.iran daily.ir/1383/2174/html/economy.htm#33453> (accessed June 11, 2007).

Kipling, Rudyard. "Recessional (1897)." *The Oxford Book of English Verse.* Originally published in 1919. <www.bartleby.com/101/867.html> (accessed June 4, 2007).

Knox, E. L. Skip. "The Crusades." <http://crusa des.boisestate.edu/> (accessed May 28, 2007).

" The Korean War Armistice." *BBC News.* <http://news.bbc.co.uk/1/hi/world/asia-pacific/2774931.stm> (accessed May 18, 2007).

"The Korean War—The Inchon Invasion." *Naval Historical Center.* <www.history.navy.mil/photos/events/kowar/50-unof/inchon.htm> (accessed May 16, 2007).

"The Kosovo Myth" <http://www.salon.com/news/1999/03/cov_25newsb.html> (accessed August 6, 2007).

Lendering, Jona. "Alexander the Great: The Ten-horned Beast." <http://www.livius.org/aj-al/alexander/alexander00.html> (accessed March 7, 2007).

———. "Alexander's successors: the Diadochi." <http://www.livius.org/di-dn/diadochi/diadochi.htm> (accessed March 7, 2007).

———. "Ammon." <http://www.livius.org/am-ao/ammon/ammon.htm> (accessed March 7, 2007).

———. "Demosthenes." <http://www.livius.org/de-dh/demosthenes/demosthenes.html> (accessed March 7, 2007).

———. "Philip II of Macedonia." <http://www.livius.org/phi-php/philip/philip_ii.htm> (accessed March 7, 2007).

———. "Porus." <http://www.livius.org/pn-po/porus/porus.htm> (accessed March 7, 2007).

———. "What Happened at Gaugamela?" <http://www.livius.org/aj-al/alexander/alexander_z7.html> (accessed March 12, 2007).

Levine, Marsha A. "Domestication, Breed Diversifi cation and Early History of the Horse." <http://www3.vet.upenn.edu/labs/equinebehavior//hvn wkshp/hv02/levine.htm> (accessed April 23, 2007).

Maihafer, Harry J. "Wars of Alexander the Great: Battle of Issus." <http://www.historynet.com/wars_conflicts/ancient_medieval_wars/30375 21.html> (accessed March 14, 2007).

May, Timothy. "Chormaqan and the Mongol Conquest of the Middle East." <http://www.historynet.com/magazines/military_history/3030386.html> (accessed April 20, 2007).

Middle East Institute. "Policy Brief: Iran, Iraq, and the Legacies of War." March 4, 2005. <http://www.mideasti.org/articles/doc342.html> (accessed June 11, 2007).

The Middle East Quarterly. "Usama bin Ladin: 'American Soldiers are Paper Tigers.'" December 1998. <http://www.meforum.org/article/435> (accessed May 7, 2007).

Mixter, John R. "Wars of Alexander the Great: Battle of the Granicus." <http://www.historynet.com/wars_conflicts/ancient_medieval_wars/3036426.html> (accessed March 13, 2007).

"Modernism and Experimentation: 1914–1945." *Outline of American Literature.* <http://usinfo. state.gov/products/pubs/oal/lit6.htm> (accessed June 6, 2007).

"The Narodna Odbrana (1911)." *World War I Document Library.* Brigham Young University Library. <http://net.lib.byu.edu/~rdh7/wwi/1914m/odbrana.html> (accessed April 22, 2007).

The National Archives: British Battles From Crimea to Korea. "After Balaklava." <http://www.national archives.gov.uk/battles/crimea/after.htm> (accessed April 18, 2007).

Paine, Thomas. "Common Sense." Reprinted at the Constitution Society. <www.constitution.org/tp/comsense.htm> (accessed March 10, 2007). Originally published in 1776.

———. "The American Crisis: 1, December 23, 1776." Reprinted at the Constitution Society. <www.constitution.org/tp/amercrisis01.htm> (accessed March 10, 2007). Originally published in 1776.

PBS.org. "Frontline: Campaign Against Terror: Interviews: Lt. Colonel David Fox." <http://www.pbs.org/wgbh/pages/frontline/shows/campaign/interviews/fox.html> (accessed September 1, 2007).

Polybius. "The Battle of Cannae, 216 B.C.E.." Internet Public History Sourcebook. <http://www. fordham.edu/halsall/ancient/polybius-cannae.html> (accessed March 22, 2007).

Rorres, Chris. "Siege of Syracuse." <http://www.math.nyu.edu/~crorres/Archimedes/Siege/Summary.html.> (accessed March 17, 2007).

Rowland, Emory. "Military Use of Elephants in the Greek and Roman Period." <http://www. clickfire.com/viewpoints/articles/political/elephants.php> (accessed March 15, 2007).

Saudi Aramco World. "Suleiman the Lawgiver." <http://www.saudiaramcoworld.com/issue/196402/.suleiman.the.lawgiver.htm> (accessed July 20, 2007).

SEPTEMBER 11, 2001 VICTIMS. <http://www.september11victims.com/september11victims/vic tims_list.htm> (accessed May 7, 2007).

Serbian Unity Congress. "Despot Djjuradj Brankovic." <http://www.serbianunity.net/culture/history/Serb_History/Rulers/Djuradj_Brankovic.html> (accessed July 10, 2007).

Serbian Unity Congress. "Serbian Rulers—Stefan Uros, Emperor (1355–1371)." <http://www.serbianunity.net/culture/history/Serb_History/Rulers/Stefan_Uros.html> (accessed July 2, 2007).

Smith, Adam. "An Inquiry into the Nature and Causes of the Wealth of Nations by Adam Smith." Project Gutenberg. <www.gutenberg. org/etext/3300> (accessed March 27, 2007). Originally published in 1776.

"South America for Visitors." <http://gosouthamerica.about.com/> (accessed July 30, 2007).

"The Story of Africa: Between World Wars (1914–1945)." *BBC.* <www.bbc.co.uk/worldservice/africa/features/storyofafrica/13chapter11.shtml> (accessed May 4, 2007).

"The Story of Africa: Independence." *BBC News.* <www.bbc.co.uk/worldservice/africa/features/storyofafrica/index_section14.shtml > (accessed May 25, 2007).

"Thomas Jefferson's Account of the Declaration." Reprinted at USHistory.org. <www.ushistory.org/declaration/account/index.htm> (accessed March 10, 2007).

Truman, Harry S. "The Truman Doctrine, President Harry S. Truman's Address Before a Joint Session of Congress, March 12, 1947." *The Avalon Project at Yale Law School.* <www.yale.edu/lawweb/avalon/trudoc.html > (accessed May 18, 2007).

Tsouras, Peter G. "Wars of Alexander the Great: Battle of the Hydaspes River." <http://www.historynet.com/wars_conflicts/ancient_medieval_wars/3027066.html> (accessed March 16, 2007).

United States Korean War Commemoration. "Allied Forces in the Korean War" <http://korea50.army.mil/history/factsheets/allied.shtml> (accessed June 20,2007).

University of Calgary. "Hunyadi's Letter to the Pope." <http://www.ucalgary.ca/applied_history/tutor/endmiddle/bluedot/varna.html> (accessed July 11,2007).

Utz, Curtis A. "MacArthur Sells Inchon." *Assault from the Sea, Amphibious Landing at Inchon.* Naval Historical Center. <www.history.navy.mil/download/i-16-19.pdf> (accessed May 17, 2007).

Van Jacob, Scott, and Ivan Jaksic. "Power and Politics in the Nineteenth Century River Plate." Available online at: <http://www.library.nd.edu/rarebooks/exhibits/riverplate/index.shtml> (accessed July 30, 2007).

The Victorian Web. "A British View of the Crimean War: Introduction." <http://www.victorianweb.org/history/crimea/intro.html> (accessed April 18, 2007).

The Victorian Web. "The Charge of the Light Brigade." <http://www.victorianweb.org/his tory/authors/tennyson/charge.html> (accessed April 18, 2007).

The Victorian Web. "General Comments on the Crimean War." <http://www.victorianweb.org/history/crimea/comment.html> (accessed April 18, 2007).

Vikings and Scandinavian History. <http://historymedren.about.com/education/history/history medren/msubvik.htm> (accessed June 3, 2007).

Voltaire. "The Philosophical Dictionary." H.I. Woolf, ed. New York: Knopf, 1924. Reprinted at Hanover Historical Texts Project <history.hanover.edu/texts/voltaire/volindex.html> (accessed March 27, 2007).

"Walton Harris Walker, General, United States Army." *ArlingtonCemetery.net.* <www.arlingtoncemetery.net/whwalker.htm> (accessed May 19, 2007).

Wars of the World: Armed Conflict Events. "Second Ashanti War, 1873-1874." <http://www.onwar.com/aced/nation/all/asante/fasante1873.htm> (accessed May 16, 2007).

Wormser, Richard. "Harry S. Truman Supports Civil Rights (1947–1948)." *PBS.* <www.pbs.org/wnet/jimcrow/stories_events_truman.html> (accessed May 24, 2007).

"WWI—The Great War Remembered." *United States Department of Defense.* <www.defenselink.mil/home/features/2005/WWI/index.html> (accessed April 22, 2007).

Index

T

U